Calamity Jane

Calamity Jane

The Woman and the Legend

James D. McLaird

University of Oklahoma Press : Norman

Library of Congress Cataloging-in-Publication Data

McLaird, James D.
Calamity Jane: the woman and the legend / James D. McLaird.
    p.   cm.
Includes bibliographical references (p.) and index.
ISBN 0-8061-3591-3 (hc: alk. paper)
1. Calamity Jane, 1852–1903. 2. Women pioneers—West (U.S.)—
Biography. 3. Pioneers—West (U.S.)—Biography. 4. Frontier and
pioneer life—West (U.S.) 5. West (U.S.)—Biography. I. Title.

F594.C2M34 2005
978.02'092—dc22
[B]
2005041723

1 2 3 4 5 6 7 8 9 10

To my entire family:
Donna, my wife
John and Steven, our sons
Rachel, our daughter-in-law
Andrew, Ceiteag, and Ashlyn, our grandchildren
and Ruby, my mother
for this opportunity comes rarely.

Contents

Illustrations

Maps

Acknowledgments

Initially, I did not plan to write a biography of Calamity Jane. Instead, it was my intention only to determine how Calamity became famous, if, as earlier biographers had suggested, she had not scouted for the army, nor been the sidekick of Wild Bill Hickok, nor ridden for the pony express, nor been an outlaw or a law officer. However, as I began researching, my long-time friend Brian Dippie of the University of Victoria suggested that it was first necessary to separate fact from fantasy in her life's story. Brian's off-hand remark cost me more than a decade of my own life.

I am indebted to Brian for his encouragement and advice as this project took shape. During our family visits, Brian and his wife, Donna, energized my effort through their passionate interest in the subject. Brian also sent important source material, gave suggestions and leads, and talked with me about western legend-making. In addition, he offered valuable advice after reading the draft for this book. If there is any merit in this work, I owe it to him.

Another scholar who provided significant help with this project was Richard W. Etulain of the University of New Mexico. I was first alerted to Dick's interest in Calamity Jane by librarians and archivists during research trips. My heart sank at the news; although I had spent several years examining documents, I feared his competition. However, after we met I learned my worry was needless. Dick's enthusiasm for the subject is contagious. Besides sharing information and sources, Dick meticulously combed through a draft, providing detailed suggestions to improve style and content. I cannot thank him enough.

Besides Brian and Dick, many others were crucial to the success of this project. Although it is painful to read editorial criticism of one's writing, the process is essential to the creative process. Three chapters in this book received careful scrutiny when they were submitted for publication in historical journals. Thanks are due to Nancy Tystad Koupal for her efforts on behalf of Chapter 13, which appeared as "Calamity Jane: The Life and the Legend" in *South Dakota History* (Spring 1994); to Chuck Rankin for his skillful editing of Chapter 15, published as "Calamity Jane's Diary and Letters: Story of a Fraud" in *Montana The Magazine of Western History* (Autumn-Winter 1995); and to Richard Etulain for helping make Chapter 5 acceptable as "Calamity Jane and Wild Bill: Myth and Reality" in *Journal of the West* (April 1998). Thanks also are due the South Dakota State Historical Society, Montana Historical Society, and *Journal of the West* for permission to reproduce them.

I owe another debt of gratitude to archivists and librarians. Researching this book was especially tedious because little documentary evidence was readily available. In fact, there were times when I doubted sufficient material could be found to reconstruct Calamity Jane's story. In order to establish her movements through the northern plains region, I began reading all the newspapers—on microfilm—from South Dakota, Montana, and Wyoming between 1875 and 1903. Often, I scanned film for hours without finding even a mention of her. When I finally located a new story, however trivial, institutional peace was disturbed by my exuberance. Without the patience and understanding of librarians and archivists, and their willingness to satisfy my unquenchable thirst for microfilm and documents, this book could not have been completed.

Thus, I wish to express my appreciation to the staffs—a cold way of referring to wonderful human beings who miraculously provide access to information—of numerous research institutions and libraries. I owe special gratitude to the librarians at Dakota Wesleyan University who made innumerable interlibrary loan requests for me for more than a decade—Linda B. Ritter, Suzanne A. Cohen, Karen M. Bruns, Judy M. Lehi, Jodie Barker, and Laurie L. Langland. I also want to thank those nameless people who responded to these requests. In addition, personnel at the following historical societies and public and university libraries, who will have to remain unnamed because there are so many, helped immensely and have my eternal gratitude. Thanks, then, to the people working at the Adams Memorial Museum, Deadwood; American Heritage Center, University of Wyoming; Billings Public Library; Buffalo and Erie County Public Library, New York; Buffalo Bill Historical Center, Cody, Wyoming; Center for Western Studies, Augustana College, Sioux Falls; Colorado Historical Society; Deadwood Public Library; Denver Public Library; Hearst Free Library, Lead, South Dakota; Mercer County Library, Princeton, Missouri; Miles City Library; Minnesota Historical Society; Montana Historical Society; Nebraska State Historical Society; Ohio Historical Society; South Dakota State Historical Society; State Historical Society of North Dakota; Wisconsin Historical Society; and the Wyoming State Archives.

Numerous individuals also made contributions, without which this book would be much less complete. Although I hesitate listing them for fear of forgetting someone due to faulty record-keeping, I owe such a debt to the following people that they deserve citation. Thanks, then, to that indefatigable researcher, William Whiteside, who located elusive information about the Canary family, including the marriage record of Martha's parents; to John D. McDermott, who sent me significant articles about Calamity and even interrupted his own work to examine records for me in Washington, D.C.; to Joseph Rosa, whose correspondence always contained valuable information about Calamity and Wild Bill Hickok; to Alan Woolworth, who steered me to Thomas Newson's publication; to Paul Hedren, who shared his military records from Crook's 1876 expedition; to Ellen Mueller, who introduced me to Elijah Canary; to Marion Nelson, descendant of Lena Canary, who shared family genealogy; to John and Grace Mickelson, who loaned dime novels and early Black Hills pamphlets; to Doug Engebretson, who sent articles from newspapers and popular western magazines; to Doris Whithorn, who corrected misinformation about Calamity Jane photographs; to Paul Fees, who located Buffalo Bill's comments about Calamity; to Paul Hutton, who loaned movie photographs; to George Atwood who sent articles about Martha and Lena Canary in Lander; to Evalyn Claggett, who called my attention to important Black Hills newspaper articles about Calamity; to Lorraine Collins, who shared her research on Jean Hickok McCormick; and to Bob Lee, who introduced me to the Society of Black Hills Pioneers. I also owe a special debt to my brother and sister-in-law, Bob and Lee McLaird at Bowling Green

University, who researched census data and located popular culture materials, and to sister-in-law Janice Roggenkamp, a psychologist, who helped me understand the complexities of alcohol addiction.

Dakota Wesleyan University granted a sabbatical that allowed me to finish this manuscript. Likewise, many colleagues—faculty, staff, administrators, and students—supported this project. Sometimes, I fear, they shammed interest as they listened to just one more Calamity Jane story, but it helped to have listeners. Especially important were those who assisted with administrative support, secretarial help, and publicity, including Dr. John L. Ewing, Jr., Dr. Robert G. Duffett, Dr. Bruce L. Blumer, Amy W. Moore, Daryl E. Beall, Lori J. Essig, Chad E. Larson, Gloria L. Hanson, and Beth Monson.

A word of appreciation is due Charles E. Rankin, editor-in-chief of the University of Oklahoma Press, whose encouragement brought this project to fruition. Managing editor Alice K. Stanton, along with editorial assistants Candice L. Holcombe, Alessandra E. Jacobi, and Bobbie Canfield, showed incredible patience as they guided me step by step through the process of publishing my manuscript. Finally, copyeditor Jay Fultz deserves commendation for his rigorous efforts to improve the final product.

Despite all this help, there are still leads to follow and bits of information in my files that need to be connected. Thus, despite the passage of many years since this project began, I wish there were more time to perfect this manuscript. However, my wife is wondering when she might once again see the surface of the dining-room table, a sure sign it is time to stop. Any shortcomings in this biography are due to my own failings and not to the people who assisted me. If this study of Calamity Jane contributes to the history of the American West and gives the reader pleasure, it will have been worth all the effort.

Calamity Jane

Introduction

"A complete and true biography of the life of Calamity Jane would make a large book, more interesting and blood-curdling than all the fictitious stories that have been written of her," remarked the editor of the *Livingston (Montana) Enterprise* in 1887, "but it would never find its way into a Sunday school library." He added that Calamity Jane at that moment "was on a ranch down in Wyoming trying to sober up after a thirty years' drunk."[1]

More than one hundred years have passed since the editor made these observations, and although numerous accounts of Martha Canary, better known as Calamity Jane, have been produced, none can be considered a "complete and true biography." Most popular accounts make Calamity Jane a gun-toting heroine, claiming she was an associate of Wild Bill Hickok and served as a frontier scout, stagecoach driver, and pony express rider. Conversely, most scholars debunk her purported legendary achievements and depict her as little more than a drunken prostitute. "With Calamity Jane we have the problem of the hero who performed no heroic deeds," said biographer J. Leonard Jennewein. Since "we must not destroy our heroes, we manufacture deeds as needed."[2]

Favorably disposed writers did indeed invent adventurous tales about Calamity Jane. And, in order to overcome her seedy reputation, they emphasized her acts of charity and lack of hypocrisy. This produced a quandary: "Was she a frontier Florence Nightingale, Indian fighter, army scout, gold miner, pony express rider, bull-whacker, and stagecoach driver," asked Merrit Cross in his essay for *Notable American Women*, "or merely a camp follower, prostitute, and alcoholic?"[3] It also became a perplexing problem to explain Calamity Jane's fame if she did nothing to deserve her reputation. The common response, that dime novels made her famous, begged the question. If she did nothing noteworthy, how did she come to the attention of dime novelists?

It was difficult for biographers to provide conclusive answers to these questions because few reliable sources were available. Since Martha Canary was illiterate, there was no personal correspondence, and few of her closest acquaintances bothered to describe their relationships with her. Although Martha, with the help of an amanuensis, published the *Life and Adventures of Calamity Jane, By Herself* in 1896, it is brief and so filled with exaggeration that it confuses as much as it explains her activities. Even such basic facts as her name and the date and place of her birth have remained controversial. As historian Richard W. Etulain aptly observes, "The paucity of solid facts and the plethora of stylized stories force the biographer to sort through thousands of bits and fragments to stitch together a story, much of it at odds with most of her previous life stories."[4]

Yet, sufficient documents have been located to allow a reasonable reconstruction of her biography. Census records establish Martha's birthdate, birthplace, and parentage and confirm that at least a portion of her *Life and Adventures* is reliable. Newly discovered published interviews and manuscripts buried in archives furnish insights into her personality and behavior. Contemporary newspaper articles, though they must be used cautiously, allow her movements to be reconstructed. Equally important, newspapers, through omission, make it possible to discredit some of her purported activities.

Although Martha Canary lived only forty-seven years, from 1856 to 1903, her life encompassed a dramatic period in the history of the American West. She experienced first-hand that era of western expansion in the late nineteenth century that has been the subject of endless romantic stories in popular fiction and history. Even though she never served as a scout, Martha accompanied military expeditions commanded by Colonel Richard Dodge in 1875 and General George Crook in 1876. Martha was not an intimate companion of Wild Bill Hickok, but she was with his party when it entered Deadwood during the gold rush of 1876. It is doubtful she ever helped construct railroads, but she did frequent the booming settlements established as the Union Pacific in Wyoming, the Northwestern in Dakota, and the Northern Pacific in Montana were built. There is no evidence that Martha ever panned for gold, but she joined mining rushes to the Black Hills, the Coeur d'Alenes, and possibly the Klondike. Like other well-known frontier figures, she occasionally joined shows touring eastern cities, where she related her role in the conquest of the West. By the latter period of her life, however, the West had changed and Martha's independent and free-spirited lifestyle was out-of-place. As the legendary Calamity Jane, Martha was welcomed when she revisited earlier haunts and proudly announced that she belonged among the founders of these communities. However, positive impressions soured when Martha engaged in drunken escapades, and she often received jail sentences and requests to leave town.

In many respects, the woman who emerges from the evidence is dramatically different from the person typically portrayed in popular biographies. Illustrations depicting Calamity Jane in male attire, combined with descriptions of her scouting, bullwhacking, stage-driving, shooting, drinking, and swearing, have obscured Martha's feminine qualities. "She dressed, after her first appearance in Deadwood, as other women dressed," wrote John S. McClintock, who knew her during the Black Hills gold rush, "and although she was the last word in slang, obscenity, and profanity, her deportment on the streets, when sober, was no worse than that of others of her class."[5] Most photographs of Calamity Jane in male clothing were taken in studios for publicity purposes. Less formal pictures show her daily attire was a dress.

Martha also was a mother, having at least one son and one daughter, and seems to have loved her children dearly. When talking about her daughter to a reporter in 1896, Martha remarked, "She's all I've got to live fer; she's my only comfort."[6] Concerned about social appearances, she referred to her various male companions as "husbands." In addition, Martha most often worked in what were then regarded as female occupations. She generally made her living as cook, waitress, laundress, dance-hall girl, and prostitute. Occasionally, she operated her own business establishments, including restaurant, laundry, saloon, and bagnio. In later life, she earned a living by exploiting her national reputation, telling her story on stage and selling her autobiography and pictures.

Martha's downfall was alcohol. In fact, Martha's enduring poverty derived from her acute alcoholism rather than from lack of enterprise. From the first newspaper story describing her in 1875 to the last day of her life, drunkenness was a constant refrain. Although she struggled to end her dependence upon alcohol, she failed. Sadly, her friends, despite understanding the hold it had on her, joined her in binges and supplied her with liquor.

The bleak details of Martha's daily life stand in stark contrast to her colorful reputation. Indeed, Martha's career offers an outstanding case study in legend-making. Minor episodes were magnified into heroic adventures and generic tales were adjusted to fit Martha's circumstances until her reputed activities bore little resemblance to reality. Despite the divergence of the Calamity Jane legend from the experiences of Martha Canary, these two strands are interrelated: being a celebrity had an impact on Martha's attitudes and behavior, and because she was famous society responded to her differently than to other women in her circumstances.

What most separated Martha from her female companions in the West were her charisma and bold actions that gained attention from the press. Even before dime novels using her name appeared, she achieved considerable regional notoriety. But it was the appearance of her name in yellowback literature that led to her national fame. Although Martha occasionally denounced the dime novel stories about her as lies, she spun similar yarns herself, expanding her role in events she knew only indirectly.

Although Martha Canary accomplished little of historical significance during her career, she warrants a full-length biography as an icon in the history of the American West. In fact, an accurate, chronological narrative of Martha Canary's life is long overdue, if for no other reason than to correct the vast amount of misinformation circulating about her. This study attempts to fill that void. Because so many of the tales popularly associated with Calamity Jane lack foundation, it seems necessary to discuss the evidence contradicting them, even when it disrupts the story line. Sadly, after romantic adventures are removed, her story is mostly an account of uneventful daily life interrupted by drinking binges.

Martha's efforts to maintain family life and her employment in menial jobs relegated to women have been overshadowed by her image as a gun-toting, swearing, hard-drinking frontierswoman. Not surprisingly, histories of women in the West emphasizing monot-onous daily chores and the difficulty of managing family, home, and work, find Calamity Jane an unacceptable model. In fact, historian Glenda Riley says that writers who roman-ticize the lives of "famous women who acted more like men than women" suffer from the "Calamity Jane syndrome."[7] Evidence showing Martha to be a caring, if incompetent, par-ent working in commonplace jobs will require that Calamity's image as "bad woman" be modified.

However, to show that Martha's daily routine resembled that of other pioneer women is not the primary focus of this biography. Martha, like Buffalo Bill, is an anomaly in the history of the West. Her importance rests not on the similarity of her life to that of other frontier women, but on the manner in which her life was reshaped to fit a mythic struc-ture glorifying "the winning of the West."

Consequently, the growth of the Calamity Jane legend needs revisiting as much as the life of Martha Canary. In addition to narrating the story of her life, then, this biog-raphy attempts to account for her reputation as a frontier scout, relate the emergence of her purported relationship with Wild Bill Hickok, clarify how she became a dime novel heroine, and explain the development of her reputation for acts of charity and nursing. These important ingredients in her legend are discussed within the chronological frame-work of her life. Extensive quotations from newspapers and other contemporary sources are included not only to suggest who the real Martha Canary was, but to reveal the intricate process of legend-making. The story of the Calamity Jane legend extends far beyond Martha's death in 1903, for after that new tales were added to meet the demands of twentieth-century audiences.

Thus, *Calamity Jane: The Woman and the Legend* tells the intertwined stories of Martha Canary, pioneer woman, and Calamity Jane, legendary heroine. Despite many years of research, gaps in the evidence remain. New information continues to appear even as this manuscript goes to press. More letters, diary entries, newspaper notices, interviews, and photographs will add to Martha's story in the future, and new ingredients will be added to her legend. Nevertheless, sufficient records exist to write the relatively "complete and true biography" called for by the Livingston editor more than a hundred years ago.

CHAPTER ONE

Princeton, Missouri
1856–1864

Martha Canary, later known as Calamity Jane, was born in the vicinity of Princeton, Missouri, in 1856, perhaps on the first of May. That virtually every published account differs concerning these simple facts illustrates the confusion that exists about the life of this famous woman. Other dates and places of birth, and even different family names, are suggested. Various writers assert that she was born in 1844, 1847, 1851, 1852, or 1860, in Burlington, Iowa; La Salle, Illinois; Salt Lake City, Utah; or near Fort Laramie in Wyoming Territory; and that her name was Dalton, Somers, Coombs, or Conarray.[1] Indeed, one of her acquaintances believed that the name Canary became attached to Calamity Jane solely because her singing resembled that of a mule, or Rocky Mountain canary.[2]

Although Martha never concealed her identity, few of her contemporaries knew her by other than her nickname "Calamity Jane" prior to the appearance in 1896 of the *Life and Adventures of Calamity Jane, By Herself.* Several acquaintances, however, recorded her correct name and age prior to her autobiography's appearance. For example, newspaperman Thomas Newson, who interviewed her in the Black Hills in 1878, accurately identified her as Martha Canary, twenty-two years of age.[3]

Martha herself is to blame for two common inaccuracies in later accounts about her, the date of her birth and the spelling of her name. In *Life and Adventures* she related, "My maiden name was Marthy Cannary, was born in Princeton, Missouri, May 1st, 1852." Concerning her family, she added, "Father and mother natives of Ohio. Had two brothers and three sisters, I being the oldest of the children."[4] While generally correct (the May first birthdate will have to be accepted on faith), the year of her birth is demonstrably wrong. The census report of 1860 for Mercer County, Missouri, in addition to suggesting the correct spelling of her name, Martha Canary, clearly indicates that she was born in 1856, for she was four years old when the census was taken.[5] The census lists her father, R. W. Canary, age thirty-five in 1860, a farmer from Ohio; her mother, Charlotte, age twenty; and Martha, the eldest child, with a brother Cilus, age three, and a sister, Lana, one year old.

Charlotte would have been sixteen years old when Martha was born. Evidently, Martha's grandfather, James, seventy-two years of age, was living with the family, for his name appears next to theirs in the census. Biographers have failed to use this census to correct information in Martha's *Life and Adventures*, accepting her "facts" even while complaining that her autobiography is unreliable.[6]

Why Martha related an incorrect date of birth in her 1896 autobiography is a matter of conjecture. Posing as older may have begun when she was orphaned at about age twelve in an attempt to prevent authorities from ending her independence, or perhaps she adjusted her chronology because she appeared older than she was. The autobiography's misdating may, of course, result from simple carelessness on her part or by a ghostwriter.

Residents of Princeton have long been aware of her origins in their vicinity. When Calamity Jane died in 1903, the *Princeton Press* carried her obituary: "The dispatches in the daily papers last week announcing her death were read with especial interest by Mercer county citizens," stated the paper, "a great many of whom remembered her father and mother and a number of whom remembered the woman herself when she was a girl here."[7] The volume on Missouri in the American Guide Series asserts that Martha Canary is the "best known, perhaps, of early-day Princeton residents."[8] Today, a sign along the highway entrance to the town announces the annual celebration of "Calamity Jane Days," a two-day sales promotion sponsored by local businessmen. Not only are there sales at "calamitous" prices, but the event has included a parade, barbeque, dance, trail ride, flea market, car show, black powder turkey shoot, and athletic contests. Excitement is added by the "Shoot-Out Gang," and a Calamity Jane Melodrama held in the Cow Palace allows the crowd to cheer heroes and boo villains. Reigning over the festivities is the winner of the "Miss Calamity Jane" contest (her escort is, of course, "Wild Bill Hickok"), and there is even a "Little Miss Calamity Jane and Wild Bill Hickok" contest for three- and four-year-olds.[9]

Nevertheless, contemporary Princeton displays only sporadic interest in its famous product. A few miles north of Princeton is the "Calamity Jane Roadside Park" developed in 1957, the town's "first attempt to claim fame as the birthplace of this famous woman of the early days." Nearly another decade passed before a sign marked the site of the farmhouse in which she was born. For several years thereafter, the local historical society published a historical paper coinciding with the celebration of "Calamity Jane Days." In 1991, a dramatic presentation based on her life titled "Calamity Jane's Return, Who Says You Can't Go Back Home," was added to the festivities. However, today a visitor has to ask for directions to find the historical marker at her birthplace outside Princeton. Calamity's controversial reputation may play a part in the town's general lack of interest. There has been some debate whether naming a local woman "Miss Calamity Jane" is appropriate, given Calamity's reputation.[10]

Reminiscences by people in Princeton who remembered the Canary family were utilized by Duncan Aikman for his 1927 biography, *Calamity Jane and the Lady Wildcats*. A flamboyant writer more concerned with colorful narrative than careful documentation, Aikman nevertheless did considerable research. However, he erred frequently by accepting reminiscences collected sixty years after the events had occurred as established fact, and he embellished stories to fit his interpretation. Unfortunately, he failed to discover the census record listing Martha and, using the 1852 birthdate from her autobiography, invented stories of her childhood to conform with his assumption that she was twelve years old before her family left Princeton. For Aikman, Martha already was an "untutored rebel" whose creed was "to hell with the consequences." Allowed to roam as she wished by indulgent or inadequate parents, the tomboyish Martha learned all the "interesting, almost awe-inspiring secrets of country depravity." Aikman related a fictitious story of Martha successfully dodging corncobs thrown by local boys while she played in the woods like a young Amazon, cursing them with profanity usually reserved for adults.[11] In contrast, Martha relates little about her childhood in her autobiography, recording only that she "had a fondness for horses," adventure, and "outdoor exercise."[12]

Aikman mentioned in his biography that he had discovered documents proving the Canary family had resided in Princeton. Land records, he asserted, showed that Bob Canary purchased 180 acres of farmland for $500.[13] When later scholars could not locate these records, Aikman's credibility was questioned. Another biographer, Roberta Beed Sollid, noted that "if deeds for this property ever did exist, they are not on hand at the present," adding that Aikman "from a few recollections of old-timers spun an elaborate tale" about Martha and her family.[14]

The land records do exist, however, and with the 1860 census data and recently discovered probate court records dating from the death of Martha's grandfather, James, considerable documentation of the Canary family's residence in Princeton is available, reawakening interest in the reminiscences utilized by Aikman. The land records from the Office of the Recorder of Deeds for Mercer County suggest the Canary family probably arrived in 1856, for on April 28 that year, Hiram Overstreet sold 320 acres for $1,775 to James Canary, Martha's grandfather.[15] If the family arrived in Missouri near the date when this land was purchased, Charlotte would have been pregnant during their trip to Missouri, and Martha would have been born only two days after Robert's father acquired his land.

Shortly after he purchased his land, James sold 40 acres to Robert Southers (Sowders?) for $50 on November 19, 1856, and another 100 acres for $400 to James Kilgore on October 8, 1859. Southers and Kilgore were sons-in-law, married to Robert's sisters, Lanny and Mary. Evidently divesting himself of his land holdings, James on October 8, 1859, sold the remaining 180 acres of the land he purchased in 1856 for $500 to Robert and Charlotte Canary, Martha's parents. Having sold his land to his children for considerably less than he paid for it, James evidently retired and lived with Robert and Charlotte.

Martha's grandfather died a few years later. The probate court records for James Canary, dated June 30, 1862, list James' nine children who were heirs to his estate: Joseph and wife Sarah, with several children, residing in Washington County, Ohio;

Joshua, residence unknown; Levina, married to William N. Jones, Wheeling, Virginia; Abner and wife, Harriet Busly, with several children, living near Parkersburgh, Virginia; Lanny, married to James Kilgore, a carpenter from Ohio, Mercer County, Missouri; James Thornton and family, Mercer County, Missouri; Rachel Ann, married to Joseph Hague, living near McConnellsville, Ohio; Mary, married to Robert Southers, Mercer County, Missouri; and Robert Willson.[16]

These records show that, in addition to Robert and his father James, three of Robert's siblings resided in Mercer County. His sister Lana, age forty-one in 1860, and her husband James Kilgore, forty-seven, lived near Robert's family in Ravenna Township. Mary, thirty-six, married to Robert Southers, forty, also resided nearby with their two children, Loretta, nine; and Sorina, three. Living in Medicine Township was Robert's brother, James Thornton, referred to simply as Thornton perhaps to eliminate confusion with his father. Thornton filed on land from the government on May 3, 1858, indicating he may have arrived in Missouri later than the others.[17] The 1860 census indicates Thornton was forty, a farmer, and married to thirty-seven-year-old Delila. Eight children are listed, including daughters Victoria, fifteen; Tabitha, fourteen; E. J., twelve; Candis, five; and S. V., two; and sons, W. E., eleven; J. M., seven; and G. W., five months.[18] The Thornton Canary family evidently resided in the Princeton area long after Calamity became a national celebrity, finally selling their land on January 18, 1882, and moving to Midvale, Idaho. The Southers and Kilgore families evidently remained in Missouri.[19]

Prior to their migration to Missouri in the 1850s, the Canary families were listed regularly in Ohio census reports. The 1850 census from Malaga Township, Monroe County, Ohio, lists James Canary, age sixty-two. With him lived his wife, Sarah, fifty-six, as well as Joshua, thirty-six, and Robert, twenty-five, these sons evidently single and living at home. Residing nearby was Thornton Canary, age thirty, with his wife Delilah, age twenty-seven, and four children. James Kilgore and Lanny were listed in the census immediately after the Thornton Canary family.[20] Clearly these families were neighbors in Ohio and probably remained in close proximity during their westward migration.

Further back in time, records provide less information, but the 1820, 1830, and 1840 censuses all report James Canary living in Malaga Township, Monroe County, Ohio. The township was organized in 1820, when James Canary was first reported there by the census.[21] Other Canary families resided throughout Ohio, some perhaps brothers and cousins of James. These census records indicate the Canary family had been long-time residents of Ohio before their trek to Missouri. Their location prior to 1820 is uncertain, but James Canary's place of origin in the 1850 census, indistinctly written, appears to be Virginia, where he would have been born in 1788. The 1830 census indicates a man between seventy and eighty years of age living with James, perhaps his father. No other contemporary records of the family from Malaga Township have yet been located.

Monroe County, Ohio, was remote and predominantly rural. In 1840, during the Canary family's residence there, the county's population was 18,544, and Malaga Township, situated in the northwest portion, had but 1,443 residents. The county seat, Woodsfield, had 262 inhabitants, causing visitor Henry Howe to conclude that it was "much out of the world." In fact, Howe thought the "entire county was quite primitive." Its residents mostly lived in cabins, which had the blessing of "saving many the worry of having so much to look after." Although the county was "away from all travel, except on the river fringe," according to Woodsfield resident Daniel Wire, its people were "generous, warm-hearted and benevolent." Monroe County was called "Dark Monroe" by Whigs, said Howe, because of its "stunning Democratic majorities." Indeed, said Wire, its people were so devoutly democratic that they allowed for "no distinction in society, no aristocratic lines drawn between the upper and lower classes."[22] From this distinctly rural and egalitarian region, the Canarys moved to an area in Missouri similarly remote from population centers.

The Canary families' migration from Ohio to Missouri in the 1850s made them typical rather than exceptional. Because there are no extant diaries or reminiscences by the Canarys, the motivation for their move from Ohio cannot be determined, but during this period there was a great population upheaval from the Old Northwest. Like others, they probably moved to improve their livelihood, enticed by stories of better and cheaper land in the West. Perhaps the death of James's wife, Sarah, added to their willingness to depart. Persistent rumors that the Canarys stopped in Iowa before settling in Missouri evidently are true. One of Thornton's children was born in Iowa, suggesting he lived there for a while. Census records also indicate James and Lanny Kilgore resided in Polk County, Iowa, between 1852 and 1856. More importantly, a June 14, 1855, Polk County marriage record for Robert W. Canary and Charlotte M. Burge was recently discovered. According to the 1850 census, the Burge family had lived in Iowa for some time. Henry and Elizabeth Burge, ages fifty-four and fifty-three, originally were from Pennsylvania, and had six children: Gideon, nineteen; Benjamin, seventeen; Andrew, fifteen; Harriet, thirteen; Charlotte, ten; and Elizabeth, eight. Although the eldest four children were born in Ohio, Charlotte was born in Illinois and Elizabeth in Iowa, suggesting the Burge family's progressive migration across the country.[23] Evidently, Charlotte and Robert met during the Canarys' brief sojourn in Iowa and were married when Charlotte was fifteen or sixteen years of age.

James Canary, accompanied by several of his children, left Iowa at least by 1856, arriving in nearby Missouri during Mercer County's early settlement period. Mercer County lies along the northern border of Missouri, about midpoint from east to west. No major river is located in the county, but there are numerous valleys with small creeks bounded, now as then, by elm, oak, hickory, ash, and beech trees that provide building material and fuel, while ridges between the streams provide prairie farmland. Besides raising livestock, early farmers grew corn, oats, wheat, and hay, and occasionally tobacco, potatoes, and sorghum for molasses. Although the first settlers arrived in Mercer County in 1837, the county's remote location caused it to be peopled somewhat slowly. Local histories suggest the slavery issue played a part in this: northern migrants preferred non-slave Iowa, while southern landseekers tended to avoid northern Missouri because of its proximity to a free state.[24] Perhaps it was to the liking of the Canarys because, like Monroe County in Ohio, Mercer County was comfortably rural. Mercer County's population was only 2,691 in 1850, and Princeton, the county seat, was not incorporated until 1853. The county's population grew to 9,300 by 1860. Ravenna Township, where James Canary located, was among the last to be populated; it was primarily prairie, and most settlers preferred timbered areas.[25]

A local resident, J. E. Fuller, recalled that Robert and his young wife, Charlotte, initially lived in a small store building near the current location of the Mercer County courthouse where, some believe, Martha may have been born.[26] No birth records were kept at that time, and reminiscences cannot be used to establish precisely Martha's birthplace. The comment in a local newspaper that "the Canary family moved several times during the years they spent in Mercer County, and that fact has given rise to disagreements as to where they lived," is an appropriate conclusion.[27] That there were several Canary families may have furthered confusion. It is possible that the young family lived in town as James finalized his land purchase, but the historical marker commemorating Martha's birth is located about five miles east of Princeton at the farm later belonging to Joseph T. Pickett; this was the land purchased by Robert from his father in 1859.

Robert Canary's young family probably lived at first with James. "The house where she [Martha] was said to have been born was a large log house with rooms upstairs," wrote local reporter Doris Thompson. Mercer County resident Elson McClaren remembered that the house was vacant when he was a boy, and that it "was later used as a corn crib. The house stood until it rotted down." Only a few decades ago, logs and stones from the Canary house still could be found and "buttons, pieces of China and an 1850 penny" were discovered there by Pickett family members.[28]

The list of James Canary's property compiled for the probate court after his death in 1862 indicates sufficient holdings for a decent livelihood. There were three horses, one a mare with a colt; a pair of oxen; three cows with calves, a yearling steer and a yearling heifer; eleven sheep; and twelve hogs. In addition to this livestock, James owned two wagons, a breaking plow, a long-handled shovel, a breakfast table, two bedsteads, two feather beds, a stove, a chest, a windmill, a sausage grinder, and other miscellaneous equipment. Interestingly, given his lack of education, James owned "One Family Bible" and "one large Testament."[29] Although this property suggests Martha's childhood environment was similar to that of other rural families, her parents may not have been typical.

Robert and Charlotte made a lasting impression in the county, being "a family the neighbors were not likely to forget," reported Doris Thompson in 1957, adding that many entertaining stories "are still related over and over."[30] These include the same colorful local accounts embellished by biographer Duncan Aikman thirty years earlier. Mrs. William Collings said that Charlotte Canary shocked the neighbors with her cigar smoking, drinking, and cursing. Once she rode past the Collings home with some red calico, and, according to Aikman, threw it to Mrs. Collings, telling her to "take that and make a dress for your damn bastard."[31] Understandably, Bob and Charlotte's relatives were relieved when the ill-behaved family left Princeton a few years later. One local historian reported in 1970 that Bob and Charlotte's descendants, still embarassed, "carefully avoid" talking about them.[32]

One of these relatives, Thornton's wife Delila, evidently supplied derogatory stories about Charlotte to her friends, who in turn told them to Aikman. Delila purportedly said that Bob Canary discovered his future wife in an Ohio bawdy house when she was in her early teens. In Aikman's version of Delila's story, Robert, "an innocent and not too shrewd farm boy" who was "bedazzled by Charlotte's beauty," hoped "to reform her," but obviously failed in his mission. Bob first worked for his father on the farm in Mercer County, Aikman added, and was considered to be lazy and dependent.[33] Local reminiscences report that Charlotte "laughed at her weak husband, neglected her children, and continued her trips to town where she sought the saloons and the company of rough men."[34] Aikman believed Charlotte's behavior later was imitated by her famous daughter. But these stories about Charlotte and Robert by hostile relatives and gossipy acquaintances must be accepted cautiously. Still, they are more convincing than accounts by other descendants who claim that Robert was a military chaplain and Methodist minister.[35] No reliable evidence indicates Robert was other than a farmer.

Perhaps reminiscences overstate Robert's laziness as well. His real estate and personal property were listed in the 1860 census at $1,500 and $400, respectively, significantly above James Kilgore's $300 and $400, and comparable to the estates of other successful neighbors. Bob, some reported, "did the best he could for his children," and Mrs. Eliza Pickett recalled Martha "as a nice child who played with the Pickett children."[36] Local histories suggest Martha was sent to a local "subscription school." If so, she likely received little support for her education at home; her mother was illiterate, as were her grandfather James and aunts Lana and Mary. Nevertheless, Winfield Keith remembered her presence in school, though her attendance must have been brief because the family left the area shortly after the farm was sold in 1862, when Martha was only six.[37]

Even though these documents and reminiscences must be interpreted carefully, evidence supports Martha's statements in her *Life and Adventures* that her birthplace was Princeton, that her family's point of origin was Ohio, and that she was the eldest child. Accounts of Calamity Jane offering different places of origin, birth dates, and family names can be dismissed. However, because most accounts of Martha include considerable misinformation on these matters, it may be worthwhile to discuss the most frequently cited versions and note their derivation. Such a digression may clarify why the identity of Calamity Jane has been so muddled in biographical sketches.

The most widespread of the inaccurate accounts of Calamity Jane's origins are the Coombs, Dalton, and Conarray versions. The earliest of these appeared in 1877, when Dr. A. R. Hendricks of Des Moines, Iowa, told a correspondent that he knew Calamity's father, B. W. Coombs, for many years pastor of the First Baptist Church in Burlington, Iowa. The doctor asserted that Calamity, the youngest of four children, was born in 1847, and had a sister and two brothers. Not surprisingly, modern researchers have discovered no record of a Coombs family in Burlington.[38] Why Hendricks told the story cannot be determined; perhaps he was spinning a yarn to gain attention. In any event, what better romantic suggestion than having the notorious Calamity Jane be a minister's daughter, now reduced by circumstances to breaking accepted moral codes.

Martha learned of Hendricks' account of her origins, and in 1878 told writer Horatio N. Maguire that she was angry about reports that she was a horse thief, highway woman, card sharp, and minister's daughter, and declared that "these are false, the last especially."[39] Despite Calamity's frustration, the minister's daughter story persisted. In fact, in a twisted rewrite of Maguire's interview with Calamity, a *Literary Digest* article in 1925 concluded that claims that Calamity Jane was a highway woman, a three-card monte sharp, and a horse thief were wrong, but the claim that she was a minister's daughter "is authentic."[40] Suggestions that Calamity's father was a minister continue to appear even today in accounts of her life.

A more widely circulated false origin story is the "Dalton" version. It claims that Calamity Jane was Jane Dalton, born near Fort Laramie, Wyoming, in 1860. The story appeared in numerous books by individuals personally acquainted with Calamity Jane, including Harry (Sam) Young, Valentine T. McGillycuddy, Estelline Bennett, and Dora Du Fran, and therefore gained credibility.[41] Calamity's father, these accounts suggest, was an enlisted soldier named Dalton whose service at Fort Laramie ended in 1861. He then moved to a "stream called the La Bontie, 120 miles from Fort Laramie," where he was killed in an attack by Indians. His wife, badly wounded, managed to carry their infant daughter to Fort Laramie, but after reaching the post, died. The infant was adopted by Sergeant Bassett of Company I, Fourteenth Infantry, and his wife, and they named her "Calamity" because of her calamitous beginnings. Jane became the pet of the soldiers at Fort Laramie, and in 1875 accompanied them on an expedition to the Black Hills that included Young and McGillycuddy among its members.[42]

It is a wonderfully romantic tale, but completely in disagreement with Calamity's own account of her origins and without documentary support. Too much traffic passed through Fort Laramie for her to have gone unnoticed there for more than a decade.[43] Additionally, biographers J. Leonard Jennewein and Roberta Beed Sollid long ago exposed plagiarism in comparing the nearly verbatim reminiscences by Young and McGillycuddy, which had been assumed to be independent accounts. Young, for example, relates that Mrs. Dalton "was shot in the eye with an arrow, destroying her sight" in that eye. "Traveling nights and hiding by day, subsisting on weeds and roots, she finally managed to reach Fort Laramie in eight days, a mere skeleton of her former self, her clothing torn in shreds. Before medical aid could be procured, she expired." McGillycuddy similarly asserts that Mrs. Dalton, after being "shot in the eye with an arrow" which destroyed half of her vision, escaped with her infant on her back, and by "travelling nights and hiding by day, subsisting on weeds and roots, she finally managed to reach Fort Laramie in eight days, a mere skeleton of her former self, and in a short time expired."[44]

Young, whose account appeared in 1915, first published the tale; Valentine T. McGillycuddy repeated it without attribution in a letter to the *Rapid City Journal* in October 1924. Julia McGillycuddy, who in 1941 used the story in her account of her husband's life, must be wrong in stating that he learned the Dalton story from Colonel Dodge in 1875. Though Young, McGillycuddy, and Dodge all met Calamity Jane when she accompanied the Black

Hills expedition in 1875, and perhaps then heard the Dalton tale, McGillycuddy clearly borrowed Young's account for his 1924 letter: the wording is derivative.[45]

But if Young first related the tale, McGillycuddy gave it respectability. From his letter, and Julia McGillycuddy's later book, the Dalton story entered a variety of other works. Doane Robinson, who presided over the South Dakota State Historical Society for a generation, included the Dalton version in his *Encyclopedia of South Dakota* (1925). His son, Will Robinson, who succeeded as the head of the Society, responded with the Dalton story to all inquiries about Calamity's origins for another generation.[46]

The other disseminations of the Dalton story, which appeared to confirm its genuineness, likewise were derived from Young and McGillycuddy. Estelline Bennett, an experienced journalist and author of *Old Deadwood Days* (1928), placed the story for reasons of style in the mouth of her uncle at a dinner conversation. Claiming that she was reporting a discussion taking place in 1895, and that an old bullwhacker (Young?) was the source of the tale told by her uncle, Bennett includes the Young-McGillycuddy story among tales derived from other Black Hills histories, making the invented conversation appear authentic.[47] Likewise, Dora Du Fran utilized McGillycuddy's 1924 letter, as her account of Jane Dalton proves: "The baby was left to the care of the soldiers' wives, and like Topsy, 'she just growed,'" wrote Du Fran. McGillycuddy in his 1924 letter had written, "She was something like Topsy in Uncle Tom's cabin, she was not exactly raised she growed."[48] Thus, the McGillycuddy, Bennett, and Du Fran accounts of Calamity's birth all have a common derivation, from Harry (Sam) Young. Whether the imaginative Young invented the story or reported a frontier tale he remembered from his experiences in 1875 cannot be determined.

A third oft-repeated version of Calamity's origins, suggesting she was Martha Jane Conarray, came from the pen of Clarence Paine. The author of several serious articles on Calamity Jane and the only early researcher to discover the existence of the 1860 Mercer County census listing the Canary family, Paine refused to accept the census information indicating that Robert and Charlotte were Martha's parents because the 1856 birthdate seemed to him too late.[49] Finding another family in Mercer County with a similar name, Conarray, Paine concluded this might be a misspelling of Canary made by the census recorder. No father was listed, but Abigail, the mother, aged forty and from Tennessee, had two daughters: M. J., sixteen; and E. E., seven.[50] The initials M. J. were beguiling to Paine, perhaps standing for Martha Jane. Though "M.J." was born in Illinois rather than Missouri, Paine speculated that Abigail might have moved her family to Princeton during the child's infancy, and Martha would have believed she was born there. Like the Robert Canary family, the Conarrays lived on a farm, attested by the inclusion with them in the census report of W. H. Walker, age seventeen, as farm laborer.

If M. J. Conarray is interpreted to be Calamity Jane, she was born in 1844, not 1852 as she stated in her *Life and Adventures*. Paine suggested the age discrepancy probably occurred because no woman would admit to her real age; thus, it would not be unusual that Calamity was eight years older than she reported. In addition, Paine believed photographs taken of Calamity in 1903, the year of her death, showed a woman more likely fifty-nine than a mere forty-seven.[51] But prolonged illness and alcoholism had taken their toll on Calamity by 1903, and Paine's point about photographic evidence is mere inference. As for his belief that the initials M. J. more readily explain her nickname "Calamity Jane," there is no evidence "Jane" ever was part of her given name. Frontier nicknames frequently were created without regard to given names. In fact, other census records of the Conarray family indicate the initials "M. J." stood for Margaret J., not Martha Jane, and that Conarray may have been Connoway.[52]

Not surprisingly, later writers were confused by these varied accounts of Calamity Jane's origins. One biographer concluded that Calamity's birthplace, birthdate, and family name never could be determined with certainty, and told her readers, "Take 'yer choice.'"[53] However, documentary evidence about the Canary family, in agreement with information in Calamity Jane's *Life and Adventures*, allows the historian to conclude beyond a reasonable doubt that Martha Canary was born in 1856 in Mercer County, Missouri.

The years when the Canary family lived in Missouri were troublesome times. Relations between the North and South reached a crisis stage, and biographer Aikman learned from informants that Charlotte was a "secesh." He believed there may have been difficulty between the Canarys and their pro-Union neighbors.[54] No evidence exists to support this assertion, however. Thornton Canary, who remained in Missouri throughout the Civil War period, evidently had no problems with his neighbors despite his brief enlistment in the state militia in 1861 when Missouri allied with the Confederate States.[55] Martha mentioned nothing in her autobiography about the Civil War or any problems concerning slavery and secession, simply reporting that in 1865 the family departed for Montana. Once again she was inaccurate in her chronology; the family left a year or two earlier.

The *Princeton Press*, upon Martha's death in 1903, recalled that Bob and Charlotte left in 1864, moving briefly to Appanoose County, Iowa, from whence they departed "to the gold fields of Montana."[56] The mining stampede to Montana began after gold was discovered in 1863 at Alder Gulch. The Montana strike was but the most recent installment in the mining rushes that had repeatedly pushed population westward, including those to California in 1849, Colorado in 1858–59, Nevada in 1859, British Columbia in 1857, and Idaho in 1860. Inevitably, these discoveries lured thousands of farmers and laborers from their homes, though seldom did they find gold or lucrative employment.

The Canary family's westward migration again would be typical. Missourians were among the largest groups departing for the Montana gold fields.[57] It is likely their primary motivation for leaving Missouri was the hope for easy wealth and adventure. However, one family recollection disagrees. Tobe Borner, the son of Martha's sister, Lena Canary, claimed that Robert became a Mormon and decided to migrate to Salt Lake City. In an embellished version of Borner's story, combined with other misinformation, biographer Glenn Clairmonte described the family's move to Kirksville, Missouri, where Robert became a minister and decided to move his family to Salt Lake City to live among the Mormons so that young Martha could get a good education. Charlotte, in Clairmonte's account, was a dutiful housewife tending the children and her garden, and only reluctantly agreed to Robert's decision to leave Missouri.[58]

Documents suggest a different motivation for Robert's decision to leave Princeton between 1862 and 1864. Land records indicate that on December 20, 1862, Robert and Charlotte sold to James Brown, for no consideration in cash, the 180 acres in Mercer County they had purchased from James Canary. In fact, Robert and Charlotte were involved in legal difficulties and had received a summons to appear in court. James Canary, who evidently died on April 12, 1862, left no will, and Hannibal Armstrong was appointed executor of the estate. He filed suit against Robert on November 4. According to court records, Robert had borrowed $600 from James in 1861, which he had never repaid. In addition, he had "by means unknown to the Plaintiff" taken possession of "Specie bank notes checks etc." valued at $417.68 and refused to turn them over to Armstrong. Finally, Robert refused to relinquish livestock, equipment, and household property valued by Armstrong at $490.50.

Accordingly, the circuit court ordered Sheriff W. B. Rogers to summon Robert to court for the March 1863 term, which the sheriff reported he did on January 2, 1863. Between the time Armstrong submitted his case to court and the summons was delivered, Robert sold his land. The March circuit court records indicate he did not appear, and the court ruled that if he did not show up by the September term, he would lose by default. Documents indicate he once again failed to appear, and it is likely he had left Missouri. Although probably a formality because there was no way to collect the money, Armstrong, on behalf of the heirs, was awarded $630.75 by the court. This probably was based on the $600 Robert had borrowed, plus interest. The documents do not mention what happened to the specie bank notes and property; perhaps they were secured earlier.[59]

Although court records suggest Robert was dishonest, this is only one of several possibilities. Perhaps he was a dutiful son who for years helped his father and expected to retain a major portion of the estate after his father's death, only to have it taken from his hands by lack of a will. We probably will never know whether he borrowed money from his father to purchase needed livestock or equipment, or whether Robert and Charlotte neglected their farm and spent James's cash in Princeton saloons. It does seem suspicious that they left Mercer County suddenly, and absconding without repaying funds owed to other family members would explain the hostility displayed in later family stories told about Robert and Charlotte.

Robert and Charlotte's departure from Princeton probably occurred in the spring of 1863. It is possible the family lingered a year in Iowa, as the Princeton newspaper later recalled, perhaps living with friends or relatives. Having found it necessary to leave, and lured by opportunity for wealth in the West, the Canary family in 1864 began its long journey to the Montana gold fields. This uprooting experience ultimately resulted in Martha's becoming an orphan far removed from relatives, friends, and familiar childhood environment.

CHAPTER TWO

To Montana and Wyoming
1864–1874

During the ten years after the Canary family departed from Missouri, Martha became an orphan and adopted habits of drinking, smoking, cursing, and wearing male clothing that became her legendary trademarks. At some point Martha also was given her famous nickname. Although this period was decisive in her character formation, few documents mention her, and surviving reminiscences are difficult to substantiate. Worse, Martha's autobiography often is unreliable, including invented episodes designed to enhance her heroic reputation. Still, sufficient evidence exists to develop an outline of her activities during these critical years.

"In 1865 we emigrated from our homes in Missouri by the overland route to Virginia City, Montana," Martha recalled in her *Life and Adventures*, "taking five months to make the journey."[1] Most likely it was in 1864, not 1865, that the Canary family left, probably joining a wagon train comprised of other midwesterners attracted to the Montana gold discoveries. No contemporary documents confirm their presence with any known group or their route. Martha, however, offered a general description of their journey: "I remember many occurrences on the journey from Missouri to Montana," she said, mentioning crossing flooded streams and lowering wagons over cliffs with ropes. "The greater part of my time was spent in hunting with the men and hunters of the party, in fact I was at all times with the men when there was excitement and adventures to be had." Martha became, in her words, "a fearless rider."[2] The fact that she was eight years old (assuming an 1856 birth and an overland trip in 1864) does not square with the impression created by writers that she was then an attractive young woman.

Martha's family typified westward-bound travelers along the overland trail. Most emigrants were young parents with children under fifteen, from Missouri or its neighboring states, farmers, and relatively poor. It would have been difficult for Martha's parents to secure adequate finances to make the trip. Traveling westward was expensive, the essential outfit for a family of four costing nearly $600.[3]

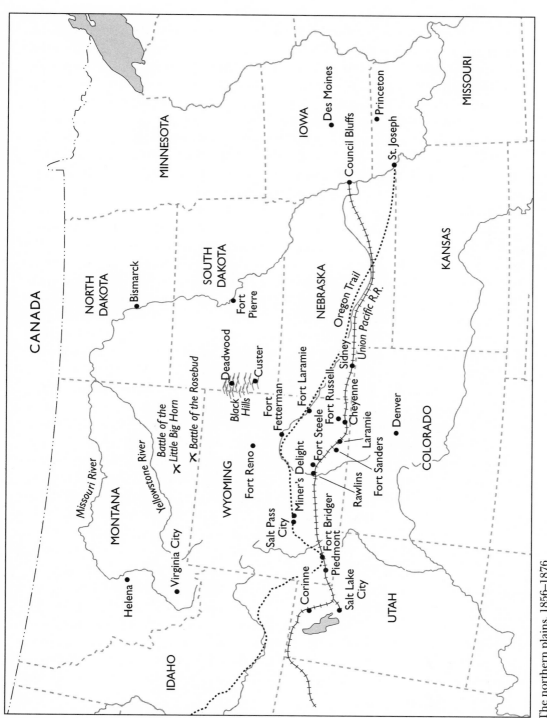

The northern plains, 1856–1876

Travelers to the Montana gold fields usually followed the overland trail along the North Platte River to Fort Laramie in Wyoming, through South Pass to Salt Lake City, Utah, and then northward to Montana. Boney Earnest, who served as a scout for the army at Fort Steele and later resided in Carbon and Natrona counties in Wyoming, recalled meeting the Canary family while they tarried at Fort Steele for about a week. He learned from Martha's father that the family was very poor, but "would go where the mining was, get a claim, and make some money." Boney said he killed an antelope for them before they pulled out for Salt Lake City and the Montana gold fields. Although important, Boney's reminiscence must be accepted with caution: he misdated their meeting (he said 1872 rather than 1864), recalled that Martha was about fifteen years old (she was eight), and remembered that the family included two other girls (there should also have been boys).[4] Nevertheless, it is likely he met the Canary family. Perhaps he confused details of his 1864 meeting with later encounters he had with Martha.

Although no further accounts mention the Canary family, other travelers to the Montana gold fields recorded travel experiences probably similar to theirs. Twenty-five-year-old Sarah Raymond maintained a diary during the westward journey with her parents in 1865. Despite their age differences, Sarah's narrative is useful to suggest what Martha's trip may have been like. The primary motivation of the Raymonds for emigrating was their hope for a better economic future, but others in their company left Missouri because of the turmoil caused by the Civil War. Whatever their motives, many midwesterners were traveling westward. Over five thousand freight wagons passed Fort Kearny in a six-week period, leading Sarah to contemplate, "wagons, wagons, wagons."

Martha recalled that the journey took five months. Sarah's took somewhat over four. The westward trip at times was difficult and dangerous. Like Martha, Sarah recalled flooded streams, and once she impressively drove the family's wagon across a swollen river. Never, however, did Sarah's wagon driving and horseback riding impinge on her feminine qualities, and men frequently asked to accompany her during the trip. On their wagon train, Sarah claimed, no profanity by the men was allowed, and behavior was always circumspect. Conversely, Sarah observed that many women accompanying other wagon trains were guilty of unladylike behavior, which did not set well with her.

From Sarah's viewpoint, except for one occasion when some rough Missourians asked to join their train, the trip raised few serious concerns. She found the journey to be comparable to an enjoyable picnic and camping excursion. Sometimes she rode with friends ahead or behind the wagon train, enjoying the freedom to visit. Forgetting the ominous possibility of Indian attacks, she even left the wagon train to ride alone and look at the beautiful scenery.[5] If twenty-five-year-old Sarah Raymond found the trip an enjoyable adventure, how much more exciting for the carefree eight-year-old Martha? Perhaps Martha's pleasant experiences, remembered by her almost thirty years later, obscured less enjoyable tasks: as the eldest child, she may have been expected to care for younger siblings.

Upon her arrival in Montana, Sarah Raymond was unimpressed with the mining settlement of Virginia City: "It is the shabbiest town I ever saw, not a really good house in it."

The Raymonds rented a log cabin with two rooms for eight dollars a month. She observed tremendous activity, like "bees around a hive," in Alder Gulch: "It seemed that not one of that great multitude stopped for one instant shoveling and wheeling dirt, passing and repassing each other without a hitch. It made me tired to look at them."[6] Into this hive of activity, a year earlier, young Martha had arrived with her parents and siblings.

In her autobiography, Martha did not discuss any of the family's activities in the Montana gold fields. However, the Canary family made an appearance in the pages of the Virginia City newspaper on December 31, 1864. They clearly had fallen on hard times: "Three little girls, who state their name to be Canary, appeared at the door of Mr. Fergus, on Idaho street, soliciting charity," the paper reported. Perhaps they were aware that James Fergus was one of the commissioners of Madison County in charge of providing for the poor. "The ages of the two elder ones were about ten and twelve respectively," the journalist continued, and "the eldest carried in her arms her infant sister, a baby of about 12 months of age." The eldest undoubtedly was Martha, though she was not yet nine. The reporter understandably might have overestimated her years, hardened as she was by a frontier journey and caring for an infant. The children were poorly dressed, each having only "a calico slip" for protection from harsh winter conditions. Fortunately, "Mrs. Fergus, Mrs. Castner, and Mrs. Moon kindly provided them with food and some clothing." The children then "returned to Nevada," a mining camp just below Virginia City, "where they have existed for some time."[7]

Concerning Robert and Charlotte, the newspaper was less than sympathetic. They were described as "inhuman brutes who have deserted their poor, unfortunate children" and the situation was a "most flagrant and wanton instance of unnatural conduct on the part of parents." The father, it continued, "is a gambler in Nevada," and the mother, who was "last seen in town, at Dr. Byam's office, a day or two since," was "a woman of the lowest grade." Hoping "Divine anger will overtake them sooner or later," the reporter suggested in the meantime that human laws be "applied to their case, and stern justice meted out to the offenders."[8]

There is no evidence that legal action was taken against Martha's parents. In fact, it cannot be absolutely proven that the newspaper was describing her family since it cites no given names. However, there are too many coincidences to allow dismissal. Martha said they were there, and the reference to her mother as "a woman of the lowest grade" agrees with hostile Princeton reminiscences. The Canary family left Missouri with few financial resources, and their destitution would have been exacerbated by extreme winter conditions in 1864–65 in Montana that caused prices of food to skyrocket. As the meager savings of many migrants quickly dwindled, they were driven to extraordinary efforts to provide satisfactory food and clothing for their families.[9]

Somehow the Canary family survived, although they evidently left Virginia City. Martha said they remained in the Montana mining camps until the spring of 1866, when her mother died in Blackfoot City, a mining settlement north of Alder Gulch. Martha would have been nine or ten when Charlotte died, precisely what she told a reporter thirty years later.[10] According to a 1903 Deadwood newspaper, older residents remembered her "as a little girl in Montana," and claimed "her mother was a washer woman at Blackfoot, Montana, for a long time."[11] Similarly, frontiersman Ben Arnold recalled seeing Martha in Montana, "a girl of thirteen," he estimated, whose "mother being poor . . . took in washing from the miners." Martha "gathered and delivered laundry for her mother, and many knew her as an attractive, vivacious girl." Arnold thought she "was led astray . . . by a man whose name one of the gold gulches still bears," a suggestive statement perhaps meant to explain later dissolute activities.[12]

Although evidence confirms Martha's claims to have traveled to the Montana mining camps with her parents in 1864–66, no documents support the legendary tales about her activities there that were formulated long after her death. Tom Brown, a miner who later became a successful businessman in South Dakota, inaccurately described her as about twenty or twenty-two years old in 1866 when he saw her robbing a grocery store to obtain food for sick miners she was nursing.[13] This story, with its Robin Hood aspect, fits neither her age nor her situation in 1866.

Another unbelievable story told about Martha, deemed significant by biographer Aikman, was told by Charles W. Bocker of Laramie, Wyoming. Bocker claimed he met Calamity Jane in 1865 in West Bannack, Montana, where she was operating a gambling and prostitution establishment in partnership with Madame Mustache. According to Bocker, when he went for water at a nearby creek, Calamity laughed at him because his bucket leaked badly. She brought him a new bucket and some doughnuts, and purchased eggs and salt from him.[14] At that time, Martha would have been only nine years old. Possibly Bocker was recalling an incident that occurred many years later, or perhaps another woman nicknamed Calamity Jane was in business there. It is possible, too, the story was wholly invented.

Aikman told one other unsubstantiated tale recounting the Canary family's Montana years, and claimed Calamity Jane herself told the story. In this version, Robert died in Montana, but Charlotte did not, and she became Madame Canary, running "an enticing bagnio in town by the subtle name of 'The Bird Cage.'" Later, he said, Charlotte remarried and lived in Salt Lake City.[15] No evidence has been found of a house of prostitution in Montana called "The Bird Cage," or of Charlotte in Salt Lake City, and there is little reason to disbelieve Martha's published statement that her mother died in Montana.

Instead, after her mother's death, Martha recalled in *Life and Adventures,* her father took the family to Utah, "arriving at Salt Lake City during the summer" of 1866. Perhaps Robert intended to return to Missouri. "Remained in Utah until 1867, where my father died," said Martha, and "then went to Fort Bridger, Wyoming Territory." No record of Robert Canary's death has been located. Although Martha did not relate what happened to her siblings, it is surmised that those who survived were adopted by families in the Salt Lake City or Fort Bridger region. Martha may have been adopted as well, but soon was on her own. After remaining at Fort Bridger for a while, Martha explained that she "then went to Piedmont, Wyoming, with U.P. Railway."[16]

If there are any remaining doubts that Martha's *Life and Adventures* includes reliable biographical information, they should be stifled by information in a special 1869 Carter

County (Wyoming) census. Martha Canary's name appears in its list of Piedmont residents. According to the document, she had been in Wyoming for five months. Although Missouri is correctly listed as her birthplace, Martha's age is given as fifteen (she would have been thirteen). No other members of the Canary family are listed.[17]

Piedmont at first seems an unlikely destination for a young woman. Although the site experienced a brief boom period, George Crofutt's 1871 tourist's guide for the transcontinental railroad describes Piedmont Station, resting at an altitude of 7,123 feet, as "unimportant," adding that "the country is rough and broken."[18] Little is known of Martha's life there, but an eighty-four-year-old resident of Scottsbluff, Nebraska, identified only as Mr. Andrews, reminisced in 1954 that his mother ran a boarding house in Piedmont and in about 1871 hired fourteen- or fifteen-year-old Martha "to tend me." Unfortunately, she "spent most evenings dancing with soldiers and, finally a neighbor told of seeing her dressed in a soldier's uniform at some party. Mother blew up and fired her." Andrews identified his stepfather, Edward Alton, as the source for his information.[19] In the 1869 Piedmont census, the names of Edward and Emma Alton, both thirty-one years of age, appear near that of Martha Canary, lending credibility to Andrews's claims. A Wyoming rancher, James Regan, confirmed the story, adding that Ed Alton had been a soldier at Fort Bridger. Regan, who remembered meeting Martha at Fort Bridger and in Piedmont, said Mrs. Alton took care of Martha until she was fourteen.[20] Martha said little about this period in her life, but in 1901 a journalist who interviewed her reported that, after her parents died, "she fell into the hands of an old woman, from whom she ran away, attaching herself to an army post."[21]

There are other possibilities, however, concerning the identity of Martha's temporary custodian. In one improbable version, she was "half adopted by the soldiers" not in Wyoming but in Butte, Montana, and they "paid an old woman to look after her." This woman neglected her, so Martha began frequenting Butte's saloons, singing to the soldiers while perched on the bar. There she "learned to drink and to swear and to play cards until the men were afraid to compete with her."[22]

Perhaps more reliable is an account describing Martha during the period between her father's death and her arrival in Piedmont. According to this story, circulating in 1885 from Lander, Wyoming, Martha Canary, age eleven, lived briefly with Major Patrick A. Gallagher and his wife, Frances, in Miner's Delight, Wyoming Territory. They "picked up the girl as they passed through Fort Bridger." In this report, "the youngster knew nothing of her parents and was a stray from infancy. She was pretty and vivacious but in a short time her escapades shocked the whole settlement." Because the Gallaghers were unable to control her, "the miners took up a collection and sent her to the railroad," where she survived on her own among "the most degenerate railroad workers and other elements of the motley population."[23]

The Gallaghers did indeed reside in Miner's Delight in 1868. Patrick Gallagher first arrived in Wyoming in the fall of 1863 in command of troops at Fort Bridger, then moved to Salt Lake City. In September 1867, he filed a claim on the Miner's Delight lode in the Wind River Mountains in western Wyoming as a gold rush commenced. As many as four or five thousand people hurried to that region by the summer of 1868 and new mining communities appeared, beginning with South Pass City, and shortly afterwards, Miner's Delight. The newspaper in April 1868 reported that Major Gallagher was en route from Salt Lake to the mines with a train of supplies, and when he returned in June, it said that he carried $15,000 in gold dust with him. In July, Gallagher again traveled to Hamilton City, as the settlement of Miner's Delight came to be called, this time accompanied by his wife. However, neither the journalist for the *Sweetwater Mines* who accompanied the Gallaghers, nor correspondent James Chisholm of the *Chicago Tribune* who visited them that September, mentioned an orphan with them.[24] Even so, Martha may have met the Gallaghers at Fort Bridger, accompanied them to Miner's Delight, and then left for Piedmont.

Martha struck Wyoming at a momentous time. "The most exciting years in Wyoming history were 1867, 1868, and 1869," observed the state's foremost historian, T. A. Larson.[25] The primary cause for the intense excitement was the arrival of the Union Pacific Railroad, which in the summer of 1868 employed perhaps six thousand men scattered over hundreds of miles in the lightly populated region. Four forts along the Union Pacific route in Wyoming protected the railroad crews from Indians and, on occasion, helped maintain law and order in the towns. Fort Russell, established in 1867, was located near Cheyenne; Fort Sanders, in 1866, near Laramie; and Fort Steele, 1868, in the vicinity of Rawlins. Fort Bridger in the west, developed earlier as a private enterprise, was purchased by the government in 1858.

While the railroad was being built, the short-lived mining boom in western Wyoming occurred. Chisholm, who journeyed west to file stories about the gold rush, found the end-of-track towns along the railroad far more interesting than the mining settlements. The 1869 special census (the same that listed Martha Canary in Piedmont) listed only 1,517 residents in the mining region. The regular census in 1870 indicated a continuing decline in population to only 1,166.[26] There was too little gold to sustain the mining boom, and Chisholm concluded that most of the miners would have been better off had they never come. Many of them, like Chisholm, probably left their cabins for the more exciting railroad centers.

There is every reason to believe that Martha, after leaving the mining settlements and working in Piedmont, joined the camp followers inhabiting the railroad towns and nearby military posts. Clement Lounsberry, editor of the *Bismarck Tribune*, extracted some information from her about this period in her life during an interview in 1877: "At first a waif in a Mormon camp, then she passed through the mining excitements in the west, now a prostitute, now striving to mend her ways."[27] Frontiersman Ben Arnold also recalled her presence among the Union Pacific towns after her parents' deaths: she "became a follower of the freighting teams, and learned to be a good driver," he said, adding that "she visited many places, and when the Union Pacific reached Corinne, Utah, she went thither and traveled up and down the line till 1875 when she went to Cheyenne and to Fort Laramie."[28] Corinne, the shipping point between the railroad and Virginia City, Montana, is a logical place for her to have headquartered.

The excitement and wanton behavior in the Union Pacific towns where Martha resided can be gleaned from Chisholm's reports and from articles in the *Cheyenne Leader* and the *Frontier Index,* a newspaper-on-wheels published in succession at Fort Sanders, Laramie City, Benton, Green River City, and Bear River City as the Union Pacific progressed westward. In November 1868, the *Index* reported that Wyoming had grown in fourteen months from a population of less than a thousand to about thirty-five thousand inhabitants concentrated in the towns along the Union Pacific. Among them, the newspaper reported, there were "adventurous and energetic men," including miners, ranchers, merchants, construction workers, and professional men, but there also were "gamblers in profusion, and a full complement of other characters who do not reflect much credit on any place they infest."[29]

Chisholm referred to the latter group as "rolling scum" and said he saw the same people in each town he visited: "the same gamblers, the same musicians playing the same old tunes to the same old dance, the same females getting always a little more dilapidated." Among them were "Mag & Moll, and gentle Annie, and Moss Agate, and the Schoolmarm, and Mormon Ann, and crazy Jane, and all the pioneers of vice, to keep the dance going till the town is danced away again to another point."[30]

Although Martha Canary is unmentioned in the *Index*'s descriptions of this floating population, the newspaper's comments concerning the women amid this crowd are of special interest. "One of the town 'mollies' was on the rampage yesterday," reported the June 12, 1868, edition. "She made the feathers fly—drunk as a 'fiddler's tincker.' She bawled and she squalled. Never before did we see the like."[31] On July 7, the Police Report included thirty-two arrests, "upon the various charges of drunkenness, disorderly conduct, firing pistols, and females on the streets in male's costume."[32] For women, wearing male attire was not only frowned upon but punishable by a fine.

Unlike most members of the transient population, Martha was working her way eastward rather than westward through the Union Pacific towns. Boney Earnest, who earlier had met the Canary family en route to Montana, said he encountered Martha again at Rawlins, near Fort Steele, looking for work. He helped find her a position with a "French lady" who kept a pool hall and believed that Martha remained there for a year before returning to Salt Lake City. He did not see her for two years, but said she eventually returned to Fort Steele near Rawlins and "knocked around there for a little while and got pretty tough and some old woman was there and she stayed with her . . . and finally fell from grace altogether."[33]

At least two other Canary children resided in western Wyoming during this period. Lena (Lana) Canary, born in 1859 according to the 1860 Mercer County (Missouri) census, lived near Lander, Wyoming. Her son, Tobe (Tobias) Borner, later wrote a family history, evidently based on his mother's stories. Although his version of the family's origins and trip west varies widely from Martha's autobiography, his assertion that his mother was Martha's sister is supported by other evidence. The discrepancies in their narratives may be explained by Lena's being very young during the family's trip west and having retained only vague memories of their life in Missouri. In addition, the Borner family's story undoubtedly was embellished over the years.

According to Borner, the Canary family left an undesignated eastern location in 1864–65 for Salt Lake City. He said that the family, besides Mr. and Mrs. Canary, consisted of three children: Martha, twelve; Lena, eight; and Elijah (or Lige) five. "Mr. Canarie [sic] was a Methodist minister," but "had heard so much of Utah, and what the Mormons were going to do in making it a paradise" that he "joined the Mormon church." Unfortunately, while crossing the plains, Martha's parents were killed during an Indian raid. Young Martha, Borner said, daringly rode back ten miles to a fort they had passed, and returned with soldiers who rescued the wagon train. After burying her parents, Martha took charge of the family's outfit and the children, and continued the trip to Salt Lake City.

After their arrival in Utah, wrote Borner, Martha took a job in a boarding house, but moved to Wyoming during the gold excitement. While working in South Pass City, she met John G. Borner, who hauled supplies between Salt Lake City and the mining camps. When John broke his leg, Martha made two trips for him while he recuperated. In return for her help, Borner secured a job for Martha at Jim Kime's hotel and found positions for Lena and Lige as well. In November 1875, said Tobe Borner, Johnnie Borner and Lena Canary were married by Justice of the Peace James Kime of South Pass City.[34]

Substantiating this information, the 1880 census of Sweetwater County lists John Borner, age forty-one, and Lena Borner, age twenty-one, with four children: Rebecca, Tobe (Tobias), Francis, and Theresa.[35] John Borner, from Saxony, Germany, emigrated to Wisconsin in 1859 and served in the Union army in the Civil War. Afterwards, he worked on a Union Pacific construction crew, then lived in Salt Lake City for two years. In 1869, he joined the gold rush to Wyoming. Between 1872 and 1874, Borner lived four miles above today's Lander, Wyoming, and his place became known as "Borner's Gardens."[36] According to Tobe, not only did John Borner marry Lena, he employed her younger brother, Lige (Elijah) Canary. Lige was "a real rough and tumble boy" when he was fifteen, wrote Tobe. "He was an excellent shot with a rifle or pistol and could ride anything that wore hair, or wasn't afraid to try."[37]

George Reeb, a pioneer of Cooke, Montana, who became acquainted with Martha in subsequent years, recalled that when he visited Evanston, Wyoming, in 1900, he met "Elisha [sic] Canary, who had just finished serving a term of five years in the Wyoming penitentiary for complicity in a scheme to exact money from the railroad by placing stolen cattle on the tracks and then filing claims after the animals' sudden demise." Reeb said "Elisha" asked him during the course of their conversation if he knew Calamity Jane, "and being informed in the affirmative," the ex-convict said "that Jane was his sister and that he was her 'baby' brother." When Reeb later told Martha of meeting "Elisha," she "broke down and sobbed like a child," and "insisted upon his taking, as a souvenir gift, a fancy glass bottle, blown in the shape of a monument, which article he still has in his possession."[38] The relationship between Martha, who then lived in Montana, and Elijah had not been publicized before Reeb related his story, and his identification of Elijah as Martha's brother is therefore important. Reeb, however, failed to acknowledge the true basis of his encounter with Elijah, which occurred not during a visit to Evanston but in the Wyoming penitentiary, where he and Elijah served concurrent sentences between 1898 and 1900.[39]

Wyoming penitentiary records show Elijah Canary beginning a five-year sentence on April 27, 1896. A resident of Uinta County, Wyoming, he was, as Reeb stated, in prison for obstructing the railway. The Evanston newspaper clarified that Elijah and William Kunz (Kuntz) "were charged with driving horses on the track of the Oregon Short Line with the intention of having them killed by trains and thereafter demanding remuneration from the railroad company." Significantly, the penitentiary record lists Elijah's birthplace as Montana. Elijah's age in 1896, when he entered prison, was listed as twenty-eight, making his birth date 1868. This is unlikely; in Martha's account, Charlotte died two years earlier. Elijah's burial record, which lists his birth date as July 1, 1862, is similarly confusing because that would mean he was born in Missouri, not Montana.[40]

According to prison records, Elijah, an uneducated laborer and ranchman, was of "medium heavy build," standing 5' 6" and weighing 154 pounds. He had a dark complexion and brown hair. Elijah had no living parents; his wife, Kate, lived in Ogden, Utah. His religious affiliation once is described as "none," but in another place is listed as Mormon.[41] Some of Lena's descendants reported that Elijah returned to Uinta County to work on a ranch after serving his prison term, lived a hermit's life during his later years, and was buried near Irwin, Idaho.[42] Inexplicably, burial records show his death occurred not in Idaho but in Roosevelt, Duchesne County, Utah, on October 20, 1922.[43]

Stories circulating in Lander, Wyoming, suggest that for a while Martha and Lena operated a laundry there.[44] Because Martha resided in western Wyoming at different times between 1884 and 1894 as well as in the years immediately after 1869, it is difficult to ascertain when they might have run this business. Lena died in 1888, and is buried in the Milford Cemetery on the north fork of Wind River.[45] Descendants of the Borners residing today in Wyoming insist that Lena's family did not appreciate the visits of their notorious relative. One recollection suggests Martha visited her sister only when she knew John Borner would not be home. If family traditions are true, Borner's response is understandable: purportedly, Martha once became so drunk in Lander that she took off her clothes and paraded naked up and down the streets while singing in a loud voice.[46]

The fate of the remaining Canary children is uncertain. One of Martha's brothers evidently accompanied her to the Black Hills in 1875. A journalist estimated that he was then sixteen and said that Martha was supporting him. Despite the age discrepancy, it may have been Elijah.[47] A Wyoming correspondent in the 1930s claimed that "two of her brothers lived, and may still do so in the Star valley, in the village of Freedom," located near the Wyoming-Idaho border.[48] Another account claims that one of Calamity's sisters lived in Idaho. According to a "ballad-singing, half-blind hermit" living "near the Golden Anchor mine alone with his memories," one brother went to a dance hall where the sister worked, intending to shoot her "because she was 'turnin' out bad.'" He did not, however, and she continued her unreformed life under the name "Lousy Liz." The hermit concluded that her "married name is best left unmentioned."[49]

Although only meager records describe Martha Canary between 1864 and 1869, existing evidence locates her in Montana and western Wyoming. Contrary claims placing her in other areas of the country during these years cannot be substantiated. The most frequently suggested alternative is Kansas, unmentioned by Martha in her autobiography. Miguel Otero, later governor of New Mexico, remembered seeing Calamity Jane in Hays City, Kansas, in 1868, an "extremely good-looking" young woman of about twenty. "After a few years she left Hays City and moved from terminal town to terminal town along the advancing Kansas-Pacific Railroad," eventually reaching Kit Carson, and then drifting to Dodge City, Granada, and La Junta.[50] Although migrating from one booming railroad town to another was behavior typical of Martha, it is unlikely this was she. Otero would hardly mistake a twelve-year-old girl for an attractive woman of twenty.

Biographer Aikman also suggested Martha was in Kansas, although he thought it might have been between 1870 and 1872. Admired so much that she gained the title "the prairie queen," according to Aikman, she nevertheless became the humorous target of a ballad singer, "Darling Bob Mackay." After he asked her "an intimate question concerning her lower lingerie," Calamity "filled the air with shrill and slightly obscene rebukes for his bawdiness, and his sombrero with warning bullets."[51]

Later romancers, of course, could not avoid connecting stories mentioning Calamity Jane in Kansas to the known presence of James Butler (Wild Bill) Hickok there. Author and actor William S. Hart wrote a tale placing Calamity in Abilene in 1869, where she warned Hickok of a plot by outlaws to kill him.[52] Jean McCormick, who in 1941 claimed to be the daughter of Hickok and Calamity Jane, included a similar incident in her fraudulent "Calamity Jane's Diary and Letters." In her version, Hickok and Calamity were married in Kansas in 1870 and had a daughter (Jean, of course).[53] Martha would have been about fourteen years old, probably was not yet known by her famous nickname, and, in any event, her *Life and Adventures* said she first met Hickok in 1876 at Fort Laramie.[54]

Even though sufficient evidence is available to reject stories about young Martha Canary between 1864 and 1869 that stray too far from established facts, there are no contemporary documents to confirm or deny stories about the next five years of her life. Compounding the problem, Martha's *Life and Adventures,* useful for her earliest years, becomes fanciful. The adventurous stories she introduced into her autobiography likely resulted from decades of telling tall tales and from efforts to promote interest during her 1896 dime museum tour. "Joined General Custer as a scout at Fort Russell, Wyoming, in 1870," Martha claimed, and "started for Arizona for the Indian campaign." It is an absurd suggestion. George Armstrong Custer was not at Fort Russell and did not participate in an Arizona campaign.[55] A question remains, of course, whether Martha might have accompanied other troops sent to the Southwest. If she did scout, she certainly was not as accomplished as she suggests, or she would have received considerable notice. "Was in Arizona up to the winter of 1871," Martha continues, "and during that time I had a great many adventures with the Indians, for as a scout I had a great many dangerous missions to perform and while I was in many close places always succeeded in getting away safely for by this time I was considered the most reckless and daring rider and one of the best shots in the western country." At a time when a woman performing traditionally male tasks was newsworthy, Martha's purported exploits in Arizona, when she was but fourteen or fifteen, went unmentioned in the press.

Martha's narrative concerning her subsequent activities from 1872 to 1874 is similarly distorted. "After that campaign I returned to Fort Sanders, Wyoming, remained there until spring of 1872, when we were ordered out to the Muscle Shell or Nursey Pursey Indian outbreak." That campaign, she said, was commanded by "Generals Custer, Miles, Terry and Crook," and "lasted until fall of 1873." This garbled account, lacking the accuracy expected of a key participant, confuses various military campaigns against the Indians. There was no conflict with the Nez Perce in 1872–73, although there was in 1877, when Chief Joseph led his people in a race for Canada; commanders included Oliver O. Howard, John Gibbon, Samuel D. Sturgis, and Nelson A. Miles. Officers George Crook, Alfred H. Terry, and George Armstrong Custer were involved in the Sioux campaign of 1876. Here Martha's *Life and Adventures* has degenerated into frontier fiction.

There are clues within Martha's recitation of events, however, that suggest her location during these years. Specific mention of Fort Russell and Fort Sanders indicate familiarity with eastern Wyoming. Combined with proof of her presence in Piedmont in 1869, her claim to have been at Fort Bridger, and the stories about her at Miner's Delight and at Fort Steele, this evidence implies she continued spending her formative teenage years in Wyoming.

In agreement with this conclusion, John P. Belding, later a deputy U.S. marshal headquartered in Deadwood, claimed he saw Martha in Cheyenne as early as 1868, when the railroad was being built, and that she was a camp follower, or prostitute. Belding thought Calamity was sixteen when she arrived in Cheyenne. Either his age estimate or his chronology must be mistaken, for she would have been twelve in 1868. In any event, Belding said she was "so dissolute that she and others of her class were forced to leave the city."[56] Martha confirmed her presence there at an early date when interviewed in 1887: "When I first came to Cheyenne there was not a respectable shelter in the place," she said, "and the proprietor of a tent was a lucky person indeed."[57]

Only a few weeks after the railroad arrived in 1867, Cheyenne's "population had grown to perhaps 6,000, among whom there may have been about 400 women and 200 children." Many were transient, intending to take advantage of opportunities during the boom period. Street fights and shootings were relatively common, and numerous prostitutes worked in the city, as indicated by the fining of forty women in the Cheyenne Police Court on September 10, 1868.[58] Typically, the prostitutes worked in dance houses and small saloons where crime was prevalent.

At some point during these years, Martha probably was associated with the Cheyenne hurdy-gurdy house operated by James McDaniels, who was known as the "Barnum of the West" because his prominent establishment included a museum, live theater, and zoo. In his promotions, he compared the "Thomas and Jerry's" drinks to "the dew on a damsel's lips," and added, "Speaking of damsels, just step into the Museum and you'll see em, large as life, besides 1,001 other sciences embracing every known subject."[59] At which of the several establishments owned by McDaniels between 1867 and 1876 Martha might have worked, and when she was employed, is uncertain, but those familiar with her career remembered her working at his places of business.[60]

In the early 1870s, Martha evidently migrated northward from Cheyenne to the "road ranches" between Fort Russell and Fort Laramie. These were sites at which travelers and soldiers typically tarried for a spell, picking up refreshments and perhaps a night's lodging. Heightened conflict with the Plains Indians in the 1870s led to heavy traffic between Cheyenne and Fort Laramie. John Hunton, who operated one of the road ranches, later wrote an uncomplimentary reminiscence about Martha that casts further light on her activities during this period. In the fall of 1873, Hunton remembered, Jules Coffey and Adolph Cuny opened a large store west of Fort Laramie called Three Mile; it included several buildings, with ice house, blacksmith shop, and billiard hall. They carried on, Hunton wrote, "quite an extensive business selling goods, running a saloon and general road ranch." However, in 1874, business slackened, and they "decided to add new attractions, and for that purpose they constructed eight two-room cottages to be occupied by women." They recruited about ten prostitutes from various cities, and one of these women, recalled Hunton, was Calamity Jane. "Her achievements have been very greatly magnified by every writer I have ever read," wrote Hunton, "for she was among the commonest of her class." Her only "redeeming trait," in Hunton's opinion, was that "she seldom spoke of what she had done or could do with a gun or a pistol." He added, "I have no recollection of ever seeing her shoot at any object, but I have seen her fire her pistol into space."[61]

Sergeant John Q. Ward, who was stationed in the vicinity of the road ranches, corroborated Hunton's recollection. Ward said his personal acquaintance with Calamity lasted about six years and he recalled that it was early in 1874 when she appeared at Cuny and Coffey's road ranch. "Coffee's [sic] Ranch was known to every soldier, mule skinner, bull whacker, cowpuncher, packer, gambler, and bad man for hundreds of miles up and down the Platte River, and it was at this place Calamity acted as entertainer—dancing, drinking much bad whisky and in various ways relieving her victims of their coin, which she spent with a free and willing hand."[62]

Martha's work as a dance-hall girl and prostitute in the "hog ranches" located in the vicinity of Fort Laramie in 1874 probably mirrored her earlier life along the Union Pacific. But it is misleading to portray young Martha as a regular occupant in a house of prostitution. If her behavior during this period was characteristic, she would have worked only intermittently at the road ranch. Often Martha roamed freely, and sometimes she established lengthy relationships with her male companions.

Although her adolescent years were difficult, Martha survived and adapted to the frontier environment. Her formative experiences presaged her future. Martha maintained ties with her siblings, but she never permanently settled down. For the remainder of her life, military posts, mining rushes, and railroad boom towns drew her as a magnet attracts steel.

CHAPTER THREE

The Black Hills Expedition of 1875

No place is associated more with Calamity Jane than the Black Hills of South Dakota. Asked by a reporter in 1896 when she first came to the Black Hills, Martha Canary emphatically answered "1875," and then added, "Wa'n't nothin' here but a few miners, an' they wouldn't have been here if me an' the soldiers hadn't come an' took 'em away from the Injuns. Yes; I was a regular man in them days. I knew every creek an' holler from the Missouri to the Pacific."[1]

Martha's claim is supported by the reminiscences of several people who were with the government's 1875 scientific party investigating the mineral resources of the Black Hills. Yet some scholars questioned her early presence there because no contemporary documents confirmed it. Roberta Beed Sollid, for example, concluded that there was no "absolute proof that she made the trip at all, even as a camp-follower."[2] Now, however, evidence exists proving her presence with the Black Hills expedition of 1875. The story deserves careful attention because it was then that the first contemporary references were made to Martha Canary bearing the nickname "Calamity Jane" and to her wearing male apparel.

How Martha Canary became known as Calamity Jane is a matter of conjecture. Nicknames were common in the West. Often they related to one's place of origin: California Joe, Missouri Jim. William F. Cody became known as "Buffalo Bill" because of his expertise in shooting buffalo. Some nicknames originated with a peculiar characteristic: "Laughing Sam" Hartman, "Poker Alice" Tubbs. Others were less definite in their source. It is difficult, for example, to ascertain why James Butler Hickok became known as "Wild Bill."

Martha told a colorful yarn about her nickname's origin in her *Life and Adventures*. She claimed her famous christening occurred during the "Nursey Pursey" (Nez Perce) outbreak of 1872–73 at Goose Creek, near the present town of Sheridan, Wyoming. According to Martha, Captain Egan was in command of an unnamed military post and during an excursion from the fort was wounded by ambushing Indians. "I was riding in advance," Martha claimed, "and on hearing the firing turned in my saddle and saw the Captain reeling in his saddle." She galloped to Egan's rescue, lifted him to her horse, and carried him back to the post. When he recovered, Egan gave her the name "Calamity Jane, the heroine of the plains." Martha told a similarly romanticized version about wearing men's clothing. Before the Arizona campaign of 1870, she said, she "had always worn the costume of my sex." But when she joined Custer's command, she "donned the uniform of a soldier. It was a bit awkward at first but I soon got to be perfectly at home in men's clothes."[3]

In fact, Martha most likely adopted male attire when she became a camp follower. Military uniforms were readily available and helped her associate more freely with soldiers. Martha also stretched the truth in her story about her naming. Presumably she is referring to Captain James Egan, who commanded the "white horse troop" of the Second Cavalry stationed at Fort Sanders, Fort Russell, and Fort Laramie between 1868 and 1876. But, although Egan was wounded in several Civil War engagements, there is no indication he was shot while stationed in the West.[4] Journalist M. L. Fox in 1903 recalled that Egan's wife wrote a letter to the *Chicago Tribune* after learning about Martha's claim to have saved her husband. According to Mrs. Egan, her husband "was never rescued by 'Calamity' and . . . no such incident ever happened."[5] Duncan Aikman claimed that Egan's only encounter with Calamity occurred when he ordered her and a female companion to leave Fort Laramie, where they were wearing uniforms and "enjoying the novelties of barrack life."[6] Even though Aikman's story, like Martha's account, is not supported by evidence, the behavior it suggests fits her documented activities better than Martha's colorful tale. As Roberta Sollid properly concluded, Egan "was a colorful personality and the kind of man with whom Calamity would have liked to be permanently linked."[7]

Many other explanations of the origin of Martha's nickname have been given. Sometimes another person is substituted for Egan. Thus, she saved "Antelope Frank" after his horse fell during a fight with Indians: "It's a good thing to have a friend like you around, Jane, in a time of calamity," he exclaimed.[8] According to the *Deadwood Pioneer-Times*, humorist Bill Nye applied the nickname to her "during the early 'seventies" when he was editor of the *Laramie Boomerang*—impossible since Nye did not arrive in the West until after Martha already carried her famous nickname. George Hoshier, one of the pallbearers at Calamity's funeral, said the sobriquet was bestowed on her because "she was always getting into trouble. If she hired a team from a livery stable she was sure to have a smash-up. . . . Calamity followed her everywhere." No evidence supports this assertion, either.[9]

Some writers suggest the nickname was derived from Martha's work as a nurse during epidemics. According to one account, the naming occurred during a "mountain fever" outbreak in General George Crook's encampment in early 1876 near Rapid City. Martha labored constantly, "answering each suffering patient's feeble beck or peevish call." Among those stricken was a "young West-pointer" who called Martha "our angel in calamity." Frontiersman Ben Arnold similarly recalled that Martha received her name from "her unselfish labors during this great calamity," but said it happened during a smallpox epidemic in Deadwood in 1878. Since Martha bore her famous nickname prior to these purported epidemics, this notion belongs to folklore.[10]

More recent writers invented other reasons for her naming. Black Hills humorist Ed Ryan said he gave her the nickname during a poker game. Typically when she lost, he said, she would cry, "What a calamity." During one game, as Ryan placed his winning cards on the table, he exclaimed, "Jane, here is another calamity," and, according to Ryan, she was known by that nickname ever after.[11] His ridiculous tale has as much authenticity, however, as most other explanations. The historian Robert Riegel suggested the name came about because "sudden death would overtake her current paramour, and under mysterious circumstances. Hence the name 'Calamity.'"[12] Riegel's explanation of its origin recalls a dime novel featuring Calamity Jane in which the heroine kills all those responsible for her guardian's death, thus gaining the famous nickname.[13] Another far-fetched version came from Black Hills historian Watson Parker, who suggested that the name resulted because "her paramours were generally visited by some venereal calamity."[14]

Calamity's nickname likely had a simpler origin. When newspapers in the late-nineteenth century reported "calamities," they typically referred to events such as earthquakes, fires, floods, and disease epidemics. Perhaps a St. Paul reporter was thinking of such a devastating force when, in 1901, he suggested her name came "from a faculty she has had of producing a ruction at any time and place and on short notice."[15] Association with misfortune also might be its source. One of her acquaintances, Valentine T. McGillycuddy, thought that her "bad luck," such as being orphaned in early childhood, led to her naming.[16]

To complicate matters, the appellations "Calamity" and "Jane" were not restricted to Martha Canary. "Jane" frequently was applied in the same manner as "Jane Doe," and "Calamity" was added to describe behavior. For example, Calamity Joe was given the name "for the calamity he raised in general."[17] Calamity Sal was hauled to jail in Cheyenne after imbibing too heavily.[18] That city also saw the presence of Columbia Jane, who wanted to attend the 1876 Centennial and, needing clothing, helped herself in a dry-goods store.[19]

In fact, several women in the West were called Calamity Jane. A Sidney, Nebraska, newspaper in 1877 described the activities of "Calamity Jane No. 2," and it is unclear from the story whether Martha Canary was considered the first or second. This Nebraska Calamity Jane evidently deserted her husband and child for a bullwhacker. Another well-known Calamity Jane was Mattie Young, killed in a buggy accident while drunk in Denver in 1878. In Montana, Annie Filmore was known as Calamity Jane No. 2 and was an alcoholic who severely abused her son. Mrs. Opie, nicknamed Kentucky Belle, alias Calamity Jane, was another alcoholic mentioned frequently by newspapers in towns along the Union Pacific. Significantly, all these Calamity Janes suffered from alcoholism, were prostitutes, and exhibited eccentric behavior.[20]

The nickname Calamity Jane first appeared, so far as known, in a Pueblo, Colorado, newspaper in April 1875: "'Calamity Jane' is a Pueblo female belonging to that class whose 'feet take hold on hell,'" the article declared. This Calamity Jane, identified as Mattie Hamilton, was almost killed by her husband, who "remonstrated with her the other day by sticking a revolver under her nose, but the weapon refused to go off, and a terrible 'Calamity' was averted."[21]

Though Mattie was a common derivative of Martha, this probably was not Martha Canary. Mattie Hamilton might be the Calamity Jane, described by Miguel Otero, who followed the railroad construction camps through Kansas, Colorado, and New Mexico, or she could be Mattie Young, who later was killed in a Denver buggy accident. Regardless of the identity of Mattie Hamilton, her story suggests the name's likely origin: the first known Calamity Jane is a frontier prostitute. In this Pueblo incident, her husband, George Hamilton, "not content with thrashing his wife in the usual way, borrowed a gun and announced his intentions to treat her as he would any other game."[22] Mattie "made complaint" before Judge Hart, saying she had married Hamilton "when she was an inmate of a house of ill-fame," and he had promised to "earn an honest living for her." Instead, he forced her to continue working, and was "now living on the earnings of her prostitution."[23] Before the law could prosecute him, Hamilton "skipped out." The reporter concluded, "The city is well-rid of him."[24] Clearly, Mattie was well-rid of him also.

The first newspaper article identifying Martha Canary as Calamity Jane appeared in June 1875 in the *Chicago Tribune*. It contains a unique version of the derivation of her nickname. According to J. R. Lane, the correspondent, "Jane" Canary in 1874 had accompanied an expedition in the Powder River country, but she wandered off, causing one of the scouts to remark, "It would be a great calamity if she should be captured or killed by the Indians." Afterwards, the soldiers called her Calamity Jane.[25] Despite its early appearance, Lane's version cannot be considered definitive, and it does not explain why other women bore the same nickname.

If Martha accompanied an expedition in 1874 as Lane suggests, she did not refer to the trip in her autobiography. Many years later, however, William F. (Buffalo Bill) Cody said that he received orders from General Sheridan in 1874 to guide a military expedition led by Captain Anson Mills. While in the Big Horn Mountains, they encountered several Montana prospectors, and with them, Cody recalled, was Calamity Jane. The Montana party accompanied the military expedition for several weeks, during which Martha spent most of her time with the scouts. Cody described Martha as a good hunter and "perfectly at home in that wild country," and added that when she wore men's clothing "she might easily be mistaken for a man" even at a short distance. Cody was certain, however, that Martha never was employed as a scout. Instead, "she would join different military expeditions as a kind of hanger on, and generally joined them so far away from the settlements that it would be cruel for a commanding officer to send her away from the command or put her under arrest. Everyone knew and liked her, and dubbed her 'mascot'; and were generally glad to have her along with the company."[26]

Cody did not call Martha a prostitute, as John Hunton, who operated a road ranch between Cheyenne and Fort Laramie, did. Although Hunton thought it was in 1875 that he first saw her, he was certain she was in the area earlier. Hunton said she often stopped at his roadhouse when she worked for Cuny and Coffey and at "other places of similar character at Fort Laramie and Fort Fetterman."[27] Sergeant John Q. Ward thought it was in 1874 that she was employed at Cuny and Coffey's road ranch and that she then moved ninety miles farther north to a similar place six miles south of Fort Fetterman. Between 1874 and 1876, said Ward, she "was constantly at one or the other of these places, leading a wild and reckless life."[28] Both Hunton and Ward remembered that she accompanied military expeditions in the region as a camp follower. It is hardly surprising, given these recollections, that in 1875 she was discovered among the soldiers during the Black Hills expedition.

Rumors of gold in the Black Hills had circulated for many years, but because the Hills were located in the midst of Sioux country miners were prevented from systematically prospecting there. This situation changed in 1874 when Lieutenant Colonel George Armstrong Custer led an expedition into the Black Hills to explore and locate an appropriate site for a fort for anticipated operations against the Sioux. His expedition is sometimes described as a "summer picnic." Soldiers picked flowers from horseback as they rode through beautiful valleys, officers drank champagne in an open tent, Custer attempted to climb Harney Peak, and William H. Illingworth took memorable photographs of the expedition and countryside. During the journey, gold was discovered along French Creek in the southern Hills and the news was flashed to the world.[29]

The announcement of the discovery of gold, eagerly awaited by prospective miners, occurred in August 1874. By October, a party of gold seekers led by John Gordon left Sioux City for the Hills, and before year's end was entrenched in a stockade at French Creek. Accompanying them was "the first white woman in the Black Hills," Annie Tallent, who later authored an account of her experience.[30] Their entrance placed the government in an awkward position. The publicity of a gold discovery and the penetration of the Hills by miners violated a treaty with the Sioux ratified in 1868 that guaranteed the region would be free from incursion. Troops were ordered to remove the Gordon Party and other miners in the vicinity. Despite initial setbacks because of severe winter conditions, the soldiers succeeded.

In 1875, the military continued its efforts to stem the mining rush, but hundreds of gold seekers evaded them. General George Crook, who personally thought miners should be allowed to seek Black Hills gold, reluctantly ordered his troops into the Hills in July 1875 to remove miners. Tactfully, he persuaded some miners to depart temporarily, guaranteeing their claims until Indian title to the region could be extinguished. Meanwhile, efforts were made to acquire the Black Hills.

The government also decided to send an expedition into the Hills to determine the extent of its mineral wealth, essential information for deciding appropriate government policy. Custer's 1874 announcement of vast amounts of gold had been disputed by several members of his expedition. As a result, even while the mining rush was in progress in 1875, the government sponsored a scientific expedition to the Black Hills to evaluate its mineral deposits. The party was headed by geologists Walter P. Jenney and Henry Newton. Accompanying the expedition were scientific specialists, including Horace P. Tuttle, astronomer, and Valentine T. McGillycuddy, engineer and topographer. Lieutenant Colonel Richard Irving Dodge, in command of four hundred soldiers, escorted the party. With the expedition in an unofficial capacity was Martha Canary.[31]

Several expedition participants, including McGillycuddy, teamster Harry (Sam) Young, and scout Moses (California Joe) Milner, later told stories about Martha's presence with the Jenney expedition. Biographer Roberta Sollid was suspicious of the tales told by Young and McGillycuddy because Young's account seemed exaggerated and McGillycuddy obviously plagiarized from Young's narrative. "Much investigation among old-timers," wrote Sollid, "failed to give a clue of anyone who might be 'Sam' Young, although this unknown author wrote as if he were an eye-witness to every event that took place in the Black Hills."[32] However, had Young wanted to gain fame by pretending he was involved in important frontier adventures, he would have selected a better known expedition to accompany, such as the 1874 Custer expedition. In any event, it is now known that Young was a teamster in the vicinity of Fort Laramie in 1874–75: his name appears with those of other freighters in John Hunton's account book.[33] In addition, proof has surfaced since Sollid published her biography of Calamity Jane that confirms Martha's presence with the party. As a result, the Young and McGillycuddy reminiscences warrant attention.

McGillycuddy remembered that on the evening of May 20, 1875, while he was sipping wine with Colonel Dodge, Henry Newton, and Horace Tuttle, he inquired about "an unusual-looking girl on the parade grounds that day, one not over sixteen and wearing spurs, chaps, and a sombrero." Dodge responded that she was Calamity Jane, "regimental mascot in spite of her name," and then related the spurious Jane Dalton tale of her origins. He added that she "had been living at the post when he had come to Fort Laramie." She was, he said, a "queer combination." She would nurse sick soldiers, mend their clothes, and cook for them. "But as for morals, she didn't know the meaning of the word." Since she "was crazy for adventure," he suspected she was planning somehow to join their expedition into the Black Hills.[34]

In fact, McGillycuddy continued, she asked him to help her do exactly this, urging him "to speak a word for her" to Dodge. Despite his disclaimer that such an effort "would be absolutely useless," she cheerfully "sauntered off toward the barracks." McGillycuddy, whose account was written after Martha became famous, does not explain why a young camp follower would request permission to accompany the expedition when, according to his own later testimony, she intended to accompany it secretly anyway.[35]

The expedition left Fort Laramie on May 25, 1875, and marched unsteadily toward the Black Hills. Accompanying them, said McGillycuddy, was "an unaccounted for young private" who became more and more daring as the post was left farther behind.[36] But the identity of this "private" finally was discovered. According to "Sam" Young, Martha, who was dressed as a soldier, crossed the parade ground and met "an officer, who was a German and a great disciplinarian, and having no chance to get by him, saluted him in true soldierly style." He returned her salute, upon which several officers began laughing. When he demanded to know why, they "told him that the soldier he had just saluted was Calamity Jane. His dignity was hurt and he immediately began an investigation and found that it was true."[37]

Just as he copied the "Jane Dalton" account of Martha's origins, McGillycuddy borrowed from Young to tell of her discovery. Thus, McGillycuddy relates that one day "Jane" walked past the officers' quarters toward the sutler's store to purchase cigars. Several officers recognized Martha, but "had no intention of betraying her." Unfortunately, she met the officer of the day, Lieutenant A. H. Von Luettwitz, and it being too late to turn back, she "straightened her shoulders and saluted with military precision." He returned the salute, causing bystanders to chuckle loudly. Luettwitz investigated and learned that "through the aid of the army tailor, who had fitted a soldier's uniform to her slim figure, Calamity Jane had been metamorphosed into a private in the United States Army."[38]

Although it is clear McGillycuddy used Young's account, he added new information, such as the name of the German officer. Young similarly included material not utilized by McGillycuddy. For example, Young related, "Calamity Jane was enamored with Sergeant Shaw, of company E, 3rd cavalry." It was Shaw who "suggested that she wear cavalry clothes" so she could accompany him. Martha spent her entire time with Shaw, said Young.[39] Possibly McGillycuddy omitted Shaw's name because he thought it incorrect; others suggest Martha's beau was Sergeant Frank Siechrist.[40]

After the officer learned of Martha's presence, wrote Young, Shaw was "severely reprimanded," and Martha was expelled from camp. She went to Young, who was one of the teamsters, "and knowing me well, asked if she could go along with us. If so, she would do the cooking for our mess." The wagon master gave permission, Young says, but she was required "to change her soldiers' clothes for citizen clothes, which we furnished her." According to Young, she traveled with them the rest of the way. He recalled that "Jane was then about fifteen years of age, quite good looking, dark complexioned, black eyes and black hair, which she wore short." Young's inaccurate determination of her age probably derived from his belief that she was born in 1860. More persuasively, Young reported that she "had no particular use for a citizen, but anybody with a blue coat and brass buttons, could catch Calamity."[41]

McGillycuddy's memory of Dodge's dismissal of Martha from camp is different from Young's, and makes McGillycuddy rather than Young central to the story. Seemingly heartless, Dodge ordered her from camp, said McGillycuddy. She appealed to him for help, but he said he could do nothing. Nevertheless, none of the soldiers "showed any special signs of uneasiness at leaving the girl alone on the prairies sixty miles from the nearest lodging with the probability of Indians lurking near." This was because they knew she would rejoin the expedition, which she did each day, followed by a repetitious ceremony in which Dodge once again ordered her from camp. It is a most unlikely rendition of events. Indeed, in his journal, Dodge did not even mention Martha being with the command.[42]

On June 4, the expedition finally reached the southwestern edge of the Black Hills, where it established Camp Jenney. While the party camped, Captain Andrew Burt returned to Fort Laramie with a wagon train for supplies. With him he carried dispatches written by the party's newspaper correspondents. Acting Assistant Surgeon J. R. Lane, who doubled as correspondent for the *Chicago Times*, sent a lengthy account of the expedition's progress, including the first contemporary description identifying Martha Canary by her famous nickname.

According to Lane, Martha's presence in the West was the result of "yielding to drink." Alcoholism had caused her to become "a homeless outcast, . . . repenting for a few months and hiring out to do housework, then being found out, returning to her vicious life, until the next periodical fit of repentence came on." This "good looking" woman had been, he asserted, "the respectable proprietress of a millinery store in Omaha" a few years earlier. But "John Barleycorn" had destroyed that career, as it had the livelihoods of many others Lane met in the West.

> Is it at all strange, then, that CALAMITY JANE should be here. Calam is dressed in a suit of soldier's blue, and straddles a mule equal to any professional blacksnake swinger in the army. Calamity also jumps upon a trooper's horse and rides along in the ranks, and gives an officer a military [salute] with as much style as the First corporal in a crack company. Calam is often taken for a trumpeter, or a bugler, but Calamity isn't any such thing. For Calamity Jane, or rather Jane Canary, is a female.

Lane said Martha already had been "all over the frontier, and on several dangerous scouts." Now she "wanted to see the Hills; so donning a suit of blue, and taking her brother, a lad of 16, whom she supports, with her, she got into a government wagon, and, with the help of drivers and soldiers, here she is." Lane concluded: "Who says women cannot endure hardships equal to a man?"[43]

Although Lane's account contains mistakes, such as his suggestion that Martha had managed a business in Omaha, his description confirms that she accompanied the Jenney expedition, albeit in an unoffical capacity. Lane's mention of Martha's caring for her brother Cilus, or possibly Elijah, indicates that she was maintaining contact with her siblings. Finally, evidence of Martha's early addiction to alcohol, vividly described by Lane, clarifies much about her behavior. Consequently, this first confirmed description of Martha Canary as Calamity Jane is of paramount significance to her history.

While the party rested at Camp Jenney, they located Custer's 1874 trail and, after the supply train arrived, followed his route to French Creek. At this site, where gold had been discovered a year earlier, Jenney's party established Camp Harney on June 15. The command took over the Gordon Stockade, built a year earlier by gold seekers who had been forcibly removed from the Hills, and used its cabins for storehouses and shops. Then Jenney began his search for gold. Nearby, "very enthusiastic" miners were busily at work. However, Jenney reported discouragingly on June 22 that the excitement of expedition members about the French Creek gold deposits dampened after "no one obtained even by several hours hard labor more than a few cents worth of gold dust."[44]

The exploration party remained at Camp Harney on French Creek for about two weeks. Additional supplies arrived from Fort Laramie on June 23, and ten wagons returned to that post on June 28. It is possible Martha was sent back to Fort Laramie with this or another returning party. Accounts differ concerning how long she remained with the expedition. McGillycuddy claimed she accompanied them for the entire journey, flitting "from camp to camp" caring for sick soldiers and mending their clothes, and "frequently striding into the hills with her rifle and bringing back a deer or an antelope."[45] But John Hunton learned that Calamity Jane only "remained with the expedition until detected" and then was sent back to Fort Laramie, "which was in a short time." Jim Duncan, the wagon master, "demurred at the order," but made certain she left.[46] Most likely, Hunton is correct that Martha was sent back with the supply train from the French Creek encampment or shortly thereafter.

However, there is no doubt that Martha accompanied the expedition at least to French Creek. While the party camped there, photographer A. Guerin of St. Louis took the earliest confirmed picture of Calamity Jane.[47] He had missed the expedition's departure because of illness, but arrived at Camp Harney on June 23 with the supply train. His photograph depicts Martha in men's clothing reclining against a large rock near French Creek. In addition to having her picture taken, Martha received further newspaper coverage. Twenty-four-year-old correspondent Thomas C. MacMillan, who signed his articles "Mac," accompanied the 1875 expedition for the *Chicago Inter-Ocean* and described Martha in his dispatch sent from French Creek. With the expedition, he said, was "a strange creature" who "has been a camp follower of the outfit since leaving Laramie," and he compared her to Bret Harte's character Cherokee Sal in "The Luck of Roaring Camp." Wrote Mac:

> This "Calamity," which high latitude nomenclature has her, is a young woman who has followed the expedition from the first until now. Her costume, I must confess, is remarkably similar to that worn by Uncle Sam's boys, and it does not appear to be the custom here for ladies to ride as they do further east. In this, I grant that I may be in error, it has been so long since we left civilization. Certain it is, however, that "Calamity" has the reputation of being a better horse-back rider, mule and bull-whacker (driver) and a more unctious coiner of English, and not the Queen's pure either, than any (other) man in the command, and it is even whispered that a certain le petit corporale knows why "Calamity" came to the Hills and how.[48]

MacMillan's report, along with Guerin's photograph, proves Martha's presence with the Jenney expedition at French Creek in the Black Hills and also suggests the reason she was with the party.

Other reminiscences of Martha by members of the expedition are anecdotal in nature, confirming her incidental role. Moses (California Joe) Milner, who accompanied the party as scout, recalled a quarrel with Martha after she childishly stole his dog. When he located her, Milner picked Martha up by her feet and shook her. Twice during the expedition, said Milner, he shot near her feet to make her dance "the tenderfoot dance . . . to keep from being pestered any further by her."[49] Likewise, teamster "Sam" Young recalled a minor mishap while Martha rode with him in his wagon. When the wagon overturned while crossing a creek, "Calamity, being under the wagon sheet, was compelled to crawl out of the hind end, and in doing so, fell into the water up to her neck. My! how she did swear at me; and she always seemed to have the idea I did it purposely, but such was not the case."[50]

The expedition left French Creek on July 18, probably without Martha. Upon reaching Spring Creek, Colonel Dodge observed that "the whole valley is filled with miners, many already camped on claims, but the large majority traveling, in wagons, on horseback and on foot, going and coming in all directions. They seem to have suddenly sprung from the earth."[51]

Official visitors arrived as the command traveled northward. First, the commissioners trying to negotiate the purchase of the Black Hills from the Indians met the Jenney party. They were escorted by Captain James Egan. Shortly afterwards, General George Crook, who was charged with removing the miners from the Hills, arrived, but rather than taking action against the miners, brought several citizens with him for a hunting excursion.[52] Meanwhile, Jenney's party continued surveying the physical features of the eastern and northern Black Hills, not returning to Fort Laramie until October 14. Their trip lasted over four months.

Jenney's report about gold deposits in the Black Hills was not overly enthusiastic: the placer mining, he observed, was "not remarkably rich," and he believed the region's prosperity would come from stock raising, not gold. His cautious report, however, did not deter promoters: the Yankton newspaper headlined Jenney's announcement, "Dakota's Mines to Eclipse the World" and Bismarck's paper added, "Gold Enough to Pay the National Debt."[53] The mining rush accelerated, and the government soon ended its efforts to stem the tide.

As miners flooded the Black Hills in the ensuing months, they preserved the memory of Martha's presence with the Jenney expedition. Captain Jack Crawford, the "poet scout" who served as Black Hills correspondent for the *Omaha Bee*, wrote a letter from Custer City in January 1876, informing the newspaper's readers about gold mining activities in the Hills. In his report, he mentioned "Calamity Bar," a "fine mining claim about three miles from Custer" that received its name "from a woman who accompanied the soldiers last summer. They called her Calamity Jane."[54] Crawford also wrote "To the Miners in Custer," versifying his news about the gold diggings. The fifth stanza began:

> Now Calamity bar is a good one,
> Yes, Calamity, that's its name;
> And it must be a great calamity,
> If its like old Calamity Jane.[55]

Martha also had a prominent elevation named for her. "Calamity Peak," wrote geographer A. T. Andreas in 1884, was named "in honor of a sporting woman, familiarly known as 'Calamity Jane.'"[56] She had made a spectacular entrance into the region's history and had been featured at age nineteen in geography, news reports, and poetry.

In her *Life and Adventures*, Martha, of course, claimed that she was a member of the military party rather than a camp follower. Yet her peripheral role in the Jenney expedition is evident from her garbled rendition of events. "We were . . . ordered to Fort Custer, where Custer City now stands, where we arrived in the spring of 1874," she claimed. Her facts are wrong: no Fort Custer ever was established in the Black Hills. Martha continued: "were ordered to Fort Russell in the fall of 1874, where we remained until spring of 1875; was then ordered to the Black Hills to protect miners, as that country was controlled by the Sioux Indians and the government had to send the soldiers to protect the lives of the miners and settlers in that section." However, no expedition was sent to protect miners. The expedition she accompanied had as its purpose to confirm or deny reports concerning quantities of gold, and the 1875 Crook expedition, which Martha did not accompany, attempted to remove miners from the Hills rather than shield them from Indian attacks. Martha's *Life and Adventures* is what might be expected from a camp follower rather than someone serving in an official capacity.[57]

Not surprisingly, later writers became confused concerning Martha's first appearance in the Black Hills. John S. McClintock's *Pioneer Days in the Black Hills*, among the most reliable reminiscences about the Black Hills gold rush, reported: "It is generally conceded by old timers, that she accompanied General Custer's army to the Hills in 1874, and also General Crook's expedition to the Hills in 1875." Author Robert Casey mistakenly reported that Calamity herself said "that she was with General Custer on his first expedition into the Hills in 1874." And Black Hills pioneers Jesse Brown and A. M. Willard erroneously reported her "dressed as a soldier" while with General Crook as he attempted to remove miners from the Hills in 1875.[58]

Other writers incorrectly concluded that she was the "first woman in the Black Hills."[59] Certainly she was among the earliest non-Native American women in the Black Hills. However, Custer's 1874 expedition had included Aunt Sally, a black cook, and the Gordon Party's Annie Tallent holds title as the "earliest white woman" in the Hills. Interestingly, newspaperman George Stokes, who was among the miners illegally sneaking into the Black Hills in 1875, excluded Martha from his list of earliest pioneers for other reasons. Stokes's party included "the wife of Hebron, a Kansas farmer," who was highly regarded by the men; she sewed on buttons and washed clothing, and party members donated food and treats for the family. "Why not?" said Stokes, "they were the first white woman and children to invade the forbidden Hills." Although he was unaware of Tallent's claim, Stokes was fully cognizant that Calamity Jane had preceded Mrs. Hebron into the Hills, but he dismissed her right to be considered the earliest because "the officers had pronounced her *persona non grata*. Mrs. Hebron was different; she was a wife and mother."[60]

Later romancers dressed up, or rather, undressed, stories about Martha's experiences during the 1875 expedition, probably to stimulate interest. Author Stewart Holbrook related that Martha was "rigged up in the baggy, shapeless clothes of the enlisted man of 1875" by Sergeant Frank Siechrist so that she could join him on the Jenney expedition. "At some stop along the way, after the party had camped one evening," Holbrook writes, "an officer strolling near a stream was struck dumb—we can presume—for Jane was right in there with the boys and she had troubled herself no more than they about a bathing suit." As a result, said Holbrook, she was sent back.[61] This story, repeated in numerous popular accounts of Calamity Jane, is sometimes placed with other military expeditions.

Whatever the truth of such anecdotes, the fact that Martha accompanied the Black Hills expedition of 1875 is now clear. Her picture was taken, newspaper correspondents described her there, numerous expedition members recalled her presence, and her name was given to a mining claim and mountain peak. Upon her return, recalled John Hunton, she "resumed her old life at the Cuny and Coffey ranch and other places of a similar character at Fort Laramie and Fort Fetterman until the organization of General Crook's army in May, 1876."[62] Martha, who entered western history by accompanying the Black Hills expedition in 1875, intended to repeat her feat with Crook in 1876.

CHAPTER FOUR

With Crook in 1876

While the nation celebrated its centennial in 1876, decisive events occurred in the northern plains. That year the Black Hills gold rush was in full progress, and the United States Army moved in force against the Sioux to crush their independence. Interestingly, both the 1876 military campaign and the mining rush to the Black Hills are remembered for the deaths of legendary participants, Lieutenant Colonel George Armstrong Custer at the Little Big Horn and James Butler (Wild Bill) Hickok in Deadwood. It was also the most eventful year in Martha Canary's career. As a camp follower, she participated in the army's campaign against the Sioux, and subsequently she accompanied Hickok to the Black Hills. Stories about her service as a scout during the Sioux wars and tales about an intimate relationship with Wild Bill Hickok became major ingredients in her legend.

The 1876 military campaign began after government officials decided in November 1875 that the Sioux must relinquish the Black Hills region. A proclamation was issued demanding the Indians come to the government's agencies by January 31, 1876, or be declared hostile and forcibly removed from their hunting grounds. Many Indians probably were unaware of the order; winter conditions forbade others from traveling to the agencies, even if so inclined. Still others simply ignored the demand or did not understand its significance. Consequently, military forces on the northern plains received orders to take action, and in March General George Crook, commanding ten companies of cavalry and two companies of infantry, marched north from Fort Fetterman, Wyoming.[1] Later that spring, troops from Montana led by Colonel John Gibbon, and forces from northern Dakota commanded by General Alfred Terry and Lieutenant Colonel George Armstrong Custer, would join the campaign. The movements of these armies were only loosely coordinated, but it was hoped their combined efforts would force the Sioux to submit.

Preparations for Crook's campaign began in February, with troops, packers, and scouts gathering at Fort Fetterman. Located near the fort were "Whiskey Gulch" and the

"Fetterman Hog Ranch," where soldiers obtained the drinks they desired. There, dance hall girls and prostitutes also plied their trade. It was at the Fetterman and Six Mile road ranches, recalled John Hunton, that Martha spent considerable time in 1876.[2] Lieutenant John G. Bourke, aide to General Crook, said that each of these "hog ranches" contained from three to six women, among the worst Bourke had ever seen. Their lanterns at night lured soldiers from the garrisons.[3] These establishments undoubtedly were busy after the 300 enlisted men and nearly 100 civilian employees who resided at Fort Fetterman were augmented by the 883 men in Crook's Big Horn and Yellowstone Expedition.

Martha planned to sneak along with Crook's troops. Isaac N. Bard, an employee of John (Portugee) Phillips at the Chugwater Ranch fifty-two miles north of Cheyenne, stopped at Fagan's road ranch during a trip to Fort Russell. There he recorded in his diary on February 21, 1876, the notorious woman's intentions:

> Tewsday (Feb. 22) Very plesant all day. Left town at 9 A.M. made a short call at Pole Creek there is 6 or 8 B.Hills teams hear. Drove over to Fagans. He is crowded full. Calamity Jane is hear going up with the troops. I think there is trouble ahead everything is crowded hear there is 7 companies on the road.[4]

Bard does not identify Martha's role, nor does he confirm that she departed with the troops. It can be assumed, however, that she joined the command as a camp follower, as she had during the Jenney expedition the previous summer.

Crook placed Colonel Joseph J. Reynolds in command of the troops while he followed with the supply train as the army marched northward from Fort Fetterman on March 1. To increase their speed, they packed only absolutely necessary supplies. When a severe snowstorm struck a few days later and temperatures plunged to below zero, the soldiers, without tents and sufficient blankets, suffered horribly. Nevertheless, on March 17 they attacked a Cheyenne and Sioux village located by the scouts. Too little permanent damage was done, however, to claim victory; it is possible that only one warrior was killed. Also, in the confusion of battle several soldiers fell into the hands of the enemy, and the Indians later recaptured most of their ponies. Because of his ineffectiveness, Reynolds was court-martialed, and General Crook, upon the army's return to Fort Fetterman, began preparations for a second offensive.[5]

Several participants in the March campaign recalled Martha's presence with the command. Stanley Lash's grandfather, who was a blacksmith at Fort Fetterman, told Stanley about the excitement when the soldiers learned that Martha had joined them: "The rumor of her discovery spread like wildfire among the restless troops," he said.[6] However, Sergeant George S. (Moccasin Joe) Howard remembered that she was with the teamsters rather than among the soldiers.[7] Another member of the party recalled her being with a female companion known as "Shingle-Headed Little Frank." The two "somehow managed to smuggle into General Crook's command," then returned to Cheyenne. Little Frank was then as notorious as Martha and was described as a "petite, pretty and vivacious woman" who "was a special favorite among the soldiers." Like Martha,

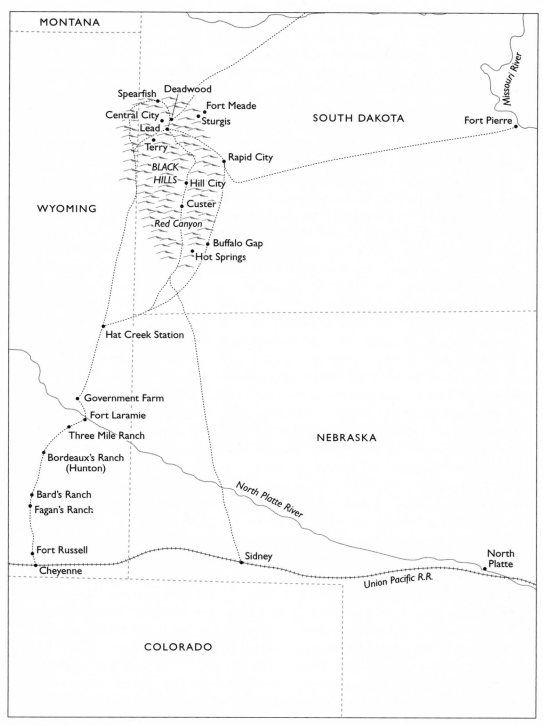

MONTANA

SOUTH DAKOTA

Missouri River

Spearfish • Deadwood
Central City • • Fort Meade
Lead • • Sturgis
Terry
BLACK
HILLS
Rapid City
Hill City
Custer
Red Canyon
Buffalo Gap
Hot Springs

Fort Pierre

WYOMING

Hat Creek Station

Government Farm
Fort Laramie
Three Mile Ranch
Bordeaux's Ranch
(Hunton)
Bard's Ranch
Fagan's Ranch

NEBRASKA

North Platte River

Fort Russell
Cheyenne

Sidney

North
Platte

Union Pacific R.R.

COLORADO

The Black Hills, 1875–1880

Little Frank wore male apparel. Carrying a small faro game, Little Frank managed to win a considerable sum from the troops. Afterwards, recalled an old-timer, the two women "went on a wild, reckless spending orgy in Cheyenne . . . with the money thus won." That spring, Martha and Little Frank were often seen together "loafing around Cheyenne or attending a variety show at McDaniels theatre."[8]

Martha evidently left Cheyenne for the Black Hills shortly thereafter. Her presence in the Hills in April 1876 has confused biographers who assumed she made only one trip there in the spring, that being with Wild Bill Hickok in June. However, several reminiscences locate her in the Hills a couple of months earlier.

Martha probably joined one of the numerous parties traveling that spring to the gold regions. By January 1876, it was estimated four thousand miners were already in the Hills, and one traveler counted two hundred wagons with fourteen hundred people on the trail between Cheyenne and Custer.[9] The latter town, located on French Creek where General Custer's 1874 expedition first discovered gold, had grown rapidly during the initial mining rush to the Black Hills. It was the natural destination for miners, and by March 1876 Custer's population was between five and six hundred, of which about twenty were women. Its boom period was brief, however. Gold discoveries in the northern Black Hills caused Custer's population to decline rapidly, and by April it was being transformed into a supply depot for miners embarking to richer fields.[10]

One of the freighters leaving Cheyenne for the Black Hills in April was Jesse Brown, captain of a train of twenty-five teams bound for Custer City. He remembered that while he was in Custer a government mule train arrived, "and Calamity Jane was driving one of the teams, dressed in buckskin suit with two Colts six shooters on a belt. She was about the roughest looking human that I ever saw." He also remembered that "the first place that attracted her attention was a saloon, where she was soon made blind as a bat from looking through the bottom of a glass."[11]

Among the people remaining in Custer in April was John W. (Captain Jack) Crawford, the "poet scout" who had popularized Calamity's name in verse after her 1875 exploits. He continued to write dispatches for the *Omaha Bee*, but also served as "chief of scouts" for the Black Hills Rangers, organized to thwart the threat of Indian marauders. In addition, he purported to be Custer's assistant marshal, and he recalled arresting Martha for intoxication and disorderly conduct.[12] Another Custer resident who remembered Martha there was Sidney J. Cornell. He described her as "a woman low down in her class," and said she had a "firey and impetuous temper." In fact, when angry, she used "language that would make the very air turn blue." According to Cornell, Martha tried to stab Roger D. Williams in a Custer store because he laughed at her.[13]

Brothel madam Dora Du Fran remembered that in later years Martha told of a dramatic incident that influenced her views of Indians. To Dora, Martha described "the terribly mutilated bodies" of a family massacred in Red Canyon near Custer City in April 1876. Martha recalled that "the woman was soon to become a mother. She had been cut open and the unborn baby's body was tied around her neck." The men were also horribly disfigured, and the family's black servant "had a stake driven through her body and was set upright against the branches of a tree." Not surprisingly, reported Du Fran, Calamity claimed "the only good Indians were dead ones."[14] Martha was describing the Metz family murders, but she may have learned the story from others since her version includes details that clash with other eyewitness accounts. Metz, a Custer baker, sold out as the Custer City boom collapsed, and departed with his wife and a small party for Laramie. With him was a teamster named Simpson, a black cook named Rachel Brigges, and W. J. (California Bill) Felton with two companions, Gresham and Beergessir. The party was attacked at Red Canyon on April 24. Riding a mile ahead of the party, Felton escaped, and managed to take his two fatally wounded friends with him. However, Metz, his wife, and their driver were all killed. The next morning, a party found the mutilated victims strewn through the gulch. Metz's black servant was not discovered until several days later. She was "leaning face forward against the bank, in an upright position, and with a single arrow piercing her back, as if she had been shot from behind while peeping over the top of the bank."[15] Although Martha may have learned about the event second-hand, her familiarity with the Metz massacre supports other evidence that she was in the Black Hills that April.

From Custer, Martha traveled northward to Rapid City. There, David Holmes, a member of an expedition of gold seekers from North Dakota, wrote in his diary on May 5, "We met a party today coming in from Cheyenne, one of the party was 'Calamity Jane.'" Holmes recalled that she was "riding horseback attired as a man with a Winchester rifle across her saddle bow."[16]

If this was Martha, she must have returned to Cheyenne shortly after Holmes saw her. The trip between Custer City and Cheyenne took approximately a week, and it would have taken a few more days from Rapid City.[17] On May 22, Martha was arrested in Cheyenne for grand larceny. The indictment charged that "Maggie Smith," a name she evidently used to obscure her identity, had on February 20 taken a linen skirt and over-skirt worth seven dollars, a pair of stockings worth fifty cents, and "one petticoat of the value of two dollars and fifty cents of the personal goods and chattels of one Minnie Clark." In addition, she stole a hat valued at two dollars, a cloth sack, black dress, pair of ladies' cuffs, and a veil from Maggie Louise.[18] "Maggie Smith" was identified as Calamity Jane by the Cheyenne newspaper when it reported that the jury reached a "not guilty" verdict in "the case of the Territory vs. Maggie Smith, alias Calamity Jane."[19]

Martha spent nearly three weeks in jail awaiting trial before her release on June 8. Reminiscences by several Cheyenne residents are evidently based on this incident and suggest she had difficulties that spring finding appropriate apparel. "During her imprison-ment here and shortly before her scheduled trial, it was revealed that she had no suitable clothing to wear in a courtroom," wrote one journalist. He added that Deputy Sheriff T. Joe Fisher's wife, Catherine, loaned Martha a dress. After her court appearance, Martha walked through the streets of Cheyenne in her new clothes, causing Mrs. Fisher considerable embarrassment because it implied familiarity.[20]

The dramatic sequel to Martha's stay in the Cheyenne jail was told in several satirical journalistic accounts. These stories show that Martha became locally notorious even before dime novels made her nationally famous. Denver's *Rocky Mountain News* described her as "an eccentric female resident" of Cheyenne at the bottom of the social scale whose weaknesses included strong drink and profanity. After her stay in jail, it said, she "snuffed the fresh air of freedom once more," and because "it was too early to repair to Church and give thanks for her deliverance from bondage," she repaired to the saloons where she "lost no time in celebrating her release by getting speedily and comfortably drunk."[21]

At the end of her Cheyenne drinking spree, Martha rented a horse and buggy from James Abney's stable, ostensibly to drive to Fort Russell only three miles away. However, the *Cheyenne Daily Leader* gibed: "Indulgences in frequent and liberal potations completely befogged her not very clear brain, and she drove right by that place."[22] Martha finally reached a road ranch on Chugwater Creek fifty miles distant, where, reported the *Rocky Mountain News*, "she astonished the border barkeeper by the liberality and munificence of her patronage, and the ease and accuracy with which she swore at him." But, said the reporter, the bartender, used to frontier life, was unconcerned. He "sold her as much whisky as she craved during the night, and next morning refilled her bottle without a murmur."[23] The imaginative correspondent for the *Daily Leader* elaborated: "Continuing to imbibe the bug juice at close intervals and in large quantities throughout the night, she woke up the next morning with a vague idea that Fort Russell had been removed but being still bent on finding it, she drove on, finally sighting Fort Laramie, ninety miles distant."[24]

Martha showed little concern about her mistake, ventured the *News*: "Fort Laramie was as welcome as Fort Russell would have been, so long as the sutler had plenty of whisky." Putting the horse out to grass, she "enjoyed camp life after her usual fashion."[25] However, when law officer Joe Rankin arrived several days later, Calamity "begged him not to arrest her, and as he had no authority to do so, he merely took charge of Abney's outfit which was brought back to this city Sunday."[26]

Since Martha's epic buggy ride from Cheyenne to Fort Laramie occurred while a military campaign against the Sioux was in progress, the reporter for the *News* mischievously inquired of Martha whether she had seen any Indians. According to the correspondent, Martha responded in the affirmative. In fact, she claimed "that a party of howling devils swooped down upon her and tried to capture her outfit, but she swore at them till they left." Cynically, the reporter concluded, "The guileless Sioux were probably awed by her profanity, or, being exceedingly superstitious they may have taken Calamity Jane for Belzebub himself, in the disguise of a Cheyenne beer-jerker."[27]

As these articles about Martha's buggy ride indicate, correspondents rarely displayed sensitivity about her alcoholism. Similar sensationalized accounts about her eccentric behavior typified newspaper coverage throughout her life. These journalists perhaps also misconstrued Martha's purpose for hurrying to Fort Laramie after her imprisonment. While she was awaiting trial, Crook's army left Fort Fetterman to begin its second campaign against the Indians, and she intended to join them.

This time Crook meant to gain a decisive victory over the Indians. His army contained more troops, having 47 officers and 1,002 men. Several reporters accompanied the army, including John Finerty of the *Chicago Times* and T. C. MacMillan of the *Chicago Inter-Ocean*, but none identified Martha in dispatches. However, several members of the command mentioned her in their reminiscences, including Lieutenant John Gregory Bourke, Captain Anson Mills, and scout Frank Grouard.

The army moved north on May 29, reaching old Fort Reno on June 2, old Fort Phil Kearny on June 5, and Goose Creek on June 11. At the latter location, they established a "permanent camp" and awaited for arrival of their Crow and Shoshone scouts. A few days later, 176 Crow and 86 Shoshone Indians augmented the command, and the enlarged force marched toward the Rosebud River in search of the Sioux. They did not have long to wait. On June 17, a several-hour engagement known as the Battle of the Rosebud was fought. Crook discovered that the Indians, among them the famous leader Crazy Horse, were a worthy match for his army. In fact, some of his units were almost overwhelmed during the battle. When the fighting ended, Crook determined that he could not continue as planned and returned to his base camp at Goose Creek to await supplies and reinforcements. His men, said one witness, expended more than twenty-five thousand shells in the encounter. Although losses were relatively light, with twenty-one wounded and ten killed, the command had taken a beating. On June 21, the wounded were returned to Fort Fetterman for medical care. Meanwhile, their Shoshone and Crow allies left, with no intention of returning, leaving Crook desperate for scouts.[28] While Crook's army recuperated in northern Wyoming, Custer's command was annihilated on June 25 at the Little Big Horn.

Martha claimed that she played an important role in Crook's campaign. "In spring of 1876," she related in her *Life and Adventures*, "we were ordered north with General Crook to join Gen'ls Miles, Terry and Custer at Big Horn river." Actually, General Crook's movements were only loosely coordinated with those military forces commanded by General Alfred Terry and Lieutenant Colonel George Armstrong Custer, and General Nelson A. Miles was not involved in the spring campaign. Martha also included a fictitious account of her activities with the command: "During the march I swam the Platte River at Fort Fetterman as I was the bearer of important dispatches. I had a ninety mile ride to make, being wet and cold, I contracted a severe illness and was sent back in Gen. Crook's ambulance to Fort Fetterman where I laid in the hospital for fourteen days."[29] Official communications to Fort Fetterman were carried by couriers whose names are cited in documents, but Martha's is not among them.[30] Perhaps she was humorously referring to her ninety-mile buggy ride when she claimed to be carrying dispatches.

But several writers besides Martha claim she served as a scout for Crook's command. One researcher, Clarence S. Paine, concluded, "Her own story that she served as scout for General Crook in the campaigns of 1876 has been ridiculed by many, yet there is evidence that she may have served in that capacity on at least one occasion." He believed she was "accustomed to such a life, capable of riding long distances and of shooting when necessary."[31] However, the only evidence supporting Paine's conclusion is from the memoirs of Frank Grouard, one of Crook's scouts.

According to Grouard, after several scouts left the command during the campaign, he hired replacements. Those he remembered employing included Charlie Chapin, Bill Zimmers, Jim Phoenix, Black Hills Frank, and Calamity Jane.[32] Sadly, Grouard's memoirs, which did not appear until 1894, were compiled by the sensationalistic journalist Joe DeBarthe and contain distortions. No military records confirm the employment of Martha Canary as a scout.[33]

However, since Calamity's scouting career is central to the development of her legend, and Grouard's testimony is uniquely supportive, it demands careful scrutiny. The employment of the additional scouts occurred, Grouard said, after the Battle of the Rosebud. Becoming impatient while waiting at the Goose Creek camp for Wesley Merritt's Fifth Cavalry to reinforce his command, Crook decided to leave his position and, recalled Grouard, "jump the hostiles with what command he had." They moved to the Tongue River, but could not locate the Indian camp. Returning to Little Goose Creek, where they finally were joined by the Fifth Cavalry, the army moved to the present site of Sheridan, Wyoming. While making preparations to pursue the Indians, remembered Grouard, "some of our scouts had to leave us," and "I got orders to hire all the scouts I could find." This statement means Martha and the others Grouard mentioned were employed after the arrival of the Fifth Cavalry on August 3 and before the command left its permanent camp on Goose Creek to search for the Indians. But other evidence suggests Martha was sent back to Fort Fetterman on June 21. Since she could not have arrived before mid-June, her scouting career, if it occurred at all, was extremely brief and not when Grouard reported it.

An examination of the other scouts Grouard claimed he employed clouds the issue even further. All are real people, but none is reported with Crook's summer expedition. Charlie Chapin, an actor, briefly performed in the Black Hills several years later. According to his memoirs, written while incarcerated in Sing Sing prison, he was not in the region in 1876; in addition, he mentioned no employment as a scout.[34] Black Hills Frank probably refers to Calamity's associate, Little Frank. It does not seem likely that Grouard employed two prostitutes as scouts without other participants in the campaign noticing. Phoenix may be the man killed at Fort Fetterman Hog Ranch in 1884, and perhaps served as a scout during the March campaign.[35] The only Zimmer identified in contemporary records appears in Hunton's diary, and no information exists about him other than the name Bill Zimmer.[36]

Furthermore, Crook's other scouts vigorously disagree with Grouard's assertion that Martha ever served as a scout. For example, Ben Arnold, who had known Martha in Montana during her childhood, declared that "the stories of her being a scout or guide are inventions of people who never knew her." She did have "many stirring adventures and many true stories could be told of her," he said, but "most of them would not look well in print."[37]

Captain Jack Crawford, who joined Crook's command after the Battle of the Rosebud, also emphatically asserted that Martha "was never employed as a scout by General Crook." In his position as General Wesley Merritt's chief of scouts, Crawford had opportunity to become "well acquainted with every scout employed by the government," and Martha "was not with the command at any time." By the time Crawford arrived at Crook's encampment, Martha was in Deadwood. Nevertheless, Crawford had opportunity to learn the truth about Martha's role from his fellow scouts. Though sexist by today's standards ("a real frontiersman" would find "absurd" the notion that any woman could scout), Crawford's testimony is convincing.[38]

Crawford did not, however, deny that Martha had been with the command. In fact, he said that Crook "gave her no recognition whatever, except to order her out of camp when he discovered she was a camp follower."[39] Other members of Crook's army also recalled her being with the command as a camp follower. According to Lieutenant John Gregory Bourke, Crook's aide-de-camp, "It was whispered that one of our teamsters was a woman, and no other than 'Calamity Jane,' a character famed in border history." She disguised herself by wearing the "raiment of the alleged rougher sex, and was skinning mules with the best of them." She was discovered, Bourke said, when she "didn't cuss her mules with the enthusiasm to be expected from a graduate of Patrick & Saulsbury's [sic] Black Hills Stage Line, as she had represented herself to be." Although Bourke's entry about Calamity Jane appears between June 9 and 14 in his chronologically arranged narrative, she could not have joined the command by that time. In fact, Bourke's hearsay account obviously was inserted long after the events occurred; she was not in 1876 "a character famed in border story." Also, had Bourke observed her driving mules, he would not have thought her profanity inadequate, it being among her strongest suits. Bourke's mention of Calamity Jane indicates only that officers became aware that the notorious woman was among the troops. Moreover, his statements are so imprecise about time that he may, in fact, have been referring to the March campaign rather than the one in June.[40]

Captain Anson Mills also recalled Martha's joining the command, but thought it was before they reached Fort Reno on June 2, an impossibility because she was still in a Cheyenne jail. Martha was "discovered and placed under guard," Mills remembered, but she still managed to embarrass him. As he walked through the wagon-master's outfit, she called out, "There is Colonel Mills, he knows me!" Because of her reputation as a camp follower, Mills's men had a good laugh at his expense. He decided that she recognized him because she once was employed as a cook by his neighbor in North Platte. Although no evidence establishes that Martha ever resided at North Platte, she could have recognized Mills from his presence at other military posts or from an earlier expedition. A married man of integrity, Mills was chagrined at Martha's familiarity, especially because, despite his protests, no one believed that he was unacquainted with her.[41]

Mills recalled that after the officers discovered Martha with the soldiers, she was detained and "placed in improvised female attire." She accompanied the troops only "until a force was organized to carry our helpless back, with which she was sent."[42] Mills's recollection suggests Martha left from the Goose Creek camp with the wounded on June 21. If so, she was sent back only days after she joined the command. According to Dr. Valentine T. McGillycuddy, who was stationed at Fort Fetterman, the wounded arrived there on June 27.[43] McGillycuddy did not mention Martha among them, but he may have been preoccupied with the large numbers of wounded men.

Mills's recollection that Martha was sent back with the wounded is supported by John Hunton. He recalled that Martha and "three other women of the same character" had been "smuggled out with the command and remained with it until found out and ordered back." Hunton, believing it was May when the women left with the army, clearly impossible in Martha's case, was certain they returned with the wounded from Rosebud. "I saw her on the way up to John Brown Ranch the same day the train arrived in Fetterman," he recalled.[44]

Sergeant John Q. Ward also remembered that Martha "and her side kicker, Frankie, procured mounts, and in the full regalia of cavalry troopers took the field with the command." Like Hunton, he mistakenly thought they might have been with the command from its departure on May 14 and believed they remained with Crook's army until after June 26, when Custer's troops were annihilated. According to Ward, Martha and Frankie were sent back to Fort Fetterman "under the escort of a discharged soldier" through the Indian-infested country.[45] The unanimity among Mills, Hunton, and Ward concerning Martha's being sent back from Crook's command to Fort Fetterman is significant. Her arrival there near June 27 also corresponds to the time of her encounter at Fort Laramie with the Hickok party traveling to the Black Hills.

That many of these witnesses made errors concerning the precise moment that Martha visited Crook's army is understandable. Few of them had personal contact with Martha and probably assumed that if they encountered a woman in male clothing, it was the notorious Calamity Jane. Moreover, there was considerable traffic to and from the army in the field that summer, and many other camp followers wearning male apparel joined the command.

In fact, correspondent Thomas C. "Mac" MacMillan of the *Chicago Inter-Ocean*, who had met Martha during the 1875 Black Hills expedition, titled one of his 1876 dispatches "Crook's Camp Followers." He confirmed that "the number of camp followers with the Big Horn expedition [was] considerable," although he did not see Martha. He did have a personal encounter with "a lad of 15 or 16," who came to the reporter's tent and asked if they "could see him through the expedition." Although "his voice and face were feminine, . . . his clothing was unmistakably that of the soldier-citizen." MacMillan added that after the correspondents gave "him (or her) some supper" and promised to allow "him (or her)" to join them "to the end of the expedition," the camp follower departed but failed to return, having "some calls to make in the other companies."[46]

Likewise, John F. Finerty, correspondent for the *Chicago Times*, reported that on July 13 "our wagon train arrived from Fetterman," and with it "also came the devil, in the shape of a peddler who sold whisky. Two abandoned females, disguised as mule drivers, also came into camp." Soon several soldiers were drunk: "General Crook got angry when he learned what was going on, ordered the whisky barrels seized and the harlots put under arrest, to be sent back with the first train."[47] Martha by this time was safely ensconced in the Black Hills. Nevertheless, some writers have incorrectly identified Martha as one of these prostitutes. Among modern historians assuming one of these women was Calamity Jane is J. W. Vaughn in his highly respected narrative, *With Crook at the Rosebud*.[48]

Because of these conflicting and imprecise memoirs about Martha's presence with Crook's command, final conclusions must remain tentative. Nevertheless, it is clear that her time with Crook's command in June 1876 was brief. She reached the Goose Creek encampment between June 15 and June 18, proximate to the Battle of the Rosebud, and probably was sent back with the wounded on June 21. Only a remote possibility exists that Grouard allowed Martha to ride with the scouts during that brief period.

Despite the improbability that she ever served as a scout, she told others that she had. In 1878, Horatio N. Maguire, a Black Hills journalist, described the notorious woman in a nationally circulated booklet. "She admits," said Maguire, "that she has dressed in male attire," and has "acted in the capacity of a scout in the Indian service." Maguire accepted her claim. Besides reporting her story, he included a sketch of Martha in male attire riding astride her horse, pistol in hand and rifle strapped to her back. The picture is labeled, "Miss Martha Canary ('Calamity Jane'), The Female Scout."[49]

Among the few historical markers that commemorate the activities of Martha Canary is one located in Sheridan, Wyoming, the site of Crook's camp at the time of the Battle of the Rosebud. In the brief history of the campaign provided on the sign, three famous members of Crook's 1876 expedition are mentioned: Buffalo Bill, Frank Grouard, and Calamity Jane.[50]

Later romancers expanded on Martha's scouting reputation. When she passed through Omaha, Nebraska, in 1892, the newspaper reported that during the past decade "no name has been more familiar to Americans than that of Calamity Jane." During her career, she "killed forty Indians and seventeen white men." And, the newspaper added, she was "a scout for the United States army and it was she who first carried the news of Custer's massacre to the old frontier forts."[51]

Clinton Wells, a Wyoming bullwhacker, exaggerated further. Wells claimed that Martha tried to warn Custer of the danger he faced. She "rode from General Crook's camp in Wyoming with a secret message for General Custer," Wells explained. The dispatch urged Custer to delay his attack until reinforcements could be sent, but Martha was held up by severe weather and contracted pneumonia. "In the interim, Custer rode over the ridge beyond the Little Big Horn—baited there by a few Indian stragglers," and encountered "a horde of Cheyenne and Sioux Indians who killed every soldier."[52]

Other writers suggested that she had accompanied Custer rather than Crook. On one occasion, a Glendive, Montana, correspondent asked Martha about her rumored involvement in the Custer fight. Always willing to satisfy reporters, and revealing a seldom-mentioned sense of humor, Martha responded: "I was with Custer for several months

and in different engagements, but if I had been with him in his last battle, I would probably be with him now." Then she added: "On the other hand, had Custer paid attention
to warnings and a message I sent him he and his brave band might be now in the land
that I am in."[53]

Reports of Martha being with Custer at the Little Big Horn led one reporter in 1902
to remark angrily that, although Martha had "a number of hair-breadth escapes" during
her life, and probably was "entitled to as much notoriety as the average frontiersman or
woman," it was an offense to real frontiersmen to suggest she was ever associated with
Custer.[54] Despite the journalist's chagrin, the stories about Martha's scouting career
have continued.

Although Martha's role with the military during the 1876 Indian campaigns has
been greatly exaggerated, her movements in the spring of 1876 did require physical
endurance and placed her in considerable personal danger. She accompanied Crook's
winter campaign in February, traveled to the Black Hills in April, served time in a
Cheyenne jail in May, hurried to northern Wyoming to join Crook's command in June,
then returned to Fort Fetterman before the end of the month. Obviously, she thrived
on adventure.

After Martha's return from the field, John Hunton recalled that she "soon left
Fetterman and I do not think returned there that year, but she was in Fetterman in
the spring of the year 1877 for a short time."[55] His recollection that she left Wyoming
in June 1876 is accurate. Once again she traveled to the Black Hills, this time for an
extended stay. "When able to ride I started for Fort Laramie where I met Wm. Hickock,
better known as Wild Bill, and we started for Deadwood, where we arrived about June,"
wrote Martha in her *Life and Adventures*.[56] Entering the Black Hills with Hickok, when added
to claims that she scouted for Crook, enhanced her legendary reputation immeasurably.

CHAPTER FIVE

With Wild Bill Hickok
in Deadwood, 1876

To this day, tourists flock to visit the graves of Martha Canary and James Butler (Wild Bill) Hickok, who lie buried near each other in Deadwood's Mount Moriah Cemetery. It is commonly supposed that the two had a long-standing relationship that ended in tragedy with Hickok's death on August 2, 1876.

Hickok's biographers, however, discount any serious relationship between the two figures, suggesting he was too fastidious a man to associate with such a dissolute woman. Frank J. Wilstach, whose 1926 biography *Wild Bill Hickok: The Prince of the Pistoleers* did much to secure Hickok's twentieth-century popularity, labeled any relationship with Calamity "gossip" and said that "the report that he [Hickok] was associated with the woman at any time seems to be pure moonshine."[1] Similarly, Joseph Rosa, the foremost modern Hickok scholar, concludes that "of all the women associated in any way with Wild Bill, she [Martha] had the least to do with him, yet she is always spoken of in the same breath when Hickok's women friends are mentioned."[2]

Stories connecting Martha Canary and James Butler Hickok began appearing even during Martha's lifetime. For example, an Omaha newspaper in 1892 referred to her as "an old side partner of Wild Bill, the notorious desperado who was assassinated in Deadwood. Jane was in Deadwood at the time and was among the first to place a pillow under the head of the dying man and minister to his wants."[3] Deadwood newspapers at the time of Martha's death on August 1, 1903, also linked her to Hickok, but showed considerable confusion. First it was suggested that Martha asked to be buried next to her old friend, and then, only a few days later, it was stated that he was her "former husband" and that they lived "as man and wife in a cabin along Deadwood gulch."[4] In the ensuing years, accounts became increasingly fanciful, with some writers even changing Martha's death date to coincide with Hickok's. For example, Harry (Sam) Young asserted that she died August 2, 1906, "the same day and month, and the same hour, Wild Bill was assassinated thirty years before."[5]

The truth concerning the relationship between Martha and Wild Bill may never be determined. Clearly, neither fantasizing romanticists nor hostile detractors are completely correct. Martha was far more attractive a personality than critics suggest, but less intimate with Hickok than romanticists imagine. Martha's *Life and Adventures* asserts in a matter-of-fact manner that she first met Hickok at Fort Laramie in June 1876 and traveled to Deadwood in his company. She refers to him in her book only as a friend.[6]

Upon her return to Fort Fetterman about June 27 after visiting Crook's army, Martha evidently meandered to Fort Laramie and the nearby road ranches. A traveler to the Black Hills, Charles Grant, recalled meeting her at Hat Creek Station, about sixty miles from Fort Laramie. They first became acquainted when "she asked me if I had any chewing tobacco," said Grant. "Fortunately for her I had some, and gave her half a plug." During that meeting, which he recalled lasted only a half-hour, she explained that she had attempted to join a military expedition (Grant thought Custer's), but "the soldiers had refused to permit her to accompany the command."[7] After talking with Grant, Martha probably wandered to Fort Laramie. Coincidently, Wild Bill Hickok, who with his friend Charles (Colorado Charlie) Utter had organized a wagon train of gold seekers to go to the Black Hills, also visited the post.

Hickok already was a well-known frontiersman. Born in Troy Grove, Illinois, on May 27, 1837, he first journeyed west with his brother, Lorenzo, in 1856. He became a spy and wagoneer for the Union during the Civil War. But it was a controversial shooting incident at Rock Creek stage station in Nebraska in 1861 that propelled him to fame. Details of the Rock Creek event are disputed, but Hickok and others at the station killed several members of the McCanles family. An exaggerated version of that incident, combined with other heroic adventures, appeared in the February 1867 *Harper's Monthly*, bringing Hickok national prominence. The author of the story, George Ward Nichols, portrayed the McCanles family as a gang of proslavery villains and claimed that Hickok single-handedly fought off his opponents with gun and knife. A few months after the appearance of Nichols's article, Hickok was featured in a dime novel, *Wild Bill, The Indian Slayer* (July 1867), helping enlarge his reputation. Later, in Hays City and Abilene, Kansas, he acted as deputy U.S. marshal, army scout, and law officer, service which also enhanced his stature.

Although many admired Hickok, others despised him for his showy dress, his itchy trigger-finger, and his compulsive gambling. Legends say he killed thirty-six men, or perhaps a hundred, but his most careful biographer, Joseph Rosa, concludes the killings numbered about ten.

Hickok spent much of his time in 1874 and 1875 in Cheyenne, Wyoming. There, on March 5, 1876, Hickok married Agnes Lake Thatcher after a long acquaintance that began in 1871 in Abilene. W. F. Warren, the Methodist minister in Cheyenne who married the couple, wrote in the remarks column of the church register, "I don't think they meant it," but he may have been mistaken. After a two-week visit to her family in Cincinnati, Ohio, Hickok returned alone to Cheyenne. He then joined the gold rush to the Black Hills, evidently intending to send for Agnes as soon as he was established.[8]

Planning to lead a wagon train of gold seekers into the Black Hills, Hickok traveled to and from St. Louis and Cheyenne several times during the spring of 1876, recruiting and organizing the proposed expedition. The Cheyenne newspaper reported on April 14 that "Wild Bill still lingers with us," spending his time "stuffing newcomers and tenderfeet of all descriptions with tales of his prowess and his wonderful discoveries of diamond caves, etc., which he describes as being located 'up north.'"[9] At some point he met Colorado Charley Utter, who intended to establish a Black Hills transportation line, and the two seem to have merged their efforts.[10] The Hickok-Utter party evidently left Cheyenne on June 27 for the Black Hills, reaching John Hunton's road ranch on June 30. Hunton dutifully noted in his diary, "Large party of B. Hillers passed with 'Wild Bill.'"[11]

Hickok and his companions tarried briefly fifteen miles north of Fort Laramie at Government Farm, a popular stopping point for wagon trains. There they hoped to join other parties for security against Indians. The party also took on an unexpected new member, Martha Canary. Joseph (White-Eye) Anderson, one of Hickok's associates, remembered that when they arrived at Fort Laramie, an officer requested they take Martha with them. It being "just after payday," she "had been on a big drunk with the soldiers and had been having a hell of a time of it." She was now residing in the guard house, "very drunk and near naked." Steve Utter, Charley's brother, agreed to take her along. Anderson added: "The officer furnished a suit of soldiers' underclothes, and the rest of us furnished her with sufficient clothes to wear," including a buckskin costume and a broad-brimmed hat. White Eye thought her reasonably attractive when she was sober, cleaned up, and dressed.

Many years later, White-Eye Anderson wrote that this "was the first time that Wild Bill had met her and he surely did not have any use for her." White Eye claimed that Martha's companion during the trip to the Hills was Steve Utter.[12] Likewise, John Hunton, who had become acquainted with Hickok in 1874–75, was convinced that Wild Bill had not met Martha before this journey by wagon train in 1876.[13]

Martha was not the only camp follower with Hickok's party. Although many of the people in the wagon train were prospectors, gamblers, and saloon men, recalled Anderson, there also were as many as fourteen "ladies of easy virtue."[14] John Gray, a member of the party who later became a prominent mining figure in the Hills, recalled that the party included Calamity Jane, Madame Moustache, and Dirty Em, "each of whom will be remembered by old-timers."[15]

The trip from Fort Laramie to the Black Hills took about two weeks, during which Anderson and Martha became well acquainted. He estimated her age to be twenty-five (she was twenty). According to Anderson, Martha could drive a team of mules as well as any man. Her bullwhacking skills proved valuable to the party, he said. She would get them over the rough places "with a black snake whip and lots of cussing." Martha also was good with a rifle and six-shooter. One day when a coyote was spotted in the distance, the men fired at it with their rifles and missed, but Martha, said Anderson, killed it "with a six-shooter when it was over one hundred yards away." Besides these "masculine" activities,

Martha helped Anderson, the party's cook, prepare the food, which led him to conclude she was a "big-hearted woman." However, he also recalled that when the party gathered near the campfire each night, she "told some of the toughest stories I ever heard and there would always be a big crowd come over to the campfire to hear her talk."[16]

According to Anderson, Hickok avoided Martha's campfire stories, but he nevertheless frequently came into contact with her during the trip. This was because Hickok had a keg of whiskey and invited his friends to help themselves. Martha "hit it more often than anyone else," recalled Anderson. But each time she wanted a drink, she had to request the tin cup from Hickok. "She would say, 'Mr. Hickok, I'm dry again.' Once he told her to go slow, that others were dry too."[17]

These anecdotes obscure the difficulty of wagon travel to the Black Hills. Only a few weeks after the Hickok party made the trip, a party of eight men including journalist Leander P. Richardson, left Fort Laramie. From the beginning, "sand-gnats" harrassed them. These pesky insects, Richardson wrote, "darted into our eyes, crawled into our nostrils, buzzed in our ears, and wriggled down our necks in a most annoying fashion." In addition, they had to cross "deep and precipitous gulches," and after a cold, drizzling rain, all of their party caught colds. The rainfall also produced mud that clung so tightly to the wheels that it became necessary every hundred yards "to dismount and pry it away with a crow-bar."[18] It is likely the Hickok party's journey was similarly demanding.

Upon reaching the southern Black Hills, the Hickok party stopped briefly in Custer City.[19] Most of the town's residents had left after learning of the gold discoveries in Deadwood. Those remaining recalled that Hickok stayed in a little house on the banks of French Creek. After the visit of "Wild Bill and his crew of depraved women in 1876," a reporter noted, Hickok was considered by the people of Custer "as a 'bum' and hard citizen who sought only the lower strata of society for associates."[20]

However, Hickok soon left Custer, arriving in Deadwood about July 12 with several companions. Newspaperman Richard B. Hughes described their spectacular parade down Deadwood's main street. Accompanying Hickok were "four other characters—also of considerable notoriety," Charley and Steve Utter, "Bloody Dick" Seymour, and Calamity Jane, "who basked chiefly in the reflected glory of their leader." Their entry was designed to attract attention, Hughes added, as they "rode the entire length of Main Street, mounted on good horses and clad in complete suits of buckskin, every suit of which carried sufficient fringe to make a considerable buckskin rope."[21] Black Hills pioneer John S. McClintock, who learned of the party's arrival the next day, remembered two women in Hickok's party, Calamity Jane and Kitty Arnold.[22] After arriving, they pitched their tents along Whitewood Creek, according to White-Eye Anderson. Martha did not remain with them, however. "Wild Bill, the Utter boys, Pie, my brother Charlie, and myself camped there," said White-Eye, "and sometimes Calamity Jane came to camp when she got hungry."[23]

Confirming Martha's presence in Deadwood, the *Black Hills Pioneer* of July 15 reported, "'Calamity Jane' has arrived."[24] Martha was the only member of the Hickok party whose arrival was announced, perhaps because she was well known from her earlier trips to the

Hills. She immediately became a dance-hall celebrity. Those who assume she was too dissolute and masculine to be attractive missed essential qualities of her character. Even detractor Captain Jack Crawford, who believed Hickok's "name should in no way be associated with Calamity Jane's," admitted that she was "a good-hearted woman and under different environments would have made a good wife and mother." But growing up in mining camps without parental supervision resulted in her living "in a wild, unnatural manner."[25]

In her *Life and Adventures*, Martha omitted her dance-hall career, instead claiming that during June she served "as a pony express rider carrying the U.S. mail between Deadwood and Custer, a distance of fifty miles, over one of the roughest trails in the Black Hills country." Although previous riders were "robbed of their packages, mail and money," Martha said she was not bothered by road agents because of her "reputation as a rider and quick shot."[26] Her story is fanciful. Charley Utter did establish an express mail service in July, perhaps the "pony express" Martha mentions, but no source indicates she rode for it or any other mail service.[27] In fact, her autobiography is somewhat contradictory. It states that she "remained around Deadwood all that summer visiting all the camps within an area of one hundred miles," which, if true, left little time to carry the mail.

White-Eye Anderson recalled the period differently. Shortly after their arrival in Deadwood, he remembered, Martha asked the members of the Hickok party for a loan. "I can't do business in these old buckskins," she explained. "I ain't got the show the other girls have." The men all contributed, said Anderson, but Hickok's $20 came with a request that she "wash behind her ears." Martha agreed and took a bath in the creek, even asking Steve Utter to "wash her body thoroughly with perfumed soap." Then she purchased "a good outfit of female clothes." When Martha returned to the Hickok camp a few days later, said Anderson, she "pulled up her dress, rolled down her stocking and took out a roll of greenbacks" and repaid the money she had borrowed. She said business had been good, but she "didn't express it in just that way." Anderson also remembered that Hickok refused repayment, saying, "At least she looks like a woman now."[28]

John S. McClintock similarly recalled that Martha figured "conspicuously in the many dance halls."[29] In these popular dance halls, or hurdy-gurdy houses, young women were made available as dancing partners. Usually there was no charge for dancing, but at the end of each dance, men took their partners to the bar to purchase drinks, with the proprietor sharing profits from the sales with the dance-hall girls. The Deadwood newspaper described the hurdy-gurdy dances in considerable detail:

> To witness a dance at one of our hurdy gurdy houses, we think would be interesting to some of our eastern friends unaccustomed to such scenes, particularly after the dance has been under way for several hours, and the participants in the dance have had sufficient time to become well filled up with the choice brands of whisky usually sold at such places. The whisky soon limbers them up and the motley crowd vie with each other in showing their own peculiar fancy steps, while their partners, the frail sisters of the town, put on their sweetest smiles and enter into the amusement with vigor.[30]

A prospector, George Stokes, said that when he saw Martha she was wearing "a ten-collar Stetson with a cowman's purple handkerchief around her neck" and "danced with everybody and promenaded to the bar, as was the custom, after every dance."[31]

Generally, these dancing establishments remained opened most of the night, and although the girls were not necessarily prostitutes, it was not uncommon for them to engage in the oldest profession. Some accounts identify E. A. Swearingen's "Gem" as the establishment where Martha initially danced in Deadwood. Swearingen had entered Deadwood with a bull team in May 1876. "He arrived on Monday and by the next Saturday he had a dance hall running," recalled the Deadwood newspaper, noting that the flimsy structure was built of lumber and canvas. That summer, he had only three women available for dancing: Mrs. Swearingen, Kitty Arnold, and Calamity Jane. Needing another dancer, a young man "was dressed in feminine garb, corseted and padded, with closely shingled hair," said the newspaper, and sold liquor as easily as the women.[32]

Swearingen's dance hall had a bad reputation. McClintock said "it would require an abler pen than mine to portray anything approaching a true picture of the inside workings of that notorious den of iniquity." Swearingen made regular trips to other towns to recruit new women, enticing them to the Hills with promises of jobs in hotels or with families. If, after reaching Deadwood, the young women refused to work in his dance hall, they had to fend for themselves. Despite the Gem's unsavory reputation, said McClintock, Swearingen drew support from Deadwood's "so-called leading citizens" as well as from "residents and floaters of the underworld." His dance hall became Deadwood's "chief attraction."[33]

Deadwood bartender Sam Young, who first met Martha during the 1875 Black Hills expedition, recalled not only that Martha worked at the Gem but said she helped Swearingen recruit other young women as well. Young became reacquainted with Martha while he was playing a game of faro in Jim Pencil's saloon. Since she was broke, Young gave her "a five-dollar greenback," which she spent immediately on drinks, "and in a short time she was in a wild state of intoxication." Young claimed that Swearingen once asked Martha to go to Sidney, Nebraska, "to white slave for him." She returned with ten girls, having "captivated them with exaggerated stories of the immense wealth in the Black Hills and the large amount of money to be made." Young also recalled that Martha's "habits were thoroughly masculine," and that she frequently danced with the girls just as the men did.[34]

William B. Lull, a Methodist minister's son who arrived in the Black Hills in 1875 in search of gold, likewise recalled Martha working in the dance halls. Lull, nicknamed "New York Billie," became the manager of Porter's Hotel, which catered to dance-hall girls and gamblers. Martha was one of the hotel's occupants. She also served refreshments at the Bella Union, remembered Lull, who characterized her as a "lone Wolf" and "born gambler" addicted to the game of faro. During the time she stayed at the hotel, Martha became seriously ill with mountain fever or typhoid. Against her will, Lull sent for a doctor and organized the other hotel girls to take turns caring for her.

Although Martha had to be forced to take her medicine, she afterwards thanked Lull and gave him a tintype of her.[35]

According to Leander Richardson, for a while Martha maintained her own sporting establishment in competition with Kitty Austin (Arnold). Richardson remembered that Martha had arrived in Deadwood with only "a suit of men's clothing and a progressive jag," so dress was a problem for her. Although Kitty "was the prettiest" and had a lavish wardrobe, Martha "could outride, outdrink, and outshoot" her, and occasionally, after consuming sufficient liquor, would ride "up and down the street howling like an Indian" and "shoot in all the windows of Miss Austin's vaunted temple of Terpsichore."[36]

White-Eye Anderson related one memorable dance-hall episode involving Martha and "Tid Bit," a redhead from Salt Lake City who, like Martha, entered the Hills with the Hickok party. Tid Bit "agreed to entertain" a fellow nicknamed Laughing Sam. But the gold dust he gave her as payment turned out to be "brass filings and black sand." Learning of the deception, Martha borrowed Charley Utter's "two big, ivory handled six-shooters," and walked to the saloon where Laughing Sam and Bummer Dan ran a faro game. Anderson and his friends followed "to see the fun." Martha, with guns in hand, informed the crowd what Laughing Sam had done. "I never heard a man get such a cussing as she gave him," Anderson said, adding that Martha forced Laughing Sam to give Tid Bit "two twenty dollar gold pieces."[37]

Another popular story identifies Martha as the culprit who disrupted a theatrical presentation. According to Leander Richardson, Jack Langrishe was performing *The Streets of New York* that summer. One scene in that play depicts two female characters deciding to commit suicide and the hero bursting into the room to save them. At this intense moment in the drama, a woman "clad in yellow silk trimmed with bright green" loudly "cleared her mouth of its cargo of tobacco juice, and cried in disdainful tones that were perfectly audible all over the house: "Oh, H——l! That's a put up job." After a "momentary lull," there was a "howl of laughter, in which even the dying actresses were forced to join."[38] However, Martha may not have been the person guilty of the expectoration and exclamation. In a later article, Richardson identified Martha's rival, Kitty Arnold, as the tobacco-spitting woman.[39]

Encounters between Martha and the first minister in the Black Hills, the Reverend Henry Weston Smith, also became the gist for legend. Sam Young recalled that during the minister's first sermon in Deadwood, five dance-hall girls attended, and Martha, in "an intoxicated condition, snatched his old hat from his hand," announcing to the listeners, "You sinners, dig down in your pokes, now; this old fellow looks as though he were broke and I want to collect about two hundred dollars for him."[40] According to White-Eye Anderson, at another service the minister talked about money being the root of all evil. Martha told him "that she didn't care very much for the money, just as long as she had plenty of the root she was satisfied."[41]

While Martha entertained in dance halls and participated in Deadwood's camp life, Hickok practiced shooting targets at his camp, perhaps did a little prospecting, and drank and gambled in Deadwood's saloons. Discomforting for Hickok biographers is the claim of John S. McClintock that the famous gunman "was frequently seen while in Deadwood, walking on the street with his two six-shooters stuck under the waist band of his pants, with no scabbards in sight, followed by his 'consort,' 'Calamity Jane.'"[42] Learning of McClintock's assertion, Frank J. Wilstach responded that it "appears to be wholly unwarranted." He added that "Wild Bill would not so lower himself" to have a relationship with Calamity Jane.[43] McClintock insisted, however, that Martha came to Deadwood with Hickok and "followed him up and down the streets, accompanied him to and from restaurants, and after he was killed, wailed over his body and invoked maledictions upon the head of his murderer."[44]

Other witnesses support McClintock's claim. Charles Grant, who shared chewing tobacco with Martha at Hat Creek Station, also saw her associating with Hickok in Deadwood. Grant said he saw Martha repeatedly in Deadwood. "When she was sober, which was only once in a while," Grant recalled, "I usually talked with her, but when she was drunk I kept as far away from her as possible, as she was considerable of a nuisance." He especially remembered her profanity: "Swear! No woman that ever breathed could beat her when she was angry, or only half angry." Grant remembered that Wild Bill interrupted one of his conversations with Martha, and he "left them to talk it out."[45]

Hickok's friend, Moses (California Joe) Milner denied there was any relationship between Martha and Wild Bill, but he evidently encountered her on the same day he met Hickok in a Deadwood saloon. Martha teasingly asked Milner if he wanted her to dance standing on her head again, referring to the time he had picked her up by her feet during the 1875 expedition. According to Milner's biographers, he looked at her scornfully, then pulled his gun and demanded she dance for the saloon crowd. When she responded with "a mocking laugh," he began firing shots near her feet to make her dance. "Whenever she showed signs of stopping Joe would hasten her movements with another bullet, to the delight of the crowd of miners." Then he lifted her atop the bar, making her continue dancing by firing shots over her head. "In the end he permitted her to stop, but warned her to keep away from him unless she wanted to dance every time they met."[46]

Even though these witnesses suggest Martha and Wild Bill maintained at least a casual friendship in Deadwood, others deny any relationship. The journalist Leander Richardson said he knew all about the last days of Wild Bill because he was a guest of the gunman and his partner, Charley Utter. Richardson denied any intimacy between Hickok and Martha. Instead, he said, her heartthrob was Colorado Charley, "the dandy of that country." Utter had long blonde hair and a mustache, and wore "beaded moccasins, fringed leggings and coat, hand-some trousers, fine linen, revolvers mounted in gold, silver, and pearl, and a belt with a big silver buckle." Martha, said Richardson, "had it as her sole ambition, aside from the consumption of all the red liquor in the gulch, to win him." Unfortunately, Richardson was in Deadwood only five days, and on the third day of his visit Hickok was shot, making his testimony less than authoritative.[47] Moreover, Martha might well have pursued Colorado Charley, followed Wild Bill around town, and spent time with other men in the dance halls as well.

Hickok's drinking and gambling brought him into regular contact with the saloon crowd. On August 2, while Hickok played cards in Number 10 Saloon, Jack McCall shot him in the back of the head, killing him instantly. McCall's motives have not been ascertained, but alcohol and a minor quarrel stemming from an earlier card game were probably factors. Others suggest McCall was hired to assassinate Hickok by lawbreakers who feared he was going to be appointed marshal, but little evidence supports this assertion.[48]

Martha claimed that she played a central role in McCall's capture. In her *Life and Adventures*, Martha recalled that Hickok "remained in Deadwood during the summer," which, if referring to the two or three weeks between mid-July and August 2, is true. While he sat "at a gambling table in the Bell Union [*sic*] saloon, in Deadwood," she continued, "he was shot in the back of the head by the notorious Jack McCall, a desperado."[49] Her memory was inaccurate; Hickok was killed not in the Bella Union but in Saloon No. 10, operated by Nuttall and Mann. This error caused biographer Roberta Sollid to comment teasingly, "No one would criticize her for confusing a saloon or two."[50]

According to Martha, after she learned of the shooting she started at once in search of the assassin, locating him in "Shurdy's [Shoudy's] butcher shop." Having forgotten her guns on her bedpost, she "grabbed a meat cleaver and made him throw up his hands," an action making little sense when one recalls that an armed McCall could easily have shot her when she approached. After McCall surrendered, she said, he was "taken to a log cabin and locked up, well secured as every one thought, but he got away." He was recaptured, however, at "Fagan's ranch at Horse Creek, on the old Cheyenne road" and then was "taken to Yankton, Dak., where he was tried, sentenced and hung."[51]

Although generally correct, Martha's description of McCall's capture, escape, trial, and execution contains serious errors and omissions. Witnesses remembered that after McCall walked out of the saloon and mounted his horse to get away, a loose cinch caused the saddle to turn and "he fell to the ground." Hurriedly he ran up the street, and, reported the *Black Hills Pioneer*, "was captured by a lively chase by many of the citizens." Even Martha's friend, Sam Young, the bartender in Saloon No. 10, did not mention her in his rendition of Hickok's death and the capture of McCall.[52] Her assertion that McCall escaped from jail is also in error. Instead, he stood trial in Deadwood, where a jury found him "not guilty," evidently based on his fabricated statement that Wild Bill had killed his brother in Kansas. Martha was correct in saying that he was later arrested in Wyoming, but it was in Laramie, not at Fagan's ranch. Because his trial had occurred outside the bounds of legally recognized government, McCall was retried and convicted for the murder of Hickok in Yankton, Dakota Territory, and hanged on March 1, 1877.[53] Captain Jack Crawford correctly concluded that the stories of Martha's involvement in the capture of Jack McCall are "another bit of fiction."[54]

If Martha made errors in her autobiography, she exaggerated even more extensively in a 1902 interview. Hickok now became her "affianced husband" and was to marry her "within a few days, when McCall shot and killed him in cold blood in Deadwood." When it seemed that there was "no prospect that the vigilantes or the authorities would take any action," Martha said she went to Yankton, "took the case before a grand jury and had McCall indicted." After his arrest, she added, McCall was tried, convicted, and hanged in Yankton. Actually, Martha played no part in McCall's Yankton trial and execution.[55]

But Martha's own account of McCall's arrest and execution was no more exaggerated than stories by some of her contemporaries. An unidentified old-timer, who claimed he knew her in 1876, confirmed her tale to the reporter and then embellished it. "I chanced to be at Yankton," he asserted, "and was one of the twenty-two who were in the enclosure where the hanging took place." Martha, dressed in her buckskin outfit, watched as the final moment approached. "McCall caught her eye," and angrily "hissed an anathema at her and expressed a wish for a gun that he might shoot her as the last act of his life."[56] This absurd fiction that Martha initiated McCall's arrest and attended his hanging in Yankton also appeared in the first movie about Calamity Jane, filmed in Nebraska in 1915.[57]

However, those who believe Martha had no contact with Hickok may be guilty of disregarding evidence.[58] Evidently, Martha sincerely mourned his death. Richard B. Hughes observed that while "the reputation of Hickok was such as to cause little mourning over his fate, and was confined chiefly to those of his kind," he did have "one sincere female mourner" and that was Martha, "whose grief for a time seemed uncontrollable."[59] John S. McClintock, who believed that Wild Bill and Calamity Jane were close, added that after Hickok's death Calamity showed no particular preference for any other man.[60] Moreover, Thomas Newson's *Drama of Life in the Black Hills*, written for the stage in 1878, describes Martha's sorrow and deserves attention because it appeared within two years of the events it depicts. Newson, a St. Paul, Minnesota, journalist who visited the Hills, claimed his dramatic piece was "drawn from living realities" that were "truthful to a degree that will challenge the criticism of those best informed." Although the drama describes no deep intimacy between Wild Bill and Martha, it nevertheless depicts her in the saloon when Wild Bill began gambling. Referring to Wild Bill as "one of my best and dearest friends," she departs shortly before McCall enters the saloon and shoots Hickok. Hearing the news, Martha rushes back to the saloon, asking, "Who shot Wild Bill?" She then

> pushes aside the crowd, who gaze upon her with astonishment. Takes the head of Wild Bill in her lap and moans: "Oh! my God! my best, my greatest friend is gone! Bill! speak to me! Bill! open your eyes! Bill! you can't be dead! When the cold world kicked me, it was you who helped me. When the heart was breaking, it was you who calmed it. Oh! my God! my God!" and Jane falls to the floor in a swoon. None touch her, but Wild Bill's body is picked up, placed upon a bench, . . . those present step back, gaze upon the scene (Calamity Jane being still upon the floor,) and the curtain falls.[61]

Although melodramatic, Newson's scene of an emotionally distraught Martha Canary matches recollections by Hughes and McClintock.

Leander Richardson, however, did not mention seeing Martha at the saloon after Hickok was killed, even though he went there immediately upon hearing the news of the shooting. Nor did he say Martha was at Hickok's funeral. Richardson said there was a large crowd at the burial because "with the better class 'Wild Bill' had been a great favorite," a conclusion at variance with the recollection of Richard B. Hughes, who said Hickok was mourned primarily by members of the lowest social order.[62] In agreement with Hughes, White-Eye Anderson remembered six or seven of the dance-hall girls present for Hickok's funeral, including Big Dollie, Tid Bit, Dirty Em, Smooth Bore, Sizzling Kate, and Calamity Jane. Martha, he said, "gathered some little blue flowers that grew beside the road and threw them into the grave before they filled it with sod."[63]

Although newspapers did not describe the funeral, they do confirm that Martha was in Deadwood the day Wild Bill was shot. They also indicate that she became involved in other emotionally charged episodes that day. Hickok's death was but one of several violent events in Deadwood in August 1876. By summer, the town's population perhaps reached ten thousand inhabitants and it seethed with activity. Several shootings took place. Besides the assassination of Hickok, at least two other people were killed, leading prospector Jerry Bryan to write in his diary: "It is getting to dangerous here to be healthy. A man is liable to be shot here any time by Some Drunken Desperado, and it is not very Safe to go out but we have decided to go tomorrow[;] any thing is better than Staying here."[64]

But it was also dangerous to leave Deadwood. Near-panic developed in the town after it was learned that Custer's command had been annihilated at the Little Big Horn. It was rumored that Indians returning from the summer's fighting were killing settlers and taking cattle and horses.

Fear of Indians brought offers of a $50 reward for an Indian's head, deemed a visible sign of progress. On the same day Hickok was killed, Brick Pomeroy, an employee of V. P. Shoun, was chased by Indians while searching for wandering stock near Deadwood. He shot one of his pursuers and hurried to warn citizens of Deadwood. A makeshift posse rode in pursuit, and one fellow, identified only as "a Mexican," cut off the head of the Indian Pomeroy had killed. After his return to Deadwood, he exhibited the gruesome trophy to an enthusiastic crowd.[65] McClintock remembered that the "excitement created by the killing of Wild Bill had already reached high pitch," when the rider arrived carrying the "gory head."[66] According to one Black Hills correspondent, Martha was a member of the rowdy crowd, and "recognized the head as belonging to a young brave of the Red Cloud agency."[67] Why she was considered able to identify the Indian is unclear, but the newspaper confirms her presence in Deadwood the day Hickok was killed.

Only two weeks later, another skirmish with Indians occurred at Centennial Valley north of Deadwood. When it was discovered that about a hundred head of horses had been taken from the "Montana herd," a Deadwood posse followed the thieves' trail. All the Indians had vanished but one. When Isaac Brown approached that warrior's hiding place, he was shot and killed. Another posse member, Charlie Holland, returned fire and, thinking he had killed the Indian, moved into the open. But Holland was wrong and he was in turn killed. The dejected party went back to Deadwood, returning the next day to recover the bodies.[68]

Adding to the hysteria, on August 20, the same day Brown and Holland were killed, Preacher Smith was murdered when he left Deadwood to deliver a sermon at Crook City. A Deadwood newspaper reported that his death "created a great excitement. Men were rushing in every direction seeking arms and cartridges, every dealer having anything of the kind, handing them out freely."[69] Several men, including Lou Mason and "Texas Jack," went to recover Smith's body. As they searched the area, Mason saw an Indian and shot at him. Believing he had killed the Indian, Mason approached. However, the Indian was still alive and, like Holland earlier, Mason was shot dead instead. Texas Jack quickly dispatched the Indian and returned to Deadwood.

After summarizing the day's events, the correspondent for the *Laramie Sentinel* added:

> It is now my duty to chronicle a horrible and barborous [*sic*] sequel to this affair. After killing the Indian, Texas Jack cut off his head, which he hung by his hair to his saddle and came riding into town with it, a frightful spectacle to behold. And with the ghastly head dangling from his saddle, Jack rode up and down the street of the town. He drank excessively, became much intoxicated, and whooped and yelled at the top of his voice until night.[70]

Texas Jack, like his predecessor two weeks earlier, hoped to claim the promised reward for the head of an Indian. But first, "in company with Calamity Jane, Dirty Em and others," he "paraded it through every saloon in town." How long the saloon-trek with the grisly trophy lasted is not recorded, but finally the "spectacle became so revolting that Seth Bullock and others took it away from him, and at night buried it in the rear of the Gem theatre."[71]

Two days later, another shooting occurred. This time it involved Martha's friend, Sam Young, bartender in Saloon No. 10. The victim was Myer Baum, known as Bummer Dan. When confronted by officers, Young said that "he thought he had shot the wrong man." Indeed, his intended victim was Laughing Sam Hartman, who had threatened to kill Young, probably because of a dispute over a woman. Evidently, Laughing Sam had induced Bummer Dan to wear his coat to Saloon No. 10. When the unfortunate man entered the rear door, Young shot him. After several hours' deliberation, the newspaper reported that the jury, "returned the usual verdict of 'not guilty.'"[72]

These turbulent conditions subsided as local government was organized. The threat of Indian raids also decreased when General Crook's army arrived in the Black Hills. Since the inglorious Battle of the Rosebud, Crook, after receiving reinforcements, had pursued his Indian opponents. Little success had attended his efforts, however, and supplies were so short his command was reduced to eating horsemeat. Desperately in need of food, Crook sent a party to the Black Hills to secure supplies. As the main command followed, they encountered the camp of American Horse, an engagement resulting in Crook's victory at the Battle of Slim Buttes on September 9.

Upon his arrival in the Black Hills, Crook received a hearty welcome. Martha possibly was among those greeting the troops. Valentine T. McGillycuddy, serving as medical officer with Crook's army, recalled that she was "blossomed out as a fully equipped border scout," with "beaded buckskin trousers, blue shirt, broad brimmed hat, Winchester rifle, mounted on a bucking broncho," and carrying "a supply of fluid ammunition in the saddle bags."[73] McGillycuddy's colorful description of Martha may be a later embellishment, however, based on hearsay. His 1876 diary suggests he was not along when the command entered Crook City, remaining instead at camp on the Belle Fourche River.[74]

Deadwood held a reception for Crook and his officers at the Grand Central Hotel. To the crowd, Crook described his command's hardships during the march and their successful destruction of the Indian village north of the Black Hills. He was frequently interrupted by cheers from the enthusiastic populace. Afterwards, a petition for continued military protection was presented to Crook, who promised to deliver it to his superiors.[75] Crook's aide, Lieutenant John G. Bourke, learned from Deadwood's citizens that four hundred unprotected citizens had been killed during the summer and even the first preacher in Deadwood had been murdered. When an Indian was killed by the whites, Bourke wrote, "Deadwood would go crazy with delight; the skull and scalp were paraded and sold at public auction to the highest bidder." No wonder "the joy of the people in the Hills knew no bounds" when the army arrived.[76]

In his account of the festivities, however, Bourke failed to describe the grand march and dance that night, which of course required women, in short supply in Deadwood. McGillycuddy rendered a detailed and probably romanticized account of the evening's events. It was Martha, he said, who "led the grand march" with Crook and afterwards placed a kiss on the general's cheek as they danced a schottische. But Deadwood residents in later years thought it was either Trixy or Dirty Em who danced with Crook that night.[77]

McGillycuddy also danced the schottische with Martha that evening. "Her legs still were steady, for she carried her liquor like a man," he said, though, according to his biographer, he "scarcely could keep his balance as they cavorted through the half-drunken mob, Martha shrieking at old pals and slapping them on the back as they passed." Finally, Martha became the dancing partner of a corporal while the doctor rested. When the festivities ended, McGillycuddy and Martha left the hall, but while he went back to camp, Martha, "looking young in spite of the sickly gray dawn, though drink was hardening her face," entered Al Swearingen's dance hall to continue her revelry.[78]

Martha did not mention these activities in her *Life and Adventures*, asserting instead that she "remained around Deadwood locating claims, going from camp to camp until the spring of 1877."[79] Nor did she mention helping an injured miner. According to John D. Vaughan, in the fall of 1876 Martha nursed Jack McCarthy, who had broken his leg. Doctor Meyer had set the bone and bound the leg in splints, but since McCarthy lived alone in a cabin on Poorman's Gulch between Central City and Lead, circumstances looked bleak for him. The doctor, stopping at Madame Mustache's Gayville establishment, mentioned McCarthy's plight. Martha overheard the story and decided to help. Vaughan held no romantic illusions about the heroine of his story, commenting that "the money earned in dancing with and luring victims to the bar, went as rapidly as it came." But on this occasion, when someone "required the services of a nurse," she "danced, and with feverish eagerness asked for checks instead of drinks. She wanted money." Madame Mustache and the other "petticoated attractions in that Gayville hell" contributed to the cause, and the next morning Martha went to Deadwood to purchase supplies and engage a packer. This deed was done with "no hope or expectation of reward, present or future," said Vaughan. "They were . . . outcasts; soiled doves, doves in the net of perdition." Martha arrived at McCarthy's cabin with the supplies in time for Thanksgiving, Vaughan said, and remained there to care for him.[80]

Although the story may be true, the chronology does not fit Martha's circumstances. She had taken a new job in November 1876, reportedly having "eschewed the wine-cup and her other minor imperfections" to "slingeth hash" in a restaurant and hotel in Custer.[81] Though her employment there may have been brief, a Sioux City journalist in 1886 remembered "the first restaurant in the Hills" located there, with "the notorious Calamity Jane" as "dining-hall girl," and said she "permitted no grumbling at the 'hash' she brought to the table."[82]

Even though Martha ended 1876 working at a menial job, it had been an eventful year for her. She had accompanied the Crook expedition against the Sioux and had ridden into Deadwood with Wild Bill Hickok. Moreover, her flamboyant behavior made it impossible for newspapers to ignore her. She made good copy. The next year, sensationalist writers extended her notoriety to a national audience.

Martha Canary (Calamity Jane), Black Hills, 1875

At age nineteen, Martha accompanied the Jenney expedition of 1875 into the Black Hills. She evidently was secreted into the party by one of the soldiers. Being with this expedition resulted in considerable publicity for her, including having her picture taken by photographer A. Guerin of St. Louis. This is the earliest known picture of Martha, who was already known as Calamity Jane. Courtesy, J. Leonard Jennewein Collection, Layne Library, Dakota Wesleyan University, Mitchell, South Dakota.

Martha Canary (Calamity Jane), Deadwood, 1876–1877

Calamity Jane rode into Deadwood in mid-July 1876 with Wild Bill Hickok's party, attracting attention in the buckskin outfit of a scout. This photograph, evidently taken in 1876 or 1877 in Deadwood, reinforces popular notions that Martha was a scout and gunfighter. The unidentified photographer took at least one other picture, showing the heavily armed Martha seated. Courtesy, Montana Historical Society (MHS 941–419).

James Butler Hickok (Wild Bill), 1869

Calamity Jane is most often associated with Wild Bill Hickok. However, the pair met only a couple weeks before they arrived in Deadwood in July 1876, and Hickok was killed August 2, making their purported relationship of short duration. This photograph of Hickok was taken a few years before he entered Deadwood. Courtesy, Adams Museum & House, Inc., Deadwood, South Dakota..

Lower Main Street, Deadwood, a.k.a. "The Badlands," 1877

The intense activity characteristic of a gold camp is still evident in this photograph taken a year after the 1876 rush began. It depicts the "badlands" district where dance halls, saloons, gambling, and prostitution were prevalent. Courtesy, Adams Museum & House, Inc., Deadwood, South Dakota.

**C. S. Stobie (Mountain Charlie), Calamity Jane, and Captain Jack Crawford,
Denver, Colorado, 1878 (?)**

In his poetry and newspaper dispatches, Captain Jack Crawford helped publicize Martha
Canary's trip with the Jenney expedition in 1875. However, the woman he is sitting
with in this photograph probably is not Martha. Instead, she might be Mattie Young,
also known as Calamity Jane, who died in a buggy accident in Denver in 1878.
Courtesy, Denver Public Library, Western History Collection (F-3908).

"Miss Martha Canary ('Calamity Jane'), The Female Scout"

The earliest illustration depicting Martha as a scout appeared in Horatio N. Maguire's *The Coming Empire* (1878). Maguire, a Black Hills booster, wrote a fanciful description of Calamity Jane in this and an earlier publication. These stories led directly to Calamity Jane being featured as a dime novel heroine. Author's collection.

Horatio N. Maguire

Journalist Horatio N. Maguire helped create Calamity Jane's legend through his color-ful descriptions about her scouting career and shooting skills. Courtesy, J. Leonard Jennewein Collection, Layne Library, Dakota Wesleyan University, Mitchell, South Dakota.

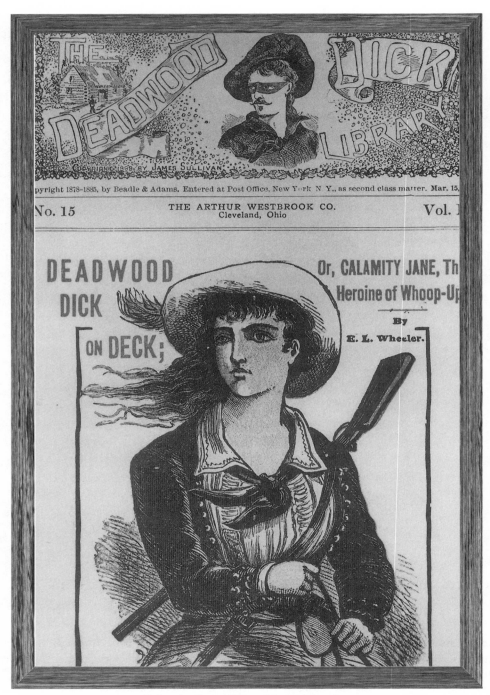

Calamity Jane, Dime Novel Heroine

Edward L. Wheeler's Deadwood Dick dime novel series, which began in 1877, elevated Calamity Jane from local notoriety to national prominence. This famous cover illustration is from a later printing of *Deadwood Dick on Deck; or, Calamity Jane, The Heroine of Whoop-Up* (1877). Author's collection.

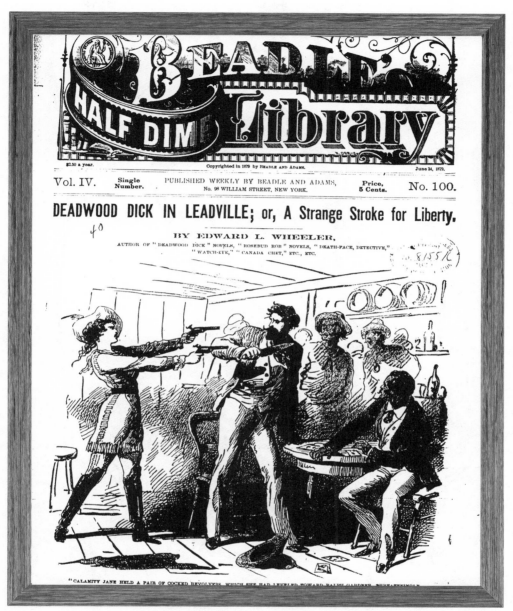

Calamity Jane, Dime Novel heroine, 1879

This is the only other dime novel by Edward Wheeler that has Calamity Jane featured on the cover. It is from *Deadwood Dick in Leadville; or, A Strange Stroke for Liberty* (1879). It shows Calamity Jane intervening to prevent a gambler from cutting off his opponent's head, which had been used as the wager in the game. Author's collection.

Edward Lytton Wheeler

The only known image of dime novelist Edward L. Wheeler, who made Calamity Jane a household name, is this sketch from the cover of one of his booklets. In his short writing career, Wheeler turned out about a hundred dime novels, including thirty-three in the Deadwood Dick series.

"Martha Canary, or Calamity Jane," 1878

Evidently made from an unknown photograph, this sketch shows Martha in 1878 when she was about twenty-two years old. It is from Thomas Newson's *Drama of Life in the Black Hills* (1878). Author's collection.

CALAMITY IN MALE ATTIRE.

"Calamity in Male Attire," 1878

Included in Thomas Newson's *Drama of Life in the Black Hills* (1878) are two unique sketches. The first shows Martha in male attire early in the evening; the second depicts her later that night wearing a dress. Author's collection.

CALAMITY IN FEMALE ATTIRE.

"Calamity Jane in Female Attire," 1878

Author's collection.

"Poor George," 1878

In this sketch from Thomas Newson's *Drama of Life in the Black Hills* (1878), Martha is shown grieving at a friend's death. Her charitable reputation as a nurse was established early in her life. Author's collection.

"One and Original 'Calamity Jane,'" Miles City, Montana, 1880–1882

Photographer L. A. Huffman took this famous picture of Martha Canary in Miles City, probably when she arrived with the Northern Pacific Railroad in 1882. She evidently operated a saloon and restaurant in that area for a while, catering to the railroad's construction crews. Courtesy, Montana Historical Society (MHS 981-573).

Martha Canary, 1880s (?)

This undated photograph of Martha Canary found in a scrapbook probably dates from the 1880s. Courtesy, Colorado Historical Society (F 50350 BPF).

CHAPTER SIX

Dime Novel Heroine, 1877

Accompanying the Crook expedition and entering the Black Hills with Wild Bill Hickok in 1876 provided an historical basis for Calamity Jane's later inclusion among the West's legendary figures, but far more significant in establishing her fame was becoming a featured character in a dime novel in October 1877.

In the late nineteenth century, dime novels played a role in popular culture similar to that of film and television today. These small pamphlets cost only five to ten cents each, and a single title might sell over sixty thousand copies in its first edition. With subsequent printings, sales of six hundred thousand copies for a single story were not uncommon. Although written primarily for working-class audiences, dime novels were read by members of all social classes and the "genre pervaded the entire culture."[1]

After becoming a figure in popular fiction, Martha was recognized everywhere as the "dime novel heroine." Fame had unexpected repercussions. Martha's new stature caused bystanders to stare at her in awe. At times she reveled in this new fame and exploited it to her advantage. Nonetheless, her day-to-day activities remained largely unchanged. As a result, journalists frequently penned cynical commentaries contrasting the woman they observed to the images of her in dime novels.

Martha's movements in the spring of 1877 immediately before she achieved celebrity status from dime novels are obscure. According to the *Cheyenne Daily Leader* in January 1877, Martha was "married and settled down at Custer City."[2] Her husband remains unidentified. How long she remained in Custer also is unclear.

As before, Martha muddied the record by inventing participation in significant events. One morning while riding about twelve miles from Deadwood, Martha recalled in her *Life and Adventures*, she met the overland stage coming from Cheyenne. Immediately, she recognized that something was amiss. "The horses were on the run, about two hundred yards from the station," she said. Then she noticed that there was no driver and that the coach containing passengers was being chased by Indians. The experienced horses even without directions took the coach to the barn. There Martha saw "the driver John Slaughter, lying face downwards in the boot of the stage, he having been shot by the Indians." Assessing the situation in a moment, Martha "removed all baggage from the coach except the mail," took the driver's position, and "with all haste drove to Deadwood, carrying the six passengers and the dead driver."[3]

Contemporary newspapers dispute her rendition of this famous incident on March 25, 1877. Road agents, not Indians, stopped the stagecoach and killed its driver. Slaughter's body was found near the road by the posse, not in the boot of the stage. When the horses bolted, preventing the robbers from securing the hoped-for loot, the driverless stage proceeded into town, not to a stage station. Finally, the names of all the participants are known, and Martha's is not among them.[4] Nevertheless, Martha probably was in the vicinity. She simply placed herself in the center of events she experienced from the periphery.

Although Martha claimed to be rescuing a besieged stage, newspapers linked her to some of the region's most notorious road agents operating along the Cheyenne–Black Hills route. In 1877, numerous Deadwood coaches were robbed, and Sheriff Seth Bullock and other law enforcement officials sought in vain for the outlaws. Finally, local residents in western Wyoming alerted law officers that seven strangers were roaming in the area. Three of these men had made inquiries about "a man and a woman dressed in men's clothes." One cried out, "by G—d he would find them as they had the 'sway.'" When the officers arrived, they arrested Frank Barker and F. P. Womack, but only after a six-mile chase which included an "interchange of shots." The third gang member, Bill Bevans, was arrested in Lander City while eating a meal. There was no doubt about his guilt; Bevans was wearing a watch stolen from one of the stage passengers. Law officers searched for the rest of the robbers with no success.

After the capture of the three outlaws, it was learned by officials that one member of the band and his female companion had disappeared with the loot. "The supposition is," reported the press, "that the man and woman alluded to are the notorious Jack Wadkins and Calamity Jane."[5]

The missing gang member was not located until a year later. Pursuing a lead, Sheriff Bullock located the road agent, named "Reddy" McKimie, or "Little Reddy", in Ohio, and he was caught and jailed. Investigation proved that McKimie not only was the missing stage robber but was responsible for John Slaughter's murder. At the time of that killing, he was with a different band of road agents, one including Joel Collins, Sam Bass, Frank Towle, and Jim Berry. These outlaws, concerned that McKimie's unnecessary murder of Slaughter would bring relentless pursuit by the law, forced him to leave their band. He then joined Bevans, Clark Pelton (alias Billy Webster), Dunc Blackburn, and James Wall and robbed three stagecoaches on three successive days in July 1877. It was after the last of these robberies that "a disreputable woman accompanied the party." Overhearing plans by gang members to kill McKimie when he returned from securing supplies in South Pass City, the woman informed McKimie of the plot, and they determined "to get the others drunk, take their booty and decamp." According to newspaper reports, their plan worked perfectly; after taking the loot, they traveled to Point of Rocks station along the Union Pacific in Wyoming, then traveled by train to St. Louis. There, a reporter learned, McKimie "gave the woman $1000 and left her." Afterwards, McKimie went to Texas, then returned to his home in Ohio, explaining that he had become rich from cattle operations in the West.[6]

Was the disreputable woman with the outlaw band Martha Canary? Only rumor, not evidence, suggests that she was McKimie's mysterious companion. Calamity's acquaintance, Sam Young, claimed that she was once stopped on a trip by Jim Wall (*sic*) and his gang, and afterwards became "enamored with one of the gang named Blackburn," joined the outlaws, and was with them when they were captured and jailed in Laramie, Wyoming. But some of his facts are wrong; Martha, for example, was not arrested with the road agents. Nevertheless, some writers speculate that Martha married outlaw Dunc Blackburn and they had a child, or that she was the companion of Bill Bevans.[7] Indeed, she might have known Bevans when she was a child in Montana, but there is no proof of a continuing relationship. Undoubtedly, Martha knew the road agents who frequented saloons and road ranches in the region. But she probably was not the woman who accompanied the outlaws. Despite her obvious presence in Cheyenne and Deadwood during the period when Bevans and McKimie were captured, law officers evidently did not seriously consider her a suspect.

Martha enjoyed tantalizing reporters by implying that she worked with the bandits. Almost a decade later, a journalist reported Calamity's version of these events. She "joined one of the most desperate gangs of road agents in the hills," he reported, and in 1877, "personally superintended the execution of a most daring and successful robbery." Afterwards, she dumped her lover, Bevans, for McKimie, then drove McKimie off as well.[8] Two years later, she told another reporter that she "embarked in a business that you nor no one else will ever learn anything about from me; but I will say that I became well acquainted with every road agent who helped to hold up a Black Hills coach."[9]

Meanwhile, Martha's local notoriety gained the attention of journalist Horatio N. Maguire who was writing a promotional booklet on the Black Hills. In an effort to "satisfy an eager public," Maguire hastily penned a pamphlet of approximately sixty thousand words describing the discovery of gold and containing information about mining, Indians, the climate, and Black Hills settlements. Buried inside the pages of Maguire's *The Black Hills and American Wonderland* (1877) is a flamboyant description of Calamity Jane, written, he said, "from personal explorations." Maguire introduced his colorful account of Calamity Jane by describing himself arriving in the Black Hills and asking Jack Baronett, "one of the pioneers of the Black Hills," how far it was to Deadwood:

> "Only a mile and a half; that girl on the horse is going there now."
> "Girl! What girl? I don't see any body on a horse but that dare-devil boy yonder."
> "Why, that's a girl on that bucking cayuse; that's 'Calamity Jane.'"

And "Calamity Jane" she was, as I ascertained in getting some items in regard to her most remarkable career of ruin, disgrace and recklessness. There was nothing in her attire to distinguish her sex, as she sat astride the fiery horse she was managing with a cruel Spanish bit in its mouth, save her small neat-fitting gaiters, and sweeping raven locks. She wore coat and pantaloons of buckskin, gayly beaded and fringed, fur-trimmed vest of tanned antelope skin, and a broad-brimmed Spanish hat completed her costume. Throwing herself from side to side in the saddle, with the daring self-confidence of a California *bucharo* in full career, she spurred her horse on up the gulch, over ditches and through reservoirs and mudholes, at each leap of the fractious animal giving as good an imitation of a Sioux war-whoop as a feminine voice is capable of.[10]

Although based on "personal explorations," Maguire's imaginative portrait is largely fiction. He mistakenly placed Calamity Jane's origins in Virginia City, Nevada, rather than Virginia City, Montana. He also said she was from "a family of respectability and intelligence." After she took "the first step of ruin," wrote Maguire, she became a nomad, joining hunting parties, mining stampedes, freight trains, and even rendering "good service as a scout in an Indian campaign." Maguire concluded: "She is still in early womanhood, and her rough and dissipated career has not yet altogether 'Swept away the lines where beauty lingers.'"[11]

Maguire's fanciful description of Martha received widespread circulation as numerous newspapers reprinted or paraphrased his description of her. Denver's *Rocky Mountain News* published the story on June 10, 1877, and the *Cheyenne Daily Leader* a few days later.[12] Moreover, it is possible Maguire's booklet was serialized in eastern newspapers. The primary significance of his account is not in its details but in its power to inspire a dime novelist to include Calamity Jane as a character in a new series of stories that summer.

Meanwhile, Martha meandered to Cheyenne. "Calamity Jane arrived here yesterday from the Black Hills," the *Daily Leader* reported on July 7. Her visit began inauspiciously with a call at Terry & Hunter's livery stable to rent a buggy. Remembering that once before "she took a horse and buggy from another stable, ostensibly to ride for Fort Russell, but did not stop until she reached Fort Laramie," Frank Hunter refused her request.[13] Martha, wearing a cavalry uniform and carrying a bullwhip, next visited the newspaper office. According to the editor, who related his encounter with her with humor and a flair for the dramatic, she cried out:

"I want to see the fighting editor. I am Calamity Jane. I'm just in from the Black Hills. Be you the fighting editor?" And she cracked her whip at a big fly on the ceiling, hitting it in the left ear and knocking it out of time.

The editor quickly fled to another room and escaped through the skylight. When he returned later his office was in a mess, and a note that Calamity Jane made the office boy write for her was pinned to the door. It read as follows:

Print in the LEADER that Calamity Jane, the child of the regiment and pioneer white woman of the Black Hills is in Cheyenne, or I'll scalp you, skin you alive, and hang you to a telegraph pole. You hear me and don't you forget it.

CALAMITY JANE.[14]

How much of the editor's description is to be believed is uncertain, but it clearly indicates Martha's increasing notoriety. Moreover, if she had just arrived from the Black Hills, it is unlikely she had been with "Reddy" McKimie or Bill Bevans because at about this time Bevans was arrested in western Wyoming, and McKimie and his female companion should have been in St. Louis.

Notwithstanding the editor's flamboyant story, Martha gained widespread attention without harrassing newspapermen. For example, the rival *Cheyenne Sun* announced that "the return of the well known frontierswoman, 'Calamity Jane,' to Cheyenne, which took place yesterday, was one of the few events of a dull, sultry July day." Her recent publicity caused the reporter to interview Dr. A. R. Hendricks of Des Moines, Iowa, who claimed to know Calamity's early history. Hendricks wove a fascinating tale, asserting that she was the daughter of a minister, B. W. Coombs, of Burlington, Iowa, and that she had left home with a young man named Washburne. The couple, he said, then went to Galesburg, Illinois, where they were married, but Mr. Washburne was killed in the Civil War. Seeking vengeance, his wife "donned male attire and entered the Union army as a scout and spy." After the war, said Hendricks, she "traveled all over the States and Territories west of the Missouri river" until her name became "as well known to the frontiersman as are those of Wild Bill, Texas Jack or Buffalo Bill." Finally, with mystical premonition, Hendricks predicted that she would be "a remarkable subject for the basis of a novel in the hands of Ned Buntline, Dr. Beadle or Sylvanus Cobb."[15] Only three months later, Calamity Jane was featured in a dime novel.

While Hendricks spun his tale, Martha returned to the Black Hills. During the trip, she had the "misfortune to get her foot badly hurt and received injuries by the recent upsetting of a wagon in which she was riding," reported the newspaper. Evidently, Martha's foot was not injured badly, for within a week she was "dancing at the Bonanza on Lee street."[16] Her presence in the Deadwood dance hall, as she was being hailed in newspapers as a hero along the lines of Buffalo Bill Cody and Wild Bill Hickok, was too much for some journalists.

Dan Scott, a reporter for Charlie Collins's *Daily Champion*, began the attack, calling her a "fraud." If she were judged on merit, "a hundred waiter girls and mop squeezers in this gulch are her superiors in anything the reader can name," he said, adding caustically that she mostly "lays around with a lot of road agents on the prairies." Scott thought "her form and features" were "not only indifferent, but repulsive." Yet "everybody who has been in the Hills knows Calamity; simply because the newspapers have thrown her up on the surface of public notice." Furthering her publicity by printing another article, even if a hostile one, wrote Scott, "makes us sick too."[17]

Shortly after the *Champion*'s scurrilous attack, an angry Martha Canary visited the newspaper office. According to Scott, the "awful girl" gave him a "fearful racket," and "cried, and swore, and danced, and bit her teeth. . . . At one time I thought she would tackle me, but I was ready to put in my best licks." She was not finished. Returning to the office several weeks later, the "notorious character, who is known from Maine to Mexico," confiscated Charley Collins's picture from the office wall, evidently taking it to the drinking establishments for a bit of vengeful fun. "Charley, upon his return, went in pursuit of her. He found her in a saloon but did not succeed in recovering his property."[18] Martha's dispute with Charley Collins became a local legend. In 1882, the *Pioneer* recalled that upon Martha's visit to the office, Collins "bounded out at the back door," and only through diplomacy was she prevented from "cleaning out the concern." For several days, Collins "remained in one of the small, uninhabited gulches," hiding until Martha's "rage had cooled."[19] It was the first in a series of bouts with the press.

Another Deadwood newspaper, the *Times*, soon followed Collins's lead in exposing so-called heroines. Its September 20 issue described "the first case of a woman being imprisoned in the Hills." The *Times* did not identify the young woman by name, but it has often been concluded that the newspaper was referring to Calamity Jane. This "young woman attired in male apparel" arrived from Hat Creek station, "the home of our Robin Hoods," it said, "and immediately on arriving here got drunk, drunker than a biled owl, and kicked up a considerable rumpus on the streets."[20] However, as ensuing stories in the *Times* suggest, this woman probably was not Martha Canary but a Mrs. Bloxsom, who had been termed a heroine by the rival *Pioneer*. "That 'heroine of the Hills,' who figured so largely in the local columns of our contemporary this morning, didn't 'pan out' very well upon investigation," the *Times* said. "She is a low down idiotic sort of a prostitute who has been herding with Indians, negroes and soldiers, for the past year."[21] Even though the *Times* was not criticizing Martha Canary in this case, she also met with scorn. In "An Idyl De Macaroni," a satirical poem printed in the *Times*, the last stanza read, "Through slushy sun and sunny rain / She sweetly babbled, 'What a name / For me to bear, Calamity Jane.'"[22]

Not all journalists shared jaundiced views of Martha. One editor visiting the Black Hills determined her to be an enjoyable companion. Colonel Clement A. Lounsberry of the *Bismarck Tribune* came to the Hills in August 1877 to report on its natural resources. In his description, he daringly related a visit he made to a Deadwood hurdy-gurdy house. In the dance halls, he asserted, members of different social classes freely mixed, "and you will find occasionally a high toned citizen tripping the light fantastic in the hurdy gurdy with Can Can Dolly, Calamity Jane or some other 'character' in the Hills as a partner." Indeed, as he entered the door of the dance hall, he observed Can Can Dolly, "a good looking woman of about twenty," entertaining customers. Although he assured readers that he "saw her but a moment," he described her wager to "kick your hat off for the drinks," at which time "a fellow six foot four accepted the wager and she was engaged in that pleasant pastime."

Martha, Lounsberry said, "waltzes on one leg and polkas on the other" and thereby "gets her living." His description of her dancing was meant to be complimentary. Evidently, he not only danced with Martha but conversed with her extensively during the evening. "Jane is not very bad and has many interesting features," he wrote. "Left in a Mormon camp without father or mother when a mere child like Topsey, she 'growed just like the corn.'" Living among rough associates, she never learned social graces. She joined mining rushes, for a while was a prostitute, attempted to "mend her ways," then joined General Crook as a scout, afterwards became "the lioness of the hills," and finally "a devoted wife." Lounsberry did not identify Martha's husband, but said that, after a fire destroyed all their belongings, Martha's comfortable life on a ranch with her spouse ended. She was then "forced by circumstances to return to her old mode of life because she knew no other." Never, he said, had he "met a person more readily brought to tears by kind words or gentle reproof for evil deeds." Lounsberry concluded, "She deserves kind words rather than reproach."[23]

Not only did Lounsberry describe Martha favorably, he evidently courted her. "Calamity Jane was on yesterday presented with an excellent photograph of Col. Lounsberry," reported the Deadwood newspaper of November 30, explaining that friends of the Bismarck editor needn't worry too much, because it was "only a slight *affaire de coeur*."[24] Lounsberry's infatuation with Martha, in stark contrast to criticisms of other journalists, suggests those correspondents might have been reacting to romanticized images that conflicted too sharply with the familiar figure in Deadwood's dance halls. Their mortification had only begun, however. That fall Martha became a dime novel heroine.

New York dime novelist Edward L. Wheeler during the summer of 1877 began writing a new series of stories with a Black Hills setting. The first appeared on October 15 as *Deadwood Dick, The Prince of the Road; or, The Black Rider of the Black Hills.* Wheeler's "Deadwood Dick" series became one of the most popular runs for Beadle and Adams, the nation's largest dime novel publishing firm. Besides Deadwood Dick, who was invented, Calamity Jane is the main character in the series. Wheeler made it seem as if he experienced the events in his stories first-hand. For example, he wrote: "The first time it was ever my fortune to see [Calamity Jane], was when Deadwood was but an infant city of a few shanties, but many tents."[25] However, Wheeler clearly borrowed his descriptions from Maguire's earlier publication. In fact, it is unlikely Wheeler derived information about Calamity Jane from any source other than Maguire.

The contribution of Horatio Maguire and Edward Wheeler to the growth of the Calamity Jane legend generally has not been recognized by biographers.[26] A comparison of Wheeler's description of Calamity Jane in his first Deadwood Dick story to Maguire's account in *The Black Hills and American Wonderland* clarifies Wheeler's dependence. Paraphrasing Maguire, Wheeler related that Calamity Jane was from Virginia City, Nevada, of a "family of respectability and intelligence." She "dressed in a carefully tanned costume of buck-skin, the vest being fringed with the fur of the mink; wearing a jaunty Spanish sombrero; boots on the dainty feet of patent leather, with tops reaching to the knees; a face slightly sunburned, yet showing the traces of beauty that even excessive dissipation could not obliterate; eyes black and piercing; mouth firm, resolute, and devoid of sensual expression; hair of raven color and of remarkable length."[27]

Edward Lytton Wheeler became a well-known author of dime novels in the 1870s and 1880s. Born in Avoca, New York, in 1854 or 1855, he was the son of Sanger and Barbara Lewis Wheeler. The family moved to Pennsylvania in the early 1870s and managed a boarding house. Wheeler evidently began his writing career early in 1877. His first published novel probably was *Hurricane Nell, the Girl Dead-Shot; or, The Queen of the Saddle and Lasso*, which featured a fictional woman who would be the prototype for his Calamity Jane stories. His career advanced rapidly, with his letterhead describing his avocation as "Sensational Novelist." Soon he was making about $950 a year. He moved to Philadelphia, there managing a theatrical company that may have featured his first Deadwood Dick story on stage. In 1878, he married Alice Fager of West Philadelphia. The Wheelers had at least one child, a boy, but little is known about the family. It is assumed Wheeler died in 1885 when, without announcement to readers, his writing halted abruptly.[28]

In his brief, prolific writing career, Wheeler authored about a hundred dime novels. Thirty-three of these made up the Deadwood Dick series, and Calamity Jane appeared in more than half of them. Even though Wheeler utilized Maguire's description, the dime novel Calamity Jane bears more similarity to Hurricane Nell than to Martha Canary. It was not uncommon for authors to use the names of actual western figures, such as Kit Carson, Wild Bill Hickok, Davy Crockett, and Buffalo Bill, but events in the dime novels usually were fictional. This was the case concerning Calamity Jane.

Besides his Deadwood Dick stories, Wheeler wrote numerous other novels, including the Rosebud Bob, Sierra Sam, Kangaroo Kit, Yreka Jim, and Denver Doll series. This astounding production was possible because by the time Wheeler began writing, a prescribed formula for the narratives had been established.[29]

Although dime novel westerns evolved from earlier fiction placed in a frontier setting, such as James Fenimore Cooper's *Leatherstocking Tales*, a steady decline in quality occurred as writers and publishers met increasing demands for cheap, popular literature. By the end of the Civil War dime novels had become the most popular form of American fiction.[30] The treatment of female characters especially illustrated the increasing sensationalism. In this trend, Wheeler played an important role. Rather than displaying "the awe-inspiring gentility of Cooper's heroines," observes Henry Nash Smith, Wheeler's heroines became Amazons "distinguished from the hero solely by the physical fact of [their] sex."[31]

Wheeler's female characters often violate society's codes for women's behavior; they smoke, drink, dress, and swear like men. Although these daring women may have appealed to adolescents in rebellion against adult standards, they were hardly emancipated, quickly returning to traditional submissiveness and domesticity when involved in relationships with men. Wheeler's Calamity Jane, for example, saves Dick's life repeatedly; she is an excellent shot, an outstanding rider, and occasionally smokes cigars. Nevertheless, after Deadwood Dick kisses her, she awaits "the appointed time to come when she should go to claim the love and protection of the only man she ever worshipped."[32]

Wheeler's dime novels tended to be about forty thousand words in length and were filled with uninterrupted action and adventures. For juvenile readers, action was all-important. As dime novel scholar Daryl Jones observed, "Often the plot of the dime novel seems nothing more than a fast-paced loosely connected sequence of fistfights, gunplay, and hairbreadth escapes strung out interminably and tied together by a happy ending."[33]

In Wheeler's stories, Deadwood Dick and Calamity Jane are involved in impossible adventures and desperate situations that they miraculously survive. Repeatedly taken captive, they escape through their own cleverness or the miraculous intervention of other heroic figures. In addition, Calamity Jane and Deadwood Dick appear in disguises so well devised that they do not recognize each other.

Finally, Wheeler's thirty-three Deadwood Dick stories are sequential in plot, similar to modern soap operas, each building on the action, events, and characters of the last. Earlier researchers who thought the action was haphazard and nonsequential undoubtedly did not read the entire series and failed to consider the order in which Wheeler wrote them.[34] Filled with fighting and intrigue, the plots also emphasize relationships between young men and women. During the series, Deadwood Dick is involved with many different women and marries four times. Calamity Jane, Dick's trusted sidekick, eventually becomes his fourth wife. Their courtship and married life are tempestuous, with both Calamity Jane and Deadwood Dick displaying deeply suspicious natures when the other has any interaction with a person of the opposite sex.

For all their turbulance, the characters in these dime novels are relatively uncomplicated. It is easy to distinguish heroes from villains. Deadwood Dick and Calamity Jane, for example, are intelligent, refined, attractive figures. They are skilled in the use of weapons, are masters of disguise, display superior horsemanship, and outwit evildoers. Thus, when Deadwood Dick is introduced by Wheeler in the first novel, he is "trim and compactly built," and shows "a grace of position in the saddle rarely equaled," making "a fine picture for an artist's brush." Villain Chet Diamond, on the other hand, is a "black, swarthy-looking" fellow, "with 'villain' written in every lineament of his countenance." In fact, Wheeler adds, villains often have black hair and eyes "owing to the condition of [their] souls."[35]

Of course, dime novels featured more than nonstop action and tumultuous characters. What binds together the sometimes complicated story lines, remarks Daryl Jones, is the quest for the ideal world. Although the stories reflected the interests of juvenile readers, they also addressed societal concerns. Nineteenth-century America was experiencing rapid industrialization and urbanization. As Jones notes, working-class Americans, targeted by dime novelists, felt impotent when they confronted job competition from immigrants willing to work for lower wages, mechanization in the workplace, and giant corporations that seemed in control. The widening gap between rich and poor, urban poverty, and high crime rate threatened their traditional ways of life and morality.

That meant dime novels frequently became vehicles for social criticism. In these stories, government and law often are controlled by rich and unscrupulous individuals, with dime novel heroes, guided by a higher justice, struggling to defeat these powerful villains. Among Wheeler's innovations was the creation of an outlaw hero, Deadwood Dick. He resembled law-abiding dime novel heroes and, like them, struggled with public morality and abuse of power. According to Jones, dime novel stories provided the American public with courageous heroes "who possessed a capacity for resolving in fantasy the otherwise insoluble conflicts of the age."[36]

In addition, Wheeler's stories reflected concerns about declining morality, especially in women's conduct. As women left the security of home for the workplace, it was feared they would face new temptations: they might be led astray by evil men, or become sexually liberated. Facing these possibilities, dime novels, observed Jones, "endorsed conventional moral values and affirmed that virtue would ultimately prevail over evil forces."[37] In most stories, there is a temptress who tries to seduce the hero. These women either die a violent death, or lose their feminity and become like Amazons. (Men in Wheeler's novels who are guilty of sexual transgressions such as bigamy are inevitably killed.) Interestingly, the fictional Calamity Jane rejects socially acceptable behavior (she smokes and dresses like a man), because she was "ruined" by a villain and made an outcast. Deadwood Dick explains that this undeserved blemish should not permanently stain her reputation, and she, like him, remains a force for good.

Wheeler's first Deadwood Dick dime novel, *Deadwood Dick, The Prince of the Road*, introduces Edward (Ned) Harris, the road agent disguised as Deadwood Dick. Harris's motive for becoming an outlaw stems from the deaths of his parents at the hands of his evil uncle, Alexander Filmore. Afterwards, Edward and his sister, Anita, are placed under the guardianship of their uncle and are beaten and half-starved. Edward tries to get help from neighbors, then goes "to the courts for protection," but, he says, "my enemy was a man of great influence, and after many vain attempts, I found that I could not obtain a hearing; that nothing remained for me to do but fight my own way." Edward takes some of the $50,000 his uncle stole from his parents' estate and escapes with his sister to the West. His uncle sends assassins to kill them, but all meet death at Ned's hand.[38]

As noted above, Calamity Jane, like Deadwood Dick, has assumed a new identity as an outcast. Her new guise is occasioned by the loss of sexual purity, forcing her to break off with the man she intended to marry. Deadwood Dick explains:

> "Hold! there are yet a few redeeming qualities about her. She was *ruined*—" and here a shade dark as a thunder-cloud passed over Ned Harris's face— "and set adrift upon the world, homeless and friendless; yet she has bravely fought her way through the storm, without asking anybody's assistance. True, she may not now have a heart; that was trampled upon, years ago, but her character has not suffered blemish since the day a foul wretch stole away her honor!"[39]

In the novel, Calamity is Dick's friend, but is not a member of his band of road agents and thus acts independently. She saves Dick's life during one scrape, and the two fight side-by-side in a barroom brawl. The saloon fight occurs while Calamity gambles with villain Cattymount Cass. Harris, standing nearby, insinuates that Cass has cheated. In the ensuing ruckus with Cass and his gang, bullets fly "like hailstones, and men [fall] to the reeking floor each terrible moment." Harris is "wounded in a dozen places and weak from the loss of blood; yet he stands up bravely and fights mechanically." Calamity Jane, whose fighting prowess equals that of Deadwood Dick, "faces the music with as little apparent fear as any of those around her."

At the novel's conclusion, loose ends are tied together. Calamity rescues Dick after he has been captured by the Filmores and the villains are hanged. Dick's sister, Anita, is happily married. Edward Harris, in love with character Alice Terry, asks her to marry him. When she refuses, he responds, "Your refusal has decided my future. A merry road-agent I have been, and a merry road-agent I shall die." Nevertheless, Dick shortly afterwards asks Calamity Jane to marry him, but she also responds, "No!" adding, "I have had all the *man* I care for. We can be friends, Dick; more we can never be!"[40]

Calamity Jane is barely mentioned in several subsequent Deadwood Dick stories. In her place is Leone Hawk, who becomes Dick's wife. Although Leone and Dick have a son, Deadwood Dick, Jr., their relationship is strained. Eventually, Leone becomes a villain and both she and Dick, Jr., are killed. Remaining in the background, Calamity continues to be Dick's trusted friend and in his absence takes charge of his band of road agents. She is independently wealthy, owning gold claims and Deadwood's largest saloon and carries more than $10,000 with her at all times. Regarding her love life, the author concludes, "I don't think [Calamity] will ever marry; her life will continue that of a dare-devil and reckless adventurer that she is, until the end."[41]

After almost disappearing from the series, Calamity Jane dramatically reappears at central stage in the eighth novel, *Deadwood Dick on Deck; or, Calamity Jane, the Heroine of Whoop-Up*, published December 17, 1878. Needing to reintroduce her to readers, Wheeler again paraphrases Maguire's description of Calamity, but adds new details. He now states, for example, that Calamity Jane was born Jane (Jennie) Forrest of Denver before moving to Virginia City, Nevada. Clearly, Wheeler was incorporating information from an article, perhaps written by newspaperman Horace Greeley, about Mountain Charley (Elsa Jane Forest), a woman in Colorado who wore men's clothing.[42]

In Wheeler's story, Jennie, while living in Denver, promises to marry Charley Davis, but loses her virtue to villain Arkansas Alf. She then disappears without informing Davis. When she meets Charley six years later, he asks her what happened. Jennie, now Calamity Jane, responds that when he last knew her, she was "a maiden, and as modest as they make 'em. But terrible changes have come since then."[43]

The dime novel Calamity Jane is an able frontierswoman. Wheeler asserts that "any person who has witnessed the dare-devil riding of this eccentric girl, in her mad career through the Black Hills country, will agree with me that she has of her sex no peer in the saddle or on horseback." Indeed, his description of her horsemanship shows her to be an incredibly remarkable rider:

> She dashed madly down through the gulch one day, standing erect upon the back of her unsaddled cayuse, and the animal running at the top of its speed, leaping sluices and other obstructions—still the dare-devil retained her position as if glued to the animal's back, her hair flowing wildly back from beneath her slouch hat, her eyes dancing occasionally with excitement, as she recognized some wondering pilgrim, every now and then her lips giving vent to a ringing whoop, which was creditable in imitation if not in volume and force to that of a full-blown Comanche warrior.
>
> Now, she dashed away through the narrow gulch, catching with delight long breaths of the perfume of flowers which met her nostrils at every onward leap of her horse, piercing the gloom of the night with her dark lovely eyes, searchingly lest she should be surprised; lighting a cigar at full motion—dashing on, on, this strange girl of the Hills went, on her flying steed.

Calamity has reason to be watchful, for the "glowing end of her cigar" is detected by waiting assassins, who declare, "She mustn't escape us this time." Nevertheless, their ambush fails once again, thanks to Calamity's markmanship, and she muses, "Reckon at least a couple of 'em bit ther dust ef not more."[44]

Although Calamity Jane wears a buckskin outfit, she is well-educated and whenever she wants to can "drop the rude vernacular of the mines." She also is beautiful and wears diamond rings, a diamond pin, a massive gold chain, and "slippers of dainty pattern upon the feet." Her blouse, open at the throat, partially reveals "a breast of alabaster purity."[45]

Calamity's former lover, Charley Davis, is now a special detective for the government, and the villain of the story is none other than Arkansaw Alf, "The Destroyer," who "ruined" her. Alf, in turn, is employed by Congressman Cecil Grosvenor, a bigamist who attempted to kill his first wife for her inheritance. At the end of the novel, Arkansas Alf is hanged by Deadwood vigilantes and Grosvenor is arrested by Charley Davis. Rumors circulate that Calamity and Charley might yet marry.[46]

For reasons Wheeler does not explain, Calamity Jane never marries Davis. Meanwhile, she and Deadwood Dick independently travel to the new mining camp of Leadville, Colorado. The cover illustration of *Deadwood Dick in Leadville* (1879), depicts Calamity with guns drawn to prevent villain Ralph Gardner from cutting off the head of his opponent at the gambling table (his opponent's head was the wager in the game). Meanwhile, Deadwood Dick, hoping to rid himself of his outlaw reputation, fights a gang of evildoers. Despite his efforts on behalf of society, his road-agent notoriety continues, so he decides to surrender to the authorities, even though this means hanging. Secretly, Dick instructs Calamity and their friend, Old Avalanche, to recover his body and "apply remedies" for his "resuscitation." He believes that once he has been declared legally dead, he will be a free man when he revives. Calamity accomplishes this task successfully. As she predicts, however, his resurrection fails to bring acceptance.[47]

Despite saving Dick's life, Calamity remains only his friend and Dick marries Stella Howell. A villain poisons Stella, however. Distraught, Dick accuses Calamity of killing Stella from motives of jealousy. But the villain is Fanny Farron, wanting revenge because Dick had refused to marry her. In *Deadwood Dick's Device*, Farron is killed, and Dick apologizes to Calamity for his unfair accusation.[48]

Dick subsequently marries Edith Yates, who now displaces Calamity Jane as a major character. Edith is killed in a later novel, however, when outlaws attack the stage in which the couple are riding. Dick, allied with Rosebud Rob, hero of another dime novel series by Wheeler, struggles against the murderers led by Captain Terrible. In the meantime, Calamity reappears and now is in love with Dick. After learning that Dick's wife is dead, Calamity turns away, "lest the yearning, hungry look in her wildly beautiful eyes should pain him." When they are imprisoned by outlaws in a cave, Calamity and Dick discover their attraction is mutual. Wheeler concludes that "in the dim future, it is not improbable that Dick and Calamity will enter into a loving partnership for life, which long delayed consummation, we believe, our readers will welcome."[49]

Their marriage, nonetheless, is repeatedly delayed. First, a hesitant Calamity wants to be certain of Dick's fidelity and, disguised as "Little Toothpick," follows him to Secret City, Colorado. When "Little Toothpick" makes negative remarks to Dick about Calamity, he angrily responds, "Cast no slur upon her character, or you will make me forget that I am a *man* and you are a weak woman. What the girl may have been concerns you not; a single misstep need not curse her for eternity." Dick successfully passes Calamity's tests, despite his aspersions on the "weaker sex," and after the unmasking departs with her "for other wild and exciting scenes of the mighty West."[50]

But in a later story, Calamity tells Kentucky Kit that just as she and Dick were about to marry, "they dissolved, by mutual consent." Kit then falls in love with Dick, but their relationship is short-lived. Kit and her mother, the Black Hills Jezebel, are both killed. Their fate is decreed since Kit is a fallen woman and her mother a bigamist.[51]

The relationship between Dick and Calamity once again blossoms in *Deadwood Dick's Doom* (1881). When the two meet, Dick tells Calamity he is "going to settle down for good, in some lonely spot." He then adds, "Come to me, at Death Notch, Calamity, and the hand you have so long sought shall be yours." She accepts his offer and they finally are married in Nevada.[52]

Their married life, however, is as turbulent as their previous relationship. In one story, Calamity is kidnapped by Captain Crack-Shot, whose devious plans are thwarted, thanks to Dick's trained dog. Then, in a later novel, Calamity is again taken captive, this time by Tra-la-lee Charlie, who nearly beats her to death when she refuses his proposition to become his companion. Left for dead, she is held prisoner by Aztecs who reside in a secret mountain stronghold. Recovered from her disabilities, Calamity escapes, and, with another heroine, Roxey Ralph, similar in dress and style to Calamity, she rides to the rescue of Deadwood Dick, who has been tied by Ponca Indians to a stake to be burned. Together again, Dick and Calamity try to find happiness by moving to a place where their identities are not known.[53]

Eventually, Calamity Jane and Deadwood Dick arrive in California. Dick continues to participate in adventures while a pregnant Calamity remains home. But when Dick returns, he sees Calamity secretly kissing an outlaw. Then, she disappears with the baby, Deadwood Dick, Jr. Swearing vengeance against his unfaithful wife, Dick follows in pursuit. He finally discovers that the outlaw he saw kissing Calamity is her evil brother, Ralph Chester. Despite her innocence, this time the couple cannot resolve their differences, and they play a game of euchre to see who gets the child. Dick wins, and when a desperate Calamity attempts to shoot herself, a bystander pushes her gun aside, causing the bullet to pierce Ralph Chester's heart. Calamity falls "in a swoon over the body of her evil brother." At the end of *Deadwood Dick's Big Deal* (1883), the twenty-fifth novel in the series, Dick leaves with his son, and, writes Wheeler, "One thing is certain—his and Calamity's paths in life henceforth lead wide apart."[54]

When Dick next meets Calamity, she is his enemy. She identifies Dick to a hostile saloon crowd, almost costing him his life, and then joins his opponents in battle. At the end of the story, however, as Dick leaves town, he finds "an inanimate form in a mountain gulch south of Faro Flats." Believing the remains are Calamity's, he weeps.[55] But Dick is mistaken in his identification. Calamity reappears in a later story disguised as Shasta Kate. The two rediscover their love for each other and Dick asks Calamity to be his wife again. "Neither of us have been angels, in the past, but, let that drop," Dick tells her. "No one ever gets any consolation looking back into a shadowed past." Thus, Calamity, Dick, and their son are reunited.[56]

Even this happy ending is temporary. In Wheeler's final story, *Deadwood Dick's Dust; or, The Chained Hand* (1885), wicked townspeople steal Dick's valuable mining claim and he declares war on the town. The villains, however, capture Calamity Jane, and before Dick can rescue her, hang her as his accomplice. Although Dick destroys the town, he also is killed during the fighting. Afterwards, Deadwood Dick and Calamity Jane are buried side-by-side in a nearby peaceful valley, ending the long-running dime novel series.

Whether Edward Wheeler was responsible for narrating the deaths of his famous hero and heroine, or whether a ghostwriter finished the series after Wheeler's death, which probably occurred at about this time, is unknown. Other writers evidently did use his name to begin a new series of Deadwood Dick, Jr., novels that continued to appear for many years.

Wheeler's Deadwood Dick stories transformed Martha Canary from a locally notorious camp follower and dance-hall girl into a nationally recognized dime novel heroine. That Calamity Jane was utilized as a character in dime novels placed her in a class with Kit Carson, Buffalo Bill, and Wild Bill Hickok. It was easily assumed that she had performed significant accomplishments to warrant this honor. But, in Martha's case, her rise to prominence was based entirely on newspaper stories about her eccentric behavior—wearing men's clothing, drinking, and swearing—and on her claims to have scouted for Crook. Only by circumstance did her name come to Wheeler's attention.

Interestingly, the stories invented by Edward Wheeler for his dime novels did not become part of Calamity Jane folklore. Legendary feats in the dime novels such as battling Cattymount Cass, being kidnapped by Tra-la-la Charlie, and resuscitating Deadwood Dick are not found in other popular accounts of Calamity Jane. Thus, even though dime novels brought Martha celebrity status, the stories in them were immaterial to her fame. Tales associated with Calamity Jane in folklore, such as scouting for Crook, riding with Wild Bill Hickok, capturing Jack McCall, or saving the Deadwood stage, are not derived from dime novels. Instead, these stories were told by Martha Canary and embellished by other storytellers. Martha's status as a dime novel heroine, however, added to the willingness of listeners to accept her tales as fact.

Most Americans realized that dime novel characters were invented. In fact, many readers assumed Calamity Jane was imagined just as Deadwood Dick was. The *Cheyenne Daily Leader* in 1885 observed, for example, that "many people think Calamity Jane is a heated myth of the disordered brain of some penny-a-liner, but she is a reality, and the pen of a half crazy imagination is not needed to enhance her actual deeds."[57]

Although Wheeler was the first and most important dime novelist to utilize the name of Calamity Jane in his stories, he was not the only one. For example, an unknown writer using the pseudonym "Reckless Ralph" produced "Calamity Jane, The Queen of the Plains," published serially in *Street and Smith's New York Weekly* in 1882. In this story, desperado Mountain Jim is shot by twenty-six vigilantes, but before he dies informs the young woman he has been raising that he is not her father and instructs her about hidden papers explaining her origins. In following years, each of the vigilantes responsible for Mountain Jim's death is killed, and the young woman becomes known as Calamity Jane because of her presence in the vicinity of their calamitous deaths. She eventually becomes the proprietress of a Deadwood gambling hall and a partner of the notorious outlaw, Jesse James. When her real father finally appears in the story, he is shocked by her dress and reckless behavior, remarking, "It is terrible to think one so beautiful should be so fallen!" But one of her friends explains, "She is not fallen, the way you mean." Her father is relieved "that but for gambling and shooting, she is pure." Clearly, the author shared Wheeler's narrow view of morality, which prohibited (or condemned) fornication but not gambling or shooting people. Ultimately, Calamity forgives her father, who had deserted her early in life, and the two depart to begin life anew in Colorado.[58]

One other dime novel is often mentioned in commentaries on Calamity Jane, even though no copy has been located. Author Lewis Freeman recalled that while an adolescent he read a "saffron-hued thriller called 'The Beautiful White Devil of the Yellowstone.'" Unlike the stories by Wheeler and Reckless Ralph, it featured Calamity Jane and Wild Bill Hickok together in romantic adventures. Freeman said he read the forbidden story in the haymow and commented that "the fragrance of dried alfalfa brings the vision of 'Calamity Jane' before my eyes even to this day."[59] Perhaps Freeman's 1922 recollection is inaccurate, but finding a secluded place to read the dime novel probably typified youthful behavior because adults disapproved.

Mirroring later anxieties about the impact of music, movies, and television on families, late-nineteenth-century society decried the influence of dime novels on the morality of their children. Many feared that reading these western adventures might cause young people to become violent and immoral. Captain Jack Crawford, the "poet scout," became a leading critic. "I wish I could sit down and take every dime novel reading little boy in America by the hand and point out to him the destination he will reach if he persists in reading the vile trash," Crawford exclaimed. These stories glorified the wrong kind of people. Many convicts in western penitentiaries, he explained, "assert unqualifiedly that they were brought to their present shame and disgrace thru reading dime novels."[60]

Thus, although dime novels preached the values of traditional morality and opposed wickedness derived from love of money, they simultaneously were perceived by members of society as undermining acceptable standards of conduct. The dime novel Calamity Jane reflected this social ambivalence. Her smoking and wearing male attire presented a daring challenge to accepted codes of behavior for women. Conversely, there were positive qualities in the dime novel Calamity Jane, including sincerity, naturalness, and individualism, standing in stark contrast to the artificiality, materialism, and conformity of the late-nineteenth-century urban, industrial East. Furthermore, despite the differences in the adventures of the dime novel Calamity Jane and those told by Martha Canary, the two women shared certain qualities. Both challenged society's standards of behavior for women, and at the same time were admired for generosity, honesty, and lack of pretentiousness. However, Martha's boasting, prostitution, and alcoholism separated her widely from the dime novel heroine. Each time Martha's contemporaries met her, they faced this disparity between the fictional heroine and the actual woman.

CHAPTER SEVEN

Life in Dakota, 1878–1881

For three years following her emergence as a dime novel heroine, Martha Canary lived in the Black Hills and at Fort Pierre in Dakota Territory. She did not have a permanent residence, seeking places instead where excitement was at its most intense. Although Martha's life could be described as seminomadic, her trail nevertheless becomes decidedly easier to follow because of her dime novel fame. Newspapers now reported her presence more frequently. Still, the existence of other Calamity Janes and inaccurate reports of her travels confuse the record.

For example, on August 4, 1877, the *Sidney (Nebraska) Telegraph* reported that Calamity Jane had arrived from the Black Hills, but immediately left with a bullwhacker, having "received a promotion on the road as assistant wagon boss." But "her husband is not a violent mourner," continued the *Telegraph*, because "if she has any conscience she took it with her, and if she had any virtue her husband did not know it. Her child is now in good hands, and the painter [husband] is happy."[1] The identification of this Sidney Calamity Jane as Martha Canary is doubtful. The newspaper clearly states that the Sidney woman is "Calamity Jane No. 2," and Martha was reported in the Black Hills at nearly the same time. Another woman nicknamed Calamity Jane lived in Denver and in August 1878 was "thrown from a buggy and seriously injured" while intoxicated. The Denver Calamity Jane died shortly after her accident. At the news of her death, Deadwood's *Times* quickly announced that this was "Not Our Calamity Jane," identifying the Denver woman as Mattie Young from Iowa. "There is but one real Calamity and she is now one of the distinguished denizens of Deadwood," the *Times* explained.[2] The death of Denver's Calamity Jane left Martha as the only serious claimant to the famous nickname, and rightly so. It was through her career that the name had become nationally known.

Inaccurate accounts of Martha's presence in other locales also make it difficult for historians to trace her movements. For example, Lieutenant Charles A. Varnum said she was in the vicinity of the fight between the army and the Nez Perce at Canyon Creek in Montana, and on September 4, 1877, nursed the wounded as they were transported from the battlefield to their Tongue River camp.[3] At precisely this time, Martha was giving chase to Dan Scott and Charley Collins in Deadwood for writing a scurrilous article about her. Most likely, Varnum, hearing in later years that Calamity Jane had lived at some time near Canyon Creek, mingled that story with his reminiscence of the Canyon Creek battle.

Instead, Deadwood continued to be Martha's primary residence between 1877 and 1879. There, Horatio N. Maguire, one of the individuals most responsible for her national prominence, again brought her before a larger audience. In his booklet, *The Coming Empire: A Complete Treatise on the Black Hills, Yellowstone and Big Horn Region* (1878), Maguire included a brief biography of Martha that mixed fanciful legend with information probably derived in part from her. In one obviously exaggerated tale, he claimed she could "throw an oyster-can into the air and put two bullet-holes into it from her revolver before it reaches the ground, and offers to bet she can knock a fly off an ox's ear with a sixteen-foot whip-lash three times out of five." More significant was her response to his query about her work in traditionally male occupations: "Hasn't a poor woman as good a right to make a living as a man?" she responded. According to Maguire, she added that "society, and not herself, [was] to blame, as she always came near to starving to death when she tried to support herself in a more womanly way."[4]

Despite Martha's assertion that society forced her into working as stage-driver, bullwhacker, and army scout, she mostly labored at jobs typically occupied by women. Moreover, she actually showed preference for domestic life with husband and home. When a reporter for the *Black Hills Daily Times* greeted her in Deadwood on December 17, 1877, she explained, "I want you to understand my name ain't Calamity Jane, its Maggie Cosgrove."[5] Her new husband, George Cosgrove, had accompanied the Hickok-Utter wagon train into the Black Hills. William Powell, a pioneer bullwhacker, remembered that George and Martha spent the winter of 1876–77 in Sherman, Wyoming, and that Martha told him she had married Cosgrove in Cheyenne. Joseph "White-Eye" Anderson also remembered her with Cosgrove at Jack Bowman's Hat Creek ranch in 1879. Martha was at the bar drinking when she exclaimed, "Boys, . . . I am married to George now and am living straight and don't do any business on the outside."[6]

Cosgrove family records indicate that George was born in Toronto, Canada, on September 12, 1853, and arrived in the United States with his parents when he was five. First settling in Michigan, the family next moved to Wyoming, and in 1876 George and his father, William, traveled to the Black Hills with the Hickok caravan. Initially, they prospected for gold; then, as experienced freighters, they hauled supplies on the Fort Pierre–Deadwood trail. The family recalled that Martha gave George a picture of herself "in the buckskin outfit she wore while freighting."[7]

In January 1878, Martha became "disgusted with Deadwood" and left for Rapid City. Her *Life and Adventures* adds that while in Rapid City she prospected for gold.[8] Her efforts to find gold must have been brief. Martha was back in Deadwood by January 22 and, according to the newspaper, had her photograph taken for the first time. It was mistaken since photographs of her exist from 1875 and 1876. This may have been her first visit to a photographic studio, however.[9] By February, she seems to have left her "husband" George Cosgrove for another man: "'Calamity' and her 'darling Jim,' and one or two other attendants at a Saturday night dance, succumbed to the green-eyed monster, and made things lively until Officer Clark put a quietus to the difficulty," one reporter wrote.[10]

The identity of "darling Jim," like many of Martha's male associates, remains a mystery. She is reported with other men during this period as well. According to John Ward, she married Frank Lacy and lived west of the Black Hills near Fort Fetterman in Wyoming. Ward said that Lacy had two bull teams and held a government contract to haul wood to the fort. While with Martha, he cut logs in the mountains and established a road ranch sixteen miles west of Fort Fetterman that furnished food, liquor, and lodging for travelers and kept the stage stock. Their establishment was located near the place where stage coaches most frequently were robbed. Once, said Ward, road agents left the mail scattered about after stopping the stage. Lacy and the stage driver picked up the mail, only to be arrested for theft. When Lacy went to the penitentiary, said Ward, Martha left once again for the Hills.[11] Freighter Samuel Smith also remembered Martha with several yoke of oxen going into the mountains to chop and haul wood, but he did not mention Lacy.[12]

While Martha meandered between Deadwood and nearby mining camps and road ranches, journalist Thomas Newson penned his *Drama of Life in the Black Hills* (1878). Calamity Jane is a central character in Newson's melodramatic play, to which was added a one-page biography of Martha Canary based on personal observations. Newson's description of Martha is among the most important early accounts of her, offering important insights into Martha's personality:

> Jane grew up among the rough and tumble of the world, and is to-day what delicate society would denominate, a strong-minded woman. She is about 22 years old; has a dark complexion; high cheek bones; an awkward walk; receding brow; black hair; rather pleasant eye, but when in passion emitting a greenish glare. Her movements are all free and unstudied, yet in no sense unbecoming. Her conversation is animated, her language good, and her heart warm and generous. She imitates no one; is an original in herself; despises hypocrisy; and is easily melted to tears. She is generous, forgiving, kind-hearted, sociable, and yet when aroused, has all the daring and courage of the lion or the devil himself . . . and when dressed in her own garments she looks comely; when equipped as a man she has all the characteristics of the sterner sex, with her pistols, bowie-knives and other weapons of death.[13]

Although Newson romanticizes Calamity's adventures, claiming she has scaled mountains, served as a scout, and fought Indians, he correctly identifies her as Martha Canary and accurately cites her age as twenty-two.

"The Recorder," a character in Newson's *Drama of Life* who might be Clement Lounsberry or Newson himself, interviews Martha, asking questions that make a modern biographer envious for the opportunity. Concerning whether she is literate, Martha responds: "Never went to school; can neither read nor write." The Recorder asks the derivation of her nickname, to which Martha answers, "Because of the calamity of my birth—I ought never to have been born. It is not my real name." Inventing fictitious military careers for her parents, Martha explains that she was "born in the army after my father's death." Her father "was a soldier," and her mother "a laundress in the army." When finally the Recorder asks, "Jane, ain't you tired of this way of living?" Martha responds with a simple "Yes." As the scene closes, "Calamity is seen on the stage with her face in her hands, crying."[14]

In other scenes, Newson offers a vivid portrait of Martha's life during her early adult years. His descriptions of her character and behavior stand in stark contrast to the dime novels then circulating. Scene VIII, Act I, introduces Martha. First, a visitor to the Black Hills, identified simply as "the Professor," sees Calamity Jane having a drink in Custer and mistakes her for a young man. Then, later that evening, she plays cards with three men and now is dressed "in the garments of a woman." She calls for another round of drinks and "quaffs her wine." When she loses, "her eyes flash, she throws down her cards, pushes back the table and pounds her fists on the bar." But the men persuade her to return. This time she is more successful, "and laughs with delight—she has beaten them all in the game."[15]

In another of Newson's scenes, Martha dances in the hurdy-gurdy house:

> Four girls can be seen in the inner room, darting about, and among them, Calamity Jane, dressed in a plain black silk dress—comely figure. A small, dappy fellow, dressed in brown velvet, appears in the front room among the men, and exclaims loudly:—"Gentlemen will please prepare for the dance." One and another take a girl and assume their places upon the floor, while the music strikes up a lively tune. Calamity comes to the bar with a rough looking man and says: "Give me a cigar."—Lights it and walks off; smokes a moment, and then throws it away. The man in velvet calls off in a loud and drawling manner, and the dance sets in. Two of the girls are drunk and stagger; the third one is noisy. Calamity is quiet, with an occasional remark; dances modestly, and at the conclusion of the dance all parties repair to the bar. The three girls drink whisky with the men; Calamity takes wine.[16]

Newson's heroine stands apart from the other dance-hall girls, quiet, serious, and even consuming a different drink.

Other scenes offer similarly unfamiliar images of Martha Canary. In one she is skipping and singing "as happily as any young girl," holding the arm of her new husband. Her unidentified companion tells her they will go to his ranch tomorrow, "where I have cattle, cows, horses, and everything necessary to make us comfortable." Martha is "glad."

She does not like giving up all her old friends, but says "I'll do it, of course I'll do it, if I say so." Then she queries her husband: "Say! Jim, what will you do if there comes another Indian war, and Crooks wants me to go as scout?" Jim agrees that she would have to go in that event, and the two continue down the street, Martha singing as they leave.[17]

Newson's *Drama of Life* also depicts her nursing a miner stricken with "mountain fever." The miner's friends ask Martha to help. "Of course, I will," she responds, remembering that the sick man, George Fullerton, "spoke kindly to me and gave me some money when I was in distress." As he dies, Martha "sobs violently."[18]

Although Newson claimed his dramatized portraits of Black Hills residents were authentic, the local press insisted that "as a picture of life in the Black Hills it is not faithful, nor does it do the bone and sinew of them justice." Evidently, it was not so much the inaccuracy of the stories that angered the newspaper as the selection of citizens featured by Newson. The book's large sales were due, the *Black Hills Daily Pioneer* asserted, to "the morbid curiosity existing in the east to see his so-called lions of the Hills, who are in fact but the most disreputable of our community."[19] In addition to Martha, Newson included sketches of the beautiful gambler Nellie Ford; Hickok's friend, Charles "Colorado Charlie" Utter; and dancer Kitty Le Roy, recently murdered by her husband.

Not surprisingly, Clement Lounsberry's newspaper reacted positively to the content of Newson's book; Lounsberry, after all, was the subject of one of the dramatized portraits. His *Bismarck Tribune* enthusiastically reported that sales were so good that a second edition was being printed now that the first ten thousand copies had been sold. Even Lounsberry found one weakness, however. "The work is full of interest," his newspaper reported, but "the illustrations are horribly executed (and the artist ought to be)." Newson responded defensively, saying that "the cuts of Calamity Jane, Charles Utter, Kitty Leroy and Col. C. A. Lounsberry, were all taken from photographs, and I am confident are excellent likenesses." Still, since the book cost a "paltry sum of 25 cents," making it "unequaled in cheapness," the portraits were "good enough" until sales were sufficient to produce better ones.[20] Lounsberry was correct; the portraits are terrible.

Nevertheless, the four illustrations of Martha are important. Three poorly drawn sketches are based on scenes from *Drama of Life.* Two of these show her in male attire early in the evening, then changing into a dress later at night, depicting her cross-dressing as no one else has done. Another shows her tending a sick miner. The final illustration, an important engraving that accompanies Newson's biography in *Drama of Life,* is based on a photograph of Martha that no longer exists and offers a unique portrait.

Other observers besides Newson have provided important images of Martha's life in the Black Hills. Dr. Henry F. Hoyt, who arrived in Deadwood in 1877 to practice medicine, remembered that one Saturday night he "heard a commotion and down the street came a woman on a horse at full gallop." It was Martha, carrying a pistol in each hand and shooting randomly while she "emitted a good imitation of an Indian war-whoop at every jump of her mount." She wore a soldier's uniform, and, recalled Hoyt, she "was the first female I had ever seen riding astride."[21] Cowboy E. C. "Teddy Blue" Abbott recalled her differently. It was in about 1878, he said, and Martha was "at the height of her fame." She was "some sort of a madam . . . running a great big gambling hall in Deadwood," and he remembered her "dressed in purple velvet, with diamonds on her and everything."[22]

In addition, several young people long remembered their first encounters with Martha. Mont Hawthorne, who accompanied his father from Nebraska to the Black Hills in 1877 to sell flour, was unimpressed when he met "the dangedest looking woman" he'd ever seen. Martha, he said, "was real tall and built like a busted bale of hay." Not only was she wearing men's clothing, she was "chewing tobacco and letting it get away from her." Worse, she had been drinking, and "she teetered, and pretty near fell on her face in my fire." He became embarrassed when she put her arm around him and told everyone he "was going to be a great freighter some day."[23] Mary Fanton, later a well-known writer and editor, also encountered Martha in Deadwood. Mary's father, William, owned a hotel and bank there from 1877 to 1879. Martha lived near their home in a cabin constructed of old logs and tin cans. Mary, who was about thirteen, visited Martha several times, despite rumors that people who talked with her suffered calamities. She said Martha treated her gently and gave her gifts.[24] Another observer, Fred Borsch, claimed it was Martha who gave him the first money he ever earned. She was upset about a dead dog lying on a Deadwood street and asked that it be buried. No one paid attention to her. Fred finally buried the animal, and she paid him five dollars for his effort.[25]

Martha also volunteered to help people who were sick or injured. In the booming mining town, violence was hardly uncommon, and the newspaper began its coverage of an 1878 stabbing incident with the headline "More Blood Letting." According to the report, Frank Warren, a Deadwood resident, met an unnamed newcomer, and for two days the two men drank heavily. Drunk, the visitor fell asleep, and Warren allegedly "went through his pockets, stealing about $16 in money, all he had." When the stranger awakened, he went in search of Warren and stabbed him. Graphically, the newspaper reported that "the knife . . . entered the unfortunate man's bowels just above the navel," and the "bloody villain" turned "the sharp blade around in order to make sure work, and then drew it upward, opening a gash of about two inches in length." Warren was rushed to the doctor's office and then moved to a cabin.[26] The next day, the *Times* reported, "the man Warren, who was stabbed on lower Main street Wednesday night, is doing quite well under the care of Calamity Jane, who has undertaken the job of nursing him." Complimenting her efforts, the correspondent added, "There's lots of humanity in Calamity, and she is deserving of much praise for the part she has taken in the particular case." Incredibly, given the description of his injuries, Warren survived.[27]

That fall after she left Deadwood, Martha once again volunteered to help an injured man, this time in the newly established town of Sturgis near Fort Meade. In her *Life and Adventures*, Martha asserted that she "went to Bear Butte Creek with the 7th Cavalry" and helped build Ft. Meade and the town of Sturgis. Although the town and fort were founded at about that time, Martha was neither with the cavalry nor a town founder.[28] Sturgis, located twelve miles from Deadwood, attracted gamblers and dance-hall girls from the latter town, especially on payday at Fort Meade. Martha was among these Deadwood residents making Sturgis their new headquarters. Describing one of Martha's trips there in September 1878, the *Deadwood Times* reported that she "was a passenger by the outgoing Bismarck coach last evening." Although "her destination is not known . . . she probably went down to see the boys in blue."[29]

Martha remained in Sturgis for some time. When in October the *St. Paul Pioneer Press* reported that Calamity Jane was living in Le Mars, Iowa, the Deadwood paper retorted, "She is now a respected resident of Sturgis City, and the proprietress of a successful laundry." Because of her fame, it continued, "every one-horsed city in the country is claiming the veritable Calamity as a resident."[30] Still a resident of the Sturgis–Fort Meade area months later, Martha clearly worked not only as a laundress but in the dance halls as well. There, according to a newspaper in February 1879, she "walloped two women." The reporter added: Martha "can get away with half a dozen ordinary pugilistic women when she turns loose, but she never fights unless she is in the right, and then she is not backward to tackle even a masculine shoulder hitter."[31]

It was during another dance-hall skirmish that Martha volunteered to nurse an injured man. The day after she punched the two women, a Fort Meade soldier named Hanlon was arrested for a "trivial offence" and confined. Somehow he induced his guard to accompany him to Sturgis, where Hanlon "had become enamored with one of the weak sisters" who carried the nickname "Scarfaced Charley." Hanlon's absence was soon noticed, and a patrol was sent to the dance house where Hanlon and his girl friend Charley were "whirling in the mazes of a dance." When Hanlon saw the soldiers, he raced out the front door, the patrol in hot pursuit. He refused to halt as ordered, so they fired. "He fell where he was shot," said the reporter, and immediately was carried back to Iler's saloon. There Martha, "with that redeeming element of sympathy for which she is noted, at once rushed to her house, stripped her bedstead of its contents and carried them over to where the wounded man was being placed in a wagon." Unfortunately, her help could not save this man; Hanlon died shortly afterwards at the military post.[32]

Wanderlust soon drove Martha elsewhere. She "was among the stage arrivals from the north, on Tuesday," reported the Rapid City newspaper on March 8, 1879.[33] She soon left Rapid City, however, and her route afterwards is lost to history. But her return to Dakota Territory in May from points unknown received newspaper attention. She was a passenger on the new luxury steamboat, the *Dacotah,* pushing northward up the Missouri River. This "magnificent floating palace," with accommodations for one hundred cabin passengers, was on its maiden voyage. It had recently left Omaha, and Martha may have boarded it there, or perhaps even farther downstream. Passing through Yankton on May 23, Martha continued up the river to Fort Pierre, and then returned to the Black Hills.[34]

According to the Yankton newspaper, Martha recently had "sold her claim in the Hills for $16,000" and planned "to open a ranche in the Black Hills." Another newspaper thought she had "started a ranche at Fort Pierre."[35] But no evidence confirms that Martha sold any claims. In any event, what was meant by a "ranche" was likely a roadhouse for

travelers with restaurant, saloon, sleeping quarters, and probably gambling and prostitution. Charles F. Hackett recalled that Martha worked in such a place along the
Missouri River, but thought it was in 1877. He said that only a month before he arrived,
it was a lively location as the headquarters of the Van Tassel and Gardner's Concord coach
line to the Black Hills. But gone now was the dance house operated by "Calamity Jane,
Red Jacket and other frail creatures of the frontier."[36]

In 1879, however, Martha evidently traveled through Yankton and Fort Pierre without
stopping. By July she was back in Deadwood. "Calamity Jane is again a resident of this
place," declared the *Daily Times*, "and graced the Gem last evening."[37] But Calamity was
not a dance-hall girl at Swearingen's Gem Variety Theatre for long. She became suddenly
and seriously ill, as noted by the newspaper on July 15. Martha "was taken very sick
yesterday afternoon, and medical aid was hurriedly summoned," it said. "Congestion of
the bowels is the difficulty, and the case is a dangerous one." Medical treatment was
successful, however, and only a few days later it was reported that Martha "was out a
short time yesterday afternoon."[38]

While Martha was ill, Deadwood's *Times*, often critical of her, printed a lengthy
editorial entitled "Calamity Jane's Virtues." It contained the community's appreciation
for her charitable work. She has "many solid friends among the best citizens of the
Hills," the newspaper reported, and her illness caused considerable concern. One man
"living up the gulch" who had never met her, sent a representative "with instructions to
ascertain her wants and provide for them fully at his expense." He did this despite her being
a "rough frontier girl, with many faults, embracing a large portion of the forbidden
precepts of the decalogue." This was because she had helped so many others. "Whenever sickness or like trouble" appeared, she volunteered her services, said the *Times*.
"The thinking portion of our people," it added, instead of dwelling on the "derogatory
elements of her life," look at her positive traits. Calling her a "rough diamond of the
border," the newspaper noted that "many a man who has been stricken with disease,
in the wild, unfrequented corners of the frontier where no woman but Calamity dared
to penetrate, owe their lives to the tender care" she provided. "These are among the
solid virtues of Calamity Jane," it concluded. "These traits of character make Calamity
solid with the good people of the west."[39]

Recovered by November 1879, Calamity made a brief trip back to Fort Pierre.
"Calamity Jane, who has been spending the fall months at Fort Pierre, one of the watering
places of this country, is now on her return to the metropolis, a passenger by La Plant's
bull train," reported the *Times*.[40] By December, she was again in Sturgis, and referred to
as "the queen of the dance house." Recalling earlier reports that she had sold mining
claims and purchased a ranch, the Cheyenne newspaper commented, "Her striking it
rich doesn't prevent her from making more money."[41] Soon she revisited Deadwood,
then went to Rapid City for the winter because, said the newspaper, "Deadwood is too
puritanical for her."[42]

She traveled even farther if reminiscences can be trusted. At some point during
the fall or winter months of 1879–80, Martha returned to the Union Pacific towns in

Wyoming. At an unspecified time during the 1879 excitement caused by the "Meeker massacre," she was seen in Rawlins. The town became the center for freighting supplies for the troops sent from Fort Steele and other posts in the region to subdue the Ute Indians after agent Nathan Meeker and most of his employees at White River Agency in northern Colorado were killed on September 30.

From October to at least December 1879, Rawlins's population "was rapidly increased by some three-hundred Bull Whackers and Mule Skinners, saloon keepers, gamblers and dance hall girls," remembered Fenimore Chatterton, who worked as a bookkeeper at the general store owned by J. W. Hugus. And, he added, "Calamity Jane was among them."[43]

M. Wilson Rankin, courier for the army during the Meeker crisis, also recalled Martha's presence there. Normally, Rawlins had a population of about eight hundred, Rankin remembered, but now "was filled to overflowing with the class of men who drift to such excitements of this nature." Among the "Distinguished Visitors" during the crisis was "no less a personality than 'Calamity Jane,' with a somewhat less notorious companion, 'Cotton Tail,' a 'dizzy blonde,' from Cheyenne, Sidney and the Black Hills area." They "made Rawlins a few days' business call during the height of the Ute excitement," remembered Rankin, and evidently departed as the excitement diminished.[44]

On trips such as this one from the Black Hills to the Union Pacific towns, Martha made unscheduled stops in other settlements. Residents later told anecdotes about her visits. Johnny Mills, a Laramie barber, thought it was 1878 when Calamity was in his business place. While she was standing in his barber shop with her head in a wash basin, "her posterior became the target for a prankster." Martha, assuming it was Mills who swatted her, smashed a pitcher of water over his head.[45]

Martha was back in Rapid City on April 20, 1880. Her visit coincided with "the session of the district court, and she manifested a good deal of delight in meeting the members of our bar there, and they were all, or most all, glad to see her," reported the newspaper.[46] Martha was probably not there because of legal difficulties, however. And it was her last known visit to the Black Hills until 1895. She was now mostly attracted to the booming town of Fort Pierre. As the Chicago and North Western Railway built westward from Minnesota across Dakota, the construction camps at track's end provided new excitement. The trains were projected to reach the Missouri River, across from Fort Pierre, that fall. The disorder accompanying the Black Hills mining rush was now mostly over, so perhaps the Deadwood newspaper was correct in suggesting their city had become too puritanical for Martha.

Once again, in her *Life and Adventures*, Martha correctly located herself at the new scene of her activities. She probably described her occupation inaccurately, however. "In 1879 I went to Fort Pierre and drove trains from Rapid City to Fort Pierre for Frank Witcher," she recalled, "then drove teams from Fort Pierre to Sturgis for Fred Evans." Calamity's familiarity with the Black Hills and Fort Pierre freight lines is evident in her identification of the freighter's names; Witcher and Evans advertised their freighting services beginning as early as 1877.[47] No evidence exists, however, that she ever worked regularly as a bullwhacker. She was listed as "a passenger by La Plant's bull train," but not as a driver, in the newspaper's first notice of her travels with the freighters. A female bullwhacker would have been newsworthy, as is evident in newspaper coverage of a Mrs. Oleson several years later. Noting Oleson's first arrival in 1886, the Deadwood newspaper reported, "A female bull-whacker was one of the novelties of Main Street yesterday. She handled the whip and with it her team as dexterously as the greatest veteran of the opposite sex, and without uttering a word, demonstrating the fact that profanity is not essential to the successful engineering of a string of cattle." Even more significantly, a subsequent paper described Oleson as "the original and only female bullwhackeress."[48]

Descriptions of Martha's bullwhacking in the Fort Pierre area probably confuse her with Oleson. For example, Mrs. M. J. Schubert, who arrived in Pierre from Wisconsin in 1883, remembered seeing "Calamity walking down the street beside the teams with her whip in hand" a number of times.[49] But Martha had left the Fort Pierre area in 1881, and no one places her in that vicinity during the next twenty years.

However, one pioneer of the area recalled Martha managing a freighting business. John Edmund Boland, who had worked on Missouri River steamboats before becoming a freighter, "found her to be a shrewd business woman" and "a lone wolf with nerve." He claimed her freighting operation had thirty teams of oxen and hauled freight between Fort Pierre and the Black Hills. Boland believed that her business manager was Dick Dunn, that they headquartered near Deadwood, and that he last saw her in 1883–84 sixty miles east of Deadwood. But Boland must be in error. Not even Martha claimed she owned a freighting business. Moreover, Charles Fales, who knew both Martha and Dick Dunn, said he "never heard of Calamity being in the freight business," but "Dick Dunn was, and had about three bull teams." When historian J. Leonard Jennewein asked Fales if Martha ever was a freighter, he said no, but recalled another woman who was.[50]

Martha undoubtedly traveled with freighters to and from the Black Hills and Fort Pierre several times in 1879–80. She might have used the whip occasionally, even if she did not draw a salary as a bullwhacker. Because so many reminiscences suggest she did, her adeptness at that avocation cannot be discounted. Nevertheless, it is doubtful she was regularly employed, and her association with bullwhackers probably involved companionship as much as transportation. According to bullwhacker William F. Hooker, bullwhackers seldom drank alcohol while working, but at the end of a freighting trip following weeks or even months of deprivation they celebrated by spending almost all their pay in gambling and sporting houses. Their spree ended only when their money ran out, at which time recruiters for freighting businesses waited outside the dance halls and gambling dens to sign them up for another trip.[51] Martha likely joined the bullwhackers in these celebrations.

Martha's more permanent residence in Fort Pierre began in July 1880 when the town's *Weekly Signal* announced: "Calamity Jane, a well known character of this western country came in from the Black Hills." Her arrival coincided with a tumultuous period in the history of the community. Within months, the railroad was expected to make its terminus in the area, so Fort Pierre was experiencing the typical excitement of a frontier boom town. "Track laying on the Northwestern railroad west of Huron, is progressing at the rate of two miles per day," reported the *Signal* the same day it announced Martha's arrival.[52] Huron was only 120 miles east of Fort Pierre, and Martha was but one of a host of individuals helping relieve laborers of their pay as the railroad neared its destination.

Far in advance of the construction crews were the graders, who by July 21 were "within about ten or twelve miles" of the Missouri River.[53] Boisterous and unruly crowds in Fort Pierre flocked to the numerous saloons and dance halls located on the east side of the river at the proposed site of the railroad terminus. The newspaper reported that one man was accidentally wounded as "the crowd were all pretty full, and were shooting off their revolvers through the roof and sides of the house."[54]

A few weeks later, the *Signal* reported another shooting. "Geo. Baker, who used to run a dance house here, went over on the railroad about three weeks ago," the story reported, "but the railroaders getting tired of him and his outfit, turned loose at them the other night, cutting their trunks and tents to pieces and shooting Baker in the leg."[55] George Baker was Martha's business partner. The Deadwood newspaper clarified that the shooting occurred sixty miles east of Fort Pierre when "George Baker, Calamity Jane and others attempted to start a bagnio."[56] The Yankton newspaper amplified that Baker "left Pierre for the west end of the Chicago & Northwestern track, accompanied by Calamity Jane and others, with the purpose of going into business. Reaching their destination a row occurred with some natives and Baker was shot through the leg making a severe but not dangerous wound." Baker's injury became serious when gangrene developed, but he eventually recovered, luckier than others who were fatally shot in the next weeks.[57]

Calamity Jane was rumored to have associated with Alexander (Arkansaw) Putello as well as with Baker. Arkansaw was involved in several shootings in Fort Pierre. Whether Calamity actively participated in these events cannot be ascertained, but they suggest her involvement with Fort Pierre's toughest element. Among those killed by Arkansaw was "George the Kid," described by the *Signal* as "a bold bad man" who had "killed two or three men already, and shot at several others." George's death was justified as self-defense because he had been in the process of drawing his revolver. After another killing, the Fort Pierre newspaper commented despairingly, "One by one they pass away, and this is the second one in less than two weeks, and the end is not in sight."[58]

The reporter's prediction was correct, causing citizens to organize as vigilantes to regulate "East Pierre." Declaring that no more shooting would be allowed on the streets, these "regulators" soon tangled with Martha's former associate, George Baker, who, with a companion named Kelly, attempted to rob George Jennings's restaurant. Jennings recognized them, causing Kelly to shoot him, though not fatally. The two outlaws were caught and a squad of regulators warned them to leave the settlement and never return. "This order was promptly obeyed and the community is rid of two bad men," the newspaper asserted.[59]

Baker and Kelly, however, only crossed the Missouri River from East Pierre to Fort Pierre. There they "enlisted Alexander McDonald Putello, alias 'Arkansaw,' in their behalf." Conceded to be the leader of the bad element in Fort Pierre, Arkansaw set out to challenge the order against shooting in the streets. He made good on his promise, but so did the vigilantes. When they ordered Arkansaw to surrender, he ran into the brush along the river, firing as he went. The vigilantes responded with a fusillade, killing Arkansaw. Afterwards, Baker and Kelly disappeared from the scene. A few weeks later the newspaper reported that "since the 'Home Guards' took the reins of government in hand and put 'Arkansaw' to sleep, everybody has been quiet and peaceful."[60]

Several pioneers in Fort Pierre recalled less adventurous aspects of Martha's life there. Among these was Albert Lot Hamlin, who came to Pierre to build sheds for hides. His stories about Calamity were undoubtedly embellished over the years, but probably correct concerning her general conduct. On his first night there, he was awakened by gunfire and, probably exaggerating the violence as he later recalled the incident, said that three men were hanging from a tree and another three bodies lay nearby the next morning. During breakfast, he remembered, someone asserted that the trouble had begun at "Calam's place." The claim was immediately challenged by other customers: "There wasn't a damn bit of trouble at her place! She gets blamed fer a lot of stuff" despite the fact that her establishment is "the best run place in town." Hamlin learned that Martha was running a saloon on the Missouri River and that her place was frequented by bullwhackers. As soon as they were paid, the freighters always "thought of 'Calam,'" said Hamlin, "and the good times they could have at her place in Pierre—where they wouldn't be robbed, over charged, or mistreated."

Hamlin and his crew decided to visit her place after supper. Noticing that "if the saloons were taken out of the town there would not have been enough left to sneeze at," they finally located her establishment, distinguished from the others by a sign over the door, "Calamity Jane's." Entering the saloon, they were confronted with "music, shouting and scuffling of hob-nail shoes." The air was also permeated by "boisterous conversation and profanity." Nevertheless, in her establishment there was "no monkey business" because she "was not a woman to trifle with and they knew it."

Fifty years later, Hamlin described "the greatest woman character of the wild West" from memory:

> Behind the bar she stood, about five foot nine inches high. She had dark brown eyes, high cheek bones (denoting possibility of some Indian blood) and a pointed chin. Her raven hair was tucked up under a brown Stetson hat. She was entirely garbed in buckskin—both trousers and coat and vest, a red bandana around her neck. A small sized pair of black high heel boots finished out her other extremity.

She weighed about 170 pounds, but it was "all frontier muscle," he said. And when she greeted her customers, "pearly teeth showed when she smiled." She was also good at her business: "As fast as the men hollered for drinks she slid them down the bar. Invariably they stopped right where she intended them to," leading one man to comment, "Gosh, if Calamity Jane's eye is as good on the rifle as it is sliding drinks she must a knocked over plenty of Sioux and Cheyenne in the Big Horn country, and when she bushwhacked on the Union Pacific railroad in Utah and Wyoming." Remarkably, Hamlin said Martha "turned down many a drink back of the bar. It seemed a personal pride with her to stay sober and 'tend to business.'" When a "wild woman" entered the bar, "blazing loose a six-shooting Colt" at a man she was chasing, Martha jumped over the bar and disarmed her. Hamlin and his men thought she was "about the fastest mover on the hoof" they ever saw.[61]

Frontiersman Zack Sutley also encountered Martha in Fort Pierre. Sutley remembered Fort Pierre as filled with "the rough element which follows a sudden boom and dance halls." But no saloons were located there because "it was on an Indian reservation." These establishments were located across the river. According to Sutley, Martha regularly traveled "back and forth to the Hills with some gambler or freighter."

Once, remembered Sutley, "we heard a hammering on our door and got up to find Calamity Jane and a liveryman from Rapid." Martha explained that she was being chased by a United States marshal "for selling whisky without a government license." On the other side of the river was a bullwhacker camp where she would be safe. Sutley loaned Martha his horse to cross the river, calling across the water to the men in the camps to hold lanterns to guide her ashore: "Before long I knew she had reached the other side, for I could hear Jane swearing and knew the horse was shaking off the water." After Sutley's horse was returned to him and stabled, the marshal arrived. Spotting Martha's driver, the lawman questioned him and Sutley concerning her whereabouts. Sutley told them she had crossed the river and offered the marshal his horse, just as he had Martha. The marshal decided to wait until morning. When he crossed the river the next morning, the bullwhackers denied she was there. Asking where she had gone, he was told that "he could go to hell before they'd tell him." The marshal, said Sutley, returned to Rapid City without his prey.

Sutley recalled one other encounter with Martha. During one of his trips on the Fort Pierre–Deadwood trail, he stopped at another party's camp and asked for something to eat. To his surprise, Martha was their cook and was just preparing breakfast. While he visited, Sutley pulled off his boot, showing a raw sore where a blister wore off: "Jane was very sympathetic, dressing my heel and binding it with a piece of cloth which she tore from her clothing." While hardly material for a dime novel, Sutley's story has a ring of truth. It led to his conclusion that Martha "had unexpectedly womanly traits and was the first to help a pilgrim family in distress or to nurse a sick miner or freighter."[62]

Many other stories were told about Martha's nursing at Fort Pierre. Charles Fales recalled that she was asked to care for his aunt, who had "mountain fever." Martha agreed, but was told she had to wear a dress and not smoke, drink, or swear, because Fales's aunt was a refined woman. For several weeks Martha did as asked, said Fales, but as soon as his aunt was well enough to take care of herself, Martha headed for the bars, "and in an hour from that time she couldn't hit the ground with her hat."[63]

But Martha's varied activities made it difficult for eyewitnesses to decide on her true nature. Zack Sutley, for example, concluded: "Any attempt to describe this picturesque character whose name is everywhere an echo of the old frontier days is certain to fall short of the truth." Differing accounts of her can be found, he said, "most of them probably true, to prove she was any kind of person one wants to call her." He considered her "a strange mixture of masculine boldness and feminine gentleness."

Sutley described Martha's complicated relationships with men. She "spent most of her life with some freighter on the trail or keeping house for some ranchman or stock tender at a stage station," he said. But her male companions were seldom true husbands. Although Martha "lived before the days of 'affinities' and 'companionate marriages,'" Sutley concluded, "these terms describe well her relationships."[64]

Other than George Baker, none of Martha's male associates in Fort Pierre have been identified. One unsubstantiated story that came to light in 1996 claims that in 1881 Martha gave birth to a daughter named Maude. According to this account, written by Maude's daughter, Ruth Shadley, Martha, unable to care for the child while she worked as a freighter, gave the infant to Sadie Beck, a cook in Pierre. Sadie, in turn, gave the child up for adoption to Joe and Mary Weir. Shadley offers as proof a similarity in appearance between Martha and Maude, a coincidence in dates between Martha's residence in Pierre and Maude's birth, and rumors during Maude's life that she was Calamity Jane's daughter. But these are insufficient to prove her case. When Sadie Beck signed the adoption papers in 1883, she said she was the mother. Also, newspapers, which regularly reported events in Martha's life, did not mention a child in Pierre. Moreover, in an 1896 interview Martha explained that she had borne two children, a boy who died and a daughter, then nine, named Jessie.[65]

Although newspapers did not mention that Martha had a child, they did report her participation in the celebration of the railroad's completion. The citizens of "East Pierre" organized a grand ball in honor of the event. Everything went "magnificently until nearly daylight," reported the Deadwood newspaper. Then, it added sarcastically, "the entire assemblage was thrown into grief and the festivities and rejoicing came to an end." This was because "the belle of the evening and of the new metropolis, by some unexplainable accident, fell down stairs and broke one of her legs. Her name is Calamity Jane."[66] The newspaper's readers undoubtedly would have understood that Martha had become too drunk to negotiate the steps successfully.

The coming of the railroad led to Martha's departure from Pierre. A few weeks after the celebration, it was reported that she had "recovered from her broken leg, and by the way of a rustication," went to Chicago. Cynically, the reporter requested the citizens of Chicago "to deal gently with this Black Hills exotic, as she is a tender plant and never could endure rough treatment."[67] Shortly afterwards, it added that Martha "at last met her affinity." She has "married and . . . settled down in St. Paul." There, the newspaper added, she "has become an ornament to society, and will remain one until some goul [*sic*] gives her away. Desiring Jane's welfare, we will not tell her new name, and hope it may never be found out."[68] The reporter need not have worried; the name of Martha's new "husband" remains unknown even today.

Martha did not mention visits to Chicago or St. Paul, or any marriage, in her *Life and Adventures*. Instead, she said simply, "In 1881 I went to Wyoming and returned in 1882 to Miles City."[69] Perhaps she did visit earlier haunts in Wyoming, but no evidence of her trip has yet surfaced. Instead, she disappeared from public notice for nearly a year, an absence easily explained by recalling that she moved frequently and often lived in remote areas. Her absence did not stop her publicity, however. In 1880, she was mentioned in Arthur Morecamp's popular novel *Live Boys in the Black Hills; or, The Young Texas Gold Hunters*. As the main characters in the story reach Deadwood, they see Calamity Jane "on horseback, riding straddle, drunk as a fool, and cutting up like a greaser on a spree."[70]

Then, after nearly a year's absence, Martha appeared on February 11, 1882, in Bismarck. There, in a saloon on Missouri Avenue, she described herself to a correspondent for Pierre's *Dakota Journal*, as "one of the founders of Pierre." The reporter added that "her maternal eye looks upon our large and still growing city with much satisfaction."[71] She had stopped in Bismarck en route to the new booming camps, such as Miles City, as the Northern Pacific railroad built westward. It would be more than a decade before she returned to Pierre or the Black Hills.

CHAPTER EIGHT

Following The Northern Pacific
1882-1884

In her *Life and Adventures*, Martha Canary asserted that in 1882 she journeyed to Miles City, Montana, where she "took up a ranch on the Yellow Stone, raising stock and cattle." She "also kept a way side inn, where the weary traveler could be accommodated with food, drink, or trouble if he looked for it."[1] Her story offers a more positive impression of her "roadside ranch" than visitors might have received. It also suggests more stability than her nomadism allowed. For three years, Martha followed the Northern Pacific as it built westward through Montana and joined a mining stampede to the Coeur d'Alenes in Idaho. In addition, Martha began making stage appearances. Though only twenty-six, she was a celebrity. As the frontier era ended in the northern plains, shows depicting life in the "Old West" began touring the country and Martha's dime novel fame made her an attraction.

Martha's initial appearance in Miles City occurred on February 11, 1882. "Calamity Jane is in town," reported the newspaper.[2] Her arrival in Miles City coincided with renewed westward construction of the Northern Pacific Railroad. Initiated in 1870, the transcontinental railway was built simultaneously eastward from Puget Sound and westward from Duluth. When the company faced bankruptcy in the Panic of 1873, however, construction from Minnesota was halted at Bismarck. Not until July 5, 1881, did the railroad reach Glendive, Montana. As it continued westward, railroad towns such as Miles City, Billings, Livingston, Bozeman, and Missoula experienced boom periods. On September 8, 1883, at Garrison in western Montana, the final spike linking the two halves of the railroad was driven before a crowd of distinguished visitors. The arrival of the Northern Pacific helped usher in the greatest population growth in Montana since the gold rush of the 1860s, a 365 percent increase between 1880 and 1890.[3]

During construction, more than 3,500 men worked in the Yellowstone valley. The typical "floating population" of saloonkeepers, gamblers, and prostitutes accompanied the railroad's progress. "As bad a crowd as ever gathered together in any country is just now assembled on the line of construction of the Northern Pacific road," reported the Helena newspaper that spring of 1882.[4] Among them was Martha Canary.

Before she took up more permanent residence in Montana, however, Martha may have returned to Wyoming. She once said she was in Rawlins "the night when Lacy and Opium Bob were strung up in the stockyards."[5] According to Fenimore Chatterton, manager of the general store in Rawlins, this event occurred in March 1882. While store-owner J. W. Hugus was in California, "a gang of thieves from Rawlins, headed by Jim Lacy, Opium Bob and H. Carter, decided that the night of a pay day at Fort Steele" was a good time to force Chatterton to open the safe for them. The night before payday, however, the gang "robbed and nearly killed a Chinese man in Rawlins." Afterwards, remembered Chatterton, vigilantes "rounded up the seven murderers and hanged them in the stockyards." The vigilantes then printed notices ordering about another sixty people of similar character out of town.[6] If Martha watched the hangings, she left shortly afterwards; she may have been one of the undesirables asked to leave town.

In June 1882, Calamity was reported "living on a ranch on Graveyard bottom, in the Yellowstone valley," the likely location she referred to in her *Life and Adventures*.[7] Located about twenty miles west of Miles City, Graveyard Bottom took its name from the numerous Indian burials there when the first white residents arrived. The town of Miles City had been established even before the railroad reached Montana. It sprang up in 1876 during the campaign against the Sioux Indians, when saloons and a gambling hall were built to take advantage of the demand created by troops stationed there. Besides catering to the soldiers stationed at Fort Keogh, built in 1878, the town became a center for marketing buffalo hides. Then, after the buffalo disappeared, cattlemen moved into the area. But the town's greatest prosperity was ushered in by the railroad's arrival. It also "brought in a new class of tough, the city rough-neck and booze-fighters, whose kind we had not had because of the splendid isolation we had enjoyed," asserted Samuel Gordon, editor of the Miles City newspaper.[8]

Even though the ranching Martha describes in her autobiography suggests an idyllic interim in her otherwise flamboyant life, she probably represented the "new class of tough" Gordon deplored. "Calamity Jane is running a saloon at Rosebud," reported newspapers in June, suggesting the nature of her establishment. Rosebud was the town established west of Miles City as the railroad built westward. In early July, the Miles City newspaper reported one of her recurring visits: "Calamity Jane came to the metropolis last week from her Rosebud ranch, and 'took in the town' in great shape. She is a queer freak of nature, and . . . looks as if she had seen hard usage of late."[9] That newspapers referred to her Rosebud saloon as a ranch suggests the loose meaning of that term in the late-nineteenth-century West.

Martha remained in Miles City for its Fourth of July festivities. Learning of her drunken revelry, the Deadwood newspaper noted that her behavior had not changed since her departure from the Black Hills. Satirically, it informed readers, "We learn from an exchange, that Calamity Jane is a prosperous rancheress in the Rose Bud valley, a pupil of the Oscar Wilde school of esthetics, an admirer of the beautiful in nature, and

The northern plains, 1880–1903

so devoted to the old flag, that she came a long distance to assist in the celebration at Miles City, on July 4th. Calamity orated."[10] It did not require a national holiday to lure Calamity to town, however. In late July she was again in Miles City, arriving "from Grave Yard Bottoms." She came "to take in the Miles City 'helephant.'" The phrase "seeing the elephant" meant to encounter perils such as epidemics or floods, or to reach one's goal. The next week the newspaper said she "meandered about the town as it were."[11]

It probably was during one of Martha's 1882 visits to Miles City that L. A. Huffman, one of the West's finest frontier photographers, took her portrait. Huffman had arrived at Fort Keogh in December 1878, and his photographs of the Yellowstone valley region, Little Big Horn battlefield, and Yellowstone National Park, made him a well-known figure. He opened his studio in Miles City in 1880–81 as the Northern Pacific approached the Yellowstone valley. Huffman did not appreciate the railroad's impact on the region, however. After it arrived, "there *was* no more West," he said; "it was a dream and a forgetting, a chapter forever closed."[12] In his photographs Huffman preserved the West before the arrival of the railroad. Among his pictures is a studio portrait of Calamity Jane, decked out in a fine dress and hat and looking every bit a brothel madam. Ironically, while her name was associated with the old frontier Huffman loved, she arrived with the railroads harboring the changes he decried.

The boom period in Miles City quickly subsided. In December 1882, Deadwood resident Al Burnham rode the stage to visit Miles City and reported that the town was "virtually dead" now that the tracks continued on westward.[13] Martha was among those who left Miles City as the boom ended. In September, she was reported in Billings. She undoubtedly recognized many earlier acquaintances: "There may be a few good people left in the Black Hills," reported the Billings newspaper, "but that they are very numerous is hard to realize, so many of the pick of the community have settled here." In November, Martha was still "doing business at Billings," probably again operating a combination saloon, hotel, restaurant, and gambling place. The Billings newspaper also described her as "the heroine in stories that have appeared in the *New York Weekly.*"[14]

Among the early residents of Billings who remembered Martha was H. B. Wiley. He had begun working for postmaster Colonel L. Whitney shortly after the post office was established in late July or early August 1882. Located in the general store, the post office was comprised of empty beer cases outfitted with glass panes. Martha once asked Wiley if there was mail for her. "I looked, but found none for her," he said, and Jane responded, "Young fellow, you are all right. I came in yesterday and that old feller, without getting up, told me there was no mail for me. I told him to get up off his lazy stern and look."[15]

Although Martha followed the railroad westward, she continued intermittently to live at Graveyard Bottom near Miles City. She lived there with an unidentified male companion, perhaps cowboy Frank King.[16] In late November, newspapers announced the birth of "little Calamity." Friends in the Black Hills learned more about Martha's baby from a member of Evans's mule train who hauled freight between Deadwood and Miles City. The freighter "assures us that she is still with her husband, living on a ranch in the

Yellowstone valley," said the newspaper. The reporter also found that Martha called her "bright looking boy baby . . . Little Calamity, as she has been unable to find a name nice enough for him." According to the newspaper's informant, Martha was "thoroughly regenerated," and now "intended to live a quiet, domestic, granger life, only visiting town occasionally to hear the band play." She now wanted only the "solid comfort in training up little Calamities for the presidency of the United States." Then, as the freighter watched, Martha raised "her little bundle of humanity to her face, and between kisses explained: 'Muzzie's yittle snoozey darling knows that much, so it does.'"[17]

Martha may sincerely have meant to reform when her son was born. Unfortunately, "little Calamity" probably died in infancy, and Martha returned to earlier habits.[18] The Miles City newspaper stated in December that she "has gone back on the turf and is running a hurdy-gurdy house at Livingston." Hearing the news, Deadwood's *Times* informed readers, "Calamity Jane, the irrepressible, has already tired of the humdrum of married life on a ranch, and is once more on the warpath. By late Montana papers we see that she is at Livingstone [*sic*], the same old Calamity as when here in '77 and '78." The Deadwood editor left little doubt what he meant. After learning that the state of Delaware was being claimed as the birthplace of Wild Bill, Persimmon Bill, and Calamity Jane, he wrote that she "was born and reared in Montana," where she currently resides, and "has never been out of it only when in Dakota and for a short time when on a bridal tour she visited St. Paul." Teasingly, he said of Delaware's claim, "The two Bills they can have, but Calamity Jane never. Jane has never breathed the air of a state yet. It would smother her, unless it was the state of inebriety."[19]

The editor's remarks typified newspaper comments describing Martha. Journalists poked fun at her drinking and unconventional behavior, probably because she was a celebrity and her eccentric ways stood in sharp contrast to her image as a frontier heroine. William D. Knight, editor of the Miles City newspaper, for example, mentioned her in his story about a new eastern fad. "The jeweled garter craze still holds out in the large cities of the east," he wrote, and "the leading jewelers of New York, Boston and Chicago keep a large assortment of such novelties always in stock." Although some "actresses and wealthy ladies" paid "as high a price as $250 for a single pair of stocking supporters," Calamity Jane, "residing in this city, is satisfied with an old pair of her husband's suspenders to hold her four dollar stockings in place." Knight, acquainted with Martha during his earlier newspaper career in the Black Hills, undoubtedly realized that his comic reference would elicit a response. Fortunately for him, Martha had already moved to Billings before his story appeared. It was the Billings editor, instead, who received her visit. "If the irate female who called on us Tuesday with a request to 'pitch into' Bro. Knight, ever reaches Miles city, it will be a 'Calamity' for the editor of the Journal," he warned.[20]

Local historians in Billings and Laurel claim that Martha lived either in a dugout or in a shack along Canyon Creek ten miles west of Billings. She worked at a nearby stage station as cook and cut cedar trees to sell to ranchers for fence posts and perhaps for firewood as well. Nearby, according to these accounts, lived two horse thieves. The Laurel town history claims the two "cutthroats" enlisted Jane "in a horse-rustling scheme beginning in 1883," ending a year later in a famous shootout in which the two horse thieves were killed. Martha, not present at their demise, "continued cutting posts, breaking horses, but drinking heavily." She gained a reputation as a rustler despite the fact none of her neighbors ever accused her of "expropriating any livestock."[21]

This description of Martha's rustling activities is of doubtful authenticity. Martha probably resided at Canyon Creek in the early 1890s rather than in 1883–84, when the horse thieves were there. One local resident, Charles Zimmerman, recalled Calamity stopping by their house several times as she and her husband hauled wood to town. However, Zimmerman did not arrive in Billings until 1890.[22] If she was there in 1882, her stay was brief. Having lived in the Miles City area between February and August 1882, she arrived in Billings in September and by December continued westward as railroad construction progressed to Livingston.

Nevertheless, the Canyon Creek cabin has been established in Montana folklore as Martha's home and the two horse thieves as her associates. Horsethief Cache is described by the *Montana State Guide* as "a high tableland surrounded by steep bluffs" located "on the south side of the canyon, across from the site of Calamity Jane's house. It has but one approach, and that is well concealed."[23]

The demise of the two outlaws purported to be Martha's companions occurred on July 4, 1884. Driving a herd of horses, probably stolen, into the Lewiston, Montana, area to trade or sell, Charley (Rattlesnake Jake) Owens got involved in an argument and struck a man across the face with his gun. He and his companion, Charles Fallon, then decided "they would run the town." After several drinks in a saloon, Jake got into another fracas and shots were fired. Aroused by the shooting, other townspeople joined the fray. Fallon was shot in the abdomen while firing his Winchester from horseback, but nevertheless managed to join Jake, who was hiding behind a building. From that vantage point, Fallon deliberately shot and killed Ben Smith, an innocent victim running to get out of the way. A responding hail of bullets killed Owen and Fallon.[24] When the *Billings Post* reported the incident, it said that "Owens lived in a dug out near Billings most of last winter, and was distinguished by his wearing his hair in the approved style of the dime novel desperado." He was "known by the name of Rattlesnake Jake, and was generally known as a 'bad' man." The report concluded that "everybody here thinks there was a good days work done in ridding the country of these two desperate characters, and only regret that an innocent man has been killed."[25]

But Martha is unmentioned in these accounts of the shooting. In later years, people who remembered that she lived at Canyon Creek probably linked her presence there to stories about the horse thieves. Martha, however, had left the area before the rustlers arrived at Canyon Creek. On January 30, 1883, she was reported "on one of her jamborees" in Muir City, a town located at the Bozeman Pass tunnel, twelve miles from Bozeman. "The company is laying track over the range, and trains will be running into Bozeman inside of two weeks," the newspaper reported. The Black Hills correspondent who relayed the story of Martha's presence for readers in Deadwood concluded, "Times are very lively here. It puts one in mind of the Hills in early days."[26]

As the construction crews marched northwestward toward Missoula, Martha followed, evidently continuing to establish hastily built road ranches where she provided food, liquor, and lodging. While northwest of Missoula, she became involved in legal difficulties. "'Calamity Jane' and a man named Kibble were arrested a couple of weeks ago at Camas Prairie, on a charge of selling liquor to Indians, and lodged in jail at Missoula," the Helena newspaper reported. Martha was fortunate this time, for she "got free owing to a technical error in the complaint."[27]

Martha remained in the Missoula area several months. The *Glendive Times* in April reported that she was "again on the war path near Missoula" and "her specialty is dexterity with a six shooter and a poker deck." In the summer of 1883, as the railroad neared completion, a correspondent writing under the pseudonym "Crayon" also mentioned Martha being in the Missoula area. Describing the large crowds gathered for the "christening festivities of Missoula's railway birth," Crayon observed that the usual undesirable elements were present. "A camp of gamblers and horse thieves, composed of men and women who hardly deserve the name, is the only object *unworthy* of notice passed on the journey," he reported. "'Calamity Jane,' 'Deadwood Dick,' and other female desperadoes who have followed the track-building for several years, reside here."[28]

Martha apparently traveled even farther west, visiting Spokane, Washington. Old-timers in 1903 recalled that she arrived with the railroad and became "the keystone around which all the excitement and life of the new town was reared." She "dealt faro bank on Main Avenue in a wooden building that stood adjacent to what is now the Owl saloon," and while she played cards would "peacefully chew tobacco and smoke a cigar at the same time." If anyone mentioned drinking, "she was always Johnnie on the spot." She drank "neat whisky." Martha was usually seen in men's clothing with her "overalls tucked in the tops of rawhide boots" and her hair "cut man-fashion." She also was rather free in "annexing new husbands." Nevertheless, one remembered, she had a good reputation because she was "the last person to hold the head and administer consolation to the troubled gambler or erstwhile bad man who was about to depart into the new country." Publisher Glen Adams said his father "used to hire an old time cowboy named Charles Wroe to cut wood in winter. Wroe said he knew Calamity, and that 'she was a good woman only she drinked.'"[29]

It is unclear when Martha returned to the Yellowstone valley towns in Montana. She may even have traveled to Iowa to make a stage appearance. Although evidence is too slight to make positive identification (an impostor may have used her famous nickname), a "Calamity Jane Combination" performed in Iowa in fall 1883. The show folded when "the manager went broke . . . kicked the pet grizzly bear over the foot lights, broke the nose of the leading lady, was arrested and fined, and having no money paid the fine by sawing wood."[30]

Whatever her itinerary, Martha probably spent most of the winter of 1883–84 in the Yellowstone valley. A number of indeterminate stories about her in Miles City and Livingston seem to date from this period. "Teddy Blue" Abbott remembered meeting her in Miles City in the fall of 1883. Plagued by a strict boss who ordered his cowboys not to drink when visiting town and forbade them to read the *Police Gazette* at the ranch, Teddy Blue decided to take action. While the boss sat in the hotel lobby, keeping an eye on the bar to prevent the cowboys from drinking, Abbott schemed with Martha to embarrass "old man Fuller," offering her two-and-a-half dollars to sit in Fuller's lap and kiss him. "And she was game. She walked up to him with everybody watching her, and sat down on his lap, and throwed both her arms around him so his arms were pinned to his sides and he couldn't help himself—she was strong as a bear. And then she began kissing him and saying: 'Why don't you ever come to see me any more honey? You know I love you.'" Abbott added to his boss's discomfort, telling him to enjoy himself while assuring him that he would not write to his folks about it. "The old man spluttered and spit and wiped his mouth on his handkerchief. And he left the hotel and that was the last we saw of him that night." Afterwards, said Abbott, "Calamity Jane told the story all over town and it was quite a joke of the time and as long as we were in town she got all she wanted to drink." Abbott said he encountered Calamity Jane once again that winter at the "Belly-Ups" stage station, the first stop when leaving Miles City for Deadwood. "Bulldog George was running the bar and Calamity Jane was cook. I stood her off for a dinner saying I will pay you sometime. She said she didn't give a darn if I ever paid her."[31]

Likewise, cowboy Luke D. Sweetman recalled seeing Calamity Jane in Miles City, though he remembered it being in 1886, unlikely since she had left the vicinity by that time. Staying for the winter in a cabin located ten miles from Miles City, Sweetman went to town to get groceries before severe weather struck. While shopping for supplies, he heard sleigh bells, and observed "a livery team drawing a fine cutter, and driven by a woman." It was Calamity Jane and another woman "out for a joy ride in their furs and robes." They stopped at a saloon and ordered drinks, then "drove around town a few blocks and stopped in front of another saloon" and repeated their act. "With voices raised in song and mirth," they continued stopping "at each of the numerous saloons as often as their systems required refreshment." And, concluded Sweetman, "when I left town they were turning corners on one runner."[32]

Another Miles City resident described Martha helping a man diagnosed with smallpox. S. W. Russell, later a Deadwood businessman, recalled her nursing a young Englishman after Dr. Fedd, the county physician in Miles City, decided to place the visitor in an improvised "pest house." Martha insisted that he be placed in her small house off Main Street, where she nursed him back to health. The Englishman, who purportedly told Russell of the incident, said that when he became well, he offered to marry Martha, but she "laughed at me and told me that was nonsense, that I was not her kind and she was not mine." She then advised him to leave Miles City, free himself from the drinking crowd, and get a job. Even though Russell's tale lacks any corroboration, it may be authentic. Certainly he was no romanticist; he also told of seeing her in later years in Deadwood "staggering up Sherman street."[33]

Other anecdotes from this period are set in early Livingston. One tale engrained in Montana folklore involves Kitty O'Leary, known as Madame Bull Dog, the proprietor of a Livingston dance hall who announced "that she would stand for no damfoolishness" in her establishment. Because of her forbidding size and strength, she "saved the wages of a bouncer by polishing off roughnecks herself." The Montana state guidebook claims that she "tipped the scales at 190, stripped. And stripped she was most of the time." Martha, who may have been Madame Bull Dog's associate in the dance hall, quarreled with her, "whereupon Madame Bulldog tossed Calamity Jane into the street, 'as easy as licking three men.'" According to the story, Martha did not fight back: "Calamity was tougher 'n hell, but she wasn't crazy!"[34]

Byron Hinckley, one of Martha's acquaintances, spun a different tale of the Madam Bull Dog fight. The saloon where the action took place, he said, was the Bucket of Blood in Livingston, and the proprietor was Mack Rickard, father of Tex Rickard, the famous fight promoter. Madame Bull Dog, weighing nearly three hundred pounds and with a projecting jaw reminding observers of a bulldog, made her reputation in demonstrations of feats of strength and wrestling matches. When Martha, who was in her early twenties, stopped by for a drink, Rickard, to the delight of bystanders, promoted a fight between the two women; the winner was to collect a purse of fifty dollars. Although outweighed by 150 pounds, Martha managed momentarily to floor her rival, but the heavier woman finally took control and prepared to spank her as she would a child. Martha then bit Madam Bull Dog's ear. Rickard stopped the fight and declared Madame Bull Dog the winner, but the crowd's sympathy was with the loser. According to Hinckley, Martha was treated to drinks by the saloon crowd for the remainder of the evening.[35]

Perhaps the stories of the fight between Calamity Jane and Madame Bull Dog are apocryphal, but Martha definitely was in Livingston during spring 1884. The *Livingston Daily Enterprise* of March 14 reported that "Calamity Jane, the most noted woman of the western frontier and the heroine of many a thrilling nickel novel, is taking in the sights in Livingston to-day." Then the newspaper added: she "pulled up stakes and joined the stampede for the Coeur d'Alenes."[36]

The Coeur d'Alene mining rush in Idaho was a natural destination for Martha. Gold was discovered near today's Murray, Idaho, in the fall of 1882 by A. J. Pritchard and his partner. The next spring another discovery was made seven miles north on Eagle Creek. The excitement brought about by the Coeur d'Alene discoveries was "intense," according to the *Bismarck Tribune*, with "two hundred men a day" arriving at the mining region in spring 1884. The new camp soon had forty-seven saloons. An Eagle City correspondent described the women arriving in the Coeur d'Alenes: some "dress stylishly and wear silks and diamonds," others dress "coarsely and slovenly," and "quite a number wear men's clothes and walk the street in garments that would excite the envy of Susan B. Anthony."[37]

Martha probably traveled to the Coeur d'Alenes twice. According to Adam Aulbach, editor of the *Coeur d'Alene Sun*, she made a trip there in February 1884 and with her came eight other "girls." Their journey was difficult and slow. The women left the railroad at Rathdrum, took a stagecoach to the Coeur d'Alene River and to Kingston, rode horseback to Jackass (located three miles above Kingston), and finally crossed the divide to Beaver and Eagle City. According to Aulbach, Martha said of the trip, "Hell, I could have gone to New York and back in the time it took to maneuver transfer points to get to Jackass Junction, and the agony on the trail was another Hell." Aulbach also told of her stage production, the first significant social event in Eagle City. It "took place in a long, tented barroom," he said. Whiskey was fifteen cents a shot, and roulette and other games of chance were available, but the "star of the evening" was Martha Canary. The "orchestra of four fiddlers" played, then "the red calico stage curtains parted" revealing her "in her mannish woolens," and she narrated "a monologue of her life," after which the "girls, more feminine, danced and the party was on." Aulbach described the scene:

> A dance was announced. The eight girls were lined up at the end of the long tent. The excess of Beau Brummells wishing to dance made a routine imperative. Each male was allowed a choice and one turn around the dance floor, then another partner took over. . . .
>
> Short tempers! Fights! The crimson silhouettes on the snow attested to this. The bouncers gave much to their manly art. Then inertia. Night became day, the hanging lamps cast a ghastly dull glow. The party was over.
>
> Calamity said goodbye in her inimitable way—a rough-housing push, a shake and a hug. She yelled above the din: "At least we ain't cooking in the hot boxes of hell. We'll be a-wishing we were when we hit the commodious Jackass Trail. I'll be back when the birds are atwittering in the spring."[38]

Aulbach's description of Martha's stage production in Eagle City is very important. Often it has been assumed that her first stage appearance occurred in 1895–96, whereas Aulbach's account indicates this aspect of her career, however embryonic, began more than a decade earlier.

Martha's second trip to the Coeur d'Alenes occurred in March 1884, and is confirmed by contemporary newspapers. As she traveled by train to the jumping-off point to the gold fields, she encountered a reporter for the *Helena Weekly Herald* intending to report on conditions in the mining region. "Among the passengers was the redoubtable Calamity Jane," he wrote, "whose name has become familiar throughout the West." Her appearance, he said, was surprising. She "seemed scarcely the character imagination would ordinarily picture. Young in years, with a clear cut profile, firm set lips and bright gray eye, her whole countenance indicates determined resolution and a courage no danger or emergency could for a moment daunt." Her gender, he thought, complicated her frontier career. "Born a man, she would probably have proved a 'Buffalo Bill,' a 'California Joe,' or a 'Wild Dick,' as it is she is simply Calamity Jane." After having dinner, the reporter and his companions adjourned to the smoking car and during the evening discussed their adventures and mining strikes. As the evening grew late, the reporter observed, "Calamity Jane has gone to sleep and most of us nod off into oblivion."[39]

According to one modern account of her visit, Martha's goal on the March trip was "to milk the miners of all the gold dust to be had." Her plans failed, however, when she encountered Molly Burdan, known as Molly b'Damn, who had the same idea. Molly, a young Irishwoman, established a popular sporting house in the gold camp; because of her accent, her name sounded like "b'Damn."

After a short visit, Martha left the Coeur d'Alenes permanently.[40] The Livingston newspaper of April 16 reported her return to their community: "Calamity Jane has successfully escaped various trials and tribulations incident to a trip to the Coeur d'Alenes, and is back in Livingston again," it said. "She has had enough of the mines and abuses that country in round terms." Happy to print her criticism of the new mining camp in hopes the boom would not negatively impact Livingston's growth, the Livingston editor added, "Jane has had a life's experience in western camps, and is able to size up a new country pretty intelligently."[41]

Other editors were less enthusiastic about Martha. The Bozeman newspaper, for example, was pleased she left for Helena. Referring to her as "ubiquitous a character as Buffalo Bill," the journalist hoped she would "find the capital city attractive enough to remain there awhile." The Helena newspaper, in turn, noted the arrival of the "distinguished" woman "whose name has become as familiar in the northwest as that of Buffalo Bill." However, this newspaper clearly considered her reputation far from "distinguished" when it reported that Richard Twoey, "a pal of Calamity Jane," had stolen a pie from the Billings bakery.[42] This story associated her with the disreputable class of citizens, not the eminent.

Another indication that her reputation was far from respectable was the press's continued ridicule of her. Concerning Martha's trip to the Coeur d'Alenes, for example, the *Bismarck Tribune* cynically commented, "How the rough miners will stare to see a beautiful, blushing damsel walk into their midst." The *Tribune*'s reporters, who regularly bantered back and forth with writers for the *Philadelphia Call*, now modified their invitation to the Pennsylvanians to come out to hunt and fish. "Since the offer was made, brethren, Calamity Jane has returned from the Coeur d'Alene mines, and it may be best for you to fly in some other direction. Mlle. Jane has a yearning love for genius and nobility, and—Well, be warned in time." Upon learning that an Iowa congressman was nicknamed "Calamity Weller," the reporter teased, "First thing he knows our own beloved, sad-eyed Jane will be after him for infringement on her title." Later, the newspaper added: Calamity Weller's beard looks "as if it had been cut with a buzz saw," and thus "resembles 'Calamity Jane's' hair."[43]

But for others, Martha's dime novel reputation was an asset. During the summer of 1884, she was enlisted to accompany Tom Hardwick's "wild west show" touring the Midwest. Hardwick was an old associate from the Black Hills, having once been deputy sheriff in Deadwood. He claimed friendship with William F. (Buffalo Bill) Cody and W. F. (Doc) Carver, both important figures in western touring exhibitions, and was supposed to have been a poker companion of James Butler (Wild Bill) Hickok. In Montana, he raised horses and achieved considerable notoriety after Indians from Canada crossed the border and stole some of his broncos. Hardwick, with his friends, tracked them and attacked their camp. He purportedly spent nearly two years in prison in Helena for violating border agreements.[44]

Hardwick's "Great Rocky Mountain Show" was one of several early efforts to establish an authentic exhibition of westerners to tour eastern cities. A number of these toured in 1884. Besides the Buffalo Bill, Pawnee Bill, and Doc Carver shows that dominated the scene in 1884, Hardwick's troupe faced competition from the Sitting Bull combination. Its "lecturer" was none other than T. N. Newson, who had written the drama about Calamity Jane in 1878. Hardwick's "combination" would feature former scouts and a party of Crow Indians. The Livingston newspaper reported that the Indians would "be arrayed in feather costumes and . . . carry with them their ponies, tepees and everything necessary to furnish a true picture of savage life and customs."[45]

The Great Rocky Mountain Show may have begun its tour in Bismarck in May. "The band of Crow Indians who under the lead of Liver Eating Johnson are starting out for a starring trip in the east, showed in Bismarck a few nights ago," reported one Montana newspaper. The legendary John (Liver-Eating) Johnson, one of the show's featured attractions, purportedly had eaten the livers of the Crow Indians he killed after they murdered his family.[46] The star, however, was Curley, the Indian billed as the only survivor of Custer's Last Stand. After playing Bismarck, the troupe's itinerary evidently continued through Minnesota and Wisconsin before finally reaching Chicago.

The show began its tour without Martha. As the caravan progressed eastward, however, Hardwick returned to Montana "to purchase more ponies and secure the service of several cowboys" as added attractions. According to the *Billings Post*, "The erratic female, known as Calamity Jane, who was one of the first stampeders into the Black Hills country, left on Monday's train to join the Liver Eating Johnson troupe." The newspaper noted, however, that "Calamity is not so attractive in appearance as she was in the early days of Deadwood."[47] Subsequently, Montana newspapers referred to the Great Rocky Mountain Show as the "Calamity Jane—Liver Eating Johnson Combination," in deference to their celebrities.

In late June, as Martha left Montana to join the show, Hardwick began encountering problems. Several Crow Indians already had decided to return home. "Old Crow, String Leg, and one who couldn't give his English name" stopped at the office of the St. Paul newspaper, it was reported, and said they were stranded. They hoped to find work "to earn their way back to Fort Custer, Montana, their home." When Hardwick was asked about the situation, he denied the show was in trouble.[48]

The enterprise was beset with financial difficulties, however. Newspapers detailed both the show's performances and its increasingly desperate straits. Advertisements preceding the arrival of the "Great Rocky Mountain Show" at Janesville, Wisconsin, on June 3, 1884, for example, described it as "a vivid and thrilling illustration of wild western life" and claimed that fully "one thousand men, women, Indians, squaws and animals are connected with this show." Highlighted in the publicity was Curley, "the only survivor of the Custer massacre." The newspaper observed, "If half that is advertised is performed, it will afford amusement enough for anyone."[49]

The festivities began with a parade to the fairgrounds, followed by afternoon and evening performances. About a hundred Crow Indians, cowboys, and animals performed "quite a number of lively and startling acts which kept the audience awake at least," the newspaper reported, "and made some of them take a good care that they did not lose their heads." The reporter seemed most impressed by the presentation of "Custer's last battle, showing the position of the troops and of the Indians, and how Curley, the scout, made his escape."[50]

The show maintained a busy schedule. Having arrived in Janesville on July 2, and presenting on July 3, the troupe departed for Milwaukee on July 4, where they repeated their performances. According to the Milwaukee newspaper, between seven and ten thousand attended the afternoon performance. A reporter, describing the attack on the emigrant train and stagecoach, said, "When the red devils bound their unfortunate captives to the stake, preparatory to burning them alive, the excitement of the vast crowd became intense; and when the daring scouts came gallantly to the rescue, dispersing the Indians and releasing the captives, they were greeted with a round of applause." Another reporter rated the show "fully equal" to the more famous "Buffalo Bill combination," and commented that the stage passengers recruited from the audience were robbed "in a manner that would do Jesse James credit."[51]

Despite good crowds and positive reviews, financial conditions worsened. Soon, newspapers reported that the exhibition was "temporarily stranded in Milwaukee." In fact, the show remained in Milwaukee for the remainder of that week, charging ten cents for a visit to the Indian camp, and an admission fee of twenty-five cents for adults, or ten cents for children.[52] The company finally left for Chicago on July 18.

Calamity Jane is not mentioned in the show's billings, though she should have arrived before the performances in Janesville and Milwaukee. She perhaps arrived too late to be featured in publicity. Although Curley continued to receive most attention from the press, Hardwick was considered the "chief attraction," giving "a graphic illustration of how he once saved a family of emigrants from being burned at the stake, after being captured by hostile redskins." The only other performer to receive individual mention was Liver-Eating Johnson, misidentified by the newspaper as "Lion-Eating Johnson," who "appeared in the scene of the rescue of the treasure-coach from the road-agents."[53]

Financial troubles soon finished the show. The cowboys added to Hardwick's problems, going on a drunken shooting spree in downtown Chicago. The police confiscated "twelve large navy revolvers and a knife" from them after they were arrested. The culprits were fined three dollars each for disorderly conduct and five dollars each for carrying deadly weapons. Martha may have been with them. That afternoon, the exhibition "gave their usual exhibition to a crowd of 12,000 people."[54]

Shortly afterward, the cowboys approached the proprietors for their wages, evidently not having been paid for some time. "Hot words were exchanged and revolvers drawn," it was reported. Once again proprietors T. W. Hardwick and William Skeigle were unable to make payment, and the partnership completely collapsed.[55] The return of the Crow Indians with "their ponies, buffaloes and other paraphernalia" was reported by the Livingston newspaper on August 8. The next week "the portly form of John Johnson, better known as Liver Eating Johnson," was again seen on the streets of Billings. "He had a good time," the newspaper reported, "but we understand that the company did not make a financial success of their exhibition." Martha's return to Montana was not mentioned, but the Livingston newspaper did report the demise of the "Calamity Jane—Liver Eating Johnson—Crow Indian—Cowboy combination called Hardwick's show," and explained that its members "were forced to sell their ponies in order to get back to Montana."[56]

After Hardwick's performers returned, newspapers announced that Martha was leaving Montana for Wyoming. The exciting Northern Pacific construction camps were a thing of the past and reports of a gold discovery near Buffalo, Wyoming, may have led to her departure. Perhaps she also thought it time to visit her brother and sister. Whatever her motives, after spending several months in Buffalo, she proceeded to Fort Washakie near Lander in November.[57] She would remain in Wyoming for the next ten years.

CHAPTER NINE

Life in Wyoming, 1884-1894

Martha Canary spent most of her time in western Wyoming between 1884 and 1894, but unscrambling her movements is sometimes difficult.[1] She frequently traveled to and from new railroad towns as extensions were built from main arteries to interior regions. Further complicating matters, two other "Calamity Janes" crossed her path, and researchers have often assumed references to them were to Martha. Finally, several people claiming to have met her misdated or invented their encounters, and Martha deliberately distorted her personal itinerary in her autobiography.

According to her *Life and Adventures*, Martha left Montana in 1883, traveled to Ogden, Utah, then spent time in San Francisco, California, and Fort Yuma, Arizona, before reaching El Paso, Texas, in fall 1884. There, Martha said, she married Clinton Burke in August 1885, "as I thought I had traveled through life long enough alone." Their daughter was born on October 28, 1887, "the very image of its father, at least that is what he said, but who has the temper of its mother." After quiet years in Texas, they moved to Boulder, Colorado, she added, where they maintained a hotel in 1893. Afterwards, they traveled through Wyoming, Montana, Idaho, Washington, and Oregon, before arriving in Deadwood in 1895.[2]

Although at some point between 1884 and 1894 Martha may have made trips to California and Texas, it is doubtful she met Burke before the 1890s, so he could not have been the father of her daughter.[3] Martha undoubtedly introduced Burke as her long-standing husband to persuade the public in 1895–96 that her male companion of that time (Burke) was her child's father. This made her daughter legitimate and her family life seem stable.

If Martha's distortions in her autobiography are not sufficiently confusing, several accounts of Calamity Jane between 1884 and 1894 refer to other women. In 1889, for example, the Laramie newspaper announced that "two women, both well-known characters, were before Justice Jahren this morning charged with drunkenness. One is known as

'Old Mother Gladdis,' and the other as 'Calamity Jane.' They were given eight and a half days each and are now in jail." There is good reason to conclude this Calamity was not Martha. Only a few weeks later, the Laramie newspaper reported: "Mrs. Ope [*sic*] alias 'Kentucky Belle' alias 'Calamity Jane' was shipped to Fort Collins this morning" and "will probably keep her ugly mug out of Laramie for some time to come." Kentucky Belle was a well-known alcoholic who, like Martha, moved through Union Pacific towns for many years.[4]

Another woman frequently confused with Martha was Annie Filmore, called "Calamity Jane No. 2." She evidently lived in Castle, Montana, in about 1890. Filmore had a vicious temper, once becoming so irate at her son that she "struck him a violent blow with an ax," crippling him for life.[5] The Annie Filmore incident most often attributed erroneously to Martha Canary involves an indictment for fornication between painter Charles Townley and Calamity Jane in Livingston on November 5, 1888.[6] After charges were made, Townley, broke and unable to paint, overdosed on morphine. "I have been ruined by a prostitute," he explained in his suicide note. "She soaked [pawned] my tools for whisky, . . . I curse the day we met." Newspapers confirm that this prostitute was Annie Filmore, not Martha Canary.[7]

Misleading reminiscences also confuse Martha's movements during the decade after 1884. Journalist Estelline Bennett, for example, recalled that she and a childhood friend met Calamity Jane in Deadwood in the 1880s, and she "asked if we didn't want some candy." Although scared, the two girls accompanied her to Goldberg's grocery to receive their treats. But the children must have met a different woman; Martha was not in Deadwood between 1879 and 1895. Pete Lemley, an Iowa farm boy, likewise was mistaken when he claimed that he met Martha in Deadwood in 1885. Making his way to Mike Russell's saloon, Pete said he "knew her as quick as I seen her," and exclaimed, "I come one thousand miles jes' to see you ma'am." Pete either was wrong about the date, met an impostor, or invented the story.[8]

When Martha left Montana in 1884, her initial destination was Buffalo, Wyoming. She evidently lingered there for the summer. Cattleman Edward Burnett remembered that she "did not run a dance hall, being more in the whiskey line than dancing." According to Burnett, she "always had something apt to say; would josh with the best of them, and they could not get her rattled." She also made strangers feel at home. Once, when she saw "some saw-mill hands who were rather shy about mixing with the crowd," recalled Burnett, she called to them, "Come up here, you Lumber-Jacks" and bought drinks for everyone.[9]

From Buffalo, Martha traveled to western Wyoming. For a while she located in Lander, where her sister Lena and perhaps brother Elijah still resided. It is possible that at this time Martha, in company with Lena, ran a laundry.[10] Not surprisingly, newspapers soon mentioned her in Rawlins, the region's most important Union Pacific shipping point. "'Calamity Jane,' the noted and notorious, . . . is in Rawlins," announced the *Carbon County Journal* in December 1884, adding: "'Calamity' is a character, and has probably crowded a little more experience and frontier life into her career of some forty odd years than any other woman in the country."[11] The newspaper was mistaken. She was twenty-eight years old, not forty. Nevertheless, she was in Rawlins, although another newspaper clarified that she was only visiting that town, having "concluded to make Lander her permanent place of abode."[12]

When she arrived in Rawlins, Martha was referred to as "Mattie King," but her "husband" was unmentioned. Saloon keeper Nicholas Kappes recalled, however, that she was "with a flashy rounder named Koenig, or King and they were married or at least lived together." Likewise, Wyoming pioneer John Fales remembered Martha with "her husband, a man who went by the name of King." However, neither of these men was precise about when they saw King and Martha together.[13]

Martha visited Rawlins again in July 1885, according to the local paper, and participated in a barroom brawl. "Miss Mattie King, the great and only Calamity Jane, became endowed with the ambition to meet any and all comers in the fistic arena last Saturday," it said, "and accordingly loaded up with a more than average supply of 'Elbow croaker.'" She had little difficulty with Blanche Daville, sending her "to the grass on the first round." But her next opponent was a policeman "who placed the gentle Maggie in durance vile until Monday morning, when Judge Edgerton scooped in the stakes and gate receipts, amounting to $19.95."[14]

A few months later, a correspondent for the *Cheyenne Daily Leader* tracked down the famous "Heroine of Yellow-Back Literature" in Lander for an interview. From residents, the reporter learned that Martha spent some of her "earliest years . . . in this section, and . . . has long been talked of among the old timers." He ferreted out information about Martha's adoption by the Gallaghers and about her "wallowing in the railroad slums for several years" before going to the Black Hills.

Titling the interview "A Sketch of the Reckless Life of This Female Bandit," the reporter naturally recorded road-agent yarns, convincingly told, it seems, by Martha herself. In the Cheyenne correspondent's account, Martha not only rode with "one of the most desperate gangs of road agents in the hills," she led it. And, in a new version of the arrest of Bill Bevans, the newspaper said the outlaws were secure until a drunken Calamity Jane inadvertently spilled the beans about the stage robbery.

Having spun a fanciful account of her career as a road agent, Martha next told about her many suitors. According to the reporter, she was "reckless in disposition, pretty in looks, and full of animal spirits," qualities that brought her "lovers by the crowd." But she kept these men only as long as they had money. "Heart and affection were to her unknown terms, and when the revenue failed so did the lover." If they did not die in quarrels over her, the reporter said, she sometimes "made away with them with her own hand." Actually, no evidence indicates any of Martha's companions ever being killed. In any event, the reporter was less flattering when describing the woman before him. She was, he said, a prostitute. "As age and exposure has ravaged her beauty and tamed her spirit, her career has become less notorious, but not less vile, and she will go to her grave the hideous ruin in appearance she always was in reality."[15]

The Lander interview with Martha was widely circulated. Such extensive publicity typically led to further newspaper attention, but this time she went unnoticed for almost a year. She probably continued to live in western Wyoming, however. A year later it was rumored that she might return to Buffalo: "Calamity Jane, . . . who held forth in Buffalo two years ago, intends to re-visit her old stamping ground in this locality," the newspaper said.[16]

Instead, Martha showed up in Crawford, Nebraska, as the Fremont, Elkhorn & Missouri Valley Railroad was being built toward Wyoming. When the tracks reached Fort Robinson in 1886, the town of Crawford immediately sprang up near the military post and the usual temporary population, including Martha, arrived. According to historian Wayne C. Lee, she "lived in a tent, as many of the first residents did, in the north side of town." With her she brought a wagon filled with cooking equipment.[17] Homesteader W. H. Cash, whose crops had dried up, began working on railroad construction in the area; he also remembered Martha visiting Chadron. Cash especially recalled her generosity when a young stranger was killed in a blasting-powder explosion. According to Cash, Martha collected more than one hundred dollars in donations to pay burial expenses, located the victim's parents, and had the remains shipped to them.[18]

Martha's visit to these railroad towns set a pattern for the next eight years. She traveled to many of them that popped up between 1886 and 1894 as railroads built into the region between the Union Pacific and Northern Pacific lines. The Fremont, Elkhorn and Missouri Valley Railroad came under the ownership of the Chicago and Northwestern before it reached Crawford. It then continued into Wyoming in 1886 and the towns of Lusk, Douglas, and Casper mushroomed. The Cheyenne and Northern Railroad constructed a line from Cheyenne to the North Platte River between 1886 and 1889, establishing Wendover, which briefly boomed as the railroad's terminus. Finally, between 1888 and 1892, the Burlington Railroad built northwestward from Alliance, Nebraska, to Billings, Montana, passing through Newcastle, Gillette, and Sheridan, Wyoming. Many of these new railroad towns "suffered through vest-pocket editions of the boom-and-bust experience so painful to Union Pacific towns of the late 1860s," wrote historian T. A. Larson. "They had their tent towns and their miniature hells on wheels (without vigilantes), and they suffered from the shrinkage that followed the construction period."[19]

Meanwhile, Martha established a lengthy, but stormy, relationship with railway brakeman William P. (Bill) Steers. Born in Honey Creek, Iowa, on March 13, 1865, Steers was nine years younger than Martha. Descendants remember that after "Uncle Will" married the famous woman, the family ostracized him.[20] The couple remained together about three years.

The first notice of the tempestuous pair came from Meeker, Colorado, directly south of Rawlins. Ed Wilber, an early resident, recalled that Martha was in Meeker with Steers "for two months or better, and of course the reputation she had, whenever I would meet her or see her I would always salute her, and that is all the acquaintance I ever had with her."[21] But bad as Martha's reputation was, Steers managed to outdo her. In September 1886, "Calamity Jane, the she son-of-a-gun, swore out a warrant for the arrest of Steers, who has acted in the capacity of husband to the noted Calamity for some time back," the newspaper reported. There was a lively trial in the attorney's office, where Martha sat "with a blossom on her lip." She said that Steers tried to stab her, then hit her with a rock. When she informed the officials that "he wasn't a true husband," Steers "said she was a d——m liar and proceeded to shed his coat." After the attorney spoke on behalf of Martha, the judge fined Steers and made him spend the night in jail.[22]

The trial over, Martha got drunk. The next morning, Steers was released and left town, but returned when "he realized that Calamity he must have to cheer him on his journey." She willingly joined him, and the two "started out Monday morning afoot, Jane carrying the pack." The reporter concluded, "They are a tough pair." Upon their arrival in Rawlins, the local editor, aware of events in Meeker, commented harshly that Steers "deserves a hangman's knot." Sympathetic to Martha, whose "post office name" was Mrs. Martha King, the editor asserted that she was "not half as bad as the human ghouls that abuse her. The victim of passion, with generous impulses, this poor pilgrim has been made the scape-goat of the outlaw, the assassin, the tin horn, and at last the outcast of man." Finally, the editor queried, "Kind Christians, what will you do with her?"[23]

Six weeks later, the Rawlins newspaper reported that Steers had beaten her once again. Martha "and her best man, one Steers, who is one of the most worthless curs unhung," declared the editor, "got into a drunken quarrel last Monday. Steers struck Calamity over the head with a monkey wrench, cutting a severe gash just above the ear." Shortly afterwards, Martha, with "a red handkerchief tied around her head, weeping and wailing," located Officer Jim Finley and made formal complaint. While Steers fled toward Colorado, Martha vented her anger and pain in the Senate saloon, where she "began to make the welkin ring with profanity and maudlin tears." Her ire was further aroused when she was escorted out of the bar, so she began throwing rocks, breaking one of the plate-glass windows. As a result, Officer Finley loaded Martha into the "transfer wagon" and hauled her to jail.[24] About a week later, Steers was captured and given a thirty-day sentence. The newspaper, pleased that Steers "received the punishment he so richly deserves," nevertheless declared that the "miserable stick" should get "a more severe punishment than a month's free board, but the law will not allow it."[25]

This incident perhaps led Martha to separate from Steers temporarily. As she meandered through Wyoming in the following months, Steers was unmentioned. Instead, Martha's drinking was featured. In fact, it is possible she had a drink named for her at Joe Adams's establishment in Rawlins, where the "bad medicine" (whiskey) was now referred to as "Calamity water."[26] In Carbon, east from Rawlins, residents remembered that Martha "strode into the saloon" saying, "I think it's about time we had a drink." She "took her whiskey neat," and when the bartender asked her if she wanted some water, she responded: "'No, . . . I'll take the same for a chaser.' And while the hard-drinking men in the saloon watched, she poured the whiskey nonchalantly down her throat."[27]

Martha spent much of 1886–87 in Douglas, one of the new booming communities along the Chicago and North Western Railroad. She probably took the stage from Rock Creek, the connecting point for traffic between the Union Pacific and Douglas. Minnie

Rietz, whose father, C. D. Griffin, drove the last stage from Rock Creek northward, remembered that Martha was a passenger on one of his final trips. Martha lacked money to pay the fare, so her heavy cowhide trunk was kept as security. Because she never reclaimed the chest, Griffin purchased it; inside the lid were pictures of Calamity Jane and Wild Bill Hickok, Minnie recalled, while the trunk itself contained only dresses, a Paisley shawl, and cheap jewelry.[28]

Martha likely arrived in Douglas some time during the summer of 1886, as Natrona County historian Alfred Mokler reported. Mokler colorfully described another stage ride she made from nearby Fort Fetterman to Douglas. When she boarded, Martha insisted upon sitting next to stage driver Jeff Crawford. "As was her custom, she had with her a plentiful supply of whiskey, which she drank as she traveled along the rough road, to wash the dust from her throat and at the same time lend cheer and courage to endure the jolts of the rickety, rocking stage coach." She also had a basket of grapes, and the combination was disastrous. "Her dress was of the Dollie Varden variety, dotted with pretty red flowers, and she also wore a red straw hat with a red feather in it," related Mokler. As they forded the Platte River, her dress got wet, causing the colors to run and dust to collect on it. When she arrived in Douglas, "Jane, with her dress of many colors, with her face and hands besmeared with grime and grape juice, with bedraggled hair, bleared eyes and sunburnt face, was a spectacle that caused many men to surround her and pass remarks not considered complimentary or pleasing to the new arrival." Martha's response to her hecklers, Mokler concluded, "need not go down in history."[29]

Another reminiscence of Martha in Douglas provides an even less appealing image. Cowboy Reuben B. Mullins recalled seeing her asleep in a dance hall during a hot afternoon. "Her slumbers were of the stertorous or jerky order," he remembered, "and occasionally she'd give a snort which caused me to believe that the end for Calamity was at hand." As she slept, he observed "flies by the hundreds" swarming "about and into her mouth and nose, yet the attack went unnoticed by Calamity, and she slumbered on and on until she got through slumbering, or, in other words, until she sobered up." The incident stuck in Mullins's mind the remainder of his life, "though I fain would forget it."[30]

After remaining in Douglas about six months, Martha traveled to Laramie in February 1887. The *Laramie Daily Boomerang* observed cynically that the whiskey of Douglas evidently "was not flavored to her taste." Martha's behavior did not improve. The newspaper, referring to her as "the wreck of what might once have been a woman," reported that she was "gloriously drunk this morning and if she didn't make Rome howl she did Laramie." As a result, "her resting place is now the soft side of an iron cell."[31]

She next visited Cheyenne after an absence of "ten or eleven years." Because she remained elusive, the reporter only learned of her presence second-hand. She was "in a very dilapidated condition judging from what is said by those who have seen her," he said. Despite her drinking, she continued to be the subject of romantic tales: it was "only a few months ago that her picture appeared in one of the New York illustrated police papers," the newspaper reported. A week later, the "irrepressible Calamity Jane . . . departed for other climes."[32]

Where Martha went after she left Cheyenne is uncertain. At some point, though, she rejoined Bill Steers, and the couple evidently visited his relatives in the Wisconsin area. Upon their return to Wyoming in June 1887, a Cheyenne reporter this time managed an interview. She was now called "Mary Jane Steers." According to Martha, she had married Mr. Steers in Rawlins two years earlier, and they had lived there "most of the time since."[33]

Martha was considered worthy of an extensive interview because of her dime novel reputation and local notoriety. The reporter affirmed this when he predicted that she would "be remembered in the annals of Wyoming long after more useful and better members of our society are forgotten." The journalist described the Martha of years past "as a beautiful and dangerous courtesan, who seemed to take a devilish delight in fascinating her victims and then casting them aside as a child does an old toy."

Stretching her age, perhaps to allow a longer career on the frontier, Martha began: "It hardly seems to me that I was born over forty years ago." She then recalled "exciting personal experiences" in Deadwood and Rawlins, but it was Bismarck that drew most of her attention in this interview. There, said Martha, she met a "pretty little army officer" who fought a duel over her with another soldier. After killing the man, Martha's lover feared a lynching. Accompanied by Martha "dressed in men's clothes and riding a broncho," he fled to Deadwood. "I tell you that was a tough trip," she said. "I lost the road and for six days ate nothing but a couple of biscuits." She also implied that this was her first time in male attire. Discovering no suitable job in Deadwood, she took work as a mule driver between the Black Hills and Cheyenne. "I made fully ten trips, and no one ever knew that I was other than just what I appeared to be," she said. Martha was, of course, distorting events. No such duel is known to have occurred, and she donned men's clothing much earlier. Continuing to exaggerate, she added that when she went to Lander, "a drunken cowboy . . . killed a storekeeper on my account. Of course I was sorry, but I couldn't help it."

The reporter turned the conversation away from the men who supposedly fought for her hand to question the accuracy of a recently published history of her life, perhaps the one that purportedly had appeared in a New York police magazine. Martha responded, "I read that. No, it was a pack of lies." She added emphatically: "I very seldom talk about myself, but when I do I tell the truth. I can prove every word I've told you by people right in this town." But, of course, she had not told the truth. Kindly, the reporter did not contradict her, but he did make a sour comment concerning her behavior in Cheyenne: her "one overruling passion now is her love for strong drink, and about 10 o'clock last night she was arrested in an Eddy street saloon." This time she escaped a stay in the local jail by presenting to the judge "a physician's certificate that she was in a rather delicate condition."[34] Martha was pregnant. Sadly, while she believed her "delicate condition" was sufficient to forestall a jail sentence, it did not deter her from making a prolonged saloon appearance.

As they left Cheyenne, Martha hoped to convince Steers to visit Lusk, "as I hear that is a lively town."[35] Her desire to visit Lusk probably was not fulfilled, but it is possible that her publicity led to an invitation to appear at the Fourth of July celebration in Oelrichs, a cattle town southeast of the Black Hills. According to writer August Schatz, town founder Harry Oelrichs decided to make the 1887 holiday a memorable event. In addition to the usual races, "almost a thousand Sioux and Cheyenne Indians" would reenact a sham battle. As an added attraction, Calamity Jane was to be one of the speakers. "By ten in the morning, the crowd began to gather in the dance pavilion where a number of noted people were to give addresses," Schatz wrote. "Mr. Oelrichs made the short address of welcome, then Calamity Jane was to give a short talk." But she failed to appear, having "visited so many saloons in town that she was dead drunk by mid-morning." Worse, "when she found the door of Shepard's saloon locked, she took out her six-shooter and shot the doorknob off the front door." As a result, said Schatz, Martha spent the holiday in the Oelrichs jail.[36]

Afterwards, Martha returned to Lander. The Buffalo, Wyoming, newspaper in September reported that "the only and original 'Calamity Jane,' she of Black Hills fame in the early days, and whose fame has long since graced the pages of dime novels, has been holding forth at the county seat of our neighboring county, Fremont, during the summer, drunk and disorderly as usual." Perhaps Martha intended to curtail her drinking, however, now that she was pregnant. According to the Lander newspaper, she stopped by the office and told them "that she would leave Lander to-day for a week's absence, the said week's absence being especially designed as a preparatory course to sobering up and behaving herself." The newspaper wished "Miss King" success "for the very large job she so bravely announces her intention of tackling."[37]

When Deadwood's *Black Hills Daily Times* received this news, the editor decided this was not Martha Canary. He mistakenly concluded that "the genuine Calamity Jane is, and has been, for four or five years a respectable married woman living with her husband on a ranch in the Yellowstone valley above Miles City."[38] But Montana newspapers long since had reported her departure and frequently printed accounts of her antics in Wyoming. The newspaper's erroneous conclusion, however, provides a useful lesson concerning how localized news was in the late nineteenth-century West. If Black Hills journalists could not establish Martha's whereabouts even when she was not distant from them, it is understandable why modern researchers have found it so difficult to reconstruct her movements.

According to Martha, on October 28, 1887, her daughter was born. Bill Steers, in whose company she remained despite frequent separations, most likely was the father. In September 1887, only a month before the child's birth, a newspaper reported that "Wm. P. Steers is the husband of the famous Calamity Jane. The pair now reside at Lander." Describing Steers as a "slightly built, sickly looking and unassuming genius, about 25 years old," the newspaper said that he and Martha "separate about four times every year, and as often reunite." The paper also published a private letter that Steers had written, attesting to his despicable nature. In the letter, Steers told his friend he had "succeeded in 'getting away with the old woman's [Calamity's] watch and chain.'"[39]

The next spring Martha once again had Steers jailed for abuse, this time in Green River, Wyoming. The newspaper reported that "'Calamity Jane,' giving her name as Mrs. Steers, had her so-called husband arrested for assault Wednesday evening and lodged in jail." Identifying her as the woman "of dime novel fame" who was "well known by many of the old timers of the Black Hills, Cheyenne, and Sweetwater mining country," the newspaper added that she too had been arrested "for being drunk and disorderly," and as a result "now occupies quarters in the county bastille."[40]

Constable Stanislaw Dankowski recalled arresting Martha, either upon this or another occasion. Dankowski had emigrated to the United States from Poland and in 1882 located in Green River, where he met Martha, "a frequent visitor" who "came into town quite often to get drunk, very drunk." In about 1886, recalled Dankowski, she became so unruly that he decided to "take her to the jail to sober up a bit." Dankowski, along with Sheriff Joseph Young and two other men, attempted to take her into custody. However, Martha "fought like a tiger." Before the four men subdued her, Martha's clothing was "practically torn off."[41]

Where Martha's daughter lived while she and Steers cavorted in saloons in western Wyoming is unclear. Probably the child was left with friends or family. Martha finally decided to get legally married, despite Steers's continued abuse. Her motivation for doing so probably was to give her daughter legitimacy. Justice of the Peace A. W. Fisher of Pocatello, Idaho, officially united in marriage William P. Steers and Miss Martha Canary, both listed as Pocatello residents, on May 30, 1888.[42] This legal proceeding is the last reference to Steers in company with Martha, suggesting a permanent separation afterwards. When Martha published her autobiography in 1896, she claimed that she married Clinton Burke in Texas in 1885 and that he, not Steers, was the father of the child, thus erasing Bill Steers from her personal history.

Several years later, stories circulated that Martha and one of her husbands were divorced in Almeda, California, with her husband receiving custody of their children. Although the tale may be spurious, it could be rooted in actuality. Martha purportedly told the judge, "I ain't no saint, and yet I might be worse; I've nursed this man that's gittin' this divorce, and I've saved his worthless life once; the law ain't givin' me a square deal—it never gives a woman a square deal, nohow."[43] The story was embellished as her legend grew. In a later version, Martha sought the divorce because her husband ran away; when the judge asked why, she responded: "Because I was after him with an axe."[44]

What happened to Martha's daughter has long puzzled biographers. Sufficient evidence now exists to suggest an answer. In an 1896 interview, a reporter learned from Martha that her daughter's name was Jessie (she then was nine).[45] After Martha's death in 1903, few people remembered her daughter. In the 1930s, however, one Jessie Oakes of Los Angeles, California, wrote letters to several historical societies, newspapers, and government offices requesting information about her "grandmother," Calamity Jane. Jessie Oakes undoubtedly was Martha's daughter, but seems to have suffered from identity confusion. In her letters, Jessie correctly cited her birthdate as October 28, 1887, and remembered being with Martha in Deadwood in 1895–96 and in the Billings area in the late 1890s. Perhaps Martha had called Jessie her granddaughter to reduce social pressure on the child affected by her notoriety. Either Martha or Jessie "invented" parents for her as well. Jessie described her mother as "a beautiful woman" and "a crack shot and a wonderful rider," and her father as "a handsome lieutenant, an Army officer." She also claimed to have a half-brother named Charles Jackson Oakes and said that they were separated when small children.[46]

Rumors persist that another child was born in Wyoming, but it seems unlikely. John Fales, a coal miner, remembered that after Martha left her first husband, King, she lived with a "Bob Sears," and finally a fellow named Stokes. His memory, fifty years afterwards, was pretty good: Sears was undoubtedly Steers, and Stokes possibly Oakes. However, his recollections at times were faulty: he described Martha as "an enormous woman, being six feet eight inches tall" and thought she "had two daughters, whom she kept in Chicago and educated." He added: "I don't think they ever knew their mother was the famous 'Calamity Jane.' They knew her only as Nell King."[47]

After her marriage, Martha evidently returned to Lander. Newspaperman Henry E. Wadsworth recalled her in the city early in 1889, "when the frost was going out of the ground, and the roads and streets in Lander were ankle-deep in mud and slush." She wore "men's clothing, with a slouch hat, and her trusty gun hanging from her waist." Wadsworth met her on the sidewalk, which consisted of two narrow boards. He moved to one side, "to give the lady the right-of-way," but for some reason she was in a surly mood and decided it was insufficient. "Get out of my way, you d—— —— —— —— ——!" she snarled. "I thereupon took it that she meant what she said, and at once stepped off into the deep mud and let her go by." This "was the last time I ever saw her," Wadsworth said, "and I thought then that if I ever saw her again it would be 'too soon.'"[48]

Bill Huntington, a young cowboy from Nebraska, also met Martha in Lander. "Her and a soldier that I think was her man was taking whiskey straight at Coulter's saloon," he remembered. He described her as "a tall, dark, striking looking woman, not much of a mixer but tended to her own business. She wore pants like a man instead of dresses."[49] While in the saloon, Huntington joined a dice game in which the winner would receive a saddle horse. No one had scored high when it was Bill's turn. "I pushed the dice box over to Calamity Jane and told her to spit on the box to make it lucky," said Huntington, but she "shook her head no, explaining, 'No Kid, I ain't lucky. If I spit in the box you would get nothing but aces and deuces.'" Instead, a freighter spat tobacco in the box which, while messy, turned the trick. Bill won the horse, but the crowd decided drinks were on the winner and after paying the bill, he was broke.[50]

Other Wyoming residents also told anecdotes recalling Martha's visits to their towns. Rock Springs pioneer George L. Erhard remembered it was 1889 when she visited there, though most likely she stopped on more than one occasion. According to Erhard, she made a living "among the wine-rooms" by inveigling "the spending boys into buying extra drinks on which she received a percentage from 'Uncle George' Harris, conductor of a variety theater." Nicholas Kappes, who operated a "beer saloon" in Rock Springs, remembered her approach with the men. She "would lean her elbow on the bar, blow smoke in their eyes and talk in confidential whispers to the strangers she flattered with her caressing words." For some reason, Martha took a liking to Kappes's establishment and "pre-empted it as a home." Even though she was kind to the "gentle owner," he considered her a nuisance. "She would bring rough men into my place and make them spend their money freely, thinking that she was boosting for my business," said Kappes. When she appropriated a cot Kappes kept in his back room for her daytime slumbers, he tossed it into the cellar. Martha began cussing and finally became "so obnoxious City Marshal George Pickering arrested her." Afterwards, she was severely reprimanded and ordered out of town.[51]

Kappes said Martha also spent much time in nearby Green River. There she "frequented the rougher saloons and entertained the tenderfoot gentry by bragging wildly about her acquaintance with noted characters of the west," including Generals Sheridan and Custer, Major Reno, Buffalo Bill Cody, Wild Bill Hickok, Seth Bullock, and Mike Russell. She also played "with the gun she always carried," bragging, "When this dog barks, somebody drops!" She especially enjoyed saloon brawls, he said, and "would rush in and knock the fighters right and left until she stood triumphantly above the sprawling mortals—supreme. Then she would calmly call for drinks, and, while stimulated, dream of her ephemeral glory." However, when she appeared before a judge, Kappes noticed, "her bravado vanished and she took her sentence meekly, with hardly a word of comment."[52]

Erhard remembered that Martha left Rock Springs for Cheyenne, then continued eastward to Sidney, Nebraska, where she remained a week before journeying to Alliance, "then wide open and a rendezvous for construction crews."[53] Although Erhard's reconstruction of Martha's movements in 1889 cannot be verified, she evidently did travel eastward to the new railroad towns. Sheila Hart recalled Martha in Field City, popularly referred to as Tubb Town, on July 4, 1889. Tubb Town was located at the Burlington railroad terminus three miles south of present Newcastle, Wyoming. When Newcastle was established in September 1889, Tubb Town immediately disappeared. During its brief existence, the community had thirty saloons and a bawdy house that included among its inhabitants, recalled Hart, "such notorious damsels as 'Jimmy the Tough, Poker Nell, Queenie and the famous Calamity Jane.[']" According to Hart, Martha's entrance into town was dramatic, "not in but on top of the stage beside the driver." She was "robed like the Queen of Sheba on her way to visit Solomon." Afterwards, Hart "watched with fascinated eyes" while Martha visited a dry-goods store and "caressed the folds of a length of shell-pink satin, draped it across a flat chest and against a wrinkled, leather brown neck," remarking as she purchased it that "it would make such a pretty evening dress—it [is] so sweet and girlish."[54]

That fall, Martha arrived in Casper with the railroad. The Casper newspaper commented: "Were it not for the occasional musical notes of 'Calamity Jane' our streets would be as orderly as any eastern city."[55] John Fales recalled meeting her in Casper when he traveled there with his father. The "first person I saw at this dance hall was Jane," who recognized him even though she had met him only once before. She bought him a drink, "then bought a bottle and took it down to camp, woke up my father and gave him a drink. It was a wild night, and the last time I ever saw Calamity Jane."[56] Cattleman Edward Burnett also encountered Martha in Casper. With Burnett were two young men from Boston. After visiting a saloon and playing whist, one member of the party asked a saloon musician to go find some girls. He brought "two of the damndest looking blisters you ever saw," said Burnett. One was called Irish, whom he described as "a whale," and the other was Calamity Jane. He "never saw a more disappointed bunch of boys," though they were "good sports."[57] They had a "hilarious time" playing cards and dancing until a marshal arrived to arrest Irish for theft. She resisted but, after a fight, was hauled off to jail, and Calamity left to pay her bail.

By midwinter Martha was again on the move. She celebrated the new year in the once-booming settlement of Wendover, the end of the railroad extension built from Cheyenne. "New Years day in Wendover has been a failure," a correspondent observed, and "the only soul who has had the temerity to come and spend the holidays . . . is Calamity Jane, the real and original, of Black Hills fame." According the the reporter, Martha said Wendover reminded her of "Deadwood with the wood sawed off." The journalist seemed most impressed by her drinking prowess:

> Calamity is one of the most amiable of women; ornery of feature though kindly of eye, and an enthusiastic bull on the whisky market. Her manner betrays an unstrung and emotional temperament, properly understood only by those who have studied the ethics of the western system of getting drunk, for at one moment she is lifted high up into heaven on the wings of a snifter and the next plunged into a sea of unutterable gloom from the reaction of a snort. But there are many worse people in the world than Old Calamity. As a female holy terror she has no living superior, and her worst enemies will not deny that she is an able drinker.[58]

Martha quickly departed for Cheyenne, where the newspaper duly noted her arrival, describing her as "the heroine of numerous sensational publications."[59]

Indeed, Martha again had become a character in "a thrilling story of the dime novel order." *Calamity Jane: A Story of the Black Hills* by William Loring Spencer, the wife of Alabama senator George Spencer (William was named for her uncle, a major-general in the Confederate army), was based on experiences derived from George and William Spencer's 1877 honeymoon in the Black Hills. Mrs. Spencer wrote at least five popular novels rooted in personal experiences, and at least three were serialized by the *New York Times*. Nothing in her Calamity Jane novel, however, shows familiarity with Martha Canary, though it is possible William saw her in Deadwood. In the story, innocent, beautiful Meg Stevens discovers Deadwood's high society to be snobbish. She becomes a friend of Calamity, who stands in stark contrast to the social elite and protects Meg and her lawyer husband as they battle corrupt officials. A tragic figure, Calamity is mortally wounded at the end of the novel. It is then Meg discovers that Calamity and the feared road agent Charley are one and the same. As she dies, Calamity refuses Meg's plea to repent because, like a modern Robin Hood, she "took from the rich only, and always gave to the poor."[60]

Romantic fiction of this sort did not win over local observers. Instead, journalists continued to use Martha as a comic figure. When a school in the Black Hills went through three teachers in a a school year because several tough boys refused discipline (the third "school marm" suffered fractured ribs), the position remained vacant. One newspaper teasingly remarked, "The directors are corresponding with Calamity Jane with a view of employing her."[61]

Meanwhile, Martha dropped from sight for the remainder of 1890 and much of 1891. Alfred Mokler said she lived near Fort Washakie in the Lander area.[62] She evidently also visited booming construction camps as the Burlington railroad built its tracks through northeastern Wyoming. Gillette, established in 1891, may have experienced her presence, although Dick Nelson, who worked for the Burlington, concluded that "Gillette's reputation was saved by her absence." However, W. H. Cash, the Nebraska homesteader who met Martha in early Crawford, said she was in Gillette when he arrived with his cows to sell milk. He also remembered that after a freighter nicknamed "Daniel Boone" became seriously ill, Martha hired a driver to rush to Sundance for a doctor. Even though the physician arrived before dawn, Boone died the next day.[63]

Martha also may have visited the town of Suggs, located on the Burlington extension between Gillette and Sheridan. Suggs was considered among the wildest of the new towns, and the Deadwood newspaper described the women there as "the lowest strain of demi monde, being classified with such aged dames as Missouri Jane, Calamity Jane and Bismarck Annie."[64]

Other writers, however, claim that Martha joined the mining rush to the new silver camp of Creede, Colorado, between 1890 and 1892. It would not be an unusual diversion for her, but no concrete evidence yet places her there. Instead, Edwin Lewis Bennett, a resident of Creede during its boom period, concluded that while Poker Alice Tubbs's presence in Creede is "pretty well authenticated," Calamity Jane probably never "got that far south."[65]

Nevertheless, Martha sometimes left Wyoming. For example, in February 1892, she unexpectedly arrived in Omaha, Nebraska. The newspaper learned that she still lived in Lander, Wyoming, and was "en route home from a visit with her relatives in Iowa." The Omaha correspondent also described her legendary career, offering a fascinating glimpse into public perceptions at this time. "For the last ten years no name has been more familiar to Americans than that of Calamity Jane," the newspaper observed. "In the early days she was a scout for the United States army and it was she who first carried the news of Custer's massacre to the old frontier forts. . . . She has a record of having killed forty Indians and seventeen white men and she is the heroine of a score of sensational novels. She has had dozens of narrow escapes from assassination and lynching."[66] Unfortunately, the article did not disclose whether this misinformation came from Martha's lips or from the reporter's imagination.

After Martha returned to Lander, her actions seemed an endless repetition of past behavior. On December 9, 1893, she arrived in Rawlins with "her usual jag." A few days later, she was in Laramie, "a west bound passenger on a pauper's ticket." The newspaper, observing that she "is more or less well known to all old timers," gave her name as "Mrs. King," confirming that Steers was no longer her companion.[67] In fact, she possibly had renewed her relationship with King. The Rawlins newspaper recalled that upon her return after a several years' absence, she had with her "a little girl she had stolen and a man named King she introduced as her husband." Town officials told her to "move on."[68]

In fact, Martha was once again preparing to move the center of her activities. She was increasingly attracted to the booming railroad towns in northeastern Wyoming, and probably made her permanent departure from the Lander area in 1893. If reminiscences can be trusted, Sheridan was among her next stops. Local historian Ida McPherren thought Martha drove bull teams there just before the arrival of the Burlington in 1893–94. Others recall her staying at the Sheridan Inn, established in 1893, the meeting place for western celebrities such as William F. (Buffalo Bill) Cody.[69] Edward Burnett, who had met her previously in Buffalo and Casper, said he encountered her for a third time in Sheridan. There, Martha entered a local drinking establishment, but the bartender refused to serve her. She argued to no avail. "Then she went and sat down on Buffalo Bill's knee," said Burnett. "She must have talked very nice to him—he soon came up to the bar and set up the drinks for the house."[70] Burnett's story, unfortunately, lacks confirmation by Cody.

It was perhaps in Sheridan that John M. White observed one of her spectacular visits: "She was dressed in leggings, short skirt and blouse, all of buckskin, and wore a sombrero on her head. Two formidable revolvers were attached to her belt, and she strode along with a firm step and careless air," indicating "her perfect familiarity with the part she was playing." He learned from informants that she had played an important role protecting other women in early mining camps: "She constituted herself the special champion of her sex, and many a less redoubtable female owes the redress of her wrongs to the significant intervention of 'Calamity Jane.'"[71]

As the Burlington extended northward from Sheridan to Billings, Martha went with it. According to her daughter, Jessie, they were in Billings by 1893.[72] The Deadwood newspaper confirmed that she was there in 1894, noting that her "presence in a mining camp in the old days was always regarded as an indication of a prosperous town." It added that she had aged: "Jane is not a society woman, and retains few traces of that beauty which had at once been her pride and fatal gift."[73]

Charles Zimmerman, whose father began ranching near Billings in 1890, remembered that Calamity hauled wood from her Canyon Creek cabin to town to sell as fuel. She was living with her husband and daughter and often would stop by their ranch during trips to town. He recalled that Calamity's daughter was about his age; indeed, Charles, like Jessie, was born in 1887. Although Charles said he "enjoyed visiting with Calamity and her daughter," he admitted that he and Jessie "didn't say much to each other." Zimmerman remembered that Calamity worked in Billings as well, cleaning hotels and saloons.[74]

Martha's residence in Billings, which lasted perhaps a year, coincided with controversial events. A depression in 1893 resulted in widespread unemployment. Members of "Coxey's Army," led by the populist reformer Jacob Coxey, intended to demonstrate in Washington for legislation aimed at helping the unemployed. When they commandeered a train in Butte, authorities attempted to stop them, and on April 24 a violent shootout in Billings left one dead and several injured. Montana's railroads again were temporarily paralyzed that summer by the Pullman strike, with railroad workers fighting wage cuts and lay-offs. Martha was present during at least one of these confrontations between federal troops and protesters: a photograph depicts her standing amid the soldiers.[75]

Martha probably traveled to other communities in the area as well. Ida McPherren, then a young woman recently arrrived in Montana, remembered her as one of the visiting celebrities at the July 4, 1894, celebration in Cinnabar, "dressed in buckskin trousers, fringed buckskin jacket and a man's wide brimmed hat; in the height of her glory because she was creating a sensation."[76]

But Martha remained in Billings only briefly, leaving that town in August 1894. The local newspaper noted her departure and described her former means of living: "Calamity Jane, who has been running a restaurant on the South side, has packed her saratoga and left our city." Two months later, "Hotel Calamity," perhaps referring to the building in which her establishment had operated, was offered for sale.[77]

From Billings, Martha traveled eastward to Miles City. There she met cowboy Wirt Newcom, who had stopped trailing herds in 1893 and found a job working in a Miles City stable. Martha, he said, lived in a "shack standing back of the old Grey Mule saloon." She told Newcom that she had now married a "fellow by the name of Burke," who was considerably younger than she was. When Newcom told Martha he thought Burke was handsome, just as Wild Bill Hickok had been, Martha responded, "I never had a fellow with a h—— of a lot of money; I always did pick a good-looker."

While in Miles City, Martha ran afoul of the law. She woke Newcom one night at the stable, explaining that she needed him to take her to Deadwood. "Ed Jackson put me in jail because I was a celebrity," she said, "and Judge Milburn fined me one hundred dollars. I haven't got any money." Martha intended "to make a run for it," Newcom said. Because Newcom was alone at the stable he couldn't leave town, but he found a cow-puncher who agreed to help her. When her rescuers stopped by her house, "Jane came out with her war bag and we carried out a cheap suitcase, and all that was good old Jane's 'forty year's' gatherings." As Martha said goodbye, she told Newcom (she called him Slim), "You tell old Jackson, the chief, Slim, he ought to be ashamed of himself. Do you know it took him and two more men to put me in jail? Tell him for me some day I am coming back here to Miles City and I will whip h—— out of him. Goodbye, Slim."[78]

But Martha did not reach her destination, Deadwood, on this trip. Instead, she was next reported at Ekalaka, Montana. There, Clinton Burke worked at Cap Harmon's 22 Ranch in 1894–95. Harmon's son, Dick, remembered that Martha "was married to one of our cowboys—Jack Burke [sic]. She had a little girl she said was her daughter with her."[79] Ida Castleberry, who lived in Ekalaka, also recalled Martha with Burke and "their daughter, a little girl about five, six or seven years old." They "lived in a tent," Castleberry remembered, and once "Calamity took care of a sick woman for a few days," making her "well liked."[80]

It was only a short distance from Ekalaka to the Black Hills, and in 1895 Martha finally finished her trip to Deadwood. It was her first visit there since her departure in 1879. The dramatic response to her visit would open a new chapter in her life.

CHAPTER TEN

A Deadwood Celebrity, 1895–1896

"'Calamity Jane!' The Fearless Indian Fighter and Rover of the Western Plains, in Deadwood," announced the *Black Hills Daily Times* on October 5, 1895. "There is probably not a newspaper nor magazine published in the United States," it added, that has not printed stories "about Calamity Jane and her thrilling experiences and exploits of the western borders."[1] Martha's extensive front-page attention in Deadwood's newspaper reflected not only her fame, however, but the editor's belief that she represented something important in the town's past. Only sixteen years had passed since she lived in the Black Hills, yet she was perceived to be from a distant and romantic age.

Martha's arrival in Deadwood evidently caught the city by surprise. On the afternoon of October 4, driver Hank Jewett had made his usual trip to the railroad depot, returning "with two passengers, one a short, heavy set, dark complexioned woman of about 42 years, clad in a plain black dress" and with her, "a little girl who has seen probably nine summers." Immediately, old-timers recognized the woman as Calamity Jane, "who was doubtless the best known character in the primitive Deadwood." As word spread through town, a reporter for the *Times* hurried to interview her. When he located her at the courthouse, she immediately "reached out her hand for a friendly grasp," he said, recalling that she was known for her "happy cordial manner." It did not matter "whether a person was rich or poor, white or black, or what their circumstances were, . . . Her purse was always open to help a hungry fellow, and she was one of the first to proffer her help in cases of sickness, accidents or any distress."[2]

Martha was invited to use Sheriff Remer's office to visit with her old friends. There, the reporter learned that her name now was "Mrs. M. Burke" and that she recently had been living on a ranch about fourteen miles from Ekalaka, Montana, with her husband and daughter. "They have been there the past summer, but Jane did not like that kind of life and came to Deadwood with the intention of residing here," the reporter said. She hoped to find "respectable employment" and wanted her daughter to have "the benefit of the schools." Her husband was not with her, however, having accompanied Martha and her daughter only as far as Belle Fourche. They came the rest of the way by train and stagecoach.[3]

When the reporter asked about her early adventures, Martha was "so flustrated from meeting former acquaintances and walking over her old stamping ground that she could hardly collect her thoughts." Regaining her composure, she narrated the tales that later would appear in her *Life and Adventures*, such as serving as a scout, being nicknamed by Captain Egan after saving his life, and capturing Jack McCall when he shot Wild Bill Hickok. She added that she had "associated with desperadoes and frequented saloons and dance halls, but seldom had any serious trouble," and while she admitted that "she drank a little," it was "never to excess." In agreement, the reporter noted that, although she had worn a fringed buckskin suit with a white hat and always was armed, she "never to our knowledge made a disturbance nor was arrested."[4]

Martha's recitation of her life story answers a question biographers have long pondered: did Martha create the stories in her *Life and Adventures*, or were they the invention of a ghostwriter? This interview proves that Martha was responsible for these tales. Probably she had been telling them to willing listeners for many years. Furthermore, she told the reporter that since her life had "never been written up, authentic," she might "narrate the numerous incidents . . . to some good writer sometime and have it published." About that possibility, the reporter responded, "Her life would make one of the most interesting and thrilling stories of western life ever put in type."[5]

Ironically, Martha added that she did "not like newspaper notoriety" because so many writers had "faked interviews with her and written up a lot of lies." She complained further that there were numerous western shows in the East "defrauding the public by advertising impostors as the original Calamity Jane." Martha thought "she could make lots of money" if she were to join a show, but did not think she would like that kind of life.[6] However, just as she already had determined to publish her autobiography, Martha obviously planned to tour the East as soon as she could make appropriate arrangements.

In fact, Martha's original intent in visiting the Black Hills was to join a show. Several months prior to her visit to Deadwood, she mailed letters asking for help with travel expenses. Her letters, probably written by Burke or another acquaintance, had come as a surprise. "It has been stated almost time without number by both the eastern and western press that Calamity Jane was dead," reported the *Rapid City Daily Journal* after learning of the correspondence.[7]

One letter, addressed to J. S. Gantz of Rapid City, suggested that Martha "would once more like to visit this section in which several years of her wild life has been passed," but stated that she was "without means having lost everything by fire some little time ago."[8] How Gantz responded is unknown, but the reaction of John Scollard of Sturgis, who received a similar letter from Martha, was clear. Scollard's letter, mailed from Butte, Montana, stated that Martha wanted to return to the Hills to "reside indefinitely." Now having a child, she needed $50 to pay her transportation costs. "Not wishing to become a general ticket agent for the numerous parties who have gone hence heretofore, the unchristainlike Scollard has lost Calamity's letter," the newspaper reported.[9]

In these letters, Martha disguised her real purpose for coming to the Hills. The Diamond Dick & Company Wild West Show was recruiting well-known frontier characters as attractions. The participants were to meet in Gordon, Nebraska, with their first exhibition scheduled for nearby Valentine. "A feature for the show has been secured that will be without question a great drawing card," reported the Rapid City newspaper, "it being none other than the only and original Calamity Jane, a character well known to old-timers in the Black Hills."[10] Martha was supposed to meet with the show's manager, Mr. Maddox, in Rapid City in early May, approximately when Gantz and Scollard received their appeals for financial aid. Her solicitations must have been unsuccessful; she evidently did not make the May appointment. Strangely, at the time of her October visit, Black Hills journalists seem to have forgotten about these requests for funds and her plans to join the Diamond Dick show.

Considering Martha's reputation, it is at first bewildering that her return to the Black Hills in 1895 should have elicited such a positive response from Deadwood's citizens. Indeed, their neighbors were far less enthusiastic. The *Custer Chronicle* was downright cynical concerning Deadwood's fascination with its lawless and colorful past and suspected financial considerations prevailed. In its notice of Martha's arrival, titled "The Cat Came Back," the Custer newspaper wryly commented that she "has now voluntarily conferred upon Deadwood the boon so anxiously, but vainly sought by others." Whereas other Black Hills communities touted natural and scenic attractions such as "plunge baths, Sylvan lakes, Spearfish canyons, Wind caves and Devils towers" Deadwood would feature a "somewhat antiquated and weather worn star of attraction."[11] Nevertheless, Deadwood residents welcomed Martha and vividly remembered her visit for the rest of their lives.

Estelline Bennett recorded those memories best in *Old Deadwood Days*. When they learned of her arrival, recalled Bennett, prominent citizens hurried to greet her. Among those she remembered being present were Seth Bullock, the first sheriff; Porter Warner, editor of the *Times*; Bill Bonham of the *Pioneer*; Mike Russell, hunting companion of Buffalo Bill; Dr. Babcock, Deadwood's first physician; and C. V. Gardner and George Ayres, merchants. All had arrived in the Hills during the gold rush.[12]

In her account of Martha's visit, Bennett tried to explain why the town's social elite greeted Martha so warmly. She believed it was because those who arrived in Deadwood during the gold rush had shared bonding experiences that superceded class, race, and gender. Bennett referred to this group as the "stagecoach aristocracy." Indeed, membership in Deadwood's Society of Black Hills Pioneers, founded in 1889, was limited to individuals who reached Deadwood during its first two years.[13]

The adhesion that developed between participants in western mining rushes has been described well by Thomas Dimsdale, who joined the earlier gold rush to Montana. These individuals, he wrote, depended "for life itself upon the ministration and tender care of some fellow traveler." Afterwards, "the memory of these deeds of mercy and kindly fellowship" bound them tightly together. Among the most helpful during trying times were the "social outcasts." In addition, women, always scarce in the camps, were held in high regard regardless of their station in life.[14] Deadwood's pioneers, then, welcomed Martha not only because of common experiences but because they remembered her friendliness and help for those who were sick or injured. Bennett's chapter title, "When Calamity Jane Came Home," can be understood only in this light.

Bennett knew about the days of '76 only through stories told by her uncle and father. She recalled that her uncle, General A. R. Z. Dawson, made a concerted effort to introduce her to Martha. Her father, Judge Granville Bennett, "didn't feel strongly enough on the subject to oppose it," said Estelline, who was "glad Mother wouldn't know about it until it was too late to object." For Estelline, Martha represented "old Deadwood" more than any other individual. "Whatever there was of evil in Calamity's life has been long since forgotten," she concluded, and "the good she did will be on men's tongues until the last of the old stagecoach aristocracy is gone."[15]

Nevertheless, Martha did not make a positive first impression. To begin with, she was not wearing the anticipated buckskin costume. "She was a plain woman," recalled Bennett, "looking older probably than she really was," wearing "a shabby dark cloth coat that never had been good, a cheap little hat, a faded frayed skirt, and arctic overshoes." Bennett's uncle attempted to polish Martha's tarnished image, saying "she doesn't belong in the kind of clothes she's wearing. She doesn't belong in this day and age. You should have known her when she wore fringed buckskin breeches and carried a gun." He concluded that now there was little opportunity "to show those rough rugged virtues that made Calamity beloved." Bennett realized that her uncle was "a little sad about these soft days that had come upon us."[16]

Bennett quickly discovered that Martha's reputation for sharing was deserved. She was wearing arctic overshoes because she had given her other footwear "to a woman comin' up on the train to Rapid City this morning. Hers was so worn out they didn't cover her feet, and anyhow I was comin' on in the stage and you know that's comfortable and she was riding out in forty miles to a ranch in an open wagon. They might get caught in a snow storm."[17]

Martha hoped to place her daughter in the Sturgis convent school for "some schooling," but did not have the necessary cash. Therefore, said Bennett, Martha's friends decided to hold a fund-raising event at the Green Front, which was located in the "badlands" district of gamblers and prostitutes. The effort gained widespread support. "Everybody's buying tickets," Martha observed happily, meaning her daughter could attend a convent school. Indeed, said Bennett, the Green Front benefit was "a howling success." Unfortunately, when the money was turned over to Martha that evening, she decided to treat the crowd to drinks for their kindness. Her friends tried to stop her, "but she forgot all about the young daughter, the convent, and higher education for women, and got roaring drunk." The party was long and loud, and her friends saved only a small portion of the proceeds for their intended purpose.[18]

Bennett could not attend the benefit, but she did hear Martha celebrating afterwards. "She was going up and down Main street and she woke me out of a sound slumber in my little bed on Forest Hill." Martha's loud voice "had a carrying quality," and Bennett said she "recognized it easily." If others had disturbed the peace to that extent they would have been arrested, Bennett thought. But "it never would have occurred to Deadwood's night policeman, nor to anyone else in authority to question Calamity Jane's pleasures, even though they woke the entire town."[19]

Brothel madam Dora Du Fran likewise recalled Martha's howling. "Her voice, Du Fran remarked, "could be heard from one end of Main street to the other and straight up about six blocks." Martha's spree lasted more than a week, Du Fran said. Afterwards, she found Martha asleep on Main Street with her feet in some water running down the gutter. "A friend and myself got her up, took her home and this was the beginning of our friendship, which lasted until death came to her," Du Fran concluded.[20]

Although Deadwood's newspapers did not mention the Green Front benefit, they confirm that Martha spent considerable time in Deadwood's bars. On the very first evening after her arrival, reported the *Evening Independent*, "Calamity had her little 'red paint brush' along with her," and "could not resist the old time temptation to do a little decorating." About a week later, a "drunken Swede" who apparently "wanted to make a record for himself[,] landed on 'Calamity Jane's' jaw," the newspaper added. She did not take kindly to his fisticuffs, and "complaint was made today and the fellow will probably have to pay a fine for the offense."[21]

Other Black Hills towns were less inclined to grant Martha leeway, as she soon learned. She was initially welcomed when she visited nearby Lead. "As Attorney H. E. Dewey was turning the bank corner about 9:30 this morning," reported the *Lead Call*, "he was much surprised to hear a woman's voice cry out 'Hello Dewey.'" Before him stood a "short, heavy set, dark complexioned woman" who "approached him with out-stretched hand." It was Calamity Jane. Dewey, who recalled her from his early days in Pierre, was soon joined by a large crowd that "gathered on the opposite corner of the bank to catch a sight of this much noted woman." The reporter noticed her "pair of steel grey eyes which seem to penetrate clear through one, and as she would recognize some of the old timers she did not hesitate to sing out their name and extend her hand for a hearty shake."[22]

Martha informed the Lead newspaper that she intended to remain for some time in the Black Hills. She also noted that Lead, with its new buildings and larger population, was far different than in 1876, when it consisted of only a few cabins. The reporter decided she too had changed: "P. A. Gashurst remembers seeing her in 1876, dressed in a buckskin suit, and said that she was a handsome woman at that time."[23] Martha quickly interrupted these romantic memories by patronizing a saloon: "She did not act like the lady most persons thought she was from the flowery account of her in yesterday's paper, and had to be assisted into a hack by Officer Geo. A. Northam, to whom she used vile language," one reporter said.[24]

There was considerable controversy after the Lead police escorted Martha from town. According to the *Deadwood Evening Independent*, when she arrived in Lead, she had already imbibed "a hilarious jag of Green Front rye, and the first thing she did was to enter a saloon, contrary to a municipal ordinance relating to such affairs." Law officers immediately "stopped her fun" and shipped her back to Deadwood. This led some people to comment that "the chief was just a little too hasty in the matter, and that if she belonged in Deadwood, there are several more of her ilk who are just as boisterous and also came from that place, who ought to be sent back."[25]

Undeterred, Martha visited Lead again two days later. "The old timers who knew her in 1876 had a desire to see her and those who had heard of the woman and had never seen her could not control their curiosity," reported the newspaper. As soon as she arrived in town, she went to a dance hall on Bleeker Street where spectators gathered to see her. There were many, the newspaper reported, "anxious to spend 25 cents to dance with her, just to have it to say they had danced with 'Calamity Jane.'" Soon Martha "had a full sized jag on board, and this, together with a vile cigar which she smoked, made her look anything but the beautiful woman which novelists and story writers have said so much about."[26]

Realizing the financial potential of being a celebrity, Martha "had a lot of pictures of herself in frontier costume taken by Locke & Peterson, and is selling them about town," reported the Deadwood newspaper. "The old timers are all buying from her," and, of course, so were younger people raised on legends. Not all the photographs were of recent vintage; one was a reproduction of a picture taken during the gold rush.[27] Martha used these photographs to provide her livelihood. For example, a surviving 1895 ledger from Jacob Goldberg's grocery store in Deadwood shows that on October 10 she charged ten cents' worth of starch, which brought her total indebtedness that year to seven dollars. The only payment she ever made to Goldberg was on October 28, when the merchant credited her account one dollar "By Picture."[28]

The photographs also were of great value in saloons. Pers Russell remembered that when Calamity Jane first arrived in Deadwood, she would place a handful of silver on the bar at the Bodega and buy drinks for everyone until she ran out of money. Then she would watch for an unwary passerby and demand he buy a round of drinks.[29] Her photographs simplified the process. According to Horry Fish, a tool-packer for mines in Terraville near Deadwood, when Martha "bounced into a saloon" she "threw her picture on the bar, collected $10 from the barkeeper and yelled out, 'Come on boys, drink.'"[30]

Even the town of Lead found Martha's appeal too great to resist. According to the Lead newspaper, since Deadwood had "given a few benefits at the Green Front," her admirers in Lead now planned to follow suit and hold a "'bloomer masquerade ball' at Rilly & Carr's Bleeker street resort."[31] The women attending the fund-raiser were to wear bloomers, although the guest of honor long had dressed in masculine clothing. When the dance was held, however, Martha failed to appear. Her absence did not seem to detract from the event held in "the tenderloin precinct" of town. There was a large crowd and the newspaper said it was "a regular calamity howler." It concluded, "The flowers which bloom in the spring are not to be compared with the bloomers which bloomed at the ball."[32]

The reason "that grand old ruin" missed the bloomer ball, reported the *Lead Call*, was that she was "in temporary retirement at Hot Springs."[33] Having discovered a new source of income, Martha was peddling her photographs in other Black Hills communities. On November 4, she left Deadwood for Rapid City "to stay a few days," reported the newspaper, "selling photos of herself taken in male attire, of buckskin. It makes a novel picture."[34] She made an equally novel picture as she rode on the train to Rapid City: "She sat in the smoker with other men, and smoked as hard as the best of them, and had a good time, but says she doesn't drink now—and those who know her say she isn't a bad woman."[35]

The Rapid City newspaper recalled that this was Martha's first visit since she resided there briefly in 1878. "She remembers all of the residents of the city at that time," asserted the reporter, "and made inquiry after many that had almost passed out of remembrance." Unlike other writers, the Rapid City correspondent thought Martha did "not look a day older than when she was a familiar figure upon our streets."[36]

From Rapid City, Martha took the Elkhorn railway to the southern Hills. She almost missed the train. Conductor Bert Cox heard a "heart-rendering shriek," and Martha, "a full block away," yelled to him to hold the train for her. The conductor kindly waited, and she gave him "a hug of affection, the trade mark of which is only known to Calamity Jane."[37] The train made a brief stop at Buffalo Gap, leading the town's newspaper to announce, "The most notorious character in the western country, was in the Gap a few minutes last Sunday evening." While in Buffalo Gap, it observed, "she was 'on the road' to intoxication and Hot Springs."[38]

A reporter for the *Hot Springs Star* was among those greeting her when she arrived. "Jane seemed very much delighted to meet us," he wrote, "and talked quite freely about nothing." But her drunkenness offended him: "'Calamity' is said to have always been kind-hearted and helpful to the sick and afflicted, and we believe it; and it is also said that she isn't tough and doesn't drink like she used to, and we're rather inclined to believe that—though it would have been a novelty to have seen how tough she was in the early days, and how much she drank then."[39] The reporter, obviously disappointed about her intoxication, hurried to disengage himself.

Afterwards, Martha caused an even greater stir. "She seemed to have an idea that she owned the town and proposed to have her way awhile—and she had it if one is to judge by the manner in which she was conducting herself on the street this afternoon," reported the *Star*. First, she attempted to borrow Jack Quigg's saddle horse for a ride, and when Quigg objected, she subjected him to "miserable abuse." Then the "miserable creature" accosted a "young lady" walking down the street, "used vile and revolting language" toward her, and might have struck her had a gentleman not intervened. Angrily, the editor concluded, "She should be given to understand that Hot Springs is governed in a different manner than was the Deadwood of '76." Although Martha warranted praise for helping pioneers who were sick, she "will have to conduct herself differently than she has in Hot Springs before she can gain much respect from respectable people." The *Star* concluded: "She should have been locked in the cooler this afternoon."[40]

Dr. C. W. Hargens, the town's mayor, remembered being informed that Martha was considerably "under the influence" in the Bodega saloon and "making a great disturbance." Hargens decided to check for himself. When he arrived at the saloon, he saw her "dressed in trousers, heavy leather jacket and wide-brimmed hat; strapped around her waist was a wide belt studded with cartridges and in the holster was a Colt revolver." The saloon owner feared that she might "cut loose" if they tried to curtail her drinking, so Hargens instructed the police chief "to just stick around and keep an eye on her." He added that when the saloon closed, she was to be offered a night's lodging at the jail. To the town's relief, Martha returned to Rapid City the next morning.[41]

Learning of the criticisms directed at her by the Hot Springs newspaper, Martha proceeded immediately to the *Rapid City Journal* office. The story of her encounter with the woman in Hot Springs was "grossly untrue in several instances," Martha said, asking the editor to report that "when a paper publishes the truth concerning her she has nothing to say, being ready to stand by her actions whatever they are." However, "she is indignant . . . when statements are made which have not truth for their foundation." What angered her most, it seems, was the remark that she had "halted a young lady on the street and used vile and revolting language." Martha claimed this was not true, declaring she had "never insulted a lady in her life—the one in question not acting in a manner which would warrant her being called a lady." The editor concluded that many people in Rapid City might agree with her, remembering that Martha always showed respect for "a true woman" in the early days.[42]

No drunken exhibition was mentioned during Martha's visit to Rapid City, which in any event was brief. She entrained by November 17 for Deadwood "for an indefinite stay."[43] That visit was equally brief, however, as she continued her town-to-town visits. The *Sturgis Record* on November 29 reported her arrival there, "selling photographs of herself," and observed happily, "She didn't get bilin' once."[44] In December, Martha left for Hill City, then proceeded to Custer, where the newspaper noted that it had been "nearly twenty years" since she last had been in town. There were few familiar faces there now, said the newspaper, but Martha too had changed: "the buckskin suit and side arms of pioneer days having given place to the apparel common to her sex." Her reason for visiting was "purely of a business nature, to turn an honest dollar by the sale of her photographs," the newspaper noted. And "her conduct . . . was in pleasing contrast with her deportment in the by gone days, and whatever may be said of her behavior in other towns visited, her actions while here were fairly within the bounds of modern female propriety."[45]

Although frequently traveling to other towns, Martha maintained a residence in Deadwood. There, reporter M. L. Fox tracked her down for an interview. She learned that Martha was living at "California Jack's" home, "a cozy little house set among the pines." When she arrived at the house, Fox inquired for Calamity Jane, and the woman who answered the door responded, "Yes; that's me. Walk right in. Rather dirty-lookin' house, but we've been 'bout sick an' let things go. I ain't combed my head to-day; looks like it, too, I 'spose." And so began one of the most notable interviews of Martha

Canary. Perhaps the fact that the journalist was a woman sparked her interest in Martha's domestic life.

While Martha gathered chairs, Fox observed her to be "of medium height, robust, rather inclined to stoutness, and looks to be in the prime of life, but I believe she is past that, though her hair, which is long, still retains its natural brown color; her eyes are dark gray, and their expressions are many. Her chin is firm and mouth decided." By this time, Martha's husband, Clinton Burke, had joined her in Deadwood. The journalist described him as "a young-looking man, whose white linen and good clothes looked rather out of place in the room, that would have been quite home-like but for its disorder."

Fox asked Martha how it felt to revisit Deadwood after so many years' absence. "It seems good to see all the folkses, fer I know a good many yet," Martha responded. "But Deadwood's growed awfully an' hain't the same. 'Long seventeen er eighteen year ago the camp was right smart." She then reminisced about the early days when she first arrived in the Hills and told Fox about her early life. She was born in Missouri, Martha said, then went to Montana with her parents when she was "quite young." Martha explained that her parents died when she was "nine year ole." When the reporter asked what she did afterwards, Martha replied: "Wal, we lived near a post, an' them soldiers took care of me. I didn't know nothing 'bout women ner how white folks lived; all I knowed was to rustle grub an' steal rides behind the stage-coaches an' camp with the Injuns."

Martha told Fox that she was now forty-three, adding several years to her age, then exclaimed, "Everybody says I don't look it, but it's 'cause I've lived outdoors so much an' had good health. I don't claim to be Injun, but I guess I'm part, fer I jest love to roam 'round an' live like 'em. I tole my husband I'd heap rather get us each a pony an' ride down to the States than go on the cars."

Martha also chatted about her recent life and marriage. "I'll tell you how 'tis, Miss. I'm honestly married to this man. I had to go to Texas to get him," she said laughing. "Nobody'd have me here." She added that they tried "to live decent." First they attempted ranching in Montana, then "lived in a loggin' camp an' kept boarders, but they didn't pay up very well." Finally, Burke "went into business in a boom town, an' when the boom died down we lost everything." After this mournful recital, Martha continued:

> I've got lots of chances to go into shows an' the like in the East. I'm gettin' old an' can't work, an' I ain't anybody nohow, so I might's well do that as anything else. All I ask is to be spared an' have my health so's to give my little girl an education, so when I do go she will have some way to support herself if she don't get married. I never had no chance to learn nothin'. I don't care what they say 'bout me, but I want my daughter to be honest an' respectable"—and she wept pitifully.

As Fox listened, Martha's daughter arrived: "There comes Jessie from school," she said. "I'm glad she's come while you're here, fer I want you to see her. She's all I've got to live fer; she's my only comfort. I had a little boy, but he died." As Jessie entered the house, the reporter saw "a neatly-dressed girl" who was "shy and embarrassed" and estimated her age to be nine. She "had a bright face, and her manners were very good for one whose opportunities had been so few."

The interview over, Fox prepared to leave, when Martha unexpectedly took her hand and exclaimed, "I'm so glad you come; it seems so good to talk to somebody decent. I've been tough an' lived a bad life, an' like all them that makes mistakes I see it when it's too late. I'd like to be respectable, but nobody'll notice me; they say, 'There's old Calamity Jane,' an' I've got enough woman left 'bout me so that it cuts to hear them say it." The reporter saw that Martha's eyes were overflowing with tears and "knew they were bitter with regret." Fox pondered "how much better anyone else would have done, placed in the same position," and concluded, "She has a kind heart, or her jolly good-natured manner belies her, and she has done a lot of good in the world."[46]

The hurt Martha experienced was shared by her daughter. According to Mrs. Osborne Pemberton, who attended school with Jessie at St. Edward's Academy in Deadwood, Jessie was teased by the other children. Pemberton remembered Jessie as being very shy and recalled that one day, as the children were returning from attending church services, some boys began throwing stones at her and chanting "Calamity Jane, Calamity Jane." Jessie left school after only a few weeks' attendance.[47]

Martha had mentioned to Fox the possibility of touring with a western show. Undoubtedly, she would attract crowds. Newspapers observed that when she arrived in the Hills, "those who knew her only by reputation stared at her in open-mouthed amazement, as though she was one of Barnum's curios," and one bystander "was heard to say a short time ago he would give $5 to see her."[48] Indeed, the managers of the Cincinnati-based Kohl & Middleton Dime Museums were already in contact with her. Martha related the circumstances in her *Life and Adventures*:

> My arrival in Deadwood after an absence of so many years created quite
> an excitement among my many friends of the past, to such an extent that
> a vast number of the citizens who had come to Deadwood during my
> absence who had heard so much of Calamity Jane and her many adven-
> tures in former years were anxious to see me. Among the many whom I
> met were several gentlemen from eastern cities, who advised me to allow
> myself to be placed before the public in such a manner as to give the
> people of the eastern cities an opportunity of seeing the Woman Scout
> who was made so famous through her daring career in the West and the
> Black Hills countries.[49]

It is possible, however, that it was Martha who initiated contact with the dime museum managers. One newspaperman reported, "Mrs. Burke (Calamity Jane) some time ago . . . asked for an engagement" to tour the dime museums of Kohl & Middleton and "was made happy by receipt of a letter accepting her and fixing dates" for appearances. "Of course, she will accept," he concluded.[50]

Charles Kohl and George Middleton, both of whom had been associated with Barnum's shows, were leading figures in midwestern entertainment. The dime museum format had grown popular in the 1880s and featured curiosities and variety shows. These "museums" scheduled up to five performances per day, though Martha would be featured only twice each day. Performances were kept appropriate for mixed audiences, and words such as "slob," "damn," and "hell" were not allowed.[51] Martha's initial contract was "for eight weeks at $50 a week and all expenses" and would include two weeks at each city on the tour.[52] It probably seemed a good salary: the wages of a working cowboy were $30–40 per month.[53] She would begin her appearances on January 20 in Minneapolis, then travel to Chicago, Philadelphia, New York, and additional unspecified cities. Her husband, Clinton Burke, was offered a salary too and would accompany her.[54]

Black Hills newspapers wished her success. A Rapid City journalist wrote: "It is hoped by her many old time acquaintances and friends that she will play to a good business, and, profiting by past experience, have something at the end of her contract to show for her work."[55] Concerns were expressed about her drinking, however. A few days before her departure for Minneapolis, one correspondent observed that "Calamity Jane has lately been partaking freely of that which leaveth its color on the nose and has been causing no little amount of disturbance." He added that if she did not arrive on time for her engagement, her contract would be voided.[56]

Meanwhile, Martha began preparations for her departure. In early January, she made arrangements to place her daughter in St. Martin's Academy in Sturgis. A. O. Burton, who in 1895–96 worked as an agent for the Chicago and North Western Railroad in Sturgis, remembered Martha stopping to purchase a ticket to Deadwood; she told him she had "brought the 'Kid' down and placed her in the Catholic school." Burton assumed the girl was adopted.[57]

Martha's preparations included putting together an appropriate western outfit. John Sohn, the Deadwood shoemaker, recalled making her a pair of boots: "Nice black boots, they were, cowboy boots, with three inch heels and cost $11.00." According to Sohn, "Calamity never paid for them; she never paid for anything, but one day one of the members of the Pioneers came in and paid me."[58] Martha also practiced with "a Winchester rifle yesterday and did some splendid shooting," reported the Deadwood newspaper, "though she has not handled a rifle much during the past 15 years." Her shooting was good indeed, if accurately reported: "At 100 paces she put 5 bullets in a 6-inch bullseye out of 8 shots." The reporter recalled that she had been a "splendid markswoman" in earlier days, when "even the most desperate outlaw feared her," and predicted a successful tour. He added, "We venture the assertion that there isn't a character of the western border who is so well known throughout the United States as Calamity Jane, and whose thrilling experiences have been read and devoured by everybody as much as hers."[59]

Martha departed from Deadwood on schedule, and soon arrived in Minneapolis, where she was billed as "The Famous Woman Scout of the Wild West," the "Comrade of Buffalo Bill and Wild Bill," and the "Terror of Evildoers in the Black Hills." Readers were enticed to "See this Famous Woman and Hear Her Graphic Description of Her Daring Exploits!" An accompanying illustration depicted Calamity in buckskins, with rifle in hand and knife between her teeth.[60] She looks "like a veritable desperado," one Black Hills newspaper observed, adding, "If she doesn't get drunk and break up the whole show it will be a surprise to those who have witnessed her orgies in Deadwood and Hot Springs during the past few months."[61]

Some biographers mistakenly concluded that was precisely what occurred. Roberta Sollid, for example, speculated that Martha "was not able to stay away from her liquor and conform to the restrictions imposed upon her by the management," and was sent back.[62] However, Martha not only completed her Minneapolis engagement but shortly afterwards appeared in Chicago. Her arrival prompted front-page attention in the *Inter-Ocean*. "The most interesting woman in Chicago at the present time arrived here Sunday night from the West," it announced, and "wears buckskin trousers and is not afraid of a mouse." Evidently, Burke no longer was with her. The newspaper reported that she was "married upwards of ten years ago, to a ranchman named Burke," but he had been dead for some years and Martha made the decision to go on tour to pay for her daughter's education.[63] Burke, however, was still alive, and their separation was only temporary.

In the recital of her life story to the *Inter-Ocean* reporter, Martha repeated the same tales she had told in Deadwood. Thus, she was christened by the wounded Captain Egan, rescued the stage driven by Johnny Slaughter, and captured Jack McCall after he killed Wild Bill. Undoubtedly, these were the same stories she related from the dime museum stage. During her tour, her autobiographical account was published as the *Life and Adventures of Calamity Jane, By Herself* and was offered for sale at her performances. What is noteworthy about Martha's account of her life is not the exaggerations, but how closely it follows the historical record. Martha was either a participant or happened to be in the vicinity of most of the events told in the *Life and Adventures*. Martha correctly placed herself with the Jenney and Crook expeditions and mentioned only a brief friendship with Hickok.

Several new wrinkles appeared in the *Inter-Ocean* version, however. In its account of her life, the *Inter-Ocean* said she had "killed scores of Indians with her rifle," helped "in lynching desperadoes," and "saved many lives." Then the reporter became confused and scrambled names. The stagecoach she rescued, he said, was traveling "from Deadwood to Wild Birch." Its driver was none other than "Jack McCaul," who had been "wounded by an arrow." Martha was the only person "with courage enough to mount the driver's seat," despite the fact "the other passengers were men." She again encountered "Jack McCaul" after he assassinated Wild Bill Hickok, and she not only captured him in a butcher shop with a meat cleaver but presided at his hanging.

The *Inter-Ocean* reporter also erroneously credited Martha as the inspiration for Bret Harte's "The Luck of Roaring Camp," a short story featuring Cherokee Sal, a prostitute who frequented mining camps. Harte's story, which appeared in 1868, when Martha Canary was but twelve years of age, does not include a character named Calamity

Jane. Nevertheless, the writer claimed that since Harte's story appeared, "the name of 'Calamity Jane' has been known to every household."[64] Because of the *Inter-Ocean*'s wide circulation, these distortions frequently reappeared in later accounts of Martha's life.

Martha also regaled the reporter with her proposed activities in Chicago. "Some day," the reporter mused, "she declares her intentions of riding over the boulevards astride her broncho, and showing the new women they are way behind the times in their advanced ideas." Furthermore, she asserted, "When I go for my ride, . . . I am going to take my rifle along, and if you are bothered with coyotes any in the suburbs, I'll kill a few of 'em off." She seemed surprised when told that they didn't have coyotes in the city. The newspaper, however, teasingly suggested that the Chicago police might employ her to locate the vandal who had been cutting off dogs' tails and the deviant "whose mania is kissing girls without permission." They warned that "Chicago may have a wild Western lynching soon."[65]

The *Deadwood Times* found Martha's Chicago interview amusing. The famous Old West woman was entertaining "thousands of visitors by shooting at flying objects with her Winchester and Colt's '45' and narrating her remarkable and thrilling experiences on the plains when skulking reds were thick as coyotes," it said. Obviously, the journalist added, "Calamity is right in her glory now." She also is proposing to ride on the boulevards, he continued, and wants a broncho rather than a tame horse so that she can "show the bloomer girls" how a western woman handles a horse.[66]

Some of Martha's western acquaintances were visiting Chicago and stopped to see her after performances. Alex Cunningham, who knew Martha in Casper, Wyoming, noticed the sign advertising "Calamity Jane, ten cents admission" while walking down State Street. Inside, he saw Martha "seated on a sort of a throne at the end of the hall." She recognized him at once and came to greet him. "She was the same old Calamity," said Cunningham, and "kept her audience entertained all the time by her bright wit."[67]

The remainder of Calamity's dime museum tour has not been established. She probably next performed in Cincinnati, then made scheduled stops in Philadelphia and New York.[68] Apparently, she continued her dime museum tour to the end of May, longer than the initial eight-week engagement. Although she probably drank and caused mischief, there is no evidence that her tour ended abruptly as a result of her drinking. Instead, the cause of her return to the Black Hills, according to one newspaper, was the receipt of a "letter informing her of the illness of her young daughter, who has been living with Mr. and Mrs. Ash of Sturgis since the mother went to Minneapolis."[69]

In fact, the *Deadwood Daily Times* reported that Martha "proved to be a drawing card" during her several-month tour with Kohl & Middleton and was expected to return to New York in October to appear with the Huber Museum Company.[70] Still, they speculated she was not what the eastern public expected. Raised with notions of a romantic, wild west heroine, audiences undoubtedly discovered the rather plain woman disappointing:

> That fearless woman of the wild and wooly west who has been one of the
> most conspicuous characters in the yellow-backed novels of the modern

day has actually appeared in life in the eastern cities, where the youth who have eagerly devoured nonsensical yarns about her exploits, could feast his eyes upon her in the dime museums, has at last lost her charms. The public has gazed upon her—simply an ordinary woman and she is no longer an attraction.[71]

It is not clear, however, whether the editor was reporting views from the East, or reflecting his own belief that Martha's tour was a disappointment to admiring readers of romantic tales.

Having returned to Deadwood by the end of May, Martha reestablished her lucrative sales career. Now, in addition to selling photographs, she was peddling her *Life and Adventures*. "During her absence she has had printed a brief sketch of her life which she is disposing of at 15 cents a copy," reported the Deadwood newspaper, adding that she "went down to Sturgis last evening."[72] Martha did not remain there long, however. Evidently, she went to Sturgis only to pick up Jessie, then left abruptly for Newcastle, Wyoming, where she "says she will reside . . . permanently."[73] But that too was only a casual visit, and soon she left for Montana. She would not return to the Black Hills for seven years.

Burke possibly accompanied Martha and Jessie on this trip; he definitely was with them in Montana for a while afterwards. However, at some point he and Martha separated and Burke returned alone to Deadwood. Even though the relationship between Martha and Burke lasted only a few years, Calamity Jane is most often identified as Mrs. Martha Burke. This is due to the fact that Burke was her companion when the *Life and Adventures* was first published. In it, Martha called herself "Mrs. Martha Burke." Also, when she died in the Black Hills in 1903, Deadwood officials printed that name on the headstone marking her grave.

Deadwood businessman John S. McClintock recalled that Burke, when he returned to the Black Hills in the late 1890s, "found employment here as a hack driver, and for several months following proved himself well adapted to the business by making good for his employer."[74] Because McClintock owned a hack line, he was in position to know these details, although he should have said several years instead of only months. Confirming McClintock's assertion, the Deadwood newspaper in 1899 described a minor accident Burke had while driving one of James Simpson's hacks to Lead.[75] Burke once again made news in August. The police were "looking for the person or persons who entered Clinton Burke's room at 125 Sherman street Wednesday and abstracted ten dollars in cash." The robbery occurred while Burke was at work. The newspaper described him as "a hard working man" and said "he has been unfortunate within the last two or three years in practically losing the use of one of his legs." As a result, he had "an enormous doctor's bill," which caused him to feel his losses in the burglary "keenly."[76]

Burke continued working faithfully in Deadwood until 1903, but then left town under a cloud. According to McClintock, Burke absconded with his employer's money "and was never again heard of by either his family or his employer."[77] Indeed, in August

1902, a "warrant was sworn out . . . charging Charles [*sic*] Burke with having stolen the sum of $175 from his employer, James Simpson." Burke had driven hack for Simpson for many years and was a trusted employee, "so it was nothing new for him to have checks drawn in favor of Mr. Simpson cashed," the newspaper explained. In this instance, he cashed a check in Lead "and since that time he has not been heard from." After Mr. Simpson learned of Burke's disappearance, he "had the warrant issued for his arrest, charging him with grand larceny."[78] Only months after Burke left Deadwood in 1903, Martha arrived for her final visit to the Black Hills.

But it was Martha's visit to the Black Hills in 1895–96 that proved most eventful in her life. As a result of that visit, she appeared on stage, sold her photographs, and published her autobiography. In her remaining years, she would eke out a meager livelihood by continuing to peddle her pictures and pamphlets and occasionally by performing in shows. Martha's visit to the Black Hills was an important moment in Deadwood's history as well, forever celebrated in Estelline Bennett's *Old Deadwood Days*. Her return coincided with the twentieth anniversary of the "days of '76," and, with Calamity Jane in their midst, newspapers reminisced about events of that era. Especially noteworthy was August 2, the anniversary of the death of Wild Bill Hickok, which occurred shortly after Martha's departure. Her recently published *Life and Adventures* suggested not only that she and Hickok were friends but that she captured his assassin, Jack McCall, in a butcher shop with a meat cleaver. "Nearly every man, woman and child in the United States has read and heard more or less about Wild Bill, the famous scout who was shot and killed in Deadwood by an outlaw, one Jack McCall," asserted Deadwood's *Times*. Most knew only that he was shot and killed, so the newspaper provided a detailed story, including an account of McCall's capture. When McCall "tried to escape," a "crowd of desperate persons" followed and captured him, "and Calamity Jane claims the honor of having disarmed McCall and taking him prisoner." But, was she telling the truth in her recent autobiography? "Many of our old timers, who still reside here, recollect distinctly that event," commented the *Times*, implying that Martha had exaggerated her role.[79]

As Deadwood's newspaper had discovered, Martha's *Life and Adventures* introduced a new version of events and a confused chronology that clouded her story as much as it answered questions. Yet, seldom did writers during her lifetime take issue with her claims. Instead, some individuals, eager to gain attention, said they participated in these events with her. Martha's autobiography forever muddied her history, causing far more confusion than the dime novels. Most readers at least realized the latter stories were fictitious, whereas they often accepted Martha's life story as the truth.

CHAPTER ELEVEN

Life in Montana, 1896–1901

Once Martha learned there was a ready market for her photographs and auto-biography during her Black Hills visit and dime museum tour in 1895–96, she returned to Montana to peddle her pictures and booklets. She also continued making stage appearances, joining mining rushes, and visiting new railroad camps. But all these activities paled before her saloon engagements.

Despite her announcement in 1896 that Newcastle would be her new home, Martha remained there only briefly. Soon she moved on to Sheridan, Wyoming, where dentist Will Frackelton heard she was "making her way with a pack outfit, selling little pamphlet autobiographies." She also planned "to revisit the scenes of her old scouting exploits with General Crook," he said, even though these memories left her "restless and unhappy." Strangely, Frackelton did not mention Martha's husband and daughter.

According to Frackelton, Martha strongly objected when a report of her registration at the Windsor Hotel was printed in the local newspaper. "In language very much to the point," she told editor Jim Gatchell "to keep her name out of his sheet" because she "already had more publicity than she wanted." Not surprisingly, Frackelton was nervous when Martha showed up at his office for dental work. But this time, he said, "the feminine side of Calamity's dual personality was uppermost and she addressed me quietly. Her teeth were hurting and would I look them over?" It took several sessions to fill her cavities; when the work was completed, she paid him in cash.

According to Frackelton, Martha was "fairly good-looking, of average size, with red hair streaked with gray." He also noticed "something about Calamity's keen eye that seemed to go right through one." Because she was poorly educated, he added, "profanity was as useful as the other words in her vocabulary." From area residents, Frackelton also learned "unconventional anecdotes that had nothing to do with her feats as a scout for Custer, as a mail carrier, or as the heroine of the Deadwood smallpox epidemic." An old mule skinner, for example, told Frackelton that Martha worked as well as any of the other freighters, but "when night came, if any of the boys wanted to go to the brush, she was always willin' to pull off a pants leg." Then the freighter reconsidered: "Doc, just forget I said that. Jane was a perfect angel sent from heaven when any of the boys was sick and gave them a mother's care till they got well."[1]

Shortly after her dental work was completed, Martha left for Montana. In August, the *Livingston Post* reported her in town "selling a little book, descriptive of her years of life upon the frontier." The reporter thought she was "considerably stouter than she was in the days when she was leading such an active life" as recounted in the *Life and Adventures*. Still, she had "the free, swinging, easy walk and bearing of a woman who has not crippled herself in early life with the harness and trappings of fashion." In fact, the reporter compared her to a champion boxer, having "the appearance of being as strong as a John L. Sullivan in that man's prime and in a contest of physical strength today could undoubtedly best most men."[2] Martha evidently did not object to the reporter's comparison of herself and a prize fighter.

Martha soon resumed her travels, reaching Helena in September. The *Helena Daily Independent* described Martha in less complimentary terms, calling her a "masculine appearing woman wearing a black sombrero and a dark-colored dress of rough material." Nevertheless, the reporter said she "attracted considerable attention on Main street." She was "selling an autobiography in pamphlet form, the proceeds to go, as she explained, toward educating her daughter." Martha's pamphets sold well, "for everyone had heard of Calamity Jane," the journalist asserted.[3]

The story of Martha's visit to Helena was embellished by an unknown correspondent whose account subsequently appeared in newspapers throughout the nation. According to the reporter, many people would be surprised to learn Martha was "tramping from house to house in Helena" selling her autobiography because it has been assumed "Calamity Jane never existed, except in the imagination." Although her life story would not qualify as a "literary gem," the journalist added, this did not "bother the authoress; all she aspires to is a sale, sufficient to clothe and feed herself until something better comes up."[4]

In the accompanying summary of Martha's life, the correspondent copied from the account that had appeared a year earlier in the *Chicago Inter-Ocean* rather than from the *Life and Adventures* that Martha was peddling. This is evident from the erroneous story of "John McCaul," stage driver, driving to "West Birch," which does not appear in the autobiography. In addition, Martha "killed more than five score Indians" and experienced "more deadly rows than falls to the lot of a hundred average men." She became the leader of the women scouts in the West.[5] Strangely, newspapers in the northern plains reprinted this story without comment.

Meanwhile, Martha continued her travels. The Anaconda newspaper on October 6 announced, "Calamity Jane Here: The Famous Old-Timer Arrived in the City Yesterday." As elsewhere, readers were informed that she was "selling a little pamphlet" about her life. It was significant, said the newspaper, because "the history of Montana has produced only one Calamity Jane."[6] A week later, a correspondent in Deer Lodge recorded her only known political statement. That fall, voters would be choosing between William Jennings Bryan, Democrat and Populist, and William McKinley, Republican, for the presidency. Bryan, the advocate of "free silver," was especially popular in mining regions. Martha insisted "that Bryan was 'jest goin' ter chaw MerKinly up and spit him aout in pesky chunks.'"[7]

Finally, Martha decided to establish a more permanent residence. According to the *Castle (Montana) Whole Truth*, Martha was opening "a nice restaurant" in a vacant building there. Burke was with her, and Jessie evidently attended the Castle school.[8] About Martha's past history, the *Whole Truth* less than truthfully added that she had been involved in "more dangerous clashes with Indians and stage robbers than ever Bill Codey [*sic*] dreamed of in his palmiest and most paradoxical days."[9]

Martha's entrepreneurship in Castle was short-lived. The newspaper reported on November 21 that both "Mr. and Mrs. M. Burk who started a restaurant here a few weeks ago, were arrested last Sunday morning" on the charge of "absconding debtors." Creditors attached a team of horses "owned" by Martha and Burke. However, a Livingston man named Dickinson (or Dixon) claimed Martha and Burke had not completed paying him for the horses. Furthermore, before the court could decide the case, it had to determine whether Dickinson ever held legal title to the team. The newspaper thought the trial might have "some interesting features." But Martha and her husband were soon released,and the case may have been settled out of court.[10]

A few days later, Martha stopped through Livingston en route to Billings. In the latter town, the newspaper, like others before, reported she was "selling a book which purports to be her 'life.'" Although the editor was cautious about accepting the stories she told as fact, he noted that "as the biography of a pioneer of Billings the work meets with a ready sale."[11]

Making Billings her new home, Martha traveled to and from Yellowstone Park to market her photographs and pamphlets. In fact, she was issued Special Permit No. 1 on July 19, 1897, to sell "postcard views of herself" in the Park.[12] Although she spent considerable time there, few Yellowstone tourists mentioned meeting her. One who did was author Burton Holmes, who took photographs of her for his *Travelogues*. Holmes's picture shows Martha fashionably outfitted in a dress and hat.[13] Another person who chanced meeting her in Yellowstone Park was Will Frackelton, the Sheridan dentist. He said he and his wife were on a packing trip in 1897 when they met Martha. Frackelton remembered Martha "swearing a blue streak" when her horses strayed.[14]

While in the area, Martha evidently visited the new settlement of Cody, Wyoming. The town was experiencing a boom as a large irrigation project was completed. One of the town's founders, George W. T. Beck, recalled that "Calamity Jane of Deadwood was a resident here for a couple of years," suggesting she had traveled to the community on more than one occasion.[15]

In June, Martha was back in Billings, where she informed a reporter that she intended to leave "about the first of August to travel through the large cities under the direction of Kohl & Middleton, the dime museum managers of Cincinnati." She said they agreed to pay her $100 a month.[16] Although Martha possibly made this second dime museum tour, no evidence yet proves it. However, Montana newspapers did not mention her for nearly a year, suggesting she did. When she resurfaced, she was a long way from her Montana haunts.

"Calamity Jane, of Deadwood and Leadville fame, and one of Wells-Fargo's most trusted detectives, is in Dawson," declared the *Klondike Nugget* on June 23, 1898. The *Nugget*'s physical description indicates it was indeed Martha: "There is a suggestion in the steel-blue eyes . . . that would warn the unwary, and a glance at the half-sad face indicates that her life has not been all sunshine." Captivated by her dime novel reputation, the reporter added that "the life of this woman has been filled with wild adventures, and on more than one occasion she has been forced to take human life in defense of her own." Nevertheless, he continued, "she is as gentle and refined as any of her Eastern sisters."[17]

Gold had been discovered in the Klondike in fall 1896, but the mining rush began only after the electrifying words "A ton of gold" were flashed through the country on July 17, 1897. Because of travel difficulties, it was not until the next spring that the mass migration occurred. By summer 1898, perhaps thirty thousand people were in the area. Among the early arrivals in Dawson was Eugene C. Allen, founder and editor of the *Klondike Nugget*.[18]

Martha's arrival was reported the first week after Allen's newspaper began publication. She probably met many old acquaintances there. For example, Captain Jack Crawford, whose poem in 1875 spread her fame, was then in town. Most gold seekers discovered that the best claims already were taken. With few prospects and high prices, discouraged miners started homeward before winter struck. Martha probably departed with them, spending only a couple of weeks in the mining settlement. Possibly she performed in one of the theaters; it has been claimed she did in Skagway, perhaps en route to or from Dawson.[19]

Martha was back in Montana in August. She "startled the tenderfoot editor out of a year's growth" when she stopped at the office of the *Livingston Post*. The newspaperman was especially surprised by her dress, for she was "togged out like the ultra type of new woman in the effete east and had an air of up-to-dative-ness about her that was worth coming miles to see." She planned to visit Yellowstone Park again, he said, selling "her photos and biography to admirers of female emancipation during the tourist season."[20]

That summer, Martha relocated once again. In September, a correspondent found her at Crow Agency, Montana, in sight of the Little Big Horn battlefield. Martha liked to talk about Custer, "whom she describes as an absolutely fearless, tireless and brave man, and over whose untimely and sudden end she has shed not a few tears," the reporter said. She could see his tomb from her house, he continued, "and to this fact may be ascribed the principal reason of her residence there." The writer repeated Martha's claim that her military career began in Custer's command, adding that when her identity was discovered Custer gave her only a "slight reprimand" because she served with such ability. Her name appeared on the muster roll as "M. Cannary." Once she was nearly captured, the journalist added, but her marksmanship served her well, and, "after wounding one of the Indians, she made her escape, and, upon reporting to Gen. Custer, was warmly praised."[21]

Area residents saw Martha involved in commonplace activities instead of heroics. A Park City resident, George Herbert, recalled that Martha used to take the train from Laurel to Rock Creek where she would get off to fish, then come back with the train when it returned.[22] Gambling was another of Martha's passions. A faro table she purportedly used during the 1890s is today displayed in a Billings museum. Newspapers mentioned Martha breaking her collarbone in November 1898 as a "result of riding a bucking broncho" in Columbus, Montana.[23] After recovering, she took a job doing laundry at the Cottage Inn in Billings. While she was working, someone stole her gold watch and some cash from her room.[24]

Although Martha's daughter was not mentioned in these stories, Billings resident Mary C. Connolly said she went to school with Jessie "and we all played hopscotch and jumped rope on the same playground." Connolly remembered Martha living in "an old house down near the sugar factory," doing housework to pay expenses. She also recalled that Martha smoked "big black cigars" and drank whiskey sometimes, but generally minded her own business.[25]

Numerous anecdotes about Martha in Billings seem to date from this period. Mrs. William Polly, whose father was in the cattle business, remembered Martha living "in a Billings stable with several companions of the rougher element." Polly recalled her father's new business partner from the East standing in front of a saloon one evening when Martha, "a little tipsy perhaps, strolled by." The visitor made some uncomplimentary remarks about Martha, said Polly, and she "turned upon the fellow in a fury." After she "eloquently presented her opinion of him," she kicked him, "landing the sharp toe of her boot deftly upon his chin and leaving a gash he did not soon forget."[26]

Another anecdote was told by Warren E. Rollins, a young artist from the West Coast who traveled to Billings to teach. Although he did not drink, Rollins supplemented his income by doing portraits in saloons. Learning that the famous Calamity Jane would soon be in town, Rollins decided to make her one of his subjects. She arrived in the saloon one evening "dressed in pants" and wearing a six-shooter. Nevertheless, Rollins thought Martha a "beautiful woman" underneath her "mask of masculinity" and asked her if he might paint her portrait. Although "hostile to the whole idea," Martha, learning Rollins was a "teetotaler," agreed to pose for him on the condition that he match her "drink for drink" as he worked. Rollins waited until she "was pretty much under the influence" before starting. Positioning himself near a large spittoon, he ordered drinks. Martha began drinking as he started painting. Feigning clumsiness, Rollins repeatedly dropped his brush. Each time he leaned down to retrieve it, he poured his whiskey into the spittoon without Calamity noticing. Thus he completed his work without a drink. Sadly, Rollins's portrait evidently was destroyed in a fire.[27]

A third anecdote, told by cowboy Bill Huntington, describes a Calamity Jane impersonator named Powder-Faced Tom. His imitation shows how Calamity Jane's barroom behavior was perceived by her associates. The event supposedly occurred in Bob Conway's saloon in Billings. There Tom "decked himself out in women's clothes with a pair of red stockings" and passed himself off as Calamity Jane. Once in the saloon, Tom "began a story about early days in Deadwood," said Huntington. "Just as the story was getting good about Wild Bill Hickok, Calamity would lose her voice and call for a drink for herself and friends which was quickly served. As the story went on the pauses for a drink came oftener and the story got wilder." Then a "a big baboon faced Irish man" learned they were poking fun at his friend Calamity Jane. He tore Tom's dress off, leaving Tom standing "in his long John underwear and red stockings." Tom raced from the saloon, and, recalled Huntington, "the last I saw of him he was going down the alley looking like a picked chicken."[28]

Meanwhile, the real Martha Canary had moved to Bridger, a small community southwest of Billings. Known earlier as Stringtown, the town boomed when the railroad reached it in 1898–99. A resident, Jordan N. Bean, remembered Martha doing laundry there in 1898. He also recalled that she was living with a man named Dorsett from Livingston, who hauled barrels of water to Bridger.[29] The Billings newspaper confirms Martha's new relationship. According to the *Gazette*, Martha stormed into Billings from Bridger in April 1899. "It is said that she is looking for her husband, who, a week ago, skipped for parts unknown with a younger and handsomer girl," the paper reported.[30]

Dorsett, like most of the men in Martha's life, is a shadowy figure. He is probably the Robert Dorsett injured in an accident in Livingston several years earlier.[31] Newly printed editions of Martha's *Life and Adventures* include the name Dorsett written after "Mrs. Martha Burk." Cowboy Andrew Malum recalled visiting Billings in May 1899 with "Bob Dorset" when they were employed by the Circle Diamond outfit. According to Malum, Dorsett spied Martha walking down the street and asked Malum if he would like to meet his wife. Malum learned later that Dorsett "had become friendly with the woman whom he so designated" and it was her habit "to call a male friend her 'husband.'" After Dorsett introduced Malum to Martha, she asked to see Malum's wallet. Finding two five dollar bills in it, she took one. "That was her manner," Malum remarked. Not wanting to leave him penniless, she was satisfied "to take half of what was found in [his] pocketbook."[32]

Martha made the town of Billings lively during her visits. Malum recalled that one evening, while the crowd was in the midst of its merrymaking at the Castle dance hall, "there appeared at the entrance . . . a form that was recognized by all present as that of Calamity Jane." Martha ordered everyone except Dorsett and Malum out of the room, then fired her revolver, shattering the plate-glass behind the bar. There was an immediate exodus. "Her eyes sparkled with mischievous intent as she walked across the floor in a triumphant attitude and strode toward the bar," said Malum. She then ordered drinks at her companions' expense, and the crowd eventually returned. The next day, a Sunday, she continued her mischief, riding a borrowed horse into the saloon. Her behavior, Malum concluded, was "merely an exhibition of individual freedom and indicative of the temperament of the day when the most unexpected was likely to happen."[33]

From Billings, Martha and Dorsett traveled northward to Fergus County. The Lewistown newspaper reported Martha's arrival there in May 1899. "Mrs. Dorset, more familiarly known as 'Calamity Jane,' and years ago a well known character in this section as well as other parts of the west, arrived from Billings last week and is seeking employment," the paper said. "She carries her years well and was recognized by several who remember seeing her last in the early 80's."[34] Martha perhaps had more plans for Lewistown than the newspaper realized. According to one resident, she intended to establish a house of prostitution there.[35] Evidently she did not succeed, for she moved elsewhere. Two months later, Martha made a "pleasant call" at the Lewistown newspaper office. After talking about "old times in the Black Hills," she informed the editor that she was now living in Utica.[36]

According to the Utica town history, Martha appropriated a vacant cabin east of town.[37] Philip Korell, a Fergus County rancher, said Martha and Dorsett remained in Utica for nearly a year. Dorsett was about thirty, he thought, and Martha considerably older. They worked for him briefly. When talking to Dorsett, Martha constantly exclaimed, "Robert Dear," Korell remembered. At one point, Martha told Korell she would like to create a disturbance at an impending dance just to show the crowd she still could handle a revolver. As Justice of the Peace, Korell warned her not to, though he confided he would have enjoyed seeing her cause a ruction.[38]

Martha also worked as cook at the Judith Hotel Cafe. According to one local story, the hotel bartender, Walter Waite, "fetched a pair of Jane's underpants out of the room she was staying in and hung them over the saloon bar." When Martha learned what he had done, she "strapped a pistol on and marched right over to the saloon." Trouble was avoided, however, after Waite diplomatically granted her a week's worth of free drinks.[39]

Martha visited nearby Gilt Edge as well. A resident, Lillian Weston Hazen, recalled Martha living there one winter, "and it was said that she was never the last up to the bar when somebody set up the drinks."[40] Another townsman, Henry Parrent, claimed Martha rescued him when he was losing money during a crooked poker game. Taking out her gun, she poked it "right into the middle of the card game," said Parrent, and "my luck began to change and I came out the winner by a whole lot." Parrent also remembered that Martha liked to sit beside the stage driver when traveling, and she "smoked big black cigars." Once, when her cigar was mostly "smoked up," she asked to use the driver's cigar to relight hers. But when she returned it, the driver discovered "he had the stub." Parrent last saw Martha in Utica, he said. She had "two tents side by side," using one to live in and the other to wash clothes "for the shearers and freighters."[41]

Another person who met Martha in Gilt Edge was cowboy "Teddy Blue" Abbott. He had borrowed money from her for a meal in Miles City in 1883, but had failed to repay her. Now Abbott reminded Martha of his fifty-cent debt. She told him to forget it, but Abbott insisted on giving her the money, so they "went and drunk it up."[42]

Inexpensive new cameras allowed amateurs to take casual snapshots of such events. Two photographs show Martha and Teddy Blue proposing a toast and then drinking. Another picture, taken in Lewistown, depicts Martha in common dress and hat, and probably is characteristic of her day-to-day appearance. Other photographs of Martha show her holding a rifle and the reins of a horse. The photographer is usually identified as Dr. W. A. Allen of Billings, a dentist who regularly traveled to Gilt Edge and Utica. But there are several variations in surviving copies of this picture, suggesting he took more than one shot or other bystanders also had cameras. Later, Martha told a writer that the horse was named Bess and that General Crook had given it to her. According to Martha, Bess was killed during a fight with Sioux Indians. But the photograph was taken in 1898–99 in Utica, long after the Indian wars had ended, and the horse most likely was borrowed.[43]

Some Utica residents were not as pleased about their famous resident. Mrs. William Polly, for example, remembered Martha as "a great borrower who always had a generous portion of her neighbors' household utensils in her own kitchen." Polly recalled Martha "living with one of her several husbands, a certain Mr. Dorsey," and said she scraped out a "meager living" as the "town washwoman." Although Polly avoided Martha when possible, she still had an unpleasant encounter. One day Dorsett knocked at her door, explaining "his wife was ill and about to die." Polly hurried to help, but discovered Martha really didn't want a nurse. Instead, Martha asked Polly to iron some clothes due to be delivered that day. Because Martha "was in a sullen and imperious mood," Polly did as told, "quaking with fear all the while." Not long afterwards, said Polly, Martha, "under cover of darkness . . . left town, leaving several hundred dollars in unpaid bills behind."[44]

Shortly afterward, Martha and Dorsett separated. It is possible Jessie went with Dorsett. According to Jessie, when she was about ten, Martha's "last husband" took her away.[45] This may have happened earlier, perhaps when they were living in Bridger. One writer claimed that Dorsett took Jessie to Livingston to be raised by his mother, but this story lacks confirmation.[46]

Martha's movements after she left the Judith Basin country in autumn 1899 are unclear. Reminiscences, however, suggest she returned to the small towns near Yellowstone Park. According to Billy Jump, bartender at the Pisor Saloon, Martha lived in Horr during the fall and winter of 1899. There she continued selling her photographs and life story. Jump found it advantageous to have her in the saloon telling tall tales because the miners who came to drink found them entertaining. She especially liked to tell about her adventures as a scout, Jump said, "including the time an Indian shot her in the back of the head and she rode 40 miles with the arrow in her." To prove her story, Martha would show her scar. Jump did not recall Martha becoming drunk in his saloon. Nor were his customers offended by her profanity. However, it bothered other town residents. Maude Rockinger Lind said her parents warned her to walk on the opposite side of the street from saloons where Martha was drinking because of the "rough talking and loud swearing." Still, many people in the town liked Martha and, according to Jump, "pooled their spare cash and supported her during that winter."[47]

Martha also spent several months in the nearby town of Aldridge. She occupied a small house near the lake, but only during the fall months because it was used for ice storage during other seasons. As in Horr, some of Martha's neighbors did not respond positively to her presence. Agnes Somerville stopped Martha from holding her little girl and singing to her. Likewise, Katherine Cotter Tribble remembered Martha being turned down when she offered to help Katherine's father after he broke his leg. Katherine's mother would not let Martha near her husband. According to Katherine, Martha left "in a huff, saying, 'I've set a damned sight better man's legs than Tim Cotter's.'"[48]

Martha's movements through other Montana communities at the end of the century cannot be timed so precisely. Writer W. G. Patterson, for example, saw Martha in Butte, but did not clarify when. She seemed strangely out of place, he said. "Imagine a town thronged with well-dressed women—for Butte is as modish in these days as Boston—and then picture the bent figure of a creature whom you guess is a woman, garbed in rough gunny-sacking, stamping along in men's boots." This was his first sighting of Martha. As he watched, Martha fell on the ice, perhaps distracted by a boy taunting her. Although Martha had "an ugly gash across her forehead," said Patterson, she seemed more upset that "impertinent youngsters" no longer gave her respect. Patterson mentally compared "the wretched creature" in Butte to an early photograph he had seen of Calamity Jane "as the saucy-faced 'soubrette' of a frontier dance-hall, bespangled and bediamonded." She now seemed only a pathetic caricature.

Before Patterson published his article about Martha for *Wide World Magazine* (1903), he interviewed other people in the area who knew her. George Martz, overseer at the Helena jail, was one informant. Martz evidently provided the vivid description of Martha's torment in the Helena jail, as recorded by Patterson. When Martha first arrived at the jail, her face was so pale that Martz decided she "would never leave the building except in a coffin." Martha told him if she recovered, she was going to reform and travel to the East with her daughter. That night, jail attendants heard Martha screaming; she was dreaming she was fighting Indians. After shouting to her imagined soldier friends, her sentences would "dwindle to an old-age quiver," Martz recalled. "We finally quieted her to some extent," he added. "She hadn't the vitality to keep that state of excitement up long."[49] This delirium undoubtedly was the result of Martha's alcoholism.

Although Martha's movements in 1900 were not reported by Montana newspapers, her arrival in Miles City on January 3, 1901, was widely advertised. The Miles City newspaper said she was looking for work:

> Jane Dorsett arrived this morning from Dickinson, North Dakota, and may remain here permanently. Few people here know Jane by this name and the item might not receive a second thought, but the announcement that Calamity Jane is in town is of interest to all old timers. She is at present a guest of the European Hotel and will remain a day or two and perhaps longer—that is if she succeeds in her mission, which is to obtain employment. For Jane is a cook and a good one and there is no reason why she shouldn't get a situation if there is any demand for cooks.

Five years had passed since her last visit to Miles City, the reporter noted. She was traveling alone. According to the writer, her daughter was attending school in Helena. Although "Calamity Jane may have ceased to be an object of much interest to those who have known her for years and are familiar with her career," the reporter continued, "she will always interest the tenderfoot who has heard lurid tales of her adventures in the Dakotas and Montana when this country was new."[50]

Martha evidently failed to land a lasting position as a cook in Miles City, so she continued westward. In Billings, she took up residence in a "hotel" operated by Yee Sam Lee.[51] Lee's establishment had an unsavory reputation; only a year earlier he was fined for renting rooms for immoral purposes.[52] Martha and Lee were soon embroiled in a dispute. "Mrs. R. S. Dorsett, better known as 'Calamity Jane,' has begun suit in Justice Fraser's court against Yee Sam Lee, proprietor of the L. & L. restaurant, to recover $300 damages," the newspaper reported. "Mrs. Dorsett claims that Lee is withholding from her a trunk containing dresses and bedding valued at $500."[53] Lee claimed Martha had used her trunk as security for her room rent. After investigating, the newspaper determined the trunk contained "only three dresses that would not bring very much at even a secondhand store."[54] But Martha won the case, "bitterly fought by counsel on either side," and then left Billings.[55]

Soon afterward, Martha arrived in Livingston. "Mrs. Robert Dorsett, known the world over as 'Calamity Jane,' is in the city this week selling pictures and a sketch of her life," reported the Livingston newspaper on January 19.[56] She remained in town a few weeks, then took the train toward White Sulphur Springs. However, this trip was cut short by severe illness.

The Bozeman newspaper on February 12 reported that "a strange woman was taken sick on the train Saturday morning . . . and is in a very precarious condition."[57] Martha was so ill she could not even identify herself to the conductor. Concerned officials met the train at the next station; because Martha had no money, she was taken to the poorhouse where the county physician examined her. According to the newspaper, she recovered quickly, was "discharged on Monday," and left "rejoicing." Despite this report about Martha's poverty, she had a means of livelihood; the Bozeman newspaper clarified that "she still has for sale copies of her picture and the little pamphlet purporting to be a history of her life."[58]

Martha's brief stay in the poorhouse gained widespread attention, providing newspapers an excuse to recount once again her life story. Denver's *Rocky Mountain News* thought her to be "about 70 years of age now" and reported that "her body bears the scars of a dozen bullets which she received in fights with road agents and Indians in the wild days of Montana." It repeated inaccurate lurid tales that Martha shot her first husband for beating her, that she killed her second husband in a dance-hall fight, and that "others of her marital companions came to bad ends and several were divorced."[59]

Deadwood's *Daily Pioneer-Times* told its readers that her illness was the result of "exposure during her long service as a government scout and Indian fighter." It depicted her as a victim of modernization: "For a number of years, until infirmities and age prevented, she also served the government as a mail carrier, but this last employment was denied when steam and electricity supplanted the horse." The *Pioneer-Times* also sympathetically portrayed her as a single mother, forced to take care of her daughter alone after the death of her husband, Clinton Burke, in 1895, a startling comment considering that Burke at that moment was living in Deadwood. The doting mother gave her daughter "all the love and tenderness the woman could muster" it said, and has "labored night and day that her daughter might be educated and grow up among cultivated and gentle people."[60]

Martha was unhappy about this publicity. According to a Billings reporter, she expressed her wrath at "the space writer in Livingston, who started the report of her being a county charge." He "narrowly missed annihilation," and "the bombardment he received from the tongue of 'Calamity' made him feel smaller than 30 cents."[61]

Nevertheless, the news that Calamity Jane had been taken to the poorhouse brought her unexpected benefits. While Martha continued her travels eastward to Big Timber and Billings, a campaign was being initiated on her behalf.[62] "She has been receiving considerable notoriety of late," a Billings newspaper explained. The Sunday edition of the *Denver Post* included "quite a sketch of her, together with her photo, and large headlines announcing that she was now in the poor house." As tales of her deteriorating health and destitution spread, friends, acquaintances, and even total strangers opened their pocketbooks. "Only a couple of days ago she received the sum of $65 from Dr. Frank Powell, better known as 'White Beaver' of St. Paul, who was well acquainted with her in the days when she was a scout," the paper noted.[63]

Learning of Martha's incarceration, Powell had immediately inquired about her condition, explaining that many old-timers would willingly "join in making her life more comfortable if she is really in dire want." According to Powell, "no matter what the 'holier than thou' set may think, she and such as she made it possible for civilization to take hold and fasten itself upon the land of the Indian and buffalo, and now that she is helpless the cloak of charity should be thrown over the unfortunate part of her life." He was certain his friend William F. Cody, whom he called Martha's "foster brother and lifelong companion," would also contribute.[64]

As contributions poured in, Montana editors tried to unscramble the events that had generated this unexpected charity. The *Anaconda Standard* explained that the initial article about Martha's stay in the poorhouse was accurately reported, but eastern correspondents in Butte then exaggerated Martha's destitution. These "imaginative writers" claimed Martha "was suffering the direst straits of poverty and her days were being passed in the gloomy occupation of looking out upon the merry world through the uncurtained windows of the Gallatin county poorhouse." Consequently, the entire country became "stirred up" about Martha's plight.[65]

These journalists, the *Standard* concluded, did Martha "an important service in spreading the news of her misfortune." Now, Martha was "firmly on her feet again financially." The reporter concluded that her stay at the poor farm was "a snap when viewed in the light of financial results."[66]

Still, Martha was unhappy about the situation. She had been placed under medical care against her will and was embarrassed by the publicity that followed. When she arrived in Red Lodge in April, she immediately contacted stage driver J. A. Virtue and left with him for Cody, Wyoming, "in order to get as far beyond the pale of civilization as possible." She may also have been attracted by the construction camps as the Toluca-Cody Branch of the Burlington railroad built from Montana to Cody.[67]

Accordingly, the *Cody Enterprise* on April 18 announced, "This morning Cody was honored by the arrival of Calamity Jane, a lady well-known all over the western country." The reporter learned that she planned to remain in town for an extended period.[68] However, Martha returned to Livingston about a week later, once again imbibing heavily in its saloons. While staggering down the street one night, she met a young correspondent, Lewis R. Freeman. Although he did not publish his account of this chance encounter until twenty years later, Freeman's interview with Martha, which lasted intermittently for a week, is important.

Freeman had recently arrived in Livingston to play baseball. Facing tough competition from neighboring towns, Livingston recruited players from outside the region. Since league rules required participants to be residents, the town provided these outsiders with jobs. Freeman worked at the Livingston newspaper. He is remembered, however, for his adventure stories.[69] *Down the Yellowstone* (1922), one of several travel books he authored, devotes an entire chapter to his meeting with Martha in Livingston in May 1901.[70]

"In every man's life there is one event that transcends all others in the bigness with which it bulks in his memory," wrote Freeman, adding that "the thunderbolt of a living, breathing 'Calamity Jane' striking at my feet . . . is my biggest thing." It began while Freeman was returning after midnight to his hotel room in Livingston. He thought he saw a cowboy "in the act of embracing a lamp-post," but it turned out to be an inebriated Martha Canary.

> A gruff voice hailed me as I came barging by. "Short Pants!" it called; "oh, Short Pants—can't you tell a lady where she lives?"
>
> "Show me where the lady is and I'll try," I replied, edging cautiously in toward the circle of the golden glow.
>
> "She's me, Short Pants—Martha Cannary—Martha Burk, better known as 'Calamity Jane.'"
>
> "Ah!" I breathed, and again, "Ah!" Then: "Sure, I'll tell you where you live; only you'll have to tell me first." And thus was ushered in the greatest moment of my life.[71]

Martha, he learned, had arrived that afternoon from Bozeman and rented a room over a saloon. After becoming drunk, she recalled only that the bartender's name was Patsy. Thus, Freeman and Martha began a bar-to-bar search for Patsy.

"It was a long and devious search," recalled Freeman, "not so much because there was any great number of saloons with outside stairways and mixologists called Patsy, as because every man in every saloon to which we went to inquire greeted 'Calamity' as a long-lost mother and insisted on shouting the house." After a round of drinks, the entire crowd would join the search; the process was repeated in every bar. When they finally located Patsy and learned where her room was, Martha had lost her key. "After a not-too-well-ordered consultation, we passed her unprotesting anatomy in through a window by means of a fire-ladder and reckoned our mission finished," Freeman said.[72]

The next morning, Freeman dropped by to see how Martha was faring. He found her smoking a cigar while cooking breakfast, and she asked him to join her. She had no recollection of their previous meeting, though she still called him "Short Pants," referring to his "omnipresent checkered knickers."[73] When Freeman asked if she would grant him an interview, she agreed. For the next week, Freeman took notes as Martha narrated her life story. He also took several photographs. One shows Martha sitting in her kitchen smoking a cigar; another depicts her seated among beer barrels telling her story.

Freeman's excitement in meeting Calamity Jane derived from his youthful consumption of dime novels. She was, he said, "the heroine of that saffron-hued thriller called 'The Beautiful White Devil of the Yellowstone.'"[74] Now his heroine stood before him. She looked to be, he thought, about fifty-five years of age (she actually was only forty-five), though he cautioned it depended where one looked. "Her deeply-lined, scowling, sun-tanned face and the mouth and its missing teeth might have belonged to a hag of seventy," he said. But when watching her walk, one might conclude she was "a thirty-year-old cowpuncher just coming into town for his night to howl." Freeman also learned that the "black scowl" on her face was deceptive. "Hers was the sunniest of souls, and the most generous."[75]

Before she began the story of her life, Martha asked Freeman to "just run down and rush a can of suds, and I'll rattle off the whole layout for you. I'll meet you down there in the sunshine by those empty beer barrels." When Freeman returned with with the beer, he found Martha "enthroned on an up-ended barrel" ready to begin.[76] He listened and responded as she narrated. Later he recorded their interplay in *Down the Yellowstone*:

> "My maiden name was Martha Cannary. Was born in Princeton, Missouri, May first, 1848." Then, in a sort of parenthesis: "This must be about my birthday, Pants. Drink to the health of the Queen of May, kid." I stopped chewing dandelion, lifted the suds-crowned bucket toward her, muttered "Many happy Maytimes, Queen," and drank deep. Immediately she resumed with "My maiden name was Martha Cannary, etc." . . . As a child I always had a fondness for adventure and especial fondness for horses, which I began to ride at an early age and continued to do so until I became an expert rider, being able to ride the most vicious and stubborn horses.[77]

She told about her journey to Montana, the deaths of her parents, scouting for Custer, and being christened with the name "Calamity" after saving Captain Egan's life. Here Freeman interrupted Martha. Her version, he said, differed from that in the dime novel he read. Martha began "swearing hard and pointedly, so hard and pointedly, in fact, that her remarks may not be quoted verbatim here," Freeman wrote. "The gist of them was that 'The Beautiful White Devil of the Yellowstone' was . . . a pack of blankety-blank lies, in fact, and of no value whatever as history." Freeman was astonished: "I realize now that she was right, of course, but that didn't soften the blow at the time."[78]

Martha resumed her story, beginning once again, "My maiden name was Martha Cannary." She recited her previous story verbatim, then told of being in the Black Hills in 1875, scouting for Crook in 1876, riding for the pony express, and capturing Jack McCall after he killed Wild Bill Hickok. Once again Freeman interrupted her, unable to reconcile her version with the dime novel account in "Jane of the Plain." As before, her response was "unfit to print." According to Martha, "'Wild Bill' had *not* expired with his head on her shoulder, muttering brokenly, 'My heart was yours from the first, oh my love!' Nor had she snipped off a lock of Bill's yellow hair and sworn to bathe it in the heart-blood of his slayer. All blankety-blank lies, just like the 'White Devil.'"[79]

For the third time, Martha began her story, "My maiden name was Martha Cannary." Freeman stopped interrupting her. "This time I kept chewing dandelions and let her run on to a finish, thereby learning the secret of her somewhat remarkable style of delivery." She was delivering her memorized dime museum lecture. "Like a big locomotive on a slippery track, she had had to back up to get going again every time she was stopped," Freeman said.[80]

Only after she finished her recitation did Freeman convince Martha to talk about her other experiences in the West. He took meticulous notes but never published this portion of the interview. It was not as exciting as her earlier tales, but nevertheless was of interest, he said. "Circulating for three decades through the upper Missouri and Yellowstone valleys" to places where the "action was liveliest and trouble the thickest," Martha "had known at close range all of the most famous frontier characters of her day," Freeman wrote. Many of her stories "seemed to throw doubt on a number of popularly accepted versions of various more or less historical events," he added. Freeman hoped someday to "cross check" her stories with other sources before publishing them.[81] It is history's loss that these notes of their conversation have not surfaced.

One day Martha failed to appear at the appointed time. When Freeman asked about her at the saloon, he learned she was last seen riding toward Big Timber early that morning. As usual, she had not paid her room bill, but Patsy said it was a "perfectly good account" because "she never failed to settle up in the end." According to Freeman, he next heard of Martha a couple years later when he read of her death.[82] It is not surprising that Martha disappeared without telling Freeman that she was leaving; unexpected departures were her pattern. More strange is that Freeman was not aware of her adventures during the year before she died. Martha's brief sojourn in the poorhouse was about to pay its greatest dividend, leading to a highly publicized trip to the Pan-American Exposition in Buffalo, New York.

Meanwhile, after leaving Livingston, Martha continued traveling, meeting friends, and drinking. Once again, she became so ill that medical help was summoned. On May 15, 1901, she was discovered asleep in the back of Taft's Saloon in Red Lodge. Observers noticed her limbs were badly swollen and, concerned that she was near death, sent for the county physician. While the doctor examined her, townspeople pondered what to do. Charley Bowlen promised money for her care, saying "no matter what kind of life 'Calamity' had led, she had given many a poor devil her last cent and that as long as he had a cent, she should not be neglected." But before any plans could be implemented, Martha vanished. Waking from her deep slumbers and "defying the ravages of disease," she had quietly boarded the evening train for Billings.[83]

Martha tarried only briefly in Billings before departing for Livingston. One Livingston reporter thought she looked "well and hearty," despite her recent illness. The journalist also learned from Martha that she was still "living high" as a result of "that story about her being committed to the poor farm." It had "proved a veritable bonanza" for her, he concluded.[84]

Relative affluence did not deter Martha from peddling her pamphlets and photographs to tourists, and they evidently bought. According to the *Livingston Post*, Martha returned from Mammoth Hot Springs in June "to secure a new lot of the pamphlets containing the weird and uncanny story of her life. She reports having had great success in 'hot airing' the tourists who are making Wonderland, and says that if she could only hold onto the money she is making she would be a bloomin' millionaire in a short time." Although the rainy spring weather sometimes curtailed her selling trips, she lost money mainly because of her alcoholic thirst. In the words of the newspaper, "She is unable to keep the proceeds of her work in this wet weather, when keeping the outside dry does no good unless the inside is kept in exactly a reverse condition."[85] Sometimes the weather really did prevent her from peddling her booklets. Once she arrived in Livingston from Horr, having found "the weather too severe for her to begin selling her books in the Park."[86]

But Martha's activities were about to be interrupted by something more significant than bad weather. Her poor-farm experience had come to the attention of a philanthropist who was en route to rescue Martha from her destitution. Martha's next adventure would equal any she experienced during her frontier years.

Martha Canary, Rawlins, Wyoming, 1880s (?)

Although the precise date, location, and name of photographer who took this picture are unknown, it evidently dates from Martha's years in Wyoming after 1884. Courtesy, Denver Public Library, Western History Collection (F-38793).

Martha Canary (Calamity Jane), Evanston, Wyoming, 1880s (?)

Taken by an unidentified photographer probably between 1884 and 1893, this studio image shows Calamity decked out in a fancy cowboy outfit, perhaps one she wore when appearing in parades and at community celebrations. Courtesy, J. Leonard Jennewein Collection, Layne Library, Dakota Wesleyan University, Mitchell, South Dakota.

Elijah Canary

Martha's brother, Elijah, lived in western Wyoming and Utah for many years. In 1896, he was convicted for driving horses across railroad tracks in southwestern Wyoming, intending to demand payment for damages. Elijah's photograph was taken while he served his sentence in the Wyoming Territorial Prison in Laramie between 1896 and 1900. Courtesy, Wyoming State Archives, Department of State Parks and Cultural Resources, Biography #13577.

Martha Canary, Billings, Montana, 1894

After spending a decade in Wyoming, Martha followed the railroad as it was built from Sheridan, Wyoming, to Billings, Montana. In 1894, she posed (fifth from end on right) in Billings with soldiers called to restore order during the Northern Pacific railroad strike. Courtesy, Montana Historical Society.

Martha Canary (Calamity Jane), Deadwood, South Dakota, 1895

When Martha visited Deadwood in 1895 after more than fifteen years' absence, she was greeted as a celebrity. Martha immediately had several photographs taken at the studio of H. R. Locke, selling them as she toured the Black Hills and dime museums in eastern cities. Besides sitting for the photographer, Martha posed while standing and facing different directions. Courtesy, Montana Historical Society (MHS 941-417).

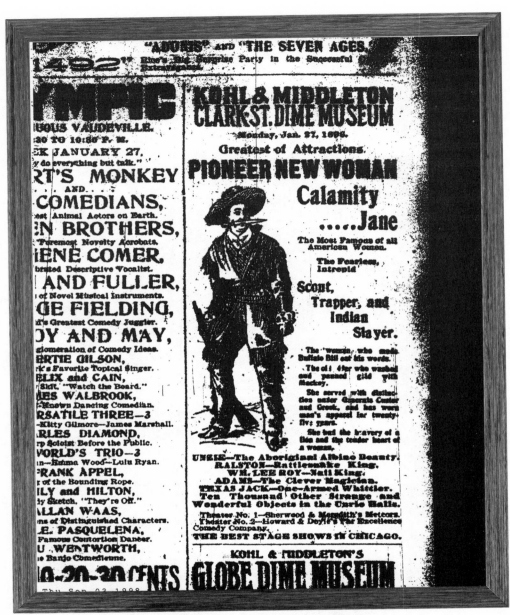

Dime Museum Advertisement, 1896

Martha followed her dime museum debut in Minneapolis in January 1896 with a two-week appearance in Chicago. There, the *Chicago Inter-Ocean* of January 27 advertised her as "The Fearless, Intrepid Scout, Trapper, and Indian Slayer." Author's collection.

Calamity Jane, Livingston, Montana, 1896–1898

After her successful dime museum tour in 1896, Martha returned to Montana where she had several photographs taken of her in the studio of C. E. Finn of Livingston. She sold these to Montana friends and Yellowstone Park tourists. Finn took several shots showing Martha facing front, right, and left. Courtesy, Montana Historical Society (MHS 941-418).

Martha Canary, Utica, Montana, 1897–1898

For about two years, Martha lived in the Utica, Montana, area, where this street photograph of her was taken. It is often misidentified. Jean Hickok McCormick, who in 1941 claimed to be the daughter of Calamity and Wild Bill, said that the horse in the photograph was named Satan, was a gift to Calamity from Wild Bill, and was dead after 1893. But Martha told another writer that the horse was a gift from General Crook, was named Bess, and was killed in 1875 or 1876 during her escape from Indians in the Black Hills. Actually, the horse was evidently borrowed from a local cowboy for the picture, and the photograph was taken in Utica, Montana, in 1897 or 1898. Courtesy, Montana Historical Society (MHS 941-411).

Martha Canary and E. C. (Teddy Blue) Abbott, Utica or Gilt Edge, Montana, 1897–1898

When Martha visited the towns of Utica and Gilt Edge, Montana, she met an earlier acquaintance, cowboy Teddy Blue Abbott. This is one of two snapshots showing the two having a reunion drink. They obviously were enjoying themselves, having exchanged hats. Courtesy, Montana Historical Society, (MHS 941-408).

Martha Canary and E. C. (Teddy Blue) Abbott, Utica or Gilt Edge Montana, 1897–1898

Courtesy, Montana Historical Society (MHS 941-409).

"CALAMITY-JANE"

Martha Canary, Yellowstone Park, 1897–1898

In 1897, Martha was issued a special permit to sell "postcard views of herself" in Yellowstone Park. She peddled her pictures and autobiography there to tourists in her later years. However, the only photograph that has been located showing her in the Park was taken by professional photographer Burton Holmes. From Burton Holmes, *Traveloques,* 1901. Author's collection.

Martha Canary, Lewiston, Montana, 1899

As cameras became more common, snapshots like this one showing Martha in everyday dress were taken. Mrs. E. G. Worden of Lewiston, Montana, has been tentatively identified as the phoptographer. Courtesy, J. Leonard Jennewein Collection, Layne Library, Dakota Wesleyan University, Mitchell, South Dakota.

Martha Canary, Montana, 1890s (?)

This studio photograph probably dates from the late 1890s in Montana, but its provenance is uncertain. It first appeared in England in W. G. Patterson's article, "Calamity Jane," in *Wide World Magazine*, August 1903. Author's collection.

Martha Canary, Livingston, Montana, 1901

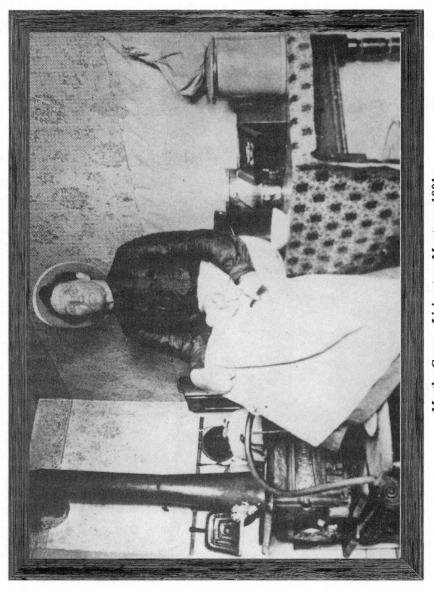

Writer Lewis Freeman managed to interview Martha intermittently for about a week in Livingston, Montana, in May 1901. After their first encounter, she invited him to join her for breakfast, when he took this picture showing her smoking a cigar while cooking. From Lewis Freeman, *Down the Yellowstone,* 1922. Author's Collection.

Martha Canary, Livingston, Montana, 1901

Martha, perched atop a beer barrel behind a Livingston saloon, narrated the story of her life to writer Lewis Freeman while she drank. There, Freeman snapped this picture, which is reproduced from Lewis Freeman, "Calamity Jane and Yankee Jim," *Sunset* magazine, July 1922. Author's Collection.

"CALAMITY JANE"

Martha Canary (Calamity Jane), at the Pan-American Exposition, Buffalo, New York, 1901

In 1901, Martha was invited by journalist and philanthropist Josephine Brake to live with her in New York, ostensibly to live out her last years in luxury. However, upon her arrival in Buffalo, New York, Martha was signed up to perform in Fred Cummins's "Indian Congress" at the Pan-American Exposition. There, a photographer captured this image of an aged Calamity Jane appearing none too pleased with her new circumstances. From Richmond Hill, *A Great White Indian Chief,* 1912. Author's collection.

CHAPTER TWELVE

The Pan-American Exposition
1901-1902

Martha celebrated Independence Day 1901 in her typical fashion. She got royally drunk. According to the Livingston newspaper, by the time she arrived in town on the train from Yellowstone Park she already had imbibed heavily. Still, she visited more saloons "where all residents were greeted with the familiar 'Hello, dear!' 'Hello, darling!' which have made her famous as well as conspicuous."[1]

Martha's physical and mental condition had deteriorated, however. Friends now "missed the light in her eye," observed the Livingston reporter, even if the profanity "with which she starts or finishes a well rounded sentence, or a well earned roast for some bystander," remained recognizable. She looked "worn and weary, twisted and bent, and on the rapid decline." It was apparent, concluded the reporter, that her days were numbered.[2]

But another major adventure awaited Martha before her demise. The news that she was an inmate in a poorhouse had come to the attention of correspondent Josephine Winifred Brake of New York. Brake was now en route to Montana to rescue the beleagured heroine. She hoped to convince Martha to leave the West and live in luxury with her in New York.[3]

Brake was described by the Livingston newspaper as "one of the foremost women journalists in the country." It added that she was "tall, dark and graceful, with a fine face that shows strength of purpose without overshadowing the charms of feminity." Her voice betrayed a slight southern accent. Brake's interest in Martha was stimulated from reading about her western adventures. She was certain anyone showing "so much daring courage and strength [had] other good qualities." But her decision to offer Martha a place to retire in ease was made only after "talking with General Egan, whose life she once saved." The identity of Brake's General Egan is unknown; the Captain Egan who, according to Martha, had claimed christened her with her famous nickname had died in 1883. Unaware of the deception, the Montana correspondent nodded approvingly, "After all these years the man whose life she saved was instrumental in providing a home for her."[4]

Brake arrived in Butte on July 9, reaching Livingston a few days later.[5] Accompanied by Dell Alderson, editor of the *Livingston Post*, Brake began her search for Martha.[6] Shortly afterwards, the *Post* reported that Brake had found Martha "ill in the hut of a negro woman on the bank of the Yellowstone." According to Alderson, Brake exclaimed: "I'se been watin', honey, watin' long for you. Come along east with me and I'll set you up in business and put you on the cushions for the rest of your natural life." At this offer, Martha wept "bitter, burning, boiling tears all over the ill-kept cot on which she was lying." Never, said the newspaperman, had the sick woman "seen anybody quite as willing to go deep down into the long sack and dig up the spondulix without getting value received." Upon accepting Brake's offer, Martha promised "to be a good girl all the rest of her life."[7]

Later, the *Post* explained the cause of Martha's most recent illness. She had been hiking three miles over the mountains each day to help a friend confined in the Aldridge hospital with blood poisoning. According to the reporter, Martha had carried fruit and other necessities to the invalid, selling her booklets and pictures to pay for the items. It was during her last trip that Martha "took to her bed, where she was found by her benefactress."[8]

Other writers reported the meeting between Martha and Brake differently. They disagreed, too, about Martha's willing acceptance of Brake's offer. The *Butte Miner*, for example, said Brake found Martha peddling her pictures and pamphlets at Mammoth Hot Springs in Yellowstone Park. When Brake returned to Livingston with Martha, said the Butte correspondent, it was learned that "considerable trouble was had in inducing the aged woman to change her habits of life and bid goodbye to western life, which she so long enjoyed."[9]

Journalists also disagreed about the sincerity of Brake's intentions. Although the *Post*'s editor suggested Martha might now "spend the rest of her days eating spring chicken and living like a prince," others suspected Brake had ulterior motives.[10] The *Billings Times* announced Martha's departure with the headline, "Gone Off In Doubtful Company." According to the *Times*, many old-timers were upset that Martha "was rail-roaded out of the state of Montana by an entire stranger." This reporter said he first became suspicious when Brake claimed she worked for the *New York Journal*, then denied it after being questioned. The *Times* suspected Martha would be used "for some advertising purpose." It continued:

> Newspaper women do not receive such magnificent salaries that they can make such journeys and burden themselves with the care of an old woman. She never saw Jane; only read about her. She has some scheme afoot and Calamity will bitterly regret leaving Montana. She will earn what she gets, but only for the woman who took her away. Some of the old pioneers ought to try and keep watch as to just where Calamity is taken.[11]

Subsequent events showed that the editor's suspicions were at least partly justified.

Other observers thought there was as much reason to be concerned with Brake's welfare as Martha's. A reporter for the *Red Lodge Picket* predicted that "the old girl won't take kindly to this eastern scheme." He continued: "Calamity, you know, likes pilgrims at about the same ratio that the devil is stuck on holy water."[12] Similarly, the *Butte Miner* thought it "doubtful if 'Calamity Jane' will take to this radical change" and guessed she would be back in Montana before year's end.[13]

In a different vein, the editor of the *Billings Gazette* mused about the irony of the situation. Martha's opportunity to retire in comfort in the East was based solely on her reputation as the legendary Calamity Jane. The unadorned Martha Canary would be considered an unwelcome guest. Thus, Martha owed "a debt of gratitude to the romancer and the writer of 'yellow backs,'" even though she denounced their stories as lies, for they were responsible for this "whim of a sentimental woman" from New York.

The Billings editor discussed at length the discrepancy between the lives of the legendary heroine, Calamity Jane, and the common woman, Martha Canary. "The true stories" of Martha "would probably be no less interesting and amusing than the fictitious ones that have given her fame and renown," he said, but "they would not be accorded space in publications having a circulation in the home and among the people of refined natures." Martha was not a scout or dispatch bearer as had been claimed, he added. Rather, she was a camp follower and mostly showed up at military posts near payday. Since she accompanied soldiers during campaigns, occasionally she became "mixed up in some scrimmage," he continued, "but the picture of 'Calamity,' clad in buckskin reining a wild charger and waving a man's hat as she led a band of dashing troopers into battle" is from the imagination of novelists. Thus, the career of the legendary Calamity Jane diverged widely from the life of Martha Canary. "The one drawn by the romancer may be more inspiring and more attractive," but it does not reflect reality, the editor concluded.

Even though the Billings editor discounted heroic tales about Martha's military career, he thought she had redeeming qualities. "Her deeds of unselfish charity and benevolence . . . atoned for many of her shortcomings," he said. In his opinion, her greatest failing was her addiction to alcohol. But "when the time comes that she must answer for her deeds on earth the good recorded to her credit will be found to balance the bad," he concluded.[14]

While editors contemplated the circumstances of her departure, Martha made preparations to leave. First, she thought it necessary to join "the boys" for a farewell drink.[15] Then, she left with her new chaperone. During a brief stop in Glendive, a reporter hurried to question Martha about her decision. "She said she had no regret in leaving the scenes that had made her famous, because no one in this part of the country cared for her now."[16]

Tension between Martha and Brake quickly surfaced, however. By the time the pair reached St. Paul and registered at the Ryan Hotel, Brake "was extremely nervous," observed a reporter, who added that traveling with Martha evidently "had been equal to a tenderfoot's first experience with a bucking broncho." Martha had agreed not to drink during the trip "except when Mrs. Brake consented," and to avoid trouble Brake had approved so often that the flask "had been worn as smooth as a nursing bottle."[17]

During their stop in St. Paul, Brake purchased new clothing for her traveling companion with comical results. After being fitted out, Martha went to her room alone to dress. She sprinkled face powder "in promiscuous fashion on her bright blue shirtwaist, black skirt, face and hair," a journalist reported, and "was a sight to behold when Mrs. Brake opened the door and surveyed her." Also eliciting comment was Martha's smoking of "long, black cigars." Putting a positive spin on the situation, Brake explained that Martha was "honesty personified" and did not pretend to be other than what she was. Nevertheless, Brake found handling Martha to be extremely difficult.[18]

Correspondents also found Martha to be problematic. When she arrived in Minneapolis, Martha showed a journalist her battered hand satchel. She said it had been damaged from striking a Montana reporter who had written untruths about her. Said Martha, "He didn't see me, and I got a good crack at him. His head was cut considerable."[19] Now she displayed her antipathy to reporters once again. This incident occurred after Brake surreptitiously arranged a meeting between Martha and a young correspondent. Brake warned the reporter about Martha's dislike of journalists, telling him a different version of the recent Montana confrontation. Martha took offense when a Helena reporter refused to smoke with her, said Brake. Throwing her satchel at him, Martha knocked off his hat and scratched his face. It was afterwards that the victim's negative impressions were published. Brake decided to introduce the Minnesota reporter to Martha as her cousin.

The "cousin" was having a "first rate interview" as he smoked with Martha in her hotel room until a rival correspondent entered the room unannounced and requested to talk with Martha. She responded curtly, "I give you to understand that I don't give no news to papers. You git right out of here." The reporter then complained, "I don't see why you won't talk to me. Our paper is just as good as the one this man represents." Learning of this deception, Martha exploded. Finding the notes the first journalist had concealed, she tore them up and ordered both reporters out of her room, adding "a few choice expletives, large octagonal ones" as they departed.[20] The episode undoubtedly exacerbated tensions between Martha and her benefactor.

Still, the pair continued their journey together to Buffalo, New York, where Brake had rented a temporary home. There, Martha became an immediate sensation. The *Buffalo Morning Express* reported on July 29 that a trip to Niagara Falls was planned. Expected to join the party were poet Ella Wheeler Wilcox and the mysterious General Egan. Martha also met "Doc" Waddell, press agent for Colonel Fred Cummins's Indian Congress then performing at the Pan-American Exposition in Buffalo. "Possibilities of new calamities undoubtedly rose in the imagination of Doc, as he gazed on Jane," remarked the newspaper.[21]

Cummins, director of the Indian Congress, had assembled representatives from thirty-one tribes in 1898 for the Trans-Mississippi Exposition and again in 1899 for the Omaha Greater American Exposition. From these successful performances, he created his Pan-American Exposition show featuring "leading chieftains from forty-two different tribes of North American Indians."[22] Among these, Geronimo received top billing.

Undoubtedly, the Indian Congress hoped to add Martha to their show. Cummins chartered the trolley car that took her to Niagara Falls. During the visit, Martha "stood on the brink of the falls and her photograph was taken as she seemed to defy the waters," the newspaper reported. Shortly afterwards, it was announced that Martha would be adopted "as one of the members of the Indian Congress."[23] The degree of involvement by Brake in these arrangements can only be surmised from later developments.[24] Evidently, Martha would receive only a portion of her wages and Brake the remainder. In addition, there were stipulations curtailing Martha's drinking and movements.

Before she joined Cummins's show, however, Martha endured a reception and banquet in her honor at the Iroquois Hotel. It is uncertain whether the event was sponsored by Brake or Cummins, but many prominent people attended the reception "anxious to see one who had passed through the stirring times of the Far West."[25] Making the best of Martha's reticence that evening, one reporter said she "made a short speech at the reception," but "would say nothing at table, following an old western scout's custom of keeping silence at public functions." That evening, it was announced Martha would drive a one hundred mule train down Buffalo's Main Street the next day. "This will be the biggest mule team ever hitched up," the newspaper reported, and "Calamity Jane will handle it just as easily as an ordinary teamster handles a span of trained horses."[26] As Montana friends had predicted, Martha's projected life of ease had vanished. In defense of Brake, she reportedly was working to secure a government pension for Martha, who was "as much entitled to a pension as any man who fought for the Government."[27]

The Pan-American Exposition, comprised of shows and exhibits from various states and countries in the Western Hemisphere, was in full swing. Among the visitors that summer were President William McKinley, Vice-President Theodore Roosevelt, Kaiser Wilhelm, Admiral George Dewey, and General Nelson A. Miles. Special days were designated to honor organizations in attendance. For example, July 31 was "Elks Day," when costumed members of the lodge would march through the city's streets. It was in this parade that Martha drove "a watering cart" drawn by one hundred mules. She was located near the end of the procession.[28] That afternoon, the Elks were treated with a special performance by the Indian Congress. Martha "was given a warm reception, and her riding was good enough to ensure her success with every audience that sees the show," said one reporter. Also featured was "Wenona, the Sioux girl sharpshooter," who spelled B.P.O.E. "on a target with rifle bullets" for visitors.[29]

Some journalists were convinced that Martha's appearance in Cummins's exhibition was proof of Brake's exploitation. These writers predicted Brake would reap most of the proceeds from people paying to see Calamity Jane. In fact, one correspondent reported that although Martha drew large, admiring crowds when she appeared in one of the side shows, she received only thirty cents, plus her meals, for her first week's work.[30]

Martha made her second parade appearance on "Midway Day" when more than one hundred thousand people attended the Exposition. Grand Marshal of the parade was

Frederick T. Cummins and the entries included the Carlisle Indian Band, Winona, and "Calamity Jane, the heroine, who wears a hero's garb," said the newspaper. Following Martha was Geronimo, described by one reporter as the "old fellow on the gray horse who was followed by three fierce Apaches in light yellow."[31]

According to Buffalo newspapers, Martha became a major asset for Cummins's western show. "The arrival of Calamity Jane at the Indian Congress has stirred things to greater activity," one journalist asserted. "Every day during the past week the congress had an attendance comprising nearly one-half of the total number of people who pass through the main entrances of the Pan-American." There were, of course, other reasons for Cummins's success. For instance, the Indian Congress attracted audiences because of its open-air performances in a "monster arena" that seated twenty-five thousand people. Its dramatic events included "expert rifle shooting, Indian races of all kinds, Wild West sports and pastimes, and a mighty sham battle participated in by 500 warriors." In addition, the Indian Congress was advertised as "one of the Government's contributions" to the Exposition because the "700 Indians which are a part of the congress are here by special permission from the United States Government."[32]

But it probably was the romantic image of the West that most attracted visitors. As one local newspaper observed, the show especially appealed "to the school boy who loves to delve into books of daring and adventure of frontier times in the old days." Most appealing of the western attractions, said the reporter, were "Geronimo, the human tiger, Winona, the wonderful Sioux rifle shot, and Calamity Jane, famous in song and story of frontier days."[33]

Nevertheless, Cummins's own publicity never mentioned Calamity Jane. Probably this was because she joined the show so late in the season and remained with it only briefly. She was featured, however, in a 1912 publication by Cummins describing his show. This publicity piece, including pictures and descriptions of the people who had starred in his various exhibitions, devotes considerable attention to Martha. Cummins's description of her is noteworthy for its inaccuracy, asserting for example that she had been a spy during the Civil War, passing as a male by wearing men's garments. The booklet's photograph of Martha, taken at the Exposition, reveals an aging and sober-looking woman, perhaps unhappy in her new environment.[34]

One of Martha's Montana friends, W. H. (Wirt) Newcom, was among the Exposition visitors. As Newcom entered the grounds with his eastern relatives, they heard shooting. Newcom recalled one family member exclaiming, "O, that is the Wild West show. Do you want to go in there with us? They have that wonderful woman with the show; I think they call her Calamity Jane. Did you ever hear of her in the west?" When Newcom admitted that he knew her, the family insisted he introduce them. Newcom said he "tried to explain that 'Jane' was a bit rough," but his relatives would not listen.

Newcom rated the show "very good." When Martha tore into the ring on horseback in her buckskin outfit she "stole the show," he said. Afterwards, he reluctantly steered his relatives toward her living quarters. When Martha saw him, she immediately yelled, "Slim. Old Slim from Miles City. Damn my skin, if it ain't. Where in h—— did you ——?" Newcom hushed her, explaining that his relatives were church-going people. Then he introduced them:

> Never will I forget poor old Jane, and never was I more amazed at any change of front in a person; never could you imagine it could by any chance be the same person I had just met in the rough, boisterous way. I stopped sweating blood. I was too delighted with her and she was as polite as any one of the party and entertained them all royally for fifteen or twenty minutes.

She also told Newcom about her problems with Brake. Martha doubted she could survive the restrictions Brake had imposed on her drinking.[35]

In fact, the strained relationship between Martha and Brake had reached a breaking point. According to one newspaper, "Jane found that she could use money, even on the Midway, so she broke with the peaceful home, the novelist, and the assured comforts for old age, repudiated the contract made for her, and made a new one with the managers of the show." By negotiating independently with Cummins, Martha "got real money" and escaped the philanthropist's regulations.[36] Afterwards, Brake no longer played a role in Martha's personal affairs, although behind the scenes she continued efforts to get a government pension for her.

In a week Martha returned to old habits. "Alas, 'Calamity Jane,' The Aged Celebrity, Overcome by Liquor, Arrested, and Released on Suspended Sentence," declared the Buffalo newspaper. "Mrs. Mattie Dorsett, the original 'Calamity Jane,' of Wild West fame," was discovered by a patrolman near the Exposition gate "reeling from side to side." Although Martha spent the night in jail, the next day she was given a suspended sentence. To her presumably naive audience, she explained that "it was the first time she had ever been arrested."[37]

Newspapers in Montana gleefully reported the predictable result of the receipt of her first paycheck. The *Livingston Post* reprinted the colorful account in the *New York Sun*: after receiving her pay, Martha "passed out of the grounds. Across from the gates the door of a saloon stood invitingly open. Jane passed in."[38] The sequel was familiar: "What Jane does in saloons is a matter of history—it need not be reported," commented the Livingston journalist.[39]

Although this time Martha received a suspended sentence, further leniency was not assured. The next day, when an Exposition guard "attempted to interfere with her personal liberty," he "was sent spinning on his head."[40] After another saloon engagement, during which she made "the atmosphere blue," she was "admonished to sin no more" by the court. One spree resulted from a broken relationship. Martha reportedly fell in love with Frederick Darlington of Batavia, New York. Realizing "the hopelessness of her passion," however, she spent three days shut in her room. When this confinement failed, she "went on the warpath in regular frontier style and made things lively around the Indian village." The spree ended only when Darlington returned. Afterwards, there were rumors the two might marry.[41]

But Martha evidently went to English Centre, Pennsylvania, instead. There she visited Byron Hinckley, an old friend from the West. Hinckley had extended her an invitation when he attended the Exposition. Her four-day visit coincided with the burning of a horse stable. According to Hinckley, Martha had become especially fond of a chestnut horse that had to be killed because of severe burns. The next morning, she was in an apologetic mood. She told Hinckley that once she visited a fortune-teller who told her, "No matter how evenly your life stream seems running, suddenly it dams up, there will always be death, fire and ruin wherever you are." Mournfully, Martha added, "I couldn't even keep my child with me." Although Hinckley never blamed Martha for the fire, her comments implied responsibility and she left shortly afterwards.[42]

In fact, Martha had decided to leave the East permanently. Newspapers in Montana reported her desire to return, but said she was short of funds. She hoped William F. Cody, scheduled to arrive in Buffalo soon with his show, might help her. After each of her public appearances, it was reported, she inquired about Cody, a needless query since newspapers publicized that Buffalo Bill's Wild West show would arrive on August 26.[43]

The "Great Parade of Buffalo Bill's Show" occurred as scheduled. Cummins's Indian Congress joined the procession, but accounts of the parade do not mention Martha.[44] Instead, newspapers reported that, upon Cody's arrival, "a very tired and despondent looking woman pushed aside the curtains" of his tent. It was Martha who told Cody, "They've got me Buffaloed, and I wanter go back. There's no room for me in the east. Stake me to a railroad ticket and the price of the meals, an' send me home." Cody purchased her a ticket, adding twenty-five dollars for food. Afterwards, reported the newspaper, "Calamity Jane disappeared, and it is supposed she is using the ticket."[45]

A year later, Cody recalled his visit with Martha. She "was anxious to leave Buffalo," but needed money. The Buffalo police were just as anxious to get rid of her, added Cody, "for her sorrows seemed to need a good deal of drowning, and she got into lots of trouble." He helped her out: "Well, of course, she was one of the pioneers. For old time's sake, you know———."[46]

Martha's departure from Buffalo occurred shortly before McKinley was scheduled to arrive for President's Day. Cummins's Indian Congress planned a special performance in his honor.[47] However, on Friday, September 6, while McKinley spoke on the Exposition grounds, anarchist Leon Czolgosz shot him. Eight days later the president was dead. It was reported Czolgosz was inspired by Emma Goldman, an anarchist leader, whose lecture he attended earlier in Cleveland. These events inspired one Montana correspondent to quip, "Calamity may not be possessed of all the feminine graces, but she is a better citizen than Emma Goldman any day in the week."[48]

Meanwhile, Martha had traveled to Chicago, where she was "stranded." Probably she had squandered Cody's gift to purchase alcohol. Needing funds, she contracted to appear at a dime museum in Chicago. When a Billings acquaintance discovered her there, she "embraced him as if she had found a long lost brother." Imploring him to help her, Martha said the New York woman had secured her "for exhibition purposes" and not for the purpose of providing her a life of comfort.[49] Not mentioning Cody's help, Martha said she had contracted with the dime museum in Chicago to "accumulate enough money to pay her railway fare back to Montana."[50] However, Martha found it difficult to gather the needed funds, and her return to the West was made only in small installments. She next was advertised as an attraction at the Palace Museum in Minneapolis, where a theatrical publication advertised: "Hear Calamity Jane tell of her wild life fighting Indians on the frontier."[51]

In an amazing coincidence, while standing at the corner of Nicollet Avenue and Second Street in Minneapolis, Martha encountered the very reporter who had pretended to be Brake's cousin a few weeks earlier. He audaciously asked her for another interview. "Not in a hundred years," she shouted, calling him a liar and pounding him with a "storm of invectives." A crowd gathered and a policeman had to intervene so Martha could continue her way safely. The newspaper reported the journalist's reaction: "Wh-e-w! Guess that's about near enough to get to her. Thought sure she was going to strike me."[52] Martha evidently left Minnesota shortly after this confrontation.

Montana newspapers, noticing Martha's slow but steady progress toward home, predicted her arrival there within a week or two. But Martha disappeared. Impulsively, she had decided to visit earlier haunts in Pierre, South Dakota. "Calamity Jane is back for a visit at her old stamping grounds when Pierre was the jumping off place for civilization and west of it was hostile country," reported a local newspaper in early November. "The old timers who she is looking up mostly agree that she is the genuine Jane who lived here twenty years ago," although, it added, "there are those who are doubtful and claim that the original Jane is dead."[53] Pierre's journalists seemed surprisingly ignorant concerning Martha's recent adventures in New York, assuming she had come "from the Hills country." A Fort Pierre reporter learned that Martha intended to remain for the winter.[54]

For a while, Martha led a "very quiet and unobtrusive life" in Pierre, reported the newspaper, but that soon changed. She "evidently does not want the public to get an idea that she is tottering over the precipitous verge of toothless decrepitude and aged decay merely because she is not so young as she used to be," wrote a Pierre journalist. After drinking "a quantity of hopified elixer," she decided to make life interesting, assaulting one fellow "with a yard or so of pyrotechnic billingsgate and vituperative epithets, which she uncoiled with the glibbest of tongues and which will make his hair crimp when he thinks of it ten years from now." The Pierre correspondent concluded, "Since her tea parties are not of the kind to meet the unqualified approval of the best society of Pierre, since it became the capital of the state, it is hoped that she will confine her operations to a limited area."[55]

"Still on Earth," announced the Livingston newspaper upon learning of Martha's escapades in Pierre. "Several weeks ago the newspapers from Buffalo to San Francisco were full of the doings of Calamity Jane," it said, but then news about her ceased. According to the paper, many people had been "inclined to think that possibly Calamity had changed her abode from earthly quarters to the ethereal regions," or that perhaps she had been given a lengthy sentence by an unsympathetic judge. But these assumptions proved "to be false alarms." Although Martha still intended to return to Montana, she remained in South Dakota for about six months.[56]

Years later, Pierre residents still remembered Martha's visit. Charles Fales recalled that she arrived wearing "feminine attire—long skirt, white waist and a monstrous flowered hat—then prevailing styles in the east."[57] Pierre photographer R. H. Kelly preserved this image of Martha Canary for posterity.[58] But her fashionable appearance belied her poverty and poor health. G. H. Grebe remembered her stealing a bottle of whiskey from a local bar. Afterwards, he said, she was laid up with broken ribs. Because of her condition, townspeople provided her with firewood that winter.[59] I. N. Walker, then a schoolgirl in Pierre, said Martha took up residence "in an old shack down near the river bottom where the poorer people lived." Usually Martha wore "an old pink gown" around town, recalled Walker, who thought Martha, when "properly dressed," looked about forty years of age. Walker perceived that Martha felt unaccepted by other women, mingling with them only if they asked her to work or help during illness.[60]

Other Pierre residents told of their personal encounters with Martha as well. Homesteader Fred L. Fairchild recalled seeing her in the Northwestern railroad freight office trying to convince the agent to let her have her bedstead, mattress, and chairs without paying freight charges. Fairchild thought her household items worth only a few dollars. When he left, Martha was sitting on the agent's knee, coaxing him to give her the items.[61] She provided further entertainment when she looked up former dance-hall friend Maggie Laughlin. Since her days in Deadwood, Maggie had reformed and married. According to Charles Fales, Maggie was entertaining a church group in her home when Martha, "drunker than a hoot owl," stopped to visit. Maggie hastily escorted Martha out of her house.[62]

Martha's stay in South Dakota may have been extended unintentionally. No railroad crossed the Missouri River at Pierre, meaning she would have to travel east and north before she could return to Montana. Severe winter storms and spring floods halted railroad traffic several times during spring 1902.[63] Perhaps due to this bad weather, Martha wandered through eastern South Dakota for several weeks. According to the *Sioux Falls Argus Leader*, she spent time in Huron and Aberdeen as well as in Pierre. She traveled by train, it said, riding in the smoking cars "where the smoke is the thickest and the drinks are passed the most frequently." The newspaper also observed she could "swear oftener and use more blood-curdling oaths in rapid firing order than any other heavyweight of her class."[64]

An Aberdeen reporter learned of her presence in town on March 14. While there, he said, she "gave none of the exciting exhibitions of recklessness which are said to have characterized her visits" elsewhere. Instead, "she remained quietly at a hotel except during a short time she spent drinking and smoking in a saloon." She attracted attention only because it was unusual to see a woman in a bar. The Aberdeen reporter thought Martha so aged that she was not likely "to do much more riding on the range clad in buckskin as a man nor participate in many more of the dare-devil escapades which are credited to her."[65]

Martha left Aberdeen on the westbound train. It is possible she next visited Evarts, a lively shipping point for cattle along the Missouri River north from Pierre. Ben Arnold, an old acquaintance who knew her in Virginia City, recalled meeting her there. At first not recognizing her because she "was old and haggard beyond her years," Arnold asked her questions to prove her identity. He called her Jane Somers, perhaps referring to the last name of one of Martha's early male companions. Arnold mentioned that she "carried photographs of herself dressed in buckskin costume, which she sold." He added that many of those she met "made small purchases and refused to take change, as they considered her a fit object of charity."[66]

While South Dakota newspapers reported Martha meandering through the eastern portion of the state, the Glasgow, Montana, newspaper of March 22 claimed that Calamity Jane was there. With the Glasgow woman was a "girl of about four years." Immediately after her arrival, this Calamity Jane stopped at the courthouse to request funds designated for the indigent. The county clerk, "who had the questionable pleasure of a previous acquaintance[,] gave her what is commonly known as 'the frozen face.'" However, a ticket was purchased for her to Great Falls, which she said was "her lawful home."[67] No record of Martha at Glasgow or Great Falls has been located, nor was she reported with a child at this time. Most likely the Glasgow Calamity Jane was a different woman.

Meanwhile, Martha arrived in Huron, South Dakota, on April 8. "'Calamity Jane,' of more or less early day fame at Pierre and in the Black Hills country, from '76 to '83, now owner of valuable cattle ranch interests in Montana and the northern Hills country, is in the city," the local paper announced.[68] Holland (Holly) Wheeler, who owned the pharmacy and general store, recalled Martha's visit to Huron. She stayed in a boxcar along the railroad tracks, he said. A family with five children, "all sick with the flu," also lived there and Martha stopped at his store to purchase medicine for them. According to Wheeler, Martha seldom drank, although she "was known to have an occasional cigar and hang out with farmers talking about crops in the saloon."[69]

After a few weeks in Huron and perhaps following brief visits to other communities, Martha reappeared in Aberdeen in mid-April. "She spent one day here," a reporter said, "and when it became known that she was in town there was much curiosity to see her, and not a few did call upon her." Still angry about her New York experience, Martha said she had been "badly cheated" by the "so-called charitable woman" who had taken her to Buffalo. Martha also regaled Aberdeen spectators with a new version of events about Wild Bill Hickok and Jack McCall. She and Hickok were planning to marry before he was shot, said Martha. Martha also claimed responsibility for McCall's subsequent indictment, trial, and hanging. Among her listeners in Aberdeen was an old-timer who had known her thirty years earlier. "She recognized him in an instant and expressed much pleasure in seeing him again," the newspaper reported. He verified her story of thwarted courtship and explained that he too witnessed McCall's hanging at the Yankton jail.[70]

But most pioneers found these fictitious accounts "amusing." One critic, interviewed by the *Sioux Falls Press*, contradicted everything Martha and the Aberdeen old-time had said. He noted, for example, that Hickok had no serious relationship with Martha, that the hanging of McCall did not occur in the Yankton jail yard, and that Martha was not at that event. He asserted that if Wild Bill were still alive, he would take umbrage at these suggestions, and the Aberdeen old-timer "might have time to drop to his knees and pray, but he would have to hurry." People should stick to the facts, the pioneer from Sioux Falls concluded, which "are doleful enough in any case."[71]

Martha probably had stopped in Aberdeen because it was the railway connection to Livingston, Montana, her destination.[72] She also had a layover at Oakes, North Dakota, the connecting point between the railroad systems of the Dakotas. According to the *Oakes Republican*, Martha was "not in a condition suitable for an interview" because she had spent about $30 in an Aberdeen saloon the day before and was "still showing the effects." Nevertheless, she offered to buy drinks. Her invitation was not accepted, the reporter asserted, causing her to remark that Oakes was "not the town" she thought it was. According to the newspaper, except for breakfast at a hotel, she spent the entire day in the men's waiting room in the depot smoking a cigar and left at midnight for Jamestown."[73]

The Jamestown newspapers reported events in Oakes differently, however. In these accounts, Martha was drinking in an Oakes saloon when "some of the boys" decided to "have a little fun with the 'old woman.'" Martha stood their derogatory comments for only a short time, then "pulled out a shootin' iron and the music began." She made them dance. When one tried to escape, she threw a billiard ball at him, commenting that, "she would tell him when school was out and he could go." The reporter also noted that, afterwards, Martha "said she enjoyed society in Oakes very much."[74] The only acknowledgment by the Oakes newspaper that any such event ever occurred was a later note that "Mack," presumably one of the boys, had "not forgotten his contact with Calamity Jane."[75]

The story of Martha's shooting exhibition in Oakes gained nationwide attention, and was often retold in a style reminiscent of dime novels. The *New York World*, for example, reported:

> She was on her way from Jamestown, N.D., to Livingston, Mont., when her birthday called for a proper celebration. This was in the cow town of Oakes. She drank much and in one saloon the cowboys began to chaff her.
>
> Calamity Jane smiled grimly and asked every one up to the bar. They howled. Two revolvers suddenly appeared in the woman's hands. She can "draw" as quick as any man who ever lived.
>
> "Dance, you tenderfeet, dance!" she commanded grimly, and she fired a few shots by way of emphasis.
>
> They danced, and with much vigor. They did other things that she commanded. Calamity Jane is not a person to be trifled with. The manner in which she shut up that saloon was powerfully convincing.[76]

When a reporter asked William F. Cody about events in Oakes he "smiled sadly," observing that "none of us on the frontier ever met any one like her." Martha shared both the merits and faults of the "old frontier types," he continued. But "there is no more frontier any more and never will be again, and that is why we like to look back, and why the few that remain of the old-timers we marched with and fought with have a warm place in our affections, whatever or wherever they may be." What Martha did in Oakes, he concluded, showed she remained "true to herself and the old days."[77]

Martha's stop in Jamestown, the next town on the railroad, was less newsworthy. A reporter for the *Daily Capital* found her "very willing to talk of herself and her checkered career," and learned she made her home in Livingston selling "curios and such" to tourists. "Sometimes she wears a buckskin suit . . . and people from the east think she is a 'b-a-d' woman with a big B," he added. However, the journalist himself saw "only a plain, medium sized woman with an unquenchable thirst" who enjoyed the public's attention. Another Jamestown writer observed that, although Martha claimed to have a ranch in Montana, she "dressed in ordinary clothing of a woman not possessed of any great amount of money."[78]

According to the *Jamestown Daily Alert*, Martha was not feeling well when she arrived in town. Nevertheless, it said, her eyes were "as keen as ever." Martha told reporters she had spent the winter in Pierre with broken ribs. In a tone similar to that sounded by Cody, Martha remarked: "Pierre is getting pretty tame." In fact, "all the west is getting tame nowadays—so different from what it was when I first came through this country." Because she was short of funds, a request was made to the county commissioners for money to purchase her a ticket to Montana.[79]

Martha's return to Montana continued to be interrupted with unscheduled visits, however. The *Mandan Pioneer* on April 18 mentioned her arrival there "to renew acquaintance with old timers with whom she was a familiar character in times when things were wild and wooly." As was her habit, Martha "proceeded to do things up brown as soon as she arrived and those who did not know of her presence in this vicinity were soon made aware of it."[80] She next stopped in Dickinson, where she accumulated "a jag of beautiful proportions and board[ed] for a time at Hotel de Sheriff Goodall."[81]

Finally, after nine months' absence, Martha reached Montana. The Billings newspaper observed that Martha, after having been in the "effete and pampered east," had learned that "only Montana and its snowcapped mountains and ozone laden prairies can appease her longings for nature, pure and untrammeled." As usual, it added, "among the first to be made aware of her return were the saloonmen. She called on a number of them."[82]

Martha told her drinking companions in Billings about her difficulties with Josephine Brake in New York. Cowboy Thomas Edgar Crawford remembered Martha relating how she sneaked from her room one day to a local bar. After having several drinks, she secreted a quart of whiskey in her clothing and took it back to her room. "It was not long before she started a roughhouse, which must have been lots of fun from the way she laughed while telling the story to me," said Crawford.[83]

Martha's excitement at being home was likely diminished after she was arrested on her first night back by "a cruel hearted policeman" for being drunk and disorderly. Although she was released in the morning, "her pride has been wounded and she finds herself disgraced," the Billings paper observed. It was hardly the kind of welcome a celebrity might expect after a lengthy absence. But the editor was unsympathetic. "Hard as it must seem to her, 'Calamity Jane' is learning that the old west, the west with which her name is linked, has been forced to give way to the west as the tenderfoot would have it," he explained. She would have to learn that "the freedom and ease of manners that prevailed in those 'good old days' are gone and conformity to accepted customs is now expected from everybody."[84]

Shortly after the Billings newspaper made its critical remarks, Martha left for Livingston. The poetic greetings from the newspaper there also carried negative undertones.

> Calamity Jane is home again from her wanderings far and wide; she longs no more for the eastern shore and the surge of the rushing tide; back to the hills of her stamping ground she has come to settle down, leaving the glare of the hated east for the mountains' restful brown. . . . Like the prodigal son she sings a song, a song of troubled verse, with a drink and a dirge, a curse and a prayer, a cow horse and a hearse. "The fatted calf was dressed for me," she sings in mournful strain, "but the husks have a greater zest for me, and I'm off for my stys again."[85]

Ignoring the press's remarks, Martha resumed her previous activities in the small communities near Yellowstone Park, where she faced less interference from law officers and the social elite. By May she was in Horr, then moved to Gardiner at the Park's northern entrance. "Calamity Jane, the notorious, drifted into Gardiner last week," announced the newspaper, and "emphasized her arrival in a manner peculiarly her own, and satisfied the average citizen that she was the original and genuine."[86]

While Martha was in Gardiner, a small-time thief named Richard Lee "performed the unmitigated, nervy and inhuman act of 'rolling' Calamity Jane," reported the Livingston paper.[87] According to one of Martha's friends, Lee stole the ring she claimed Wild Bill Hickok had given her; it was shaped "like a striking rattlesnake with several complete coils around the finger." Martha notified the sheriff who located the ring and arrested Lee.[88] But when the time arrived for Lee's arraignment, Martha failed to appear, "and as there was no evidence against the defendant he was discharged."[89]

Meanwhile, Martha returned to "her shack" in Gardiner, where she continued selling her autobiography to Park tourists. In late May, however, serious illness once again interrupted her activities. At the county's expense, she was taken by train to Livingston, where officials planned to place her in the Park County Poor Farm. But Martha refused. Deciding Livingston was no longer the place for her, "she borrowed enough money to buy a few drinks of whisky and a ticket to Lombard," the newspaper said. The county commissioners, it added, not wanting responsibility for her, chose to "place no obstacle in her way if she wants to leave the county."[90]

Martha missed the train, however, participating in one more spree in Livingston. After making her rounds through the saloons, she "had a jag aboard that would have taxed the capacity of an elephant, not to speak of a woman who is now cavorting around in the horizon of her seventieth sunrise," the newspaper reported. The editor's estimation of her age was long by nearly twenty-five years. When the police found Martha in a drunken slumber on one of the benches in front of the Albemarle Hotel, she was arrested. Soon, the newspaper said, she "was engaged in her old time occupation of playing checkers on a window grate at the county jail."[91]

After promising to leave town, Martha was released the next day. The Livingston paper hoped she would not come back "to this inhospitable clime for sometime."[92] Two weeks later, Martha surfaced in Lewistown. Acting as though she had just arrived from New York, she expressed "no use for the type of civilization encountered in the east." She then spent a couple of days celebrating "in true western style."[93]

From Lewistown, Martha took the stage to nearby Kendall. She "insisted on a seat beside Johnney Harvey on the front boot," the Lewistown paper reported, and tried to take the reins. "Johnney had to do some tall talking to keep the ribbons," it added. En route, Martha visited the saloon at Spring Creek station, there awaiting the afternoon coach before completing her trip.[94] She probably remained in the Kendall and Lewistown area that summer. By November, however, she had returned to Red Lodge near Yellowstone Park. "The famous female scout, Calamity Jane, arrived in the city last Saturday," announced the *Red Lodge Picket*, "and for the past week has been renewing acquaintances with the friends of early days over the flowing bowl." As she departed on the train for Billings, Martha admitted to friends that she was "not in the best of health."[95] A Billings reporter confirmed Martha's sickly appearance, adding that her New York experiences had "just about soured her on the human race."[96]

As Martha's health deteriorated, efforts once again were being made on her behalf. Josephine Brake, now in Chicago, was still trying to secure a government pension for her.[97] Many newspapers in the northern plains joined the campaign. Lewistown's *Fergus County Argus*, for example, believed Brake's effort should be supported by circulating petitions. These "would receive a hundred thousand signatures west of the Missouri river," the editor predicted. Also, Montana's congressional representatives should "render what aid they could in that direction." In fact, he suggested, if constitutional, "a small appropriation" for Martha should be granted by the state legislature. After all, despite her personal failings, she "was as brave and intrepid as any of the great Custer's troopers." He was certain the pension campaign would be championed by the public. When Martha recently visited Lewistown, people "stopped in crowds to gaze upon her," he said. For them, she revived memories of "the stirring events in which she was a prominent figure."[98]

But those against an annuity for Martha were equally persuasive. Whereas editors supporting a pension were enamoured of Calamity Jane's heroic legend, opponents emphasized Martha's faults as a woman. The *Lewistown Democrat* for example, said it was "an open question as to whether or not this frolicsome lady" deserved any financial consideration. In this editor's opinion, Martha already had received more than was justified. First, she had "unbounded freedom in her exploitation of those peculiar gifts which distinguish her from the average woman," he said. In addition, having had a "myriad of romances" written about her that assured "the perpetuation of her name in the temples of historical fame," she had been wined and dined "by those who looked upon her as a wild west heroine." The editor did not see that she deserved more.[99]

Nevertheless, the petition movement gained momentum. Among those signing were people "of influence and wealth," reported the Billings newspaper. But since the government already had rejected any subsidy for Martha (no records indicated that she performed military service), the petitions now being circulated asked the government to reverse its decision. Supporters realized that giving Martha an unrestricted stipend invited disaster, however, for she would simply spend the money on alcohol. "It is pitiable to see the old girl now on one of her twisters," said one. "She has worn ragged holes in her credit in every saloon from Glendive to Kalispell." To counter this difficulty, pension advocates urged that Martha be given "a guardian, just as if she were a child" and be given funds "only at such times as she is in actual want and when she guarantees that she will not spend it over the bar treating every sheep herder she meets." The difficulty with helping Martha improve her life, one petitioner remarked, was that "you might as well try to make a pet out of a timber wolf. She has been foot-loose all her life, and the quickest way to break her heart would be to take away her peculiar and eccentric ideas of liberty."[100]

But advocates for a government annuity did not gain their point. Moreover, despite pervasive images of the legendary Calamity Jane that caused many westerners to forgive Martha's current sins, their sympathy had limits. Increasingly, she was viewed as a burden to society, an unwelcome holdover from the frontier past. She was more acceptable in memory than in reality. This situation was difficult for Martha to accept, for she too was captivated by romantic notions of the past and expected to be treated as a celebrity.

These arguments about Martha's legacy would resurface a year later when she died in Deadwood. Editors, acquaintances, and casual observers once again would attempt to assess her role in history. Meanwhile, Martha was about to embark on her last journey.

CHAPTER THIRTEEN

Death in the Black Hills, 1903

"Jane On The Warpath," declared the Billings newspaper on November 21, 1902. For no apparent reason, "save that suggested by a mind more or less disordered by too free indulgence in her favorite tipple," Martha attacked a young store clerk in Billings. With hatchet held high, she threatened to chop the woman to pieces. Although the reporter thought Martha might have intended her threat as a practical joke, the victim did not appreciate her humor. Another salesperson disarmed Martha and escorted her out of the store. Surprisingly, no formal complaint was made. After Martha made another disturbance the next morning, however, she was arrested. The reporter predicted the judge would sentence her to a long stay in the county jail to give her sufficient time "to get the liquor out of her system."[1]

Observers in Billings had noticed Martha becoming more unruly the past few weeks. "The sad truth of the matter is that Jane has been drinking quite freely of late," explained one journalist. Breaking a vow of total abstinence she had made that summer, Martha returned to old habits during the fall political campaign. When she boarded the Republican election special to Columbus, mainly for free drinks and companionship, Martha already had "a good sized jag." She also drank heavily in Laurel and Red Lodge before returning to Billings. Ever since, the paper added, she had continued to imbibe heavily and some of her friends feared "age and strong drink" had affected her mind.[2]

The newspaper's prediction that Martha would be given jail time was accurate: the judge sentenced her to sixty days, hoping to give her "time to recruit up, as she is in a bad way physically."[3] Martha did not serve her full sentence, however. When she complained of sickness, a physician was called and she was diagnosed with severe rheumatism. As a result, Martha was sent to the hospital. Having survived "all kinds of enemies, from Indians to sutlershop whiskey," a Billings reporter commented, Martha finally was "compelled to lower her colors to a foe as silent as he is merciless—disease."[4]

After regaining her health and sobriety, Martha was given her freedom. She immediately resumed drinking, however, and soon was "in a condition which those addicted
to the use of the language of the street would designate as 'jagged,' but which a lady of
her own refinement would probably describe as 'overcome,'" the newspaper commented.
Deciding that Billings "had become too much of a tenderfoot town," Martha told a
reporter she was going to return to the Black Hills, "where she had friends and . . .
would be appreciated for her real worth." Following her pledge, Martha boarded the
Burlington train on December 12 and left Montana forever.[5]

The "noted female character" made it only to Sheridan before she once again
"loaded up on whiskey and remained drunk several days," the Billings newspaper
learned.[6] The Wyoming community was aware of her reputation for causing a ruction.
The Sheridan editor teasingly commented after Martha registered at the hotel, "The
management of the hostelry are polishing up their guns and imploring the marshal for
protection."[7] The townspeople were probably happy that Martha immediately resumed
her trek to the Black Hills. When she boarded the train all she carried was a small
satchel, according to Burlington railroad conductor Dick Nelson. She rode in the men's
smoking car, "poorly dressed, dirty and unkempt, and down in the dumps." She claimed
friends had given her a ticket, but could not produce it. However, when her identity
became known, several passengers took a collection, paid her fare, and gave her some
cash for expenses.[8] After a brief stop in Custer, she continued by train to Deadwood.[9]

"Calamity Jane Returns," announced the *Deadwood Evening Independent* on December
15. The reporter, who referred to her as "the leading western scout," said old-timers
remembered her with gratitude, for they were "never turned from her door hungry as
long as she had food." Martha was wearing a brown derby, the reporter noticed, and her
face had more wrinkles than previously. He also commented on her "noticeably slender
figure," suggesting Martha might have lost weight since her previous visit. Nevertheless,
the reporter said, she was "the same Jane as of old."[10] A writer for the *Deadwood Pioneer-
Times* was not as generous. "Age is telling on her, and her hair is becoming streaked with
gray," he said, "and she is not the same vivacious Jane of years agone." Martha informed
the reporters that after she visited "old friends," she might return to Montana.[11]

As was her habit, Martha interrupted her stay in Deadwood with visits to neighboring communities. Local newspapers duly reported her departures and returns. "Mrs.
Burke, alias 'Calamity Jane,' was a passenger on last evening's outgoing train, after looking
over the city for several days," the *Evening Independent* stated on December 19. She
returned on Christmas Day "to spend a few of the holidays in her favorite resorts."[12]
One of her drinking sprees gained widespread attention. A dispatch from Cheyenne
on January 7 to the *Denver Post* noted that Martha was again "on the rampage." This
surprised the journalist because he thought she had been living "a life of quiet respectability" since her return from New York. In fact, he continued, "the public had almost
forgotten her when she broke loose in celebration of the glad Christmastide." However,
these antics were no longer acceptable, and "Jane finds herself in the lock-up, where she
is now, and scheduled among the plain drunk."[13]

A few weeks later, Martha journeyed to the town of Belle Fourche, located immediately north of the Black Hills. The *Belle Fourche Bee* on January 15 announced her intention to live there permanently: "She says she is tired of travelling and desires to locate somewhere, where she can lead a quiet life, earn her living in an honorable manner and spend the balance of her days in peace and quiet." With her, the *Bee* said, was her daughter. The circumstances of her daughter's arrival in Belle Fourche remain unknown. Instead of describing Jessie, the newspaper advertised Martha's need for a job. She could do "washing, cooking or nursing," it asserted, and hoped to "support herself and daughter in a proper manner." Martha's abilities as a nurse received especially favorable recommendation from the newspaper. "When others passed by on the other side, she, of her own accord, visited the sick and took care of them."[14]

Belle Fourche, a shipping point for cattle, was filled with cowboys. These reminded Martha "of old times, then getting pretty tame in other places," remarked Dora Du Fran, the brothel madam who hired Martha as cook and laundress. According to Du Fran, Martha arrived in Belle Fourche with everything she owned "in a dilapitated old suit case." It included only her buckskin outfit, two calico dresses, and some underwear. Like the newspaper, Du Fran praised Martha for her "many hundreds of deeds of kindness" accomplished without pay and in a disapproving society. Having grown up without guidance and among bad associates, Martha was "a product of the wild and wooly west," said Du Fran, and "was not immoral; but unmoral."[15]

Another Belle Fourche resident, Samuel G. Mortimer, remembered Martha stopping at his hardware store. As soon as she heard his name, she asked if he was related to the George Mortimer she had known in Montana. When he confirmed that George, now dead, was his father, Martha warmed to him. She informed Mortimer that she "was going to do laundry work for the girls in the Red Light District," but needed equipment. Mortimer provided her washtubs, a flatiron, and other necessities. She made small payments to Mortimer as she received her wages. However, Martha missed payments when she began drinking again. According to Mortimer, "When she was 'in her cups,' she was pretty much of a nuisance . . . and swore like a trooper." These drinking sprees always left her broke and repentent, he said. Then she would ask Mortimer for a small loan to purchase food and other necessities. She repaid all her bills except for three dollars still due when she died, Mortimer recalled.[16]

Dora Du Fran also remembered Martha's drinking sprees. Martha had remained sober about six weeks when "the old urge overcame her good resolutions," Du Fran said. The day after payday, no breakfast was served at the "boarding house." In the distance, Du Fran heard Martha's "wild howls." After celebrating for five days, Martha returned to work.[17]

According to Du Fran, Martha always began her drinking sprees by donning "her buckskin suit, high-heeled boots and Stetson hat, a wide ammunition belt and two forty-fours, holstered at each side." Although Martha never shot anyone, said Du Fran, she scared people by drawing her guns "when in a peevish fit." However, she was easily pacified. An apology and a drink "made her forget any differences in a moment."[18]

Martha preferred hard liquor to beer, recalled Du Fran. When ordering a drink, she always exclaimed, "Give me a shot of booze and slop her over the brim." She would drink until she reached the "howling stage." Since "nothing could quell the howling completely," said Du Fran, one of her friends "would escort her home with a quart of whiskey hugged to her breast to act as a night cap and put her to sleep." Her sprees often lasted for days. If someone was sick, however, Martha would stop drinking and within a day be at work. But, said Du Fran, "about six weeks was her sober limit."[19]

According to Du Fran, one of Martha's drinking sprees in Belle Fourche ended prematurely after a practical joke by her cowboy friends. While Martha was sleeping, the cowboys powdered her face with charcoal. Unaware of her new appearance, Martha wandered into the post office. The clerk, fearing a robbery, fainted. The postmaster scolded Martha so severely that she decided to sober up, said Du Fran, and "peace came once more to the city."[20]

Martha worked at Du Fran's establishment only about a month. In early March, the *Belle Fourche Bee* reported that she "pulled out for a ranch," where she had "obtained employment for the season."[21] Martha later explained to a reporter that she had cooked at "a Belle Fourche hotel," but the work was "rather hard" for her at her age and she quit.[22] It is a reasonable explanation. In fact, rather than immediately going to work on a ranch, Martha traveled to Hot Springs in the southern Hills. Although she told the newspaper she was there to visit old friends, the town was noted for its healthful baths.[23] The warm mineral waters would have soothed aches and pains symptomatic of rheumatism, and one newspaper confirmed that she spent "a few weeks for her health" there.[24]

Martha could not stay away from liquor, however, even while recuperating. John Stanley, later editor of the *Lead Daily Call*, recalled being in Hot Springs carrying important papers to the courthouse when a friend told him Calamity Jane was at the Bodega saloon. They ought at least to to "get a glimpse of her," the friend told Stanley. When they entered the saloon, Martha greeted Stanley like an old acquaintance, even though he had never met her before. She was wearing her "early-day buckskin garb, with red belt and cowboy hat," he remembered. As Martha shook Stanley's hand, she grabbed his papers, returning them only after he bought a round of drinks for the house.[25]

Shortly afterward, Martha left for Rapid City, where she decided to remain several weeks to attend the city's carnival. The newspaper termed her visit "particularly fortunate" because Calamity Jane was "one of the most widely celebrated characters in the west" and would enhance their April festivities.[26] Health problems continued to plague her, however. She became sufficiently ill to require medical attention. The nature of her illness is unknown, but Dr. R. J. Jackson said that when Martha came to see him, she was in "bad shape" and "beyond help," so he gave her "some harmless medicine" and sent her on her way.[27] When she recovered, Martha returned to Deadwood. Before she left, she announced her intention to come back to Rapid City for the celebration.[28]

The Rapid City newspaper advertised the eleventh annual meeting of the Western South Dakota Stockgrowers' Association and accompanying "carnival of western sports" as the "Biggest Event of Years." According to the paper, the town "was decorated from stem to stern and everybody was out for a good time." There were roping contests, cowboy races, dances, a parade, concerts, and orations. But Martha failed to appear.[29]

Perhaps Martha had gone to work at a ranch outside the Hills, as she had planned. In mid-June, she surfaced in Sundance, Wyoming. Her trip there from Aladdin, colorfully related in the Deadwood newspaper, was probably typical of her other travels. Riding in a hack with a young driver, she accosted bystanders with requests for whiskey or cigars. She surprised two young men playing cards near their herd of horses, shouting, "High, low Jack and the game," and "Got a bottle?" When they responded negatively, she asked for a "smoke," and when they again said they had none, requested a "chew." "One of them produced a plug of Climax and she took a chew that would make a Kentuckian ashamed of himself." Her seventeen-year-old driver had "a novel experience to relate afterwards," said the paper.[30]

It was Martha's first trip to Sundance. Storekeeper William R. Fox remembered her as a plain woman who looked nearer to eighty years of age than her actual forty-seven. "Dressed in a dark-colored garment of poor material; her stringy gray hair twisted into a careless knot at the nape of her neck; her skin wrinkled and sallow, she was indeed an object of pity," he said. Apparently believing she was entitled to handouts because of her own generosity, Martha "had no scruples about asking for anything she wanted." She took a room in the vacant American House hotel; Fox supplied her with furniture from his store. Others provided a stove, groceries, and spending money. Finally, the seven saloons in Sundance "furnished her with whiskey all the time she lived there," Fox recalled. Not surprisingly, he remembered her "groggy with liquor most of the time." To his dismay, she made his furniture store her "loafing place." Fox ignored her "fabulous stories of the early days," which differed little, he said, from the tall tales he had heard many times before. According to Fox, Martha claimed she was in Sundance looking for her husband, who was supposed to be living there. This story he also discounted because "she had claimed so many different men as her husbands."[31]

Barbara Henderson Fox, a youngster at the time, vividly recalled Martha striding down the street with a "five pound lard pail full of foaming beer." Unlike William Fox, Barbara found Martha appealing. She admired the "careless grace" of the tall, gaunt, good-looking woman who bravely ignored town gossip. "The fact that she would have nothing to do with the women of the town added to her attractiveness." Martha also lived up to her reputation for kindheartedness, attending to an old freighter at his deathbed. After he died, Barbara remembered, Martha sat beside his body all night "while she drank quantities of beer and wept copiously."[32]

Several weeks later, without giving notice, Martha departed. Once again she drifted through various Black Hills communities. Dora Du Fran recalled a "last big spree" in Belle Fourche that summer. When Du Fran wrote her book in 1932, she could "still remember the wild yells" Martha made "as she topped the hill," riding behind a cowboy heading for Spearfish. Martha had another three-day spree in Spearfish, said Du Fran, then "caught a ride to Deadwood on the Spearfish stage."[33] Confirming Du Fran's recollection, the Spearfish newspaper on July 8 reported that "Calamity Jane, the one and only, really and gracious Calamity, blew in from Belle Fourche Monday and is telling her old Spearfish friends what she thinks of them."[34] Afterwards, Martha visited Lead. There the police invited her "to take a hike," reported the newspaper, and "she compromised by taking the first train she could catch that was headed for Deadwood."[35]

Martha chose an auspicious time to return to the city that had become linked with her name in dime novels. The National Editorial Association had selected Deadwood as a point of interest on its annual excursion and town leaders wanted to make a positive impression. The editor of the *Daily Pioneer-Times* devoted nearly two columns of space in the July 12, 1903, paper touting Deadwood's attributes, including its schools, churches, and industries. His editorial, entitled "Coaching the Editors," admonished citizens to downplay Deadwood's "Old West" image. The visitors "will expect to find the Deadwood of romance of twenty-five years ago," he wrote. Instead, they should discover that "Wild Bill sleeps peacefully in Mount Moriah cemetery," and because bad men no longer shoot up the town, "the county jail and city calaboose are . . . largely ornamental now."[36]

By coincidence, Martha, a living reminder of the town's frontier period, appeared in Deadwood as the editors visited town. Traveling to Deadwood by train, she rode in "the men's smoker." When word circulated of her presence, many of the journalists filed through to see her. Although "she is not as robust nor as picturesque as she was ten or fifteen years ago," the *Daily Pioneer-Times* reported, "she possesses all her original traits and characteristics." Noting the visiting editors' fascination with Martha, the Deadwood paper quickly changed its tune, praising her as a reminder of the city's gold rush days and calling her "one of the truly unique characters of the West." To its surprise, the newspaper learned that Martha's daughter, now married, was living in North Dakota and had two children. "It seems rather odd to think of Calamity Jane as a grand-mother," said the reporter, "but she says it is true nevertheless."[37] The reporter may have misunderstood, however; no evidence has surfaced that shows Martha ever had any grandchildren.

Shortly after Martha's Deadwood visit, the *Rapid City Daily Journal* reported that the "distinguished, notable and typical plains woman of '76 fame" was again their guest. Her presence attracted considerable attention. A Rapid City reporter noted, "There is hardly enough rubber now in people's necks it seems to allow them to stretch it far enough to get a good look at Jane."[38] A few days later, Martha returned to Deadwood for what would be her last visit. There, John B. Mayo, owner of a liquor business and an amateur photographer, took a memorable photograph of her standing next to the grave of Wild Bill Hickok, further mingling the pair in popular imagination. Mayo said he first asked her for this favor when he met her at a saloon in Sundance. Martha agreed, explaining she would be in Deadwood after July 4. A week later, Mayo, accompanied by Jake Kump, a boarder at his home, searched for Martha in Deadwood's saloons and flophouses. Finally locating Martha "in the shade sitting on a keg behind a saloon," the two men proceeded to the cemetery with the inebriated woman. Mayo proposed hiring a hack, but Martha, he recalled, insisted on walking, exclaiming, "Anytime I can't walk up there to lay a rose on poor Bill's grave, I'll let yuh know it. Come on." Their path took them up a rather steep trail and across a ravine. "I sweated blood getting Jane across that canyon," Mayo recalled. "Jane was woozy, panting, and weaving as she plodded along on the high track, which was nothing but a narrow bridge, and we had our hands full of equipment. I half expected her to take a header off the trestle into the gulch bottom."

After reaching Mount Moriah Cemetery, Mayo still had a difficult time getting his photograph. "The grave had an iron rail fence around it and the gate was locked," Mayo remembered, "so I decided to take a picture of Jane standing in front of the grave holding the flower that I brought along." While Mayo positioned the camera and adjusted the lens, Martha, he said, "fell asleep on me—standing up." Next, she objected to Mayo's artificial flower. "What would poor old Bill think of [me] placing a phony rose on his grave?" she asked. After resolving this concern, Mayo put his head under the camera's cloth cover to recheck the focus, only to hear Martha exclaim, "What in hell yuh hidin' yer head for?" She had assumed he wanted to have his picture taken with her. "Any damn time I'm too old to have a picture taken with a young whipper-snapper, I'm too old to have any picture taken," she complained. To appease her, Mayo stood beside her and had his companion take the picture. Afterwards, he managed to get a picture of her standing alone by the gravesite.[39]

Charles Haas also photographed Martha that summer, although under entirely different circumstances. As he walked down a street in nearby Whitewood to a family gathering, he met Martha, who noticed his camera and asked him to take her picture. "I hopped off this old board sidewalk and took the picture," Haas recalled. Then Martha said, "Now how about a couple of drinks?" Haas agreed and the two went to Jackson and Gustine's saloon, an establishment she patronized regularly. His photograph depicts an aged, ordinary-looking woman, a stark contrast to the romanticized image captured by Mayo at Hickok's grave.

Nevertheless, Haas shared in that romantic view. While at the saloon, he decided to get a souvenir. "The saloon had those tokens that you paid with, and I thought I'd like to keep the token that I paid for her drink with," he said. When he switched tokens, Martha asked for an explanation. After he told her he wanted a remembrance of her, she responded, "Oh, that's very nice." Haas said he wore the token on his watch fob, along with a copy of the picture he took, for the rest of his life. "Lots of us in Whitewood, and here in Deadwood, too, knew the better side of Calamity," he said.[40]

Haas related several stories about Martha's charitable work to explain his positive impressions of her. He said a young grocery clerk told him Martha once entered his store with a basket on her arm; after filling it, she left without paying. When the clerk told the owner, he was informed that Martha could have whatever she wished because these were supplies for the sick or destitute. It was this reputation that motivated Haas to get a souvenir. Unfortunately, he added, sometimes Martha "would go to these bawdy houses and dance halls and it was whoopee and soon she was drunk and then, well, things just sort of went haywire with old Calamity."[41]

That Martha was ailing, as suggested by Haas's photograph, was confirmed by the newspaper. She had not been feeling well when she arrived in Deadwood, and, according to the reporter, announced "that she was 'going to cash in.'"[42] Still, she continued drinking.

While "fairly heavy with liquor," she joined several Burlington railroad men who were visiting on a street corner in Deadwood across from the Bodega Bar. Joe Hilton, an engineer, remembered that someone purposefully set her off by mentioning Buffalo Bill. She "started to give [Cody] a tongue lashing," because she had been "stranded in New York and was pretty mad about it." Martha then told the men she planned to go to Terry the next morning. Since Hilton was the engineer, he gave her instructions concerning when and where the train would depart. The next morning she was there waiting. "We got off the engine where Calamity was and we talked to her for a few minutes and we told her that when we pulled up to where she was, why she could get on," explained Hilton, "and that's the last I saw of her."[43] Hilton recalled that she had been drinking and looked terrible. Martha rode "on the last car of the ore train, a boxcar converted into a sort of day-car" usually used by the trainmen. Hilton liked to remember that it was he who "gave Calamity Jane her last ride."[44]

Martha arrived in Terry on July 24. Shortly thereafter, the *Terry News-Record* reported that "the heroine of many a lurid tale of the Black Hills, and whose name is interwoven with the early history of this region as a daring government scout and bull-whacker," was seriously ill. An acquaintance, H. A. Scheffer, took her to his hotel and arranged for Dr. Richards to see her.[45] She told several friends who called on her during the week that "all my old pards have gone over the divide and I am ready to go too." According to one reporter, Martha did not take kindly to the services of the physician—"and when he became impatient she was inclined to assert the old time vindictiveness and her weakened condition alone, kept her from adding another combat to her record."[46] Despite the doctor's efforts, Martha died on August 1, 1903, at 5:00 in the afternoon, of "inflammation of the bowels."[47] Undoubtedly, her life-long drinking contributed to her death. Although she was but forty-seven years of age, her appearance led some observers to estimate her age as seventy-three.[48]

According to the Deadwood newspaper, Martha had requested W. R. Monkman, editor of the *Terry News-Record*, to send her trunk, which she left in Spearfish, to Lottie Stacey, daughter of a Deadwood pioneer, at Belle Fourche. Monkman, who visited Martha in the waning hours of her life, may have been the source of much of the information in her obituary. This included the claim that Martha had a married daughter in North Dakota whose address she refused to divulge, alluding to "an estrangement." Monkman also was asked to make final arrangements. When death neared, he hurried to Deadwood to elicit the support of the Society of Black Hills Pioneers, which had been assisting with funerals of early settlers for several years. The *Pioneer-Times* soon reported that "F. X. Smith, one of the Pioneers, will go to Terry today to take charge of the remains" and the services would be held in Deadwood.[49]

Members of the Society of Black Hills Pioneers were not Martha's usual associates. Smith, Jack Gray, and J. W. Allen, for example, were highly respected citizens. But these old-timers remembered "her acts of kindness when there was no other woman in the gulch and when those in distress must have perished but for her thoughtfulness," the newspaper asserted. Accordingly, the Pioneers intended to give her "the best funeral their means [would] command."[50]

An embellished version of the funeral arrangements later appeared, reminiscent of earlier invented episodes in Martha's career. In this account, some of Deadwood's citizens were drinking together in Mike Russell's saloon when they learned of Martha's death. They "decided to give her a big last sendoff." The more they drank, the more elaborate their plans became. Soon "word was sent forth calling on all business houses to close during the services." Then came the momentous decision: where should she be buried? The inebriated party decided she should be buried next to Wild Bill Hickok: "Now Wild Bill had absolutely no use for Jane, but this distinguished self appointed committee decided it would be a good joke on the old boy to make him 'layup' with her for all eternity," the storyteller related.[51]

Instead, contemporary newspapers suggest that the decision to bury Martha near Hickok was made during her final days. "At her request," Deadwood's *Pioneer-Times* reported, "the remains will be buried in Mount Moriah cemetery at Deadwood beside those of William Hickok, 'Wild Bill' her former consort, who was murdered in Deadwood in 1876."[52] It is possible, however, that members of the Society of Black Hills Pioneers played a part in this decision.

Before Martha's funeral could be held, her body had to be transported from Terry to Deadwood. Reminiscences suggest it was a macabre trip. Her body was loaded into either a wagon or a buggy for the eight-mile trip. The driver evidently was accompanied by several of Martha's friends, and the party increased in numbers as the trip progressed. At least one, and perhaps several, unscheduled stops were made to celebrate her final journey to Deadwood. According to Mrs. John Traul, on at least one occasion the party delayed several hours at a saloon, leaving the body unattended in the wagon.[53]

Burial preparations were in the hands of C. H. (Charlie) Robinson, Deadwood's mortician, who worked with his father, Henry. Many years later, Charlie told how he had been called to prepare Martha's body for burial on an earlier occasion as well. The first time turned out to be a practical joke by the saloon crowd, always trying to find someone to purchase drinks. One of them had come to Robinson's door, telling him that his services were needed because Calamity Jane had passed away. When Robinson arrived at the saloon to tend the body, the local prostitutes were all present and having trouble keeping a straight face. According to Robinson, Martha was covered with a sheet, her hands folded across her body and her face covered with enough flour "to make a batch of biscuits." Realizing it was a prank, Robinson asked for a knife to determine if Martha was really dead. Martha immediately revived, yelling, "Dam you Jack, you ain't going to cut me full of holes. I'll shoot you, if you come near me." Despite his cleverness, Robinson was coerced into buying drinks for the crowd.[54]

When Martha's body was brought to Robinson after her real death on August 1, he said it would be available for viewing "for three days with someone by her side to protect the body from any harm."[55] According to one eyewitness, a guard was necessary because "numbers of curious women came to look upon her, and many clipped locks of hair from the head, to the extent of defacing the remains." In fact, this witness recalled, they had to use a wire screen to protect her head.[56] Robinson took at least two pictures of the body at the mortuary. He perhaps took a personal interest in the preparation of Martha's body; it was later claimed that Martha had cared for his younger sister in 1878 when she was terminally ill with typhoid fever.[57]

Martha's funeral was held at the Deadwood Methodist Church with its pastor, Dr. Charles B. Clark, preaching the funeral sermon. This was done, reported the *Daily Pioneer-Times*, despite the fact "Jane had not been a church goer and her life had been characterized by frequent debauches from church ways." The service on August 4 was packed with spectators and mourners, many of them old settlers. Her casket was almost concealed with "masses of floral offerings," reported the Deadwood newspaper.[58] The minister handled the difficult task charitably, emphasizing Martha's humanitiarian acts during Deadwood's early years. Echoing popular sentiment, Clark asked, "How often amid the snows of winter did this woman find her way to the lonely cabin of the miner" to help one suffering from illness? The minister predicted that when the history of the Black Hills was written in future years, "Jane Burke will, in all the deeds which kindness and charity dictated in those early days, be the heroine." After his message, several hundred persons viewed the body and the Deadwood band led the funeral procession to Mount Moriah Cemetery, where Martha was interred near Wild Bill Hickok.[59] According to Mrs. A. M. Workman, a Black Hills resident who attended the funeral, as the mourners returned to town, someone yelled, "Let's go and have a drink on Calamity." Before the day was over, many of those who had attended the funeral were drunk.[60]

Although no one at the time of Martha's death seems to have protested the location of Martha's grave, the family and friends of James Butler Hickok expressed their concerns shortly afterwards. Lorenzo B. Hickok wrote to Lawrence County officials to complain about the proximity of her grave to that of his brother. The clerk of courts, Sol Star, responded that the "records show that a lot was purchased alongside and outside of the lot (fenced) of your Brother's for the burial of Calamity Jane," assuring Lorenzo that "said lot does in no wise conflict or disturb the resting place of J. B."[61] Captain Jack Crawford lodged a more public protest several months later. He insisted that Hickok's name "should in no way be associated with Calamity Jane's." They met only a few weeks before Hickok's death, he said, and newspaper reports that her dying request was "to sleep by the side of the man she first loved" were, in his opinion, nonsense.[62]

In the days following the funeral, rumors abounded that one of Martha's husbands had attended the funeral, weeping copiously. Upon investigation, the newspaper learned that a man named Saunders declared "that he and Jane passed vows of eternal constancy upon their separation" when he was sent to the penitentiary in Michigan, and he "came back to the Black Hills to get her, not knowing she was dead." None of the Deadwood old-timers could remember the man and the newspaper unsympathetically pronounced him an imposter.[63]

The fake husband was not the only charlatan attempting to take advantage of Martha's fame. After her burial, the local "Hindoo seer" claimed that he had prophesied the time of her death "to within a week." She had visited him to have her fortune read, he said, and received his forecast with resignation. "I think you're right," he reported her as saying, "because I've felt since coming to the Black Hills this time that I probably wouldn't get away." The seer, who had been predicting profitable mining ventures for investors, now exploited Martha's death for advertising purposes.[64]

Befitting that of a national celebrity, Martha's death received widespread newspaper attention. Local editors dealt with Martha's controversial reputation in a variety of ways. The Deadwood newspaper commented that Martha Burke, "the 'Calamity Jane' of border fiction," was "one of the most unique feminine characters of the Western frontier" and "died as she had lived, in defiance of all traditions." The reporter then wove a fictionalized version of her western career. As a youth in Montana's gold fields, she was "slender and of a beauty that bewildered the western miners," he said. She was allowed to run free and became the familiar of freighters, hunters, and trappers. Then she enlisted in an expedition, "a step towards a career that few American women have equaled." The reporter repeated familiar stories about Martha serving as a scout and messenger for the army, living with Wild Bill in Deadwood in 1876, and capturing Jack McCall after he killed Hickok. However, he added new details to the latter event, claiming that when she cornered McCall with a meat cleaver from the butcher shop, she "would have severed his head from his body but for the intervention of bystanders." But, said the writer, Martha also displayed feminine qualities, and "constituted doctor, nurse, and cook to many of the miners who became afflicted with smallpox and other diseases." Because of this, he concluded, pioneers of the Hills "speak her name almost reverently."[65]

The Lead newspaper showed fewer romantic notions in its summary of Martha's career. It agreed that she had assisted in caring for the sick during an epidemic of fever in early Deadwood. But, it added, she "was never taken seriously by the people of the Black Hills" except when she was under suspicion of helping road agents. Most of the deeds attributed to her, the Lead editor explained, came from "the doubtful romancers of the east" who "allowed their imagination to run riot."[66]

Newspapers outside the Black Hills often used the Deadwood obituary as a source, but added local stories, material from other published accounts, interviews with people who allegedly knew her, and information of dubious origin. The *New York Times*, for example, featured her as the "Woman Who Became Famous as an Indian Fighter." It claimed she served with Generals Custer and Miles and also became "a carrier of the Government mails in those dangerous times, when men would not venture to make the trip across the prairies." As a result of her fame, the *Times* continued, "thousands of tourists went miles out of their way to see her," and "speculators fenced in her house and charged an admission fee to tourists."[67]

For its notice of Martha's death, the *London Star* interviewed William F. Cody, then touring in England. Cody accurately informed the London reporter that Martha never was employed by the government as a scout, although she sometimes accompanied the troops as a "mascot." He also told the reporter, "Whenever she could get hold of any whisky she was pretty sure to paint the town red." However, Cody continued with stories about Martha's career reminiscent of the dime novels. During skirmishes with Indians, "Jane was always up on the firing line," he asserted. But, Cody added, her "best work" was not accomplished during the Indian wars; it occurred when law officers asked her for help capturing criminals, a task at which she was eminently successful.[68]

Because Cody's name attracted readers and lent veracity, many newspapers cited his testimony. However, instead of using the recent interview in the London newspaper for information about Martha's career, editors turned to a version published a year earlier. In this account, Cody reported mistakenly that she first traveled west with her parents to Virginia City, Nevada, rather than to Virginia City, Montana. At the age of ten, he continued, she was separated from her father and brothers during an Indian attack. Eventually, she became a skilled frontierswoman. "Before she was 20 General Cook [sic] appointed her a scout under me," said Cody, after which "her life was pretty lively all the time." Exhibiting a touch of chauvinism, he added, "Though she did not do a man's share of the heavy work, she has gone in places where old frontiersmen were unwilling to trust themselves, and her courage and good-fellowship made her popular with every man in the command." He probably made the last comment tongue-in-cheek, for Cody knew Martha had been a camp follower.[69]

Inaccurate material from an 1896 summary of Martha's life in the *Chicago Inter-Ocean* also was perpetuated in many obituaries. Martha had taken part "in every lynching bee" in early Deadwood, it said, and saved the Deadwood stage when its driver, "Jack McCaul, was wounded by an arrow." Although none of the male passengers "had nerve enough to take the ribbons," she bravely drove the stage to "West Birch." After "McCaul" recovered, he murdered Wild Bill. Martha, using only a butcher's cleaver, captured the assassin and soon "McCaul's body was swinging from the limb of a cottonwood tree."[70] Through these obituaries, this false information about Martha's life was further perpetuated.

A chorus of voices joined these newspaper stories to help romanticize Martha's career. Only days after her funeral, a poem by George W. Hale dedicated to her memory appeared in the Deadwood paper:

> No more wild oaths, no pistol crack,
>> No games of death with mountain men;
> The broncho and the dear old shack,
>> I have no further use for them.[71]

Another poem, "Epitaph," written by E. P. Corbin, told of the enduring love between Wild Bill Hickok and Calamity Jane:

> In spirit land they have met and kissed,
> Billing and cooing over all they missed.
> Closed for aye, this earthen door,

Man must never open more.

Alas and alack, such love as thine

Wild, unchaste, in constancy almost Divine.[72]

These extravagant claims and romantic notions finally proved too much for Deadwood's newspaper editor. On August 23 an editorial headline pleaded, "Let them Rest." The editor insisted that neither the passing of Wild Bill nor of Calamity Jane, with their checkered pasts, was worth the great indulgence in maudlin sentiment then appearing. Because the first request of visitors to Deadwood was information on the pair, the topic had become a "red rag to the editorial bull," he admitted. He called for citizens to emphasize the more positive features of the town, exhorting them to let Calamity Jane and Wild Bill Hickok "rest in their graves." The editor concluded: "They are dead now and there was nothing in the lives of either with which to make a hero or point a moral."[73]

In support of its assessment, the Deadwood newspaper printed a critical account of Martha's career by M. L. Fox, who had interviewed her eight years earlier. Fox attributed the dead woman's notoriety entirely to "eccentric habits and 'penny dreadful' story writers," rather than to any heroic deeds. Although Fox allowed Martha was kindhearted and "ready to nurse the sick or give her last penny to anyone who needed it," she did not deserve her fame. She never served as a government scout, wrote Fox, nor had she "killed either an Indian or a white man." Instead, she was "an ignorant woman of most unwomanly habits" who frequented dance halls and saloons. Although she "dressed in the garb of a man, carried revolvers and a knife in her belt and a Winchester rifle," she was undeserving of "any notoriety beyond what I have stated," Fox concluded.[74]

Nevertheless, a few newspapers defended Martha. The *Rapid City Journal*, though admitting Martha's fame came about "only because she did so many things unusual for a woman to do," thought she deserved better press. "Calamity drank the wine of life, draining the cup to its dregs," but she nonetheless accomplished "many kindly, womanly things," and "when she stands before the Great Judge she will be on equal footing."[75]

Most newspapers in the northern plains supported Deadwood's editor. For example, Rapid City's *Black Hills Union* did not think Martha would be well received in the heavenly abode, as the *Journal* had suggested. In an editorial, "The Cup and Its Dregs," the *Union* challenged newspaper accounts about Martha's "charity, her goodness of heart and her glittering career." Instead, asserted the editor, her life "was one of wanton waywardness and debauchery." The *Union* had no sympathy with those who excused Martha's behavior as an effect of her social environment. In its opinion, her early life was no worse than that of thousands of other young women who managed to lead honorable lives. Martha, the editor continued, was simply a coward who avoided the truly "brave acts" of working, getting an education, and leading a respectable life. Even her humanitarianism was grossly exaggerated, for "thousands of virtuous girls" risked their lives nursing victims of contagious diseases or wounded soldiers on the battlefield without reward or notice.

The *Union's* editor gave a harsh tongue-lashing to those who had whitewashed the life of Calamity Jane. "The worst sample of the silly slush being published just now," he wrote, "is from the pen of some water-brained ninny by the name of George Walter Hale, of Central." Objecting to Hale's poem as "hero worship," the editor countered, "Ask the honest pioneer what Jane was famous for and he will tell you that she was noted for the amount of bad whiskey she could get away with and for being so low and debased that she was fit company only for dogs." Her "noble escort, Wild Bill," he added, also was "a good for nothing lout whose handsome person and cleverness at murdering innocent people gained him some dime novel notoriety." The editor concluded with a tirade against "the sort of scum that are held up to our girls and boys as being noble-hearted and heroic men and women whom unavoidable circumstances compelled to adopt the lives they lived. What rank falsehood! What puerile and nauseating stuff!"[76]

The *Gardiner (Montana) Wonderland* joined the *Union* in its caustic assessment of Martha. It announced her death with the headline, "Calamity Jane Finally Does the Proper Thing."[77] The newspaper in White Sulphur Springs, Montana, similarly was unwilling to concede any virtues to Martha. Its editor could not understand why her obituary was being published in most newspapers. He urged that the "facts" be considered. "'Calamity Jane,' as she was vulgarly and perhaps properly called, was a notorious prostitute who had lived in every town of the state as long as the citizens would allow her to," he asserted. She associated with "roughs, rogues, rounders, robbers and highwaymen," and "her natural haunts were in the red light or bad land districts." She never served as a scout, he added. In fact, the only thing Martha did to earn her notoriety was to "drink bad whiskey" and "use obscene, boisterous and indecent language." Condemning the adulation of Martha in the newspapers, the editor concluded, "If the press of the state cannot find a more respectable person to eulogize through its columns for the delectation of its respectable readers, better that it 'pi' its forms, throw its presses in the dump pile and embark in the cultivation of rattlesnakes."[78]

But even these formidable attacks on the legend of Calamity Jane could not stem the tide of romantic sentiment her death inspired. As the *Belle Fourche Bee* observed only a few days after her funeral, Martha "was buried beside 'Wild Bill' Hickok, one of her old consorts, in the cemetery at Deadwood, and now Deadwood will have a double attraction to exhibit to visitors from the east."[79]

CHAPTER FOURTEEN

Building a Legend, 1903–1953

For nearly two decades after Martha Canary's death in 1903, it seemed that she might be forgotten. Only sporadic stories were published about her and memorials commemorating Calamity Jane were uncommon. Except for her gravesite in Deadwood, there were few reminders of her activities in the West. Nevertheless, she continued to be remembered in local folkore. In Montana, Bill Huntington and his cowboy companions named a wild mare "Calamity Jane" after it dumped its rider into a cactus patch. And during the First World War, South Dakota soldiers in France fired the last artillery shot of the war from their cannon named "Calamity Jane."[1]

Published accounts of Calamity Jane, even though few in number, varied greatly. Some writers related wildly fictionalized stories about her; others insisted that her fame rested on flimsy foundations. The first story about Martha to appear after her death, W. G. Patterson's "'Calamity Jane,' A Heroine of the Wild West," was published in *Wild World Magazine* (1903), an English periodical targeting younger readers. Patterson's biography included several imaginary tales of Calamity Jane's heroic adventures. In one of his stories, Calamity is carrying the mail through a narrow pass in the hills when a mountain lion leaps on the shoulders of her horse. Fearlessly, she puts "the muzzle of a six-shooter right into the animal's ear" and shoots "the brute dead." In another of Patterson's tales, Calamity is pursued by two Sioux warriors. In the chase, her horse stumbles and breaks its leg. With only two cartridges remaining in her revolver, Calamity uses one to shoot her horse, then kills the closest Indian with the other. She bluffs the remaining warrior into surrendering by threatening him with her empty revolver.

Patterson related an even more impressive escape by Calamity when she was pursued by Black Elk's band of Indians. An "edict had gone forth in the Sioux camp" that Calamity must be captured, wrote Patterson. "She had shot too many braves, escaped too many ambushes, proved her intrepidity in too many ways, to make her a desirable person to leave longer at liberty." Shortly afterwards, the Indians give chase when they find Calamity removing a rock from her horse's hoof, but she gallops away, eluding them until she arrives at the edge of a cliff so steep it "would have scarcely furnished secure foothold to a Rocky Mountain goat." Still, Calamity once again escapes by finding a narrow trail down the cliff, and her pursuers decide she is protected "by the Great Spirit."[2]

Patterson's stories were too far-fetched to be accepted as genuine. However, similarly fictitious tales told by several of Martha's western acquaintances were assumed to be authentic. In *Adventures with Indians and Game* (1903), Dr. William A. Allen reminisced about an encounter with Martha near Spearfish in 1877. "As we passed up the valley," wrote Allen, "we were surprised to see a white woman riding toward us at full gallop." It was Calamity Jane carrying dispatches to Custer City, he said. She tells Allen that Indians are attacking a party farther up the trail and he leads his men to their rescue. Meanwhile, Martha continues her important trip through hostile territory. Like Patterson, Allen concluded that Martha's "daring intrepidity, her rapidity of movement and her deadly skill with firearms" caused Indians to believe she was "possessed of supernatural powers."[3]

Allen's tale about Martha, accompanied by a brief, inaccurate biography, circulated widely. Shortly after Allen's book was printed, his publisher, A. W. Bowen of Chicago, included Allen's account of Calamity Jane in its new reference work, *Progressive Men of the State of Wyoming* (1903). The editor evidently concluded that Martha's adventures were sufficiently masculine to warrant her inclusion among that state's leading male citizens.[4]

Some of Martha's acquaintances challenged these sensationalized accounts. For example, George Hoshier, one of the pallbearers at Martha's funeral, told a reporter that Martha never served as a scout nor engaged in gunfights. The only reason for her notoriety, he said, "was partly because she was always doing some crazy thing, and partly because she wanted to be notorious." Although he discounted all fanciful tales, Hoosier acknowledged Calamity's generosity. She was "a fine nurse," he said, and once helped a stranger who had smallpox in Deadwood when no one else would go near him.[5] Similarly, Judge W. L. Kuykendall, who had presided at Jack McCall's Deadwood trial, denounced tales of Martha's riding with outlaws and lawmen as fictitious. In his *Frontier Days* (1917), Kuykendall speculated that many of these stories emanated from fun-loving residents of the Black Hills spinning yarns to "eastern writers" foolish enough to believe them.[6] He would have been even more concerned had he been writing a few years later, when a flood of exaggerated tales about Calamity Jane poured out.

By the 1920s, Americans began looking back to the frontier period with increasing nostalgia. It was remembered proudly as a time when civilization overcame savagery. However, during that period America's rural-based values declined as industrialization, urbanization, and modern technology triumphed. Now it seemed as if American society was dominated by materialism. The popularity of legendary western figures reflected both of these themes. They were associated both with the conquest of the West and with fighting the greed and corruption associated with modernization.

The *New York Tribune* began an outpouring of stories about Calamity Jane in 1921 with journalist Josiah M. Ward's "A Wild West Heroine the Movies Overlook." Calamity Jane deserved to be featured in western films, Ward declared, because she was "the boldest, fiercest, tenderest, most unconventional and best known figure in the old west." In fact, she was "the only woman scout Custer ever had," and, except for Wild Bill Hickok, was the champion dead shot of the northern plains. In addition, Calamity could outride almost everyone on the western range, and was the terror of Indians, desperadoes, law officers, and bartenders alike. The only reason Ward could discover for her omission in films was that too many people thought she was a completely fictional character. He decided it was his duty to provide "some new lights on one of the old West's most picturesque figures" that might inspire movie makers.

Ward certainly cast new light on Martha's career. In her younger days, he said, she "was a beautiful woman of the purely feminine type" and "loved fine clothes and diamonds," the money for which she "won in gambling." Concerning her later career, Ward cited reminiscences by old-timers to prove Calamity was a member of Dutch Henry's gang, prospected for gold in California and Nevada, and died in Butte at the age of seventy-three. Ward also eradicated blemishes from her record. About the rumor that as a young girl she lived with the Gallaghers but later turned her back on her adoptive family and led a dissolute life, Ward countered that "there have been a number of bogus Calamity Janes, and Major Gallagher's protege was probably one of them."[7]

Other colorful accounts about Martha soon followed. A story in the *Casper Tribune-Herald* in 1921 asserted that women, as well as men, "played important parts in the building of the great empire west of the Missouri." The most famous of these, it said, was Calamity Jane. Casper resident John Fales described her for the reporter, but his portrait was entirely fictional, even though he had known Martha personally. She was "beautiful, of splendid physique, being more than six feet in height, with a clear complexion and raven black hair." Born in Pennsylvania, she had during her youth "many of the opportunities and refinements that graced the life of a gentlewoman," but left home after a romantic relationship ended painfully. Afterwards, said Fales, Calamity worked as a cowboy in Nebraska until her gender was discovered, then became a scout with Buffalo Bill.

Like the authors of dime novels, Fales described Calamity's use of "a variety of disguises" that made it difficult for even her closest friends to identify her. To change her appearance, she cut her hair short, wore false mustaches and beards, and dressed as a man. Once she dared a sheriff to try to handcuff her, and he left "with more haste than grace." On other occasions, Calamity wore an auburn wig, becoming dance-hall girl Nell King. In her feminine role, Calamity dropped "the roughness of her speech" and people "listened to her in rapt admiration, vaguely sensing the natural superiority of her intellect."[8]

Many accounts of Calamity Jane written in the 1920s associated her with Wild Bill Hickok, thus adding to her acceptance as a genuine heroine of the West. Filmmakers especially doted on this association between Calamity Jane and James Butler Hickok. As early as 1915, the Black Hills Feature Film Company of Chadron, Nebraska, produced *Wild Bill and Calamity Jane in the Days of '75 and '76*, starring local actor Freeda Hartzell Romine as Calamity Jane and A. L. Johnson as Wild Bill Hickok. In this film Calamity always wears a dress, even scouting in a buckskin skirt. Jack McCall, the archvillain, cheats at cards, robs stagecoaches, and salts gold claims. Calamity, beginning life as Jane Cassidy, lives with her mother in Butte, Montana. There Jane meets Hickok when he intervenes to halt unwanted advances by Jack McCall. Hickok again comes to the family's rescue when Jane's mother, a poor washerwoman, is unable to pay her rent. Eventually, Jane and Wild Bill are engaged to be married. At this moment, however, Hickok is summoned by General Custer to scout. Jane, unable to stand life without Hickok, secretly follows him and saves him from an ambush by Indians. Her bravery is rewarded with an appointment as co-scout. After Wild Bill and Calamity marry, they take military leave to prospect for gold in the Black Hills. In Deadwood, a vengeful McCall shoots Wild Bill; devastated, Jane weeps over his body. She then pursues legal channels to have McCall arrested in Yankton, where he is found guilty of murder and executed. This film's influence was limited by its localized circulation, but it inaugurated a trend in movies to romanticize the association between Calamity and Wild Bill.[9]

The first nationally distributed film to feature Wild Bill Hickok and Calamity Jane starred William S. Hart and Ethel Grey Terry. Although no copy of *Wild Bill Hickok* (Paramount, 1923) survives, the existing script shows that the relationship between Hickok and Calamity Jane was central to the film's plot. Calamity is in love with Wild Bill and for a while works as "lookout" when Hickok deals faro in a Dodge City saloon. But Hickok shows affection only for Elaine Hamilton, recently arrived from the East. Complicating the situation, Jack McCall, leader of an outlaw band, is in love with Calamity Jane and jealous of her feelings for Hickok. When Hickok learns that Elaine is married, he gives up women forever and leaves Kansas. Calamity, believing she can never gain Hickok's affection, rejects womanhood and begins wearing men's clothing, smoking, drinking, and gambling. During the Black Hills gold rush, Calamity and Wild Bill travel, coincidentally, to Deadwood. There, Hickok, who is going blind, suggests to Calamity that perhaps they might try life together. However, before they complete arrangements Hickok is killed by McCall. As the film closes, the tragic heroine is shown weeping over Hickok's body.[10]

Considerable screen license was employed in having Calamity Jane, Wild Bill, and Jack McCall meet in Kansas. The film also provided an imaginative motive for McCall's murder of Wild Bill and for Calamity's decision to act and dress in a masculine manner. However, the film's significance is not in its historical authenticity, or lack thereof, but in its promotion of an intimate and long-standing relationship between Wild Bill and Calamity.

Other tales about Calamity Jane that appeared in the 1920s also added to her status as a western heroine. Sioux Falls businessman Thomas Brown transformed her into a female Robin Hood. Brown claimed he witnessed Calamity Jane stealing groceries in 1866 in the Montana gold fields. It was an unselfish act, however, as the foodstuffs were intended for a sick miner.[11] Brown's tale, like stories of the Wild Bill–Calamity Jane association, was quickly accepted by other writers who, however, changed the time and location of the robbery to suit their needs.

Many popular tales then circulating about Calamity were collected by Jesse Brown and A. M. Willard, two Black Hills pioneers. In *The Black Hills Trails* (1924), Brown and Willard explained that because so many "fantastic yarns" had been told about Calamity Jane, they intended to "set forth a few of the real facts as to her life and picture her in her true light." However honorable the intentions of the two authors, they mostly printed unreliable reminiscences and fanciful stories.

Seizing upon an old newspaper article, Brown and Willard decided that Martha Canary had been born in Burlington, Iowa, in 1851 and that her father was a Baptist minister. In their account, she traveled to Sidney, Nebraska, with an army lieutenant; accompanied her mother and stepfather (named Hart) to Salt Lake City; became an inmate of bawdy houses in Rawlins and Green River, Wyoming; married a wealthy Denver man named White; joined various military expeditions in an unofficial capacity; and arrived in the Black Hills with General Crook in 1875 to remove miners.

Among the enduring tales Brown and Willard related was one involving a visitor to one of Deadwood's houses of prostitution. Afterwards, he discovered that he had been "rolled" and made complaint against Calamity Jane, who worked there. When Deadwood's justice of the peace asked Calamity whether she had taken the man's thirty dollars, she admitted to the theft. She "found the fool drunk under one of the tables," she explained, adding that she used the money to pay hospital expenses "for a young girl who was lying sick there without funds, or friends." The judge "promptly turned her free and scored the sporty gentleman who was so unwise as to carry money with him to a dive and expect to take it away with him."

Other stories collected by Brown and Willard told how Calamity Jane saved men from Indians. In one, "Antelope Frank" (also called "Buckskin Frank") was scouting with Calamity when Indians fired upon them. Frank's horse fell, leaving him afoot. Rather than escape, as urged to do by Frank, Calamity joined him in a buffalo wallow, exclaiming, "Damned if I will, Buck, I will stay right with you and we will see how many of those red——we can drop." Five Indians were killed, recalled Frank, "Jane having done her share of the execution."

Despite these descriptions of Calamity's heroic achievements, Brown and Willard concluded that she "was nothing more than a common prostitute, drunken, disorderly and wholly devoid of any element or conception of morality." Nor did they believe she was "the consort of 'Wild Bill'" because he was not the kind of man that was attracted to a woman of Jane's class." Nevertheless, they still believed she belonged in their list of important Black Hills personages because of her humanitarianism. The most important instance of her charitable nature occurred in 1878 when a "terrible scourge of smallpox" struck Deadwood and "hundreds were prostrated upon their rude beds." Other women in Deadwood would not help, fearing for their lives. "In the hour of terror and death, there came to the front, a willing volunteer, the mule-skinning, bull-whacking, and rough, roving woman from the depths, Calamity Jane." She cared for the sick "day and night" and "for week after week ministered to their wants or smoothed the pillow for the dying youth whose mother or sweetheart perhaps was watching and waiting for the one never to return." She did this, they said, without thought of reward or honor.

Martha's nursing activities became a cornerstone of the Calamity Jane myth. Besides her help during the purported smallpox epidemic, Calamity aided a family in Pierre stricken by black diptheria and nursed the Robinson child with typhoid, said Brown and Willard. Interestingly, they failed to cite any of the incidents mentioned in early Black Hills newspapers when Calamity was complimented for her charity.[12]

South Dakota author O. W. Coursey added that Calamity's humanitarianism applied to animals as well. When an abusive muleskinner with a government packtrain kicked one of his mules "viciously with his heavy army boots," Calamity Jane, who "stood near, dressed as a government scout," ordered him to stop. Angry at her interference and unaware who she was, the muleskinner knocked her hat on the ground with his whip. "Quicker than a flash, Calamity jerked out her big Colt's [sic] revolver, stuck the muzzle firmly under his nose and commanded: 'Put that hat where you got it!'" The mule-skinner did as he was told, said Coursey, and later became one of Calamity's friends.[13]

By the mid-twenties, these stories about Calamity Jane were incorporated with tales from Martha's *Life and Adventures of Calamity Jane* to formulate a heroic biography that would become standard. Author Francis W. Hilton began this process in 1925 with a short sketch for *Frontier Magazine*, calling her "one of the thousands of women whose misfortune it was not to have been born a man." According to Hilton, by age sixteen Martha "had undergone a complete metamorphosis" and, except for "a woman's tenderness," became "a man at heart." Attesting to her masculine achievements was her ability to fill a can tossed into the air with bullets before it landed. She also could "flick a fly off a mule with a sixteen-foot whip-lash." In Hilton's biography, Calamity rescues Captain Egan, saves the Deadwood stage, confronts a muleskinner abusing his animals, and cares for victims in a smallpox epidemic. Finally, she dies on August 2, "twenty seven years to the day after 'Wild Bill.'" To defend his heroine from reports that she lived a depraved life in dance halls along the Union Pacific, Hilton declared that these "wild-eyed and ludicrous tales" involved a different woman, who died in Denver in 1878.[14]

Journalist Seymour G. Pond similarly used these tales to summarize Martha's career in a 1925 article for the *New York Times Magazine*. "Into the setting sun of the Old West there sinks from view one of the most romantic characters of frontier days—'Calamity Jane,'" Pond began. "She was a tough, hard swearing, hard riding, hard drinking and hard-headed gunwoman." He added that Calamity Jane scouted for Crook and Custer, rescued Captain Egan, carried mail over "one of the most dangerous Pony Express routes," saved the Deadwood stage, fought alongside Buckskin Frank, intervened when a muleskinner abused his animals, and cared for smallpox victims. When she died, her body bore the "scars of a dozen bullets from Indians and highwaymen." Pond's account in *Literary Digest* was summarized by the title, "Calamity Jane as a Lady Robin Hood." It featured Thomas Brown's tale about Calamity Jane robbing a grocery store to get food for sick miners, but placed the event in Deadwood.[15]

Most remarkable about these accounts of Calamity Jane is how quickly they became accepted sources for other writers. The tales told by Jesse Brown and A. M. Willard, O. W. Coursey, and Thomas Brown immediately were utilized by Hilton and Pond. Still other writers expanded on the stories told by Hilton and Pond, and these new versions became sources for later authors. For example, in a 1926 story that appeared in many Montana newspapers, Don Conway told how Calamity saved the Deadwood stage driven by "Jack McCaul," intervened when a teamster whipped his animals, saved Antelope Frank during a skirmish with Indians, and captured Hickok's assassin. Wild Bill's death left her with a broken heart, resulting in "her careless wild and wicked life during the years that followed," Conway concluded.[16] Only a decade later, Conway's account of Calamity Jane reappeared verbatim under the authorship of John K. Standish, and ten years after that, the article by Standish became a primary source for W. S. Kimball of Casper, Wyoming. In his article, Kimball commented: "The reader is asked to please bear in mind that this recital is not fiction, but a true account of the life and adventures of an intelligent but unfortunate woman in an age and under conditions that may never exist again." With little passage of time, legendary tales had become regarded as primary historical sources.[17]

Meanwhile, Calamity Jane became the subject of a full-length biography. Duncan Aikman's *Calamity Jane and the Lady Wildcats* (1927) was a debunking, yet frolicking account. An El Paso, Texas, newspaperman, Aikman seriously researched his subject. Finding evidence that proved the Canary family lived in Princeton, Missouri, he was able to verify Martha's origins. But Aikman found little to support the legendary tales circulating about her name: "The closer one comes to the actual scene of Jane's heroic performances, the more they vanish," he asserted. She was a camp follower, not a scout, did not save the Deadwood stage, and never rode for the pony express. Nor could he find evidence that she ever nursed victims in a smallpox epidemic: "Among dozens of her surviving contemporaries I could find but one able, out of either positive knowledge or credible hearsay, to remember the name of a single beneficiary of her attentions. Yet almost invariably the west gives her credit for having saved hundreds, with all the harrowing details one wants[,] provided one will accept them [as] vague."

Yet, for all his debunking, Aikman himself related inaccurate information and hearsay accounts. In one of Aikman's stories, Calamity and a Texas cowboy confront each other with bowie knives in a saloon; fortunately, the crowd separates them before either is hurt. In another, she knocks out a bartender when he attempts to stop her rough-housing. Aikman made these minor events seem important. He also sacrificed fact when he reported that Calamity Jane died on August 2, 1903, the twenty-seventh anniversary of Hickok's death.

Central to Aikman's flamboyant account is Calamity's relationship with Wild Bill Hickok. Aikman was certain that Calamity was in love with Hickok, even if this interest was not reciprocated. In his version, they first meet in Kansas, then again in Cheyenne before they enter the Black Hills together in 1876. Hickok's companions deliberately clothe Calamity as a scout to attract attention to their party as they ride into Deadwood, and from that moment she gains notoriety as Hickok's protégé. His death at McCall's hand is devastating for her because she realizes that never again will she be regarded as the "Prairie Queen." Aikman's conclusion was perhaps more accurate than his facts. Calamity, he said, declined from "a delectable novelty, a vivid and genial allegory of an era's hearty rowdiness," to "a jovial sot . . . a hag of Rabelaisian glamor and burlesque eccentrities." For the remainder of her life, Aikman asserted, she was "tolerated mainly for the sake of the condescending amusement she afforded."[18]

Despite his debunking, Aikman's popular biography helped Calamity become one of the West's legendary figures. Afterwards, she was a featured figure in many histories of the West. In *Fighting Red Cloud's Warriors: True Tales of Indian Days When the West Was Young* (1926), journalist E. A. Brininstool devoted an entire chapter to this "most-talked-of frontier woman." Mostly, he reprinted stories from her autobiography and from Brown and Willard's history of the Black Hills.[19] Writer Edwin L. Sabin's *Wild Men of the Wild West* (1929) combined Aikman's debunking with popular stories about Calamity Jane. In his account, Calamity told tall tales, yet saved Buckskin Frank from Indians. She also became the Florence Nightingale of the 1878 smallpox epidemic. In Cameron Rogers's *Gallant Ladies* (1928), Calamity became one of ten women whose lives showed "courage, resource, and character."[20]

Not surprisingly, given Calamity Jane's increased status, the town of Deadwood found her, like Wild Bill Hickok, to be useful in promoting tourism. According to booster P. D. Peterson, by 1929 "thousands of visitors" came to see the graves of these "early idols."[21] That same year, the Deadwood Chamber of Commerce was organized and Nell Perrigoue, executive director, encouraged the use of Deadwood's early history in the town's advertising. This process had begun even earlier. The "Days of '76" celebration, an annual event that included a parade with participants dressed as Calamity Jane, Wild Bill Hickok, and other Black Hills characters, had been established before Perrigoue took over. And in 1928 a dramatization of the "Trial of Jack McCall" had been added to the town's festivities.[22]

Numerous popular histories of the Black Hills were published to exploit the expanding tourist traffic. Almost all included sketches about Calamity Jane, but few added new information. Typical was S. Goodale Price's *Black Hills: The Land of Legend* (1935), which repeated stories that Calamity was born in Burlington, Iowa, stopped a muleskinner from beating his animals, saved Antelope Frank from Indians, and nursed smallpox victims during the 1878 epidemic. Echoing other recent publications, Price concluded: "Beneath that rough exterior was a heart of gold, the answer as to why Calamity Jane has lived on in history."[23]

A guidebook compiler, Leland Case, was less certain that Calamity deserved so much attention. Still, Case agreed that "Deadwood always has had a fondness for Calamity dating from the time she[,] with mixed tenderness and gruffness[,] cared for small-pox patients."[24] Walter Shelley Phillips, who wrote under the pseudonym El Comancho, expanded on this: "No man can say a word against Jane in the hearing of any old-timer up there without starting a war, for the old-timer still sees, not Calamity Jane of blood-and-thunder stories, but the woman who fearlessly nursed stricken men, with death on all sides, and made good."[25]

Calamity's growing legend caused difficulties for admirers of Wild Bill Hickok. Popular histories now assumed a serious relationship between Calamity Jane and their hero. Hickok biographers were certain that this perception was not true. Nonetheless, they accepted Calamity's heroic status. For example, Frank Wilstach, whose 1926 biography helped establish Hickok's twentieth-century reputation, denounced suggestions that Calamity was Wild Bill's consort. But he believed Calamity to be "quite a remarkable person," who spent "one of the most amazing lives among the men and women who lived through the romance of the plains." Wilstach not only believed that Calamity Jane had been a scout, he even repeated the discredited tale that she became deathly ill while carrying dispatches to General Custer. "This journey almost cost Jane her life," he claimed, "yet saved it, for otherwise she would have been with Custer in his last tragic battle on the Little Big Horn."[26]

Biographer William Elsey Connelley elevated Calamity's role even more. Despite his caution in *Wild Bill and His Era* (1933) that "the tendency of the modern romancer . . . is to drape a veil of illusion over all," making the men handsome and the women "unfailingly young, charming, and of dazzling beauty," his Calamity Jane was largely romanticized. Although Connelley acknowledged she could "out-chew, out-smoke, out-swear, and out-drink most of her masculine companions," he accepted Martha's claim that Captain Egan nicknamed her after she rescued him from Indians and concluded that "it is doubtful if Custer ever had a better scout."[27]

But Calamity's shining moment, Connelley maintained, occurred in 1879 when she "laid aside her guns and became a nurse" during the smallpox epidemic in Deadwood. "Out of her own small resources, she took money for food and medicines for those too poor to buy their own . . . going constantly from one house to another on her errands of kindness." After the epidemic was contained, she requested a thirty-day leave from the army "to revisit her old home in Missouri," only to discover that the women in the "little stagnant Missouri town" were repulsed by her masculine behavior. Discouraged, she returned to Deadwood and became a pony express rider, then joined the mining rush to Central City, Colorado, where she arrested a claim jumper.

Such a heroic woman was a suitable associate for Wild Bill. Although Connelley insisted that it was "absolutely untrue that [Hickok] ever, at any time, was in love with her," he was certain "they liked and admired each other immensely." Connelley embellished Martha's unlikely tale of capturing Jack McCall. When Hickok was killed, Calamity was "among the first to reach the spot," said Connelly. Even though she had forgotten her guns, Calamity "started into raging, fiery-hearted action." Finding McCall in a butcher shop, she seized a meat cleaver and "flew at him like a wildcat," holding him "until her more timid associates" arrived."[28]

Connelley went so far as to categorize Calamity Jane with Queen Elizabeth of England and Empress Catherine of Russia, both "great half-masculine, half-feminine queens, who thought and ruled with the brains of men." Both Elizabeth and Catherine "would have understood and liked plain Calamity Jane," he asserted, because they were so similar. "Such women as these three loom together in force and character against the back drop of time!"[29]

Although these biographers hoped to quash the rumored romance between Calamity and Wild Bill, the film industry continued to link the couple romantically. The most significant movie of this period popularizing their association was *The Plainsman* (Paramount, 1937), starring Gary Cooper as Wild Bill Hickok and Jean Arthur as Calamity Jane. In this movie, Calamity Jane, Wild Bill Hickok, and Buffalo Bill Cody make their headquarters in Hays City, Kansas, shortly after the Civil War. Calamity Jane, a stagecoach driver, is in love with Wild Bill. Although Hickok seems offended by Calamity's masculine dress and aggressive pursuit, he secretly carries her picture in his watch cover. While staying with Buffalo Bill's wife, Calamity is coaxed into wearing a dress instead of her buckskin outfit and is transformed into a beautiful woman. After Calamity is taken captive by Sioux warriors, Hickok attempts to rescue her, only to be taken captive himself. To make Hickok reveal the location of a cavalry unit, the Indians begin roasting him alive. Still he refuses to talk. But Calamity, desperately wanting to save Hickok's life, reveals the route taken by the troops. Her disclosure leads to an ambush of the squad and Hickok tells Calamity that he will never be able to forgive her. Nevertheless, when they later meet in Deadwood, Wild Bill confides to Calamity that it might be time for him to settle down. He implies he would like her to join him. Instead, Jack McCall, who believes that the man who kills Hickok will become famous, shoots Wild Bill. As the film ends, a devastated Calamity Jane weeps over his body.

Despite claims by director Cecil B. DeMille that *The Plainsman* was historically authentic, the plot and characterizations in the film are mostly fictional. DeMille's efforts at accuracy were primarily confined to details. For example, he required Jean Arthur "to learn how to manipulate a 10-foot bullwhip as competently as Calamity Jane did when she was driving a stagecoach." Arthur used DeMille's wrist as a target during her practice sessions, and he "bore lash marks" for days afterwards. Another effort at historical realism concerned the film's conclusion. According to DeMille, motion picture executives wanted a happy ending with Gary Cooper riding "off into the sunset with Jean Arthur," or at least an ending with someone other than the cowardly McCall killing him. DeMille concluded with satisfaction that "history was adhered to, and the audience did not object to the much more effective, as well as truer, tragedy of Hickok's having been killed by a 'little rat' rather than by a more manly villain."[30]

But journalists on the northern plains were not impressed with *The Plainsman*'s characterization of Calamity Jane. According to one Montana newspaper, old-timers were unanimous that the film's Calamity Jane was "definitely not a life-like portrait." The old-timers who knew Calamity Jane, the reporter said, "declare that although legend pictures her as a wonderful rifle shot, she was probably a better cook than she was a gun woman." Although the reporter agreed that the talented Jean Arthur "did her best" in the role of Calamity Jane, he thought it would be difficult for any actress to "successfully recreate the many-sided, bizarre character" of Calamity.[31] Certainly, she was not "the peaches and cream sweetheart" depicted on the film. Perhaps, however, the journalist's criticism of Arthur's portrayal was unfair. Even though the petite, attractive Jean Arthur was physically miscast as the real Calamity Jane, she may have been a appropriate actress to dramatize the legendary heroine.

The film remained one of Arthur's career favorites. In fact, she had accepted the role because she was convinced that her character "was a symbol of emancipated womanhood." Arthur elaborated on her views in an article for *Screen and Radio Weekly* titled "Who Wants to Be a Lady?" Calamity Jane belonged in the "list of women who blazed the trail toward emancipation" Arthur said. She smoked (as did Arthur), and "whenever she felt in need of a stimulating nip, she went into a bar and got good service by banging the wood with a revolver butt." And, Arthur added approvingly, "she wore trousers."[32]

Others, too, viewed Calamity as a woman ahead of her time. In 1936, journalist Glendolin Wagner took offense at writers who portrayed Calamity "as a rough, ignorant wholly bad woman" and made her "the butt of ridicule in poetry and songs." In Wagner's opinion, Calamity was a person who "had the courage to live her own unconventional life—a colorful life in which we find much that is uncouth, perhaps unwomanly, but with no hint of little meannesses anywhere." To prove her case, Wagner cited testimony by Dr. William A. Allen of Billings, one of Calamity's acquaintances. Even though Calamity drank, swore, and wore men's clothing, said Allen, her eccentrities would hardly be noticed today. Whereas in her time "poor Calamity attracted unsavory attention," he concluded, she would now "be thought of merely as 'modern.'"[33]

Meanwhile, now that Calamity Jane had become an accepted figure in western history and folklore, writers exaggerated her adventures with little regard to historical accuracy. H. C. Everett explained in an article for the *Pony Express Courier* that Calamity had a dual personality. "Almost in the wink of an eye she could change from a soft and tender woman, protecting the weak and nursing the sick, to a whiskey-drinking gun fighter, as terrible as the West has ever known." Although Calamity Jane and Wild Bill Hickok never married, Everett added, they were "almost inseparable." Hickok "valued her for her skill with arms and for her bravery," and she helped him bring law and order to the West.[34]

According to Big Chief White Horse Eagle, whose purported adventures were recorded by Edgar Von Schmidt-Pauli, Hickok was "only one of [Calamity's] many lovers." She flirted with Buffalo Bill only weeks before Wild Bill was killed, said White Horse Eagle, and a drunken Hickok confronted Buffalo Bill, exclaiming, "You've stolen my girl. I give you a minute to make your miserable peace with God." Buffalo Bill expressed his innocence, informing Hickok that he last saw Calamity in the bar sitting on the knee of a "gold-digger." Hickok hurried to the saloon, concluded White Horse Eagle, where he soon added another notch to his gun.[35]

Another fantastic tale about Calamity Jane was told by cowboy "Jack" Thorp. In this story, a stranger challenged Calamity to a horse race, claiming his horse "could outrun hers under any conditions, for money, marbles, or whiskey." Calamity accepted, proposing that they ride into a saloon, have a drink, then exit through the back door, and repeat this pattern until they had raced through the town's eleven saloons. "Calamity Jane won the race by three saloons and four drinks," Thorp concluded, explaining that her horse had been trained at this task and could even "take a bottle in his teeth, up-end it, and drink just like a man—and with about the same physical consequences."[36]

Even as Calamity's historical adventures were embellished, she became a featured character in novels. Some of these were more accurate than recent histories that had appeared. The most sophisticated piece of fiction featuring Calamity Jane during this period was Ethel Hueston's *Calamity Jane of Deadwood Gulch* (1937). In this story, the central character is Phoebe Norcutt, daughter of a missionary to the Sioux. Len Wade, the officer she loves, joins her in a struggle for better treatment of Indians. Meanwhile, the hard-drinking Calamity Jane swaggers her way through the Black Hills spinning tall tales as she goes. Phoebe, who becomes Calamity's friend, develops a rule concerning stories she hears about Calamity's adventures: if Calamity is the source of the tale, it is not true. Conversely, if someone else tells a story about Calamity, Phoebe assumes it is true. Thus, Calamity did not save the stage when Johnny Slaughter is killed and she was not a scout for Crook because Calamity tells these tales herself. Despite Calamity's propensity to spin tall tales, she is more good than bad in Hueston's novel, as exemplified by her nursing of victims in a Deadwood smallpox epidemic. And when Calamity dies, Phoebe contemplates her ascent into heaven. "The angels are going to be surprised when she gets there," she muses.[37]

Most writers who featured Calamity Jane in their stories were less concerned than Hueston about historical accuracy. In Tom Curry's "Raiders of Deadwood," the Rio Kid (Bob Pryor) and his companion Celestino Mireles join Calamity Jane and Bat Masterson in a money-making venture to sell supplies in Deadwood. There, they encounter a cut-throat outlaw band formed of ex-guerillas from Quantrill's raiders who rob a government payroll, steal cattle, and plot to control all Deadwood's mines. The Rio Kid, helped by Wyatt Earp and troops led by General Alfred Terry, thwarts their efforts. Although Calamity joins the battle against the outlaws, in Curry's story she is a secondary character. She also is not emancipated, helping the other women prepare a meal when it is time for the men to eat.[38]

Having had her reputation whitewashed, Calamity Jane became an appropriate heroine even in juvenile fiction. John Mueller's *Heroes of the Black Hills* (c. 1934) features an eighteen-year-old woman, Ella Custer, who, like Calamity Jane, dresses in buckskins and is an excellent shot. In Deadwood, Ella meets Calamity, who saves Preacher Smith from a hostile crowd upset by his sermons against vice. Then Calamity and Ella join forces to battle Indians and outlaws, protecting the stagecoach driven by Deadwood Dick. Calamity, who speaks refined English and owns a ranch in Montana, had traveled to the Black Hills to marry Wild Bill Hickok. After he is killed, Calamity returns to her home near Laurel, Montana, and Ella marries Lieutenant George Powell, her beau. In Bruce Kafaroff's *Deadwood Gulch* (1941), Deadwood Dick struggles against a bandit organization terrorizing the region. Calamity Jane, a stagecoach guard, joins him in his fight against stagecoach robbers.

She also befriends two youngsters, one a reporter for his father's newspaper and the other a young cowboy who hopes someday to become a peace officer. Both boys help Deadwood Dick and Calamity Jane bring the outlaws to justice.

Poets also lauded Calamity's heroic deeds. In *The Beacon Light and Other Poems* (1927), Murray Ketcham Kirk rhapsodized about the "Dark queen of the gold-camp and plain," who shrinks "not from danger nor death."[39] Similarly, Charles P. "Soldier" Green penned a tribute to Calamity in his *Ballads of the Black Hills* (1931):

> To the Hills there rode with Custer—,
> One lone woman in that train,
> Garbed in buckskin suit and leggins,
> No one else than dear, brave Jane.

Although Calamity has her rough side, playing poker and drinking,

> When some poor, lone stage-driver,
> Lay out wounded on the trail
> Jane would mount her fiery broncho
> Bring him in and save the mail.

In Green's poem, Calamity Jane wins fame when Wild Bill marries her. But most of all, Calamity deserves honor because

> In the hearts of all old-timers
> Who have ranged about the Hills,
> There is kindly recollection
> When she nursed them thru their ills.[40]

Will Wickersham called her "The Unpolished Nugget" in his *Pa-Ha-Sa-Pa* (1948), depicting her as both adept with a gun and aiding "those in distress and disease."[41] Likewise, in Mae Urbanek's *High Lights of the Hills* (1954), Calamity Jane is "As unfettered as the wind,/ Blowing hot or strangely mild;/ Shooting and out-cursing men,/ Caring for a lonely child."[42] And physician Nolie Mumey in his 1950 poem observed, "If there be calamity, Jane will be waiting there." She was "A product of the West" and a "Young, unprotected girl/who worked, did her best. . . ." Like Ethel Hueston's Calamity Jane, Mumey's heroine could expect heavenly reward: "When the last trumpet sounds, She will be waiting there."[43]

Likewise, film and radio were unconcerned with historical accuracy. In fact, the character of Calamity Jane could be adapted to suit any situation. In *Young Bill Hickok* (Republic, 1940), starring Roy Rogers as Wild Bill, Calamity Jane (Sally Payne) joins George "Gabby" Hayes as Hickok's comic sidekick. She helps Wild Bill combat conspirators aiming to separate California from the Union to secure its gold. Calamity also serves as bridesmaid at Hickok's wedding. Like Roy Rogers, Payne sings several songs during the show, one to distract the saloon crowd while Hickok searches for incriminating evidence.

Calamity Jane again was paired with Hickok on April 10, 1944, for a segment in the Lone Ranger radio series. Uniquely, this show mentioned Calamity's Princeton, Missouri, childhood, claiming that it was there she was given her famous nickname after youth-ful escapades. As an adult, Calamity meets Wild Bill, the Lone Ranger, and Tonto in Kansas City, where she helps prevent Jack McCall from ambushing Hickok. Years later, in Deadwood, Calamity marries Wild Bill, but the marriage is kept secret because of Calamity's insatiable need for attention. To be married to the famous gunfighter would relegate her to secondary status. Devoted to Calamity, Hickok defers to her constantly, even asking Custer to hire her as a scout instead of himself. After Hickok is assassinated, the Lone Ranger chastises Calamity for causing Wild Bill's death at Jack McCall's hand because she always took the limelight, making him careless about his safety. A crest-fallen Calamity Jane afterwards informs a crowd that from now on she is to be known as Mrs. Hickok.

In several films, Calamity is involved with men other than Hickok. In *Badlands of Dakota* (Universal, 1941), stage driver Calamity Jane (Frances Farmer) falls in love with the owner of the Bella Union saloon in Deadwood, Bob Holliday (Broderick Crawford), but Bob plans instead to marry beautiful Ann Grayson. When Ann marries Bob's brother, Bob joins Jack McCall in stage and bank robberies. In a dramatic showdown, Calamity shoots Bob Holliday as he threatens to kill his own brother. She cries briefly over Bob's body, but recovers quickly and asks one of the men, "Don't you know when a lady needs a drink?"

Calamity is again the odd person out in a love triangle in *Calamity Jane and Sam Bass* (Universal, 1949), starring Yvonne De Carlo and Howard Duff. Calamity is in love with Bass, but he has eyes only for Kathy, the sister of the Denton, Texas, sheriff. Bass becomes an outlaw when he is cheated after betting on a horse race in Abilene, Kansas. Although Calamity joins Bass and his gang, and comforts Bass after he is fatally shot by a posse, he still has thoughts only for Kathy.[44]

These romanticized images of Calamity Jane in history, fiction, poetry, and film did not go unchallenged. Black Hills pioneer John S. McClintock, whose memoirs were published in 1939, disputed these "highly fictitious and laudable stories told of her by sensational writers." In his account of Calamity, McClintock discounted every heroic tale attributed to her.[45] Two years later, Deadwood newspaperman Edward L. Senn expanded on McClintock's statements. According to Senn, Black Hills old-timers were unanimous that Calamity accompanied military expeditions only as a camp follower, that she did not save the Deadwood stage after its driver was killed, and that even her nursing activities were exaggerated. Despite his caustic assessment of Calamity's career, Senn said his version was "more charitable than the comments of many pioneers of the Black Hills who had personal acquaintance and knowledge."[46]

Historian Harold E. Briggs joined the fray in 1940, devoting a section in *Frontiers of the Northwest* to "The Calamity Jane Myth." In recent years, Briggs wrote, Calamity Jane had "been depicted by numerous writers and even in moving pictures, as a picturesque and romantic border character, a 'heroine of the plains,' having most of the qualities of the good Samaritan and of a feminine Robin Hood." But such tales, Briggs said, were "pure fabrications." Calamity, he added, was personably responsible for many of these stories. Indeed, Briggs thought she would be a good subject for a a psychologist because of her efforts to cover "the drab adventures of her youth, when her only claim was her absolute lack of respectability."[47]

Even the film industry momentarily spoofed popular notions about the romantic and heroic West. In *The Paleface* (Paramount, 1948), a comedy starring Jane Russell as Calamity Jane and Bob Hope as "Painless Peter Potter," a dentist, Calamity becomes a secret government agent assigned to ferret out white renegades who are smuggling guns to the Indians. Needing a "husband" as a cover for her work, she latches on to the cowardly Potter. They join a wagon train traveling toward Buffalo Flats and are attacked by Indians. In the fight, Potter shoots blindly, but each time he fires, Indians drop. He and the others are unaware that Calamity Jane is firing simultaneously from her hiding place. Because of his imagined marksmanship, Potter becomes a hero, the "successor to Wild Bill Hickok and Buffalo Bill." In this role, he unknowingly helps distract the renegades as Calamity investigates. At the end of the film, in a scene reminiscent of *The Plainsman*, Calamity and Potter are captured by Indians working with the gunrunners. When Potter manages their escape, he becomes a real hero and Calamity marries him.

Confronted by these varied images of Calamity Jane, writers at midcentury seemed unable to decide her true nature. Journalist Robert J. Casey described this confusion in *The Black Hills and Their Incredible Characters* (1949): "Long ago somebody asked me, 'Who was Calamity Jane?' And the answer was simple," he said. "I had the legend pat, complete with names, dates, addresses and bibliography." However, wrote Casey, if asked the same question now, his answer would be "I don't know." In fact, he said, she was causing "considerably more controversy dead than she ever did in life." Those who believe she was a great humanitarian "get very angry when you mention that she ran around with a lot of strange company," and the "opposing faction is just as cocksure and just as bigoted," at times even vicious, suggesting that she "was just another one of the girls . . . only a little uglier." Casey concluded that the truth probably was somewhere between these two extremes.[48]

Thus, as the fiftieth anniversary of Calamity's death neared, the same controversy that raged in 1903 (whether Calamity Jane deserved her status as western heroine) seemed further away than ever from a conclusion. Appropriately, at this moment the film industry released the musical *Calamity Jane* (Warner, 1953), starring Doris Day in the title role and Howard Keel as Wild Bill Hickok in a delightfully romantic relationship. Even before the movie's release, South Dakota newspaperman Bob Lee predicted, "If the movie, 'Calamity Jane,' is as accurate as most Hollywood historical films, it will portray Calamity as a woman and that's about all."[49]

Doris Day later described the film as one of her favorite musicals: "I loved portraying Calamity Jane, who was a rambunctious, pistol-packing prairie girl (I lowered my voice and stuck out my chin a little)."[50] Included in the film were such memorable songs as "The Deadwood Stage," "Just Blew in from the Windy City," "Higher Than a Hawk," "A Woman's Touch," "The Black Hills of Dakota," and, of course, the Oscar-winning "Secret Love." The tomboyish Calamity Jane dresses in buckskins, drives the stage, and noisily brags, but is cleansed of her worst transgressions. She drinks only sarsaparilla, curses without profanity, and in cleaning up and changing her dress is transformed into a beautiful woman. By the end of the movie, her "secret love," Wild Bill Hickok, "is no secret any more."

The *Rocky Mountain News* thought the actual Calamity Jane would have a good laugh if she saw the movie. "The real old rip-snortin' western gal knowed as Calamity Jane probly woundn't reconize herself in this here movie," it said. "But what the movie ain't got in historical facts, its sure got in shootin' and hollerin' and scratchin' and kickin'."[51]

Another critic was not so amused. When the film was scheduled to premiere in Rapid City, Black Hills boosters asked South Dakota Governor Sigurd Anderson to proclaim "Calamity Jane Week" for publicity purposes. Anderson refused, explaining that he did not like "to have the history of the state portrayed incorrectly by the movies." Besides, he said, Calamity Jane was too notoriously a bad woman to deserve such an honor. His decision led to considerable friction. One South Dakota editor observed that advocates of "Calamity Jane Week" would have publicized "Typhoid Mary as Florence Nightingale if it would help the tourist trade." Ultimately, the governor prevailed, but the editor of the *Huron Plainsman* concluded that his opposition probably had an unintended result: "The movie and the legend and the Hills and the governor—all four—are receiving considerably more publicity than any one of them would with a routine proclamation."[52] It had been so throughout Calamity Jane's life. Even her detractors managed to promote her by calling attention to her.

In fact, despite efforts by her critics, fifty years after her death Calamity Jane's fame remained intact. Movies, fiction, poetry, and popular history had elevated her into a important western heroine. Most of these portrayals of Calamity Jane were about as accurate as the dime novels written in the late nineteenth century. For most Americans the film images of Calamity Jane were stronger than critiques by disgruntled pioneers and scholars. Indeed, that so much was being published about Calamity Jane, even if hostile, reinforced the belief that she had been an important western figure. Images of Calamity working in traditonally male occupations increased her popularity in an age when women were making strides toward equality with men, and accounts of her charitable work as a nurse showed that women need not lose their feminine qualities even as they entered the so-called man's world. Finally, at a time when America seemed beset by enemies both abroad and within, the country was more interested in appreciating its heroic past than in debunking it. At midcentury, there was little reason to doubt the security of Calamity Jane's status in western history.

CHAPTER FIFTEEN

Of Daughters, Letters, and a Diary

An entirely new dimension was added to the Calamity Jane story on May 6, 1941, when Jean Hickok McCormick of Billings, Montana, announced on the CBS radio program "We the People" that she was the daughter of Calamity Jane and Wild Bill Hickok. To substantiate her paternity, she produced a diary and letters purportedly written by Calamity Jane.[1] Although the diary and letters were clumsy forgeries, McCormick's tale was accepted by many scholars and now has become an integral part of the Calamity Jane legend.

That McCormick chose just then to identify herself as the daughter of Calamity Jane and Wild Bill Hickok is understandable. By 1941, Calamity was associated in popular culture with Wild Bill and both were regarded as noted scouts. In addition, Martha Canary's role as wife and mother had long been forgotten except by a handful of close acquaintances. Since Calamity Jane's legend did not include her parenting a child, McCormick's restoration of this aspect of Martha's life, even if fictional, struck a popular chord.

The lack of documented information in 1941 about Martha Canary made it difficult for contemporaries to contradict the tale told in McCormick's diary and letters. In retrospect, it is surprising how little was known about Calamity Jane at that time. Even Martha's autobiography, *Life and Adventures of Calamity Jane, By Herself,* had mostly been forgotten. Occasionally, a copy was found amid the relics of an old-timer, and local newspapers in the northern plains, regarding it as a long lost document of the past, would reprint the booklet in its entirety.[2] Thus, when McCormick first made her claim to be the daughter of Calamity Jane, *Billings Gazette* editor Oscar Chaffee observed: "Despite literally hundreds of stories concerning Calamity Jane, little is known regarding her life." Chaffee noted that discrepancies regarding her birthdate alone ranged from 1848 to 1860.[3]

There was another reason radio listeners readily accepted the authenticity of McCormick's 1941 Mother's Day pronouncement. Gabriel Heatter of the "We the People" program declared he "had indisputable proof of her birth," including Calamity Jane's diary, a "deathbed confession," and "a message from the daughter of a minister who purportedly married the couple near Abilene."[4] In addition, when the contents of the diary became known, some information in them seemed impossible for anyone but Calamity Jane to know. For example, the diary mentions her early Montana acquaintances and tells about her cabin outside Billings. This led one writer to conclude that, if the documents were not genuine, "someone who knew a great deal about Calamity Jane must have written these letters."[5]

According to Jean McCormick, she was born on September 25, 1873, at Benson's Landing, Montana, later the site of Livingston. Her mother, Calamity Jane, was supposedly alone at the time of the Jean's birth, and befriended only by James O'Neil, a sea captain who nursed Calamity back to health. He generously offered to raise the infant as his daughter and provide her with an education and cultural experiences unavailable in the American West. A few months later, desiring to do what was best for her child, Calamity traveled by ox-drawn wagon to Omaha, the nearest rail point, where Mr. and Mrs. O'Neil awaited them. From Omaha, baby Jean and the O'Neils traveled by train to the O'Neil residence in Richmond, Virginia. McCormick identified O'Neil as a captain for the Cunard Steamship Line, and said he took her to Liverpool, England. She received her education and training in both Richmond and Liverpool, and said she never knew the identities of her real parents.

Calamity, meanwhile, was said to have returned alone to the West to continue her adventurous, nomadic life. Unknown to anyone, McCormick related, Calamity carried with her an old photograph album in which she occasionally addressed entries to her daughter, Jean, who was referred to in the album-diary as "Janey." Combined with correspondence between herself and James O'Neil, plus additional diary entries on loose sheets of paper, the "Diary and Letters of Calamity Jane" were, upon Calamity's death in 1903, purportedly sent to O'Neil, who in turn presented them to Jean shortly before his death in 1912. The album contained fifteen entries dated 1877 to 1902 and informed daughter "Janey" that Calamity and Wild Bill Hickok had been legally married. However, after a falling out Calamity granted Hickok a divorce, and in 1876 he had married Agnes Lake.[6]

McCormick's documents went on to relate the bitter loneliness Calamity suffered after Wild Bill's death and her motherly concern for the child she had given up for adoption. In addition, album entries tell about Calamity's adventures driving the Deadwood stage, touring with Buffalo Bill's Wild West show in the East and in Europe, meeting outlaw Frank Dalton, marrying Charley Burke, purchasing a cabin on Canyon Creek next to horse thieves, and living in early Montana towns such as Coulson and Stringtown. Letters to O'Neil concern "Janey's" education and experiences, indicating that Calamity kept posted on her daughter's progress. Appended to the diary is a bizarre "confession." In it, Calamity claims Belle Starr was her sister and that Starr had a daughter named Jesse Elizabeth Oakes, whom Calamity raised and passed off as her own daughter. Starr was even said to have married a cousin of Wild Bill Hickok. The twelve entries dating between

1879 and 1903 that were written on loose sheets of paper, as well as three purported letters between O'Neil and Calamity Jane, provide further details of Calamity's experiences and acquaintances. Calamity mentioned friends such as Will Lull, her terrible treatment by the women of Deadwood, her meeting with Hickok in Abilene, her lack of education and efforts to improve her reading and writing, and accounts of her life and family. One entry indicates that Calamity's father was a preacher.

According to the diary and letters, Jean met Calamity Jane twice, but remained ignorant of their relationship. Once, when Jean was eight, Calamity visited Richmond, bringing ten thousand dollars she purportedly had won in a poker game with Northern Pacific Railroad officials to O'Neil for Janey's education. Ten years later, in 1893, Calamity again visited Janey. This time she was traveling with Buffalo Bill's Wild West Show, then said to have been exhibiting in Richmond. Afterwards, Calamity accompanied the O'Neils (and Jean) to England, where the show was scheduled to appear next.

Jean provided only sketchy information about her adult years. She claimed to have married a Virginia state senator named Burkhart, but they divorced in 1916 after eighteen years of married life. The reason Burkhart left her, Jean said, was that he inadvertently discovered the diary and letters in the flour bin where she had hidden them. According to Jean, Burkhart feared that if the public learned his wife was the daughter of Wild Bill Hickok and Calamity Jane, his political career would be ruined. Afterward, Jean added, she served for three years as a volunteer nurse in France during World War I. On November 11, 1918, she married Ed McCormick, a hospitalized American aviator who, she said, died of combat wounds shortly after their wedding.

However, details in McCormick's accounts of her life varied each time she was interviewed, calling her credibility into question. The Billings newspaper in 1941 announced that she was the daughter of Calamity Jane and "James Butler Hickok, a cousin of James Butler (Wild Bill) Hickok," but in subsequent reports she claimed to be the daughter of Wild Bill. She once said that when Captain O'Neil was in Montana in 1873 investigating the death of a brother, "a report came to him that his brother had been killed by Howling Wolf, a Sioux chief." After locating "the place where his brother had been buried," he "chanced on the cabin Calamity Jane had been hiding in," a version decidedly different from one in which Captain O'Neil was said to have been in the "Montana wilderness on a hunting expedition." Although in early statements Jean reported that she married the bedridden Ed McCormick, who died shortly after their wedding, a later article reported that Ed "was killed only 40 minutes after the ceremony when his plane was shot down," presumably while flying a mission over France. She added that she had known Ed earlier in Richmond and reported that, in a dramatic coincidence, Senator Burkhart's yacht had struck the McCormick yacht in Virginia and Jean's son, Bobby, had been killed. In Chicago, she told Clarence S. Paine, a librarian from Beloit College in Wisconsin, that a daughter born during her marriage to Burkhart was kidnapped in infancy and never located, but mentioned no son. In other accounts, the kidnapped daughter was from her first marriage to Jack Oakes, who was unmentioned in earlier interviews.[7]

Unfortunately, McCormick's obscure life left little documentation for the historian to reconstruct her story. However, what is known about her sometimes discredits her claims. If she was married to Burkhart, a state senator in Virginia, it is surprising that she and her husband are unmentioned in public records. Instead, one interviewer learned from Jean that she taught penmanship in the Butte, Montana, schools between 1898 and 1902. This was precisely when she supposedly married Burkhart in Virginia. In the 1920s and 1930s, she evidently resided in the Billings area, but sometimes worked as a cook and nurse at dude ranches in Montana, Wyoming, and Washington. It was while she was at one of these ranches, presumably in the 1930s, that Jean McCormick privately revealed her parentage. "Friends who knew her identity," wrote *Billings Gazette* editor Chaffee, "notified a radio program, which asked Mrs. McCormick to appear on the program after submitting proof" of it.[8]

Glimpses into Jean's character can be gleaned from letters she wrote to people interested in her claims after her 1941 radio interview. Evidently quite poor, she expressed concern over minor expenses such as postage stamps and complained of long hours of work. When librarian Clarence Paine proposed a trip to Montana to visit her, she replied: "I hope you won't make the trip here too early. I am holding down a job 8 hrs. per day . . . so I would have to plan to see you folks after 8 P.M. or early morning." Despairing of her situation, she added, "I shall always have to work for a living, I guess. It will be alright if I don't live too long."[9]

Claiming to be the daughter of Calamity Jane and Wild Bill Hickok immediately transformed McCormick's life. Paine interviewed her in Chicago in 1941 during her homeward trip from New York and proposed to write a biography of Calamity Jane utilizing her information. Jean, he said, could have all the profits. She agreed and granted Paine access to documents, which she sent to him piecemeal for several years.[10]

Jean was invited on June 13, 1941, to ride in the parade at the "Wild Bill Frontier celebration" in Abilene, Kansas. She arrived there with the "old diary written by her mother" and an 1862 revolver "given to her mother by Wild Bill himself." Received at the Abilene Chamber of Commerce office, Jean related that Calamity first met Hickok near Abilene in about 1870. Having learned of a plot to kill Hickok, Calamity warned him just in time and nursed his wounds after his gunfight with the would-be assassins. "Then he asked her to go to Deadwood, South Dakota," said Jean. But soon "tongues began to wag. They called her Bill's consort." Owing to the displeasure of the Hickok family, their marriage was not made public. "They never lived together after I was born," said Jean. Instead, Calamity Jane traveled to the East "till she was granted a divorce. So when Wild Bill married Alice [*sic*] Lake, the woman so much older than he, he was at liberty to do so."[11]

After her visit in Abilene, McCormick made several other appearances in rodeos that summer as Calamity Jane's daughter. Then she traveled by bus from Billings to La Crosse, Wisconsin, in September 1941 to attend the Hickok family reunion. En route, she paused in the Black Hills, where the *Rapid City Journal* reported that Jean "tenderly placed [flowers] on the graves of Wild Bill Hickok and Calamity Jane in Mt. Moriah cemetery." To a correspondent, Helen Smith, Jean privately added:

> Was it a lonely, drab old place? I'll admit I cried when I placed an armfull of flowers on the graves and if any one had been near they could have heard "Well, here I am at last. I hope you both are on some not too far distant land still able to look back and *know* that I am trying to exonerate you. Yes, trying to piece together, before a rotten doubting world, what little proof I have left, after evil tongues took one by one the desirable qualities you possessed leaving for me something obnoxious in exchange.[12]

A Rapid City correspondent described Jean as "a little woman five feet, four inches tall and weighing perhaps 100 pounds whose appearance belies her age of 68 years." The reporter also said she dressed for the role, wearing "buckskin skirt and jacket, red silk shirt, yellow neckerchief, cowboy boots and a gray sombrero."[13]

The *La Crosse Tribune*'s announcement of Jean's arrival included a picture of her "decked out in her cowgirl outfit" in the company of two of Hickok's second-cousins. She "seems paradoxical to her parentage for she is soft-spoken, slender and pretty," the *Tribune* reported, adding that her life story "would make an author of westerns look at his fiction with disgust." She "leads a quiet life," the *Tribune* continued, occasionally "appearing in rodeos, teaching penmanship in graded schools in Montana and nursing."[14] Jean remembered that the Hickok family "welcomed me with tears and kisses and were true aristocrats. I loved them all. I was so glad to find I had a family, after so many lonely years thinking I had no one." The Hickoks intended to have their next reunion, she said, with her in the West.[15]

McCormick, meanwhile, was locating proper sites for the momentos she said had once belonged to Calamity Jane. J. Almus Russell, curator for the Middle Border Museum in Mitchell, South Dakota, inquired in February 1942 whether McCormick might donate items for their collection, commenting that the museum wanted to honor Calamity "in a more dignified way than it has heretofore been done." Jean was pleased to offer them some of her mother's belongings. She also gave them permission to copy the diary because she too wanted her mother portrayed with dignity. Ever since her radio declaration of her parentage, McCormick said, she had been "picked to pieces" by disbelievers. The museum soon received a package containing Calamity Jane's handkerchief, hat-pin, and dress comb, as well as a lock of Hickok's hair and a tintype of Jean as a child that purportedly was in Wild Bill's pocket when he was killed.[16]

Other items were sent to the Pioneer Museum in Fort Collins, Colorado. There, local historian Carl Anderson became interested in Jean's story after viewing a photostatic copy of the Hickok–Calamity Jane marriage certificate she had sent to the museum. This supposed record of the marriage between Calamity Jane and Wild Bill Hickok on September 1, 1870, was written on a page ripped from a Bible. Anderson wrote to officials of the "We the People" program asking whether they believed McCormick's claims were true. "Our local historical society has challenged the authenticity of this certificate," he explained, "and claims Mrs. McCormick is an imposter." He received a response from Vivien Skinner of "We the People," who said she "would be willing to swear that [McCormick] isn't the type of person who could forge those letters." Moreover, wrote Skinner, McCormick had brought "reams and reams of writing by Calamity Jane on old and yellowed paper" with her, and she didn't believe McCormick had "the criminal shrewdness to forge them."[17]

Convinced, Anderson proceeded to write newspaper articles and letters advocating the diary's genuineness. Soon, McCormick donated further articles to the Fort Collins museum, including the album-diary and supplementary pages, Wild Bill's favorite pistol and holster, Calamity Jane's prayer book, and a lock of Wild Bill's hair. Accompanying these items were numerous photographs, depicting the Reverend Warren; the Reverend William Canary and Mrs. Canary, Calamity's father and mother; Calamity and her favorite horse; Janey at age eighteen; Janey at Richmond, Virginia, in her forties; her deceased husband, Ed McCormick; her five-year-old son Bobby, who was killed when Senator Burkhart's yacht collided with the McCormick yacht on Chesapeake Bay; Betty Jane, daughter of her first husband, Jack Oakes, kidnapped at age two; and Janey in her nurse's uniform in France during World War I.

Also included in the donated items was a manuscript by Jean McCormick titled "Beside Lonely Campfires with Wild Bill Hickok and Calamity Jane," which she intended to expand into a book. In this story, Jean embellished her earlier sketchy statements about her birth, creating a narrative such as found in nineteenth-century romantic novels. It relates that when Calamity Jane went to the Yellowstone country to have her baby, she "built a small cabin well hidden from prying eyes under an immense overhanging rock." Only two days after the baby was born, none other than Wild Bill Hickok arrived, explaining, "I love you Jane, more than anything on earth, but I'm a coward, too much of a coward to verify our marriage. You won't object should I name the baby Jane, will you? I have some money for you but other than that I am helpless." Shortly after Hickok departed, James O'Neil supposedly stumbled upon the cabin and, assisted by an Indian woman sent back by Hickok, helped Calamity. O'Neil left after a few weeks, and Calamity departed with the baby for Omaha "six months later." After a tearful parting in Omaha between mother and infant, O'Neil took the baby by train to the East, while Calamity "turned to bull team toward the west to make of life what she could or would. Quiet and unassuming, at the head of the wagon rode the sky pilot, the Rev. Sipes, who had been her faithful friend and counselor for years and would be to the end."[18]

Meanwhile, Jean pursued other options to profit from her documents. She had hoped to establish a "Wild Bill Hickok Lodge" with dining room and display area in Deadwood, but changed her mind after business leaders challenged her claim to be the daughter of Wild Bill and Calamity Jane.[19] She next considered taking over the "old stage station" in Virginia Dale, Colorado, hoping her famous parentage would attract business, but this plan also was never realized.[20] Searching for work in 1947, she inquired whether promoters in Virginia City, Montana, might want her there "reading excerpts from Jane's diary," though she was willing to accept work even as nurse or hotel clerk."[21] Eventually, Don C. and Stella Foote employed her in their Wonderland Museum in Billings, Montana, purchasing McCormick's relics and the diary and letters for display. Selected portions of McCormick's documents were published in a small booklet titled *Copies of Calamity Jane's Diary and Letters.*[22]

McCormick died in Billings on February 21, 1951, a decade after she made her dramatic announcement. She was seventy-seven years old, if her stated birthdate was accurate. Her death resulted "from heart disease after a short illness," according to an obituary notice in the *Billings Gazette*. The newspaper added that McCormick had lived in Billings most of the time since 1922 and that she had no survivors. The obituary repeated her alleged relationship to Calamity Jane and printed excerpts from the "diary and letters," but added no new information about Jean, leaving her as mysterious in death as she had been when she first made her radio announcement.[23]

Despite McCormick's complaints that she constantly faced skepticism after her 1941 proclamation, many writers accepted her story. Nolie Mumey reprinted McCormick's documents in their entirety in his *Calamity Jane* (1950). He also cited a handwriting expert who determined the documents were genuine. The analyst compared the handwriting in the diary and loose-page entries to the letters purportedly written by Calamity Jane to Captain O'Neil and concluded that all were written by the same individual. Of course, this meant all these documents could have been written by the same forger. Nevertheless, his conclusion was applauded by enthusiastic supporters of McCormick's claims. Author Homer Croy, for example, entertained "no doubt" about the diary's authenticity because "Government handwriting experts have agreed that these are Calamity's own words."[24]

Another writer who accepted McCormick's documents was Montana correspondent Kathryn Wright. In her articles about Calamity Jane, Wright even agreed with McCormick's pronouncement that a studio portrait of Calamity actually was that of a look-alike model selected by tour sponsors. "Calamity refused to sit for publicity photos while touring eastern museums and lecturing on her frontier life," McCormick told Wright.[25] McCormick's documents also were used by author Glenn Clarimonte to develop a full-length biography of Martha Canary. Clairmonte's *Calamity Was the Name for Jane* (1959) was based on fairly extensive research about Martha, but it mixed information about her with stories from McCormick's diary and letters, producing a confusing narrative. To flesh out Calamity's story, Clairmonte invented conversations.

It is curious that these writers so readily accepted McCormick's documents since the woman described in them bears little resemblance to the real Calamity Jane. Martha Canary's *Life and Adventures of Calamity Jane* tells a very different story from that in the diary and letters. Martha relates the events, authentic and imagined, that she thought to be important up to 1896 when her autobiography was published. Oddly, McCormick's diary and letters allude neither to the adventures Martha described in the story of her life nor to documented historical events after 1896 in which she participated. The diary and letters, for example, do not mention Calamity's claims of scouting for Crook, capturing Jack McCall, saving the Dead-wood stage, or serving as a Black Hills pony express rider. Nor do McCormick's documents tell about Calamity's forced visit to the Gallatin County poorhouse, her trip to the Pan-American Exposition, or her selling of her pamphlets and photographs in Yellowstone Park.

In fact, the tenor of McCormick's Calamity differs dramatically from that in Martha's 1896 autobiography and in the historical record. For example, McCormick's Calamity seems far more educated than documents show Martha to have been. In contrast to the simple language of the autobiography, the diary and letters includes phrasing such as "the staccato wail of Indian dogs," "the sunshine crept softly down between the tree branches seeming to spread a glory of radiant light about the group of friends gathered there . . . like a benediction," "a large building with brilliantly illuminated windows," "something divine above me," and "an avaricious old age."[26]

This wording is remarkable since it is unlikely Martha Canary could read and write. *Life and Adventures* was dictated by her, and evidently friends read newspapers and letters to her. "There is not in existence so far as I can determine, an authenticated piece of Calamity's handwriting," declared biographer J. Leonard Jennewein, who wrote to auto-graph dealers and collectors, searched hotel registers, and questioned old-timers.[27] His statement, made in 1953, is still true today. An undisputed letter by Calamity Jane would bring a high price at auction, yet none has been located. One signature, an "X" at the bottom of a photograph, is touted as genuine by autograph expert Charles Hamilton, and if he is correct leaves little chance for the diary and letters to be authentic.[28]

Also militating against the genuineness of McCormick's documents and mementoes is evidence that at least twice during Calamity's lifetime it was reported that she lost all her possessions in fires. In addition, no reminiscence mentions her having carried a diary. When Calamity Jane arrived in the Black Hills in 1903, her friend Dora Du Fran said her only possessions were her buckskin suit, a couple of dresses, and underwear. McCormick's claim that the diary was sent to James O'Neil at the time of Calamity's death in August is also problematic. The detailed newspaper accounts of Calamity's last days report that she asked that her belongings be sent to Lottie Stacey in Belle Fourche.[29]

In fact, the author of McCormick's diary and letters had only limited knowledge of the real Martha Canary. Much of the personal information in McCormick's version of Martha's life is incorrect. The diary clearly addresses "Janey" as her only child, whereas Martha said she had a son born in 1884 and a daughter, named Jessie, born in 1887. Upon her death, Calamity mentioned an estrangement with her daughter and refused to divulge her address for notification, reflecting a relationship very different from that portrayed by McCormick. The diary and letters also inaccurately relate the story of Calamity's husbands, definitely stating that there only were two, Hickok and Burke. Calamity's long relationship with Bill Steers and her legal marriage to him, are unmen-tioned, as are other male companions she called husbands, such as George Cosgrove and Robert Dorsett.

Besides this misinformation, Jean McCormick's diary has internal inconsistencies and numerous factual errors. McCormick, for example, says she was born in 1873, then claims she was eighteen in 1893 when she met Calamity Jane in Richmond, Virginia. In another instance, Jean claims that Calamity left Wild Bill in Deadwood in 1873 three years before the town even existed. And, according to McCormick's documents, Calamity Jane joined Buffalo Bill's Wild West Show on a tour of England in 1893. But Calamity Jane never toured with Cody's show, nor did it go to England that year.[30]

Not only do the documents contain mistakes, they show clear evidence of purposeful deception. For example, records of the Cunard Line show it never employed a captain named O'Neil. The photograph McCormick produced of "Captain O'Neil" is from a newspaper and actually is a picture of Captain A. C. Greig, who sailed for the Cunard Line from 1906 to 1945. In a different diary entry, McCormick tells about a horse named Satan, purportedly given to Calamity Jane by Wild Bill. According to the diary, Satan became Calamity's constant companion until his death, reported in the entry of May 10, 1893. "I had him buried up in the hills near Deadwood," Calamity supposedly wrote, and "here I am wetting this old album with my tears over my poor faithful pet." McCormick even provided a picture of Calamity Jane standing with Satan, "believed to have been taken in 1880 at Coulson, a Montana river bank settlement now faded from existence." But Dr. William A. Allen said he took this photograph in 1897 or 1898, five years after Satan's reported death.[31]

Clearly, the diary and letters are forgeries, and there is considerable evidence suggesting that Jean McCormick was the forger. Paine, the librarian who worked through McCormick's documents in the 1940s, concluded after studying the style and legibility of the diary that the album-diary was written "perhaps in a single night." Paine, however, thought it possible that Calamity Jane, not McCormick, had performed the task. Indeed, so much did Paine want to believe in the genuineness of the documents that he explained away evidence showing them to be forged. For example, after discovering that dates in the original diary entries had been changed, Paine decided that since the changes were not carefully covered up, they supported the diary's authenticity because a forger would have made a concerted effort to conceal the changes. "If the diary is a forgery," Paine concluded, "it is either the cleverest or the most bungled attempt of which I know."[32]

It was, in fact, a bungled attempt, as Paine himself became increasingly aware in studying the documents. First, he discovered that the marriage certificate was fraudulent. Then he learned that Jean was adding to the documents even as he was reading them. In her "desperation" to prove her parentage, Paine informed a correspondent, she complicated his efforts to prove the diary's authenticity by "continually coming up with manuscripts purportedly in the hand of Calamity" to support her claims.[33] Paine was correct, and today Jean McCormick's production of the various documents supposedly by Calamity Jane can be reconstructed to a considerable degree. The album-diary was written first, and probably, as Paine suggested in 1944, was done in one sitting. The loose-page entries to the diary were added after Jean made her announcement in 1941 as she gained new information about Calamity Jane.

The first material written by Jean in the fifteen album entries generally is focused on Montana, but also includes the stories about traveling with Buffalo Bill to New

York, Richmond, and England.[34] The Montana stories in the album that at first seemed inaccessible to anyone not a contemporary of Calamity Jane actually were readily available in Billings area newspapers in the 1930s when McCormick resided there. It is likely these were major sources for McCormick's documents. These articles included accounts of such places as early Coulson and Stringtown and such western characters as Packsaddle Ben Greenough, Dr. W. A. Allen, and Teddy Blue Abbott. It is precisely those people, places, and events that appear in McCormick's diary. Moreover, acquaintances of Calamity Jane who do not appear in these 1930s Montana articles, such as Harry (Sam) Young, Thomas Newson, Clement Lounsberry, Tom Hardwick, Dora Du Fran, and Josephine Brake, also are unmentioned in the diary. Similarly, Calamity's documentable sojourns in places such as Casper, Cheyenne, Custer, Douglas, Fort Laramie, Fort Steele, Lander, Pierre, Rawlins, and Sturgis remain unmentioned in most 1930s Montana newspaper articles. They also are absent from McCormick's diary, which assumes Calamity lived in only three places: Abilene, Deadwood, and the Billings area.[35]

But there is also information in the diary not from newspapers, such as the description of Madame Etta Feeley's house of prostitution in Billings and Calamity's marriage to Clinton Burke, which the diary places in 1891.[36] It is likely these details came from informants or personal knowledge. One of Jean's associates who might have possessed such information was Pearl McDaniels, who traveled to New York with Jean when she made her radio pronouncement.[37] Although it may be coincidental, a woman named Olive Warren McDaniels was employed by Madame Feeley (Mrs. Alice M. Leach) in 1897 in Billings, and later became a prominent brothel madam there herself. Olive, who knew Calamity Jane well, has been identified as the young woman Calamity chased with a hatchet in Yegen Brothers department store in 1902.[38]

Another informant may have been the notorious fraud J. Frank Dalton, who is reported to have visited the Yellowstone country of Montana in the late 1930s. This imposter changed his fantastic stories repeatedly, claiming at one time to have been a member of the Dalton gang and ending his career with the claim that he was Jesse James.[39] Interestingly, McCormick's documents include passages claiming that Jesse James survived after being fatally shot by Bob Ford in 1882, living afterwards under the assumed name Dalton. Calamity, in a letter purportedly written to James O'Neil in 1889, says she just met Jesse James who was "passing under the name of Dalton but he couldn't fool me." "He is quite a character—you know he was killed in '82," she added. "His mother swore that the body that was in the coffin was his but it was another man. . . . Jesse sang at his own funeral." The latter tale parallels a story told in 1937 by a Jesse James imposter who claimed that, "in disguise, he had attended his own funeral."[40]

McCormick also solicited information about Calamity Jane from local residents in Montana. L. W. Randall, magazine writer and local Montana historian, remembered that McCormick approached his Uncle Billy in the late 1930s seeking stories about what he termed "the controversial character, Calamity Jane." McCormick carried "affidavits" for him to sign, Randall said, but Uncle Billy "termed her an out-and-out hoax." Nevertheless, McCormick spent considerable time talking with him. A few weeks later, Uncle

Billy, "chuckling gleefully" while speaking with his nephew, recalled the interview "I told her what I knew and a lot of things others had told me, straight, without any covering up, but what I can't understand is why anyone would want to claim an old renegade like Calamity Jane as their mother."[41]

Another resident who visited with McCormick was cowboy "Packsaddle Ben" Greenough. McCormick "came out to my Ranch to see me and I met her in Billings several times," Greenough recalled. "I have quite a few letters now that she wrote me telling about her mother Calamity Jane." Greenough told McCormick stories about his encounters with Calamity in Billings in 1886. For his trouble, Greenough received favorable mention in "Calamity's" diary. In an entry dated July 25, 1893, Calamity supposedly wrote to Jean: "I want to tell you about a young kid I met the other day—These old cow pokes like to torment him. If he lives to be an old man and you come out in this country and ever find a real honest to God man who you ever hear speak a good word for me you ask that man his name and I bet it will prove to be Ben Greenough. He isn't so low minded that he gossips about your mother like some of these men do—You find him someday and tell him thanks for his kindness."[42]

The loose-page additions to the diary reveal even better than the album-diary how McCormick forged the documents. After she announced that Calamity and Wild Bill were her parents, several people claiming acquaintance with Calamity wrote her. Each time she received a new piece of information from these correspondents, McCormick added an entry to the diary on a loose sheet of paper. Jean meant the new entries to prove the diary's authenticity. Ironically, comparison of loose-page entries to information given to her in these letters shows similarities that defy independent invention and prove McCormick was the diary's author.

Among the first to write to McCormick was William Lull of Yonkers, New York. Lull told McCormick of his adventures with Calamity Jane during the Black Hills gold rush. Nearly eighty-seven years old, Lull said he was only twenty when he met Calamity in Deadwood. There he worked for a man named Porter from New Orleans in a hotel near the No. 10 Saloon where Jack McCall killed Hickok. "I knew your mother probably better than anyone," Lull declared. "She rented a room in the hotel" and waited tables for Tom Miller, who owned the Variety Theater next to the hotel. When Calamity "had an attack of Mountain Fever," Lull said, he found a doctor for her. Calamity often gambled, he added, and when he sometimes "staked her to a five spot," she would return in the morning "with a thousand or more."[43]

A loose-page insert to the purported diary, dated July 1880 in Coulson, Montana, reads: "I met a man here today from Deadwood who knew my best friend there, Mister Will Lull. I was sick with a fever of some sort while rooming at his Hotel." The insert adds that Lull had taken over the hotel "from a New Orleans man, Porter." Another loose-page entry, dated January 1882, adds: "I miss my friend Will Lull to stake me . . . One night he loaned me a 5 spot & when I saw him the next morning I had $1000."[44] The information in the loose pages conveys precisely the information contained in Lull's 1941 letter to McCormick.

Likewise, in her personal correspondence McCormick mentioned that Jack Lloyd had written to her, claiming to be one of the last people alive who was present at Hickok's murder. "Captain" Lloyd, who likely invented his experiences, also claimed that Calamity Jane took care of him for about four years in Deadwood when he was a boy. Not surprisingly, a loose-page entry purportedly by Calamity Jane asserts, "I am looking after a little boy. His name is Jackie."[45] When Paine began ink and paper tests to determine if the pages dated from the nineteenth century, a new loose-page entry explained why the tests might be inconclusive. In it, "Calamity" writes, "I sometimes find it impossible to carry the old album to write in so you will find now & then extra pages. My ink has been frozen so many times it is almost spoiled."[46] Not only did the entry provide an explanation why Calamity was writing on separate pages, it suggested why ink tests might not be conclusive proof of forgery!

Frequently, Jean McCormick used her loose-page entries to punish those who questioned her claims. Conversely, she rewarded those who supported her with positive comments in new diary pages. When Jean asked for help to establish a tourist business in Deadwood, Nell Perrigoue of the Deadwood Chamber of Commerce demanded proof of her parental claims. In private correspondence, McCormick told one acquaintance, "That woman Nell Perrigoue rules the roost there, and she is even trying to keep me from locating in or near Deadwood." She added that "when I *do* start on her she'll change her plans of branding before the public my parents as 'siwash'."[47] In a new loose-page entry to the diary, Calamity warns her daughter: "Now thats Deadwood for you & when you come out here, if you ever do Janey & any of them stick up their nose at you because of your parents & if they bury me beside your Father you move our bodies to Abilene Kansas or where ever you wish."[48] Removal of the bodies from graves that were a prime Deadwood tourist attraction would have been the ultimate revenge against Deadwood's Chamber of Commerce. In contrast, when Jean took her documents and relics to Fort Collins, among the people who supported their genuineness was Mrs. Bauder, a member of the Colorado town's Pioneer Society who as a former resident of Deadwood had known Calamity Jane. Not surprisingly, a loose-page entry dated July 1880 comments about Deadwood, "There is only 1 woman in that mess of crums & that is Missus Bauder."[49]

Like Nell Perrigoue, Tobe Borner, nephew of Calamity Jane, stated publicly that McCormick's claims were "utterly groundless." As in the case of others who questioned McCormick's parentage, Borner was the target in a new loose-page entry. "They [the Borners] live down in Wyoming where their brat was born. I helped them out because they were too poor to hire a midwife." Vengefully, she added: "Dont bother Janey to ever look them up. Their name is Borner & the lieingest outfit you ever saw. I had it out with Toby one day. When I got through he knew what he was. They dont know anything about you Janey. They arent fit to mention your name to."[50]

Most interesting of all the entries written by McCormick is the strange "confession" of Calamity Jane purportedly written on June 3, 1903, in Deadwood. It contends that Belle Starr was Calamity's sister and was married to William Hickok, a cousin of James Butler "Wild Bill" Hickok. The "confession" also asserts that Belle Starr posed as

Calamity's daughter in later years, and Belle's child, Jessie Elizabeth, as Calamity's grand-daughter. According to the document, Jessie Elizabeth was born at Benson's Landing, Montana, the same place Jean McCormick claimed she was born. After William Hickok ended his relationship with Belle, she lived with Jack Oakes of Fort Pierre. Starr and Oakes supposedly had a son, Charley Oakes, a half-brother of Jessie Elizabeth.[51]

This "confession" obviously was written by Jean in an effort to reconcile her claim to be Calamity Jane's only daughter with assertions made in earlier letters published in area newspapers by Jessie Elizabeth Murray, Calamity's actual daughter. Beginning in 1933 and continuing for several years thereafter, Jessie solicited information about Calamity Jane from newspapers, libraries, historical societies, and government agencies in the northern plains. She also inquired about a missing half-brother named Charley Oakes. Jessie's letters exhibit considerable identity confusion. In her correspondence, Jessie claimed to be the granddaughter of Calamity Jane. In one letter, she said that when she was ten years old Calamity's "last husband," presumably Robert Dorsett, took her away from her "grandmother." To prove her claims, Jessie listed as references people who had known her in childhood. These included Etta Feeley, the brothel madam in Billings, and Mrs. Jordan Bean, an early resident of Bridger, Montana. According to Jessie, her stepfather, Jack Oakes, killed a man near Fort Pierre and died in 1893 in an accident in Pueblo, Colorado. Her "stepmother" was Bell Oakes.[52]

By 1937, details in Jessie's letters changed. Although she continued to claim Calamity Jane was her grandmother, her father now became "Two Gun Hickok," a U.S. marshal in Dakota in the 1880s who was not to be confused with his cousin, Wild Bill Hickok. Her mother now became Belle Starr, the famous Oklahoma bandit, who in turn had been raised by Ben Waddell, the owner of the overland freighting business, and his wife. This made Calamity Jane the mother of Belle Starr.[53]

Clearly, Jean McCormick decided she had to confront the information given in Jessie's letters because it did not conform to her claims. Initially, in an entry in her album-diary dated July 25, 1893, McCormick denied the fantastic Belle Starr relationship described in Jessie's letters. Later, however, McCormick incorporated Jessie's strange information by adding the "confession," reversing her earlier denial.[54] Perhaps her decision to switch stories was made when Montana pioneers asked about the child they recalled with Calamity Jane in Bridger in 1898. That girl, about twelve years old, could not have been Jean, who would have been twenty-five at that time. This discrepancy was addressed by Helen S. Meldrum after she interviewed Jean McCormick in Buffalo, Wyoming, on May 13, 1941. Meldrum concluded that the "confession" shown to her by McCormick straightened out this confusion: the girl raised by Calamity in Bridger was the daughter of her sister, Belle Starr.[55] The bizarre "confession" may have helped clarify Meldrum's confusion, but it stands today as another glaring example of McCormick's forgery.

Interestingly, Jessie changed her story again as well. In 1942, by which time Jessie and Jean had corresponded, Jessie now claimed Calamity Jane was her aunt rather than her grandmother, and that Belle Starr was Calamity's sister rather than her daughter. In this manner, her story agreed with the one related by McCormick in the "confession."

Jessie then used the confession as evidence of her birth so she could get a pension in California. Evidently, this was deemed sufficient proof, and she received financial assistance until her death on March 14, 1980.[56]

McCormick also utilized the "confession" in the diary to prove her birthdate for old-age assistance. She petitioned the Yellowstone County, Montana, Department of Public Welfare for support in 1941. Before granting Jean's request, county officials inquired of the "We the People" personnel whether Jean's September 23, 1873, birthdate was legitimate. Based on the radio manager's belief that McCormick's documents were genuine, Jean's pension was granted.[57]

Besides getting government welfare, McCormick's motivations for writing the diary and letters included fame and personal identity. Becoming a celebrity made it possible for her to gain employment and be paid for public appearances. There can be no doubt that McCormick, who regularly complained of poverty and hard work, hoped to profit from her diary and letters.[58] However, McCormick's primary motivation may have been her psychological need for an identity. In a loose-page entry dated January 1882, the diarist (supposedly Calamity Jane) suggests that her daughter (Jean) read the novels by Mary Jane Holmes. There is reason to believe these actually were McCormick's favorites. Holmes's novels repeat a familiar theme: a child is deserted by her parents, usually for noble reasons; she is reared by kind but common people who die, leaving her orphaned; she is denied love due to unknown parentage, then redeemed and rewarded with wealth, love, and fame after an important relative is discovered. Holmes's stories also frequently involve sea captains sailing ships to Liverpool, England. The amazing tale of a sea captain adopting Calamity Jane's child, of the daughter's fantastic discovery of her parentage later in life, and of a husband ending their marriage because of her dishonorable parentage, carries themes befitting a Holmes novel. Perhaps McCormick was an orphan who wished all her life for a famous parent to rescue her from obscurity and poverty. Though speculative, such a conclusion may not be without foundation.[59]

Whatever her motives, McCormick's sincerity, combined with the existence of the diary and letters, was convincing to many people. As a result, these documents have caused lasting confusion in the historical record, and the story told in the diary and letters has become an integral part of Calamity Jane folklore. Ever since, numerous histories of the American West have utilized McCormick's documents in their portrayals of Calamity Jane. For example, writer Earl Schenck Miers, in *Wild and Woolly West* (1964), claimed that to "know the truth about Wild Bill," you had to "see him through the eyes of the one person who understood him thoroughly, the immortal Calamity Jane." She "must have her good points," he added, because Wild Bill married her, though he deserted her after she gave birth "to a child in a wilderness cave."[60]

McCormick's fabricated Calamity Jane also has inspired filmmakers. In 1984, CBS television produced *Calamity Jane*, starring Jane Alexander. The film is mostly taken from McCormick's documents. In the movie, Calamity joins Wild Bill Hickok in Kansas, and afterward they are married by the Reverends Warren and Sipes. However, in this instance the scriptwriters modified the story told in McCormick's documents: the ministers are drunk when they perform the ceremony. Because of this, Hickok does not take the vows seriously. In fact, he warns the clergymen that if they ever mention the incident, he will inform their superiors of their drunkenness. But Calamity believes her marriage is legal. She only agrees to keep it secret after Hickok explains that no town would ever hire him as marshal if they knew he was married. To appease her, Hickok buys her a new buckskin outfit and gives her a horse named Satan. But Calamity realizes that Hickok has distanced himself from her, and consequently does not tell him of her pregnancy and the birth of their daughter, Jean (Janey). Instead, the child is given up for adoption to Captain James and Helen O'Neil. Twice, after Hickok's death, Calamity meets Janey, but does not identify her relationship. Instead, Calamity continues her life in the West, a strong independent woman who refuses to be trapped by social conventions. Reflecting feminist concerns of the 1980s, Calamity advises her daughter that any woman who "goes her own way" is "damn lucky" if she "ends up with some self-respect."

In 1995, CBS again produced a film based to a considerable degree on McCormick's diary and letters. Although ostensibly a film version of Larry McMurtry's novel *Buffalo Girls*, changes were introduced to more closely follow McCormick's documents. Once again Calamity Jane and Wild Bill Hickok are married and have a child, Jean, who is given up for adoption to Captain O'Neil. In addition, in this film Calamity Jane joins Buffalo Bill's Wild West Show on its English tour, and while over there visits her daughter, who is unaware of their relationship.

That same year, McCormick's diary and letters became the basis for a full-length biography of Calamity Jane. The author, Stella Foote, had employed McCormick at the Wonderland Museum in Billings. In her account of Calamity Jane, *A History of Calamity Jane, Our Nation's First Liberated Woman*, Foote fails to address any of the criticisms about McCormick's documents that had appeared since their initial appearance in 1941. For example, Foote reproduces the phony photograph of Captain O'Neil without mentioning that it has been proven to be a photo of Captain Greig. She also ignores the inconsistencies between documented information about Calamity and the story told in McCormick's documents. Foote's biography suggests that proponents of McCormick's claims will ignore the evidence proving her diary and letters forgeries, and continue using her documents as source material for the history of Calamity Jane. Indeed, a film producer recently purchased McCormick's documents at auction for an astounding $55,000, intending to further perpetuate her story.[61]

Thus, the Calamity Jane portrayed in Jean McCormick's diary and letters has become an integral part of the Calamity Jane legend. McCormick's spurious tale now appears in a variety of popular culture mediums. In 1992, *Ms.* magazine's "Ms. Quiz" on "Women of Letters" asked readers to identify the correct title of the book of letters by Calamity Jane. The correct answer, it said, was *Calamity Jane's Letters to Her Daughter.*[62] Now, Gillian Robinson has told McCormick's story of Calamity Jane in poetry in *The Slow Reign of Calamity Jane* (1994). And McCormick's documents have even been set to music. Composer Libby Larson's *Songs from Letters: Calamity Jane to Her Daughter Janey, 1880–1902*, has gained considerable public attention, and soprano Dora Ohrenstein's rendition of the music is available on compact disc.[63]

There remains the question why McCormick's diary and letters have gained such popularity despite being obvious forgeries. The answer, it seems, has to do with the character of Calamity Jane in legend. Prior to McCormick's documents, this Calamity Jane was primarily masculine, scouting, riding, smoking, and drinking her way through the West. Evidently, this image was inadquate to fully captivate the public imagination, for early in the twentieth century Calamity's nursing and charity were increasingly emphasized, giving her feminine qualities. Calamity's humanitarianism quickly became one of the most compelling aspects of her legend. In 1941, Jean McCormick added motherhood to Calamity's character, reinforcing her femininity. McCormick's Calamity Jane has since become so popular that she often displaces the actual Martha Canary in histories of the West.

Writers utilizing McCormick's diary and letters for their portrayals of Calamity Jane provide revealing comments to support this shift. For example, journalist Kathryn Wright titled her account of McCormick's claims "Series of Letters to Daughter Reveal Feminine Side of Calamity Jane." Similarly, Suzanne Clauser, who wrote the script for the 1984 television movie *Calamity Jane*, commented: "I love the lady who's in those diaries. She's a fascinating woman." And scholar Elizabeth Stevenson in *Figures in a Western Landscape* (1994) noted how the letters "move the reader." They "create a character who is believable and haunting," she explained. In her opinion, McCormick's documents could not be "a cheap or cunning fraud for the letters have the authenticity of art."[64]

The appeal of McCormick's Calamity Jane is no more evident than in the production of the CBS movie *Buffalo Girls*. In Larry McMurtry's novel of the same name, Calamity writes letters in a diary to her imaginary daughter, Janey. However, at the end of the novel the reader learns that Janey is a product of Calamity's imagination. Furthermore, in his conclusion McMurtry employs a speculation by Clarence Paine that Calamity was a hermaphrodite, unable to bear children. Evidently, filmmakers found the story told in McCormick's diary and letters more compelling; in the film version of McMurtry's novel, Calamity's daughter is real.[65]

Nevertheless, history, if not popular culture, must respect the truth. The diary and letters are fraudulent. McCormick's Calamity Jane is vastly different from the actual Martha Canary. Yet, despite McCormick's factual errors, misinformation, and personal vendettas, her documents have secured a permanent place in Calamity Jane folklore, an amazing feat for a clumsy forgery.

CHAPTER SIXTEEN

Challenging the Myth, 1953–2003

Midpoint in the twentieth century, no one had yet produced a satisfactory, full-length biography of Calamity Jane. The subject invited scholarly attention because she was so famous and many exaggerated tales had been added to her story during the fifty years since her death. The fraudulent documents produced by Jean McCormick also demanded scholarly examination.

Several historians began seriously researching the Calamity Jane story in the 1940s and 1950s. Among those beginning biographical studies of Calamity Jane was librarian Clarence S. Paine, who had been analyzing Jean McCormick's diary and letters for a decade. Paine never finished his proposed full-length biography, but in his published essays about Calamity he dismissed any suggestions of an intimate relationship between Calamity Jane and Wild Bill Hickok.[1] Another researcher, Colorado doctor Nolie Mumey, completed his book, *Calamity Jane, 1852–1903* (1950), but his uncritical compilation of newspaper stories and unverified reminiscences, including the complete text of McCormick's "diary and letters" which he believed to be genuine, failed to settle disputes or establish Calamity's life story.

The two biographical studies of Calamity Jane that gained most scholarly respect were those by South Dakota historian J. Leonard Jennewein and by Montana State University graduate student Roberta Beed Sollid. Jennewein's *Calamity Jane of the Western Trails* (1953) was first to be published. According to Jennewein, a good case could be made "in favor of not saying anything about Calamity," who was "a disreputable old harridan, a disgrace to womankind." Nevertheless, he began reconstructing Calamity's story by interviewing people who remembered her and carefully analyzing contradictory evidence about her birth, scouting career, nursing activities, and relationship with Wild Bill Hickok. Jennewein concluded that she was an alcoholic braggart, occasional prostitute, and generally flamboyant character. "She dressed like a man," and "drank whiskey in saloons with men, before such practice was socially acceptable," he wrote.

In addition, she carried a gun, swore, chewed tobacco, and traveled with bull trains. Her unique behavior "set her apart," and "made people talk about her." She did everything "with a flair, with exuberance, with a native sense of showmanship" creating "episodes calculated to remain on the memory of the witnesses."[2]

Although Jennewein did not intend to resolve all the controversies about Calamity, he showed in his discussion of her death how such a task might be accomplished. Numerous writers had reported that she died on August 2, the anniversary of Hickok's murder. Although the "written record of the life of Calamity Jane is a maze of contradiction, errors and suppositions," wrote Jennewein, "there is no excuse for an incorrect reporting of the date of her death," a mistake made, he noted, by Duncan Aikman, Estelline Bennett, E. A. Brininstool, Jesse Brown and A. M. Willard, Robert J. Casey, O. W. Coursey, Stewart Holbrook, Nolie Mumey, Albert Williams, and Harry (Sam) Young. "We did take the trouble to read an old newspaper or two; we checked the date against all local sources," said Jennewein. "The date on her tombstone is correct." Jennewein hammered home the lesson this error provided: "Very little research, even of an elementary nature, has been applied to much of the writing about Calamity," he declared. "Writers have accepted the word of previous authors without checking original sources." In the case of her death, popular writers postponed it one day so it coincided with Hickok's, and, concluded Jennewein, even "serious writers apparently went right along with the idea."[3]

Simultaneously, Roberta Sollid, unaware of Jennewein's research, completed her master's thesis on Calamity Jane, afterwards published as *Calamity Jane: A Study in Historical Criticism* (1958). She found a different prevailing attitude about Calamity Jane among pioneers than romancers had claimed. Whereas they insisted Calamity's contemporaries would not say a bad word against her, Sollid discovered upon her arrival in Deadwood that old-timers "were not pleased to know that further research was being made on such a person as Calamity Jane" because they "thought her of no consequence and not at all important in Deadwood history."[4]

Sollid began her book with a frontal attack on the stories about Calamity Jane that had appeared in recent decades. Although Calamity during her lifetime had "gained notoriety and a certain amount of fame as a character, enough at least so that the newspapers mentioned her when she was in town," wrote Sollid, her legendary status really developed only "some twenty years after her death in 1903 and after the death of those who knew her best." It was then, said Sollid, that "for some unknown reason, sensation-writers and historians began to take an interest in her." Once begun, "prodigious quantities of material containing a paucity of truth were written about her." If uncertain of the facts, writers invented them: "No one could prove them false." It was Sollid's intent to locate contemporary newspaper records and documents to ascertain the truth. Her "study in historical criticism" would separate imagined tales and mistaken information from documented facts. Sollid's skepticism was immediately apparent: of the fifty people she interviewed during her travels through the northern plains, she concluded that only "about ten can be credited with dependable contributions."[5]

The major hurdle Sollid faced was locating sufficient information to determine the truth about disputed events. "No career is so elusive to the historian as that of a loose woman," she asserted. "Calamity Jane was that sort of woman," leaving "little behind in the way of tangible evidence which could be used by historians to reconstruct the story of her checkered career." With no personal letters by Calamity and only meager legal records, Sollid relied primarily on contemporary newspaper articles that at least established Calamity's location at particular times. These also suggested "a pattern or trend which may be used to determine the truth of her own stories or of those repeated by other people." On this basis, Sollid determined that Calamity's account of saving the stage when Johnny Slaughter was killed was a complete fabrication. She also noticed that Deadwood newspapers did not mention Calamity Jane's presence when Jack McCall was captured. Brown and Willard's description of Calamity's nursing hundreds of small-pox victims in 1878 was greeted with the query, "Why did the *Black Hills Daily Times* not 'sing her praises' during the times when the smallpox epidemics struck Deadwood?" Although Sollid acknowledged that Calamity performed charitable acts, she believed "drunkenness, whoring and violence" were the dominant features in Calamity's life.[6]

These midcentury publications about Calamity Jane revealed a significant shift toward careful research and critical analysis. Sollid and Jennewein harshly criticized less careful constructions of Calamity Jane's career. In 1957, for example, Jennewein challenged the editors of *Encyclopedia Americana* about their entry on Calamity Jane, commenting that he doubted "that a single sentence of your entry is completely true." Indeed, their error-ridden biographical sketch mistakenly described Calamity Jane as "an aide to General Custer and General Miles in numerous campaigns" and "the government mail carrier between Deadwood, S.D., and Custer, Mont." The editors accepted Jennewein's offer to write a more accurate description.[7]

The appearance in 1959 of Glenn Clairmonte's *Calamity Was the Name for Jane*, constructed from Calamity's autobiographical stories, unverified reminiscences, liberal use of McCormick's diary and letters, and invented conversations, opened the door wide for further criticism. Jennewein angrily submitted an extensive list of questions to the author and publisher for which he demanded proof. "This book, described by the publisher as 'distinguished biography,' should be classified as fiction," he declared. Similarly, Sollid, who reviewed Clairmonte's book for *Montana: The Magazine of Western History*, denounced it as having "more misinformation . . . per square page than . . . most western fiction novels." Concerning Clairmonte's reputation as a "darning needle," due to her alleged careful research, Sollid asserted: "the darning needle dropped its first stitch on page one and had failed to pick it up by the time it reached the last page fifteen chapters later." She suggested "embroidery needle" would be a better description.[8]

The academic community was strongly influenced by Jennewein and Sollid. Historian Howard Roberts Lamar, in his essay on Calamity Jane in *The Reader's Encyclopedia of the American West* (1974), showed this impact. "Apocryphal stories about her childhood and the source of her nickname are nearly as numerous as those about her supposed love affair with Wild Bill Hickok," Lamar said, adding that McCormick's diary and letters lacked documentation.[9] Likewise, in his *History of South Dakota* (1961) Herbert Schell complained that the early history of the Black Hills gold rush has "been romanticized and exploited in dime novels and Wild West shows and on movie and television screens," making "characters of such dubious repute as Wild Bill Hickok and Calamity Jane . . . into legends."[10] Another apparent change occurred in new editions of Robert E. Riegel's textbook, *America Moves West*. In earlier printings, Calamity was described as "the best-known woman of the plains," even though she was a "big, coarse, strong, vulgar, lewd, promiscuous" female who "wore men's clothes, could swear with the best, chew a sizable cud of tobacco, and drink most men under the table." Now, in the extensively revised 1964 edition of Riegel's text, the "best-known woman of the plains" was no longer mentioned.[11]

Scholars in the burgeoning new field of women's history also found Calamity Jane of little interest. According to historian Glenda Riley, earlier writers about the American West generally focused on unique females such as Calamity Jane "who acted more like men" rather than on typical western women. Riley called this tendency the "Calamity Jane syndrome." Scholar Sandra Myres similarly concluded that Calamity Jane personified "the soiled dove or female bandit . . . who drank, smoked, and cursed and was handy with a poker deck, a six-gun, and a horse." Stories about women like Calamity Jane, Myres concluded, "stood out because they differed from the lives of most pioneer women."[12] It is not surprising, then, that Calamity Jane was omitted in most scholarly histories of women. For example, Calamity Jane does not appear in June Sochen's *Herstory: A Woman's View of American History* (1974) or in *The Women's West* (1987), edited by Susan Armitage and Elizabeth Jameson.[13]

Biographers of Wild Bill Hickok were similarly upset that Calamity Jane was considered a significant western figure, but their hostility was directed at her association with Hickok rather than her unique qualities. After all, Wild Bill was hardly a typical pioneer, either. Thus, biographer Richard O'Connor included a chapter entitled "Calamity Jane and other Fables" in his *Wild Bill Hickok* (1959) in which he denounced movie versions and McCormick's documents presenting a close relationship between Wild Bill and Calamity Jane. "The drab truth is that Hickok and Calamity Jane were intimate enough to exchange a handshake or a slap on the back—nothing more," O'Connor concluded. "That she was buried near Wild Bill was "the crowning irony of his career," he added, for it meant "that he would be linked eternally for all the world to see, with the uncouth and unromantic creature whom he had known only as an occasional drinking companion."[14]

Likewise, Hickok biographer Joseph G. Rosa assailed efforts to associate the famous gunfighter with Calamity Jane. Furthermore, in his careful study, *They Called Him Wild Bill: The Life and Adventures of James Butler Hickok* (1964), Rosa entirely discounted Calamity's role in western history: "She was said to be able to outshoot, outshout, and outswear most men—although contemporary evidence does little to substantiate this portrait."[15]

This crusade to de-glamorize Calamity Jane was also evident in fiction and film. In *Miss Morissa: Doctor of the Gold Trail* (1956), Mari Sandoz describes the tribulations of Dr. Morissa Kirk to gain acceptance as a medical doctor in the West. In Sandoz's novel,

Calamity is loud and frequently drunk, having unkempt hair and a "sodden, dissolute face." When Morissa first meets her, she recognizes Calamity as a childhood friend from Missouri whom she once envied. But now Martha, who recalls that Morissa was an illegitimate child, is a rough woman and hurts Morissa deeply by calling her a "bastard" in front of a crowd.[16]

Calamity's reputation also was viewed dimly by the film industry in *This Is the West That Was* (1974), starring Kim Darby as Calamity Jane. In this movie, Calamity, a masterful spinner of tall tales, single-handedly creates Wild Bill's reputation as a gunfighter with her saloon stories of his battle with the McCanles gang (in the film he is not even an active participant), and she gives both Wild Bill Hickok and Buffalo Bill Cody their nicknames. Calamity manufactures a heroic role in western events for herself as well. About these inflated reputations, the film's narrator comments with sarcasm belying the words: "Becoming a legend in your own lifetime is a rare achievement, but Buffalo Bill Cody, and Calamity Jane, and Wild Bill Hickok achieved it, and because they did they are now a part of our heritage and history."

Even though these attacks on the Calamity Jane legend were formidable, they were buried in an avalanche of new popular publications repeating old tales. Mari Sandoz observed in 1961 when discussing famous characters of the northern plains: "Although the three gaudiest, Wild Bill Hickok, Buffalo Bill Cody, and Calamity Jane, actually existed, their actuality vanished with practically the first word of the mythmakers, who, ninety, one hundred years later are still at work and, curiously, with perhaps greater impact."[17] Historian Kent Ladd Steckmesser speculated why these romantic stories persisted. "Once a popularizer got hold of a promising character," he said, "the legends were extremely difficult to correct" because they "became embedded in a number of subsequent accounts and by simple repetition came to be accepted as the truth." Since many readers "seem to believe that proof of the reliability of a story lies in the number of times it has been repeated, without stopping to consider the source from which it came," the mere fact that legends about Calamity Jane had been circulating for a long time impaired scholarly efforts to deny them. "Serious historians lost the western field by default," concluded Steckmesser. By omitting colorful characters such as Calamity Jane from their studies, scholars left a vacuum filled by "the popularizers."[18]

The voices of the legend-makers were legion. John Burke's "The Wildest Woman in the West" in the inaugural issue of *True Frontier* magazine (1967) proclaimed that Calamity Jane "could out-cuss, out-drink, out-shoot, and often out-fight any man around." Although paraphrasing liberally from Jennewein's account ("She drank in saloons with men before such practices were acceptable"; her actions "set her apart, made people talk about her"), Burke paid little attention to Jennewein's conclusions. In Burke's version, Calamity was born Jane Dalton at Fort Laramie in 1860, was orphaned when her parents were killed by Indians, and, with soldiers as her role models, "embarked on a career which in a few years left her shorn of all decency and most womanly virtues."

Burke creatively embellished the granting of her famous nickname by Captain Egan during a skirmish with Indians. Though half of his scouting party command was killed in the initial attack, "Calamity and Egan were still alive, fighting back-to-back against the fierce Indians." Just as the chief of the band "was about to let an arrow fly straight for Captain Egan, Calamity lowered her rifle and fired with deadly aim," causing the other Indians to flee and Egan to nickname her, "Calamity Jane, The Heroine of the Plains."

According to Burke, Calamity wandered the plains until her path crossed that of Hickok in 1867. Afterwards, the pair spent nearly ten years together "in more or less 'constant association'" until his death in 1876. If born in 1860, as Burke claimed, Calamity would have only been seven when she met Hickok, a chronological difficulty that did not deter Burke from recounting their stirring adventures together. In one instance, Calamity and Wild Bill pursued outlaws who had robbed the Rapid City bank in 1873, three years before the town existed. After a fierce fight, Burke continued, Wild Bill and Calamity captured the robbers and collected a $5000 reward, resulting in a "drinking and hell-raising spree that is still talked about in Rapid City today." Compounding his errors, Burke changed the place and date of Calamity's death: "the wildest woman in the West" now died in Belle Fourche on August 3, 1903.[19]

Another popularizer, Ed Earl Repp, complained that no other woman in western history had as many fictionalized episodes attributed to her as Calamity Jane. Then in an article in *Golden West* titled "The Lady Was a Cavalryman!" (1972), Repp proceeded to invent new versions. In this account, Calamity Jane joins Wild Bill Hickok, Colorado Charley Utter, and Bloody Dick Seymour in a Black Hills theatrical production in 1876. "She was probably egotistical enough to believe she was a great actress, and of a certainty hammed it up," Repp asserted. Unfortunately, "her taste for bottled, barreled and sometimes canteened refreshments" caused problems, and though at times she "brought the house down" with her excellent shooting skills, her relationship with her stage companions was stormy. Eventually, said Repp, Calamity was dismissed from the cast. Repp also gave a new twist to Calamity's nursing during an 1878 epidemic in Deadwood: the reason she did not contract the disease herself was due to "her pickled constitution."[20]

Writers for mass-circulation western magazines were not alone in popularizing Calamity Jane. Local authors in the northern plains also continued featuring their regional heroine. In direct contrast to what Roberta Beed Sollid was told by Deadwood pioneers, Nebraska writer Martha McKelvie claimed that "the old-timers who knew her best have always hoped that someday the 'good' side of Jane would be known. Not one of them will permit an unkind word said about her." These pioneers "cannot forget that Jane once traveled two hundred miles alone in a covered wagon to nurse an old pal miner back to life," wrote McKelvie, who had Calamity travel farther and work harder to help the sick than previous writers had.[21] Black Hills author Helen Rezatto included the "Robin Hood story" in her rendition of Calamity's nursing activities, telling how Calamity robbed a grocery store to get food for sick miners. Rezatto concluded: "Probably the storekeeper would have let her charge it if she had asked politely, but Calamity always thought it was fun to wave a gun around."[22]

Thus, despite the critical studies by Jennewein and Sollid, popular stories of Calamity Jane abounded. These tales found their way into an increasingly wide range of books.

For example, histories of women in the West targeting general audiences, unlike those by academics, featured Calamity Jane. For these writers, Calamity represented the "bad woman" of the frontier, joining Belle Starr, Cattle Kate, Lola Montez, Mattie Silks, Diamond Lil, and Madame Moustache. With attention-getting titles such as *The Gentle Tamers* (1958), *Shady Ladies of the West* (1964), *Notorious Ladies of the Frontier* (1969), and *Wily Women of the West* (1972), these books seldom discredited legendary tales.[23]

Popular accounts of the western medical profession also included Calamity Jane. Robert F. Karolevitz, in *Doctors of the Old West* (1967), asserts that, although Calamity "didn't qualify by training or general reputation," her nursing of the ill and injured proves the inclusiveness of "Florence Nightingale's statement that 'at one time or another every woman is a nurse.'" Although Karolevitz did not entirely exaggerate Calamity's nursing, writer Richard Dunlop threw caution to the wind. In *Doctors of the American Frontier* (1965), Dunlop describes Calamity as an associate of Dr. Valentine T. McGillycuddy at Fort Laramie in 1875. In Dunlop's imaginative version, McGillycuddy came to rely so heavily on Calamity's help that he "regretted leaving her behind at the fort when the troopers took to the field."[24]

Calamity became a fixture in nonfiction works on western outlaws and lawman as well. These had been primarily a male domain. James D. Horan and Paul Sann's *Pictorial History of the Wild West: A True Account of the Bad Men, Desperadoes, Rustlers and Outlaws of the Old West—and the Men Who Fought Them to Establish Law and Order* (1954) now included Calamity Jane, "the woman most popularly associated with the western frontier." The authors believed she had been "tragically miscast by nature" and "should have been a man." Similarly, Lea F. McCarty's *The Gunfighters* (1959) places Calamity with a generally all-male cast, including Jesse James, Billy the Kid, Wild Bill Hickok, Doc Holliday, and Wyatt Earp. All are legendary frontier figures, and McCarty's biographies of the male outlaws and lawmen describe their famous gunfights. But McCarty's summary of Martha's life relates only that she served as a scout, shot up a few saloons, and spit tobacco on an actress. For McCarty, it seems, Calamity's unladylike behavior was sufficient to warrant her admission into his select club of western gunfighters.[25]

Charles Chilton's *The Book of the West: An Epic of America's Wild Frontier—and the Men Who Created Its Legends* (1962), written for younger readers, calls Calamity Jane "the most famous of all women outlaws" and says she was married to Wild Bill Hickok. Although Calamity's "favorite haunts were the saloons and her favorite company well-known outlaws," she "did occasionally carry a gun for the law," according to Chilton. Once, he says, she "helped to round up a whole gang of cattle thieves on Fort Pierce [*sic*] in Dakota Territory."[26]

Like these prose popularizers, poets boasted of Calamity's achievements. South Dakotan Georgene Conley hoped her poetic tribute, "A Toast to Calamity Jane," would help Calamity's legend survive. Although she depicted Calamity as a scout, freighter, markswoman, and legendary swearer, Conley thought it was Calamity's nursing of the 1878 smallpox victims that most deserved celebration: "She took care of the men with loving care,/ Almost all of them lived, fully cured." Montana poet Carol Myers echoed these sentiments in *Montana: Where My Treasure Is* (1964). Even though Calamity worked as a man and "broke her own mustangs to ride," she also "nursed rough men in illness and grief,/ When whiskey was medicine, pain's relief." In *Echoes from the Black Hills* (1984), Marianne McFarland McNeil, a Texas poet with roots in the Black Hills, portrayed Calamity as an early feminist who "lived her days, Rebelling 'gainst men's domineering ways." Still, McNeil was upset by Calamity's bragging about her relationship with Wild Bill. In her poem, after Hickok is killed, Calamity announces "they'd been lovers all along;/ Poor Bill could not declare her statement wrong." And after Calamity's deathbed wish that she be buried next to him, "many claim that they would make a bet,/ That 'Old Wild Bill' is spinning, spinning yet."[27]

The most thorough poetic tribute, however, was written and illustrated by Sidne and Stan Lynde. Their narrative poem, Calamity Jane (1975), features most of the popular tales about Calamity. The Lyndes begin with her story-telling:

> The stories that Calam could tell
> Would raise your hair on end.
> She didn't care if they were true or not,
> And neither should you, my friend.

The Lyndes relate Calamity's capture of Jack McCall after he kills Hickok, and tell about her nursing efforts in a Deadwood smallpox epidemic. They also focus on Calamity's nonconformity and independent spirit:

> She didn't care what folks said about her.
> She did just what she pleased.
> An' ridin', an' shootin' an' drinkin'
> Were just her cup of tea
> (Or Red-Eye as the case may be)[28]

As versifiers lauded Calamity Jane's greatness, western novelists told her fictional-ized adventures on the frontier. Although these writers occasionally described her in less than heroic terms, they usually had her fight on the side of law and order. In novelist Hank Mitchum's story about Deadwood in his Stagecoach Station series, the action centers on a confrontation between the owner of the stagecoach line, Tom Murdock, and outlaw leader Johnny Varnes. In this tale, it is Varnes who hires Jack McCall to kill Hickok. Calamity, described as an unattractive woman with skin "burned dark and leathery" and a "masculine swagger," brags about her scouting and bullwhacking adventures. Although Hickok gives her the cold shoulder, after his death Calamity claims "he'd been her man." Still, in the final confrontation with the Varnes gang, Calamity proves her worth. She grabs a gun dropped by the outlaw and "with lightning speed" spins around and takes him captive.[29]

The prolific English author J. T. Edson devoted an entire series of books to Cala-mity Jane's western adventures. Edson's Calamity is independent and good-looking, and very modern in her morals. In each story she becomes physically involved with

one of the other leading characters, but this lovemaking does not result in a permanent relationship. Edson also has Calamity fight another powerful woman in each of his
stories; during these brawls the combatants tear each others' clothes off and fight until
totally exhausted.

Interestingly, Edson created a fictionalized background for his Calamity Jane: after
her husband deserts the family, Martha's mother, Charlotte, leaves her children in a St.
Louis convent. But Martha runs away and joins a freighting outfit. At first she cooks for
the freighters, then learns how to use a bullwhip and gun. During her western travels,
she is constantly involved in calamitous events, resulting in her famous nickname. In
each story, she is allied with one of Edson's other heroic characters, such as Belle Starr,
Mark Counter, and the Ysabel Kid. Calamity is always friendly and generous, once helping
a family financially and in another case lying to cover for the mistakes of an excellent,
but inexperienced, military officer. Edson's Calamity also represents the West, being
open, honest, and hard-working. These qualities stand in direct contrast to those of elit-
ist easterners. Thus, in one story a friend of Calamity's advises a young woman from
the East, "People out here don't care that you come from the best Back Bay stock, that
your father is a congressman and that you have two uncles who are generals. It's what
you are that counts with a girl like Calamity."[30]

Another kind of novel, the adult western, also featured Calamity Jane. In these
stories the heroes spend as much time in bedrooms as in gunfights. Authors of these
novels, however, seemed uncertain whether Calamity was more suited for fighting or
loving. In Jake Logan's *Dead Man's Hand* (1979), Wild Bill Hickok and series hero John
Slocum battle Tom Varney's gang in Deadwood in 1876. Calamity Jane, who carries
dispatches between Deadwood and Rapid City, is Hickok's companion, living with him
in a cabin near Deadwood. Knowing he is going blind, she begs him not to accept an
offer to be sheriff of Deadwood. When she tells him she makes enough money from
carrying the mail to pay expenses for both of them, Hickok responds, "I don't want to
live off a woman, Calam, I never have and I'm a little too old to start now." When Hickok
becomes Deadwood's chief law officer, he inevitably engages in Varney's gang in a gun-
battle. In the final showdown, Hickok wins, but only with help. Calamity captures one
gang member by trickery rather than gunfighting skills; wearing a dance-hall girl's dress,
she propositions the villain, and as he undresses, she gets the drop on him. Another
adult western, *Longarm in Deadwood* (1982) by Tabor Evans, depicts Calamity Jane less
attractively. A stage driver, she swears profusely, propositions almost every man she
meets, brags that she has killed innumerable outlaws, and claims that she was Hickok's
sweetheart. Worse, in the story she receives her nickname because her lovers develop
venereal disease. Still, when the stage is attacked Calamity proves to be resourceful and
courageous, and like Deputy Marshal Custis Long, she kills an assailant. Afterwards, Long
deputizes Calamity and asks her to recruit trustworthy men, showing he considers her
a dependable associate.[31]

Film and television joined popular history, fiction, and poetry in disseminating
fanciful characterizations of Calamity Jane as her character permeated western folklore.

Most productions followed the pattern set by romantic movies such as *The Plainsmen* and the musical *Calamity Jane*, rather than spoofs like *This Is the West that Was*. In 1963, Carol Burnett starred in a remake of the popular Doris Day musical.[32] Another reworked film featuring Calamity Jane was *The Plainsman* (1966), starring Abby Dalton as Calamity Jane. It generally followed DeMille's earlier script, but significant changes weakened the plot. The dramatic moment in the earlier film when Calamity saved Hickok's life by revealing the location of a cavalry troop, thus earning his enmity, was eliminated. And, rather than ending with Hickok's assassination, the 1966 film closes with Calamity Jane and Wild Bill riding together "into the sunset." A new film, *The Raiders* (1966), also teamed Calamity Jane (Judi Meredith) with Wild Bill Hickok and Buffalo Bill Cody. In this film, the trio fight Texas cattlemen attempting to prevent the building of a railroad in Kansas. In a comic ending, Calamity drives away in her wagon pulled by two horses she has named Wild Bill and Buffalo Bill.

Although no television series was based on Calamity Jane, she appeared in several programs. One 1963 episode of *Bonanza* has Doc Holliday in love with Calamity Jane (Stephanie Powers). When he suspects "Little Joe" Cartwright is courting her, Holliday demands a showdown. Fortunately, the issue is resolved before anyone gets killed. Calamity Jane also showed up in episodes of *Colt .45* (played by Dody Heath) and *Death Valley Days* (Fay Spain).[33]

As these shows suggest, the Calamity Jane of legend could be adapted to a variety of roles and mediums. An example of her adaptability can be seen in a 1967 *Kid Colt Outlaw* comic book. In a tale titled "The Wild Ones!", Calamity Jane teaches bullies a lesson. Biggie Beckert and Little Poison terrorize a saloon in South Gulch and pick a fight with a young person quietly watching in the background. The bullies are surprised when the stranger shoots their guns from their hands. Afterwards, they learn they just faced Calamity Jane, "the fastest and deadliest shot in the Territory!" Biggie and Little Poison beg forgiveness and promise to pay for damages. If not sufficiently evident, the lesson of the story is clarified in the conclusion when Biggie remarks to Calamity, "We're gonna behave ourselves from now on! No tellin' when we'll run up to someone like you again!"

Meanwhile, realizing the drawing power of Old West myths and legends, town promoters explored how to further exploit Calamity's popularity. In 1960, Livingston, Montana, considered a Calamity Jane pageant. "Calamity Jane's story captures world-wide imagination," the newspaper reported, and "in view of this there must be some way that Livingston can take advantage of . . . this woman's story."[34] Newspaperman Fred Martin asked Livingston residents to "stop to think of what value Buffalo Bill has been to Cody, General Custer to Mandan, the Four Eyes Theater to Medora, the western atmosphere which Charley Bovey has created in Virginia City, and similar promotional efforts in other communities throughout the West." Calamity Jane, he asserted, might do the same for Livingston. "What would it mean if it would result in an additional occupancy for each of say 50 days for each hotel, motel or trailer park in Livingston?" Martin asked, adding that a Calamity Jane attraction also would help restaurants, service stations, and gift shops. In addition to a pageant, the town considered restoration of the cabin in which Calamity once lived, as well as a museum, library, and theater.[35] Although most of these projects never were realized, Livingston today sponsors an annual Calamity Jane Rodeo with a Calamity Jane Look-A-Like contest in which the winner receives a gift certificate to the Calamity Jane Steak House. Likewise, in the 1960s Princeton, Missouri, began its celebration of "Calamity Jane Days" and a local restaurant added a Calamity Jane Dining Room. There also was a souvenir shop located at Calamity Jane Junction.[36]

But it was Deadwood that led the way in promoting Calamity Jane for the tourist market, continuing its strategy begun in the 1920s. Rarely did Black Hills tourist publications fail to mention Calamity Jane, usually in association with Wild Bill Hickok. Advertisements still announce that thousands of people arrive annually "to pay their respects to these two notables." One recent brochure describes historic Mount Moriah Cemetery as "home to Wild Bill and Deadwood's wildest party girl, Calamity Jane."[37]

This local interest in Livingston, Princeton, and Deadwood led to new publications about Calamity Jane telling about her activities there. Although most repeated popular tales, some uncovered long-overlooked information about Calamity. Among the most significant was Bill and Doris Whithorn's *Calamity's in Town*, a compilation of stories about Calamity from early Livingston newspapers. Local historian Ellen Crago Mueller also found previously unnoticed Black Hills newspaper articles and interviewed descendants of Lena Canary for her biography, *Calamity Jane* (1981). Additionally, in Princeton the local historical society reprinted census information about Martha Canary's family and published recollections of the family by local residents.[38]

Despite these indications that Calamity Jane had become a fixture in western folklore, interest in her and the American West was actually declining in the 1970s and 1980s. Western movies and television programs decreased dramatically, and many magazines glorifying popular western heroes disappeared from the magazine racks. These changes probably stemmed from the controversial Vietnam War, the conscience-raising civil rights movement, and the resurgent feminist movement. Narratives about the American frontier experience had generally ignored minorities and women, as well as the destruction of the environment. Histories glorifying the "conquest of the West" increasingly came under assault. The Calamity Jane legend featuring a masculine frontierwoman who fought Indians was now less acceptable. Calamity Jane seemed an unsympathetic exponent of conquest.

As the reputations of once-popular western heroes declined, several novelists described them harshly. In *Deadwood* (1986), Pete Dexter portrays Calamity Jane and Wild Bill Hickok austerely. Hickok suffers from venereal disease and is going blind. But Calamity Jane is even worse. One character describes her as having "a man's face. Not a man you'd want to know." Her body odor is nauseating, and she has green mold growing in the creases on her neck. She also distorts the truth. A bartender remarks to Colorado Charley Utter, "Jane was the worst. . . . Ain't nobody told the lies she did." When he adds, "Whoever named her Calamity knew what they was doing," Utter replies, "She named herself." Calamity especially brags of her relationship to Hickok: "She had said they were pards, she had said they fought Indians together, she had said they were married." Although Hickok detests her, after his death she claims she is his widow, and while drunk even threatens Agnes Lake Hickok, Hickok's real widow, at a reception. Calamity Jane's only redeeming trait in Dexter's story is her willingness to nurse small-pox victims. But even these good deeds are given a dark side, for Calamity actually is spreading the disease. The epidemics in Sidney, Deadwood, and Cheyenne all occur about two weeks after her arrival.[39]

Similarly, Larry McMurtry's *Buffalo Girls* (1990) depicts Calamity Jane and other western figures as less than heroic. In this novel, an elderly Calamity Jane wanders through the West with two old trappers searching for beaver now driven almost to extinction. Like Dexter, McMurtry describes Calamity Jane as a braggart who claims she scouted for various generals, rode for the pony express, and was Wild Bill's love. Cowboy Teddy Blue tells Calamity's friend, Dora Du Fran, that "the drunker she gets, the more she lies." This saddens Dora because it means that "Calamity hadn't actually done much of anything except wander here and there on the plains," her stories being "mainly based on whiskey and emptiness." Consequently, Teddy Blue is bewildered when Calamity and her companions are asked to join Buffalo Bill's Wild West Show for a tour of England: "She can't ride and she can't shoot—about all she does is drink and tell lies," Blue remarks. "Why should the Queen want to hear a bunch of Calamity's lies?" Sure enough, Calamity Jane, while drunk, falls off the stagecoach during her perfor-mance before the monarch. Completing this bleak portrait, McMurtry has Calamity write letters to her daughter, Janey, throughout the novel, but in his conclusion reveals that the daughter is imagined because Calamity is a hermaphrodite, unable to bear children.[40]

Movie reviewers reflected on McMurtry's somber image of the West. Margaret Carlson, for example, noted the important role that Calamity's imaginary letters played in his novel: "Full of regret for never settling down, aching with loneliness, Calamity Jane dreams up a child to give meaning to her senseless life." In fact, in one letter to Janey Calamity admits that the life she invented in her correspondence "is the opposite of the life I have lived out here in this mess they call the West." Carlson concludes in *Buffalo Girls*, that "the West does not seem as mythic as it used to be. Perhaps it never was."[41]

These dreary images of Calamity Jane and the frontier West also found their way into verse. In *Soft Voices* (1980) and *The Hills Aren't Black* (1980), poet Larry Nelson says Calamity "led a low life all her life" and was "Bull whacker and Bull shitter, Le Dame; Le Bitch."[42] Similarly, Gary David's *A Log of Deadwood: A Postmodern Epic of the South Dakota Gold Rush* (1993) has Calamity claim she was General Crook's scout during a stage appearance in Chicago in 1893. "She'll wander the rest of her days, dazed / this way," writes David, adding, "That she believes / she is she echoes / down the midway all the way / back to Deadwood, resounding."[43]

Likewise, dark images of Calamity Jane were evident at the 1989 annual conference of the Montana History Society, which included a session called "Speaking Ill of the Dead: Jerks in Montana History." The most discussed presentation in newspaper reports was "Calamity Jane: Sleaze of the Frontier." The Helena newspaper, summarizing the session, explained that "the legend of Calamity Jane as a swashbuckling frontier woman who rode with Custer and captured Wild Bill Hickok's killer is almost completely a hoax." Calamity Jane was merely an "uneducated, uncultured woman who survived as best she could." According to the newspaper, the "Jerks in Montana History" session was so popular that it "had to be moved to a larger room," drawing about two hundred people. Only about twenty-five listened to other papers. Even though pleased by the attendance, the conference organizer was "distressed that much of the scholarly work of the conference would go unnoticed" with this popular session upstaging the scholars.[44]

But these put-downs did not slow the growth of Calamity Jane's popularity, any more than editorial railings had during her lifetime. The power of the Calamity Jane legend is no more evident than in the movies made from the novels written by Dexter and McMurtry. The film *Wild Bill* (United Artists, 1995) acknowledges Dexter's novel as its inspiration, and was considered by reviewer Richard Schickel among the "dankest and most claustrophobic westerns ever made."[45] Yet, it temporizes Dexter's bleak depiction of Calamity Jane. Gone is the ugly, dirty, bragging, disease-carrying female scorned by Wild Bill. Although Ellen Barkin, who plays Calamity Jane in the film, may not have the peaches-and-cream image of Doris Day, she is attractive. The movie again suggests Hickok and Calamity Jane were much more than casual friends. In fact, it is during their lovemaking that a band of assassins led by Jack McCall momentarily gains advantage over Wild Bill. Similarly, the CBS television film *Buffalo Girls* (1995), though for the most part following McMurtry's plot, ignores his conclusion that Calamity Jane was unable to bear children. Instead, in the filmed version Calamity and Wild Bill are married and have a daughter.

Besides these films, a variety of popular media featured Calamity more favorably. Some followed the lead of the movies *Wild Bill* and *Buffalo Girls*, incorporating sordid images of Calamity even while portraying her as a western heroine. A few emphasized positive qualities, especially depicting her as an early feminist. And many simply repeated stories, without change, that had appeared decades earlier. Typical of the latter were stories in mass-circulation magazines. The July 1996 issue of *True West* included a "Bonus Poster" of Calamity Jane as part of its "True West Legends" series, and an article, "Calamity Jane Lived Up to Her Name" by John C. Russell in *Wild West* magazine in 1994, told her story as if her popularity had never waned. For example, Russell explained that whatever Calamity's faults were as a woman, they were "forgiven during the smallpox epidemic of 1878 when her tireless efforts to nurse the sick earned her the nickname 'The Black Hills Florence Nightingale.'" Likewise, Calamity Jane was featured on the cover of Richard Mancini's *American Legends of the Wild West* (1992) as representative of the book's heroic figures.[46]

One novelist who incorporates derogatory images of Calamity Jane while giving her a heroic role is Judd Cole. In a new series of novels, Cole relates the fictionalized adventures of Wild Bill Hickok. In these stories, Calamity Jane pursues Hickok relentlessly because she believes they have a common destiny. Having been raised a Bible-carrying Methodist, she also hopes to make Hickok a believer. Although she saves his life repeatedly, Wild Bill does not appreciate her efforts and takes evasive action each time he sees her.

He has good reason to dislike Calamity. In *Wild Bill: Santa Fe Death Trap* (2000), she is described by Cole as "a stout young woman" so ugly that her "face terrified buzzards," and stinking so hotly she "could raise blood-blisters on new leather." Nevertheless, she once again saves Hickok's life, riding to his rescue with her camel brigade.[47]

Other writers made Calamity Jane a feminist forerunner. In a postcript to *Wildcat* (1993), romance novelist Sharon Ihle explains that, although many historians dismiss Calamity as nothing more than a drunken prostitute, in her opinion she "was simply ahead of her time with regard to career matters and men." In her story, Calamity Jane's sister, Ann Marie Cannary, arrives in Deadwood in search of her notorious sibling, hoping Martha will join her in a search for their brothers and sisters. But Martha, who lives in a cabin with Wild Bill Hickok and his companion, Lucky Luke McCanles, has adopted an independent lifestyle and is uncertain she wants to reestablish family connections. Calamity explains to her sister, "I ain't exactly what the ladies call acceptable, but it don't bother me none. Really, it don't. I like what I am and what I do. . . . There ain't no man who can drive an ox team better than me, or shoot or ride better for that matter, and it's cause that's what I like to do!"[48]

This interpretation of Calamity Jane as an early feminist became increasingly popular in the late twentieth century. In *Women of the West* (1990), children's author A. I. Lake included Calamity Jane with Annie Oakley, Carrie Nation, Sacajawea, and Narcissa Whitman. Although, in Lake's account, Calamity scouted for General Custer and received her nickname after saving Captain Egan from Indians, her daring nonconformity is central to the story. To no avail, Deadwood's virtuous women try running her out of town when she works as a bartender.

Similarly, Doris Faber's biography written for young people highlights Calamity Jane's refusal to accept narrowly defined rules for women. Although she tries working at "proper female occupations like cooking or washing clothes," these jobs do "not suit her." To escape "the many rules restricting girls and women," she pretends to be a boy. Interestingly, given her audience, Faber presents the sophisticated concept that Calamity's legend is based more on storytelling and dime novels than on reality. She even mentions that Calamity may have been a camp follower and discusses her numerous "husbands."[49]

A novel published by Disney Press, *Calamity Jane at Fort Sanders* (1992), makes an even stronger statement for Calamity's nonconformity. The story opens in Piedmont, Wyoming, where young Martha Cannary [*sic*], dressed in men's clothing and carrying a Colt revolver and bowie knife, drives the stagecoach. "You couldn't be in Piedmont long without knowing Jane Cannary, the wildest woman west of the Mississippi," the authors exclaim. Women from the Piedmont Temperance Society, led by the mayor's wife, force Calamity to leave town. Before her departure, Martha tells the women:

> "I've driven bull trains and been a cook. I worked the railroads and did
> just about anything else a man can do—and did it better! So don't you go
> telling me what a woman *ought* to be. This is 1873! There are women
> teachers, doctors, lawyers, and newspaper writers. If I wanted to be a

psalm-singin', prissy, do-nothin', bustle-wearing fuss-budget, I'd move to Boston. This here's Wyoming Territory. As a female person, I can vote and hold office. Why, I could run for president . . . Maybe I will!"

When her comments are greeted with laughter, Martha angrily wonders "why women and girls were supposed to shut themselves up in a house all day acting like they were made of china." Afterwards, Martha goes to Fort Sanders, disguises herself as a man, and scouts for Captain Egan. When one member of the command foolishly starts a fight with an approaching party of Sioux, Egan is wounded and captured. Alone, Martha tracks the Indians and learns that the Sioux never intended battle; they only meant to ask the troops to expel two prospectors illegally trespassing in the Black Hills. Daringly, Martha enters the Indian camp, arrests the miners who have been cornered in a cave by the Indians, and, gaining the friendship of the Sioux, secures Egan's release. Afterwards, Egan remarks that she is good to have around in a calamity, and Martha, liking the sound of it, takes the name Calamity Jane.[50]

A modern Calamity Jane also became the basis of an animated television series for children. Although it was short-lived, *The Legend of Calamity Jane* (1997), with actress Barbara Scaff providing the voice of Calamity, introduced the heroine as "a lone crusader for justice, bringing fear to the hearts of outlaws everywhere and keeping the spirit of the wild West alive and kicking." Regarded by *TV Guide*'s David Hiltbrand as "the seasons's most idiosyncratic cartoon, and its most intriguing," the cartoon's Calamity Jane uses her whip rather than guns as a weapon. Although this Calamity Jane plays poker in the saloon, she does not swear, and when she wears a dress, is beautiful. Hiltbrand accurately described the series as "a revisionist Western with . . . feminist overtones."[51]

Recent stage characterizations also feature an emancipated Calamity Jane. Best known of the individuals making "first-person" presentations is Glenda Bell, who contracts independently out of Windsor, Colorado. She has performed at fairs, festivals, and conferences throughout the northern plains in programs including "Calamity Jane Tells Her Tale" and "Calamity Jane's Survival Skills for 20th Century Women." Likewise, Dr. Joyce Thierer, affiliated with the Center for Great Plains Studies at Emporia State University in Kansas, makes stage presentations as a modern Calamity Jane. And Norma Rose Slack, Calamity's great-grandniece, performs at the Wyoming Territorial Park in Laramie, Wyoming. Slack bases her dramatizations on personal interpretations of "Calamity's thoughts and feelings about being an adventurous, independent woman in the rough and rugged 19th century West." According to a local newspaper advertisement, her program "is especially popular with the children."[52]

Thus, Calamity Jane remains popular as her character adapts to changing conditions. Today tourists continue to flock to the Black Hills to stand before Calamity Jane's grave. En route, they view sculptured representations of her in Wall, South Dakota. In Deadwood, where gambling has been legalized, they play slot machines at "Calamity Jane's." There are Calamity Jane postcards, Calamity Jane songs, Calamity Jane t-shirts, Calamity Jane decals for car windows, Calamity Jane dolls, and even commemorative Calamity

Jane whiskey bottles. At the National Finals Rodeo in 2000, the bareback riding event featured a horse named Calamity Jane. And, for those who want to go camping, there is even a special Calamity Jane sleeping bag designed for women who are shorter in length, wider at the hips, and narrower at the shoulders.[53]

When, in August 1989, officials at the Buffalo Bill Historical Center in Cody, Wyoming, announced they had discovered Calamity Jane's buckskit outfit in their collections, the story received national attention. Her coat, vest, and trousers, a part of the Frederic Remington collection of western memorabilia, were deemed especially important because she "left behind few personal possessions to pique the interest of modern museum visitors." In fact, "not a museum in the country could honestly say that it had any of Calamity Jane's belongings."[54] The actual Martha Canary might be astounded to learn how important her clothing has become. Indeed, there is even a new line of western wear called "Calamity Jeans." According to the label, they have been designed to capture Calamity Jane's "adventurous, proud, independent" spirit. The clothing advertisement continues, "In Calamity Jeans you will find a natural blend of form and function, style and comfort" that carries "a passion for the challenges of the new Wild West . . . and beyond."

Lost in the vast array of popular presentations of Calamity Jane is the actual Martha Canary. Her legend, which has grown steadily through the past century, completely obscures the nineteenth-century woman who carried that famous nickname. The exaggerated tales told during her lifetime and the stories invented by dime novelists pale before the imaginative accounts developed in the twentieth century. It is doubtful Calamity's role in the folklore of the American West will ever diminish. Instead, the Calamity Jane legend will be remolded to meet the needs of each generation.

Conclusion

Several months before the scheduled airing of *Buffalo Girls* by CBS television in 1995, I received a call from the producer of a proposed documentary on Calamity Jane to be shown immediately before the movie. He wondered what locations might have Calamity Jane interest and what available memorabilia might help demonstrate the historical basis of their film. During the course of our conversation, I remarked that McMurtry's *Buffalo Girls* was, of course, fiction, not history, but he insisted it was based on actual events. After he listed several "facts," which I discounted, he exclaimed, with some exasperation, that at least it was true that Calamity Jane went to England with Buffalo Bill's Wild West Show! When I again responded negatively, he politely ended the conversation, saying, "We'll get back to you." He never did.

Perhaps this incident proves the adage that historians know how to ruin a good story. Although accurate history should be as interesting as fable, fiction, and film, historian Kent Ladd Steckmesser properly observes in his study of western legends that there is "something cold and abstract" about truth. Conversely, romance and legend "are warm and colorful."[1] Besides providing enjoyment, legends contain important meaning. This explains why replacing them with truth can be unpopular. Scholars such as J. Leonard Jennewein and Roberta Beed Sollid who attempted to correct common misconceptions about Calamity Jane found their conclusions largely ignored in popular accounts. Theirs was an exercise in futility; legends cannot be destroyed by pointing out historical errors. It is relatively simple to prove that Calamity was not a significant participant in major western events, but the persistence of legendary tales has little to do with historical accuracy.

Indeed, the adventurous stories attributed to Martha Canary bear only a remote relationship to actual events in her life. Her career, in fact, may offer the best case study of legend-making in the history of the American West simply because there was so little on which to build: she arrested no outlaws, robbed no banks, and killed no Indians.

Instead, hers is the bleak story of poverty, alcoholism, and an unsteady domestic life. She worked as dance-hall girl, prostitute, waitress, bartender, and cook; she lived with various men she called husbands and expressed affection for her children. Rather than displaying legendary ingredients, her life illustrates a part of western history not often told, the existence of the poor. Most writers attempting to narrate Martha Canary's life, however, have been so overwhelmed by her legend that they have been unable to acknowledge the commonplace conditions of her life. If it were not for her legendary fame as Calamity Jane, the story of Martha Canary would hold little popular interest.

Still, that Martha's life was uneventful does not mean her legend was without roots in her experiences. As Steckmesser observes, the "historical framework around the western hero has made many of the legends more believable."[2] Indeed, Calamity's life and legend have become so intertwined that historians have spent considerable effort trying to separate them. For example, when historians suggest that Wild Bill and Calamity Jane had no significant association, they must face the fact that the two entered Deadwood together in 1876 and that their graves are side-by-side in Mount Moriah Cemetery. Clearly, historical events provided the rich ground from which legendary stories could grow; without that fertile soil, the legends would never have appeared.

That has been the central focus of this study: to show how the legend of Calamity Jane emerged from its historical roots. Popular explanations of her rise to fame tend to be grossly oversimplified, suggesting, for example, that she became well known because she selected a catchy nickname. As a young woman, Martha attracted attention because of her unusual dress, dance-hall engagements, colorful antics, and drunken bouts. However, it was the publicity she received while a camp follower with the 1875 expedition to the Black Hills that began her serious ascent to fame; it led to her inclusion in Captain Jack Crawford's widely publicized poem and in dispatches sent to Chicago newspapers. Perhaps it was mere chance that she received this attention, but her charisma undoubtedly helped her gain more notice than her associates.

But it was Horatio Maguire's fanciful portrayal of Martha in his Black Hills promotional booklet in 1877, including his identification of her as Crook's scout, that provided the impetus leading to her national prominence. His stories led to Edward Wheeler using her name in his new Deadwood Dick dime novel series. This publicity, in turn, made her more newsworthy. A cyclical pattern developed in which newspaper publicity led to appearances in other publications, which in turn led to further newspaper attention. Thus, in the 1870s and 1880s the press both reflected her growing fame and helped to create it. Ultimately, hundreds of newspaper notices described her daily activities as she traveled to and fro across the northern plains. Readers naturally assumed there had been heroic accomplishments to cause such widespread attention.

The relationship between Calamity Jane and Wild Bill Hickok was not featured in the earliest stories printed about her. Nor is there evidence, despite popular claims, that she immediately exploited her relationship with him to increase her reputation. Initially, the most important component in stories about Calamity was her avocation as scout, followed by rumors of her association with Black Hills bandits. However, once she became a dime novel heroine, as Hickok had been before she met him, mingling her career with Hickok's was natural. It was, after all, only a minor step to move Calamity from association with Deadwood Dick to companionship with Wild Bill Hickok.

Martha's own story about her achievements, finally published in 1896, reflects typical frontier exaggerations. For the most part, her claims are rather modest. Aside from suggesting that she served as a scout, saved the Deadwood stage, carried mail in the Black Hills, and captured Jack McCall, her autobiography is a rather mundane narrative. She claimed only friendship with Hickok, for example. Historians who conclude Calamity's storytelling was the primary reason she became famous exaggerate the significance of her stories in her rise to fame. Even though her claim to have scouted for Crook was important in early publications, most contemporaries viewed it as a tall tale. It probably would have been forgotten if not for other conditions.

In his study, Steckmesser examined four legendary figures: Kit Carson, mountain man; Billy the Kid, outlaw; Wild Bill Hickok, gunfighter; and George Armstrong Custer, soldier. Before their legends could take hold, Steckmesser observed, there had to be a receptive audience. "The professional hero makers must bear only part of the responsibility for the persistence of legends," he explained. "They have simply supplied what the people have demanded."[3] Flamboyant stories about unique western characters were commonplace long before Horatio Maguire described Calamity Jane, and dime novels featuring women in male roles were popular before Edward Wheeler included Calamity Jane in his Deadwood Dick series. Other women wore men's clothing and accompanied troops in the field, and Martha was but one of several women who accompanied Hickok's wagon train into Deadwood in 1876. Thus, one must look beyond Martha's personality and behavior to understand her rise to fame. If her story had not held significance for society, she would be remembered only as a notorious regional character.

Martha's violations of lines dividing the sexes, both in fiction and real life, held beguiling interest. "But the basic appeal of the legendary heroes is that they served good causes," asserted Steckmesser. "They were servants of justice and truth, defenders of the meek and oppressed" and became "actors in the great allegory of Good versus Evil."[4] Calamity Jane's ascent to legendary status began when she joined her male dime novel companions in battles against the abusive power of corrupt politicians and the wealthy. In these stories, she also fought outlaws and Indians, who were viewed as opposing the progress of civilization. In addition, the legendary Calamity Jane embodied traits deemed important by Americans, including independence, charity, courage, cleverness, sincerity, physical strength, resourcefulness, and self-reliance.

Only a few of these qualities can be found in early accounts of Calamity Jane. However, stories that enhanced her reputation were added later. Some of Martha's contemporaries, once she became famous, were anxious to claim association with her and invented participation in adventures with her, all of which added to the confusion between legend and history. More importantly, tales from folklore and legend were incorporated into her life story. Steckmesser's observation that most stories about western heroes have "a common pattern of anecdote and characterization which is literary and folkloric rather than historical in nature" is clearly true of the legends surrounding Calamity Jane.[5]

Indeed, the stories associated with Calamity Jane follow a common pattern found by Steckmesser in popular narratives about other western legendary figures. Like them, Calamity was an actual historical figure and that helped to establish a framework for her story. But, as Steckmesser notes, "the body of the narrative commonly incorporates exploits, traits, and evaluations which are inflated and legendary."[6] Although authentic information about Martha Canary is used in popular versions of her life, most of her adventures are exaggerations. She emerges unfettered by society's bonds, whether as Jane Dalton, whose parents were killed by Indians at Fort Laramie; as a minister's daughter, who fled home with a soldier; as Jennie Forrest, who was ruined in adolescence by a villain; or as the actual Martha Canary, who was orphaned in the West. Throughout her career, the mythic Calamity stands apart, wearing unique attire and engaging in activities not typical for women. She displays exceptional skills and strength, and is able to outdrink, outswear, outride, and outshoot almost any man. It is Calamity who rescues Captain Egan after he is wounded by Indians, resulting in her christening. Later, when male passengers cower inside, afraid to take the reins after Indians kill the stage-driver, Calamity climbs atop the stage and successfully completes the run. She outwits Indians, outlaws, and lawmen, once taking a Sioux captive by bluffing him with an unloaded revolver. She likewise protects the weak, preventing a muleskinner from abusing his animals; and, like Robin Hood, she robs from the rich to get food for the ill.

Before one protests that Calamity is often portrayed as a prostitute or an outlaw, it must be noted that Steckmesser found similar contradictions in accounts of other legendary figures. For instance, Custer is claimed to be both military hero and glory hunter; Billy the Kid is portrayed as both saintly and satanic; and Wild Bill Hickok is considered both civilizer and cold-blooded killer. "These contradictions facilitate the growth of legends," observes Steckmesser, "because every Western fan can create a hero after his own ideas."[7] But in the case of Calamity Jane, even those who dismiss her as an alcoholic prostitute and highlight her profanity, smoking, drinking, and gambling usually find redeeming attributes that make up for her bad behavior. Indeed, so-called respectable women fall short when compared to Calamity Jane. She was authentic rather than pretentious and, beneath her rough exterior, the guardian of true feminine virtue. Undoubtedly, the most important ingredient in the Calamity Jane legend is her nursing of smallpox victims; few accounts of Calamity Jane fail to record these charitable acts. That she actually cared for people who were ill and injured once again adds to the difficulties of trying to separate legend and fact.

Over time, Martha Canary became featured in fiction, radio, movies, television, and in a wide range of popular culture from comic books to advertising. "It is the range of mediums in which the legend appears over a period of time which entitles the hero to legendary stature," wrote Steckmesser.[8] Thus, Calamity Jane emerged as the quintessential female gunfighter, military scout, pony express rider, and nurse in western folklore. Her stature in frontier history is evident from the people with whom she is associated. For example, she is portrayed as gunfighter second only to Wild Bill Hickok. Simultaneously, she is also included with important women of the West such as Annie Oakley, Belle Starr, Elizabeth Custer, and Sacajawea.

Another sign that Calamity Jane has reached legendary status is the adaptability of the stories about her. For example, in 1941 Jean McCormick found a receptive audience when she ascribed motherly qualities to Calamity Jane. Martha also is heralded as a pioneer in the struggle for equality of women. Actress Jean Arthur viewed Calamity Jane's smoking, drinking, and wearing of male apparel as symbols of emancipation. And by the end of the twentieth century, the image of Calamity Jane as a feminist forerunner even found its way into a children's novel published by Disney Press. Undoubtedly, other new meanings will be given to old tales as the twenty-first century unfolds.

As the gap between Calamity Jane in western folklore and Martha Canary in history widened, professional scholars found the subject difficult to ignore. Particularly beguiling was the interplay between the creators of popular culture and their audience, leading to intriguing changes in characterizations of Calamity Jane. As a result, several serious studies about Martha Canary and her legend were recently inaugurated. Especially noteworthy are the essays by historian Richard Etulain. In "Calamity Jane: Independent Woman of the West," he examines the woman hidden behind "the mythological figure of popular attire." Rather than being either a dime novel heroine or a western sleaze, Etulain explains, Calamity was "a gritty pioneer endeavoring to hold onto her reputation as a woman who defined and lived in a sphere of her own making." In another study, "Calamity Jane: The Making of a Frontier Legend," Etulain traces the transformation of Martha Canary into the legendary Calamity Jane.[9]

These recent scholarly accounts, combined with appearances of Calamity Jane in popular culture, attest to the continued strength of her legend. How such a commonplace woman as Martha Canary came to receive this much attention even a hundred years after her death is a remarkable story. During her lifetime, those who knew her best never mixed fantasy and reality. She was, they believed, a kind woman, and, except for her eccentric habits, a common woman. Bewildered at the notoriety she continued to achieve after her death, one of the pallbearers at her funeral commented, "Now who in the world would think that Calamity Jane would get to be such a famous woman."[10]

Martha Canary, Pierre, South Dakota, 1901–1902

As she traveled homeward after performing at the Pan-American Exposition in Buffalo, New York, in 1901, Martha stopped in Pierre, South Dakota, to visit old friends. She remained in Pierre for the winter, where photographer R. L. Kelley took this picture of Martha dressed in her eastern finery. Courtesy, Montana Historical Society (Haynes Collection).

**Martha Canary with photographer John B. Mayo at Wild Bill's grave,
Deadwood, South Dakota, 1903**

Amateur photographer John B. Mayo persuaded Martha to pose for him in front of Wild Bill's grave in Mount Moriah Cemetery in Deadwood, about a month before her death. However, when they arrived at the site, Martha insisted that Mayo stand beside her, so Mayo's assistant took the picture. Afterwards, Mayo managed to get Martha to stand alone in front of the grave as well. Photo Courtesy of the South Dakota State Historical Society—State Archives.

**Martha Canary posing for John B. Mayo at Wild Bill's grave,
Deadwood, South Dakota, 1903**

Courtesy, Montana Historical Society (MHS 941-415).

© Chas. C. Haas

Martha Canary, Whitewood, South Dakota, 1903

Charles Haas met Martha on the street in Whitewood, South Dakota, only a few weeks before her death. After snapping her picture, Haas and Martha had a drink together in a nearby saloon. Having been ill, she appeared much older than her forty-seven years. Postcard, Author's collection.

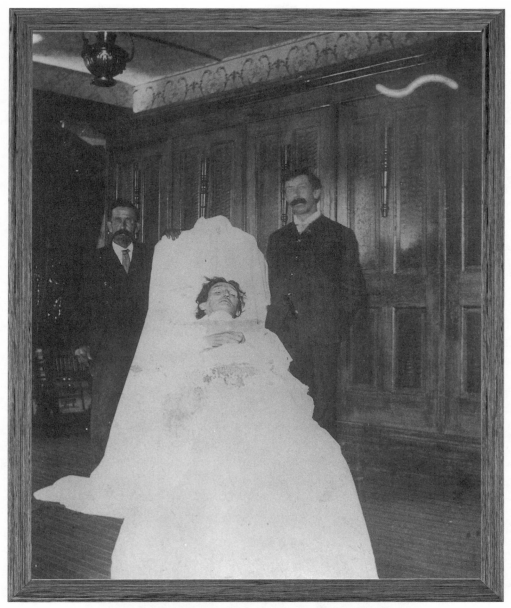

Calamity Jane in coffin, Deadwood, South Dakota, 1903

Undertakers Henry and Charles H. Robinson posed beside Martha's casket on August 4, 1903, three days after her death. Courtesy, Denver Public Library, Western History Collection (F-23387).

Calamity Jane's funeral, Deadwood, South Dakota, 1903

According to Deadwood residents, Martha's funeral was the largest in the town's history. This photograph, taken at her burial, verifies that a sizeable crowd attended the services. Courtesy, Denver Public Library, Western History Collection (F-12210).

The graves of Calamity Jane and Wild Bill Hickok, Mount Moriah Cemetery, Deadwood, South Dakota

Martha was buried near Wild Bill Hickok, whose gravesite had to be fenced to secure it from tourists who chipped the stone monuments for souvenirs. The statue of Hickok in this photograph was placed there in 1903; this picture was clearly taken shortly after Martha's death on August 1. Photo Courtesy of the South Dakota State Historical Society—State Archives.

Calamity Jane's Emerging Legend

By the time of Martha's death in 1903, legendary feats were already being attributed to her. In this engraving, Calamity Jane shoots a mountain lion that has leaped on her horse as she rides through a canyon. From W. G. Patterson, "Calamity Jane," *Wild World Magazine*, August 1903. Author's collection.

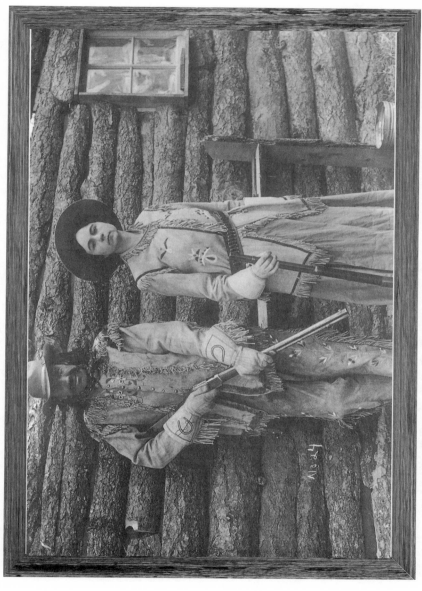

Freeda Hartzell Romine as Calamity Jane. *In the Days of '75 and '76 (1915)*

The first motion picture featuring the character of Calamity Jane was produced by the Black Hills Feature Film Company of Chadron, Nebraska. It starred Freeda Hartzell Romine (right) as Calamity Jane and A. L. Johnson as Wild Bill Hickok. In this movie, the famous pair not only scouted together, they were married. Courtesy, Nebraska State Historical Society, Lincoln, Moving Image Collections.

Calamity Jane as a Deadwood tourist attraction

Beginning in the 1920s, Deadwood deliberately promoted its legendary characters from the days of the gold rush to attract tourists. A stage production, *The Trial of Jack McCall*, was enacted regularly for visitors. In this picture from 1953, Calamity Jane is in the witness chair, pistol drawn, ready to protest the "not guilty" verdict given by the jury to McCall after he had shot Wild Bill Hickok from the back. Postcard, Brian Dippie Collection, Black Hills Postcard Co., ca. 1953.

Jean Hickok McCormick

In 1941, Jean Hickok McCormick announced to radio listeners of the "We the People" program that she was the daughter of Calamity Jane and Wild Bill Hickok. McCormick's fraudulent claims were probably rooted in movies and articles romantically associating these famous western figures. Courtesy, Denver Public Library, Western History Collection (F-24918).

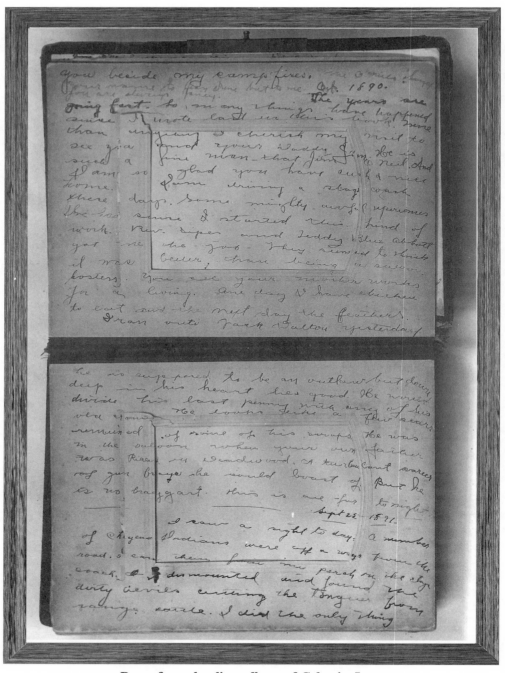

**Pages from the diary-album of Calamity Jane
produced by Jean Hickok McCormick**

The handwriting in these open pages of the photograph album that Jean Hickok McCormick claimed was that of Calamity Jane bears an uncanny resemblance to the handwriting of McCormick who taught penmanship in Montana schools. Author's Collection.

Jean Arthur as Calamity Jane, *The Plainsman* **(1937)**

The most celebrated of the early films protraying Calamity Jane featured Jean Arthur as the famous heroine and Gary Cooper as Wild Bill Hickok. In this pose, Arthur holds her whip, used not only for driving the stage but to get Hickok's attention when he ignored her. Courtesy, Paul Hutton Collection.

Jane Russell as Calamity Jane, *The Paleface* (1948)

Bob Hope and Jane Russell were paired in this comic spoof about legend-making in the West. Hope plays Painless Peter Potter, a cowardly dentist, who becomes a local hero after killing Indians; however, the shooting actually was done by Calamity Jane (Jane Russell) who was hiding nearby. Author's collection.

Doris Day in *Calamity Jane* **(1953)**

Fifty years after Martha's death, Doris Day starred in the delightful musical *Calamity Jane,* singing the Oscar-winning "Secret Love." During the movie, Calamity manages to win the affection of her secret love, Wild Bill Hickok, played by Howard Keel. Author's collection.

Jane Alexander as Calamity Jane, 1984

In a CBS television movie, Jane Alexander starred as Calamity Jane. The script was based largely on the fraudulent "diary and letters of Calamity Jane" produced by Jean McCormick. Author's collection.

Notes

INTRODUCTION

1. *Livingston Enterprise*, 17 September 1887.

2. J. Leonard Jennewein to Mr. Drake de Kay (senior editor, *Encyclopedia Americana*), 18 February 1958. J. Leonard Jennewein Collection, Layne Library, Dakota Wesleyan University.

3. Cross, "Burk, Martha Cannary," 1:267–68.

4. Etulain, "Calamity Jane: Independent Woman," 72.

5. McClintock, *Pioneer Days in the Black Hills*, 118.

6. [Fox], "Calamity Jane": 312.

7. Riley, "Images of the Frontierswoman": 1–11.

CHAPTER 1: PRINCETON MISSOURI, 1856–1864

1. *Cheyenne Sun*, 7 July 1877; Young, *Hard Knocks*, 169–70; Lewis F. Crawford, *Rekindling Camp Fires*, 272; Sutley, *Last Frontier*, 93; Paine, "Wild Bill Hickok and Calamity Jane," 168–69; and *South Dakota Guide*, 112.

2. Du Fran [D. Dee], *Low Down on Calamity Jane*, 3.

3. Newson, *Drama of Life*, 39.

4. [Canary], *Life and Adventures*, 1.

5. Bureau of the Census, 1860, Mercer County, Mo.

6. Sollid, *Calamity Jane*, 1–2, 9; Jennewein, *Calamity Jane of the Western Trails*, 14, 36.

7. *Princeton Press*, 12 August 1903.

8. *Missouri: A Guide*, 474.

9. *Mercer County Pioneer-Traces*, 3:197–98.

10. Doris Thompson, "Princeton Claims Fame as Calamity Jane Birthplace," *Princeton Post-Telegraph*, 25 July 1957; *Mercer County Pioneer Press* (Princeton: Mercer County Historical Society, 1 October 1966); *Princeton Overland Courier*, 4 September 1991. The controversy over naming the contest winner "Calamity Jane" was disclosed in personal interviews.

11. Aikman, *Calamity Jane*, 3–5, 17–21.

12. [Canary], *Life and Adventures*, 1.

13. Aikman, *Calamity Jane*, 15, 21.

14. Sollid, *Calamity Jane*, 12.

15. See also Clarence S. Paine Collection. Aikman, *Calamity Jane*, 14, states that James Canary purchased 280 acres in the "Collings church district" of Mercer County in May 1855, but this has not been confirmed.

16. Probate Records, Circuit Court of Mercer County, Mo., March 1863. Also, United States Census, 1850, Malaga Township, Monroe County, Ohio.

17. Aikman, *Calamity Jane*, 15, asserts that Thornton arrived earlier than the others, but does not cite evidence to support his conclusion.

18. Bureau of the Census, 1860, Mercer County, Mo. The graves of Martha's cousins— Valeria, Tabitha, and Sarah V.—are located in the Brantley cemetery in Mercer County. *Mercer County Pioneer Press*, 1 October 1966.

19. William R. Whiteside, "Martha Canary Family," *Mercer County Pioneer Traces* (Princeton, Mo.: Mercer County Geological Society, 1997), 1:151. Thornton and Delila sold their land on 18 January 1882 to Mike Scannell and Edward Peterson, but journalist Doris Thompson concluded that they left for Montana "some time after 1867." She also related that their son, Milt, whose leg was buried in their orchard, returned a few years later and dug up his leg to take with him to Montana. Thompson, "Princeton Claims Fame."

20. Bureau of the Census, 1850, Malaga Township, Monroe County, Ohio.

21. Bureau of the Census, 1820, 1830, 1840, 1850, Malaga Township, Monroe County, Ohio.

22. Henry Howe, *Historical Collections of Ohio* (Cincinnati: State of Ohio, 1907), 2:260–69.

23. The marriage license for Robert Canary and Charlotte Burge was taken on the 14th, and returned on the 16th. Whiteside, "Chronology: Canary Families in Iowa," August 1998.

24. *Reprint of the Original 1888 History of Harrison and Mercer County, Missouri*, 385–402; *Rogers' Souvenir History of Mercer County, Missouri*, 9–20; and Winters, *Brief History of Mercer County, Missouri*, 6–20.

25. *Reprint of the Original 1888 History*, 400–401.

26. Helen Owen, "Calamity Jane: Heroine or Outcast," TS, 11 November 1965, 2. Mercer County Library, Princeton, Mo.

27. *Mercer County Pioneer Press*, 1 October 1966.

28. Thompson, "Princeton Claims Fame."

29. The inventory of James Canary's property was compiled by Hannibal Armstrong, administrator of the estate, 4 November 1862. Probate Records, Circuit Court of Mercer County, Mo., March 1863.

30. Thompson, "Princeton Claims Fame."

31. Aikman, *Calamity Jane*, 10–11.

32. *Mercer County Pioneer Press*, 30 December 1970.

33. Aikman, *Calamity Jane*, 9, 15.

34. *Mercer County Pioneer Press*, 30 December 1970.

35. Descendant Elva Douthat reported that Robert served as chaplain at an undetermined military post for at least five years before 1856, and again during the Civil War. Douthat, "J. (James) Thornton Canary," 1:150.

36. Thompson, "Princeton Claims Fame."

37. Ibid.

38. *Cheyenne Sun*, 7 July 1877; Mueller, *Calamity Jane*, 5–6.

39. Maguire, *Coming Empire*, 64.

40. "Calamity Jane as a Lady Robinhood": 46.

41. Young, *Hard Knocks*, 169–70; McGillycuddy, *McGillycuddy Agent*, 25–27; Bennett, *Old Deadwood Days*, 234–35; and Du Fran, *Low Down on Calamity Jane*, 1.

42. Young, *Hard Knocks*, 169–70.

43. Had she lived at Fort Laramie from 1862 to 1875, commented biographer J. Leonard Jennewein, "it is inconceivable that those who have written of their days at the Fort might not have recorded the fact." Jennewein, *Calamity Jane*, 12.

44. Young, *Hard Knocks*, 169–70; McGillycuddy to Editor, *Rapid City Journal*, 1 October 1924. For analysis of this plagiarism, see Jennewein, *Calamity Jane*, 10–12, and Sollid, *Calamity Jane*, 5–9.

45. McGillycuddy, *McGillycuddy Agent*, 27. Sollid did not believe Young's stories in *Hard Knocks* had any value because she found most of them to be "contrary to accepted history." Sollid, *Calamity Jane*, 7. Jennewein, who believed strongly in McGillycuddy's integrity, refused to concede that he might have plagiarized Young's account. Instead, he thought Young might have learned the story from McGillycuddy during private correspondence between the men. See Jennewein, *Calamity Jane*, 12.

46. Robinson, *Encyclopedia of South Dakota*, 106. In 1951, Will Robinson told J. Leonard Jennewein that claims stating Calamity Jane was Martha Canary and born in Missouri were nonsense. He believed that Calamity lied about everything. Will Robinson to J. Leonard Jennewein, 11 December 1951. Jennewein Collection.

47. Bennett, *Old Deadwood Days*, 234–35. Textual comparisons suggest that portions of Bennett's dinner conversation are derived from Brown and Willard, *Black Hills Trails*, 412.

48. Du Fran, *Low Down on Calamity Jane*, 1; McGillycuddy to Editor, *Rapid City Journal*, 1 October 1924.

49. Paine, "Wild Bill Hickok and Calamity Jane," 168–69.

50. Bureau of the Census, 1860, Mercer County, Mo.

51. Paine, "Wild Bill Hickok and Calamity Jane," 168–69.

52. The 1850 Census, Appanoose County, Iowa, lists John M. Connoway and Abigail, born in Tennessee, and Margaret J., age six, born in Illinois. Connoway (Conarray) was a chairmaker from Illinois, and like Abigail was thirty years old in 1850. See Whiteside, "Chronology: Canary Families in Iowa."

53. Klock, *Here Comes Calamity Jane*, 6.

54. Aikman, *Calamity Jane*, 22–23.

55. Thornton "was mustered out soon afterward, when the command of the militia was assumed by the opposing state government." Paine, "Wild Bill Hickok and Calamity Jane," 169.

56. *Princeton Press*, 12 August 1903. One writer asserts instead that the Canary family moved from Missouri to Wisconsin, and that Martha's father, named John, was abusive and a hard drinker. McClintock, *Pioneer Days*, 115.

57. Paul, *Mining Frontiers*, 140; Faragher, *Women and Men on the Overland Trail*, 16, 189.

58. Clairmonte, *Calamity Was the Name For Jane*, 11–19.

59. Probate Records, Circuit Court of Mercer County. Armstrong did not complete his work until July 1865, when he finally advertised that he would be making final settlement of the James Canary estate the next month.

CHAPTER 2: TO MONTANA AND WYOMING, 1864–1874

1. [Canary], *Life and Adventures*, 1.

2. Ibid.

3. Faragher, *Women and Men on Overland Trail*, 189–93.

4. Earnest, "Reminiscences," Robert Beebe David Collection. Boney's brother, Frank Earnest, along with E. E. Bennett, operated the Emigrant Ferry on the North Platte River twenty miles from Fort Steele. Beebe, *Reminiscing along the Sweetwater*, 69–74.

5. Settle and Settle, *Overland Days*, 44, 50, 59, 80, 83, 99, 103, 106, 110–13, 145, 162–63.

6. Ibid., 172–73.

7. *Virginia City Montana Post*, 31 December 1864.

8. Ibid., 30 September 1865. Although the Canary family was not again mentioned in news articles, the name "R. Connary" did appear in the list of letters to be picked up at the post office.

9. Johnson, "Flour Famine in Alder Gulch": 18–27.

10. [Fox], "Calamity Jane."

11. *Deadwood Daily Pioneer-Times*, 2 August 1903.

12. Despite his inaccurate estimate of her age, it is significant that Arnold remembered her as young girl, not a grown woman. He thought her name was Jane Somers. To be certain of her identity when he met her at the turn of the century, he asked if she knew "Bill Blivens at Virginia City in 1864," implying that Blivens was the individual who led young Martha astray. She responded, "I can go to his grave as straight as an Indian goes to dog soup." Lewis Crawford, *Rekindling Camp Fires*, 272.

13. Brown, *Romance of Everyday Life*, 41–44. John S. McClintock, who knew Martha in later years, said that he was in Confederate Gulch soon after 1866, and "heard the names of many who were or had been in this vicinity but recalled no mention of this gun-woman." He added, "It appears that Mr. Brown was misinformed as to the identity of the woman in the incident he relates." McClintock, *Pioneer Days*, 116.

14. Charles W. Bocker, interview by Grace Raymond Hebard, Laramie, Wyoming, 9 August 1927, and Hebard to Duncan Aikman, 20 July 1927, 23 August 1927, and 7 September 1927, American Heritage Center. See also, Aikman, *Calamity Jane*, 43–44.

15. Aikman, *Calamity Jane*, 43–44.

16. [Canary], *Life and Adventures*, 2.

17. Bureau of the Census, 1869, Carter County, Wyoming.

18. Crofutt, *Trans-Continental Tourist's Guide*, 86.

19. *Sioux City Journal*, 25 January 1954.

20. Unidentified newspaper clipping, 1942. Fremont County Pioneer Museum, Lander, Wyoming.

21. *Helena Evening Herald*, 16 July 1901, citing *St. Paul Dispatch*.

22. *Great Falls Daily Tribune*, 18 January 1903.

23. *Cheyenne Democratic Leader*, 3 November 1885. Another version of this story suggests that "Calamity Jane was born of poor parents at Fort Washakie, this territory, and was adopted into the family of an officer stationed there, but ran away and entered upon a life of shame when only 13 years of age." *Cheyenne Daily Leader*, 21 June 1887.

24. *Sweetwater Mines*, Wyo., 1 April, 27 May, 17 June, 11 July, 8 August, and one undated article, 1868; and *Frontier Index*, Wyo., 25 and 28 August 1868. See also, Robert A. Murray, *Miner's Delight*, and Thomas, "Miner's Delight": 36–40. Chisholm said that, during his visit with the Gallaghers, there were only three women in Miner's Delight. Homsher, *South Pass, 1868*, 70–71, 104–5. Clarence Paine rejected the story that Martha lived with the Gallaghers because Chisholm failed to mention her. Paine, "Calamity Jane: Man? Woman? or Both?": 70–71. South Pass pioneer Peter Sherlock incorrectly identified Martha as "a niece of Major Gallagher." Sherlock, *South Pass*, Introduction.

25. Larson, *History of Wyoming*, 53.

26. Ibid., 113.

27. *Bismarck Tri-Weekly Tribune*, 17 August 1877.

28. Lewis Crawford, *Rekindling Camp Fires*, 272.

29. *Frontier Index*, Bear River City, Wyo., 3 November 1868.

30. Homsher, *South Pass*, 101.

31. *Frontier Index*, 12 June 1868.

32. Ibid., 7 July 1868.

33. Earnest, "Reminiscences."

34. Tobe Borner, "Calamity Jane," American Heritage Center; "Former Basinite Tells Facts about Calamity Jane's Early History," *Basin Republican-Rustler*, 18 September 1941. According to relatives interviewed by Jean Mathisen, John Borner secured a job for Lena with the James I. Patten family at Camp Brown on the Little Wind River before he married her. These descendants also said Lena was blind in one eye. Mathisen, "Calamity's Sister": 25, 29. Tobe Borner's account of his mother and father contains numerous errors. Kime's hotel was in Miner's Delight, not South Pass, and John Borner himself said he and Lena were married by Judge Edward Lawn at Lander on 20 August 1875. "Pioneer Profiles: John and Lena Canary Borner": 32–34.

35. John Borner's obituary in 1919 listed seven children: Hannah Alderdice, Greybull, Wyo.; Mrs. May (Rebecca May) Hutton, Calgary, Alberta, Canada; Mrs. Theresia Van Alstine, Okotoks, Alberta, Canada; William Borner, Twin Falls, Idaho; Tobias (Tobe) Borner, Shell, Wyo.; Frank E. Borner, Greybull, Wyo.; and Mrs. Bertha Wilkinson, Greybull, Wyo. See Mathisen, "Calamity's Sister": 23–30.

36. "Borner's Gardens" near Lander is described in *Rawlins Carbon County Journal*, 21 February 1885. For additional biographical information on John Borner, who lived in Greybull, Wyo., until his death on 18 December 1919, see Mathisen, "Calamity's Sister": 24–28, and "Pioneer Profiles: John and Lena Borner": 2, 32–34.

37. Tobe Borner, "Calamity Jane," American Heritage Center.

38. *Livingston Park County News*, 16 June 1922.

39. George Reeb, age twenty-seven, was convicted of robbing Yellowstone Park coaches on 14 August 1897, and was sentenced to two years and five months. He was released, with time allowed for good behavior, on 22 June 1900. Frye, *Atlas of Wyoming Outlaws*, 195.

40. Burial records were provided by William R. Whiteside.

41. *Description and History of Convicts in State Penitentiary at Laramie City, Wyoming*. Wyoming State Archives. Also, *Docket No. 93, District Court, Uinta County, State of Wyoming, vs. Elijah Canary, 3 December 1895*; "Description List, Uinta County, State of Wyoming, 26 April 1896"; and, *Report of Convicts Discharged, No. 253, 12 August 1900*. Elijah's crime is described in *Evanston News-Register*, 11 April 1896, and Frye, *Atlas of Wyoming Outlaws*, 167. Elijah was released on 12 August 1900, having served four years and three months, with time off for good conduct. In a letter petitioning the Wyoming governor to release Elijah early, attorneys claimed Elijah was in the employment of William Kuntz and only following orders; they added that his wife and child needed him for support, and if released, he would join his family in San Francisco. Allen & Allen, San Francisco, Calif., to Governor D. W. Richards, 26 January 1899. Wyoming State Archives.

42. These relatives also believed Elijah rode with Butch Cassidy's "Wild Bunch," and after his release from prison worked at the Dave Dean ranch in Uinta County, Wyoming. Mathisen, "Calamity's Sister": 28–29.

43. Besides Elijah's burial records, William R. Whiteside discovered that Elijah's son, Frank Canary, born 8 July 1896, died on 19 April 1916, and was buried in Panguitch, Garfield County, Utah.

44. Mathisen, "Calamity's Sister": 29.

45. According to William (Bill) Wilkensen, the great-nephew of Calamity Jane, Lena was injured while feeding her livestock and died afterwards from complications. Mueller, *Calamity Jane*, 8. Lena's obituary asserted: "She was one of the most industrious women in the valley and one whom all her acquaintances held in the highest respect. Her pride was in her children and her home." *Fremont Clipper*, 17 October 1888, quoted in Mathisen, "Calamity's Sister": 26.

46. Mathisen, "Calamity's Sister": 29; Mueller, *Calamity Jane*, 8; Marion Nelson to author, 10 February 1995.

47. *Chicago Tribune*, 19 June 1875.

48. Myfanwy Thomas Goodnough, "Calamity Jane," *Rock Springs Miner*, 20 October 1933.

49. Ross, *Westward the Women*, 133–34.

50. Interestingly, Otero recalled another prostitute in that vicinity named "Lousy Liz." See Otero, *My Life on the Frontier*, 22.

51. Aikman, *Calamity Jane*, 61–63.

52. Hart and Hart, *—And All Points West!*, 1–11.

53. "Calamity Jane's Diary and Letters" is reprinted in Mumey, *Calamity Jane*, 109ff; *Copies of Calamity Jane's Diary*.

54. [Canary], *Life and Adventures*, 4.

55. In 1870 Custer was writing his memoirs at Fort Leavenworth, Kansas, after which he took a leave to visit his wife in New York. He returned that summer to participate in hunting excursions with tourists. Sollid, *Calamity Jane*, 24.

56. McClintock, *Pioneer Days*, 116. Belding probably crossed paths with her several times because he was in Montana in 1864, in Miner's Delight in 1868, was a construction worker on the Union Pacific, and joined the Black Hills gold rush in 1876. Doane Robinson, *History of South Dakota*, 2: 1293–94.

57. *Cheyenne Daily Leader*, 21 June 1887.

58. Larson, *History of Wyoming*, 44–46.

59. Ibid., 53; *Wyoming: A Guide*, 138–39; Dial, *A Place to Raise Hell*, 32, 34. Although no documents provide details about Martha working at McDaniels' establishment, one writer fancifully related that Calamity met Wild Bill Hickok there in the early 1870s and that they watched a stage production and drank together. Eisele, *Real Wild Bill Hickok*, 261–74.

60. *Billings Daily Gazette*, 13 July 1901.

61. *Torrington Goshen News and Fort Laramie Scout*, 7 June 1928. Unfortunately, Martha's name does not appear in Hunton's daily diary entries. See Flannery, *John Hunton's Diary*, 2: 109–11. For a description of the Cuny & Coffey road ranch, see Spring, *Stage and Express Routes*, 111–13.

62. [John Q.] Ward to the Editor, 8 January 1927, *Western Story Magazine*. Typescript, Paine Collection.

Chapter 3: The Black Hills Expedition of 1875

1. [Fox], "Calamity Jane," 312.

2. Sollid, *Calamity Jane*, 27.

3. [Canary], *Life and Adventures*, 3.

4. Vaughn, "Captain James Egan": 1–3, 6–7, 18. Vaughn does not mention the purported encounter between Martha and Egan. James Egan died in 1883. Stella Foote, however, contends that it was Pat Egan, not James, who gave Martha her nickname, and that Pat sent money to help Martha in 1901 when she needed medical attention. Further confusing the story, Foote claims that "Pat" Egan commanded the "grey horse" troop. She is mistaken, for this was James Egan's troop. See Foote, *History of Calamity Jane*, 37, 141.

5. Fox believed Martha's rescue story was impossible: only a "very strong man" could have lifted Egan from his horse as he was falling without dismounting, she said, and Martha "was small and never could have lifted a child, weighing fifty pounds, as she claimed to have lifted Captain Egan." M. L. Fox, "A Land of Romance," *Deadwood Daily Pioneer-Times*, 5 September 1903.

6. Aikman, *Calamity Jane*, 66–67.

7. Sollid, *Calamity Jane*, 36.

8. Coursey, *Beautiful Black Hills*, 104.

9. *Deadwood Daily Pioneer-Times*, 2 August 1903. Edgar Wilson (Bill) Nye did not arrive in Wyoming until 1876, and did not establish the *Laramie Boomerang* until 1881. See Larson, *Bill Nye's Western Humor*, Introduction; Sollid, *Calamity Jane*, 37–38. Hoshier thought that it was not Nye but P. P. Poulton, editor of the *Cheyenne Sun*, who gave Martha her nickname, but he said the naming occurred when Poulton served as guest editor for Nye. This is impossible because Martha already had her nickname before 1876. *Sioux Falls Argus Leader*, 9 July 1906.

10. *Midland (S.Dak.) Mail*, 14 November 1929; Lewis Crawford, *Rekindling Camp Fires*, 274. James L. Sherlock suggests her nickname was given after she nursed epidemic victims in Miner's Delight. Although the timing would not exclude that possibility, his account was not published until 1978 and probably is derived from earlier tales. Sherlock, *South Pass and Its Tales*, Introduction.

11. Ryan, *Me and the Black Hills*, 47.

12. Riegel, *America Moves West*, 539.

13. Reckless Ralph, "Calamity Jane, Queen of the Plains": 3; Sollid, *Calamity Jane*, 33–34.

14. Parker, *Gold in the Black Hills*, 167.

15. *Helena Evening Herald*, 16 July 1901, citing *St. Paul Dispatch*.

16. McGillycuddy, *McGillycuddy Agent*, 27.

17. Johnston, *Last Roundup*, 116.

18. *Cheyenne Daily Leader*, 16 May 1883.

19. *Ibid.*, 11 April 1876.

20. *Sidney Telegraph*, 4 August 1877; *Cheyenne Daily Sun*, 23 August 1878; *Livingston Daily Enterprise*, 12 June 1886; *Laramie Daily Boomerang*, 25 and 26 September 1889.

21. *Denver Rocky Mountain News*, 2 May 1875.

22. Ibid.

23. *Pueblo Colorado Daily Chieftain*, 27 April 1875.

24. Ibid., 30 April 1875.

25. *Chicago Tribune*, 19 June 1875.

26. *London Star*, 7 August 1903, in "Buffalo Bill 1903 Clipping Book," Buffalo Bill Museum, Cody, Wyo. Cody's presence with Anson Mills's Big Horn Expedition in 1874 is described in Russell, *Lives and Legends of Buffalo Bill*, 209–12. However, Anson Mills did not mention this meeting with Martha: see his *Big Horn Expedition* and *My Story*, 155.

27. Flannery, *John Hunton's Diary* 2: 109–11.

28. Ward, Letter to Editor of *Western Story Magazine*, 8 January 1927.

29. See Jackson, *Custer's Gold*.

30. Tallent, *The Black Hills*, 18–100.

31. See Turchen and McLaird, *Black Hills Expedition*; Kime, *Black Hills Journals*.

32. Sollid, *Calamity Jane*, 7.

33. Hooker, *Bullwhacker*, 163.

34. McGillycuddy, *McGillycuddy Agent*, 25–27. In this story, Martha's age probably was adapted to fit the 1860 Dalton version of her birthdate, making her sixteen rather than nineteen. Elsewhere, Valentine T. McGillycuddy said Martha was "matured for her years." McGillycuddy to Editor, *Rapid City Journal*, 1 October 1924.

35. McGillycuddy, *McGillycuddy Agent*, 25–29.

36. Ibid., 33.

37. Young, *Hard Knocks*, 171.

38. McGillycuddy, *McGillycuddy Agent*, 33–34.

39. Young, *Hard Knocks*, 170.

40. Aikman, *Calamity Jane*, 70.

41. Young, *Hard Knocks*, 170–72.

42. McGillycuddy, *McGillycuddy Agent*, 33–38; Kime, *Black Hills Journals*, 21.

43. *Chicago Tribune*, 19 June 1875.

44. Turchen and McLaird, *Black Hills Expedition*, 15–16, 43.

45. McGillycuddy, *McGillycuddy Agent*, 38.

46. Flannery, *John Hunton's Diary* 2: 109–11.

47. Kime, *Black Hills Journals*, 96. The St. Louis photographer is identified as Fritz W. Guerin in Mautz, *Biographies of Western Photographers*, 782. This photograph of Calamity Jane is sometimes attributed to Valentine T. McGillycuddy. However, McGillycuddy clarified to Noah H. Rose, Berkeley, California, in 1926: "This is a photo of our Calamity, for I was present and saw the picture made in July, 1875, on Lower French Creek, in the Black Hills." See Hunter and Rose, *Album of Gun-Fighters*, 47.

48. *Yankton Daily Press and Dakotaian*, 6 July 1875. For a description of MacMillan, see Knight, *Following the Indian Wars*, 171.

49. Milner and Forrest, *California Joe*, 233.

50. Young said this incident occurred at Spring Creek; if so, Martha continued with the expedition after it left Camp Harney. Young, *Hard Knocks*, 171–72.

51. Turchen and McLaird, *Black Hills Expedition*, 47.

52. Ibid., 49–50.

53. Ibid., 6, 24.

54. *Cheyenne Daily Leader*, 24 February 1876.

55. *Sidney Telegraph*, 12 February 1876. Interestingly, the poem and accompanying article were signed "Calamity Jack." A later version of the poem is in Captain Jack Crawford, *Poet Scout*, Notes.

56. Andreas, *Andrea's Historical Atlas*, 118.

57. [Canary], *Life and Adventures*, 3.

58. McClintock, *Pioneer Days*, 117; Casey, *Black Hills and Its Characters*, 179; and Brown and Willard, *Black Hills Trails*, 414.

59. Tacetta R. Walker, "Calamity Jane, Frontier Belle," unidentified clipping, 14 June 1937. Montana Historical Society, Helena.

60. Stokes, *Deadwood Gold*, 47.

61. Holbrook, *Little Annie Oakley*, 32–33. Aikman said this event occurred during the Crook expedition in 1876. Aikman, *Calamity Jane*, 76. The story seems to have first appeared in Brown and Willard, *Black Hills Trails*, 413–14, but these authors did not specify when the purported event occurred.

62. Flannery, *John Hunton's Diary* 2: 109–11.

Chapter 4: With Crook in 1876

1. Vaughn, *Reynolds Campaign*, 26–27.

2. Flannery, *John Hunton's Diary* 2: 109–11.

3. Butler, *Daughters of Joy*, 8.

4. Spring, "Diary of Isaac N. Bard," 11: 173, 186.

5. Vaughn, *Reynolds Campaign*, 20–26, passim.

6. Reneau, *Adventures of Moccasin Joe*, 23, 161.

7. Ibid., 23.

8. Unidentified Denver newspaper article, 24 February [1901], quoted in Eisele, *Real Wild Bill Hickok*, 267. Considerable confusion exists about the identity of Little Frank, who probably was known also as Black Hills Frank, Soldier's Frank, and Shingle-Headed Little Frank. Her surname is given as O'Dare, O'Day, and Adair. See Spring, *Stage and Express Routes*, 216. John Ward also remembered that in 1876 Martha "formed an acquaintance with a woman named Frankie Glass and for some time they were inseparable companions." Ward, Letter to the Editor of *Western Story Magazine*, 8 January 1927. George Hoshier, a pallbearer at Martha's funeral, recalled "Frank Adair" in company with Martha in early spring 1876 and said "Frank had as much title to be called a scout as Calamity." He meant that neither woman deserved that designation, for he added that Martha "was no more a scout than I was." *Sioux Falls Argus Leader*, 9 July 1906.

9. Parker, *Gold in the Black Hills*, 71–72.

10. Ibid., 73–77.

11. Brown and Willard, *Black Hills Trails*, 76.

12. Captain Jack Crawford, "Truth about Calamity Jane": 333. According to Darlis A. Miller, in *Captain Jack Crawford*, 26–52, Crawford was in the Black Hills region between mid-1875 and July 1876.

13. Doane Robinson to Joe Schulze, 22 April 1922. H-74-9. South Dakota State Historical Society, Pierre. See also, Cornell, "Opening of the Black Hills": 171–75.

14. Du Fran, *Low Down on Calamity Jane*, 6.

15. Brown and Willard, *Black Hills Trails*, 96–97; Parker, *Gold in the Black Hills*, 135–36.

16. Greenwood, "Diary of D.M. Holmes," 5: 77.

17. According to the Cheyenne newspaper, Captain C. V. Gardner made the round trip to Custer in fifteen-and-a-half days, and said he could return to Custer with a load of merchandise in six-and-a-half days. *Cheyenne Daily Sun*, 27 April 1876.

18. *Territory of Wyoming vs. Maggie Smith, Indictment for Grand Larceny. A True Bill, No. 269.* 24 May 1876. Paine Collection. The identity of Maggie Louise is unknown, but within a month of Martha's arrest, Maggie Louise was tried for "having assaulted the prosecuting witness with a pen-knife." The jury found her not guilty. *Cheyenne Daily Leader*, 20 June 1876.

19. *Territory of Wyoming vs. Maggie Smith, Verdict No. 269.* Paine Collection. See also, *Cheyenne Daily Leader*, 9 June 1876.

20. In a different version, Martha was arrested "on charges of immorality" along with a soldier from Camp Carlin before Mrs. Fisher loaned her the clothing. *Cheyenne Wyoming State Tribune*, 23-26 July 1940. One reporter said that in later years, after her embarrassment receded, the story of loaning Calamity Jane her clothes became one of Catherine Fisher's "favorite anecdotes." She liked to say that "Calamity Jane not only made such a favorable impression in court that she was discharged from custody, but afterward made the gown famous by parading down the street in it." *Denver Post*, 2 November 1943.

21. "Calamity Jane. A Long and Lonely Journey into the Indian Land—An Unprotected Female Rivals Sheridan's Ride," *Denver Rocky Mountain News*, 25 June 1876.

22. "Jane's Jamboree," *Cheyenne Daily Leader*, 20 June 1876. J. C. Abney's Stage, Mail, and Express is advertised in the *Cheyenne Daily Sun*, 8 March 1876.

23. "Calamity Jane. A Long and Lonely Journey."

24. "Jane's Jamboree."

25. "Calamity Jane. A Long and Lonely Journey."

26. "Jane's Jamboree."

27. "Calamity Jane. A Long and Lonely Journey."

28. Mangum, *Battle of the Rosebud*, 28–91; Vaughn, *With Crook at the Rosebud*, 153, passim. After the fight at the Rosebud on 16 June, it was reported: "Scouts hard to obtain. Have no one as yet who has been on the Powder river trail." *Yankton Daily Press and Dakotaian*, 27 June 1876.

29. [Canary], *Life and Adventures*, 3–4.

30. According to Roberta Sollid, official communications to Fort Fetterman were carried by a courier named Harrison. Sollid, *Calamity Jane*, 31.

31. Paine, "Wild Bill Hickok and Calamity Jane," 170.

32. DeBarthe, *Life and Adventures of Frank Grouard*, 294.

33. J. Leonard Jennewein thought it possible that Grouard hired Martha, but paid her from a miscellaneous fund that left no permanent record. Jennewein, *Calamity Jane*, 17.

34. Chapin, *Charles Chapin's Story*, 20–32.

35. Vaughn, *Reynolds Campaign*, 22–23, 65.

36. Flannery, *John Hunton's Diary*, 3: 188, 191, 194.

37. Lewis Crawford, *Rekindling Camp Fires*, 272–73.

38. Captain Jack Crawford, "Truth about Calamity Jane."

39. Ibid.

40. Bourke, *On the Border with Crook*, 299–300. Bourke's comments about Calamity Jane do not appear in his daily journals of the expedition, indicating they were inserted in his autobiographical account. See Charles M. Robinson III, ed., *The Diaries of John Gregory Bourke: Volume One, November 20, 1872–July 28, 1876* (Denton, Tex.: University of North Texas Press, 2003).

41. Mills, *My Story*, 401. Roberta Sollid thought Mills's tale about Calamity was embellished: "Without questioning his ability as an army officer, or integrity as a person, it is easy to imagine that he threw in the fanciful tale of Calamity Jane to liven up a somewhat gloomy subject." Sollid, *Calamity Jane*, 30.

42. Ibid.

43. Spring, "Dr. McGillycuddy's Diary," 284.

44. The usually reliable Hunton incorrectly remembered that the wounded arrived shortly after General Merritt joined Crook with the Fifth Cavalry, which was in early July; the wounded actually returned on 27 June. Flannery, *John Hunton's Diary* 2:111.

45. About Martha's claim to have carried important dispatches for Crook, John Ward exclaimed, "What bunk! What rot!" Ward, Letter to the Editor of *Western Story Magazine*, 8 January 1927.

46. *Cheyenne Daily Leader*, 23 June 1876. Although MacMillan did not mention Martha in his June 23 dispatch, he may have met her later. For health reasons, he "was compelled to go back with the wounded to Fort Fetterman several days after the Rosebud battle." Martha also was sent back to the fort at that time. See Vaughn, *With Crook at the Rosebud*, 177.

47. Finerty, *War-Path and Bivouac*, 199–200.

48. Vaughn, *With Crook at the Rosebud*, 158.

49. Maguire, *Coming Empire*, 49, 65.

50. Unidentified clipping, Sheridan, Wyo., [1975]. Wyoming State Archives.

51. *Omaha Morning World-Herald*, 3 February 1892.

52. Brinker, "The Bull Whacker": 39–40.

53. *Billings News*, 13 July 1901.

54. *Billings Daily Gazette*, 19 April 1902.

55. Flannery, *John Hunton's Diary* 2: 111.

56. [Canary], *Life and Adventures*, 4.

CHAPTER 5: WITH WILD BILL HICKOK IN DEADWOOD, 1876

1. Wilstach, *Wild Bill Hickok*, 254.

2. Rosa, *They Called Him Wild Bill*, 227.

3. *Omaha Morning World-Herald*, 3 February 1892.

4. *Deadwood Daily Pioneer-Times*, 8 August 1903.

5. Young, *Hard Knocks*, 206–7. Other writers suggest she died on the same day twenty-seven years after Hickok's death. Jennewein, *Calamity Jane*, 8.

6. [Canary], *Life and Adventures*, 4.

7. *Colorado Springs Colorado State Journal*, 4 September 1903.

8. Rosa, *They Called Him Wild Bill*, passim. The marriage of Agnes Lake Thatcher and Wild Bill Hickok was reported in the *Cheyenne Daily Sun*, 8 March 1876.

9. *Cheyenne Daily Leader*, 14 April 1876.

10. The *Cheyenne Daily Sun*, 28 March 1876, mentioned Utter's plans to develop a Black Hills transportation line. See also Rosa, *They Called Him Wild Bill*, 280–84, and Spring, *Colorado Charley*, 88–95.

11. Flannery, *John Hunton's Diary* 2: 115.

12. Secrest, *I Buried Hickok*, 99.

13. Flannery, *John Hunton's Diary* 2: 115. Captain Jack Crawford similarly reported that Hickok told him "in June '76, in Cheyenne, that up to that date he had never met her." See Jack Crawford, "Truth about Calamity Jane," *The Journalist*, 5 March 1904, 333.

14. Secrest, *I Buried Hickok*, 93. In another version of White Eye Anderson's adventures, twenty-six sporting women were said to be with the party. Thorp, "White-Eye": 6–10, 46, 48.

15. Doane Robinson, *History of South Dakota* 2:1767. Dirty Em remains obscure, but Eleanore Dumont (Madame Moustache, 1829–79), nicknamed for the hair under her nose, was already a well-known card dealer in San Francisco in the 1850s. She worked in, or operated, gambling establishments and brothels for over twenty years in towns such as Fort Benton, Virginia City, Bannack, and Helena, Montana. In 1879, she returned to California and, destitute, took poison and ended her life.

16. Secrest, *I Buried Hickok*, 93–95.

17. Thorp, "White-Eye": 10.

18. Richardson, "A Trip to the Black Hills": 749–54.

19. Duncan Aikman thought it was in Custer, not Fort Laramie, that Martha joined Hickok's party, and colorfully related how the men dressed her in a scout's outfit for their dramatic parade into Deadwood. Aikman, *Calamity Jane*, 81–83.

20. *Deadwood Black Hills Daily Pioneer*, 28 July 1886.

21. Hughes, *Pioneer Years in the Black Hills*, 159–61.

22. McClintock said that he saw Hickok's party "shortly after their arrival." McClintock, *Pioneer Days*, 15.

23. According to Anderson, Pie and Steve Utter soon returned to Colorado. Secrest, *I Buried Hickok*, 97–99. Elsewhere, Anderson said that Martha briefly shared a tent with Steve Utter. Thorp, "White-Eye": 46.

24. *Deadwood Black Hills Pioneer*, 15 July 1876.

25. Jack Crawford, "Truth about Calamity Jane."

26. [Canary], *Life and Adventures*, 4.

27. Utter's pony express riders are named in *Yankton Daily Press and Dakotaian*, 9 August 1879. See also Spring, *Colorado Charley*, 97–98; *Stage and Express Routes*, 154–56.

28. Secrest, *I Buried Hickok*, 102; Thorp, "White-Eye": 46.

29. McClintock, *Pioneer Days*, 117.

30. *Deadwood Black Hills Daily Times*, 2 October 1877.

31. Stokes, *Deadwood Gold*, 61.

32. *Deadwood Daily Pioneer-Times*, 20 December 1899.

33. McClintock, *Pioneer Days*, 69–70.

34. Young, *Hard Knocks*, 205–6.

35. McLaird, "Writings of William B. Lull": 53–65.

36. "Tragedies of '76: They Were Performed on the Stage in Deadwood," *St. Paul Pioneer Press*, 12 March 1894. McClintock also remembered that Martha had her own sporting establishment in 1876 and 1877. See *Pioneer Days*, 117. According to one report, Kitty Arnold "wore the regular buckskin suit, trousers and all," and took her turn as a guard, with rifle, as the party trekked to the Hills. Like Martha, she was "generally found in dance halls," and "commanded respect" because of her "acts of charity." *Deadwood Black Hills Daily Times*, 7 May 1892.

37. Laughing Sam later became a well-known road agent in the Black Hills. Secrest, *I Buried Hickok*, 102. William Lull told a similar story with several variations. McLaird, "Writings of William B. Lull": 63–64.

38. *Cheyenne Daily Leader*, 17 August 1876, quoted in Secrest, *I Buried Hickok*, 112. Actor Charles Chapin falsely claimed he was present at the spitting incident, which he said occurred in 1879 during the play *East Lynne*. Chapin, *Chapin's Story*, 30–32.

39. "Tragedies of '76."

40. Young, *Hard Knocks*, 209.

41. Secrest, *I Buried Hickok*, 103.

42. McClintock, *Pioneer Days*, 106.

43. Wilstach, *Wild Bill Hickok*, 254.

44. McClintock, *Pioneer Days*, 106.

45. *Colorado Springs Colorado State Journal*, 4 September 1903.

46. Like many of the stories about Calamity Jane, California Joe's tale about making her do the "tenderfoot dance" in a Deadwood saloon cannot be verified. It is certain, however, that Milner's biographers are mistaken that he met Hickok in the Sixty-Six saloon on 20 June. Wild Bill didn't arrive in Deadwood until mid-July. Milner and Forrest, *California Joe*, 247–48.

47. Richardson, "Last Days of a Plainsman": 22. See also McLaird, "Leander P. Richardson Reports": 239–68.

48. *Deadwood Black Hills Pioneer*, 5 August 1876; Rosa, *They Called Him Wild Bill*, 279–337; *Wild Bill Hickok*, 187–213; *Jack McCall, Assassin*.

49. [Canary], *Life and Adventures*, 4.

50. There are discrepancies in accounts about which saloon was the scene of Hickok's death; in addition to Saloon No. 10, the Bella Union, the El Dorado, the I.X.L., the Saratoga Gambling House, the Sixty-Six, and the One Hundred and Ten are given as the site. Sollid, *Calamity Jane*, 99.

51. [Canary], *Life and Adventures*, 4–5.

52. *Deadwood Black Hills Pioneer*, 5 August 1876. Young recalled that after the crowd surrounded McCall, a man named Tom Mulquinn pinned his arms from behind while others then disarmed the assassin. Young, *Hard Knocks*, 219–22. When McCall was interviewed by Bill Nye in Laramie, he said that several hundred men gathered around him and "he saw that resistance was useless and gave himself up to arrest." *Laramie Sentinel*, 30 August 1876.

53. Rosa, *Jack McCall, Assassin*.

54. Captain Jack Crawford, "Truth about Calamity Jane": 333.

55. *Aberdeen Daily News*, 16 April 1902.

56. Ibid.

57. This early movie was *In the Days of '75 and '76* (Chadron, Nebr.: Black Hills Feature Film Company, 1915; reissue, Lincoln: Nebraska State Historical Society, 1989), videocassette.

58. Harry Sinclair Drago, for example, wrote incorrectly that "there is not one whit of evidence" that Hickok ever saw Calamity in Deadwood. See Drago, *Road Agents*, 110.

59. Hughes, *Pioneer Years*, 162–63.

60. McClintock, *Pioneer Days*, 118.

61. If Martha cried over Hickok's body as Newson suggests, she could not have helped capture McCall as she claimed. Newson, *Drama of Life*, 2, 63.

62. Richardson, "Trip to the Black Hills": 755; Hughes, *Pioneer Years*, 162–63.

63. Secrest, *I Buried Hickok*, 121. Elsewhere, Anderson described several women, not just Martha, picking wildflowers and placing them on the coffin. Thorp, "White-Eye": 48.

64. Walton, *An Illinois Gold Hunter*, 35–36.

65. Brown and Willard, *Black Hills Trails*, 101–3. One correspondent said the Mexican meant to scalp the Indian, but knew nothing about the procedure of scalping, so "just cut the whole head off." *Yankton Daily Press and Dakotaian*, 18 August 1876. The "Mexican" has been identified as Francisco Mores. See McFarling, "Calamity Jane." TS. Lloyd McFarling Papers. South Dakota State Historical Society.

66. McClintock, *Pioneer Days*, 109. According to one account, "about sixty-six dollars" in gold dust was contributed to the Mexican; that night he was killed in a quarrel. V. P. Shoun, owner of the herd of cattle, insisted that his employee, Brick Pomeroy, deserved the reward. After Shoun found the head in the possession of a saloon keeper, he scalped it and gave the head to Dr. Schultz. See Brown and Willard, *Black Hills Trails*, 101–3.

67. *Yankton Daily Press and Dakotaian*, 18 August 1876.

68. Brown and Willard, *Black Hills Trails*, 103–5.

69. *Deadwood Black Hills Daily Times*, 25 September 1883.

70. The correspondent added, "Many of the citizens are indignant at the barbarous display—this being the second one of the kind since my arrival here—and they are determined not to tolerate a third display of that description." *Laramie Sentinel*, 2 September 1876.

71. *Deadwood Black Hills Daily Times*, 25 September 1883. In his description, Sam Young probably mixed the two occasions during which Indian heads were paraded through the town. He said a man called "Black Jack" suggested "that we have a celebration," and "we then started on a visit to all the saloons. Jack and Calamity Jane led the way, Jack carrying the head and Calamity doing the yelling, haranguing the crowd." The next morning, said Young, "Calamity suggested that we hoist the head up on the flagstaff," after which they "formed a great circle" and performed a "war dance." Young, *Hard Knocks*, 211–12.

72. *Deadwood Black Hills Pioneer*, 26 August 1876.

73. Valentine T. McGillycuddy to Editor, *Rapid City Journal*, 24 October 1924. Correspondent John Finerty accompanied the party as it reached Crook City, and though he did not mention Martha, he said they were met by "a fair-sized crowd of hairy men and bilious women" who welcomed them loudly, and soon they were "forcibly dismounted and led to an attack on Black Hills whisky, which we found more formidable than either Sitting Bull or Crazy Horse." Finerty, *War-Path and Bivouac*, 277.

74. McGillycuddy, despite his diary notation, could easily have ridden from camp to join in the festivities. Spring, "Dr. McGillycuddy's Diary," 292–93.

75. *Deadwood Black Hills Pioneer*, 23 September 1876.

76. Bourke, *On the Border with Crook*, 380–81.

77. *Deadwood Black Hills Daily Times*, 10 August 1883.

78. McGillycuddy, *McGillycuddy Agent*, 62–64.

79. [Canary], *Life and Adventures*, 5.

80. John D. Vaughan, "Hearts Are Pretty Much Alike the World Around: True Story of a Thanksgiving Day Episode in the Black Hills Twenty-Three Years Ago," *Denver Times*, 30 November 1899.

81. *Cheyenne Daily Leader*, 23 November 1876.

82. *Deadwood Black Hills Daily Pioneer*, 28 July 1886.

CHAPTER 6: DIME NOVEL HEROINE, 1877

1. Jones, *Dime Novel Western*, 7–8, 14.

2. *Cheyenne Daily Leader*, 26 January 1877.

3. [Canary], *Life and Adventures*, 5.

4. *Yankton Daily Press and Dakotaian*, 13 April 1877; Sollid, *Calamity Jane*, 101–2.

5. *Cheyenne Daily Sun*, 11 and 15 July 1877; *Cheyenne Daily Leader*, 15 July 1877.

6. *Cheyenne Daily Leader*, 30 January 1878. See also, Engebretson, *Empty Saddles*, 54–62, 155–62; Bridwell, *Life and Adventures of Robert McKimie*, 4–11.

7. Young thought it strange that, although the other outlaws "received long sentences," Calamity "was not prosecuted." See, *Hard Knocks*, 206. Frontiersman Ben Arnold implied that Bevans was the man who "ruined" young Martha in Virginia City and that they had maintained a relationship since that time. Lewis Crawford, *Rekindling Camp Fires*, 272. Bevans had been successful in the Montana gold fields, reported one newspaper, but was "led astray by wily gamblers," and "soon sunk from his high estate, and became a drunken, degraded ruffian." He was jailed in Laramie for stealing horses in Wyoming. After escaping prison, he began robbing travelers in the Black Hills region. *Cheyenne Daily Leader*, 10 July 1877. The rumor that Calamity Jane and Dunc Blackburn had a son is reported in Nash, *Encyclopedia of Western Lawmen*, 47.

8. *Cheyenne Daily Leader*, 3 November 1885.

9. Ibid., 21 June 1887.

10. Maguire, *Black Hills and American Wonderland*, 304.

11. Ibid.

12. "'Calamity Jane' Is Strangely Like One of Bret Harte's Heroines," *Denver Rocky Mountain News*, 10 June 1877; *Cheyenne Daily Leader*, 14 June 1877.

13. *Cheyenne Daily Leader*, 7 July 1877.

14. Ibid., 7 July 1877.

15. *Cheyenne Daily Sun*, 7 July 1877.

16. *Yankton Daily Press and Dakotaian*, 26 July 1877; *Deadwood Black Hills Daily Times*, 1 August 1877. The *Cheyenne Daily Leader*, 7 August 1877, likewise reported, "Calamity Jane is 'tripping the light fantastic toe' in a Deadwood dance-house."

17. *Yankton Daily Press and Dakotaian*, 8 August 1877, citing *Deadwood Daily Champion*.

18. Ibid., 3 September 1877.

19. *Deadwood Black Hills Daily Pioneer*, 12 December 1882.

20. *Deadwood Black Hills Daily Times*, 20 September 1877; Mumey, *Calamity Jane*, 61–62.

21. Unable to resist a final jab at their competitor, the *Times* added: "The reason that we failed to discover the '*peculiarities*' of the *Pioneer*'s 'Heroine of the Hills' is easily explained. We refused to cultivate the same intimacy with her that the presiding genius of that romantic sheet did." *Deadwood Black Hills Daily Times*, 21, 22 September 1877. The *Pioneer*'s "Heroine of the Hills" was identified as Mrs. Bloxsom in the *Times* on 18 March 1878. The *Times* stopped its criticisms only upon Mrs. Bloxsom's death in December 1879. *Deadwood Black Hills Daily Times*, 9, 12, 24, 25 April; 17, 25 May; 5, 15 June 1878; 10 December 1879.

22. Ibid., 19 October 1877.

23. *Bismarck Tri-Weekly Tribune*, 17 August 1877. Lounsberry's arrival in Deadwood was announced in *Deadwood Black Hills Daily Times*, 30 July 1877.

24. *Deadwood Black Hills Daily Times*, 30 November 1877. The presentation was made on behalf of Lounsberry by "Gerry" Cooke, a railroad agent for the Chicago & North Western. Ibid., 27, 28 November 1877. The *Central City Black Hills Champion*, on 2 December 1877, remarked at Lounsberry's expense that Calamity "like many other illustrious females, has a natural weakness for Bohemians."

25. Wheeler, *Deadwood Dick on Deck*, 4. For the fictional Deadwood Dick, see Durham and Jones, *The Negro Cowboys*, 189–205; and Fielder, *Deadwood Dick*.

26. The only biographer recognizing the importance of Maguire and Wheeler in the creation of Martha's national reputation is Etulain, "Calamity Jane: Independent Woman," 83–84. Sometimes dime novelist Ned Buntline is mistakenly given credit for making Martha famous. Writer Mildred Fielder even concluded that Wheeler and Buntline were pseudonyms used by Edward Zane Carroll Judson. Fielder, *Deadwood Dick*, 7.

27. Wheeler, *Deadwood Dick, Prince of the Road*, 4.

28. Johannsen, *House of Beadle and Adams*, 2: 293–98. Wheeler's, *Hurricane Nell* was first published in *Frank Starr's Ten Cent Pocket Library* on May 4, 1877. It was reissued as *Bob Woolf, The Border Ruffian; or, The Girl Dead-Shot* (New York Beadle and Adams, 1878).

29. Kent, "Formal Conventions of the Dime Novel": 37–47.

30. Jones, *Dime Novel Western*, 5–9.

31. Smith, *Virgin Land*, 112, 119.

32. Wheeler, *Deadwood Dick's Doom*, 13.

33. Jones, *Dime Novel Western*, 135.

34. Henry Nash Smith, for example, concluded: "The relations between Deadwood Dick and Calamity Jane are hard to make out." Smith, *Virgin Land*, 117.

35. Wheeler, *Prince of the Road*, 3–4.

36. Jones, *Dime Novel Western*, 11–14, 75–76, 98, 137.

37. Ibid., 162.

38. Wheeler, *Deadwood Dick, The Prince of the Road*, 13.

39. Ibid., 4.

40. Ibid., 13.

41. Wheeler, *The Double Daggers*, 31.

42. Wheeler, *Deadwood Dick on Deck*, 24; Mazzulla and Kostka, *Mountain Charley*, Introduction.

43. Wheeler, *Deadwood Dick on Deck*, 24.

44. Ibid., 4.

45. Ibid., 4, 16.

46. Ibid., 25–26, 31.

47. Wheeler, *Deadwood Dick in Leadville*, 30–31.

48. Wheeler, *Deadwood Dick's Device*, 27–28.

49. Wheeler, *Blonde Bill*, 12, 15.

50. Wheeler, *A Game of Gold*, 14, 15.

51. Wheeler, *Deadwood Dick's Ward*, 8. In the 1881 publication, the title and subtitle are reversed.

52. Wheeler, *Deadwood Dick's Doom*, 13.

53. Wheeler, *Captain Crack-Shot; Deadwood Dick Trapped*. The latter novel appeared in 1882 as *Gold-Dust Dick. A Romance of Roughs and Toughs*.

54. Wheeler, *Deadwood Dick's Big Deal*, 15.

55. Wheeler, *Deadwood Dick's Claim*, 16.

56. Wheeler, *Deadwood Dick in Dead City*, 14, 15.

57. *Cheyenne Daily Leader*, 3 November 1885.

58. Reckless Ralph, "Calamity Jane, The Queen of the Plains," *Street and Smith's New York Weekly*, 16, 23, 30 January; 20, 27 February; and 13 March 1882. Newspapers reported that Montana pioneer Henry Horr wrote one of the earliest Calamity Jane dime novels; he might be Reckless Ralph, or perhaps he authored a yet undiscovered story. *Livingston Enterprise*, 17 September 1887.

59. Freeman, *Down the Yellowstone*, 78.

60. *Deadwood Daily Pioneer-Times*, 12 May 1901.

Chapter 7: Life in Dakota, 1878–1881

1. *Sidney Telegraph*, 4 August 1877.

2. *Deadwood Black Hills Daily Times*, 28 August 1878; 5 September 1878.

3. Greene, *Nez Perce Summer 1877*, 230; Lucullus V. McWhorter, "Unpublished Incidents in 'Calamity Jane's' Life." TMs, n.d. Folder 196. Lucullus V. McWhorter Papers. Manuscripts, Archives and Special Collections. Holland Library, Washington State University.

4. Maguire, *Coming Empire*, 65.

5. *Deadwood Black Hills Daily Times*, 17 December 1877.

6. Briggs, "Recollections of Pioneers Who Knew Calamity Jane." WPA Subject #46, TS, 1936. Wyoming State Archives. White Eye Anderson recalled that Cosgrove was "one of the boys who had come to the hills with our train," and dated his meeting with Calamity and Cosgrove in October 1879. Secrest, *I Buried Hickok*, 103. In 1881, when Cosgrove was questioned in the grand jury trial of Sam Dougherty, who was suspected of stealing government mules from Fort Meade, he admitted that he once had lived with Calamity Jane. No indication was given why this line of questioning was made, but it probably resulted from rumors of Martha's association with suspected outlaws. *Deadwood Black Hills Daily Times*, 10 February 1881.

7. Cosgrove claimed he heard the shot that killed Hickok from across the street and attended Hickok's funeral. In later years, Cosgrove served as U.S. deputy marshal in Deadwood and worked on ranches north of the Black Hills. He died in 1936. *Pioneer Footprints*, 217.

8. *Deadwood Black Hills Daily Times*, 3 January 1878; [Canary], *Life and Adventures*, 5.

9. *Deadwood Black Hills Daily Times*, 22 January 1878.

10. Ibid., 18 February 1878.

11. Ward, Letter to the editor of *Western Story Magazine*, 8 January 1927; Frye, *Atlas of Wyoming Outlaws*, 65.

12. Smith's testimony is suspect, however; he said he worked for Calamity Jane for several months and claimed Wild Bill Hickok died in her gambling establishment. Samuel Smith, interview by Dr. Grace R. Hebard, TS, 10 April 1917. Paine Collection.

13. Newson, *Drama of Life*, 39. Newson's description of Martha also appeared in the *St. Paul and Minneapolis Press*, 18 December 1877.

14. Newson, *Drama of Life*, 37–38.

15. Ibid., 33–35.

16. Ibid., 35–37.

17. Ibid., 38.

18. Ibid., 47–49.

19. *Deadwood Black Hills Daily Pioneer*, 6 June 1878. Newson presented his "Life in the Black Hills" in Deadwood in Langrishe's opera house as a dramatic lecture supplemented with music, and he planned similar presentations in a tour of eastern cities. *Central City Black Hills Champion*, 18 November, 23 December 1877.

20. *Bismarck Tri-Weekly Tribune*, 21 March 1878; 6 April 1878.

21. Hoyt, *Frontier Doctor*, 38–39. Hoyt's arrival in Deadwood from Bismarck is noted in the *Deadwood Black Hills Daily Times*, 12 May 1877.

22. Abbott (Teddy Blue) and Smith, *We Pointed Them North*, 74.

23. McKeown, *Them Was the Days*, 205–6.

24. Roberts, "Point of View," 16–17, Mary Fanton Roberts Papers (1900–1956), Roll D161, Archives of American Art, Smithsonian Institution, Detroit.

25. Fielder, *Silver Is the Fortune*, 179.

26. "More Blood Letting," *Deadwood Black Hills Daily Times*, 27 June 1878.

27. Ibid., 28 June 1878; 25 July 1878. The article of 28 June 1878 is misdated as 13 July 1876 in many sources, causing confusion in the story. See for example, Sollid, *Calamity Jane*, 66.

28. [Canary], *Life and Adventures*, 5; Lee, *Fort Meade*, 18–52.

29. *Deadwood Black Hills Daily Times*, 24 September 1878.

30. Ibid., 28 October 1878.

31. Ibid., 8 February 1879.

32. *Deadwood Black Hills Daily Pioneer*, 9 February 1879.

33. *Rapid City Black Hills Journal*, 8 March 1879.

34. *Yankton Daily Press and Dakotaian*, 22, 23 May 1879. A Yankton correspondent boarded the *Dacotah* and wrote regular reports describing its progress up the Missouri River, but did not mention Calamity Jane. Ibid., 28 May and 2, 5, 10 June 1879.

35. Ibid., 23 May 1879; *Cheyenne Daily Leader*, 6 June 1879.

36. Hackett, "Along the Upper Missouri," 38.

37. *Deadwood Black Hills Daily Times*, 4 July 1879.

38. Ibid., 15 and 18 July 1879. Initially the story misidentified the sick person as "Calamity Jones"; later issues clarified that it was Calamity Jane who was ill.

39. "Calamity Jane's Virtues," *Deadwood Black Hills Daily Times*, 20 July 1879.

40. Ibid., 18 November 1879. Another newspaper reported, "Calamity Jane is on her way to Deadwood to spend the winter." *Yankton Daily Press and Dakotaian*, 26 November 1879.

41. *Cheyenne Daily Leader*, 10 December 1879.

42. *Deadwood Black Hills Daily Times*, 10 December 1879.

43. Chatterton later became a partner, then owner, of the J. W. Hugus and Company Store, and eventually governor of Wyoming. See Chatterton, *Yesterday's Wyoming*, 24, 29.

44. Rankin, "Meeker Massacre": 140–41.

45. *Douglas Enterprise*, 26 December 1939.

46. *Deadwood Black Hills Daily Times*, 20 April 1880.

47. [Canary], *Life and Adventures*, 5; Sollid, *Calamity Jane*, 69–70.

48. *Deadwood Black Hills Daily Times*, 4 July, 21 September 1886. A photograph of Mrs. Oleson, the female bullwhacker, incorrectly identified as "Mrs. Knutson," is reproduced in Schmitt and Brown, *Settler's West*, 96–97.

49. Quoted in Sollid, *Calamity Jane*, 73.

50. Hall, "John Edmund Boland, Riverman," 216. Charles Fales, interview by J. Leonard Jennewein, TS, 6 June 1959, Jennewein Collection.

51. Hooker, *Bullwhacker*, 7–14, 99–105. In agreement, the Deadwood newspaper noted, "Fred Evans last evening paid off his teamsters, and as a natural result, the dance halls were in full blast last night." *Deadwood Black Hills Daily Times*, 11 December 1878.

52. *Fort Pierre Weekly Signal*, 21 July 1880.

53. Ibid.

54. Ibid., 28 July 1880.

55. Ibid., 18 August 1880.

56. *Deadwood Black Hills Daily Times*, 27 August 1880.

57. *Yankton Daily Press and Dakotaian*, 21 August; 4, 9 September; 19 November 1880.

58. *Fort Pierre Weekly Signal*, 25 August, 1 September 1880. Also, Engebretson, "Pierre's 'Men for Breakfast'": 47–48, 54.

59. *Yankton Daily Press and Dakotaian*, 19 November 1880. Later, the Yankton newspaper reported that Kelly and Baker had been rescued "by a band of roughs" rather than being ordered out of town by regulators. Ibid., 29 November 1880. George Baker did not, however, leave the area and was indicted in 1881 for "selling whiskey at Ft. Pierre." He received a light sentence: "one hour's imprisonment in the county jail" and a $75 fine. *Deadwood Black Hills Daily Times*, 2 and 3 February; 6 March 1881.

60. *Fort Pierre Weekly Signal*, 24 November, 8 December 1880.

61. Hamlin, "Calamity Jane": 14–15.

62. Sutley said he first met Martha in Deadwood and thought she was "born of Mormon parents in Salt Lake City, but had run away with a freighter when she was a girl of fifteen." From 1865 until her death, he said, she "spent most of her life on the trail." Sutley added that he "saw her first in Salt Lake in 1868" driving "an old Concord stagecoach" into town; Martha, age twelve in 1868, could not have driven a stage as he described, a story indicating his willingness to exaggerate. Sutley, *Last Frontier*, 93, 151, 169–70, 266–69.

63. Charles Fales, interview by J. Leonard Jennewein, TS, 6 June 1959. Jennewein Collection.

64. Sutley, *Last Frontier*, 267–68.

65. Shadley, *Calamity Jane's Daughter*.

66. *Deadwood Black Hills Daily Times*, 9 November 1880.

67. Ibid., 24 November 1880.

68. Ibid., 14 January 1881.

69. [Canary], *Life and Adventures*, 6.

70. Morecamp, *Live Boys in the Black Hills*, 293.

71. *Pierre Dakota Journal*, 11 February 1882. See also Schuler, *A Bridge Apart*, 131–32. Schuler mistakenly identified Pierre as the location of this interview, rather than Bismarck.

CHAPTER 8: FOLLOWING THE NORTHERN PACIFIC, 1882–1884

1. [Canary], *Life and Adventures*, 6.

2. *Miles City Yellowstone Journal*, 11 February 1882. The *Bismarck Tribune*, reported on 10 February 1882 that "Calamity Jane has gone to Montana," and the *Glendive Times*, on 9 February 1882, that the "ex-female scout, bullwhacker and hard citizen of the Black Hills passed through" Glendive "one day last week, en-route to Miles City."

3. *Montana: A State Guide Book*, 53, 90–91. Also, Briggs, *Frontiers of the Northwest*, 430–36.

4. L. L. Perrin, "Building of N.P. Gave Montana First Year-Round Rail Link With East, West," *Billings Gazette*, 7 December 1941; *Helena Independent*, 14 May 1882.

5. *Cheyenne Daily Leader*, 21 June 1887.

6. Chatterton, *Yesterday's Wyoming*, 30.

7. *Miles City Yellowstone Journal*, 3 June 1882.

8. Gordon, *Recollections of Old Milestown*, 37.

9. *Helena Daily Independent*, 24 June 1882; *Miles City Yellowstone Journal*, 8 July 1882, quoted in Brown, *Plainsmen of the Yellowstone*, 351.

10. *Deadwood Black Hills Daily Times*, 18 July 1882. Oscar Wilde (1854–1900), an Irish-born poet and novelist, was a leader in an aesthetic movement advocating "art for art's sake," and became notorious for his long hair and eccentric dress. That Calamity Jane was not a part of the official celebration is proven by the absence of her name in the detailed account in the *Miles City Daily Press*, 7 July 1882.

11. *Miles City Daily Press*, 29 July 1882; *Miles City Yellowstone Journal*, 5, 12 August 1882.

12. Brown and Felton, *L. A. Huffman, Photographer of the Plains*, 26. The photograph of Calamity Jane is dated 1880, prior to her known arrival. Karson, *L. A. Huffman, Pioneer Photographer*, 5–15, provides updated information concerning Huffman's arrival in Montana and his photographs.

13. *Deadwood Black Hills Daily Pioneer*, 3 March 1883.

14. *Miles City Yellowstone Journal*, 2 September, 11 November 1882; *Billings Post*, 15 July 1882. The latter newspaper mistakenly said the dime novels were "from the pen of Ned Buntline."

15. Wiley, "First Billings Postoffice and Calamity Jane": 66.

16. "In 1881, she [Martha] traveled to Miles City with a rancher named Frank King, and the couple set up housekeeping near town." Gilles, "Calamity Jane," in *Laurel's Story*, by Johnston, 44. Sheridan dentist Will Frackelton also heard that she "lived with a man named Frank King on a ranch on Powder River," but dated it later. See Frackelton, *Sagebrush Dentist*, 125.

17. "Calamity Jane, it is positively stated, has turned from her wild ways and is now the virtuous wife of a well-to-do farmer, living on a ranch in the Yellowstone valley. She has become the mother of a bright boy baby, which she calls 'Little Calamity.'" *Miller Hand County Press*, 6 December 1882. The freighter's story is in *Custer City Chronicle*, 18 November 1882.

18. Calamity told the reporter, "I had a little boy, but he died," but did not specify when. [Fox], "Calamity Jane": 312. Because the child is never again mentioned in newspapers or reminiscences, and Martha resumed her life in the Northern Pacific railroad camps, it is probable that the child died in infancy.

19. *Miles City Yellowstone Journal*, 16 December 1882; *Deadwood Black Hills Daily Times*, 15, 21 December 1882.

20. *Miles City Yellowstone Journal*, 9 December 1882; *Billings Post*, 16 December 1882. Knight was not the only Montana editor to earn Martha's wrath. One newspaper reported that the editor of the *Billings Herald* "received a call from Calamity Jane, and she gave the editor a piece of her mind for certain remarks he had made about her." *Helena Daily Independent*, 21 December 1882.

21. Gilles, "Calamity Jane," 43–46. Gilles mistakenly suggests that Martha still lived at Canyon Creek in 1886, marrying Robert Dorset who "headed a territory-wide rustling ring," then left in 1887 to marry Clinton Burke before returning to Canyon Creek in 1889. He also identifies the horse thieves as Curley O'Neill and Rattlesnake Jake Fallon, at variance with contemporary newspaper accounts.

22. Zimmerman, *Along the Zimmerman Trail*, 39.

23. *Montana: A State Guide Book*, 194, incorrectly identifies the horse thieves as Charles Rattlesnake Jake Fallon and Edward Longhair Owen.

24. *Livingston Daily Enterprise*, 14 July 1884; Johnson, "Independence Day, 1884!": 2–7.

25. *Billings Post*, 17 July 1884.

26. *Deadwood Black Hills Daily Pioneer*, 17 February 1883. Muir City, the "tunnel town," grew up where the Bozeman tunnel was being constructed.

27. *Helena Daily Independent*, 6, 20 February 1883. This story was reprinted in many newspapers with added comments. For example, the *Deadwood Black Hills Daily Times*, 16 February 1883, reported: "It seems that every since Calamity Jane has left the Hills she has been running against trouble and bad luck in all its phases. It is now reported that she is once more in the toils of the law for selling whisky to the Indians in Missoula county, Montana."

28. *Glendive Times*, 7 April 1883; *Helena Weekly Herald*, 26 July 1883.

29. *Spokane Spokesman-Review*, 6 August 1903; Adams, "Afterword," in *Life and Adventures of Calamity Jane*, 8.

30. *Deadwood Black Hills Daily Times*, 16 November 1883.

31. Abbott and Smith, *We Pointed Them North*, 74–75. An earlier version of Teddy Blue's story contains variations from Helena Huntington Smith's edited narrative. For example, Teddy Blue instructs Martha "to scare our boss out of the lobby," and she devises the plan to sit on the boss's lap. Also, instead of Teddy Blue telling the boss that he would not write his parents about the incident, one of the other cowboys does. Abbott, "When I First Met 'Calamity Jane,'" in O'Donnell, *Montana Monographs*.

32. Sweetman, *Back Trailing*, 98.

33. Russell, "Calamity Jane," TS, Hearst Free Library, Lead, S.Dak.

34. *Montana: A State Guide Book*, 200; Straus, "Madame B's Bucket of Blood," 65–66. Madame Bull Dog was among the Black Hills residents who arrived in Miles City in 1883, and like others evidently moved westward with the railroad. *Deadwood Black Hills Daily Pioneer*, 3 March 1883.

35. Shoemaker, *Byron Hinckley Tells a Tale, It is of a Wrestling Match between Calamity Jane and Madame Bull Dog, Which Jane Would Have Won But for the Madame's Repeated Foul Tactics*. TS (Harrisburg: 1952), 1–7. Jennewein Collection. Another version of the Calamity Jane—Madam Bull Dog fight appears in Thane, *High Border Country*, 191–92.

36. *Livingston Daily Enterprise*, 14 March 1884.

37. *Bismarck Tribune*, 7, 28 March 1884.

38. Wendell Brainard, "Calamity Jane Brought Her Girls to Murray," *Shoshone County (Idaho) News-Press*, 27 July 1986.

39. *Helena Weekly Herald*, 10 April 1884.

40. *Coeur d'Alene Press*, 20 April 1990. "Molly b'Damn Days" are still celebrated in Murray, Idaho. Molly, like Calamity, is remembered for her help to ill and injured miners.

41. *Livingston Daily Enterprise*, 16 April 1884.

42. *Bozeman Weekly Chronicle*, 23 April 1884; *Helena Daily Independent*, 15 April, 25 June 1884. The latter newspaper added, "The pie didn't cost Richard very much; but Yellowstone county will have to foot a bill of $75 for it, that being the cost of trying him for larceny, and boarding him till his fine of $10 and court fees is worked out according to law."

43. *Bismarck Tribune*, 14 December 1883; 21, 28 March, 25 April 1884.

44. *Deadwood Daily Pioneer-Times*, 16 February, 28 June 1901.

45. *Livingston Daily Enterprise*, 3 May, 12 September 1884.

46. *Helena Daily Independent*, 10 May 1884; Thorp and Bunker, *Crow Killer.*

47. *Bismarck Tribune*, 27 June 1884; *Billings Post*, 26 June 1884.

48. *Livingston Daily Enterprise*, 25 June 1884; *Bismarck Tribune*, 27 June 1884.

49. *Janesville Gazette*, 2 July 1884.

50. *Janesville Daily Recorder*, 4 July 1884. Curley, one of the Crow Indians who scouted for Custer, was the first to report the command's defeat. How he escaped from the battlefield remains controversial. Hardwick probably depicted the popular, but unlikely, version showing Curley leaving the battlefield wrapped in a Sioux blanket.

51. *Milwaukee Sentinel*, 3, 5 July 1884; *Milwaukee Journal*, 5 July 1884.

52. *Deadwood Black Hills Daily Times*, 13 July 1884; *Milwaukee Sentinel*, 8 July 1884.

53. *Chicago Times*, 19 July 1884.

54. Ibid., 22 July 1884; *Billings Post*, 24 July 1884.

55. *Billings Post*, 7 August 1884.

56. *Livingston Daily Enterprise*, 8, 16 August 1884; *Billings Post*, 14 August 1884.

57. *Cheyenne Democratic Leader*, 25 November 1884. Rumors of gold discoveries in the Buffalo, Wyoming, area were reported, and discounted, by the *Helena Daily Independent*, 19 September 1884.

CHAPTER 9: LIFE IN WYOMING, 1884–1894

1. For a tangled list of appearances, see Klock, *Here Comes Calamity Jane*, 26–28.

2. [Canary], *Life and Adventures*, 6.

3. Researchers have searched in vain for evidence of Martha in Texas. Robert Casey was disappointed that she "didn't rate three lines in the society columns" in El Paso when she got married. See Casey, *The Texas Border*, 75–76, 82. Despite the lack of any contemporary references to Martha, one writer created a detailed account of her life in El Paso. Lenore Dils, "Calamity Jane Spent Happy Years in El Paso," *El Paso Times*, 24 May 1964.

4. *Laramie Daily Boomerang*, 30 August; 25, 26 September 1889; *Cheyenne Daily Sun*, 25 February 1892.

5. "For Justice's Sake," *Livingston Post*, 25 July 1901. Either Annie Filmore or another woman nicknamed Calamity, while living in a Montana brothel in 1885, threw her naked three-year old child into a snowbank in January. *Bozeman Weekly Chronicle*, 7, 14 January 1885.

6. *Territory of Montana against Charles Townley and Jane Doe alias Calamity Jane, Indictment for Fornication, November 5, 1888*, Vertical File, Montana Historical Society. Biographer Roberta Sollid assumed it was Martha Canary who had inadvertently caused Townley's death. Sollid, *Calamity Jane*, 86–88. Stella Foote embellished the story, suggesting "some nosey and prissy ladies" discovered Martha and Townley together, and that the sheriff was forced to arrest them because of the complaint. Foote, *History of Calamity Jane*, 109–11.

7. Because of a technical error, the verdict was "not guilty." *Livingston Enterprise*, 7, 9, 11 November 1888; 26 January, 2 February 1889.

8. Bennett *Old Deadwood Days*, 220–21; Warren, *Badlands Fox*, 1–2.

9. *Big Horn Sentinel*, 15 November 1884; Edward Burnett, "Calamity and Irish Entertain For Bostonians, And Other Recollections," WPA Subject #64, TS, 1936. Wyoming State Archives.

10. L. L. Newton to Tobe Borner, 28 December 1940, American Heritage Center.

11. *Rawlins Carbon County Journal*, 20 December 1884.

12. *Cheyenne Democratic Leader*, 21 March 1885.

13. George L. Erhard, "Calamity Jane," *Rock Springs Rocket*, 18 January 1929; John H. Fales, interview, WPA, Subject #705, TS, n.d. Wyoming State Archives.

14. *Rawlins Carbon County Journal*, 25 July 1885.

15. *Cheyenne Daily Leader*, 3 November 1885.

16. *Buffalo Sentinel*, 7 August 1886. Another newspaper, upon learning this news, remembered that "three years ago she settled on a ranch near Billings, and frequently came in to paint the town red," a "branch of the fine arts" in which she "was unexcelled." *Livingston Enterprise*, 14 August 1886.

17. Lee, *Wild Towns of Nebraska*, 98; *Nebraska: A Guide*, 322.

18. W. H. Cash, "Hunting and Trapping in the Early Days," WPA, Subject #90, TS, n.d. Wyoming State Archives.

19. Larson, *History of Wyoming*, 159–60, 298.

20. William P. Steers's birth and death dates are from family records in the Pioneer Museum, Lander, Wyoming. Evidently, he never remarried after his relationship with Martha ended. Steers died on 15 February 1933, and was buried in Inglewood Park Cemetery, Inglewood, Calif.

21. Wilber claimed he first saw Martha in Routt, Colorado, in 1883. See Wilber, "Reminiscences of the Meeker Country": 277.

22. *Rawlins Carbon County Journal*, 18 September 1886.

23. Ibid.

24. Ibid., 30 October 1886.

25. Ibid., 6 November 1886.

26. Ibid., 13 November 1886.

27. Old-timers recalled Martha visiting Carbon in 1883, prior to her known arrival in Wyoming from Montana. *History of the Union Pacific Coal Mines*, 38. Pence and Homsher, *Ghost Towns*, 69, relate that Martha purchased a "bolt of silk just arrived from the East" for a dress, but the women of Carbon shook their heads and commented, 'Clothes don't make the lady.'"

28. Minnie A. Rietz, "Old Rock Creek," WPA, Subject #933, TS, 1936, Wyoming State Archives. Another old-timer claims Martha used her trunk to get fare for a ride from Buffalo to Fort Fetterman, Wyoming, in 1884. "'Bill Me Collect on My Trunk,'" *Buffalo Bulletin*, 16 August 1956. It is possible these tales have a common derivation.

29. Mokler, *History of Natrona County*, 433–34.

30. Mullins, *Pulling Leather*, 134.

31. *Laramie Daily Boomerang*, 28 February 1887.

32. *Cheyenne Democratic Leader*, 12, 20 March 1887.

33. *Cheyenne Daily Leader*, 21 June 1887.

34. Ibid.

35. Ibid.

36. Schatz, *Longhorns Bring Culture*, 57.

37. *Buffalo Sentinel*, 3 September 1887.

38. *Deadwood Black Hills Daily Times*, 6 September 1887.

39. *Sundance Gazette*, 2 September 1887.

40. *Deadwood Black Hills Weekly Times*, 28 April 1888.

41. Stanislaw Dankowski, interview, WPA, Subject #672, TS, 1936–1937, Wyoming State Archives.

42. Certificate of Marriage, County of Bingham, Territory of Idaho, 30 May 1888.

43. *Livingston Enterprise*, 13 April 1901.

44. Anderson, *Experiences and Impressions*, 211.

45. [Fox], "Calamity Jane": 312.

46. Bessie M. Kennedy, "Calamity Jane Starts Argument," *Rapid City Daily Journal*, 2 August 1934. Also, Jessie E. Hickok (Oakes) Murray, Los Angeles, California, to Byron Crane, Works Progress Administration of Montana, 27 November 1937 CH74–180, South Dakota State Historical Society.

47. Fales, interview.

48. Wadsworth was mistaken either about the date or the purpose of Martha's visit to Lander. She was there, he said, to visit her sister, Lena, but Lena had died on October 17, 1888. He also thought Martha's given name was Clementine Canary. Wadsworth, "Unknown History of Calamity Jane": 9.

49. Huntington said he worked in the Lander region about 1894, but it is evident from his descriptions that he met Martha there considerably earlier. Huntington, *Good Men and Salty Cusses*, 46.

50. Huntington, *Both Feet in the Stirrups*, 60–61.

51. Erhard, "Calamity Jane," *Rock Springs (Wyo.) Rocket*, 18 January 1929.

52. Ibid.

53. Ibid.

54. Sheila Hart, "Reminiscence of Early Wyoming," *Riverton Review*, 4 October 1928. Another account claims that Martha began a new fashion in Tubb Town when she hired Mrs. Nelson to make her a pink silk wrapper; afterwards, the other prostitutes all wanted similar dresses. Pence and Homsher, *Ghost Towns*, 156–57.

55. *Casper Weekly Mail*, 11 October 1889.

56. Fales, interview.

57. Burnett, "Calamity and Irish."

58. *Cheyenne Daily Sun*, 3 January 1890.

59. *Cheyenne Daily Leader*, 3 January 1890.

60. Spencer, *Calamity Jane*, Introduction, 171.

61. *Sundance Gazette*, 8 November 1889.

62. After being in Casper in 1889, said Mokler, "she went to some of the soldiers' camps in the interior and finally went to Billings." Mokler, *History of Natrona County*, 434.

63. Dick Nelson, *Only a Cow Country*, 89; Cash, "Hunting and Trapping."

64. *Deadwood Black Hills Daily Times*, 17 August 1892. That the prostitutes named in this article were actually in Suggs is indicated by the *Sundance Gazette*, 6 September 1889, which reported Missouri Jane being arrested in Field City for selling liquor without a license.

65. Feitz, *A Quick History of Creede*, 21; Robertson and Harris, *Soapy Smith*, 103; Bennett, *Boom Town Boy*, 29.

66. *Omaha Morning World-Herald*, 3 February 1892.

67. *Rawlins Carbon County Journal*, 9 December 1893; *Evanston News-Register*, 16 December 1893.

68. *Rawlins Republican*, 5 August 1903.

69. McPherren, *Empire Builders*, 10; *Wyoming: A Guide*, 212.

70. Burnett, "Calamity and Irish."

71. White claims he observed Martha ride into Deadwood in 1894, impossible since she did not return to that city until 1895. Most likely he saw Martha in a neighboring Wyoming town,

perhaps Sheridan, and then, while writing of his trip from his notes, transposed the location to coincide with his story of Wild Bill's grave. White, *The Newer Northwest*, 104.

72. Jessie wrote the newspaper to refute Dora Du Fran's assertion that she had seen Martha in Chicago in 1893: "She was not in Chicago in 1893 and she and I were in Billings, Mont." *Rapid City Daily Journal*, 2 August 1934. See also, Du Fran, *Low Down on Calamity Jane*, 9.

73. *Deadwood Black Hills Daily Times*, 26 May 1894.

74. Zimmerman, *Along the Zimmerman Trail*, 1, 39.

75. Clinch, "Coxey's Army in Montana": 2–11, claims the photograph was taken in July 1894 during the Pullman strike in Billings. Stella Foote, however, identifies it as being taken on 16 April 1894 and says it shows "Hogan's army," the Montana contingent of Coxey's army. Foote, *History of Calamity Jane*, 88.

76. McPherren, *Imprints on Pioneer Trails*, 273.

77. *Billings Weekly Times*, 16 August, 25 October 1894.

78. W. H. (Wirt) Newcom, "Quick Exit from City Recalled When Order to Move Is Issued: Wirt Newcom Writes Interesting Account of His Experience with Frontier Character," *Miles City Daily Star*, 24 May 1934. If the records reporting the death of a Clinton E. Burke in Houston, Texas, on 9 November 1929 refer to Martha's husband, he was born on 5 October 1867 in Missouri, making him eleven years younger than she. Bureau of Vital Statistics, Houston Health and Human Service Department, City of Houston, Texas.

79. William (Cap) Harmon had about eighty buildings and four thousand cattle on his ranch. J. R. (Dick) Harmon to Tom Figg, February 1960, quoted in *Shifting Scenes*, 310. Also, Orestad, *He Named It Powderville*, 113, says Martha and Burke "lived in Broncho Sam's cabin in northeast Ekalaka" one winter.

80. Quoted in Klock, *Here Comes Calamity Jane*, 12–13.

CHAPTER 10: A DEADWOOD CELEBRITY, 1895–1896

1. *Deadwood Black Hills Daily Times*, 5 October 1895.

2. Ibid.

3. The newspaper initially reported that Martha had "two children, two bright little girls, one of whom is with her." This misinformation may have resulted from Martha commenting about having had two children. Ibid.

4. Ibid.

5. Ibid.

6. Ibid. The *Bismarck Tribune*, 11 April 1884, described one Calamity Jane imposter: "Chicago has a woman who claims to be Calamity Jane. If the genuine Jane hears of this the Chicago fraud had better climb a telegraph pole and pull the pole up after her."

7. *Rapid City Daily Journal*, 30 April 1895.

8. Ibid.

9. *Deadwood Black Hills Daily Times*, 4 May 1895. In Butte, the newspaper, uncertain of Martha's presence in the city, asked, "Is 'Calamity Jane' in Butte?" *Butte Miner*, 13 May 1895. John Scollard, who came to the Black Hills during the 1876 gold rush, was owner of Hotel Scollard in Sturgis and served two terms as mayor. Robinson, *History of South Dakota*, 2: 1275.

10. *Rapid City Daily Journal*, 7 May 1895. "Diamond Dick" was the nickname of Richard Tanner of Norfolk, Nebraska.

11. *Custer Chronicle*, 12 October 1895.

12. Bennett, *Old Deadwood Days*, 222.

13. Parker, *Deadwood*, 171.

14. Dimsdale, *Vigilantes of Montana*, 17–18.

15. Bennett, *Old Deadwood Days*, 218–25.

16. Ibid., 221, 232.

17. Ibid., 229.

18. Ibid., 229–31, 241–42. Shoemaker John Sohn also recalled the Green Front benefit dance, and said "Big-hearted Calamity started buying drinks and treating the crowd" after being given the money. See Lois Miller, "Vet Deadwood Shoemaker Served Teddy, Calamity." Clipping, Billings Public Library, Billings, Montana.

19. Bennett, *Old Deadwood Days*, 241–42.

20. Du Fran said she first met Martha in Deadwood in 1886, but undoubtedly meant 1895–96. She also said that Martha "ran a little restaurant in Deadwood for a few months, but all the gang of rounders, as they called the mooching class of saloon hangers-on, ate up all the profits and left her in debt, so she was forced to close up." Du Fran, *Low Down on Calamity Jane*, 7–9.

21. *Deadwood Evening Independent*, 5, 15 October 1895.

22. *Lead Evening Call*, 5 October 1895.

23. Ibid.

24. *Deadwood Black Hills Daily Times*, 6 October 1895.

25. *Deadwood Evening Independent*, 5 October 1895.

26. *Lead Evening Call*, 7 October 1895.

27. *Deadwood Evening Independent*, 24 October 1895; *Lead Evening Call*, 9 November 1895. Pers Russell, who was associated with the Bodega saloon, remembered that Martha wanted Charlie Peterson to photograph her holding a rifle and wearing her buckskin outfit, but she had no gun. Russell said he had to borrow a rifle for her from Will Sasse at the butcher shop. Pers Russell, interview by J. Leonard Jennewein, TS, 7–8, Jennewein Collection.

28. Ledger Book, Jacob Goldberg's store. Adams Museum, Deadwood, S.Dak. Some writers claim that Martha sold "bachelor buttons" as well as photographs. See Parker, *Deadwood*, 199, and Jennewein, *Calamity Jane*, 33. Parker and Jennewein are surely mistaken: another woman was reported selling buttons at the same time Martha visited the Black Hills. Like Martha, she entered saloons "without any hesitancy whatever." *Lead Evening Call*, 26 October 1895.

29. Russell, interview, 8.

30. Lois Miller, "Spearfish Pioneer Recalls Old Day of Calamity Jane," *Sioux Falls Argus Leader*, 6 August 1950.

31. *Lead Evening Call*, 9 November 1895.

32. Ibid., 11 November 1895.

33. Ibid.

34. *Deadwood Black Hills Daily Times*, 5 November 1895.

35. Ibid., 9 November 1895. Martha probably stopped at other towns as well; the Custer newspaper clarified that she was "visiting the towns along the Elkhorn, as far as Rapid," selling her photographs and meeting old friends. *Custer Chronicle*, 9 November 1895.

36. *Rapid City Daily Journal*, 5 November 1895.

37. Quoted in Foote, *History of Calamity Jane*, 130.

38. *Buffalo Gap Republican*, 16 November 1895.

39. *Hot Springs Star*, 12 November 1895.

40. Ibid.

41. Hargens, *Black Hills Doc*, 103–4; *Hot Springs Star*, 14 November 1895. Hargens mistakenly dated this event as 1898. The Buffalo Gap newspaper added that Martha had Hot Springs "jumping sideways for three days and four nights," and "when she departed for the upper Hills Thursday morning the sigh of relief that went up from Hot Springs was so pronounced it might have been heard at this place." *Buffalo Gap Republican*, 16 November 1895.

42. *Rapid City Daily Journal*, 16 November 1895.

43. Ibid., 17 November 1895.

44. *Sturgis Weekly Record*, 29 November 1895.

45. *Deadwood Black Hills Daily Times*, 14 December 1895; *Custer Chronicle*, 21 December 1895.

46. [Fox], "Calamity Jane."

47. Mrs. Osborne Pemberton, interview by J. Leonard Jennewein, 7 June 1960. TS, Jennewein Collection. Pemberton correctly identified Martha's daughter as Jessie Burke. She is the only person to publish a reminiscence about Jessie's attendance at the convent school in Deadwood. Also, see Mary Belle Pemberton Guthrie to J. Leonard Jennewein, 24 June [1953], Jennewein Collection. St. Edward's Academy was a tuition-supported school operated by the Sisters of the Holy Cross in Deadwood between 1884 and 1897. Duratschek, *Builders of God's Kingdom*, 71.

48. Quoted in Foote, *History of Calamity Jane*, 128.

49. [Canary], *Life and Adventures*, 6–7.

50. *Deadwood Black Hills Daily Times*, 21 December 1895.

51. Gilbert, *American Vaudeville*, 19–23; Laurie, *Vaudeville*, 235, 348–49; and Green and Laurie, *Show Biz*, 4, 92, 161.

52. *Deadwood Black Hills Daily Times*, 9 January 1896.

53. Huntington, *Good Men and Salty Cusses*, 205. Carpenters, plumbers, and house painters made about $12 a week. Gilbert, *American Vaudeville*, 19.

54. *Deadwood Black Hills Daily Times*, 9 January 1896. Duncan Aikman claimed Martha also appeared in St. Louis and Kansas City. Aikman, *Calamity Jane*, 118–19.

55. *Rapid City Daily Journal*, 24 December 1895.

56. Ibid., 1 January 1896.

57. A. O. Burton to Gale Heatter, "We the People Program," 9 May 1941. Paine Collection. Dora Du Fran thought that the child placed in the Sturgis convent was Martha's stepdaughter. See Du Fran, *Low Down on Calamity Jane*, 9. Jessie challenged Du Fran's comment in Kennedy, "Calamity Jane Starts Argument." The Sturgis newspapers do not mention the daughter, but do confirm Martha was in town. *Sturgis Weekly Record*, 10 January 1896; *Sturgis Black Hills Press*, 10 January 1896.

58. Jennewein, *Calamity Jane*, 33–34.

59. *Deadwood Black Hills Daily Times*, 9 January 1896.

60. Ibid., 16 January 1896; *Minneapolis Journal*, 20 January 1896.

61. *Spearfish Queen City Mail*, 29 January 1896.

62. Sollid, *Calamity Jane*, 78. Sollid cannot be faulted for her effort; she surmised that Martha was sent back because the *Chicago Tribune* did not note her presence. However, the rival *Inter-Ocean* gave Martha front-page coverage.

63. *Chicago Inter-Ocean*, 28 January 1896.

64. Ibid.

65. Ibid.

66. *Deadwood Black Hills Daily Times*, 30 January 1896.

67. Burnett, "Calamity and Irish."

68. A private autograph collector recently informed me that he had purchased the envelope in which the *Life and Adventures of Calamity Jane, By Herself* was mailed to the Library of Congress. The letter's place of origin was Cincinnati and it was dated February 1896. The name "Calamity Jane" is written across the end of the envelope.

69. *Deadwood Black Hills Daily Times,* 30 May 1896. Jessie probably stayed with the Henry C. Ash family of Sturgis. Henry Ash joined the Black Hills gold rush in 1876 and was U.S. deputy marshal from 1862 to 1878. He moved to Sturgis in 1877. Doane Robinson, *History of South Dakota,* 2: 1718–19.

70. *Deadwood Black Hills Daily Times,* 30 May 1896. According to the Custer newspaper, Martha returned from her tour "dead broke, but as gay and hilarious as ever." *Custer Chronicle,* 6 June 1896.

71. *Deadwood Black Hills Daily Times,* 9 June 1896.

72. Ibid., 30 May 1896.

73. Ibid., 9 June 1896.

74. McClintock, *Pioneer Days,* 119.

75. *Deadwood Daily Pioneer Times,* 19 July 1899.

76. Ibid., 19 August 1899.

77. McClintock, *Pioneer Days,* 119.

78. *Deadwood Daily Pioneer Times,* 9 August 1902. Where Burke went is unclear. He probably is the Clinton E. Burke who died in Houston, Texas, 6 November 1929, at age sixty-two. He had been working as a watchman before his death. His middle initial might account for the *E.* on Martha's grave marker (Mrs. M. E. Burke). Bureau of Vital Statistics, Houston Health and Human Service Dept., City of Houston, Texas.

79. *Deadwood Black Hills Daily Times,* 2 August 1896.

Chapter 11: Life in Montana, 1896–1901

1. Frackelton's chronology is in error; Martha's visit to Sheridan must have been in 1896. Frackelton, *Sagebrush Dentist,* 127. Frackelton's dental practice is mentioned in the *Sheridan Post,* 16 July 1896. Prince Albert Gatchell was editor of the *Sheridan Daily Journal,* but no copies of these 1896 newspapers have been located. Ida McPherren also recalled Martha's 1896 Sheridan visit in *Empire Builders,* 37.

2. *Livingston Post,* 12 August 1896.

3. *Helena Daily Independent,* 18 September 1896.

4. *Butte Miner,* 11 October 1896; *Anaconda Standard,* 30 October 1896, citing the *Baltimore American.*

5. *Butte Miner,* 11 October 1896.

6. *Anaconda Recorder,* 6 October 1896.

7. *Deer Lodge New Northwest,* 16 October 1896.

8. *Castle Whole Truth,* 31 October 1896. See also, Willard, *Adventure Trails,* 145. Novelist Richard Wheeler similarly heard that "Castle was, for a while, the home of Calamity Jane, and that Calamity's daughter attended school there." Wheeler, "Author's Note" in *Cashbox,* 434. The Livingston newspaper claimed that Martha had lived in Castle several years earlier as well, but probably was confusing her with Annie Filmore, "Calamity Jane No. 2." See *Livingston Enterprise,* 28 November 1896.

9. *Castle Whole Truth,* 17 October 1896.

10. Ibid., 21 November 1896. The Livingston newspaper explained that Martha's "team was attached by creditors and she is now endeavoring to get things straightened out. A man by the name of Dixon, who lives at Livingston, claims the team and says he only loaned it to the lady in question, but that she was to own it as soon as she paid him the price. Up to that time she had turned in nothing on account." *Livingston Enterprise*, 28 November 1896.

11. *Livingston Post*, 3 December 1896; *Billings Times*, 29 April 1897.

12. Martha's permit, issued by order of Colonel S. B. M. Young, is recorded in "Record of Property Purchased, Expended," Yellowstone National Park Archives. Haines, *Yellowstone Story*, 2: 405n30.

13. Holmes, *Travelogues*, 6: 38–39. Holmes does not provide a precise date for his encounter with Calamity Jane, but he evidently met her in 1897 or 1898; his photograph of her was included in a presentation he made at Association Hall in Brooklyn, New York, in January 1899. *Brooklyn Eagle*, 24 January 1899.

14. Frackelton, *Sagebrush Dentist*, 126.

15. George W. T. Beck, "Personal Reminiscences of the Beginning of Cody, 1895–1896," January 1936. TS, George W. T. Beck Collection, American Heritage Center.

16. *Billings Gazette*, 11 June 1897.

17. Bankson, *Klondike Nugget*, 151. Bankson reproduces numerous articles from the newspaper, including the 23 June 1898, article on Calamity Jane. Also, see Berton, *Klondike: Last Great Gold Rush*, 354–58.

18. Bankson, *Klondike Nugget*, 11, 81, 119.

19. Morgan, *Good Time Girls*, 271.

20. *Livingston Post*, 11 August 1898.

21. *Denver Illustrated Rocky Mountain Globe*, 22 September 1898.

22. Stella A. Foote, "Calamity Jane." Notes taken at Historical Society meeting, 7 March 1955, vertical file, Montana Historical Society.

23. *Billings Times*, 24 November 1898; *Billings Gazette*, 22 November 1898.

24. *Billings Gazette*, 17 February 1899.

25. Mary C. Connolly, to the Editor, *Livingston Park County News*, 8 December 1960.

26. Mrs. William Polly quoted in Walter Ed Taylor, "Film Makers Had Many Sleepless Nights Finding Suitable Character to Play the Role of 'The Canary Who Sang Bass.'" Clipping, 5 August 1937. Montana Historical Society.

27. Rollins said he sketched Martha's portrait in 1901. "The Billings Club," which contained his picture, was destroyed by fire. See W. Theteford LeViness, "Painting Calamity Jane. Even at 100, Warren Rollins Could Never Forget Billings," *Billings Gazette*, 22 April 1962.

28. Huntington, *Both Feet in the Stirrups*, 123–24.

29. Quoted in McFarling, "Calamity Jane," ch. 17.

30. *Billings Gazette*, 4 April 1899.

31. Dorsett was hauling hay when his team became frightened, and the wagon wheel passed over his leg, breaking it. *Livingston Post*, 19 November 1891; *Livingston Enterprise*, 21 November 1891.

32. Mon Tana Lou Grill, "Calamity Jane," *Cut Bank Pioneer Press*, 11 April 1930.

33. Martha was also blamed for shooting out a street light that night, but denied it "and dared any person to accuse her to her face of the act." Ibid.

34. *Lewistown Fergus County Argus*, 10 May 1899.

35. Walter Lehman to J. Leonard Jennewein, 29 July 1952. Jennewein Collection. Martha's alleged attempt to establish a house of prostitution in Lewistown was not mentioned in a local account of her stay there. A Lewistown newspaper recalled that Martha spent a winter in town

selling her booklets and "doing housework and sewing." *Lewistown Democrat-News*, 27 December 1927.

36. *Lewistown Fergus County Argus*, 12 July 1899.

37. *Utica, Montana*, 230.

38. Philip Korell to Miss Thurston, 6 February 1934, Montana Historical Society (SC 351).

39. Waite, *Silver Dollar Tales*, 23–24.

40. Litz, "Lillian's Montana Scene": 61.

41. Quoted in Wolle, *Montana Pay Dirt*, 357.

42. Abbott and Smith, *We Pointed Them North*, 75–76, mistakenly date Abbott's visit with Martha as 1907, four years after her death.

43. The Montana Historical Society dates the photograph as 1897–98. Background buildings in this photograph prove it was taken in Utica. Bill and Doris Whithorn, *Calamity's in Town*, 27. Martha's story of "Bess" is told in Patterson, "Calamity Jane": 450, 454. Andrew Malum said Martha "usually borrowed a horse from some friend." In fact, he said she did just that in May 1899. She "decked herself out in her feminine clothes, took a horse and gun and posed for her picture." Grill, "Calamity Jane."

44. Mrs. William Polly quoted in Taylor, "Film Makers Had Many Sleepless Nights."

45. *Deadwood Black Hills Weekly Times*, 28 July 1933.

46. Tacetta B. Walker, "Scenes from the Old West," TS, 9. American Heritage Center.

47. Whithorn, *Calamity's in Town*, 40.

48. Ibid., 40–44.

49. Patterson, "'Calamity Jane,'" 450–55.

50. *Miles City Yellowstone Journal*, 3 January 1901.

51. The Billings paper recalled that it had "been only a little over a year since she was at work in this city." *Billings Daily Gazette*, 5 January 1901.

52. Lee was told "to clean his establishment of all the immoral aspects and the Chinaman readily obeyed." Ibid., 22 September 1899.

53. Ibid., 26 January 1901.

54. Ibid., 29 January 1901.

55. *Billings News*, 30 January 1901.

56. *Livingston Enterprise*, 19 January 1901. The *Livingston Post*, on 17 January 1901, reported simply, "Calamity Jane is in town."

57. *Bozeman Gallatin County Republican*, 12 February 1901.

58. *Bozeman Avant Courier*, 16 February 1901.

59. *Denver Rocky Mountain News*, 25 February 1901.

60. *Deadwood Daily Pioneer-Times*, 27 February 1901.

61. *Billings Daily Gazette*, 17 March 1901.

62. Ibid., 17 March 1901; *Livingston Enterprise*, 9 March 1901.

63. *Billings Daily Gazette*, 20 March 1901. Dr. David Franklin Powell, who claimed friendship with William F. Cody, is discussed in Sorg, "Brother's Trails": 40–45, and Russell, *Lives and Legends of Buffalo Bill*, 286, 307–8, 423–24.

64. *Butte Miner*, 16 March 1901.

65. *Livingston Enterprise*, 13 April 1901.

66. Ibid.

67. *Red Lodge Carbon County Democrat*, 24 April 1901. The town of Cody celebrated the completion of the railroad connection in November. *Billings Times*, 2 May, 6 June, 15 November 1901.

68. Quoted in Patrick, *The Best Little Town by a Dam Site*, 41.

69. Newspapers reported the 1901 Livingston baseball season in detail, and list Freeman as the team's left-fielder. *Livingston Post*, 16, 19, 23, 30 May; 13, 27 June; 4 July; and 1 August 1901. The *Post*, on 18 July 1901, also reported that Freeman and two others "made the trip from this city to Big Timber last Sunday in a flat bottomed boat." The hazardous fifty-mile trip was made in a little over six hours without mishap. The reporter added that Freeman "has had some considerable experience in boating in Alaska."

70. Freeman, *Down the Yellowstone*. See also, Freeman, "Calamity Jane and Yankee Jim": 22–25, 52, 54.

71. Freeman, *Down the Yellowstone*, 77–79.

72. Ibid., 79.

73. Ibid., 80.

74. Ibid., 78.

75. Ibid., 80–81.

76. Ibid., 81.

77. Ibid., 82.

78. Ibid., 84–85.

79. Ibid., 86–87.

80. Ibid., 87–88.

81. Ibid., 88–90.

82. Ibid., 90.

83. *Red Lodge Carbon County Democrat*, 15 May 1901. See also, Owens, *Characters of the Past*, 20–21.

84. *Livingston Post*, 30 May 1901.

85. Ibid., 13 June 1901.

86. *Livingston Enterprise*, 15 June 1901.

CHAPTER 12: THE PAN-AMERICAN EXPOSITION, 1901–1902

1. *Livingston Enterprise*, 13 July 1901.

2. Ibid.

3. Ibid.; *Deadwood Daily Pioneer-Times*, 13 July 1901.

4. *Livingston Enterprise*, 13 July 1901.

5. Josephine Winifred Brake's name was on the record of registrants at the Thornton Hotel in Butte. *Butte Miner*, 9 July 1901.

6. *Livingston Enterprise*, 13 July 1901.

7. *Livingston Post*, 11 July 1901; *Denver Times*, 12 July 1901.

8. *Livingston Post*, 25 July 1901.

9. *Butte Miner*, 11 July 1901.

10. *Livingston Post*, 11 July 1901.

11. *Billings Times*, 18 July 1901.

12. *Red Lodge Picket*, 12 July 1901.

13. *Butte Miner*, 11 July 1901.

14. *Billings Gazette*, 16 July 1901.

15. *Bozeman Avant Courier*, 20 July 1901.

16. *Billings News*, 13 July 1901.

17. *Livingston Enterprise*, 20 July 1901, citing *St. Paul Dispatch*. Another paper added that Calamity "is no stranger to corn juice and about four times a day she imbibes, after giving notice of her intention." *Billings Daily Gazette*, 19 July 1901.

18. *Billings Daily Gazette*, 19 July 1901, citing *St. Paul Dispatch*.

19. Ibid.

20. *Minneapolis Journal*, 19 October 1901.

21. *Buffalo Morning Express*, 29 July 1901.

22. Hill, *Great White Indian Chief*, 13.

23. *Buffalo Morning Express*, 30 July 1901. The photograph of Martha taken at Niagara Falls has not been located.

24. Cummins "heard of the presence of Calamity Jane in Buffalo" and then "secured her as an attraction at his show last night." Buffalo Pan-American Exposition Scrapbook, vol. 15, clipping dated 30 July 1901. Buffalo Library, Buffalo, N.Y.

25. The *Buffalo Morning Express*, 30 July 1901, said manager Cummins invited people to the reception and dinner, where he "acted as toastmaster." However, the *Buffalo Evening News*, 30 July 1901, suggested the dinner was sponsored by Mrs. Brake. The *Evening News*, 30 July 1901, added that "the reception was attended by a number of prominent people who were anxious to see the heroine of the plains, who had masqueraded as a man and who fought the Indians with Gen. Custer, Buffalo Bill, Gens. Crook, Terry and Miles, for 10 years before her sex was discovered."

26. Buffalo Pan-American Exposition Scrapbook, clipping, 30 July 1901.

27. *Buffalo Evening News*, 30 July 1901.

28. *Buffalo Morning Express*, 1 August 1901. It was also reported that there would be a special performance for the Elks at the Indian Congress at five o'clock that afternoon. *Buffalo Morning Express*, 31 July 1901.

29. *Buffalo Evening News*, 1 August 1901.

30. *Billings Times*, 24 September 1901, citing *Chicago Inter-Ocean*.

31. *Buffalo Morning Express*, 4 August 1901.

32. *Buffalo Evening News*, 4 August 1901.

33. *Buffalo Morning Express*, 4 August 1901.

34. The pamphlet said incorrectly that "she was never connected with any other public exhibition." Hill, *Great White Indian Chief*, 14–15.

35. Newcom, "Quick Exit from City Recalled."

36. *Billings Times*, 24 September 1901, citing *Chicago Inter-Ocean*.

37. *Buffalo Evening News*, 9 August 1901.

38. *Livingston Enterprise*, 21 September 1901, citing *New York Sun*.

39. *Livingston Post*, 19 September 1901.

40. *Livingston Enterprise*, 21 September 1901, citing *New York Sun*.

41. *Billings Times*, 5 September 1901.

42. Shoemaker, *Pennsylvania Recollections of Calamity Jane*, 4–5, TS. Jennewein Collection.

43. *Livingston Enterprise*, 21 September 1901, citing *New York Sun*; *Buffalo Morning Express*, 11 August 1901.

44. *Buffalo Evening News*, 26 August 1901. Combined ceremonies involving the two shows do not mention Martha, suggesting she no longer was present. *Buffalo Morning Express*, 26, 31 August 1901.

45. *Livingston Enterprise*, 21 September 1901, citing *New York Sun*.

46. *Denver Times*, 1 June 1902, citing *New York World*.

47. *Buffalo Evening News*, 1 September 1901.

48. *Lewistown Fergus County Argus*, 2 October 1901.

49. *Billings Daily Gazette*, 22 September 1901.

50. Ibid.

51. *Livingston Post,* 10 October 1901.

52. *Minneapolis Journal,* 19 October 1901.

53. *Pierre Weekly Capital-Journal,* 1 November 1902.

54. *Miller Pioneer Press,* 28 November 1901, citing *Ft. Pierre Stock Journal.*

55. *Livingston Enterprise,* 21 December 1901; *Spearfish Queen City Mail,* 11 December 1901, citing *Pierre Free Press.*

56. *Livingston Enterprise,* 21 December 1901.

57. *Philip Pioneer Review,* 29 July 1937.

58. R. H. Kelly Collection (H-90-61), South Dakota State Historical Society.

59. G. H. Grebe to Will G. Robinson, 25 January 1965; Clipping dated 16 October 1941, Biographical File—Calamity Jane, South Dakota State Historical Society.

60. *Great Falls Tribune,* 22 March 1931.

61. Grace Fairchild, Fred's stepmother, said that when her husband, Sly, went to Ft. Pierre for supplies, he met Martha in Fred Rowe's hardware store. When bystanders made uncomplimentary remarks, Martha "pulled out her gun, and started shooting at their feet, clearing the store in a hurry." No contemporary source reports this newsworthy event. Fred L. Fairchild to Bill Secrest, 19 December 1953. Jennewein Collection; Wyman, *Frontier Woman,* 59.

62. Fales, interview, 9.

63. The "Worst Storm in Years" lasted sixty hours and forced railroads to halt traffic. Snowdrifts "three feet on the level" covered the region from Dickinson to Fargo, North Dakota, and reached as far south as Huron. When the snow melted, the Northern Pacific was again forced to halt traffic due to floods. *Bismarck Weekly Tribune,* 21, 28 March 1902; *Billings Times,* 18 March 1902.

64. *Deadwood Daily Pioneer-Times,* 14 October 1902, citing *Sioux Falls Argus Leader.*

65. *Aberdeen Daily News,* 14 March 1902.

66. Arnold quoted in Lewis Crawford, *Rekindling Camp Fires,* 272–73. It is possible Arnold's meeting with Martha occurred a year later.

67. *Glasgow North Montana Review,* 22 March 1902.

68. *Huron Daily Huronite,* 8 April 1902.

69. Crystal Pugsley, "Reminiscing on a Bygone Era in Huron: Wheeler Family Relates History of Early Business," *Huron Plainsman,* 14 July 1996.

70. Although Martha visited Aberdeen before she traveled to Oakes and Jamestown on 11–12 April, the Aberdeen newspaper reported her visit several days later. *Aberdeen Daily News,* 16 April 1902.

71. *Fort Pierre Fairplay,* 11 September 1903, citing *Sioux Falls Press.*

72. *Aberdeen Daily News,* 16 April 1902.

73. *Oakes Republican,* 11 April 1902.

74. *Jamestown Daily Capital,* 12 April 1902; *Jamestown Daily Alert,* 12 April 1902. According to the latter newspaper, Martha exclaimed, "You have had your fun and now it's my turn. . . . You fellows don't know as much as the calves out on my Montana ranch."

75. *Oakes Republican,* 16 April 1902. A Jamestown newspaper teasingly commented that the "Oakes Republican fails to confirm the story of Calamity Jane's fun with sports there so the scene must have been in a better town." *Jamestown Daily Capital,* 14 April 1902. The Oakes newspaper only mentioned the story in a column, "Crimes and Criminals," which included brief notices of criminal activities throughout the nation. *Oakes Republican,* 25 April 1902.

76. *Denver Times,* 1 June 1902, citing *New York World.*

77. Ibid.

78. *Jamestown Daily Capital*, 12 April 1902; *Jamestown Daily Alert*, 12 April 1902.

79. *Jamestown Daily Alert*, 12 April 1902; *Jamestown Daily Capital*, 12 April 1902.

80. *Mandan Pioneer*, 18 April 1902.

81. *Jamestown Daily Capital*, 21 April 1902. Later, the *Daily Capital*, 17 April 1902, clarified that she "spent a night in jail" in Dickinson.

82. *Billings Daily Gazette*, 16 April 1902.

83. [Crawford], *West of the Texas Kid*, 102.

84. *Billings Daily Gazette*, 18 April 1902.

85. *Livingston Post*, 24 April 1902.

86. *Livingston Enterprise*, 10 May 1902; *Gardiner Wonderland*, 17 May 1902.

87. *Livingston Enterprise*, 24 May 1902.

88. Whithorn, *Calamity's in Town*, 40.

89. *Livingston Enterprise*, 31 May 1902. While Lee waited in jail, two other prisoners, Jack Shell and Charles Adams, confided to him they had burglarized a gun shop, telling Lee where they had stashed the stolen weapons. Lee divulged the information to the police during an interrogation, leading to convictions for Shell and Adams. *Livingston Enterprise*, 3, 31 May; 7, 28 June; 16 August; 20, 27 September 1902; and, *Livingston Post*, 5, 19, 26 June; 31 July; 7, 14, 27 August; 25 September 1902.

90. *Helena Montana Daily Record*, 3 June 1902.

91. *Livingston Enterprise*, 7 June 1902. No jail records have been located showing Martha spent time serving a sentence there.

92. *Livingston Enterprise*, 7 June 1902; *Livingston Post*, 5 June 1902.

93. *Lewistown Fergus County Argus*, 18 June 1902.

94. Ibid.

95. *Red Lodge Picket*, 7 November 1902.

96. *Livingston Post*, 13 November 1902.

97. *Livingston Enterprise*, 21 June 1902.

98. *Lewistown Fergus County Argus*, 25 June 1902.

99. *Lewistown Democrat*, 11 July 1902.

100. *Billings Daily Gazette*, 11 September 1902.

CHAPTER 13: DEATH IN THE BLACK HILLS, 1903

1. *Billings Daily Gazette*, 21 November 1902. The rival *Times* teasingly compared Martha's hatchet attack to the efforts of Carrie Nation, the temperance activist who traveled around the country smashing saloons. It also clarified that Martha had been "ejected from a south side saloon" before making a "merry disturbance" in Yegen's harness department. *Billings Times*, 25 November 1902.

2. *Billings Times*, 25 November 1902.

3. *Billings Daily Gazette*, 22 November 1902.

4. Ibid., 26 November 1902.

5. Ibid., 12 December 1902. A Livingston newspaper amusingly warned that arresting Martha was risky business; if the "venerable old lady" became offended, Billings might lose "the only diversion [it] has had for many moons." *Livingston Post*, 18 December 1902.

6. *Billings Daily Gazette*, 20 December 1902.

7. *Sheridan Press*, 15 December 1937.

8. Nelson, "Calamity Jane's Last Ride": 27.

9. *Custer County Chronicle*, 16 December 1902.

10. *Deadwood Evening Independent*, 15 December 1902.

11. *Deadwood Daily Pioneer-Times*, 16 December 1902.

12. *Deadwood Evening Independent*, 19, 26 December 1902.

13. *Denver Post*, 11 January 1903.

14. *Belle Fourche Bee*, 15 January 1903.

15. Du Fran, *Low Down on Calamity Jane*, 9–11.

16. *Belle Fourche Daily Post*, 11 April 1990.

17. Du Fran added that Martha "would mount any horse she got near," which was "not so dangerous as it seemed" since the cowboys rode only safe horses to town. Du Fran, *Low Down on Calamity Jane*, 9–11.

18. Du Fran probably mixes observations of Martha's drinking sprees in 1895 and 1903. Ibid., 6–7.

19. According to Du Fran, Calamity "howled" at other times, not just when drinking. When she camped on the trail with companions, "the howl of lurking coyotes set her nerves to quivering—she wanted to join the chorus," and she did, to the dismay of those attempting to sleep. More than once her companions treated her "to a bucket of cold water." Du Fran added that Calamity's howling put coyotes to shame. Ibid., 6–7.

20. Ibid., 10.

21. *Belle Fourche Bee*, 5 March 1903.

22. Martha said it was "last fall" that she worked in a Belle Fourche hotel, illustrating how mistaken her chronology could be. *Rapid City Daily Journal*, 20 March 1903.

23. *Hot Springs Weekly Star*, 20 March 1903.

24. *Rapid City Daily Journal*, 20 March 1903.

25. O. W. Coursey, "'Days of 76' Recall Pal of Wild Bill; A Dual Personality," *Sioux Falls Daily Argus-Leader*, 30 August 1924.

26. *Rapid City Daily Journal*, 20 March 1903.

27. Ibid., 24 March 1903; R. J. Jackson, *Memory's Trail* (n.p., [1953]), 35. Dr. Jackson added, "She was a hard looking old wreck and not worth saving anyway."

28. Ibid., 7 April 1903. Similarly, the *Rapid City Black Hills Union*, 27 March 1903, reported, "Calamity Jane—the real and original Calamity—arrived in Rapid City about a week ago. She was taken quite sick Sunday, but is improving again. She intends remaining until after the big stock association meeting next month, so it is said."

29. *Rapid City Black Hills Union*, 17 April 1903.

30. *Deadwood Daily Pioneer-Times*, 25 June 1903.

31. William R. Fox, "Interview," WPA, Subject #46, TS, 1936–1938, Wyoming State Archives. According to Elizabeth Ann Zane Fox (Mrs. W. R. Fox), the man Martha claimed was her husband did live in Sundance, and his name was "Chrissy." Martha cared for him there during his illness. Clarence S. Paine, notes from a letter by Elizabeth Ann Zane Fox, 26 April 1948, Paine Collection. The Sundance newspaper did not mention Martha's presence in town until after her death. It then commented that her old acquaintances were not surprised to hear of her demise, for she had become a "habitual drunkard of recent years." *Sundance Crook County Monitor*, 7 August 1903.

32. Barbara Henderson Fox, "Interview," WPA, TS, 1936–1938, Wyoming State Archives. A lard bucket was commonly used for hauling beer from saloons to home. Marshall, *Swinging Doors*, 91.

33. Du Fran, *Low Down on Calamity Jane*, 11. Evidently, Martha made more than one trip from Belle Fourche to Spearfish in July; the Lead newspaper said she arrived in Terry from Spearfish "a week ago Friday," which places that trip on about July 24. *Lead Daily Call*, 1 August 1903.

34. Martha must have arrived in Spearfish on July 6 since this is the Wednesday edition of the newspaper. *Spearfish Queen City Mail*, 8 July 1903.

35. The *Lead Daily Call*, 11 July 1903 reported Martha was "in town this morning for a short time."

36. *Deadwood Daily Pioneer-Times*, 12 July 1903. The editor was not pleased with articles written by the visiting editors after their departure. He later commented that most moralized "on the wickedness of Deadwood." Ibid., 12 August 1903.

37. The newspaper incorrectly claimed Calamity's daughter was fifteen in 1895. Ibid., 15 July 1903. Among the editors was R. E Dowdell of Artesian, S.Dak., who was traveling with his two daughters. One of the children, Ethel, later described meeting Martha on this trip. Abild, "Calamity Jane—Woman of Mystery," 419–20; *Deadwood Daily Pioneer-Times*, 14 July 1903.

38. *Rapid City Daily Journal*, 16 July 1903; *Rapid City Black Hills Union*, 17 July 1903.

39. In later years, Mayo claimed the photographs taken about ten days before Martha's death remained unpublished until 1952 because he feared his young bride-to-be would not understand why he had been in company with the notorious woman. Joe Koller, "Calamity Jane Photograph Uncovered After 49 Years," *Rapid City Daily Journal*, 28 September 1952; Joe Koller, 27 October 1952, and John B. Mayo, 9 November 1952, to J. Leonard Jennewein. Jennewein Collection. Mayo's recollection was inaccurate; one of the pictures he took was published the year after it was taken. *Black Hills Pictured History. Deadwood Souvenir Edition*, 1905. 40.

40. Jennewein, *Calamity Jane*, 32–33. Haas noted in an interview that the photograph was taken in front of the millinery store, which in 1952 was the "county work shop" next to the post office. Charles Haas, interview by J. Leonard Jennewein (ca. 1951), TS, Jennewein Collection.

41. Haas, interview.

42. *Deadwood Daily Pioneer-Times*, 2 August 1903. Dora Du Fran said that when she had talked with Martha about death a few months earlier, Martha said, "I don't know anybody who would even plant a cactus on my grave." Du Fran then promised Martha she would care for her burial site. Du Fran, *Low Down on Calamity Jane*, 11. That Martha realized death was close also was evident from comments made to a Spearfish reporter in July; she reportedly said that she had "come back to the Hills, from Montana, to die." *Spearfish Queen City Mail*, 5 August 1903.

43. Jennewein, *Calamity Jane*, 9.

44. Hilton explained that the trip from Deadwood to Terry on the ore train took from one to more than three hours, depending upon what work was required on the trip. Joe Hilton to J. Leonard Jennewein, 12 October 1952, Jennewein Collection.

45. "This Past Week at Terry," *Lead Daily Call*, 1 August 1903. Sheffer and Jay's Saloon included a bar, rooming house, and restaurant on the first floor, and rooms on the second floor. Initially, Martha was taken to the Calloway Hotel, but Sheffer moved her to his establishment for medical care. Klock, *Here Comes Calamity Jane*, 15–16. Another physician, Dr. F. S. Howe, said he was called to attend Calamity, but because of another medical commitment and the cost to rent a buggy to Terry, he declined. Thus, he added, "$4 came between me and fame." Howe, *Deadwood Doctor*, 47.

46. *Deadwood Daily Pioneer-Times*, 8 August 1903.

47. Biographer Roberta Beed Sollid found Martha's cause of death in a book containing death records in Deadwood, but this ledger now seems to be missing. Sollid, *Calamity Jane*, 106–7.

48. *Cheyenne Daily Leader*, 3 August 1903.

49. *Deadwood Daily Pioneer-Times*, 2 August 1903. According to Jessie, the chief of police wrote to inform her of her mother's death. *Rapid City Daily Journal*, 2 August 1934.

50. *Deadwood Daily Pioneer-Times*, 4 August 1903.

51. Russell Thorp said he heard the story from Sam Tillet, a railroad engineer, who named the drinking companions as Albert Malter, Frank Ankeney, Jim Carson, Anson Higby, and Mike Russell. Russell Thorp, 22 October 1959, quoted in Flannery, *John Hunton's Diary*, 6:179–80.

52. *Deadwood Daily Pioneer-Times*, 2 August 1903. The August 8 edition of this newspaper adds that Hickok was her "former husband."

53. Fred Lockley, "Impressions and Observations of the Journal Man," *Portland Sunday Journal*, 25 March 1934.

54. *Yankton Missouri Valley Observer*, 12–18 June 1997.

55. Ibid.

56. Brown and Willard, *Black Hills Trails*, 418.

57. Ibid., 415.

58. *Deadwood Daily Pioneer-Times*, 8 August 1903.

59. The newspaper provided a detailed account of the funeral, including the text of Clark's sermon and the names of musicians and pallbearers. The latter included George S. Hopkins, Curley Simmons, L. R. Baxter, George Hoshier, and William Hanley. Ibid., 5 August 1903. J. Leonard Jennewein later identified an unnamed sixth pallbearer, George Leeman. Jennewein, *Calamity Jane*, 10. Because Martha's funeral turned into a memorable event, many people later told their stories about attending it. For example, Helen Fowler, who as a teenager played the organ at the funeral, had her story published in the *Lead Daily Call*, 31 July 1973. Not everyone was pleased to be associated with Martha's funeral. Badger Clark, son of the minister and later poet laureate of South Dakota, regretted that people remembered his father more for having eulogized Calamity Jane than for his years of work in the ministry. *Sioux Falls Daily Argus-Leader*, 20 May 1951.

60. *Lander Wyoming State Journal*, 30 November 1933. L. R. Chrisman of Deadwood remembered that it was the saloon element that turned out for her funeral and that even her pallbearers were bartenders. After Martha's burial, the crowd went from saloon to saloon with the band playing before each one; free drinks were served until everyone became completely drunk. Dunlap, *Riding Astride*, 69.

61. Rosa, *Wild Bill Hickok*, 209.

62. Captain Jack Crawford, "Truth about Calamity Jane," 333.

63. *Deadwood Daily Pioneer-Times*, 6 August 1903.

64. The promotional nature of the article was obvious: "Every one should consult him. His rooms are in the Syndicate block. . . . If you do not have time to wait, telephone, . . . or use the mails to arrange a date with him." *Deadwood Weekly Pioneer-Times*, 6 August 1903.

65. *Deadwood Daily Pioneer-Times*, 8 August 1903.

66. *Lead Daily Call*, 7 August 1903.

67. *New York Times*, 2 August 1903.

68. *London Star*, 7 August 1903.

69. Examples of newspapers including Cody's comments include *Livingston Enterprise*, 8 August 1903, and *Bozeman Avant Courier*, 7 August 1903. Typical of summaries of Deadwood's obituary was *Billings Times*, 3 August 1903. The *Denver Times*, 1 June 1902, also served as a primary source for information about Martha. Uniquely, the Pierre newspaper wondered if reports of her death were true since it "has been announced several times" in the past. *Pierre Daily Capital Journal*, 4 August 1903.

70. *Livingston Enterprise*, 8 August 1903; *Chicago Inter-Ocean*, 28 January 1896.

71. *Deadwood Daily Pioneer-Times*, 9 August 1903.

72. *Deadwood Weekly Pioneer-Times*, 20 August 1903.

73. *Deadwood Daily Pioneer-Times*, 23 August 1903.

74. Ibid., 5 September 1903. In a similar vein, the Lead newspaper copied an interview with A. D. Balcombe, the man who arrested Jack McCall in Laramie and transported him to Yankton, confirming that McCall was not lynched by Calamity as some obituaries claimed. *Lead Daily Call*, 18 August 1903.

75. *Rapid City Daily Journal*, 4 August 1903.

76. *Rapid City Black Hills Union*, 14 August 1903.

77. *Gardiner Wonderland*, 6 August 1903.

78. *White Sulphur Springs Meagher Republican*, 14 August 1903.

79. *Belle Fourche Bee*, 6 August 1903.

CHAPTER 14: BUILDING A LEGEND, 1903–1953

1. Huntington, *Both Feet in the Stirrups*, 129–31; Hanson, *South Dakota in the World War*, 320–21.

2. Patterson, "'Calamity Jane'," 455–57.

3. Allen, *Adventures with Indians and Game*, 32–34.

4. *Progressive Men*, 965. Wyoming newspaper columnist John C. Thompson later commented that this entry on Calamity Jane was "unadulterated balderdash." John C. Thompson, "In Old Wyoming," undated clipping, American Heritage Center.

5. *Sioux Falls Argus Leader*, 9 July 1906.

6. Kuykendall, *Frontier Days*, 190–91.

7. Josiah M. Ward, "A Wild West Heroine the Movies Overlook," *New York Tribune*, 16 October 1921.

8. *Casper Tribune-Herald*, 25 November 1921.

9. Eisloeffel and Paul, "Hollywood on the Plains": 13–19.

10. The film script "William S. Hart in Wild Bill Hickok," is in the files of the William S. Hart Museum in the Natural History Museum of Los Angeles County, Los Angeles, Calif. For a hostile critique of the movie, see Wilstach, *Wild Bill Hickok*, 256–57.

11. Brown, *Romance of Everyday Life*, 41–43.

12. Brown and Willard, *Black Hills Trails*, 411–18.

13. O. W. Coursey, "Days of 76' Recall Pal of Wild Bill; A Dual Personality," *Sioux Falls Argus Leader*, 30 August 1924; *Beautiful Black Hills*, 103–16.

14. Hilton, "Calamity Jane": 105–9.

15. Pond, "Frontier Still Recalls 'Calamity Jane'": 9; "Calamity Jane as a Lady Robin Hood": 46.

16. Dan R. Conway, "Calamity Jane, " Montana News Association, 4 October 1926, Montana Historical Society.

17. John K. Standish, "Calamity Jane Often Traveled over Cheyenne & Deadwood Stage Line; Notorious Character," *Lusk Herald*, 28 May 1936; W. S. Kimball, "Ye 'Good Old Days.' Historical Reminiscences of Early Day Casper," *Casper Tribune-Herald*, 28 April 1946. Another popular rendition of these tales is given in Tacetta B. Walker, "Calamity Jane, Belle of the Frontier," Montana News Association, 14 June 1937. Montana Historical Society.

18. Aikman, *Calamity Jane*, 59, 89–93, 106.

19. Brininstool, *Fighting Red Cloud's Warriors*, 333–53.

20. Rogers, *Gallant Ladies*, 12, 347–63; Sabin, *Wild Men of the Wild West*, 328–42. Even authors critical of Calamity Jane repeated popular tales. Doane Robinson, executive secretary of the South Dakota State Historical Society, asserted that she was "promiscuous in her affections" and a coarse and vulgar woman. Yet, Robinson's Calamity Jane was "kindhearted and when sober enough frequently nursed miners down with mountain fever." Doane Robinson, *Encyclopedia of South Dakota*, 106.

21. Peterson, *Through the Black Hills*, 88.

22. Bob Lee, *Gold–Gals–Guns–Guts*, 218; Parker, *Deadwood*, 239–43.

23. Price, *Black Hills*, 109–10; *Ghosts of Golconda*, 61–62. See also, Bellamy and Seymour, *Guide to the Black Hills*, 28. Scott, *Black Hills Story*, 62–64, similarly noted, "It is necessary in this Black Hills Story to include under more or less famous names one woman, Calamity Jane—because of what she did contribute to the settling of the Hills." Scott added her name "has endured along with [names of] other pioneers" because of her nursing of smallpox victims.

24. Case, *Lee's Official Guide Book*, 88.

25. El Comancho, *Old-Timer's Tale*, 30–31, 46.

26. Wilstach, *Wild Bill Hickok*, 253–65.

27. Connelley, *Wild Bill and His Era*, 184.

28. Ibid., 185–93.

29. Ibid., 197.

30. Hayne, *Autobiography of Cecil B. DeMille*, 350–52.

31. Taylor, "Film Makers Had Many Sleepless Nights."

32. Oller, *Jean Arthur*, 93–96.

33. Glendolin Damon Wagner, "Calamity Jane," Clipping, *Choteau Acantha*, [c. 1936],. Montana Historical Society.

34. Everett, "Calamity Jane": 7, 10, 16. Cowboy Bill Walker described a different Wild Bill–Calamity Jane relationship. Walker claimed that Hickok married Calamity when she was only fifteen and taught her how to shoot. But, according to Walker, Hickok was a "counterfeit" who got his gunfighter reputation "by shooting men in the back." No one mourned his passing except Calamity Jane, and Walker wondered why since Hickok "made a good profit off of her for several years, then dropped her to shift for herself." Baber, *Longest Rope*, 198–202.

35. Von Schmidt-Pauli, *We Indians*, 219–35.

36. Thorp, *Pardner of the Wind*, 116. Another invented story of Calamity Jane and horse racing involved Broncho Charlie Miller, Calamity Jane, Bat Masterson, and Poker Alice Tubbs in a saloon in Dodge City, Kansas. There, Calamity purportedly bet twenty dollars that Miller could ride a bucking horse named "Old Mex." See Erskine, *Broncho Charlie*, 199–200.

37. Hueston, *Calamity Jane of Deadwood Gulch*, 306. So convincing was Hueston's fiction that *The Columbia Encyclopedia* recommended Huston's novel in its list of biographies of Calamity Jane. See Bridgwater and Sherwood, *Columbia Encyclopedia*, I: 295.

38. Curry, "Raiders of Deadwood": 9–63.

39. Kirk, *Beacon Light*, 31.

40. Green, *Ballads*, 126–28.

41. Wickersham, *Pa-Ha-Sa-Pa*, 25.

42. Urbanek, *High Lights*, 33.

43. Mumey, *Calamity Jane*, 138.

44. Calamity Jane is located in Texas in another western film, *The Texan Meets Calamity Jane* (1950), starring Evelyn Ankers. One critic described the film as "perhaps the worst Grade Z western ever made." Scheuer, *TV Key Movie Guide*, 345.

45. McClintock, *Pioneer Days*, 115.

46. Senn, *"Deadwood Dick" and "Calamity Jane,"* 7–15.

47. Briggs, *Frontiers of the Northwest*, 75–82. Also, Bruce Nelson, *Land of the Dacotahs*, 162–67.

48. Casey, *The Black Hills and Their Incredible Characters*, 175–76. Likewise, Albert N. Williams stated, "All stories of Deadwood in the Black Hills come, eventually, to the great riddle of Martha Jane Cannary . . . known as Calamity Jane." She "has been the subject of more controversy and speculation than almost any other early-day character." Williams, *Black Hills*, 107–14. Archer B. Gilfillan also noted that Calamity was among "the most controversial figures and easily the most famous woman in South Dakota history." Gilfillan, *A Goat's Eye View*, 19–23.

49. *Rapid City Daily Journal*, 18 October 1953.

50. Hotchner, *Doris Day*, 119.

51. *Denver Rocky Mountain News*, 19 November 1953.

52. *Huron Plainsman*, 26 October 1953.

CHAPTER 15: OF DAUGHTERS, LETTERS, AND A DIARY

1. Vivien Skinner of "We the People," to Clarence S. Paine, 12 August 1942, Paine Collection.

2. *Buffalo Bulletin*, 2 May 1935; *Kalispell Times*, 2 March 1939.

3. Oscar Chaffee, "Billings Woman Announces That She Is Daughter of Famous Calamity Jane," *Billings Gazette*, 15 June 1941.

4. *Rapid City Daily Journal*, 12 September 1941.

5. Horan, *Desperate Women*, 200.

6. A double-spaced typescript of the album-diary is forty-two pages in length, and the loose-page entries are another forty-odd pages. Because the diary entries are addressed "Dear Janey," they are sometimes referred to as "letters," confusing the fact that there were letters as well as a diary and that the diary consisted of both an album and loose pages. The original album, letters, and loose pages were owned until recently by Stella Foote of Billings, Montana, who in her recent book prints the complete contents of these documents. Foote, *History of Calamity Jane*, 173, 185–209. Another important copy of the diary and loose pages is found in Mumey, *Calamity Jane*, 84–126, which separates album entries from loose pages, allowing for examination of each independently. Other editions of the diary and letters include *Copies of Calamity Jane's Diary and Letters* and *Calamity Jane's Letters to Her Daughter*.

7. Chaffee, "Billings Woman Announces That She Is Daughter"; Jean McCormick, 1947, letter quoted in Horan, *Desperate Women*, 196–200; Carl Anderson, "Calamity Jane, Wild Bill Relics Now at Museum," and "Daughter of Calamity Jane Born in Secluded Mountain Cabin in 1873, Diary Says," undated typescripts, Paine Collection; Clarence Paine, "Report of an Interview with Mrs. Jean Hickok McCormick, Self-styled Daughter of Jane Hickok, 'Calamity Jane,' Chicago, May 11, 1941," Paine Collection; *LaCrosse Tribune*, 15 September 1941; Foote, *History of Calamity Jane*, 214–17.

8. Chaffee, "Billings Woman Announces That She Is Daughter"; Helen S. Meldrum, "Daughter of 'Calamity' Jane Interviewed; Recollects Mother. Mrs. Jean McCormick Returns From Radio Broadcast," Buffalo, Wyo., 13 May (1941), reprinted in Mumey, *Calamity Jane*, 78; Paine, "Report of an Interview"; Foote, *History of Calamity Jane*, 214–17.

9. Jean McCormick to Mr. and Mrs. Paine, 21 August 1941, Paine Collection.

10. Paine, "Report of an Interview"; Clarence S. Paine to Jean Hickok McCormick, 11 July 1941, Paine Collection.

11. *Abilene Daily Chronicle*, 13 June 1941. According to Ted Viola, who arranged McCormick's Abilene appearance, she also led Abilene's "Wild Bill Hickok celebration" parade in 1946. Ted Viola to J. Leonard Jennewein, 19 February 1953, Jennewein Collection.

12. *Rapid City Daily Journal*, 12 September 1941; Jean Hickok McCormick to Helen Smith, 15 February 1942, Paine Collection. According to the *Billings Gazette*, 19 June 1941, McCormick, who had just returned from her appearance in Abilene, would be "a guest at the rodeo in Salina, Kan., in July."

13. *Rapid City Daily Journal*, 12 September 1941.

14. *La Crosse Tribune*, 15 September 1941.

15. McCormick to Smith, 15 February 1942.

16. J. Almus Russell (Friends of the Middle Border) to Jean Hickok McCormick, 3 February 1942; McCormick to Russell, 8 February 1942; McCormick to Russell, undated letter. The correspondence between Russell and McCormick continued for about a year. Jennewein Collection.

17. Carl Anderson to "We the People," 8 August 1942; Vivien Skinner to Anderson, 15 September 1942, Paine Collection.

18. Anderson, "Calamity Jane, Wild Bill Relics Now at Museum" and "Daughter of Calamity Jane." Earlier, McCormick claimed she had written a manuscript called "Calamity Jane Exposed," supposedly in the hands of a publisher in May 1941. See Meldrum, "Daughter of 'Calamity' Jane Interviewed," in Mumey, *Calamity Jane*, 78. The directors of the Fort Collins museum were not as enthusiastic as Anderson to have McCormick's relics on display and generally kept the items out of public view. Richard S. Baker to J. Leonard Jennewein, 26 January 1954. Jennewein Collection.

19. McCormick to Smith, 15 February 1942.

20. McCormick to Russell, undated letter.

21. Jean Hickok McCormick to Mr. and Mrs. Charles Bovey, 23 June 1947, George O. Simmons Papers (SC 747), Montana Historical Society.

22. Foote, *History of Calamity Jane*, 216–17. Also, Kathryn Wright, "What Kind of a Woman Was Calamity Jane? Series of Letters to Daughter Reveal Feminine Side of Frontier Woman," *Great Falls Tribune*, 20 November 1955. At least six printings of *Copies of Calamity Jane's Diary and Letters* were issued, with a total of 100,000 copies. A document in the Fort Collins Museum indicates the items received there on 15 January 1943 were returned to McCormick at her request on 11 July 1950, after she had been injured in an accident and hoped to sell the diary for needed cash. Untitled inventory list at Fort Collins Pioneer Museum, Fort Collins, Colo.

23. *Billings Gazette*, 23 February 1951. Foote, *History of Calamity Jane*, 214–17, provides a more recent biographical sketch of McCormick, but it too adds little new information.

24. The handwriting expert was Rowland K. Goddard, "Chief of the United States Secret Service in this district for many years." Mumey, *Calamity Jane*, 83–84. Goddard also compared the handwriting of Rev. W. F. Warren on Jean's "marriage certificate" to that in the Cheyenne Methodist Church marriage records. Although Goddard decided they were the same, he qualified his judgments: in McCormick's marriage certificate, he said, the minister was "undoubtedly laboring under most difficult conditions and with inadequate materials" and "had not yet acquired the skill he later shows." The writer "did not join his initials in this writing, later shown as a permanent writing habit, but he may have adopted this habit later," Goddard added. Mumey, *Calamity Jane*, 141–42. Croy, "Calamity Jane's Romantic Diary": 20.

25. Kathryn Wright, "What Kind of Woman was Calamity Jane?"

26. Foote, *History of Calamity Jane*, 186, 197, 198, 206, 208.

27. Jennewein, *Calamity Jane*, 28.

28. Hamilton, *Signature of America*, 3.

29. Du Fran, *Low Down on Calamity Jane*, 9; *Rapid City Daily Journal*, 12 September 1941.

30. Foote, *History of Calamity Jane*, 197, 209; Chaffee, "Billings Woman Announces That She Is Daughter"; *LaCrosse Tribune*, 15 September 1941; Sollid, *Calamity Jane*, 44–45; *Abilene Daily Chronicle*, 13 June 1941; Don Russell, *Lives and Legends of Buffalo Bill*, 383.

31. Horan, *Desperate Women*, 198; Rosa, *They Called Him Wild Bill*, 230–33; Cunard Steam-ship Company, Limited, to Joseph Rosa, 12 December 1957 and 8 December 1960, loaned to author by Rosa; Foote, *History of Calamity Jane*, 90, 199; Wright, "What Kind of Woman Was Calamity Jane?" For the correct date of the photograph, see Montana Historical Society to J. Leonard Jennewein, 3 January 1952, Jennewein Collection.

32. Paine also considered the error in the dating of Buffalo Bill's appearance in Richmond to be in favor of authenticity: "If the document is forged, why did the forger dwell so long upon a point which could so obviously be checked? None but the rankest amateur would have committed such a blunder." Paine, "She Laid Her Pistol Down," 9–21.

33. Clarence S. Paine to Helen T. Smith, 1 December 1954, Paine Collection.

34. Foote, *History of Calamity Jane*, 185, 199–200, 203.

35. Articles circulated by the Montana News Association (MNA) in the 1930s include: Tacetta Walker, "Calamity Jane, Belle of the Frontier," 14 June 1937, claiming Calamity Jane's father was a minister and that Belle Starr was the child of Hickok and Calamity; and Glendolin Damon Wagner, "Calamity Jane," undated clipping from *Chouteau Acantha*, containing information on W. A. Allen and Teddy Blue Abbott. Montana Historical Society.

36. Foote, *History of Calamity Jane*, 197–99.

37. *Buffalo Bulletin*, 1, 15 May 1941.

38. Kathryn Wright, "The Lucky Diamond," *Billings Gazette*, 20 June 1982. Evidently, Olive McDaniels forgave the department-store incident. In 1934, she said that she had known Calamity Jane and her daughter well and kept in touch with them for several years after they left Billings. *Billings Gazette*, 6 April 1934.

39. A correspondent from the historical society in Wibaux, Montana, alerted me to Frank Dalton's presence in the Yellowstone Valley region. One researcher suspected Dalton might have inspired McCormick to compile the diary and letters. Eng, "The Great Outlaw Hoax": 22.

40. Foote, *History of Calamity Jane*, 195, 197; Croy, *Jesse James Was My Neighbor*, 249.

41. Randall, *Footprints along the Yellowstone*, 40–41.

42. Packsaddle Ben Greenough to H. Hamlin, 21 February 1951, reprinted in *Pony Express*, April 1951: 6; Foote, *History of Calamity Jane*, 202.

43. William B. Lull to Jean Hickok McCormick, 4 July 1941, Paine Collection.

44. Foote, *History of Calamity Jane*, 187, 191.

45. McCormick to Smith, 15 February 1942; Foote, *History of Calamity Jane*, 186.

46. Paine, "She Laid Her Pistol Down," 11; Foote, *History of Calamity Jane*, 186.

47. McCormick to Smith, 15 February 1942.

48. Foote, *History of Calamity Jane*, 195.

49. Mrs. Bauder's support for McCormick is mentioned in Carl Anderson to L. R. Hafen, 14 August 1943, loaned to me by Joseph Rosa; Foote, *History of Calamity Jane*, 187.

50. "Calamity Jane," clipping, 1941, Denver Public Library, Western History Department, Denver, Colo.; Foote, *History of Calamity Jane*, 196.

51. Foote, *History of Calamity Jane*, 209.

52. *Deadwood Black Hills Weekly Times*, 28 July 1933; *Cody Enterprise*, 28 March 1934; *Lander Wyoming State Journal*, 5 April 1935; *Rapid City Daily Journal*, 2 August 1934.

53. Jessie E. Hickok (Oakes) Murray to Byron Crane, 27 November 1937, (H74-180), South Dakota State Historical Society. Although, earlier, Jessie had mentioned a William Hickok and said he was not to be confused with Wild Bill, she had not suggested any relationship to him. *Deadwood Black Hills Weekly Times*, 28 July 1933.

54. Foote, *History of Calamity Jane*, 202, 209.

55. Meldrum, "Daughter of 'Calamity' Jane Interviewed," in Mumey, *Calamity Jane*, 75.

56. Jessie Murray to L. L. Newton (ed.), *Lander Wyoming State Journal*, 12 March, 14 July 1942, American Heritage Center; *South Dakota Daily Transcript*, 24 June 1941, from the *Los Angeles Daily Journal*; McCormick to Smith, 15 February 1942; Jessie Murray, Certificate of Death, State of California, Department of Health Services.

57. Vivien Skinner to Marian D. Schumacher (Yellowstone County, Department of Public Welfare, Billings, Mont.), 6 August 1941. Paine Collection; Wright, "The *Real* Calamity Jane": 23. Stella Foote claims that McCormick brought the diary to the welfare agency much earlier (1936–37) to verify her birthdate to get assistance, and says she saw the diary at that time. Foote, *History of Calamity Jane*, 216.

58. One correspondent said Jean was paid $100 for her New York radio appearance. Anderson to Hafen, 14 August 1943.

59. Foote, *History of Calamity Jane*, 191–92. Mary Jane Holmes authored at least sixty-eight titles: among those perused by this writer were *Cousin Maude and Rosamond* (1888), *Madeline* (1881), *Tempest and Sunshine* (n.d.), *Edith Lyle* (1876), *Mildred; or, The Child of Adoption* (n.d.), *Meadow Brook* (n.d.), and *Marian Grey* (n.d.).

60. Miers, *Wild and Woolly West*, 122–25. Similarly, McLoughlin, *Wild and Woolly: An Encyclopedia*, 75–77, 221–26, used the diary and letters for his entry on Calamity Jane, and even gave Jean Hickok her own listing.

61. Saar, "Calamity Jane Trumps Buffalo Bill": 18–19.

62. Susan Hawthorne, "The Ms. Quiz: Women of Letters," *Ms.*, 2 (March-April 1992): 93.

63. The 1993 CD is *Urban Diva*, Dora Ohrenstein, Soprano, with music by Ben Johnston.

64. Wright, "What Kind of a Woman Was Calamity Jane?"; Eric Zorn, in "Lies, Lore, Myths Mold the Legend of the Old West," *Chicago Tribune*, 6 March 1984, quotes Suzanne Clauser, who added that she chose to follow the diary and letters because "the truth didn't matter in terms of the story we wanted to tell"; Stevenson, *Figures in a Western Landscape*, 172.

65. McMurtry, *Buffalo Girls*, 350, passim.

Chapter 16: Challenging the Myth, 1953–2003

1. Paine, "Wild Bill Hickok and Calamity Jane," 151–76. Another writer, South Dakotan Lloyd McFarling, drafted a several-hundred-page manuscript, "The Legend of Calamity Jane," which never was published. It is largely a critique of published reminiscences. McFarling Papers (H73-1), South Dakota State Historical Society.

2. Jennewein, *Calamity Jane*, 6–7.

3. In addition to utilizing contemporary records to establish Calamity Jane's date of death, Jennewein discredited the Jane Dalton account of her origins, Jean McCormick's documents, and claims that Calamity served as a scout. Although he believed that Calamity did care for the ill, because he had "talked with too many persons who relate the good deeds of Calamity, with specific names and places, to do any high-handed debunking," he thought some of these accounts were exaggerated. Ibid.

4. Sollid, *Calamity Jane*, Preface.

5. *Ibid.*

6. *Ibid.*, Preface, 6–7, 32, 65, 99–102, 124.

7. Jennewein to *Encyclopedia Americana*, 26 December 1957. Jennewein Collection. Jennewein was criticizing the 1947 edition of the encyclopedia.

8. Jennewein, *Calamity Jane*, 41; Sollid, review of *Calamity Was the Name for Jane*, 70.

9. Lamar, *Reader's Encyclopedia*, 146–47.

10. Schell, *History of South Dakota*, 150.

11. Riegel, *America Moves West*, 3rd ed., 539; Riegel and Athearn, *America Moves West*, 4th ed.

12. Riley, "Images of the Frontierswoman": 191; Myres, *Westering Women*, 4, 11.

13. Sochen comments, "In stories of white men conquering the West, and cowboys riding the range, there were no evil or treacherous deeds, only deeds of courage and valor. . . . The myth of the West was largely a male dream—an adventure of danger, risk, excitement, and high stakes. Neither women nor Indians counted." Sochen, *Herstory*, 194.

14. O'Connor added that, although Hickok "may not have been the most fastidious of men," photographs "indicate that [Calamity] was not the sort to arouse any great flare-up of romantic passion." O'Connor, *Wild Bill Hickok*, 236–67.

15. Rosa, *They Called Him Wild Bill*, 227.

16. Sandoz also comments in the novel about Calamity's nursing, "She went anywhere if there was a jug of whiskey to keep her company." Sandoz, *Miss Morissa*, 77–78, 201.

17. Sandoz, *Love Song to the Plains*, 208.

18. Steckmesser, *Western Hero in History and Legend*, 246–47. An additional reason it was difficult to discredit legendary accounts of Calamity Jane was the lack of documentary evidence about her. Andrew Blewitt noted in 1962 that it was still difficult "to unravel the facts about Calamity from the mass of half-truths, hearsay, legend, and downright lies with which, over the years, they have become entangled." Blewitt, "Calamity Jane": 1–9.

19. Burke, "Wildest Woman in the West": 12–13, 44–45. Other popular renditions include Robbins, "Hellcat in Leather Britches": 12–21; and Holding, "Wildcat's Kitten": 32–35.

20. Repp, "Lady Was a Cavalryman!": 12–13, 55–57.

21. McKelvie, *Hills of Yesterday*, 48–50.

22. Rezatto, *Tales of the Black Hills*, 200–7.

23. Brown, *Gentle Tamers*, 256–57; Miller, *Shady Ladies of the West*, 112–17; Drago, *Notorious Ladies of the Frontier*, 208–22; Ray, *Wily Women of the West*, 84–89.

24. Karolevitz, *Doctors of the Old West*, 159, 164; Dunlop, *Doctors of the American Frontier*, 76.

25. Horan and Sann, *Pictorial History of the Wild West*, 127–30; McCarty, *Gunfighters*, 40–41.

26. Chilton, *Book of the West*, 250.

27. Conley, *Cowboy Poetry*, 2–3; Myers, *Montana*, 8; McNeil, *Echoes from the Black Hills*, 11.

28. Sidne and Stan Lynde, *Calamity Jane*, 3, 20.

29. Mitchum, *Stagecoach Station 11*, 59–61, 176–77.

30. Edson, *Trouble Trail*, 46. Among the books in Edson's Calamity Jane series are *The Cow Thieves*, *The Bull Whip Breed*, *White Stallion, Red Mare*, *Cut One, They All Bleed*, and *Texas Trio*.

31. Logan, *Dead Man's Hand*, passim; Evans, *Longarm in Deadwood*, 64–84, 134–62.

32. According to Burnett, she "could recite almost every word of dialog before we went into rehearsal" because as a college student she had worked as a theater usher and had seen the original film at least sixty-five times. "Carol Burnett as 'Calamity Jane," *TV Guide*, 8.

33. Buscombe, *BFI Companion*, 76.

34. *Livingston Park County News*, 29 December 1960.

35. Ibid., 1 December 1960.

36. *Princeton Overland Courier*, 4 September 1991.

37. *Destination Deadwood*, 4 (May 1994), 4; South Dakota Department of Tourism, *South Dakota Vacation Guide 1996–1997*, 98. Deadwood has even been able to poke fun at its famous characters, producing a melodrama, *Desperate Damsels of Deadwood; or Virtue, Villains & Vixens*, starring Wild Bill Hick-hop, Delapity Jane, and Miss Kitty Litter. See *Visitor Magazine*, 13 (June 1996): 136.

38. Whithorn, *Calamity's in Town*; Mueller, *Calamity Jane*. An annual historical newspaper, the *Mercer County Pioneer Press* published in Princeton, Missouri, began on 1 October 1966, and continued appearing for several years afterward.

39. Dexter, *Deadwood*, 47, 49, 251, 325–26, 343–44, passim.

40. McMurtry, *Buffalo Girls*, 37, 129, passim.

41. Carlson, "Unhappy Trails," *Time* 136 (29 October 1990): 100.

42. Nelson added that one elderly Black Hills resident told him Calamity "was the drunkenest, filthiest, vilest woman" he had ever known.

43. David, *A Log of Deadwood*, 79.

44. *Helena Independent Record*, 26, 28 October 1989. The conference papers later became the basis for a book edited by Dave Walter, *Speaking Ill of the Dead: Jerks in Montana History* (2000).

45. Schickel, "Out West on a Bad Star Trip." 87.

46. "True West Legends: Calamity Jane": 31–34;   Russell, "Calamity Jane Lived Up to Her Name": 42–48; Mancini, *American Legends*, 74.

47. Cole, *Wild Bill: Sante Fe Death Trap*, 58, 164.

48. Ihle, *Wildcat*, 188–89. Another romance novel featuring Calamity Jane is Dorothy Dixon, *Yellowstone Jewel: Leather and Lace # 9*.

49. Faber, *Calamity Jane*, 12.

50. Fontes and Korman, *Calamity Jane at Fort Sanders*, 3, 7.

51. Hiltbrand, "No Plain Jane": 41.

52. [Bell and Fisher], *Wild West Legend Calamity Jane and Barb Wire* and *"The Whole Shebang;* [Thierer], *Ride into History*; Thierer, "Calamity Jane and Annie Oakley," 29; *1995 Visitor's Guide, Wyoming Territorial Park*, 17. Slack published five pamphlets about Calamity Jane containing the material she uses in her dramatizations. These are based primarily on the recollections of Calamity's nephew, Tobe Borner, but incorporating portions of McCormick's diary and letters. See Slack, *Westward Journey, How I Became Known as Calamity Jane, Calamity Jane's Cantankerous Reputation, Calamity Jane Builds a Cabin*, and, *The Capture of Calamity Jane's Heart*.

53. Advertisement, *Outdoor Life*. 82. The resurgence of Calamity Jane's popularity is not confined to the United States. In summer 2003, London's Shaftesbury Theatre featured Toyah Willcox in a stage version of the 1953 Doris Day movie, *Calamity Jane*. *London Times*, 27 June 2003.

54. The clothing matched a photograph of Calamity Jane taken at the Potter and Benjamin studio in Livingston, Montana, probably in 1896. However, researchers have been unable to prove when and where the artist acquired her outfit. Legend has it that she undressed in a saloon when Remington asked for her clothing, and was paid sufficient money for her outfit to buy drinks. Brink, "Clothing Calamity Jane": 20–24.

CONCLUSION

1. Steckmesser, *Western Hero in History and Legend*, 249.

2. Ibid., 250.

3. Ibid., 249.

4. Ibid., 255.

5. Ibid., 241.

6. Ibid., 252.

7. Ibid., 242.

8. Ibid., 247.

9. Etulain, "Calamity Jane: Independent Woman," 72–92; "Calamity Jane: Making of a Frontier Legend," 177–95. Another example of recent scholarly interest in Calamity Jane is Furlong, "Gold-Dust and Buckskins," P.h.D. diss., 1991.

10. This remark was made by pallbearer George Leeman. Jennewein, *Calamity Jane*, 9. In the 1930s, William R. Fox similarly concluded: "Today, Calamity Jane is apparently considered quite a famous character in the early West. To us, who knew her in everyday life, this has come somewhat as a surprise." William R. Fox, interview.

Bibliography

MANUSCRIPT COLLECTIONS

Biographical File–Calamity Jane. American Heritage Center, University of Wyoming, Laramie.

———. Billings Public Library, Billings, Mont.

———. Denver Public Library, Western History Department, Denver, Colo.

———. Fremont County Pioneer Museum, Lander, Wyo.

———. South Dakota State Historical Society, Pierre.

———. Wyoming State Archives and Research Division, Cheyenne.

Biographical File–Jean McCormick. Fort Collins Pioneer Museum, Fort Collins, Colo.

J. Leonard Jennewein Collection, Layne Library, Dakota Wesleyan University, Mitchell, S.Dak.

R. H. Kelly Collection (H90-61). South Dakota State Historical Society, Pierre.

Lloyd McFarling Papers (H73-1). South Dakota State Historical Society, Pierre.

Clarence S. Paine Collection, The Center for Western Studies, Augustana College, Sioux Falls, S.Dak.

George O. Simmons Papers (SC 351, 747). Montana Historical Society, Helena.

Vertical File–Calamity Jane. Montana Historical Society, Helena.

DOCUMENTS

Anderson, Carl. "Calamity Jane, Wild Bill Relics Now at Museum," and "Daughter of Calamity Jane Born in Secluded Mountain Cabin in 1873, Diary Says." Undated typescripts from *Fort Collins (Colo.) Express Courier.* Clarence S. Paine Collection, Augustana College, Sioux Falls, S.Dak.

Beck, George W. T. "Personal Reminiscences of the Beginning of Cody, 1895–1896." TS, January 1936. George W. T. Beck Collection, American Heritage Center, University of Wyoming, Laramie.

Bocker, Charles W. Interview by Grace Raymond Hebard, Laramie, Wyo., 9 August 1927. TS. Biographical File–Calamity Jane, American Heritage Center, University of Wyoming, Laramie.

Borner, Tobe. "Calamity Jane." Biographical File–Calamity Jane, American Heritage Center, University of Wyoming, Laramie.

Briggs, Laura. "Recollections of Pioneers Who Knew Calamity Jane." WPA Subject # 46, 1946. TS. Wyoming State Archives and Research Division, Cheyenne.

"Buffalo Bill 1903 Clipping Book." Buffalo Bill Museum, Cody, Wyo.

Buffalo Pan-American Exposition Scrapbook, vol. 15, unidentified clipping, 30 July 1901. Buffalo Library, Buffalo, N.Y.

Bureau of the Census. 1820, 1830, 1840, 1850, Census, Malaga Township, Monroe County, Ohio; 1860 Census, Mercer County, Missouri; 1869 Census, Carter County, Wyoming.

Burke, Clinton. Death Records, Bureau of Vital Statistics, Houston Health and Human Services Department, City of Houston, Tex.

Burnett, Edward. "Calamity and Irish Entertain for Bostonians, and Other Recollections." WPA Subject # 64, 1936. TS. Wyoming State Archives and Research Division, Cheyenne.

Canary Family Land Deeds. Office of the Recorder of Deeds, Mercer County Court House, Princeton, Mo.

Canary, James. Probate Records, Circuit Court of Mercer County, Missouri, 4 November 1862–July 1865.

Canary, Martha. Certificate of Marriage, County of Bingham, Territory of Idaho, 30 May 1888.

Cash, W. H. "Hunting and Trapping in the Early Days." WPA Subject # 90, n.d. TS. Wyoming State Archives and Research Division, Cheyenne.

Dankowski, Stanislaw. Interview, WPA Subject # 672, 1936–1937. TS. Wyoming State Archives and Research Division, Cheyenne.

Description and History of Convicts in State Penitentiary at Laramie City, Wyoming. Wyoming State Archives and Research Division, Cheyenne.

Docket No. 93, District Court, Uinta County, State of Wyoming April 26, 1896. Wyoming State Archives and Research Division, Cheyenne.

Earnest, Boney. Reminiscences. Robert Beebe David Collection, Casper College, Casper, Wyo.

Fales, Charles. Interview by J. Leonard Jennewein, 6 June 1959. TS. J. Leonard Jennewein Collection, Layne Library, Dakota Wesleyan University, Mitchell, S.Dak.

Fales, John. Interview, WPA Subject # 705, n.d. TS. Wyoming State Archives and Research Division, Cheyenne.

Foote, Stella. "Calamity Jane." Notes taken at Historical Society meeting, 7 March 1955. Vertical File–Calamity Jane, Montana Historical Society, Helena, Mont.

Fox, Barbara Henderson. Interview, WPA, 1936–1938. TS. Wyoming State Archives and Research Division, Cheyenne.

Fox, William R. Interview, WPA. 1936–1938. TS. Wyoming State Archives and Research Division, Cheyenne.

Goldberg, Jacob. Ledger Book. Adams Museum and House, Inc., Deadwood, S.Dak.

Haas, Charles. Interview by J. Leonard Jennewein, n.d. TS. J. Leonard Jennewein Collection, Layne Library, Dakota Wesleyan University, Mitchell, S.Dak.

Hart, William S. "William S. Hart in Wild Bill Hickok." N.p., 1923. TS. William S. Hart Museum, Natural History Museum of Los Angeles County, Los Angeles, Calif.

McFarling, Lloyd. "Calamity Jane," and "The Legend of Calamity Jane." TS. Lloyd McFarling Papers (H73-1). South Dakota State Historical Society, Pierre.

McWhorter, Lucullus V. "Unfinished Incidents in 'Calamity Jane's' Life." n.d. TS. Folder 196. Lucullus v. McWhorter Papers. Manuscripts, Archives and Special Collections, Holland Library, Washington State University, Pullman.

Mercer County Pioneer Press. Princeton, Mo.: Mercer County Historical Society, 1 October 1966 and 30 December 1970. Biographical File–Calamity Jane. Mercer County Library, Princeton, Mo.

Miller, Lois. "Vet Deadwood Shoemaker Served Teddy, Calamity." Unidentified clipping. Biographical File–Calamity Jane, Billings Public Library, Billings, Mont.

Murray, Jessie. Certificate of Death, State of California, Department of Health Services.

Owen, Helen. "Calamity Jane: Heroine or Outcast." TS, 11 November 1965. Mercer County Library, Princeton, Mo.

Paine, Clarence S. "Report of an Interview with Mrs. Jean Hickok McCormick, Self-Styled Daughter of Jane Hickok, 'Calamity Jane,' Chicago, May 11, 1941." Clarence S. Paine Collection, The Center for Western Studies, Augustana College, Sioux Falls, S.Dak.

Pemberton, Mrs. Osborne. Interview by J. Leonard Jennewein, 7 June 1960. TS. J. Leonard Jennewein Collection, Layne Library, Dakota Wesleyan University, Mitchell, S.Dak.

Reitz, Minnie A. "Old Rock Creek." WPA Subject # 933, 1936. TS. Wyoming State Archives and Research Division, Cheyenne.

Report of Convicts Discharged, No. 253, August 12, 1900. Wyoming State Archives and Research Division, Cheyenne.

Roberts, Mary Fanton. "Point of View." Mary Fanton Roberts Papers (1900–1956), Roll D161, Archives of American Art, Smithsonian Institution, Detroit, Mich.

Russell, Pers. Interview by J. Leonard Jennewein, n.d. TS. J. Leonard Jennewein Collection, Layne Library, Dakota Wesleyan University, Mitchell, S.Dak.

Russell, S. W. "Calamity Jane." TS. Phoebe Apperson Hearst Library, Lead, S.Dak.

Shoemaker, Henry W. *Byron Hinckley Tells a Tale, It is of a Wrestling Match Between Calamity Jane and Madam Bull Dog, Which Jane Would Have Won But for the Madame's Repeated Foul Tactics.* Harrisburg: n.p., 1952. TS. J. Leonard Jennewein Collection, Layne Library, Dakota Wesleyan University, Mitchell, S.Dak.

———, compiler. *Pennsylvania Recollection of Calamity Jane, as told by George Henry Dunkle, Born October 12, 1860, and is Pittsburg's Venerable Historian and Chronicler. With a Footnote by the Late Byron Hinkley of English Centre, Lycoming County, A Pioneer of the Old West.* Harrisburg: n.p., 1952. TS. J. Leonard Jennewein Collection, Layne Library, Dakota Wesleyan University, Mitchell, S.Dak.

Smith, Samuel. Interview by Grace Raymond Hebard, 10 April 1917. TS. Biographical File–Calamity Jane, American Heritage Center, University of Wyoming.

Taylor Walter Ed. "Film Makers Had Many Sleepless Nights Finding Suitable Character to Play the Role of 'The Canary Who Sang Bass.'" Unidentified clipping, 5 August 1937. Biographical File–Calamity Jane, Montana Historical Society, Helena, Mont.

Territory of Montana Against Charles Townley and Jane Doe Alias Calamity Jane, Indictment for Fornication, November 5, 1888. Vertical File–Calamity Jane, Montana Historical Society, Helena, Mont.

Territory of Wyoming vs. Maggie Smith, Indictment for Grand Larceny. A True Bill, No. 269, 24 May 1876, and, *Territory of Wyoming vs. Maggie Smith, Verdict No. 269*. Clarence S. Paine Collection, The Center for Western Studies, Augustana College, Sioux Falls, S.Dak.

Thompson, John C. "In Old Wyoming." Undated clipping, Biographical File–Calamity Jane, American Heritage Center, University of Wyoming, Laramie.

Wagner, Glendolin Damon. "Calamity Jane." Undated clipping, *Chouteau (Mont.) Acantha*, [1936?]. Vertical File–Calamity Jane, Montana Historical Society, Helena, Mont.

Walker, Tacetta B. "Calamity Jane, Belle of the Frontier." Unidentified clipping, 14 June 1937. Vertical File–Calamity Jane, Montana Historical Society, Helena.

———. "Scenes form the Old West." TS. American Heritage Center, University of Wyoming, Laramie.

Ward, [John Q.]. Letter to the Editor, 8 January 1927, *Western Story Magazine*. TS. Clarence S. Paine Collection, Center for Western Studies, Augustana College, Sioux Falls, S.Dak.

Whiteside, William R. "Chronology: Canary Families in Iowa." TS. August 1998. Author's Collection.

Books

Abbott, E. C. (Teddy Blue) and Helena Huntington Smith. *We Pointed Them North: Recollections of a Cowpuncher*. 1939. Reprint, Norman: University of Oklahoma Press, 1955.

Adams, Ramon F. *The Legendary West: An Exhibit by the Friends of the Dallas Public Library*. Dallas Public Library, 1965.

———. *Six-Guns and Saddle Leather: A Bibliography of Books and Pamphlets on Western Outlaws and Gunmen*. Rev. ed. Norman: University of Oklahoma Press, 1969.

Aikman, Duncan. *Calamity Jane and the Lady Wildcats*. New York: Henry Holt and Co., 1927.

Allen, Dr. William A. *Adventures with Indians and Game, or Twenty Years in the Rocky Mountains*. Chicago: A. W. Bowen & Co., 1903.

Anderson, A. A. *Experiences and Impressions: The Autobiography of Colonel A. A. Anderson*. New York: Macmillan Co., 1933.

Andreas, A. T. *Andrea's Historical Atlas of Dakota*. Chicago: R. R. Donnelley & Sons, 1884.

Armitage, Susan, and Elizabeth Jameson, eds. *The Women's West*. Norman: University of Oklahoma Press, 1987.

Athearn, Robert G. *High Country Empire: The High Plains and Rockies*. New York: McGraw-Hill Book Co., 1960.

Baber, D. F., and Bill Walker. *The Longest Rope: The Truth about the Johnson County War*. Caldwell, Idaho: Caxton Printers, 1940.

Bakken, Stephen C. *The Bet On It! Book of South Dakota Trivia*. Sioux Falls, S.Dak.: Ex Machina Publishing Co., 1992.

Bankson, Russell A. *The Klondike Nugget*. Caldwell, Idaho: Caxton Printers, 1935.

Beebe, Lucius, and Charles Clegg. *The American West: The Pictorial Epic of a Continent*. New York: E. P. Dutton & Co., 1955.

Beebe, Ruth. *Reminiscing along the Sweetwater.* Boulder, Colo.: Johnson Printing Co., 1973.

Bellamy, Paul E., and G. D. Seymour. *A Guide to the Black Hills.* N.p.: Black Hills Transportation Co., 1927.

Bennett, Edwin Lewis. *Boom Town Boy in Old Creede, Colorado.* Chicago: Sage Books, 1966.

Bennett, Estelline. *Old Deadwood Days.* New York: J. H. Sears & Co., 1928.

Berton, Pierre. *The Klondike Fever: The Life and Death of the Last Great Gold Rush.* New York: Alfred A. Knopf, 1958.

———. *Klondike: The Last Great Gold Rush, 1896–1899.* Rev. ed. Toronto: McClelland and Stewart, 1972.

Black, A. P. (Ott). *The End of the Long Horn Trail.* Selfridge, N.Dak.: Selfridge Journal, n.d.

Black Hills Pictured History. Deadwood Souvenir Edition, 1905. Lead, S.Dak.: Lead Daily Call, [1905].

Blake, Herbert Cody. *Blake's Western Stories.* Brooklyn, N.Y.: by the author, 1929.

Botkin, B. A., ed. *A Treasury of Western Folklore.* New York: Crown Publishers, 1951.

Bourke, John G. *On the Border with Crook.* New York: Charles Scribner's Sons, 1891.

Bracke, William B. *Wheat Country.* New York: Duell, Sloan & Pearce, 1950.

Bridgwater, William, and Elizabeth J. Sherwood, eds. *The Columbia Encyclopedia.* Vol. 1, 2d ed. New York: Columbia University Press, 1958.

Bridwell, J. W. *The Life and Adventures of Robert McKimie, Alias "Little Reddy," from Texas, The Dare-Devil Desperado of the Black Hills Region, Chief of the Murderous Band of Treasure Coach Robbers.* 1878. Reprint, Houston: Frontier Press of Texas, 1955.

Briggs, Harold E. *Frontiers of the Northwest: A History of the Upper Missouri Valley.* 1940. Reprint, New York: Peter Smith, 1950.

Brininstool, E. A. *Fighting Red Cloud's Warriors: True Tales of Indian Days When the West Was Young.* 1926. Reprint, *Fighting Indian Warriors: True Tales of the Wild Frontiers.* Harrisburg, Pa.: Stackpole Co., 1953.

Brown, Dee. *The Gentle Tamers: Women of the Old Wild West.* New York: G. P. Putnam's Sons, 1958.

Brown, Jesse, and A. M. Willard. *The Black Hills Trails: A History of the Struggles of the Pioneers in the Winning of the Black Hills.* Edited by John T. Milek. Rapid City, S.Dak.: Rapid City Journal Company, 1924.

Brown, Larry K. *The Hog Ranches of Wyoming: Liquor, Lust, and Lies Under Sagebrush Skies.* Glendo, Wyo.: High Plains Press, 1995.

Brown, Mark H. *The Plainsmen of the Yellowstone: A History of the Yellowstone Basin.* New York: G. P. Putnam's Sons, 1961.

Brown, Mark H., and W. R. Felton. *Before Barbed Wire: L. A. Huffman, Photographer on Horseback.* New York: Henry Holt and Co., 1956.

———. *The Frontier Years: L. A. Huffman, Photographer of the Plains.* New York: Henry Holt and Co., 1955.

Brown, Thomas Henderson. *The Romance of Everyday Life.* Mitchell, S.Dak.: Educator Supply Co., 1923.

Brownlow, Kevin. *The War, The West, and The Wilderness.* New York: Alfred A. Knopf, 1979.

Burt, Struthers. *Powder River, Let 'er Buck.* New York: Rinehart & Co., 1938.

Buscombe, Edward, ed. *The BFI Companion to the Western.* New York: Atheneum, 1988.

Butler, Anne M. *Daughters of Joy, Sisters of Misery: Prostitutes in the American West, 1865–90.* Urbana: University of Illinois Press, 1985.

Bye, John O. *Back Trailing in the Heart of the Short-Grass Country.* Everett, Wash.: Alexander Printing Co., 1956.

Calamity Jane's Letters to Her Daughter, Martha Jane Cannary Hickok. Lorenzo, Calif.: Shameless Hussy Press, 1976.

[Canary, Martha]. *Life and Adventures of Calamity Jane, By Herself.* N.p.: [1896].

Carter, Captain Robert G. *The Old Sergeant's Story, Fighting Indians and Bad Men in Texas from 1870 to 1876.* 1926. Reprint, Bryan, Tex.: J. M. Carroll & Company, 1982.

Case, Lee. *Lee's Official Guide Book to the Black Hills and the Badlands.* Sturgis, S.Dak.: Black Hills and Badlands Association, 1949.

Case, Leland D. *Preacher Smith, Martyr.* Rev. ed. Mitchell, S.Dak.: Friends of the Middle Border, 1961.

Casey, Robert J. *The Black Hills and Their Incredible Characters.* Indianapolis: Bobbs-Merrill Co., 1949.

———. *The Texas Border and Some Borderliners.* Indianapolis: Bobbs-Merrill Co., 1950.

Chapin, Charles. *Charles Chapin's Story Written in Sing Sing Prison.* New York: G. P. Putnam's Sons, 1920.

Chatterton, Fenimore C. *Yesterday's Wyoming: The Intimate Memoirs of Fenimore C. Chatterton, Territorial Citizen, Governor and Statesman.* Aurora, Colo.: Powder River Publishers, 1957.

Chilton, Charles. *The Book of the West: An Epic of America's Wild Frontier—and the Men Who Created Its Legends.* Indianapolis: Bobbs-Merrill Co., 1962.

Clairmonte, Glenn. *Calamity Was the Name for Jane.* Denver: Sage Books, 1959.

Cole, Judd. *Wild Bill: Dead Man's Hand.* New York: Leisure Books, 1999.

———. *Wild Bill: Santa Fe Death Trap.* New York: Leisure Books, 2000.

Conley, Georgene. *Cowboy Poetry.* N.p.: n.d.

Connelley, William Elsey. *Wild Bill and His Era: The Life and Adventures of James Butler Hickok.* New York: Press of the Pioneers, 1933.

Copies of Calamity Jane's Diary and Letters. N.p.: Don C. and Stella A. Foote, 1951.

Coursey, O. W. *Beautiful Black Hills.* Mitchell, S.Dak.: Educator Supply Co., 1926.

Crawford, Captain Jack. *The Poet Scout: Being a Selection of Incidental and Illustrative Verses and Songs.* San Francisco: H. Keller & Co., 1879.

Crawford, Lewis F. *Rekindling Camp Fires: The Exploits of Ben Arnold (Connor). An Authentic Narrative of Sixty Years in the Old West as Indian Fighter, Gold Miner, Cowboy, Hunter, and Army Scout.* Bismarck, N.Dak.: Capital Book Co., 1926.

[Crawford, Thomas Edgar]. *The West of the Texas Kid, 1881–1910: Recollections of Thomas Edgar Crawford, Cowboy, Gun Fighter, Rancher, Hunter, Miner.* Edited by Jeff C. Dykes. Norman: University of Oklahoma Press, 1962.

Crofutt, George A. *Crofutt's Trans-Continental Tourist's Guide.* Rev. ed. [New York: American News Co.], 1871.

Croy, Homer. *Jesse James Was My Neighbor.* New York: Duell, Sloan and Pearce, 1949.

Crutchfield, James, Bill O'Neil, and Dale L. Walker. *Legends of the Wild West.* Lincolnwood, Ill.: Publications International, 1995.

Cunningham, Eugene. *Triggernometry: A Gallery of Gunfighters.* Caldwell, Idaho: Caxton Printers, 1941.

David, Gary. *A Log of Deadwood: A Postmodern Epic of the South Dakota Gold Rush.* Berkeley, Calif.: North Atlantic Books, 1993.

DeBarthe, Joe, ed. *The Life and Adventures of Frank Grouard.* St. Joseph, Mo.: Combe Printing Company, 1894.

[DeMille, Cecil B.]. *The Autobiography of Cecil B. DeMille.* Edited by Donald Hayne. Englewood Cliffs, N.J.: Prentice-Hall, 1959.

Dexter, Pete. *Deadwood.* New York: Random House, 1986.

Dial, Scott. *A Place to Raise Hell: Cheyenne Saloons.* Boulder, Colo.: Johnson Publishing Company, 1977.

Dimsdale, Thomas J. *The Vigilantes of Montana, or Popular Justice in the Rocky Mountains.* 1866. Reprint, Norman: University of Oklahoma Press, 1953.

Dixon, Dorothy. *Yellowstone Jewel: Leather and Lace # 9.* New York: Zebra Books, 1983.

Drago, Harry Sinclair. *Notorious Ladies of the Frontier.* New York: Dodd, Mead & Co., 1969.

————. *Road Agents and Train Robbers: Half a Century of Western Banditry.* New York: Dodd, Mead & Co., 1973.

Du Fran, Dora. [D. Dee, pseud.]. *Low Down on Calamity Jane.* Rapid City, S.Dak.: n.p., 1932.

Dunlap, Patricia Riley. *Riding Astride: The Frontier in Women's History.* Denver, Colo.: Arden Press, 1955.

Dunlop, Richard. *Doctors of the American Frontier.* Garden City, N.Y.: Doubleday & Co., 1965.

Duratschek, Sister M. Claudia. *Builders of God's Kingdom: The History of the Catholic Church in South Dakota.* Yankton, S.Dak.: Benedictine Sisters of Sacred Heart Convent, 1985.

Durham, Philip, and Everett L. Jones. *The Negro Cowboys.* New York: Dodd, Mead & Co., 1965.

Edson, J. T. *The Bull Whip Breed.* London: Corgi Books, 1968.

————. *The Cow Thieves.* London: Transworld Publishing, 1968.

————. *Cut One, They All Bleed.* New York: Charter Books, 1988.

————. *Texas Trio.* New York: Charter Books, 1989.

————. *White Stallion, Red Mare.* London: Transworld Publishing, 1970.

Eisele, Wilbert E. *The Real Wild Bill Hickok: Famous Scout and Knight Chivalric of the Plains—A True Story of Pioneer Life in the West.* Denver, Colo.: William H. Andre, 1931.

El Comancho. [Walter Shelley Phillips]. *The Old-Timer's Tale.* Chicago: Canterbury Press, 1929.

Elston, Allan Vaughan. *Treasure Coach from Deadwood.* Philadelphia: J. B. Lippincott Co., 1962.

Engebretson, Doug. *Empty Saddles, Forgotten Names: Outlaws of the Black Hills and Wyoming.* Aberdeen, S.Dak.: North Plains Press, 1982.

Erskine, Gladys Shaw. *Broncho Charlie: A Saga of the Saddle. The Life Story of Broncho Charlie Miller, The Last of the Pony Express Riders.* New York: Thomas Y. Crowell Co., 1934.

Etulain, Richard W. *Telling Western Stories: From Buffalo Bill to Larry McMurtry*. Albuquerque: University of New Mexico Press, 1999.

Evans, Tabor. *Longarm in Deadwood*. New York: Jove Books, 1982.

Faber, Doris. *Calamity Jane: Her Life and Her Legend*. Boston: Houghton Mifflin Co., 1992.

Faragher, John Mack. *Women and Men on the Overland Trail*. New Haven: Yale University Press, 1979.

Feitz, Leland. *A Quick History of Creede: Colorado Boom Town*. Colorado Springs: Little London Press, 1969.

Fielder, Mildred. *Deadwood Dick and the Dime Novels*. Lead, S.Dak.: Bonanza Trails Publishers, 1974.

———. *Silver Is the Fortune*. Aberdeen, S.Dak.: North Plains Press, 1978.

———. *Wild Bill and Deadwood*. Seattle: Superior Publishing Co., 1965.

Finerty, John F. *War-Path and Bivouac: The Conquest of the Sioux*. Chicago: Donohue & Henneberry, 1890.

Flanagan, Mike. *Out West*. New York: Harry N. Abrams, 1987.

Flannery, L. G. (Pat), ed. *John Hunton's Diary 1876–'77*. Vol. 2. Lingle, Wyo.: Guide-Review, 1958.

———. *John Hunton's Diary, 1878–'79*. Vol. 3. Lingle, Wyo.: Guide-Review, 1960.

———. *John Hunton's Diary, Wyoming Territory, 1885–1889*. Vol. 6. Glendale, Calif.: Arthur H. Clark Co., 1970.

Fontes, Ron, and Korman, Justine. *Calamity Jane at Fort Sanders: A Historical Novel*. New York: Disney Press, 1992.

Foote, Stella. *A History of Calamity Jane: America's First Liberated Woman*. New York: Vantage Press, 1995.

Frackelton, Dr. Will. *Sagebrush Dentist*. Edited by Herman Gastrell Seely. Chicago: A. C. McClurg & Co., 1941.

Freeman, Lewis R. *Down the Yellowstone*. New York: Dodd, Mead and Co., 1922.

Friggins, Paul. *Gold and Grass: The Black Hills Story*. Boulder, Colo.: Pruett Publishing Co., 1983.

Frye, Elnora L. *Atlas of Wyoming Outlaws at the Territorial Penitentiary*. Laramie, Wyo.: Jelm Mountain Publications, 1990.

Gilbert, Douglas. *American Vaudeville: Its Life and Times*. 1940. Reprint, New York: Dover Publications, 1968.

Gilfillan, Archer B. *A Goat's Eye View of the Black Hills*. Rapid City, S.Dak.: Dean & Dean, Publishers, 1953.

Gordon, Samuel. *Recollections of Old Milestown*. 1918. Reprint, North St. Paul, Minnesota: Ken Crawford—Books, 1985.

The Great Northwest: A Guide-Book and Itinerary for the Use of Tourists and Travelers Over the Lines of the Northern Pacific Railroad. St. Paul: Northern News Co., 1888.

Green, Abel, and Joe Laurie, Jr. *Show Biz, from Vaude to Video*. New York: Henry Holt and Co., 1951.

Green, Charles P. (Soldier). *Ballads of the Black Hills*. Boston: Christopher Publishing House, 1931.

Greene, Jerome A. *Nez Perce Summer 1877. The U.S. Army and the Nee-Me-Poo Crisis*. Helena: Montana Historical Society Press, 2000.

Gregory, Lester. *True Wild West Stories.* London: Andrew Dukers, n.d.

Haines, Aubrey L. *The Yellowstone Story: The History of Our First National Park.* 2 vols. Yellowstone Park, Wyo.: Yellowstone Library & Museum Association, 1977.

Hamilton, Charles. *The Signature of America: A Fresh Look at Famous Handwriting.* New York: Harper & Row, 1979.

Hanson, Joseph Mills. *South Dakota in the World War, 1917–1919.* [Pierre]: South Dakota State Historical Society, 1940.

Hargens, C. W. *Black Hills Doc, 1892–1945: A History of Pioneer Medical Practice in the Southern Black Hills.* Rapid City, S.Dak.: Grelind Printing Center, 1990.

Hart, William S., and Mary E. Hart. *—And All Points West!* N.p.: Lacotah Press, 1940.

Havighurst, Walter. *Wilderness for Sale: The Story of the First Western Land Rush.* New York: Hastings House, 1956.

Hill, Richmond C. *A Great White Indian Chief: Thrilling and Romantic Story of the Remarkable Career, Extraordinary Experiences Hunting, Scouting and Indian Adventures of Col. Fred Cummins, "Chief La-Ko-Ta."* N.p.: Col. Fred T. Cummins, 1912.

History of the Union Pacific Coal Mines 1868 to 1940. Omaha, Nebr.: Colonial Press, 1940.

Holbrook, Stewart H. *Little Annie Oakley and Other Rugged People.* New York: Macmillan Co., 1948.

Holmes, Burton. *Burton Holmes Travelogues, with Illustrations from Photographs By the Author.* Vol. 6. New York: McClure Co., 1901.

Holmes, Mary Jane. *Cousin Maude and Rosamond.* New York: G. W. Dillingham, 1888.

———. *Edith Lyle.* New York: G. W. Dillingham, 1876.

———. *Madeline.* New York: G. W. Carleton & Co., 1881.

———. *Marian Grey.* Chicago: M. A. Donohue & Co., n.d.

———. *Meadow Brook.* New York: Federal Book Co., n.d.

———. *Mildred; or, The Child of Adoption.* Chicago: M. S. Donohue & Co., n.d.

———. *Tempest and Sunshine.* New York: J. H. Sears & Co., n.d.

Homsher, Lola M., ed. *South Pass, 1868: James Chisholm's Journal of the Wyoming Gold Rush.* Lincoln: Nebraska State Historical Society, 1960.

Hooker, William Francis. *The Bullwhacker: Adventures of a Frontier Freighter.* Yonkers-on-Hudson, N.Y.: World Book Co., 1924.

Horan, James D. *Desperate Women.* New York: G. P. Putnam's Sons, 1952.

———, and Paul Sann. *Pictorial History of the Wild West: A True Account of the Bad Men, Desperadoes, Rustlers and Outlaws of the Old West—And the Men Who Fought Them to Establish Law and Order.* New York: Crown Publishers, 1954.

Hotchner, A. E. *Doris Day: Her Own Story.* New York: William Morrow and Co., 1976.

Howe, F. S. *Deadwood Doctor.* N.p.: n.d.

Howe, Henry. *Historical Collections of Ohio in Two Volumes: An Encyclopedia of the State.* Vol. 2. 1888. Reprint, Cincinnati: C. J. Kerhbiel & Co., 1907.

Hoyt, Henry F. *A Frontier Doctor.* Boston: Houghton Mifflin Co., 1929.

Hueston, Ethel. *Calamity Jane of Deadwood Gulch.* Indianapolis: Bobbs-Merrill Co., 1937.

Hughes, Richard B. *Pioneer Years in the Black Hills.* Edited by Agnes Wright Spring. Glendale, Calif.: Arthur H. Clark Co., 1957.

Hunter, J. Marvin, and Noah H. Rose. *The Album of Gun-Fighters.* N.p.: by the authors, 1951.

Huntington, Bill. *Both Feet in the Stirrups.* Billings, Mont.: Western Livestock Reporter Press, 1959.

————. *They Were Good Men and Salty Cusses.* Billings, Mont.: Western Livestock Reporter, 1952.

Hutchens, John K. *One Man's Montana: An Informal Portrait of a State.* Philadelphia: J. B. Lippincott, 1964.

Ihle, Sharon. *Wildcat.* New York; HarperPaperbacks, 1993.

Jackson, Donald. *Custer's Gold: The United States Cavalry Expedition of 1874.* New Haven: Yale University Press, 1964.

Jackson, R. J. *Memory's Trail.* N.p. [1953].

Jennewein, J. Leonard. *Calamity Jane of the Western Trails.* Huron, S.Dak.: Dakota Books, 1953.

Jensen, Delwin. *Fort Pierre—Deadwood Trail: Route to the Gold Fields of the Black Hills.* Pierre, S.Dak.: State Publishing Co., 1989.

Johannsen, Albert. *The House of Beadle and Adams and Its Dime and Nickel Novels: The Story of a Vanished Literature.* Norman: University of Oklahoma Press, 1950.

Johnston, Harry V. *The Last Roundup.* Minneapolis: H. V. Johnston Publishing Co., n.d.

————. *My Home on the Range: Frontier Ranching in the Bad Lands.* Saint Paul, Minn.: Webb Publishing Co., 1942.

Jones, Daryl. *The Dime Novel Western.* Bowling Green, Ohio: Popular Press, 1978.

Kafaroff, Bruce. *Deadwood Gulch.* New York: Alfred A. Knopf, 1941.

Karolevitz, Robert F. *Doctors of the Old West: A Pictorial History of Medicine on the Frontier.* Seattle: Superior Publishing Co., 1967.

Karson, Terry. *L. A. Huffman, Pioneer Photographer.* Billings, Mont.: Yellowstone Art Center, 1990.

Kime, Wayne R., ed. *The Black Hills Journals of Colonel Richard Irving Dodge.* Norman: University of Oklahoma Press, 1996.

Kirk, Murray Ketcham. *The Beacon Light and Other Poems.* New York: Harold Vinal, 1927.

Klock, Irma H. *All Roads Lead to Deadwood.* Lead, S.Dak.: by the author, 1979.

————. *Here Comes Calamity Jane.* Deadwood, S.Dak.: Dakota Graphics, 1979.

————. *Yesterday's Gold Camps and Mines in the Northern Black Hills.* Lead, S.Dak.: Seaton Publishing Co., 1975.

Knight, Oliver. *Following the Indian Wars: The Story of the Newspaper Correspondents among the Indian Campaigners.* Norman: University of Oklahoma Press, 1960.

Kuykendall, Judge W. L. *Frontier Days: A True Narrative of Striking Events on the Western Frontier.* N.p.: J. M. and H. L. Kuykendall, Publishers, 1917.

Lackmann, Ron. *Women of the Western Frontier in Fact, Fiction and Film.* Jefferson, N.C.: McFarland & Co., 1997.

Lake, A. I. *Women of the West.* Vero Beach, Fla.: Rourke Publications, 1990.

Lamar, Howard Roberts, ed. *The Reader's Encyclopedia of the American West.* New York: Harper & Row, 1977.

Larson, T. A. *Bill Nye's Western Humor.* Lincoln: University of Nebraska Press, 1968.

————. *History of Wyoming.* Lincoln: University of Nebraska Press, 1965.

Laurie, Joe, Jr. *Vaudeville: From the Honky-Tonks to the Palace.* New York: Henry Holt and Co., 1953.

Lawrence County Historical Society. *Some History of Lawrence County.* Pierre, S.Dak.: State Publishing Co., 1981.

Lee, Bob. *Fort Meade and the Black Hills.* Lincoln: University of Nebraska Press, 1991.

————, ed. *Gold–Gals–Guns–Guts.* N.p.: Deadwood-Lead '76 Centennial, 1976.

Lee, Wayne C. *Wild Towns of Nebraska.* Caldwell, Idaho: Caxton Printers, 1988.

Leedy, Carl H. *Golden Days in the Black Hills.* Rapid City, S.Dak.: Holmgren's, 1961.

Levenson, Dorothy. *Women of the West.* New York: Franklin Watts, 1973.

Linn, Mary C. *Linn's 1976 History of Mercer County, Missouri.* N.p.: [1976].

Lloyd, Dave. *Pardners: A Tale of Eastern Montana in the 1880s.* Miles City, Mont.: H & T Quality Printing, 1989.

Logan, Jake. *Dead Man's Hand.* New York: Playboy Paperbacks, 1979.

Lynde, Sidne, and Stan Lynde. *Calamity Jane: Queen of the Plains.* Billings, Mont.: Montanacrafts and Rimrock Publishing Co., 1975.

Lyon, Peter. *The Wild, Wild West.* New York: Funk and Wagnalls, 1969.

Maguire, H. N. *The Black Hills and American Wonderland.* Chicago: Donnelley, Lloyd and Company, 1877.

————. *The Coming Empire. A Complete and Reliable Treatise on the Black Hills, Yellowstone and Big Horn Regions.* Sioux City, Iowa: Watkins & Smead, 1878.

Mancini, Richard. *American Legends of the Wild West.* Philadelphia: Courage Books, 1992.

Mandat-Grancey, Le Baron E. de. *Buffalo Gap: A French Ranch in Dakota: 1887.* Hermosa, S.Dak.: Lame Johnny Press, 1981.

Mangum, Neil. *Battle of the Rosebud: Prelude to the Little Bighorn.* El Segundo, Calif.: Upton & Sons, 1987.

Marshall, Jim. *Swinging Doors.* Seattle: Frank McCaffrey, 1949.

Mautz, Carl. *Biographies of Western Photographers: A Reference Guide to Photographers Working in the 19th Century West.* Nevada City, Calif.: Carl Mautz Publishing, 1997.

Mazzulla, Fred and Jo. *Outlaw Album.* Denver, Colo.: A. B. Hirschfield Press, 1966.

McAllister, Laura Kirley. *Gumbo Trails.* N.p.: n.d.

McCarty, Lea F. *The Gunfighters.* Berkeley, Calif.: Mike Roberts Color Productions, 1959.

McClintock, John S. *Pioneer Days in the Black Hills: Accurate History and Facts Related by One of the Early Day Pioneers.* Edited by Edward L. Senn. Deadwood, S.Dak.: by the author, 1939.

McCreight, M. I. *Firewater and Forked Tongues: A Sioux Chief Interprets U.S. History.* Pasadena, Calif.: Trail's End Publishing Co., 1947.

McGillycuddy, Julia B. *McGillycuddy Agent: A Biography of Dr. Valentine T. McGillycuddy.* Stanford University, Calif.: Stanford University Press, 1941.

McKelvie, Martha Groves. *The Hills of Yesterday.* Philadelphia: Dorrance & Co., 1960.

McKeown, Martha Ferguson. *Them Was the Days: An American Saga of the '70s*. New York: Macmillan Co., 1950.

McLoughlin, Denis. *Wild and Woolly: An Encyclopedia of the Old West*. Garden City, N.Y.: Doubleday & Co., 1975.

McMurtry, Larry. *Buffalo Girls*. New York: Simon and Schuster, 1990.

McNeil, Marianne McFarland. *Echoes from the Black Hills*. Amarillo, Tex.: Eagle Print, 1984.

McPherren, Ida. *Empire Builders. A History of the Founding of Sheridan*. Sheridan, Wyo.: Star Publishing Co., 1942.

————. *Imprints on Pioneer Trails*. Boston: Christopher Publishing House, 1950.

Mercer County Pioneer-Traces. Princeton, Mo.: Mercer County Geneological Society, 1997.

Miers, Earl Schenck. *Wild and Woolly West*. Chicago: Rand McNally & Co., 1964.

Miller, Darlis A. *Captain Jack Crawford: Buckskin Poet, Scout, and Showman*. Albuquerque: University of New Mexico Press, 1993.

Miller, Ronald Dean. *Shady Ladies of the West*. Tucson, Ariz.: Westernlore Press, 1964.

Mills, Anson. *Big Horn Expedition, August 15 to September 30, 1874*. N.p., n.d.

————. *My Story*. Edited by C. H. Claudy. Washington, D.C.: Byron S. Adams, 1918.

Milner, Joe E., and Earle R. Forrest. *California Joe, Noted Scout and Indian Fighter*. Caldwell, Idaho: Caxton Printers, 1935.

Missouri: A Guide to the "Show Me" State. Compiled by Workers of the Writers' Program of the Works Projects Administration in the State of Missouri. New York: Duell, Sloan and Pearce, 1941.

Mitchum, Hank. *Stagecoach Station 11: Deadwood*. New York: Bantam Books, 1984.

Mokler, Alfred James. *History of Natrona County, Wyoming, 1888–1922*. Chicago: R. R. Donnelley & Sons, 1923.

Montana: A State Guide Book. Compiled and Written by the Federal Writers' Project of the Works Projects Administration for the State of Montana. New York: Viking Press, 1939.

Morecamp, Arthur. *Live Boys in the Black Hills; or, The Young Texan Gold Hunters*. Boston: Lee and Shepard, 1880.

Morgan, Lael. *Good Time Girls of the Alaska-Yukon Gold Rush*. Fairbanks: Epicenter Press, 1998.

Mueller, Ellen Crago. *Calamity Jane*. Laramie: Jelm Mt. Press, 1981.

Mueller, John Theodore. *Heroes of the Black Hills: A Tale of the Conquest of the Black Hills in 1876*. Columbus, Ohio: Book Concern, [1934].

Mullins, Reuben B. *Pulling Leather: Being the Early Recollections of a Cowboy on the Wyoming Range, 1884–1889*. Edited by Jan Roush and Lawrence Clayton. Glendo, Wyo.: High Plains Press, 1988.

Mumey, Nolie. *Calamity Jane, 1852–1903: A History of Her Life and Adventures in the West*. Denver: Range Press, 1950.

Murray, Robert A. *Miner's Delight, Investor's Despair*. Sheridan, Wyo.: Piney Creek Press, 1972.

Myers, Carol. *Montana: Where My Treasure Is*. Billings, Mont.: Western Litho-Print, 1964.

Myres, Sandra L. *Westering Women and the Frontier Experience, 1800–1915*. Albuquerque: University of New Mexico Press, 1982.

Nash, Jay Robert. *Encyclopedia of Western Lawmen and Outlaws.* New York: Paragon House, 1992.

Nebraska: A Guide to the Cornhusker State. Compiled by the Federal Writers' Project of the Works Progress Administration for the State of Nebraska. New York: Viking Press, 1939.

Nelson, Bruce. *Land of the Dacotahs.* Minneapolis: University of Minnesota Press, 1946.

Nelson, Dick. *Only a Cow Country at One Time—Wyoming Counties of Crook, Weston, and Campbell 1875 to 1951.* San Diego, Calif.: Pioneer Printers, 1951.

Nelson, Larry C. *The Hills Aren't Black.* Hermosa, S.Dak.: Lame Johnny Press, 1980.

———. *Soft Voices: Poetry of the Black Hills.* Hermosa, S.Dak.: Lame Johnny Press, 1980.

Newson, Thomas McLean. *Drama of Life in the Black Hills.* Saint Paul: Dodge & Larpenteur, 1878.

O'Connor, Richard. *Wild Bill Hickok.* Garden City, N.Y.: Doubleday & Co., 1959.

Oller, John. *Jean Arthur: The Actress Nobody Knew.* New York: Limelight Editions, 1977.

Orestad, Helen Brewer. *He Named It Powderville.* N.p., 1994.

Otero, Miguel Antonio. *My Life on the Frontier, 1864-1882: Incidents and Characters of the Period When Kansas, Colorado, and New Mexico Were Passing Through the Last of Their Wild and Romantic Years.* New York: Press of the Pioneers, 1935.

Owens, Harry J. *Characters of the Past.* Red Lodge, Mont.: by the author, 1989.

Parker, Watson. *Deadwood: The Golden Years.* Lincoln: University of Nebraska Press, 1981.

———. *Gold in the Black Hills.* Norman: University of Oklahoma Press, 1966.

Patrick, Lucille Nichols. *The Best Little Town by a Dam Site, or, Cody's First Twenty Years.* Cody, Wyo.: by the author, 1968.

Paul, Rodman Wilson. *Mining Frontiers of the Far West, 1848–1880.* New York: Holt, Rinehart and Winston, 1963.

Peavy, Linda, and Ursula Smith. *Pioneer Women: The Lives of Women on the Frontier.* New York: Smithmark Publishers, 1996.

Pence, Mary Lou, and Lola M. Homsher. *The Ghost Towns of Wyoming.* New York: Hastings House, 1956.

Peterson, P. D. *Through the Black Hills and Bad Lands of South Dakota.* Pierre, S.Dak.: J. Fred Olander Co., 1929.

Pioneer Footprints. Belle Fourche, S.Dak.: Black Hills Century Club, 1964.

Price, S. Goodale. *Black Hills: The Land of Legend.* Los Angeles: DeVorss & Co., 1935.

———. *Ghosts of Golconda: A Guide Book to Historical Characters and Locations in the Black Hills of Western South Dakota.* Deadwood, S.Dak.: Western Publishers, 1952.

———. *Saga of the Hills.* Hollywood, Calif.: Cosmo Press, 1940.

———. *Smoke Signals over the Dakotas.* Deadwood, S.Dak.: Seaton Publishing Co., 1960.

Progressive Men of the State of Wyoming. Chicago: A. W. Bowen & Co., 1903.

Quiett, Glenn Chesney. *Pay Dirt: A Panorama of American Gold-Rushes.* 1936. Reprint, Lincoln, Nebr.: Johnsen Publishing Co., 1971.

Randall, Leslie Watson (Gay). *Footprints along the Yellowstone.* San Antonio, Tex.: Naylor Co., 1961.

Ray, Grace Ernestine. *Wily Women of the West.* San Antonio, Tex.: Naylor Co., 1972.

Regli, Adolph. *Fiddling Cowboy in Search of Gold.* New York: Franklin Watts, 1951.

Reneau, Susan C. *The Adventures of Moccasin Joe: The True Life Story of Sgt. George S. Howard.* Missoula, Mont.: Blue Mountain Publishing, 1994.

A Reprint of the Original 1888 History of Harrison and Mercer Counties, Missouri, First Published by the Goodspeed Publishing Co., St. Louis and Chicago, February 1888. Princeton, Mo.: Mercer County Historical Society, 1972.

Rezatto, Helen Graham. *Mount Moriah: "Kill a Man—Start a Cemetery".* Aberdeen, S.Dak.: North Plains Press, 1980.

———. *Tales of the Black Hills.* Aberdeen, S.Dak.: North Plains Press, 1983.

Riegel, Robert E. *America Moves West.* Rev. ed. New York: Henry Holt and Co., 1951.

———. *America Moves West.* 3d ed. New York: Henry Holt and Co., 1956.

———, and Robert G. Athearn. *America Moves West.* 4th ed. New York: Holt, Rinehart and Winston, 1964.

Roberts, J. R. *The Gunsmith 146: Return to Deadwood.* New York: Jove Books, 1994.

Robertson, Frank C., and Beth Kay Harris. *Soapy Smith: King of the Frontier Con Men.* New York: Hastings House, 1961.

Robinson, Charles M. III, ed. *The Diaries of John Gregory Bourke.* Volume One, November 20, 1872–July 28, 1876. Denton, Tex.: University of North Texas Press, 2003.

Robinson, Doane. *Encyclopedia of South Dakota.* Pierre: by the author, 1925.

———. *History of South Dakota.* 2 vols. Chicago: B. F. Bowen & Co., 1904.

Robinson, Gillian. *The Slow Reign of Calamity Jane.* Kingston, Ontario: Quarry Press, 1994.

Rogers, Cameron. *Gallant Ladies.* New York: Harcourt, Brace and Co., 1928.

Rogers' Souvenir History of Mercer County, Missouri, and Dictionary of Local Dates. Trenton, Mo.: W. B. Rogers Printing Co., 1911.

Rosa, Joseph G. *Jack McCall, Assassin: An Updated Account of His Yankton Trial, Plea for Clemency, and Execution.* N.p.: English Westerners Society, 1998.

———. *They Called Him Wild Bill: The Life and Adventures of James Butler Hickok.* Rev. ed. Norman: University of Oklahoma Press, 1974.

———. *Wild Bill Hickok: The Man and His Myth.* Lawrence: University Press of Kansas, 1996.

Rosen, Rev. Peter. *Pa-Ha-Sa-Pah, or The Black Hills of South Dakota. A Complete History.* St. Louis: Nixon-Jones Printing Co., 1895.

Ross, Nancy Wilson. *Westward the Women.* New York: Alfred A. Knopf, 1944.

Russell, Don. *The Lives and Legends of Buffalo Bill.* Norman: University of Oklahoma Press, 1960.

Ryan, Ed. *Me and the Black Hills—By The Old Prospector, Man Mountain Ed Ryan.* Custer, S.Dak.: by the author, 1951.

Sabin, Edwin L. *Wild Men of the Wild West.* New York: Thomas Y. Crowell Co., 1929.

Sandoz, Mari. *Love Song to the Plains.* New York: Harper & Brothers, 1961.

———. *Miss Morissa: Doctor of the Gold Trail.* New York: McGraw-Hill Book Co., 1955.

Schatz, August H. *Longhorns Bring Culture.* Boston: Christopher Publishing House, 1961.

Schell, Herbert S. *History of South Dakota.* Lincoln: University of Nebraska Press, 1961.

Scheuer, Steven H., ed. *TV Key Movie Guide.* New York: Bantam Books, 1966.

Schmitt, Martin F., and Dee Brown. *The Settlers' West.* New York: Charles Scribner's Sons, 1955.

Schuler, Harold H. *A Bridge Apart: History of Early Pierre and Fort Pierre.* Pierre, S.Dak.: State Publishing Co., 1987.

Scott, George W. *The Black Hills Story.* Ft. Collins, Colo.: by the author, 1953.

Secrest, William B., ed. *I Buried Hickok: The Memoirs of White Eye Anderson.* College Station, Tex.: Creative Publishing Co., 1980.

Senn, Edward L. *"Deadwood Dick" and "Calamity Jane": A Thorough Sifting of Facts from Fiction.* Deadwood, S.Dak.: by the author, 1939.

———. *"Preacher Smith," Martyr of the Cross.* Deadwood, S.Dak.: by the author, 1939.

Settle, Raymond W., and Mary Lund Settle, eds. *Overland Days to Montana in 1865: The Diary of Sarah Raymond and Journal of Dr. Waid Howard.* Glendale, Calif.: Arthur H. Clark Co., 1971.

Shadley, Ruth. *Calamity Jane's Daughter: The Story of Maude Wier, A Story Never Before Told.* Caldwell, Idaho: Caxton Printers, 1996.

Sherlock, James L. *South Pass and Its Tales.* New York: Vantage Press, 1978.

Shifting Scenes: A History of Carter County, Montana. Ekalaka, Mont.: Carter County Geological Society, 1978.

Slack, Norma. *Calamity Jane Builds a Cabin.* Laramie, Wyo.: Calamity Jane Enterpises, 1992.

———. *Calamity Jane's Cantankerous Reputation.* Laramie, Wyo.: Calamity Jane Enterprises, 1992.

———. *The Capture of Calamity Jane's Heart.* Laramie, Wyo.: Calamity Jane Enterprises, 1992.

———. *How I Became Known as Calamity Jane.* Laramie, Wyo.: Calamity Jane Enterprises, 1992.

———. *Westward Journey of the Canary Family.* Laramie, Wyo.: Calamity Jane Enterprises, 1992.

Smith, Henry Nash. *Virgin Land: The American West as Symbol and Myth.* Cambridge: Harvard University Press, 1950.

Sochen, June. *Herstory: A Woman's View of American History.* New York: Alfred Publishers, 1974.

Sollid, Roberta Beed. *Calamity Jane: A Study in Historical Criticism.* [Helena]: Historical Society of Montana, 1958.

A South Dakota Guide. Compiled by The Federal Writers' Project of the Works Progress Administration, State of South Dakota. Pierre: South Dakota Guide Commission, 1938.

Souvenir Edition of the 59th Annual Stock Growers Convention, Fort Pierre, South Dakota, June 1–2–3, 1950. N.p.: Fort Pierre Verendrye Benevolent Association, [1950].

Spencer, William Loring. *Calamity Jane: A Story of the Black Hills.* 1887. Reprint, Mitchell, S.Dak.: Dakota Wesleyan University Press, 1978.

Spring, Agnes Wright. *The Cheyenne and Black Hills Stage and Express Routes.* Glendale, Calif.: Arthur H. Clark Co., 1949.

———. *Colorado Charley, Wild Bill's Pard.* Boulder, Colo.: Pruett Press, 1968.

Steckmesser, Kent Ladd. *The Western Hero in History and Legend.* Norman: University of Oklahoma Press, 1965.

Stevenson, Elizabeth. *Figures in a Western Landscape: Men and Women of the Northern Rockies.* Baltimore: Johns Hopkins University Press, 1994.

Stokes, George W. *Deadwood Gold: A Story of the Black Hills.* Yonkers-on-Hudson, N.Y.: World Book Company, 1926.

Stoll, William T. *Silver Strike: The True Story of Silver Mining in the Coeur d'Alenes*. 1932. Reprint, Moscow, Idaho: University of Idaho Press, 1991.

Sulentic, Joe. *Deadwood Gulch: The Last Chinatown*. Deadwood, S.Dak.: Deadwood Gulch Art Gallery, 1975.

Sutley, Zack T. *The Last Frontier*. New York: Macmillan Co., 1930.

Sweetman, Luke D. *Back Trailing on Open Range*. Caldwell, Idaho: Caxton Printers, 1951.

Tallent, Annie D. *The Black Hills: or, The Last Hunting Ground of the Dakotahs*. St. Louis, Mo.: Nixon-Jones Printing Co., 1899.

Tarbeaux, Frank. *The Autobiography of Frank Tarbeaux*. Edited by Donald Henderson Clarke. New York: Vanguard Press, 1930.

Thane, Eric. *High Border Country*. New York: Duell, Sloan & Pearce, 1942.

Thorp, N. Howard, and Neil M. Clark. *Pardner of the Wind: Story of the Southwestern Cowboy*. Caldwell, Idaho: Caxton Printers, 1945.

Thorp, Raymond W., and Robert Bunker. *Crow Killer: The Saga of Liver-Eating Johnson*. Bloomington: Indiana University Press, 1969.

Turchen, Lesta V., and James D. McLaird. *The Black Hills Expedition of 1875*. Mitchell, S.Dak.: Dakota Wesleyan University Press, 1975.

Urbanek, Mae. *High Lights of the Hills*. Lusk, Wyo.: Lusk Herald, 1954.

Utica, Montana. N.p., 1968.

Vaughn, J. W. *The Reynolds Campaign on Powder River*. Norman: University of Oklahoma Press, 1961.

———. *With Crook at the Rosebud*. Harrisburg, Pa.: Stackpole Co., 1956.

Von Schmidt-Pauli, Edgar. *We Indians. The Passing of a Great Race. Being the Recollections of the Last of the Great Indian Chiefs, Big Chief White Horse Eagle*. New York: E. P. Dutton & Co., 1931.

Waite, Walter F. *Silver Dollar Tales*. [Conrad, Mont.]: [1996].

Waldo, Edna LaMoore. *Dakota: An Informal Study of Territorial Days*. Caldwell, Idaho: Caxton Printers, 1936.

Walter, Dave, ed. *Speaking Ill of the Dead: Jerks in Montana History*. Helena, Mont.: Falcon Publishing, 2000.

Walton, Clyde C., ed. *An Illinois Gold Hunter in the Black Hills: The Diary of Jerry Bryan, March 13 to August 20, 1876*. Springfield: Illinois State Historical Society, 1960.

Warren, Margaret Lemley. *The Badlands Fox*. Edited by Renee Sansom Flood. Hermosa, S.Dak.: by the author, 1991.

Weston County Wyoming. Dallas, Tex.: Weston County Heritage Group and Curtis Media Corporation, 1988.

Wheeler, Edward L. *Hurricane Nell, the Girl Dead-Shot; or, The Queen of the Saddle and Lasso*. 4 May 1877. Reprint, *Bob Woolf, The Border Ruffian; or, The Girl Dead-Shot*. New York: Beadle and Adams, 1878.

Wheeler, Richard S. *Cashbox*. New York: Forge, 1994.

Wheeler, Sylvia Griffith. *Counting Back: Voices of the Lakota and Pioneer Settlers*. [Kansas City]: BkMk Press, University of Missouri–Kansas City, 1992.

White, John M. *The Newer Northwest: A Description of the Health Resorts and Mining Camps of the Black Hills of South Dakota and Big Horn Mountains in Wyoming.* St. Louis, Mo.: Self-Culture Publishing Co., 1894.

Whithorn, Bill, and Doris Whithorn. *Calamity's in Town: The Town Was Livingston, Montana.* [Livingston]: [Enterprise], n.d.

Wickersham, Will. *Pa-Ha-Sa-Pa.* Boston: Chapman & Grimes, 1948.

Willard, John. *Adventure Trails in Montana.* Helena: State Publishing Co., 1964.

Williams, Albert N. *The Black Hills, Mid-Continent Resort.* [Dallas]: Southern Methodist University Press, 1952.

Wilstach, Frank J. *Wild Bill Hickok: The Prince of Pistoleers.* Garden City, N.Y.: Garden City Publishing Co., 1926.

Winters, N. A. *A Brief History of Mercer County, Missouri.* 1883. Reprint, Princeton, Mo.: Joe D. and Mary Casteel Linn, 1980.

Wolle, Muriel Sibell. *The Bonanza Trail: Ghost Towns and Mining Camps of the West.* Bloomington: Indiana University Press, 1953.

———. *Montana Pay Dirt. A Guide to the Mining Camps of the Treasure State.* Denver: Sage Books, 1963.

Wright, Kathryn. *Billings: The Magic City and How It Grew.* Billings, Mont.: Reporter Printing & Supply Co., 1953.

Wyman, Walker D. *Frontier Woman: The Life of a Woman Homesteader on the Dakota Frontier.* [River Falls, Wisc.]: University of Wisconsin—River Falls Press, 1972.

Wyoming: A Guide to Its History, Highways, and People. Compiled by the Federal Writers' Program of the Works Progress Administration. 2d ed. New York: Oxford University Press, 1946.

Yost, Nellie Snyder, ed. *Boss Cowman: The Recollections of Ed Lemmon, 1857–1946.* Lincoln: University of Nebraska Press, 1969.

Young, Harry (Sam). *Hard Knocks: A Life Story of the Vanishing West.* Portland, Ore.: Wells & Co., 1915.

Zimmerman, Charles. *"Along the Zimmerman Trail."* N.p.: by the author, 1977.

THE DEADWOOD DICK DIME NOVELS BY EDWARD L. WHEELER

(All were published by Beadle and Adams, New York, and are listed by date of publication.)

Deadwood Dick, The Prince of the Road; or, The Black Rider of the Black Hills. October 15, 1877.

The Double Daggers; or, Deadwood Dick's Defiance. A Tale of the Regulators and Road-Agents of the Black Hills. December 21, 1877.

Buffalo Ben, The Prince of the Pistol; or, Deadwood Dick in Disguise. February 5, 1878.

Wild Ivan, The Boy Claude Duval; or, The Brotherhood of Death. March 26, 1878.

The Phantom Miner; or, Deadwood Dick's Bonanza. A Tale of the Great Silverland of Idaho. May 14, 1878.

Omaha Oll, The Masked Terror; or, Deadwood Dick in Danger. July 2, 1878.

Deadwood Dick's Eagles; or, The Pards of Flood Bar. August 27, 1878.

Deadwood Dick on Deck; or, Calamity Jane, The Heroine of Whoop Up. December 17, 1878.

Corduroy Charlie, The Boy Bravo; or, Deadwood Dick's Last Act. January 14, 1879.

Deadwood Dick in Leadville; or, A Strange Stroke for Liberty. A Wild, Exciting Story of the Leadville Region. June 24, 1879.

Deadwood Dick's Device; or, The Sign of the Double Cross. A Wild, Strange Story of the Leadville Mines. July 22, 1879.

Deadwood Dick as Detective. A Story of the Great Carbonate Region. August 26, 1879.

Deadwood Dick's Double; or, The Ghost of Gordon's Gulch. A Tale of Wild-Cat City. January 13, 1880.

Blonde Bill; or, Deadwood Dick's Home Base. A Romance of the "Silent Tongues". March 16, 1880.

A Game of Gold; or, Deadwood Dick's Big Strike. June 1, 1880.

Deadwood Dick of Deadwood; or, The Picked Party. A Romance of Skeleton Bend. July 20, 1880.

Deadwood Dick's Dream; or, The Rivals of the Road. A Mining Tale of Tombstone. April 19, 1881.

The Black Hills Jezebel; or, Deadwood Dick's Ward. May 31, 1881. Reprinted as *Deadwood Dick's Ward; or, The Black Hills Jezebel.* March 30, 1887.

Deadwood Dick's Doom; or, Calamity Jane's Last Adventure. A Tale of Death Notch. June 28, 1881.

Captain Crack-Shot, The Girl Brigand; or, Gypsy Jack From Jimtown. A Story of Durango. September 20, 1881. Reprinted as *The Jimtown Sport; or, Gypsy Jack in Colorado.* February 1, 1888.

Sugar-Coated Sam; or, The Black Gowns of Grim Gulch. A Deadwood Dick Episode. October 18, 1881. Reprinted as *The Miner Sport; or, Sugar-Coated Sam's Claim.* March 14, 1888.

Gold-Dust Dick. A Romance of Roughs and Toughs. January 3, 1882. Reprinted as *Deadwood Dick Trapped; or, Roxey Ralph's Ruse.* April 24, 1899.

Deadwood Dick's Divide; or, The Spirit of Swamp Lake. August 8, 1882. Reprinted as *Deadwood Dick's Disguise; or, Wild Walt, the Sport.* July 17, 1889.

Deadwood Dick's Death Trail; or, From Ocean to Ocean. September 12, 1882. Reprinted as *Deadwood Dick's Mission; or, Cavie, the Kidnapped Boy.* October 9, 1889.

Deadwood Dick's Big Deal; or, The Gold Brick of Oregon. June 26, 1883.

Deadwood Dick's Dozen; or, The Fakir of Phantom Flats. September 18, 1883.

Deadwood Dick's Ducats; or, Rainy Days in the Diggings. March 18, 1884.

Deadwood Dick Sentenced; or, The Terrible Vendetta. A Nevada Tale. April 15, 1884.

Deadwood Dick's Claim; or, The Fairy Face of Faro Flats. July 1, 1884.

Deadwood Dick in Dead City. April 28, 1885.

Deadwood Dick's Diamonds; or, The Mystery of Joan Porter. June 2, 1885.

Deadwood Dick in New York; or, "A Cute Case." A Romance of To-Day. August 18, 1885.

Deadwood Dick's Dust; or, The Chained Hand. A Strange Story of the Mines. Being the 35th and Ending Number of the Great "Deadwood Dick" Series. October 20, 1885. (Despite the subtitle, there were only thirty-three stories in the Deadwood Dick series.)

ARTICLES

Abbott, E. C. (Teddy Blue). "When I First Met 'Calamity Jane.'" In *Montana Monographs,* edited by I. D. O'Donnell. Vol. 1, n.p., 1928–29.

Abild, Ethel Dowdell. "Calamity Jane—Woman of Mystery." In *Papers of the 14th Dakota History Conference, April 2–3, 1982,* edited by H. W. Blakely. Madison, S.Dak.: Dakota State College, 1983.

Adams, Glen. Afterword to *Life and Adventures of Calamity Jane, By Herself.* [1896]. Reprint, Fairfield, Wash.: Ye Galleon Press, 1969.

Blewitt, Andrew. "Calamity Jane." *English Westerners' Brand Book* 5 (January 1963): 1–9.

Boyle, Lamoine E. "Facing Up to Calamity." *Westways* (April 1979): 20–23, 86.

Brink, Elizabeth A. "Clothing Calamity Jane: An Exercise in Historical Research." *True West* 37 (November 1990): 20–24.

Brinker, Maud. "The Bull Whacker." *Old Travois Trails* 3 (July–August 1942): 37–40.

"Buffalo Bill and Calamity Jane." *New Buffalo Bill Weekly No. 177.* New York: Street & Smith, 29 January 1916.

Burke, John. "The Wildest Woman in the West." *True Frontier* 1 (June 1967): 12–13, 44–45.

"Calamity Jane as a Lady Robinhood." *Literary Digest* (14 November 1925): 46.

Carlson, Margaret. "Unhappy Trails." *Time* 136 (29 October 1990): 100.

"Carol Burnett as 'Calamity Jane.'" *TV Guide* 11 (9 November 1963): 6–9.

Clinch, Thomas A. "Coxey's Army in Montana." *Montana: The Magazine of Western History* 15 (October 1965): 2–11.

Cornell, Sidney J. "The Opening of the Black Hills." *Monthly South Dakotan* 1 (March 1899): 171–75.

Crawford, John W. (Captain Jack). "The Truth about Calamity Jane." *Journalist* (5 March 1904): 333.

Cross, Merrit. "Burk, Martha Canary." In *Notable American Women 1607-1950: A Biographical Dictionary*, edited by Edward T. James, Janet Wilson James, and Paul S. Boyer. Vol. 1: 267–68. Cambridge: Belknap Press of Harvard University, 1971.

Croy, Homer. "Calamity Jane's Romantic Diary." *American Weekly* (1 June 1958): 20–22.

Curry, Tom. "Raiders of Deadwood." *Rio Kid Western* 22 (March 1951): 9–63.

Douthat, Elva Pratt. "J. (James) Thornton Canary." In *Mercer County Pioneer Traces.* Vol. 1: 150. Princeton, Mo.: Mercer County Genealogical Society, 1997.

Eisloeffel, Paul J., and Andrea I. Paul. "Hollywood on the Plains: Nebraska's Contribution to Early American Cinema." *Journal of the West* 33 (April 1994): 13–19.

Eng, Stephen. "The Great Outlaw Hoax." *True West* 33 (February 1986): 16–22.

Engebretson, Doug. "Pierre's 'Men for Breakfast.'" *Real West* 225 (December 1982): 47–48, 54.

Etulain, Richard W. Afterword to *Calamity Jane: A Study in Historical Criticism*, by Roberta Beed Sollid, 149–63. 1958. Reprint, Helena: Montana Historical Society Press, 1995.

———. "Calamity Jane: Independent Woman of the Wild West." In *By Grit and Grace: Eleven Women Who Shaped the American West*, edited by Glenda Riley and Richard W. Etulain, 72–92. Golden, Colo.: Fulcrum Publishing, 1997.

———. "Calamity Jane: The Making of a Frontier Legend." In *Wild Women of the Old West*, edited by Glenda Riley and Richard W. Etulain, 177–95. Golden, Colo.: Fulcrum Publishing, 2003.

Everett, H. C. "Calamity Jane." *Pony Express Courier* (November 1940): 7, 10, 16.

[Fox, M. L.] "Calamity Jane." *Illustrated American* (7 March 1896): 312.

Freeman, Lewis R. "Calamity Jane and Yankee Jim, Historic Characters of the Old Yellowstone." *Sunset* 49 (July 1922): 22–25, 52, 54.

Gilles, T. J. "Calamity Jane." In *Laurel's Story, A Montana Heritage,* edited by Elsie P. Johnston, 43–46. Laurel, Mont.: by the editor, 1979.

Greenwood, Grace, ed. "Diary of D. M. Holmes." In *Collections of the State Historical Society of North Dakota,* edited by O. G. Libby, Vol. 5: 23–84. Grand Forks: [State Historical Society of North Dakota], 1923.

Hackett, Charles F. "Along the Upper Missouri." In *South Dakota Historical Collections.* Vol. 8: 27–55. Pierre: State Publishing Co., 1916.

Hall, Bert, ed. "John Edmund Boland, Riverman." In *South Dakota Historical Collections.* Vol. 23: 212–24. Pierre: State Publishing Co., 1947.

Hamlin, Albert Lot. "Calamity Jane." *Pony Express Courier* (December 1939): 3, 14–15.

Hart, George. "Just Plain Jane. M. J. Conarray before the 'Calamity.'" In *The Prairie Scout,* 3: 98–103. Abilene: Kansas Corral of the Westerners, 1975.

Hawthorne, Susan. "*Ms. Quiz* Women of Letters." *Ms.* 2 (March–April 1992): 93.

Hiltbrand, David. "No Plain Jane." *TV Guide* (4 October 1997): 41.

Hilton, Francis W. "Calamity Jane." *Frontier Magazine* (September 1925): 105–9.

Hofstede, David. "The Many Lives and Lies of Calamity Jane." *Cowboys and Indians* 9 (June 2001): 83–86.

Holding, Vera. "Calamity Jane, Wildcat's Kitten." *Westerner* 1 (March–April 1969): 32–35.

Johnson, Dorothy M. "Flour Famine in Alder Gulch, 1864." *Montana: The Magazine of Western History* 7 (Winter 1957): 18–27.

———. "Independence Day, 1884!" *Montana: The Magazine of Western History* 8 (July 1958): 2–7.

Kent, Thomas L. "The Formal Conventions of the Dime Novel." *Journal of Popular Culture* 16 (Summer 1982): 37–47.

Kohl, Edith Eudora. "The Truth about Wild Bill and Calamity." *Rocky Mountain Empire Magazine* (1 January 1950): 2.

Larson, T. A. "Women's Role in the American West." *Montana: the Magazine of Western History* 24 (July 1974): 2–11.

Litz, Joyce H. "Lillian's Montana Scene." *Montana: The Magazine of Western History* 24 (Summer 1974): 58–69.

Mathisen, Jean A. "Calamity's Sister." *True West* 43 (December 1996): 23–30.

Mazzulla, Fred M., and William Kostka, Introduction to *Mountain Charley, or the Adventures of Mrs. E. J. Guerin, Who Was Thirteen Years in Male Attire.* Norman: University of Oklahoma Press, 1968.

McInnes, Elmer D. "Wyatt Earp's Coeur D'Alene Comrade." *Old West* 32 (Spring 1996): 50–53.

McLaird, James D. "Calamity Jane and the Black Hills Gold Rush in the Writings of William B. Lull." *South Dakota History* 28 (Spring–Summer 1998): 53–65.

———. "Calamity Jane: The Life and the Legend." *South Dakota History* 24 (Spring 1994): 1–18.

———. "Calamity Jane and Wild Bill: Myth and Reality." *Journal of the West* 37 (April 1998): 23–32.

———. "Calamity Jane's Diary and Letters: Story of a Fraud." *Montana: The Magazine of Western History* 45 (Autumn–Winter 1995): 20–35.

———. "I Know . . . Because I Was There": Leander P. Richardson Reports the Black Hills Gold Rush." *South Dakota History* 31 (Fall–Winter 2001): 239–68.

Nelson, D. J. (Dick). "Calamity Jane's Last Ride." Edited by Kathryn Wright. *The West* 17 (September 1973): 26–27, 61.

Paine, Clarence. "Calamity Jane. Man? Woman? or Both? *Westerners Brand Book, 1945–46.* (Chicago: [Westerners], 1947): 69–82.

———. "She Laid Her Pistol Down; or, The Last Will and Testament of Calamity Jane." *Westerners Brand Book 1944.* (Chicago: Westerners, 1946): 9–21.

———. "Wild Bill Hickok and Calamity Jane." In *The Black Hills*, edited by Roderick Peattie, 151–76. New York: Vanguard Press, 1952.

Patterson, W. G. "'Calamity Jane.' A Heroine of the Wild West." *Wide World Magazine* 11 (September 1903): 450–57.

"Pioneer Profiles: John and Lena Borner." *Wind River Mountaineer* V (October–December 1989): 2, 32–34.

Pond, Seymour G. "Frontier Still Recalls 'Calamity Jane." *New York Times Magazine* (18 October 1925): 9.

Pratt, Grace Roffey. "Gold Town of the Coeur D'Alenes." *True West* 12 (September–October 1964): 28–29, 69–70.

Rankin, M. Wilson. "The Meeker Massacre." *Annals of Wyoming* 16 (July 1944): 87–145.

Reckless Ralph. "Calamity Jane, Queen of the Plains." *Street and Smith's New York Weekly,* January 16, 23, 30, February 20, 27, and March 13, 1882.

Repp, Ed Earl. "The Lady Was a Cavalryman!" *Golden West* 8 (June 1972): 12–13, 55–57.

Richardson, Leander. "Last Days of a Plainsman." *True West* 13 (November–December 1965): 22–23, 44–45.

———. "A Trip to the Black Hills." *Scribner's Monthly* 13 (April 1877): 748–56.

Riley, Glenda. "Images of the Frontierswoman: Iowa as a Case Study." *Western Historical Quarterly* 8 (April 1977): 189–202.

Robbins, Peggy. "Calamity Jane: Hellcat in Leather Britches." *America History Illustrated* 10 (June 1975): 12–21.

Russell, John C. "Calamity Jane Lived Up To Her Name." *Wild West* 7 (August 1994): 42–48.

Saar, Meghan. "Calamity Jane Trumps Buffalo Bill." *True West* 51 (October 2004): 18–19.

Schickel, Richard. "Out West on a Bad Star Trip." *Time* (4 December 1995): 87.

Sollid, Roberta Beed. Review of *Calamity Was the Name for Jane*, by Glenn Clairmonte. *Montana: The Magazine of Western History* 10 (July 1960): 70.

Sorg, Eric V. "Brother's Trails." *True West* 43 (January 1996): 40–45.

Spring, Agnes Wright, ed. "Diary of Isaac N. Bard (1875–1876)." *1955 Brand Book of the Denver Posse of Westerners*, edited by Alan Swallow. Vol. 11, 171–204. [Denver]: Westerners, 1956.

———. "Dr. McGillycuddy's Diary." *Denver Brand Book, 1953*, edited by Maurice Frink. Vol. 9, 284–93. Denver: Westerners, 1954.

Straus, Karen. "Notorious Calamity" and "Madame B's Bucket of Blood." In *Centennial Scrapbook: A Collection of Stories Celebrating the 100th Anniversary of Livingston, Montana*, 60–64, 65–66. Livingston, Mont.: Livingston Enterprise, 1982.

Thomas, Daniel. "Miner's Delight." *Real West* 144 (March 1976): 36–40.

Thorp, Raymond W. "White-Eye, Last of the Old-Time Plainsmen." *True West* 12 (March–April 1965): 6–10, 46, 48.

"True West Legends: Calamity Jane." *True West* 43 (July 1996): 31–34.

Vaughn, J. W. "Captain James Egan." *Westerners' Brand Book, New York Posse* 13 (1966): 1–3, 6–7, 18.

Wadsworth, Henry Elmer. "Unknown History of Calamity Jane." *Pony Express* 13 (April 1947): 9.

Whiteside, William R. "Martha Canary Family." In *Mercer County Pioneer Traces.* Vol. 1: 151. Princeton, Mo.: Mercer County Geneaological Society, 1997.

Wilber, Ed P. "Reminiscences of the Meeker Country." *Colorado Magazine* 23 (November 1936): 273–83.

Wiley, H. B. "First Billings Postoffice and Calamity Jane." *Montana: The Magazine of Western History* 3 (Autumn 1953): 66.

Wright, Kathryn. "The *Real* Calamity Jane." *True West* 5 (November–December 1957): 22–25, 28, 41–42.

Newspapers

Aberdeen (S.Dak.) Daily News

Abilene Daily Chronicle

Anaconda (Mont.) Recorder

Anaconda (Mont.) Standard

Basin (Wyo.) Republican-Rustler

Belle Fourche (S.Dak.) Bee

Belle Fourche Daily Post

Big Horn (Wyo.) Sentinel

Billings Daily Gazette

Billings News

Billings Post

Billings Times

Bismarck Tribune

Bozeman (Mont.) Avant Courier

Bozeman Chronicle

Bozeman Gallatin County Republican

Brooklyn Eagle

Buffalo (N.Y.) Evening News

Buffalo (N.Y.) Morning Express

Buffalo (Wyo.) Bulletin

Buffalo (Wyo.) Sentinel

Buffalo Gap (S.Dak.) Republican

Butte Miner

Casper Tribune-Herald

Casper Weekly Mail

Castle (Mont.) Whole Truth

Central City (Dak.) Black Hills Champion

Cheyenne Daily Leader

Cheyenne Daily Sun

Cheyenne Democratic Leader

Cheyenne Wyoming State Tribune

Chicago Inter-Ocean

Chicago Times

Chicago Tribune

Cody (Wyo.) Enterprise

Coeur d'Alene (Idaho) Press

Colorado Springs Colorado State Journal

Custer (S.Dak.) Chronicle

Cut Bank (Mont.) Pioneer Press

Deadwood Black Hills Champion

Deadwood Black Hills Daily Times

Deadwood Black Hills Pioneer

Deadwood Daily Pioneer-Times

Deadwood Evening Independent

Deer Lodge (Mont.) New Northwest

Denver Illustrated Rocky Mountain Globe

Denver Post

Denver Rocky Mountain News

Denver Times

Douglas (Wyo.) Enterprise

El Paso Times

Evanston (Wyo.) News-Register

Fort Pierre Fairplay

Fort Pierre Weekly Signal

Fremont (Wyo.) Clipper

Frontier Index (Wyo.) A migratory press, located at Fort Sanders, Laramie, Green River City, and Bear River City (1865–68).

Gardiner (Mont.) Wonderland

Glasgow North Montana Review

Glendive (Mont.) Times

Great Falls Daily Leader

Great Falls Daily Tribune

Helena Daily Independent

Helena Evening Herald

Helena Independent Record

Helena Montana Daily Record

Helena Weekly Herald

Hot Springs (S.Dak.) Star

Huron (S.Dak.) Daily Huronite

Huron Plainsman

Jamestown (N.Dak.) Daily Alert

Jamestown Daily Capital

Janesville (Wisc.) Daily Recorder

Janesville Gazette

Kalispell (Mont.) Times

LaCrosse (Wisc.) Tribune

Lander Wyoming State Journal

Laramie Daily Boomerang

Laramie Sentinel

Lead (S.Dak.) Daily Call

Lead Evening Call

Lewistown (Mont.) Democrat

Lewistown Democrat-News

Lewistown Fergus County Argus

Livingston (Mont.) Daily Enterprise

Livingston Park County News

Livingston Post

London Star

London Times

Lusk (Wyo.) Herald

Mandan (N.Dak.) Pioneer

Midland (S.Dak.) Mail

Miles City (Mont.) Daily Press

Miles City Daily Star

Miles City Yellowstone Journal

Miller (Dak.) Hand County Press

Miller (S.Dak.) Pioneer Press

Milwaukee Journal

Milwaukee Sentinel

Minneapolis Journal

New York Times

New York Tribune

Oakes (N.Dak.) Republican

Omaha Morning World-Herald

Philip (S.Dak.) Pioneer Review

Pierre Daily Capital Journal

Pierre Dakota Journal

Portland Oregon Sunday Jounal

Princeton (Mo.) Overland Courier

Princeton Post-Telegraph

Princeton Press

Pueblo Colorado Daily Chieftain

Rapid City Black Hills Journal

Rapid City Black Hills Union

Rapid City Daily Journal

Rawlins (Wyo.) Carbon County Journal

Rawlins (Wyo.) Republican

Red Lodge (Mont.) Carbon County Democrat

Red Lodge (Mont.) Picket

Riverton (Wyo.) Review

Rock Springs (Wyo.) Miner

Rock Springs (Wyo.) Rocket

Sheridan (Wyo.) Post

Shoshone County (Idaho) News Press

Sidney (Nebr.) Telegraph

Sioux City Journal

Sioux Falls Argus-Leader

Spearfish Queen City Mail

Spokane Spokesman-Review

St. Paul Pioneer Press

St. Paul and Minneapolis Pioneer Press

Sturgis (S.Dak.) Black Hills Press

Sturgis Weekly Record

Sundance (Wyo.) Crook County Monitor

Sundance Gazette

Sweetwater Mines (Wyo.) A migratory press, located at Fort Bridger, South Pass City, and Bryan City (1868–69).

Torrington (Wyo.) Goshen News and Fort Laramie Scout

Virginia City Montana Post

White Sulphur Springs (Mont.) Meagher Republican

Yankton Daily Press and Dakotaian

Yankton Missouri Valley Observer

Popular Culture

Advertisements and Programs

Advertisement. Sierra designs Calamity Jane sleeping bag. *Outdoor Life* (June 1996): 82.

[Bell, Glenda, and Barb Fisher]. *Wild West Legend Calamity Jane and Barb Wire, A Sharp Woman with Many Fine Points.* Windsor, Colo.: n.d. Advertising brochure.

————. *"The Whole Shebang, Ol' Calamity Howls Again.* Windsor, Colo.: n.d. Brochure.

Destination Deadwood 4 (May 1994).

41st Annual Missouri Valley History Conference, March 12–14, 1998, University of Nebraska-Omaha.

1995 Visitor's Guide, Wyoming Territorial Park and Wyoming Scenic Railroad. Laramie Boomerang, Sunday Supplement, May 7, 1995.

South Dakota Vacation Guide, 1996–1997. South Dakota Department of Tourism.

[Thierer, Joyce]. *Ride into History.* Admire, Kans.: N.p., n.d. Advertising brochure.

Visitor Magazine 13 (June 1996).

Comic Books

Sol Brodsky and Tom Sutton, "The Wild Ones!" in *Kid Colt Outlaw* 1 (New York: Leading Magazine Corp. Marvel Comics Group, September 1967).

Films and Tapes

Badlands of Dakota. Universal, 1941. (Frances Farmer as Calamity Jane)

Bonanza. "Calamity over the Comstock." NBC-TV series.

Buffalo Girls. CBS-TV, 1995. (Anjelica Huston)

Calamity Jane. Warner Brothers, 1953. (Doris Day)

Calamity Jane. CBS-TV, 1984. (Jane Alexander)

Calamity Jane and Sam Bass. Universal, 1949. (Yvonne De Carlo)

Deadwood Dick. Columbia, 1940. (Marin Sais)

In the Days of 75 and 76. Black Hills Feature Film Company. Chadron, Nebr., 1915. (Freeda Hartzell Romine)

The Legend of Calamity Jane. 1997. (Barbara Scaff, voice) Animated television cartoon series.

The Lone Ranger Meets Calamity Jane. Cassette tape, 10 April 1944.

The Paleface. Paramount, 1948. (Jane Russell)

The Plainsman. Paramount, 1937. (Jean Arthur). Remake, 1966 (Abby Dalton)

The Raiders. Universal, 1964. (Judi Meredith)

The Texan Meets Calamity Jane. Columbia, 1950. (Evelyn Ankers)

This Is the West That Was. NBC-TV, 1974. (Kim Darby)

Wild Bill. MGM/UA, 1995. (Ellen Barkin)

Young Bill Hickok. Republic, 1940. (Sally Payne)

Musical Scores and Compact Discs

Larsen, Libby. *Songs from Letters: Calamity Jane to Her Daughter Janey, 1880–1902 for Soprano and Piano.* (New York: Oxford University Press, 1989).

Urban Diva (1993). Dora Ohrenstein, soprano, with music by Ben Johnston. CD, Emergency Music, 1993.

Unpublished Manuscripts

Furlong, Leslie Anne. "Gold-Dust and Buckskins: An Analysis of Calamity Jane as a Symbol of Luck and Womanhood in the Black Hills." Unpublished Ph.D. diss., Department of Anthropology, University of Virginia, 1991.

Index